Data Mining

Third Edition

Data Mining
Practical Machine Learning Tools and Techniques

Third Edition

Ian H. Witten

Eibe Frank

Mark A. Hall

AMSTERDAM • BOSTON • HEIDELBERG • LONDON
NEW YORK • OXFORD • PARIS • SAN DIEGO
SAN FRANCISCO • SINGAPORE • SYDNEY • TOKYO
Morgan Kaufmann Publishers is an imprint of Elsevier

Morgan Kaufmann Publishers is an imprint of Elsevier
30 Corporate Drive, Suite 400, Burlington, MA 01803, USA

This book is printed on acid-free paper.

Library of Congress Cataloging-in-Publication Data
Witten, I. H. (Ian H.)
    Data mining : practical machine learning tools and techniques.—3rd ed. /
Ian H. Witten, Frank Eibe, Mark A. Hall.
        p. cm.—(The Morgan Kaufmann series in data management systems)
    ISBN 978-0-12-374856-0 (pbk.)
1. Data mining.   I. Hall, Mark A.   II. Title.
QA76.9.D343W58 2011
006.3′12—dc22   2010039827

British Library Cataloguing-in-Publication Data
A catalogue record for this book is available from the British Library.

For information on all Morgan Kaufmann publications, visit our
website at *www.mkp.com* or *www.elsevierdirect.com*

Transferred to Digital Printing in 2013

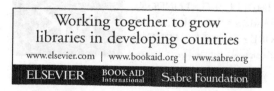

Contents

PART I INTRODUCTION TO DATA MINING

PART II   ADVANCED DATA MINING

PART III   THE WEKA DATA MINING WORKBENCH

List of Figures

List of Tables

Preface

The convergence of computing and communication has produced a society that feeds on information. Yet most of the information is in its raw form: data. If *data* is characterized as recorded facts, then *information* is the set of patterns, or expectations, that underlie the data. There is a huge amount of information locked up in databases—information that is potentially important but has not yet been discovered or articulated. Our mission is to bring it forth.

Data mining is the extraction of implicit, previously unknown, and potentially useful information from data. The idea is to build computer programs that sift through databases automatically, seeking regularities or patterns. Strong patterns, if found, will likely generalize to make accurate predictions on future data. Of course, there will be problems. Many patterns will be banal and uninteresting. Others will be spurious, contingent on accidental coincidences in the particular dataset used. And real data is imperfect: Some parts will be garbled, some missing. Anything that is discovered will be inexact: There will be exceptions to every rule and cases not covered by any rule. Algorithms need to be robust enough to cope with imperfect data and to extract regularities that are inexact but useful.

Machine learning provides the technical basis of data mining. It is used to extract information from the raw data in databases—information that is expressed in a comprehensible form and can be used for a variety of purposes. The process is one of abstraction: taking the data, warts and all, and inferring whatever structure underlies it. This book is about the tools and techniques of machine learning that are used in practical data mining for finding, and describing, structural patterns in data.

As with any burgeoning new technology that enjoys intense commercial attention, the use of data mining is surrounded by a great deal of hype in the technical—and sometimes the popular—press. Exaggerated reports appear of the secrets that can be uncovered by setting learning algorithms loose on oceans of data. But there is no magic in machine learning, no hidden power, no alchemy. Instead, there is an identifiable body of simple and practical techniques that can often extract useful information from raw data. This book describes these techniques and shows how they work.

We interpret machine learning as the acquisition of structural descriptions from examples. The kind of descriptions that are found can be used for prediction, explanation, and understanding. Some data mining applications focus on prediction: They forecast what will happen in new situations from data that describe what happened in the past, often by guessing the classification of new examples. But we are equally—perhaps more—interested in applications where the result of "learning" is an actual description of a structure that can be used to classify examples. This structural description supports explanation and understanding as well as prediction. In our experience, insights gained by the user are of most interest in the majority of practical data mining applications; indeed, this is one of machine learning's major advantages over classical statistical modeling.

The book explains a wide variety of machine learning methods. Some are pedagogically motivated: simple schemes that are designed to explain clearly how the basic ideas work. Others are practical: real systems that are used in applications today. Many are contemporary and have been developed only in the last few years.

A comprehensive software resource has been created to illustrate the ideas in this book. Called the Waikato Environment for Knowledge Analysis, or Weka[1] for short, it is available as Java source code at *www.cs.waikato.ac.nz/ml/weka*. It is a full, industrial-strength implementation of essentially all the techniques that are covered in this book. It includes illustrative code and working implementations of machine learning methods. It offers clean, spare implementations of the simplest techniques, designed to aid understanding of the mechanisms involved. It also provides a workbench that includes full, working, state-of-the-art implementations of many popular learning schemes that can be used for practical data mining or for research. Finally, it contains a framework, in the form of a Java class library, that supports applications that use embedded machine learning and even the implementation of new learning schemes.

The objective of this book is to introduce the tools and techniques for machine learning that are used in data mining. After reading it, you will understand what these techniques are and appreciate their strengths and applicability. If you wish to experiment with your own data, you will be able to do this easily with the Weka software.

The book spans the gulf between the intensely practical approach taken by trade books that provide case studies on data mining and the more theoretical, principle-driven exposition found in current textbooks on machine learning. (A brief description of these books appears in the Further Reading section at the end of Chapter 1.) This gulf is rather wide. To apply machine learning techniques productively, you need to understand something about how they work; this is not a technology that you can apply blindly and expect to get good results. Different problems yield to different techniques, but it is rarely obvious which techniques are suitable for a given situation: You need to know something about the range of possible solutions. And we cover an extremely wide range of techniques. We can do this because, unlike many trade books, this volume does not promote any particular commercial software or approach. We include a large number of examples, but they use illustrative datasets that are small enough to allow you to follow what is going on. Real datasets are far too large to show this (and in any case are usually company confidential). Our datasets are chosen not to illustrate actual large-scale practical problems but to help you understand what the different techniques do, how they work, and what their range of application is.

The book is aimed at the technically aware general reader who is interested in the principles and ideas underlying the current practice of data mining. It will also

---

[1] Found only on the islands of New Zealand, the weka (pronounced to rhyme with "Mecca") is a flightless bird with an inquisitive nature.

be of interest to information professionals who need to become acquainted with this new technology, and to all those who wish to gain a detailed technical understanding of what machine learning involves. It is written for an eclectic audience of information systems practitioners, programmers, consultants, developers, information technology managers, specification writers, patent examiners, and curious lay people, as well as students and professors, who need an easy-to-read book with lots of illustrations that describes what the major machine learning techniques are, what they do, how they are used, and how they work. It is practically oriented, with a strong "how to" flavor, and includes algorithms, code, and implementations. All those involved in practical data mining will benefit directly from the techniques described. The book is aimed at people who want to cut through to the reality that underlies the hype about machine learning and who seek a practical, nonacademic, unpretentious approach. We have avoided requiring any specific theoretical or mathematical knowledge, except in some sections that are marked by a box around the text. These contain optional material, often for the more technically or theoretically inclined reader, and may be skipped without loss of continuity.

The book is organized in layers that make the ideas accessible to readers who are interested in grasping the basics, as well as accessible to those who would like more depth of treatment, along with full details on the techniques covered. We believe that consumers of machine learning need to have some idea of how the algorithms they use work. It is often observed that data models are only as good as the person who interprets them, and that person needs to know something about how the models are produced to appreciate the strengths, and limitations, of the technology. However, it is not necessary for all users to have a deep understanding of the finer details of the algorithms.

We address this situation by describing machine learning methods at successive levels of detail. The book is divided into three parts. Part I is an introduction to data mining. The reader will learn the basic ideas, the topmost level, by reading the first three chapters. Chapter 1 describes, through examples, what machine learning is and where it can be used; it also provides actual practical applications. Chapters 2 and 3 cover the different kinds of input and output, or *knowledge representation*, that are involved——different kinds of output dictate different styles of algorithm. Chapter 4 describes the basic methods of machine learning, simplified to make them easy to comprehend. Here, the principles involved are conveyed in a variety of algorithms without getting involved in intricate details or tricky implementation issues. To make progress in the application of machine learning techniques to particular data mining problems, it is essential to be able to measure how well you are doing. Chapter 5, which can be read out of sequence, equips the reader to evaluate the results that are obtained from machine learning, addressing the sometimes complex issues involved in performance evaluation.

Part II introduces advanced techniques of data mining. At the lowest and most detailed level, Chapter 6 exposes in naked detail the nitty-gritty issues of implementing a spectrum of machine learning algorithms, including the complexities that are necessary for them to work well in practice (but omitting the heavy mathematical machinery that is required for a few of the algorithms). Although many readers may want to ignore such detailed information, it is at this level that the full, working, tested Java implementations of machine learning schemes are written. Chapter 7 describes practical topics involved with engineering the input and output to machine learning—for example, selecting and discretizing attributes—while Chapter 8 covers techniques of "ensemble learning," which combine the output from different learning techniques. Chapter 9 looks to the future.

The book describes most methods used in practical machine learning. However, it does not cover reinforcement learning because that is rarely applied in practical data mining; nor does it cover genetic algorithm approaches, because these are really an optimization technique, or relational learning and inductive logic programming because they are not very commonly used in mainstream data mining applications.

Part III describes the Weka data mining workbench, which provides implementations of almost all of the ideas described in Parts I and II. We have done this in order to clearly separate conceptual material from the practical aspects of how to use Weka. At the end of each chapter in Parts I and II are pointers to related Weka algorithms in Part III. You can ignore these, or look at them as you go along, or skip directly to Part III if you are in a hurry to get on with analyzing your data and don't want to be bothered with the technical details of how the algorithms work.

Java has been chosen for the implementations of machine learning techniques that accompany this book because, as an object-oriented programming language, it allows a uniform interface to learning schemes and methods for pre- and postprocessing. We chose it over other object-oriented languages because programs written in Java can be run on almost any computer without having to be recompiled, having to go through complicated installation procedures, or—worst of all—having to change the code itself. A Java program is compiled into byte-code that can be executed on any computer equipped with an appropriate interpreter. This interpreter is called the *Java virtual machine*. Java virtual machines—and, for that matter, Java compilers—are freely available for all important platforms.

Of all programming languages that are widely supported, standardized, and extensively documented, Java seems to be the best choice for the purpose of this book. However, executing a Java program is slower than running a corresponding program written in languages like C or C++ because the virtual machine has to translate the byte-code into machine code before it can be executed. This penalty used to be quite severe, but Java implementations have improved enormously over the past two decades, and in our experience it is now less than a factor of two if the virtual machine uses a *just-in-time compiler*. Instead of translating each byte-code individually, a just-in-time compiler translates whole chunks of byte-code into machine code, thereby achieving significant speedup. However, if this is still too slow for your application, there are compilers that translate Java programs directly into machine code, bypassing the byte-code step. Of course, this code cannot be executed on other platforms, thereby sacrificing one of Java's most important advantages.

UPDATED AND REVISED CONTENT

We finished writing the first edition of this book in 1999, the second edition in early 2005, and now, in 2011, we are just polishing this third edition. How things have changed over the past decade! While the basic core of material remains the same, we have made the most opportunities to both update it and to add new material. As a result the book has close to doubled in size to reflect the changes that have taken place. Of course, there have also been errors to fix, errors that we had accumulated in our publicly available errata file (available through the book's home page at *http://www.cs.waikato.ac.nz/ml/weka/book.html*).

Second Edition

The major change in the second edition of the book was a separate part at the end that included all the material on the Weka machine learning workbench. This allowed the main part of the book to stand alone, independent of the workbench, which we have continued in this third edition. At that time, Weka, a widely used and popular feature of the first edition, had just acquired a radical new look in the form of an interactive graphical user interface—or, rather, three separate interactive interfaces—which made it far easier to use. The primary one is the Explorer interface, which gives access to all of Weka's facilities using menu selection and form filling. The others are the Knowledge Flow interface, which allows you to design configurations for streamed data processing, and the Experimenter interface, with which you set up automated experiments that run selected machine learning algorithms with different parameter settings on a corpus of datasets, collect performance statistics, and perform significance tests on the results. These interfaces lower the bar for becoming a practicing data miner, and the second edition included a full description of how to use them.

It also contained much new material that we briefly mention here. We extended the sections on rule learning and cost-sensitive evaluation. Bowing to popular demand, we added information on neural networks: the perceptron and the closely related Winnow algorithm, and the multilayer perceptron and the backpropagation algorithm. Logistic regression was also included. We described how to implement nonlinear decision boundaries using both the kernel perceptron and radial basis function networks, and also included support vector machines for regression. We incorporated a new section on Bayesian networks, again in response to readers' requests and Weka's new capabilities in this regard, with a description of how to learn classifiers based on these networks and how to implement them efficiently using AD-trees.

The previous five years (1999–2004) had seen great interest in data mining for text, and this was reflected in the introduction of string attributes in Weka, multinomial Bayes for document classification, and text transformations. We also described efficient data structures for searching the instance space: kD-trees and ball trees for finding nearest neighbors efficiently and for accelerating distance-based clustering. We described new attribute selection schemes, such as race search and the use of support vector machines, and new methods for combining models such as additive regression, additive logistic regression, logistic model trees, and option trees. We also covered recent developments in using unlabeled data to improve classification, including the co-training and co-EM methods.

Third Edition

For this third edition, we thoroughly edited the second edition and brought it up to date, including a great many new methods and algorithms. Our basic philosophy has been to bring the book and the Weka software even closer together. Weka now includes implementations of almost all the ideas described in Parts I and II, and vice versa—pretty well everything currently in Weka is covered in this book. We have also included far more references to the literature: This third edition practically triples the number of references that were in the first edition.

As well as becoming far easier to use, Weka has grown beyond recognition over the last decade, and has matured enormously in its data mining capabilities. It now incorporates an unparalleled range of machine learning algorithms and related techniques. This growth has been partly stimulated by recent developments in the field and partly user-led and demand-driven. This puts us in a position where we know a lot about what actual users of data mining want, and we have capitalized on this experience when deciding what to include in this book.

As noted earlier, this new edition is split into three parts, which has involved a certain amount of reorganization. More important, a lot of new material has been added. Here are a few of the highlights.

Chapter 1 includes a section on web mining, and, under ethics, a discussion of how individuals can often be "reidentified" from supposedly anonymized data. A major addition describes techniques for multi-instance learning, in two new sections: basic methods in Section 4.9 and more advanced algorithms in Section 6.10. Chapter 5 contains new material on interactive cost–benefit analysis. There have been a great number of other additions to Chapter 6: cost-complexity pruning, advanced association-rule algorithms that use extended prefix trees to store a compressed version of the dataset in main memory, kernel ridge regression, stochastic gradient descent, and hierarchical clustering methods. The old chapter Engineering the Input and Output has been split into two: Chapter 7 on data transformations (which mostly concern the input) and Chapter 8 on ensemble learning (the output). To the former we have added information on partial least-squares regression, reservoir sampling, one-class learning, decomposing multiclass classification problems into ensembles of nested dichotomies, and calibrating class probabilities. To the latter we have added new material on randomization versus bagging and rotation forests. New sections on data stream learning and web mining have been added to the last chapter of Part II.

Part III, on the Weka data mining workbench, contains a lot of new information. Weka includes many new filters, machine learning algorithms, and attribute selection algorithms, and many new components such as converters for different file formats and parameter optimization algorithms. Indeed, within each of these categories Weka contains around 50% more algorithms than in the version described in the second edition of this book. All these are documented here. In response to popular demand we have given substantially more detail about the output of the different classifiers and what it all means. One important change is the inclusion of a brand new Chapter 17 that gives several tutorial exercises for the Weka Explorer interface (some of them quite challenging), which we advise new users to work though to get an idea of what Weka can do.

Acknowledgments

Writing the acknowledgments is always the nicest part! A lot of people have helped us, and we relish this opportunity to thank them. This book has arisen out of the machine learning research project in the Computer Science Department at the University of Waikato, New Zealand. We received generous encouragement and assistance from the academic staff members early on in that project: John Cleary, Sally Jo Cunningham, Matt Humphrey, Lyn Hunt, Bob McQueen, Lloyd Smith, and Tony Smith. Special thanks go to Geoff Holmes, the project leader and source of inspiration, and Bernhard Pfahringer, both of whom also had significant input into many different aspects of the Weka software. All who have worked on the machine learning project here have contributed to our thinking: We would particularly like to mention early students Steve Garner, Stuart Inglis, and Craig Nevill-Manning for helping us to get the project off the ground in the beginning, when success was less certain and things were more difficult.

The Weka system that illustrates the ideas in this book forms a crucial component of it. It was conceived by the authors and designed and implemented principally by Eibe Frank, Mark Hall, Peter Reutemann, and Len Trigg, but many people in the machine learning laboratory at Waikato made significant early contributions. Since the first edition of this book, the Weka team has expanded considerably: So many people have contributed that it is impossible to acknowledge everyone properly. We are grateful to Remco Bouckaert for his Bayes net package and many other contributions, Lin Dong for her implementations of multi-instance learning methods, Dale Fletcher for many database-related aspects, James Foulds for his work on multi-instance filtering, Anna Huang for information bottleneck clustering, Martin Gütlein for his work on feature selection, Kathryn Hempstalk for her one-class classifier, Ashraf Kibriya and Richard Kirkby for contributions far too numerous to list, Niels Landwehr for logistic model trees, Chi-Chung Lau for creating all the icons for the Knowledge Flow interface, Abdelaziz Mahoui for the implementation of K*, Stefan Mutter for association-rule mining, Malcolm Ware for numerous miscellaneous contributions, Haijian Shi for his implementations of tree learners, Marc Sumner for his work on speeding up logistic model trees, Tony Voyle for least-median-of-squares regression, Yong Wang for Pace regression and the original implementation of M5', and Xin Xu for his multi-instance learning package, *JRip*, logistic regression, and many other contributions. Our sincere thanks go to all these people for their dedicated work, and also to the many contributors to Weka from outside our group at Waikato.

Tucked away as we are in a remote (but very pretty) corner of the southern hemisphere, we greatly appreciate the visitors to our department who play a crucial role in acting as sounding boards and helping us to develop our thinking. We would like to mention in particular Rob Holte, Carl Gutwin, and Russell Beale, each of whom visited us for several months; David Aha, who although he only came for a few days did so at an early and fragile stage of the project and performed a great service by his enthusiasm and encouragement; and Kai Ming Ting, who worked with us for two years on many of the topics described in Chapter 8 and helped to bring us into the mainstream of machine learning. More recent visitors include Arie Ben-David, Carla Brodley, and Stefan Kramer. We would particularly like to thank Albert Bifet, who gave us detailed feedback on a draft version of the third edition, most of which we have incorporated.

Students at Waikato have played a significant role in the development of the project. Many of them are in the above list of Weka contributors, but they have also contributed in other ways. In the early days, Jamie Littin worked on ripple-down rules and relational learning. Brent Martin explored instance-based learning and nested instance-based representations, Murray Fife slaved over relational learning, and Nadeeka Madapathage investigated the use of functional languages for expressing machine learning algorithms. More recently, Kathryn Hempstalk worked on one-class learning and her research informs part of Section 7.5; likewise, Richard Kirkby's research on data streams informs Section 9.3. Some of the exercises in Chapter 17 were devised by Gabi Schmidberger, Richard Kirkby, and Geoff Holmes. Other graduate students have influenced us in numerous ways, particularly Gordon Paynter, YingYing Wen, and Zane Bray, who have worked with us on text mining, and Quan Sun and Xiaofeng Yu. Colleagues Steve Jones and Malika Mahoui have also made far-reaching contributions to these and other machine learning projects. We have also learned much from our many visiting students from Freiburg, including Nils Weidmann.

Ian Witten would like to acknowledge the formative role of his former students at Calgary, particularly Brent Krawchuk, Dave Maulsby, Thong Phan, and Tanja Mitrovic, all of whom helped him develop his early ideas in machine learning, as did faculty members Bruce MacDonald, Brian Gaines, and David Hill at Calgary, and John Andreae at the University of Canterbury.

Eibe Frank is indebted to his former supervisor at the University of Karlsruhe, Klaus-Peter Huber, who infected him with the fascination of machines that learn. On his travels, Eibe has benefited from interactions with Peter Turney, Joel Martin, and Berry de Bruijn in Canada; Luc de Raedt, Christoph Helma, Kristian Kersting, Stefan Kramer, Ulrich Rückert, and Ashwin Srinivasan in Germany.

Mark Hall thanks his former supervisor Lloyd Smith, now at Missouri State University, who exhibited the patience of Job when his thesis drifted from its original topic into the realms of machine learning. The many and varied people who have been part of, or have visited, the machine learning group at the University of Waikato over the years deserve a special thanks for their valuable insights and stimulating discussions.

Rick Adams and David Bevans of Morgan Kaufmann have worked hard to shape this book, and Marilyn Rash, our project manager, has made the process go very smoothly. We would like to thank the librarians of the Repository of Machine Learning Databases at the University of California, Irvine, whose carefully collected datasets have been invaluable in our research.

Our research has been funded by the New Zealand Foundation for Research, Science, and Technology and the Royal Society of New Zealand Marsden Fund. The Department of Computer Science at the University of Waikato has generously supported us in all sorts of ways, and we owe a particular debt of gratitude to Mark Apperley for his enlightened leadership and warm encouragement. Part of the first edition was written while both authors were visiting the University of Calgary, Canada, and the support of the Computer Science department there is gratefully acknowledged, as well as the positive and helpful attitude of the long-suffering students in the machine learning course, on whom we experimented. Part of the second edition was written at the University of Lethbridge in Southern Alberta on a visit supported by Canada's Informatics Circle of Research Excellence.

Last, and most of all, we are grateful to our families and partners. Pam, Anna, and Nikki were all too well aware of the implications of having an author in the house ("Not again!"), but let Ian go ahead and write the book anyway. Julie was always supportive, even when Eibe had to burn the midnight oil in the machine learning lab, and Immo and Ollig provided exciting diversions. Bernadette too was very supportive, somehow managing to keep the combined noise output of Charlotte, Luke, Zach, and Kyle to a level that allowed Mark to concentrate. Among us, we hail from Canada, England, Germany, Ireland, New Zealand, and Samoa: New Zealand has brought us together and provided an ideal, even idyllic, place to do this work.

About the Authors

Ian H. Witten is a professor of computer science at the University of Waikato in New Zealand. His research interests include language learning, information retrieval, and machine learning. He has published widely, including several books: *Managing Gigabytes* (1999), *Data Mining* (2005), *Web Dragons* (2007), and *How to Build a Digital Library* (2003). He is a Fellow of the ACM and of the Royal Society of New Zealand. He received the 2004 IFIP Namur Award, a biennial honor accorded for "outstanding contribution with international impact to the awareness of social implications of information and communication technology," and (with the rest of the Weka team) received the 2005 SIGKDD Service Award for "an outstanding contribution to the data mining field." In 2006, he received the Royal Society of New Zealand Hector Medal for "an outstanding contribution to the advancement of the mathematical and information sciences," and in 2010 was officially inaugurated as a "World Class New Zealander" in research, science, and technology.

Eibe Frank lives in New Zealand with his Samoan spouse and two lovely boys, but originally hails from Germany, where he received his first degree in computer science from the University of Karlsruhe. He moved to New Zealand to pursue his Ph.D. in machine learning under the supervision of Ian H. Witten, and joined the Department of Computer Science at the University of Waikato as a lecturer on completion of his studies. He is now an associate professor at the same institution. As an early adopter of the Java programming language, he laid the groundwork for the Weka software described in this book. He has contributed a number of publications on machine learning and data mining to the literature and has refereed for many conferences and journals in these areas.

Mark A. Hall was born in England but moved to New Zealand with his parents as a young boy. He now lives with his wife and four young children in a small town situated within a hour's drive of the University of Waikato. He holds a bachelor's degree in computing and mathematical sciences and a Ph.D. in computer science, both from the University of Waikato. Throughout his time at Waikato, as a student and lecturer in computer science and more recently as a software developer and data mining consultant for Pentaho, an open-source business intelligence software company, Mark has been a core contributor to the Weka software described in this book. He has published a number of articles on machine learning and data mining and has refereed for conferences and journals in these areas.

Introduction to Data Mining

What's It All About?

Human in vitro fertilization involves collecting several eggs from a woman's ovaries, which, after fertilization with partner or donor sperm, produce several embryos. Some of these are selected and transferred to the woman's uterus. The challenge is to select the "best" embryos to use—the ones that are most likely to survive. Selection is based on around 60 recorded features of the embryos—characterizing their morphology, oocyte, and follicle, and the sperm sample. The number of features is large enough to make it difficult for an embryologist to assess them all simultaneously and correlate historical data with the crucial outcome of whether that embryo did or did not result in a live child. In a research project in England, machine learning has been investigated as a technique for making the selection, using historical records of embryos and their outcome as training data.

Every year, dairy farmers in New Zealand have to make a tough business decision: which cows to retain in their herd and which to sell off to an abattoir. Typically, one-fifth of the cows in a dairy herd are culled each year near the end of the milking season as feed reserves dwindle. Each cow's breeding and milk production history influences this decision. Other factors include age (a cow nears the end of its productive life at eight years), health problems, history of difficult calving, undesirable temperament traits (kicking or jumping fences), and not being pregnant with calf for the following season. About 700 attributes for each of several million cows have been recorded over the years. Machine learning has been investigated as a way of ascertaining what factors are taken into account by successful farmers—not to automate the decision but to propagate their skills and experience to others.

Life and death. From Europe to the Antipodes. Family and business. Machine learning is a burgeoning new technology for mining knowledge from data, a technology that a lot of people are starting to take seriously.

1.1 DATA MINING AND MACHINE LEARNING

We are overwhelmed with data. The amount of data in the world and in our lives seems ever-increasing—and there's no end in sight. Omnipresent computers make it too easy to save things that previously we would have trashed. Inexpensive disks and online storage make it too easy to postpone decisions about what to do with all this stuff—we simply get more memory and keep it all. Ubiquitous electronics record our decisions, our choices in the supermarket, our financial habits, our comings and goings. We swipe our way through the world, every swipe a record in a database. The World Wide Web (WWW) overwhelms us with information; meanwhile, every choice we make is recorded. And all of these are just personal choices—they have countless counterparts in the world of commerce and industry. We could all testify to the growing gap between the *generation* of data and our *understanding* of it. As the volume of data increases, inexorably, the proportion of it that people understand decreases alarmingly. Lying hidden in all this data is information—potentially useful information—that is rarely made explicit or taken advantage of.

This book is about looking for patterns in data. There is nothing new about this. People have been seeking patterns in data ever since human life began. Hunters seek patterns in animal migration behavior, farmers seek patterns in crop growth, politicians seek patterns in voter opinion, and lovers seek patterns in their partners' responses. A scientist's job (like a baby's) is to make sense of data, to discover the patterns that govern how the physical world works and encapsulate them in theories that can be used for predicting what will happen in new situations. The entrepreneur's job is to identify opportunities—that is, patterns in behavior that can be turned into a profitable business—and exploit them.

In *data mining*, the data is stored electronically and the search is automated—or at least augmented—by computer. Even this is not particularly new. Economists, statisticians, forecasters, and communication engineers have long worked with the idea that patterns in data can be sought automatically, identified, validated, and used for prediction. What is new is the staggering increase in opportunities for finding patterns in data. The unbridled growth of databases in recent years, databases for such everyday activities as customer choices, brings data mining to the forefront of new business technologies. It has been estimated that the amount of data stored in the world's databases doubles every 20 months, and although it would surely be difficult to justify this figure in any quantitative sense, we can all relate to the pace of growth qualitatively. As the flood of data swells and machines that can undertake the searching become commonplace, the opportunities for data mining increase. As the world grows in complexity, overwhelming us with the data it generates, data mining becomes our only hope for elucidating hidden patterns. Intelligently analyzed data is a valuable resource. It can lead to new insights, and, in commercial settings, to competitive advantages.

Data mining is about solving problems by analyzing data already present in databases. Suppose, to take a well-worn example, the problem is fickle customer loyalty in a highly competitive marketplace. A database of customer choices, along with customer profiles, holds the key to this problem. Patterns of behavior of former customers can be analyzed to identify distinguishing characteristics of those likely to switch products and those likely to remain loyal. Once such characteristics are found, they can be put to work to identify present customers who are likely to jump ship. This group can be targeted for special treatment, treatment too costly to apply to the customer base as a whole. More positively, the same techniques can be used to identify customers who might be attracted to another service the enterprise provides, one they are not presently enjoying, to target them for special offers that promote this service. In today's highly competitive, customer-centered, service-oriented economy, data is the raw material that fuels business growth—if only it can be mined.

Data mining is defined as the process of discovering patterns in data. The process must be automatic or (more usually) semiautomatic. The patterns discovered must be meaningful in that they lead to some advantage, usually an economic one. The data is invariably present in substantial quantities.

And how are the patterns expressed? Useful patterns allow us to make nontrivial predictions on new data. There are two extremes for the expression of a pattern: as a black box whose innards are effectively incomprehensible, and as a transparent box whose construction reveals the structure of the pattern. Both, we are assuming, make good predictions. The difference is whether or not the patterns that are mined are represented in terms of a structure that can be examined, reasoned about, and used to inform future decisions. Such patterns we call *structural* because they capture the decision structure in an explicit way. In other words, they help to explain something about the data.

Now, again, we can say what this book is about: It is about techniques for finding and describing structural patterns in data. Most of the techniques that we cover have developed within a field known as *machine learning*. But first let us look at what structural patterns are.

Describing Structural Patterns

What is meant by *structural patterns*? How do you describe them? And what form does the input take? We will answer these questions by way of illustration rather than by attempting formal, and ultimately sterile, definitions. There will be plenty of examples later in this chapter, but let's examine one right now to get a feeling for what we're talking about.

Look at the contact lens data in Table 1.1. It gives the conditions under which an optician might want to prescribe soft contact lenses, hard contact lenses, or no contact lenses at all; we will say more about what the individual features mean later. Each line of the table is one of the examples. Part of a structural description of this information might be as follows:

```
If tear production rate = reduced then recommendation = none
Otherwise, if age = young and astigmatic = no then
recommendation = soft
```

Structural descriptions need not necessarily be couched as rules such as these. Decision trees, which specify the sequences of decisions that need to be made along with the resulting recommendation, are another popular means of expression.

This example is a very simplistic one. For a start, all combinations of possible values are represented in the table. There are 24 rows, representing three possible

Table 1.1 Contact Lens Data

Age	Spectacle Prescription	Astigmatism	Tear Production Rate	Recommended Lenses
young	myope	no	reduced	none
young	myope	no	normal	soft
young	myope	yes	reduced	none
young	myope	yes	normal	hard
young	hypermetrope	no	reduced	none
young	hypermetrope	no	normal	soft
young	hypermetrope	yes	reduced	none
young	hypermetrope	yes	normal	hard
pre-presbyopic	myope	no	reduced	none
pre-presbyopic	myope	no	normal	soft
pre-presbyopic	myope	yes	reduced	none
pre-presbyopic	myope	yes	normal	hard
pre-presbyopic	hypermetrope	no	reduced	none
pre-presbyopic	hypermetrope	no	normal	soft
pre-presbyopic	hypermetrope	yes	reduced	none
pre-presbyopic	hypermetrope	yes	normal	none
presbyopic	myope	no	reduced	none
presbyopic	myope	no	normal	none
presbyopic	myope	yes	reduced	none
presbyopic	myope	yes	normal	hard
presbyopic	hypermetrope	no	reduced	none
presbyopic	hypermetrope	no	normal	soft
presbyopic	hypermetrope	yes	reduced	none
presbyopic	hypermetrope	yes	normal	none

values of age and two values each for spectacle prescription, astigmatism, and tear production rate ($3 \times 2 \times 2 \times 2 = 24$). The rules do not really generalize from the data; they merely summarize it. In most learning situations, the set of examples given as input is far from complete, and part of the job is to generalize to other, new examples. You can imagine omitting some of the rows in the table for which the tear production rate is *reduced* and still coming up with the rule

```
If tear production rate = reduced then recommendation = none
```

This would generalize to the missing rows and fill them in correctly. Second, values are specified for all the features in all the examples. Real-life datasets invariably contain examples in which the values of some features, for some reason or other, are unknown—for example, measurements were not taken or were lost. Third, the preceding rules classify the examples correctly, whereas often, because of errors or *noise* in the data, misclassifications occur even on the data that is used to create the classifier.

Machine Learning

Now that we have some idea of the inputs and outputs, let's turn to machine learning. What is learning, anyway? What is *machine* learning? These are philosophical questions, and we will not be too concerned with philosophy in this book; our emphasis is firmly on the practical. However, it is worth spending a few moments at the outset on fundamental issues, just to see how tricky they are, before rolling up our sleeves and looking at machine learning in practice.

Our dictionary defines "to learn" as

- To get knowledge of something by study, experience, or being taught.
- To become aware by information or from observation
- To commit to memory
- To be informed of or to ascertain
- To receive instruction

These meanings have some shortcomings when it comes to talking about computers. For the first two, it is virtually impossible to test whether learning has been achieved or not. How do you know whether a machine has got knowledge of something? You probably can't just ask it questions; even if you could, you wouldn't be testing its ability to learn but its ability to answer questions. How do you know whether it has become aware of something? The whole question of whether computers can be aware, or conscious, is a burning philosophical issue.

As for the last three meanings, although we can see what they denote in human terms, merely committing to memory and receiving instruction seem to fall far short of what we might mean by machine learning. They are too passive, and we know that computers find these tasks trivial. Instead, we are interested in improvements in performance, or at least in the potential for performance, in new situations. You can commit something to memory or be informed of something by rote learning without being able to apply the new knowledge to new situations. In other words, you can receive instruction without benefiting from it at all.

Earlier we defined data mining operationally, as the process of discovering patterns, automatically or semiautomatically, in large quantities of data—and the patterns must be useful. An operational definition can be formulated in the same way for learning:

- Things learn when they change their behavior in a way that makes them perform better in the future

This ties learning to *performance* rather than *knowledge*. You can test learning by observing present behavior and comparing it with past behavior. This is a much more objective kind of definition and appears to be far more satisfactory.

But still there's a problem. Learning is a rather slippery concept. Lots of things change their behavior in ways that make them perform better in the future, yet we wouldn't want to say that they have actually *learned*. A good example is a comfortable slipper. Has it learned the shape of your foot? It has certainly changed its behavior to make it perform better as a slipper! Yet we would hardly want to call this *learning*. In everyday language, we often use the word *training* to denote a mindless kind of learning. We train animals and even plants, although it would be stretching the word a bit to talk of training objects such as slippers, which are not in any sense alive. But learning is different. Learning implies thinking and purpose. Something that learns has to do so intentionally. That is why we wouldn't say that a vine has learned to grow around a trellis in a vineyard—we'd say it has been trained. Learning without purpose is merely training. Or, more to the point, in learning the purpose is the learner's, whereas in training it is the teacher's.

Thus, on closer examination the second definition of learning, in operational, performance-oriented terms, has its own problems when it comes to talking about computers. To decide whether something has actually learned, you need to see whether it intended to, whether there was any purpose involved. That makes the concept moot when applied to machines because whether artifacts can behave purposefully is unclear. Philosophical discussions of what is really meant by *learning*, like discussions of what is really meant by *intention* or *purpose*, are fraught with difficulty. Even courts of law find intention hard to grapple with.

Data Mining

Fortunately, the kind of learning techniques explained in this book do not present these conceptual problems—they are called *machine learning* without really presupposing any particular philosophical stance about what learning actually is. Data mining is a topic that involves learning in a practical, nontheoretical sense. We are interested in techniques for finding and describing structural patterns in data, as a tool for helping to explain that data and make predictions from it. The data will take the form of a set of examples, such as customers who have switched loyalties, for instance, or situations in which certain kinds of contact lenses can be prescribed. The output takes the form of predictions about new examples—a prediction of whether a particular customer will switch or a prediction of what kind of lens will be prescribed under given circumstances. But because this book is about finding *and* describing patterns in data, the output may also include an actual description of a structure that can be used to classify unknown examples. As well as *performance*, it is helpful to supply an explicit representation of the *knowledge* that is acquired. In essence, this reflects both definitions of learning considered above: the acquisition of knowledge and the ability to use it.

Many learning techniques look for structural descriptions of what is learned—descriptions that can become fairly complex and are typically expressed as sets of rules, such as the ones described previously or the decision trees described later in this chapter. Because they can be understood by people, these descriptions serve to explain what has been learned—in other words, to explain the basis for new predictions. Experience shows that in many applications of machine learning to data mining, the explicit knowledge structures that are acquired, the structural descriptions, are at least as important as the ability to perform well on new examples. People frequently use data mining to gain knowledge, not just predictions. Gaining knowledge from data certainly sounds like a good idea if you can do it. To find out how, read on!

1.2 SIMPLE EXAMPLES: THE WEATHER AND OTHER PROBLEMS

We will be using a lot of examples in this book, which seems particularly appropriate considering that the book is all about learning from examples! There are several standard datasets that we will come back to repeatedly. Different datasets tend to expose new issues and challenges, and it is interesting and instructive to have in mind a variety of problems when considering learning methods. In fact, the need to work with different datasets is so important that a corpus containing around 100 example problems has been gathered together so that different algorithms can be tested and compared on the same set of problems.

The set of problems in this section are all unrealistically simple. Serious application of data mining involves thousands, hundreds of thousands, or even millions of individual cases. But when explaining what algorithms do and how they work, we need simple examples that capture the essence of the problem but are small enough to be comprehensible in every detail. We will be working with the datasets in this section throughout the book, and they are intended to be "academic" in the sense that they will help us to understand what is going on. Some actual fielded applications of learning techniques are discussed in Section 1.3, and many more are covered in the books mentioned in Section 1.7, Further reading, at the end of the chapter.

Another problem with actual real-life datasets is that they are often proprietary. No one is going to share their customer and product choice database with you so that you can understand the details of their data mining application and how it works. Corporate data is a valuable asset, the value of which has increased enormously with the development of data mining techniques such as those described in this book. Yet, we are concerned here with understanding how the methods used for data mining work, and understanding the details of these methods so that we can trace their operation on actual data. That is why our illustrative datasets are simple ones. But they are not *simplistic*: They exhibit the features of real datasets.

The Weather Problem

The weather problem is a tiny dataset that we will use repeatedly to illustrate machine learning methods. Entirely fictitious, it supposedly concerns the conditions

Table 1.2 Weather Data

Outlook	Temperature	Humidity	Windy	Play
Sunny	hot	high	false	no
Sunny	hot	high	true	no
Overcast	hot	high	false	yes
Rainy	mild	high	false	yes
Rainy	cool	normal	false	yes
Rainy	cool	normal	true	no
Overcast	cool	normal	true	yes
Sunny	mild	high	false	no
Sunny	cool	normal	false	yes
Rainy	mild	normal	false	yes
Sunny	mild	normal	true	yes
Overcast	mild	high	true	yes
Overcast	hot	normal	false	yes
Rainy	mild	high	true	no

that are suitable for playing some unspecified game. In general, instances in a dataset are characterized by the values of features, or *attributes*, that measure different aspects of the instance. In this case there are four attributes: *outlook, temperature, humidity*, and *windy*. The outcome is whether to play or not.

In its simplest form, shown in Table 1.2, all four attributes have values that are symbolic categories rather than numbers. Outlook can be *sunny, overcast*, or *rainy*; temperature can be *hot, mild*, or *cool*; humidity can be *high* or *normal*; and windy can be *true* or *false*. This creates 36 possible combinations ($3 \times 3 \times 2 \times 2 = 36$), of which 14 are present in the set of input examples.

A set of rules learned from this information—not necessarily a very good one—might look like this:

```
If outlook = sunny and humidity = high then play = no
If outlook = rainy and windy = true   then play = no
If outlook = overcast                 then play = yes
If humidity = normal                  then play = yes
If none of the above                  then play = yes
```

These rules are meant to be interpreted in order: The first one; then, if it doesn't apply, the second; and so on. A set of rules that are intended to be interpreted in sequence is called a *decision list*. Interpreted as a decision list, the rules correctly classify all of the examples in the table, whereas taken individually, out of context, some of the rules are incorrect. For example, the rule *if humidity = normal then play = yes* gets one of the examples wrong (check which one). The meaning of a set of rules depends on how it is interpreted—not surprisingly!

In the slightly more complex form shown in Table 1.3, two of the attributes—temperature and humidity—have numeric values. This means that any learning

---

Table 1.3 Weather Data with Some Numeric Attributes

Outlook	Temperature	Humidity	Windy	Play
Sunny	85	85	false	no
Sunny	80	90	true	no
Overcast	83	86	false	yes
Rainy	70	96	false	yes
Rainy	68	80	false	yes
Rainy	65	70	true	no
Overcast	64	65	true	yes
Sunny	72	95	false	no
Sunny	69	70	false	yes
Rainy	75	80	false	yes
Sunny	75	70	true	yes
Overcast	72	90	true	yes
Overcast	81	75	false	yes
Rainy	71	91	true	no

scheme must create inequalities involving these attributes rather than simple equality tests as in the former case. This is called a *numeric-attribute problem*—in this case, a *mixed-attribute problem* because not all attributes are numeric.

Now the first rule given earlier might take the form

```
If outlook = sunny and humidity > 83 then play = no
```

A slightly more complex process is required to come up with rules that involve numeric tests.

The rules we have seen so far are *classification rules*: They predict the classification of the example in terms of whether to play or not. It is equally possible to disregard the classification and just look for any rules that strongly associate different attribute values. These are called *association rules*. Many association rules can be derived from the weather data in Table 1.2. Some good ones are

```
If temperature = cool                   then humidity = normal
If humidity = normal and windy = false  then play = yes
If outlook = sunny and play = no        then humidity = high
If windy = false and play = no          then outlook = sunny and
                                        humidity = high
```

All these rules are 100% correct on the given data; they make no false predictions. The first two apply to four examples in the dataset, the third to three examples, and the fourth to two examples. And there are many other rules. In fact, nearly 60 association rules can be found that apply to two or more examples of the weather data and are completely correct on this data. And if you look for rules that are less than 100% correct, then you will find many more. There are so many because, unlike classification rules, association rules can "predict" any of the attributes, not just a specified class, and can even predict more than one thing. For example, the fourth rule predicts both that *outlook* will be *sunny* and that *humidity* will be *high*.

Contact Lenses: An Idealized Problem

The contact lens data introduced earlier tells you the kind of contact lens to prescribe, given certain information about a patient. Note that this example is intended for illustration only: It grossly oversimplifies the problem and should certainly not be used for diagnostic purposes!

The first column of Table 1.1 gives the age of the patient. In case you're wondering, *presbyopia* is a form of longsightedness that accompanies the onset of middle age. The second gives the spectacle prescription: *Myope* means shortsighted and *hypermetrope* means longsighted. The third shows whether the patient is astigmatic, while the fourth relates to the rate of tear production, which is important in this context because tears lubricate contact lenses. The final column shows which kind of lenses to prescribe, whether *hard*, *soft*, or *none*. All possible combinations of the attribute values are represented in the table.

A sample set of rules learned from this information is shown in Figure 1.1. This is a rather large set of rules, but they do correctly classify all the examples. These rules are complete and deterministic: They give a unique prescription for every conceivable example. Generally this is not the case. Sometimes there are situations in which no rule applies; other times more than one rule may apply, resulting in

```
If tear production rate = reduced then recommendation = none.
If age = young and astigmatic = no and tear production rate = normal
   then recommendation = soft
If age = pre-presbyopic and astigmatic = no and tear production
   rate = normal then recommendation = soft
If age = presbyopic and spectacle prescription = myope and
   astigmatic = no then recommendation = none
If spectacle prescription = hypermetrope and astigmatic = no and
   tear production rate = normal then recommendation = soft
If spectacle prescription = myope and astigmatic = yes and
   tear production rate = normal then recommendation = hard
If age = young and astigmatic = yes and tear production rate = normal
   then recommendation = hard
If age = pre-presbyopic and spectacle prescription = hypermetrope
   and astigmatic = yes then recommendation = none
If age = presbyopic and spectacle prescription = hypermetrope
   and astigmatic = yes then recommendation = none
```

FIGURE 1.1

Rules for the contact lens data.

conflicting recommendations. Sometimes probabilities or weights may be associated with the rules themselves to indicate that some are more important, or more reliable, than others.

You might be wondering whether there is a smaller rule set that performs as well. If so, would you be better off using the smaller rule set, and, if so, why? These are exactly the kinds of questions that will occupy us in this book. Because the examples form a complete set for the problem space, the rules do no more than summarize all the information that is given, expressing it in a different and more concise way. Even though it involves no generalization, this is often a very useful thing to do! People frequently use machine learning techniques to gain insight into the structure of their data rather than to make predictions for new cases. In fact, a prominent and successful line of research in machine learning began as an attempt to compress a huge database of possible chess endgames and their outcomes into a data structure of reasonable size. The data structure chosen for this enterprise was not a set of rules but a decision tree.

Figure 1.2 shows a structural description for the contact lens data in the form of a decision tree, which for many purposes is a more concise and perspicuous representation of the rules and has the advantage that it can be visualized more easily. (However, this decision tree, in contrast to the rule set given in Figure 1.1, classifies two examples incorrectly.) The tree calls first for a test on the *tear production rate*, and the first two branches correspond to the two possible outcomes. If the *tear production rate* is *reduced* (the left branch), the outcome is *none*. If it is *normal* (the right branch), a second test is made, this time on *astigmatism*. Eventually, whatever the outcome of the tests, a leaf of the tree is reached that dictates the contact lens recommendation for that case. The question of what is the most natural and easily understood format for the output from a machine learning scheme is one that we will return to in Chapter 3.

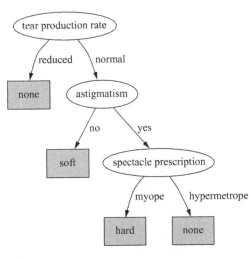

FIGURE 1.2

Decision tree for the contact lens data.

Irises: A Classic Numeric Dataset

The iris dataset, which dates back to seminal work by the eminent statistician R. A. Fisher in the mid-1930s and is arguably the most famous dataset used in data mining, contains 50 examples of each of three types of plant: *Iris setosa*, *Iris versicolor*, and *Iris virginica*. It is excerpted in Table 1.4. There are four attributes: *sepal length*,

Table 1.4 Iris Data

	Sepal Length (cm)	Sepal Width (cm)	Petal Length (cm)	Petal Width (cm)	Type
1	5.1	3.5	1.4	0.2	Iris setosa
2	4.9	3.0	1.4	0.2	Iris setosa
3	4.7	3.2	1.3	0.2	Iris setosa
4	4.6	3.1	1.5	0.2	Iris setosa
5	5.0	3.6	1.4	0.2	Iris setosa
...					
51	7.0	3.2	4.7	1.4	Iris versicolor
52	6.4	3.2	4.5	1.5	Iris versicolor
53	6.9	3.1	4.9	1.5	Iris versicolor
54	5.5	2.3	4.0	1.3	Iris versicolor
55	6.5	2.8	4.6	1.5	Iris versicolor
...					
101	6.3	3.3	6.0	2.5	Iris virginica
102	5.8	2.7	5.1	1.9	Iris virginica
103	7.1	3.0	5.9	2.1	Iris virginica
104	6.3	2.9	5.6	1.8	Iris virginica
105	6.5	3.0	5.8	2.2	Iris virginica
...					

sepal width, *petal length*, and *petal width* (all measured in centimeters). Unlike previous datasets, all attributes have values that are numeric.

The following set of rules might be learned from this dataset:

```
If petal-length < 2.45 then Iris-setosa
If sepal-width < 2.10 then Iris-versicolor
If sepal-width < 2.45 and petal-length < 4.55 then Iris-versicolor
If sepal-width < 2.95 and petal-width < 1.35 then Iris-versicolor
If petal-length ≥ 2.45 and petal-length < 4.45 then Iris-versicolor
If sepal-length ≥ 5.85 and petal-length < 4.75 then Iris-versicolor
If sepal-width < 2.55 and petal-length < 4.95 and
   petal-width < 1.55 then Iris-versicolor
If petal-length ≥ 2.45 and petal-length < 4.95 and
   petal-width < 1.55 then Iris-versicolor
If sepal-length ≥ 6.55 and petal-length < 5.05 then Iris-versicolor
If sepal-width < 2.75 and petal-width < 1.65 and
   sepal-length < 6.05 then Iris-versicolor
If sepal-length ≥ 5.85 and sepal-length < 5.95 and
   petal-length < 4.85 then Iris-versicolor
If petal-length ≥ 5.15 then Iris-virginica
If petal-width ≥ 1.85 then Iris-virginica
If petal-width ≥ 1.75 and sepal-width < 3.05 then Iris-virginica
If petal-length ≥ 4.95 and petal-width < 1.55 then Iris-virginica
```

These rules are very cumbersome, and we will see in Chapter 3 how more compact rules can be expressed that convey the same information.

CPU Performance: Introducing Numeric Prediction

Although the iris dataset involves numeric attributes, the outcome—the type of iris—is a category, not a numeric value. Table 1.5 shows some data for which both the outcome and the attributes are numeric. It concerns the relative performance of computer processing power on the basis of a number of relevant attributes; each row represents one of 209 different computer configurations.

The classic way of dealing with continuous prediction is to write the outcome as a linear sum of the attribute values with appropriate weights, for example,

$$\text{PRP} = -55.9 + 0.0489 \text{ MYCT} + 0.0153 \text{ MMIN} + 0.0056 \text{ MMAX}$$
$$+ 0.6410 \text{ CACH} - 0.2700 \text{ CHMIN} + 1.480 \text{ CHMAX}$$

(The abbreviated variable names are given in the second row of the table.) This is called a *regression equation*, and the process of determining the weights is called *regression*, a well-known procedure in statistics that we will review in Chapter 4. However, the basic regression method is incapable of discovering nonlinear relationships (although variants do exist—indeed, one will be described in Section 6.4), and in Chapter 3 we will examine different representations that can be used for predicting numeric quantities.

In the iris and central processing unit (CPU) performance data, all the attributes have numeric values. Practical situations frequently present a mixture of numeric and nonnumeric attributes.

Labor Negotiations: A More Realistic Example

The labor negotiations dataset in Table 1.6 summarizes the outcome of Canadian contract negotiations in 1987 and 1988. It includes all collective agreements reached in the business and personal services sector for organizations with at least 500 members (teachers, nurses, university staff, police, etc.). Each case concerns one contract, and the outcome is whether the contract is deemed *acceptable* or *unacceptable*. The acceptable contracts are ones in which agreements were accepted by both labor and management. The unacceptable ones are either known offers that fell through because one party would not accept them or acceptable contracts that had been significantly perturbed to the extent that, in the view of experts, they would not have been accepted.

There are 40 examples in the dataset (plus another 17 that are normally reserved for test purposes). Unlike the other tables here, Table 1.6 presents the examples as columns rather than as rows; otherwise, it would have to be stretched over several pages. Many of the values are unknown or missing, as indicated by question marks. This is a much more realistic dataset than the others we have seen.

Table 1.5 CPU Performance Data

| | Cycle Time (ns) | Main Memory (Kb) | | Cache (KB) | Channels | | Performance |
| | | Min | Max | | Min | Max | |
	MYCT	MMIN	MMAX	CACH	CHMIN	CHMAX	PRP
1	125	256	6000	256	16	128	198
2	29	8000	32,000	32	8	32	269
3	29	8000	32,000	32	8	32	220
4	29	8000	32,000	32	8	32	172
5	29	8000	16,000	32	8	16	132
...							
207	125	2000	8000	0	2	14	52
208	480	512	8000	32	0	0	67
209	480	1000	4000	0	0	0	45

Table 1.6 Labor Negotiations Data

Attribute	Type	1	2	3	...	40
duration	(number of years)	1	2	3		2
wage increase 1st year	percentage	2%	4%	4.3%		4.5
wage increase 2nd year	percentage	?	5%	4.4%		4.0
wage increase 3rd year	percentage	?	?	?		?
cost-of-living adjustment	{none, tcf, tc}	none	tcf	?		none
working hours per week	(number of hours)	28	35	38		40
pension	{none, ret-allw, empl-cntr}	none	?	?		?
standby pay	percentage	?	13%	?		?
shift-work supplement	percentage	?	5%	4%		4
education allowance	{yes, no}	yes	?	?		?
statutory holidays	(number of days)	11	15	12		12
vacation	{below-avg, avg, gen}	avg	gen	gen		avg
long-term disability assistance	{yes, no}	no	?	?		yes
dental plan contribution	{none, half, full}	none	?	full		full
bereavement assistance	{yes, no}	no	?	?		yes
health plan contribution	{none, half, full}	none	?	full		half
acceptability of contract	{good, bad}	bad	good	good		good

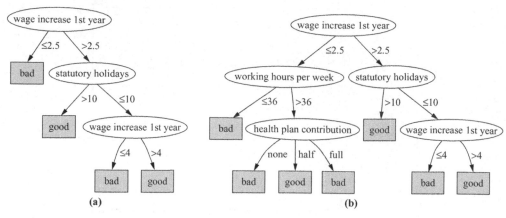

FIGURE 1.3

Decision trees for the labor negotiations data.

It contains many missing values, and it seems unlikely that an exact classification can be obtained.

Figure 1.3 shows two decision trees that represent the dataset. Figure 1.3(a) is simple and approximate—it doesn't represent the data exactly. For example, it will predict *bad* for some contracts that are actually marked *good*. However, it does make intuitive sense: A contract is bad (for the employee!) if the wage increase in the first year is too small (less than 2.5%). If the first-year wage increase is larger than this, it is good if there are lots of statutory holidays (more than 10 days). Even if there are fewer statutory holidays, it is good if the first-year wage increase is large enough (more than 4%).

Figure 1.3(b) is a more complex decision tree that represents the same dataset. Take a detailed look down the left branch. At first sight it doesn't seem to make sense intuitively that, if the working hours exceed 36, a contract is bad if there is no health-plan contribution or a full health-plan contribution, but is good if there is a half health-plan contribution. It is certainly reasonable that the health-plan contribution plays a role in the decision, but it seems anomalous that half is good and both full and none are bad. However, on reflection this could make sense after all, because "good" contracts are ones that have been accepted by *both* parties: labor and management. Perhaps this structure reflects compromises that had to be made to reach agreement. This kind of detailed reasoning about what parts of decision trees mean is a good way of getting to know your data and thinking about the underlying problem.

In fact, Figure 1.3(b) is a more accurate representation of the training dataset than Figure 1.3(a). But it is not necessarily a more accurate representation of the underlying concept of good versus bad contracts. Although it is more accurate on the data that was used to train the classifier, it may perform less well on an independent set of test data. It may be "overfitted" to the training data—following it too slavishly. The tree in Figure 1.3(a) is obtained from the one in Figure 1.3(b) by a process of pruning, which we will learn more about in Chapter 6.

Soybean Classification: A Classic Machine Learning Success

An often quoted early success story in the application of machine learning to practical problems is the identification of rules for diagnosing soybean diseases. The data is taken from questionnaires describing plant diseases. There are about 680 examples, each representing a diseased plant. Plants were measured on 35 attributes, each one having a small set of possible values. Examples are labeled with the diagnosis of an expert in plant biology: There are 19 disease categories altogether—horrible-sounding diseases such as diaporthe stem canker, rhizoctonia root rot, and bacterial blight, to mention just a few.

Table 1.7 gives the attributes, the number of different values that each can have, and a sample record for one particular plant. The attributes are placed in different categories just to make them easier to read.

Here are two example rules, learned from this data:

```
If    leaf condition = normal and
      stem condition = abnormal and
      stem cankers = below soil line and
      canker lesion color = brown
then
      diagnosis is rhizoctonia root rot

If    leaf malformation = absent and
      stem condition = abnormal and
      stem cankers = below soil line and
      canker lesion color = brown
then
      diagnosis is rhizoctonia root rot
```

These rules nicely illustrate the potential role of prior knowledge—often called *domain knowledge*—in machine learning, for in fact the only difference between the two descriptions is *leaf condition is normal* versus *leaf malformation is absent*. Now, in this domain, if the leaf condition is normal then leaf malformation is necessarily absent, so one of these conditions happens to be a special case of the other. Thus, if the first rule is true, the second is necessarily true as well. The only time the second rule comes into play is when leaf malformation is absent but leaf condition is *not* normal—that is, when something other than malformation is wrong with the leaf. This is certainly not apparent from a casual reading of the rules.

Research on this problem in the late 1970s found that these diagnostic rules could be generated by a machine learning algorithm, along with rules for every other disease category, from about 300 training examples. These training examples were carefully selected from the corpus of cases as being quite different from one another—"far apart" in the example space. At the same time, the plant pathologist who had produced the diagnoses was interviewed, and his expertise was translated

Table 1.7 Soybean Data

	Attribute	Number of Values	Sample Value
environment	time of occurrence	7	July
	precipitation	3	above normal
	temperature	3	normal
	cropping history	4	same as last year
	hail damage	2	yes
	damaged area	4	scattered
	severity	3	severe
	plant height	2	normal
	plant growth	2	abnormal
	seed treatment	3	fungicide
	germination	3	less than 80%
seed	condition	2	normal
	mold growth	2	absent
	discoloration	2	absent
	size	2	normal
	shriveling	2	absent
fruit	condition of fruit pods	3	normal
	fruit spots	5	—
leaves	condition	2	abnormal
	leaf spot size	3	—
	yellow leaf spot halo	3	absent
	leaf spot margins	3	—
	shredding	2	absent
	leaf malformation	2	absent
	leaf mildew growth	3	absent
stem	condition	2	abnormal
	stem lodging	2	yes
	stem cankers	4	above soil line
	canker lesion color	3	—
	fruiting bodies on stems	2	present
	external decay of stem	3	firm and dry
	mycelium on stem	2	absent
	internal discoloration	3	none
	sclerotia	2	absent
roots	condition	3	normal
diagnosis		19	diaporthe stem canker

into diagnostic rules. Surprisingly, the computer-generated rules outperformed the expert-derived rules on the remaining test examples. The correct disease was ranked at the top 97.5% of the time compared with only 72% for the expert-derived rules. Furthermore, not only did the learning algorithm find rules that outperformed those of the expert collaborator, but the same expert was so impressed that he allegedly adopted the discovered rules in place of his own!

1.3 FIELDED APPLICATIONS

The examples that we opened with are speculative research projects, not production systems. And the previous figures are toy problems: They are deliberately chosen to be small so that we can use them to work through algorithms later in the book. Where's the beef? Here are some applications of machine learning that have actually been put into use.

Being fielded applications, the examples that follow tend to stress the use of learning in performance situations, in which the emphasis is on the ability to perform well on new examples. This book also describes the use of learning systems to gain knowledge from decision structures that are inferred from the data. We believe that this is as important—probably even more important in the long run—a use of the technology as making high-performance predictions. Still, it will tend to be under-represented in fielded applications because when learning techniques are used to gain insight, the result is not normally a system that is put to work as an application in its own right. Nevertheless, in three of the following examples, the fact that the decision structure is comprehensible is a key feature in the successful adoption of the application.

Web Mining

Mining information on the World Wide Web is an exploding growth area. Search engine companies examine the hyperlinks in web pages to come up with a measure of "prestige" for each web page and web site. Dictionaries define *prestige* as "high standing achieved through success or influence." A metric called PageRank, introduced by Google's founders and also used in various guises by other search engine developers, attempts to measure the standing of a web page. The more pages that link to your web site, the higher its prestige, especially if the pages that link in have high prestige themselves. The definition sounds circular, but it can be made to work. Search engines use PageRank (among other things) to sort web pages into order before displaying the results of your search.

Another way in which search engines tackle the problem of how to rank web pages is to use machine learning based on a training set of example queries—documents that contain the terms in the query and human judgments about how relevant the documents are to that query. Then a learning algorithm analyzes this training data and comes up with a way to predict the relevance judgment for any document and query. For each document, a set of feature values is calculated that depends on the query term—for example, whether it occurs in the title tag, whether it occurs in the document's URL, how often it occurs in the document itself, and how often it appears in the anchor text of hyperlinks that point to the document. For multiterm queries, features include how often two different terms appear close together in the document, and so on. There are many possible features—typical algorithms for learning ranks use hundreds or thousands of them.

Search engines mine the content of the Web. They also mine the content of your queries—the terms you search for—to select advertisements that you might be interested in. They have a strong incentive to do this accurately because they get paid by advertisers only when users click on their links. Search engine companies mine your clicks because knowledge of which results you click on can be used to improve the search next time. Online booksellers mine the purchasing database to come up with recommendations such as "users who bought this book also bought these ones"; again, they have a strong incentive to present you with compelling, personalized choices. Movie sites recommend movies based on your previous choices and other people's choices—they win if they make recommendations that keep customers coming back to their web site.

And then there are social networks and other personal data. We live in the age of self-revelation: People share their innermost thoughts in blogs and tweets; their photographs, their music and movie tastes, their opinions of books, software, gadgets, and hotels; their social life. They may believe they are doing this anonymously, or pseudonymously, but often they are incorrect (see Section 1.6). There is huge commercial interest in making money by mining the Web.

Decisions Involving Judgment

When you apply for a loan, you have to fill out a questionnaire asking for relevant financial and personal information. This information is used by the loan company as the basis for its decision as to whether to lend you money. Such decisions are typically made in two stages. First, statistical methods are used to determine clear "accept" and "reject" cases. The remaining borderline cases are more difficult and call for human judgment.

For example, one loan company uses a statistical decision procedure to calculate a numeric parameter based on the information supplied in their questionnaire. Applicants are accepted if this parameter exceeds a preset threshold and rejected if it falls below a second threshold. This accounts for 90% of cases, and the remaining 10% are referred to loan officers for a decision. On examining historical data on whether applicants did indeed repay their loans, however, it turned out that half of the borderline applicants who were granted loans actually defaulted. Although it would be tempting simply to deny credit to borderline customers, credit industry professionals point out that if only their repayment future could be reliably determined, it is precisely these customers whose business should be wooed; they tend to be active customers of a credit institution because their finances remain in a chronically volatile condition. A suitable compromise must be reached between the viewpoint of a company accountant, who dislikes bad debt, and that of a sales executive, who dislikes turning business away.

Enter machine learning. The input was 1000 training examples of borderline cases for which a loan had been made that specified whether the borrower had finally paid off or defaulted. For each training example, about 20 attributes were extracted from the questionnaire, such as age, years with current employer, years at current address, years with the bank, and other credit cards possessed. A machine learning procedure was used to produce a small set of classification rules that made correct predictions on two-thirds of the borderline cases in an independently chosen test set. Not only did these rules improve the success rate of the loan decisions, but the company also found them attractive because they could be used to explain to applicants the reasons behind the decision. Although the project was an exploratory one that took only a small development effort, the loan company was apparently so pleased with the result that the rules were put into use immediately.

Screening Images

Since the early days of satellite technology, environmental scientists have been trying to detect oil slicks from satellite images to give early warning of ecological disasters and deter illegal dumping. Radar satellites provide an opportunity for monitoring coastal waters day and night, regardless of weather conditions. Oil slicks appear as dark regions in the image, the size and shape of which evolve depending on weather and sea conditions. However, other look-alike dark regions can be caused by local weather conditions such as high wind. Detecting oil slicks is an expensive manual process requiring highly trained personnel who assess each region in the image.

A hazard detection system has been developed to screen images for subsequent manual processing. Intended to be marketed worldwide to a wide variety of users—government agencies and companies—with different objectives, applications, and geographical areas, this system needs to be highly customizable to individual circumstances. Machine learning allows the system to be trained on examples of spills and nonspills supplied by the user and lets the user control the tradeoff between undetected spills and false alarms. Unlike other machine learning applications, which generate a classifier that is then deployed in the field, here it is the learning scheme itself that will be deployed.

The input is a set of raw pixel images from a radar satellite, and the output is a much smaller set of images with putative oil slicks marked by a colored border. First, standard image-processing operations are applied to normalize the image. Then suspicious dark regions are identified. Several dozen attributes are extracted from each region, characterizing its size, shape, area, intensity, sharpness and jaggedness of the boundaries, proximity to other regions, and information about the background in the vicinity of the region. Finally, standard learning techniques are applied to the resulting attribute vectors.

Several interesting problems were encountered. One was the scarcity of training data. Oil slicks are (fortunately) very rare, and manual classification is extremely costly. Another was the unbalanced nature of the problem: Of the many dark regions in the training data, only a very small fraction were actual oil slicks. A third is that the examples grouped naturally into batches, with regions drawn from each image forming a single batch, and background characteristics varied from one batch to another. Finally, the performance task was to serve as a filter, and the user had to be provided with a convenient means of varying the false-alarm rate.

Load Forecasting

In the electricity supply industry, it is important to determine future demand for power as far in advance as possible. If accurate estimates can be made for the maximum and minimum load for each hour, day, month, season, and year, utility companies can make significant economies in areas such as setting the operating reserve, maintenance scheduling, and fuel inventory management.

An automated load forecasting assistant has been operating at a major utility supplier for more than a decade to generate hourly forecasts two days in advance. The first step was to use data collected over the previous 15 years to create a sophisticated load model manually. This model had three components: base load for the year, load periodicity over the year, and the effect of holidays. To normalize for the base load, the data for each previous year was standardized by subtracting the average load for that year from each hourly reading and dividing by the standard deviation over the year.

Electric load shows periodicity at three fundamental frequencies: diurnal, where usage has an early morning minimum and midday and afternoon maxima; weekly, where demand is lower at weekends; and seasonal, where increased demand during winter and summer for heating and cooling, respectively, creates a yearly cycle. Major holidays, such as Thanksgiving, Christmas, and New Year's Day, show significant variation from the normal load and are each modeled separately by averaging hourly loads for that day over the past 15 years. Minor official holidays, such as Columbus Day, are lumped together as school holidays and treated as an offset to the normal diurnal pattern. All of these effects are incorporated by reconstructing a year's load as a sequence of typical days, fitting the holidays in their correct position, and denormalizing the load to account for overall growth.

Thus far, the load model is a static one, constructed manually from historical data, and it implicitly assumes "normal" climatic conditions over the year. The final step was to take weather conditions into account by locating the previous day most similar to the current circumstances and using the historical information from that day as a predictor. The prediction is treated as an additive correction to the static load model. To guard against outliers, the eight most similar days are located and their additive corrections averaged. A database was constructed of temperature, humidity, wind speed, and cloud cover at three local weather centers for each hour of the 15-year historical record, along with the difference between the actual load and that predicted by the static model. A linear regression analysis was performed to determine the relative effects of these parameters on load, and the coefficients were used to weight the distance function used to locate the most similar days.

The resulting system yielded the same performance as that of trained human forecasters but was far quicker—taking seconds rather than hours to generate a daily forecast. Human operators can analyze the forecast's sensitivity to simulated changes in weather and bring up for examination the "most similar" days that the system used for weather adjustment.

Diagnosis

Diagnosis is one of the principal application areas of expert systems. Although the handcrafted rules used in expert systems often perform well, machine learning can be useful in situations in which producing rules manually is too labor intensive.

Preventative maintenance of electromechanical devices such as motors and generators can forestall failures that disrupt industrial processes. Technicians regularly inspect each device, measuring vibrations at various points to determine whether the device needs servicing. Typical faults include shaft misalignment, mechanical loosening, faulty bearings, and unbalanced pumps. A particular chemical plant uses more than 1000 different devices, ranging from small pumps to very large turbo-alternators, which until recently were diagnosed by a human expert with 20 years or more of experience. Faults are identified by measuring vibrations at different places on the device's mounting and using Fourier analysis to check the energy present in three different directions at each harmonic of the basic rotation speed. This information, which is very noisy because of limitations in the measurement and recording procedure, is studied by the expert to arrive at a diagnosis. Although handcrafted expert system rules had been developed for some situations, the elicitation process would have to be repeated several times for different types of machinery; so a learning approach was investigated.

Six hundred faults, each comprising a set of measurements along with the expert's diagnosis, were available, representing 20 years of experience. About half were unsatisfactory for various reasons and had to be discarded; the remainder were used as training examples. The goal was not to determine whether or not a fault existed but to diagnose the kind of fault, given that one was there. Thus, there was no need to include fault-free cases in the training set. The measured attributes were rather low level and had to be augmented by intermediate concepts—that is, functions of basic attributes—which were defined in consultation with the expert and embodied some causal domain knowledge. The derived attributes were run through an induction algorithm to produce a set of diagnostic rules. Initially, the expert was not satisfied with the rules because he could not relate them to his own knowledge and experience. For him, mere statistical evidence was not, by itself, an adequate explanation. Further background knowledge had to be used before satisfactory rules were generated. Although the resulting rules were quite complex, the expert liked them because he could justify them in light of his mechanical knowledge. He was pleased that a third of the rules coincided with ones he used himself and was delighted to gain new insight from some of the others.

Performance tests indicated that the learned rules were slightly superior to the handcrafted ones that had previously been elicited from the expert, and this result was confirmed by subsequent use in the chemical factory. It is interesting to note, however, that the system was put into use not because of its good performance but because the domain expert approved of the rules that had been learned.

Marketing and Sales

Some of the most active applications of data mining have been in the area of marketing and sales. These are domains in which companies possess massive volumes of precisely recorded data, which, it has only recently been realized, is potentially extremely valuable. In these applications, predictions themselves are the chief interest: The structure of how decisions are made is often completely irrelevant.

We have already mentioned the problem of fickle customer loyalty and the challenge of detecting customers who are likely to defect so that they can be wooed back into the fold by giving them special treatment. Banks were early adopters of data mining technology because of their successes in the use of machine learning for credit assessment. Data mining is now being used to reduce customer attrition by detecting changes in individual banking patterns that may herald a change of bank, or even life changes, such as a move to another city, that can result in a different bank being chosen. It may reveal, for example, a group of customers with above-average attrition rate who do most of their banking by phone after hours when telephone response is slow. Data mining may determine groups for whom new services are appropriate, such as a cluster of profitable, reliable customers who rarely get cash advances from their credit cards except in November and December, when they are prepared to pay exorbitant interest rates to see them through the holiday season.

In another domain, cellular phone companies fight *churn* by detecting patterns of behavior that could benefit from new services, and then advertise such services to retain their customer base. Incentives provided specifically to retain existing customers can be expensive, and successful data mining allows them to be precisely targeted to those customers who are likely to yield maximum benefit.

Market basket analysis is the use of association techniques to find groups of items that tend to occur together in transactions, typically supermarket checkout data. For many retailers this is the only source of sales information that is available for data mining. For example, automated analysis of checkout data may uncover the fact that customers who buy beer also buy chips, a discovery that could be significant from the supermarket operator's point of view (although rather an obvious one that probably does not need a data mining exercise to discover). Or analysis may come up with the fact that on Thursdays customers often purchase diapers and beer together, an initially surprising result that, on reflection, makes some sense as young parents stock up for a weekend at home. Such information could be used for many purposes: planning store layouts, limiting special discounts to just one of a set of items that tend to be purchased together, offering coupons for a matching product when one of them is sold alone, and so on.

There is enormous added value in being able to identify individual customer's sales histories. Discount or "loyalty" cards let retailers identify all the purchases that each individual customer makes. This personal data is far more valuable than the cash value of the discount. Identification of individual customers not only allows historical analysis of purchasing patterns but also permits precisely targeted special offers to be mailed out to prospective customers—or perhaps personalized coupons can be printed in real time at the checkout for use during the next grocery run. Supermarkets want you to feel that although we may live in a world of inexorably rising prices, they don't increase so much *for you* because the bargains offered by personalized coupons make it attractive for you to stock up on things that you wouldn't normally have bought.

Direct marketing is another popular domain for data mining. Bulk-mail promotional offers are expensive and have a low—but highly profitable—response rate. Anything that helps focus promotions, achieving the same or nearly the same response from a smaller sample, is valuable. Commercially available databases containing demographic information that characterizes neighborhoods based on zip codes can be correlated with information on existing customers to predict what kind of people might buy which items. This model can be trialed on information gained in response to an initial mailout, where people send back a response card or call an 800 number for more information, to predict likely future customers. Unlike shopping-mall retailers, direct-mail companies have complete purchasing histories for each individual customer and can use data mining to determine those likely to respond to special offers. Targeted campaigns save money by directing offers only to those likely to want the product.

Other Applications

There are countless other applications of machine learning. We briefly mention a few more areas to illustrate the breadth of what has been done.

Sophisticated manufacturing processes often involve tweaking control parameters. Separating crude oil from natural gas is an essential prerequisite to oil refinement, and controlling the separation process is a tricky job. British Petroleum used machine learning to create rules for setting the parameters. This now takes just 10 minutes, whereas previously human experts took more than a day. Westinghouse faced problems in their process for manufacturing nuclear fuel pellets and used machine learning to create rules to control the process. This was reported to have saved them more than $10 million per year (in 1984). The Tennessee printing company R. R. Donnelly applied the same idea to control rotogravure printing presses to reduce artifacts caused by inappropriate parameter settings, reducing the number of artifacts from more than 500 each year to less than 30.

In the realm of customer support and service, we have already described adjudicating loans and marketing and sales applications. Another example arises when a customer reports a telephone problem and the company must decide what kind of technician to assign to the job. An expert system developed by Bell Atlantic in 1991 to make this decision was replaced in 1999 by a set of rules developed using machine learning, which saved more than $10 million per year by making fewer incorrect decisions.

There are many scientific applications. In biology, machine learning is used to help identify the thousands of genes within each new genome. In biomedicine, it is used to predict drug activity by analyzing not just the chemical properties of drugs but also their three-dimensional structure. This accelerates drug discovery and reduces its cost. In astronomy, machine learning has been used to develop a fully automatic cataloging system for celestial objects that are too faint to be seen by visual inspection. In chemistry, it has been used to predict the structure of certain organic compounds from magnetic resonance spectra. In all of these applications, machine learning techniques have attained levels of performance—or should we say skill?—that rival or surpass those of human experts.

Automation is especially welcome in situations involving continuous monitoring, a job that is time consuming and exceptionally tedious for humans. Ecological applications include the oil spill monitoring described earlier. Other applications are rather less consequential—for example, machine learning is being used to predict preferences for TV programs based on past choices and to advise viewers about available channels. Still other applications may save lives. Intensive-care patients may be monitored to detect changes in variables that cannot be explained by circadian rhythm, medication, and so on, raising an alarm when appropriate. Finally, in a world that relies on vulnerable networked computer systems and is increasingly concerned about cybersecurity, machine learning is used to detect intrusion by recognizing unusual patterns of operation.

1.4 MACHINE LEARNING AND STATISTICS

What is the difference between machine learning and statistics? Cynics, looking wryly at the explosion of commercial interest (and hype) in this area, equate data mining to statistics plus marketing. In truth, you should not look for a dividing line between machine learning and statistics because there is a continuum—and a multidimensional one at that—of data analysis techniques. Some derive from the skills taught in standard statistics courses, and others are more closely associated with the kind of machine learning that has arisen out of computer science. Historically, the two sides have had rather different traditions. If forced to point to a single difference of emphasis, it might be that statistics has been more concerned with testing hypotheses, whereas machine learning has been more concerned with formulating the process of generalization as a search through possible hypotheses. But this is a gross oversimplification: Statistics is far more than just hypothesis testing, and many machine learning techniques do not involve any searching at all.

In the past, very similar schemes have developed in parallel in machine learning and statistics. One is decision tree induction. Four statisticians (Breiman et al., 1984) published a book, *Classification and regression trees*, in the mid-1980s, and throughout the 1970s and early 1980s a prominent machine learning researcher, J. Ross Quinlan, was developing a system for inferring classification trees from examples. These two independent projects produced quite similar schemes for generating trees from examples, and the researchers only became aware of one another's work much later.

A second area where similar methods have arisen involves the use of nearest-neighbor methods for classification. These are standard statistical techniques that have been extensively adapted by machine learning researchers, both to improve classification performance and to make the procedure more efficient computationally. We will examine both decision tree induction and nearest-neighbor methods in Chapter 4.

But now the two perspectives have converged. The techniques we will examine in this book incorporate a great deal of statistical thinking. Right from the beginning, when constructing and refining the initial example set, standard statistical methods apply: visualization of data, selection of attributes, discarding outliers, and so on. Most learning algorithms use statistical tests when constructing rules or trees and for correcting models that are "overfitted" in that they depend too strongly on the details of the particular examples used to produce them (we have already seen an example of this in the two decision trees in Figure 1.3 for the labor negotiations problem). Statistical tests are used to validate machine learning models and to evaluate machine learning algorithms. In our study of practical techniques for data mining, we will learn a great deal about statistics.

1.5 GENERALIZATION AS SEARCH

One way of visualizing the problem of learning—and one that distinguishes it from statistical approaches—is to imagine a search through a space of possible concept descriptions for one that fits the data. Although the idea of generalization as search is a powerful conceptual tool for thinking about machine learning, it is not essential for understanding the practical schemes described in this book. That is why this section is set apart (boxed), suggesting that it is *optional*.

Suppose, for definiteness, that *concept descriptions*—the result of learning—are expressed as rules such as the ones given for the weather problem in Section 1.2 (although other concept description languages would do just as well). Suppose that we list all possible sets of rules and then look for ones that satisfy a given set of examples. A big job? Yes. An *infinite* job? At first glance it seems so because there is no limit to the number of rules there might be. But actually the number of possible rule sets is finite. Note first that each rule is no greater than a fixed maximum size, with at most one term for each attribute: For the weather data of Table 1.2 this involves four terms in all.

Because the number of possible rules is finite, the number of possible rule *sets* is finite too, although extremely large. However, we'd hardly be interested in sets that contained a very large number of rules. In fact, we'd hardly be interested in sets that had more rules than there are examples because it is difficult to imagine needing more than one rule for each example. So if we were to restrict consideration to rule sets smaller than that, the problem would be substantially reduced, although still very large.

The threat of an infinite number of possible concept descriptions seems more serious for the second version of the weather problem in Table 1.3 because these rules contain numbers. If they are real numbers, you can't enumerate them, even in principle. However, on reflection the problem again disappears because the numbers really just represent breakpoints in the numeric values that appear in the examples. For instance, consider the *temperature* attribute in Table 1.3. It involves the numbers 64, 65, 68, 69, 70, 71, 72, 75, 80, 81, 83, and 85—12 different numbers. There are 13 possible places in which we might want to put a breakpoint for a rule involving temperature. The problem isn't infinite after all.

So the process of generalization can be regarded as a search through an enormous, but finite, search space. In principle, the problem can be solved by enumerating descriptions and striking out those that do not fit the examples presented. A positive example eliminates all descriptions that it does not match, and a negative one eliminates those it does match. With each example the set of remaining descriptions shrinks (or stays the same). If only one is left, it is the target description—the target concept.

If several descriptions are left, they may still be used to classify unknown objects. An unknown object that matches all remaining descriptions should be classified as matching the target; if it fails to match any description it should be classified as being outside the target concept. Only when it matches some descriptions but not others is there ambiguity. In this case if the classification of the unknown object were revealed, it would cause the set of remaining descriptions to shrink because rule sets that classified the object the wrong way would be rejected.

Enumerating the Concept Space

Regarding it as search is a good way of looking at the learning process. However, the search space, although finite, is extremely big, and it is generally quite impractical to enumerate all possible descriptions and then see which ones fit. In the weather problem there are $4 \times 4 \times 3 \times 3 \times 2 = 288$ possibilities for each rule. There are four possibilities for the *outlook* attribute: *sunny, overcast, rainy*, or it may not participate in the rule at all. Similarly, there are four for *temperature*, three each for *windy* and *humidity* and two for the class. If we restrict the rule set to contain no more than 14 rules (because there are 14 examples in the training set), there are around 2.7×10^{34} possible different rule sets. That's a lot to enumerate, especially for such a patently trivial problem.

Although there are ways of making the enumeration procedure more feasible, a serious problem remains: In practice, it is rare for the process to converge on a unique acceptable description. Either many descriptions are still in the running after the examples are processed or the descriptors are all eliminated. The first case arises when the examples are not sufficiently comprehensive to eliminate all possible descriptions except for the "correct" one. In practice, people often want a single "best" description, and it is necessary to apply some other criteria to select the best one from the set of remaining descriptions. The second problem arises either because the description language is not expressive enough to capture the actual concept or because of noise in the examples. If an example comes in with the "wrong" classification because of an error in some of the attribute values or in the class that is assigned to it, this will likely eliminate the correct description from the space. The result is that the set of remaining descriptions becomes empty. This situation is very likely to happen if the examples contain any noise at all, which inevitably they do except in artificial situations.

Another way of looking at generalization as search is to imagine it not as a process of enumerating descriptions and striking out those that don't apply but as a kind of hill climbing in description space to find the description that best matches the set of examples according to some prespecified matching criterion. This is the way that most practical machine learning methods work. However, except in the most trivial cases, it is impractical to search the whole space exhaustively; most practical algorithms involve heuristic search and cannot guarantee to find the optimal description.

Bias

Viewing generalization as a search in a space of possible concepts makes it clear that the most important decisions in a machine learning system are:

- The concept description language
- The order in which the space is searched
- The way that overfitting to the particular training data is avoided

These three properties are generally referred to as the *bias* of the search and are called *language bias*, *search bias*, and *overfitting-avoidance bias*. You bias the learning scheme by choosing a language in which to express concepts, by searching in a particular way for an acceptable description, and by deciding when the concept has become so complex that it needs to be simplified.

Language Bias

The most important question for language bias is whether the concept description language is universal or whether it imposes constraints on what concepts can be learned. If you consider the set of all possible examples, a concept is really just a division of that set into subsets. In the weather example, if you were to enumerate all possible weather conditions, the *play* concept is a subset of possible weather conditions. A "universal" language is one that is capable of expressing every possible subset of examples. In practice, the set of possible examples is generally huge, and in this respect our perspective is a theoretical, not a practical, one.

If the concept description language permits statements involving logical *or*—that is, *disjunctions*—then any subset can be represented. If the description language is rule-based, disjunction can be achieved by using separate rules. For example, one possible concept representation is just to enumerate the examples:

```
If outlook = overcast and temperature = hot and humidity = high
    and windy = false then play = yes
If outlook = rainy and temperature = mild and humidity = high
    and windy = false then play = yes
If outlook = rainy and temperature = cool and humidity = normal
    and windy = false then play = yes
If outlook = overcast and temperature = cool and humidity = normal
    and windy = true then play = yes
...
If none of the above then play = no
```

This is not a particularly enlightening concept description: It simply records the positive examples that have been observed and assumes that all the rest are negative. Each positive example is given its own rule, and the concept is the disjunction of the rules. Alternatively, you could imagine having individual rules for each of the negative examples, too—an equally uninteresting concept. In either case, the concept description does not perform any generalization; it simply records the original data.

On the other hand, if disjunction is *not* allowed, some possible concepts—sets of examples—may not be able to be represented at all. In that case, a machine learning scheme may simply be unable to achieve good performance.

Another kind of language bias is that obtained from knowledge of the particular domain being used. For example, it may be that some combinations of attribute values can never happen. This would be the case if one attribute implied another. We saw an example of this when considering the rules for the soybean problem described in Section 1.2. Then it would be pointless to even consider concepts that involved redundant or impossible combinations of attribute values. Domain knowledge can be used to cut down the search space. Knowledge is power: A little goes a long way, and even a small hint can reduce the search space dramatically.

Search Bias

In realistic data mining problems, there are many alternative concept descriptions that fit the data, and the problem is to find the "best" one according to some criterion—usually simplicity. We use the term *fit* in a statistical sense; we seek the best description that fits the data reasonably well. Moreover, it is often computationally infeasible to search the whole space and guarantee that the description found really is the best. Consequently, the search procedure is heuristic, and no guarantees can be made about the optimality of the final result. This leaves plenty of room for bias: Different search heuristics bias the search in different ways.

For example, a learning algorithm might adopt a "greedy" search for rules by trying to find the best rule at each stage and adding it to the rule set. However, it may be that the best *pair* of rules is not just the two rules that are individually found best. Or when building a decision tree, a commitment to split early on using a particular attribute might turn out later to be ill-considered in light of how the tree develops below that node. To get around these problems, a *beam search* could be used where irrevocable commitments are not made but instead a set of several active alternatives—the number of which is the *beam width*—are pursued in parallel. This will complicate the learning algorithm quite considerably but has the potential to avoid the myopia associated with a greedy search. Of course, if the beam width is not large enough, myopia may still occur. There are more complex search strategies that help to overcome this problem.

A more general and higher-level kind of search bias concerns whether the search is done by starting with a general description and refining it or by starting with a specific example and generalizing it. The former is called a *general-to-specific* search bias; the latter, a *specific-to-general* one. Many learning algorithms adopt the former policy, starting with an empty decision tree, or a very general rule, and specializing it to fit the examples. However, it is perfectly possible to work in the other direction. Instance-based methods start with a particular example and see how it can be generalized to cover other nearby examples in the same class.

Overfitting-Avoidance Bias

Overfitting-avoidance bias is often just another kind of search bias. However, because it addresses a rather special problem, we treat it separately. Recall the disjunction problem described previously. The problem is that if disjunction is allowed, useless concept descriptions that merely summarize the data become possible, whereas if it is prohibited, some concepts are unlearnable. To get around this problem, it is common to search the concept space starting with the simplest concept descriptions and proceeding to more complex ones: simplest-first ordering. This biases the search in favor of simple concept descriptions.

Using a simplest-first search and stopping when a sufficiently complex concept description is found is a good way of avoiding overfitting. It is sometimes called *forward pruning* or *prepruning* because complex descriptions are pruned away before they are reached. The alternative, *backward pruning* or *postpruning*, is also viable. Here, we first find a description that fits the data well and then prune it back to a simpler description that also fits the data. This is not as redundant as it sounds: Often the best way to arrive at a simple theory is to find a complex one and then simplify it. Forward and backward pruning are both a kind of overfitting-avoidance bias.

In summary, although generalization as search is a nice way to think about the learning problem, bias is the only way to make it feasible in practice. Different learning algorithms correspond to different concept description spaces searched with different biases. This is what makes it interesting: Different description languages and biases serve some problems well and other problems badly. There is no universal "best" learning method—as every teacher knows!

1.6 DATA MINING AND ETHICS

The use of data—particularly data about people—for data mining has serious ethical implications, and practitioners of data mining techniques must act responsibly by making themselves aware of the ethical issues that surround their particular application.

When applied to people, data mining is frequently used to discriminate—who gets the loan, who gets the special offer, and so on. Certain kinds of discrimination—racial, sexual, religious, and so on—are not only unethical but also illegal. However, the situation is complex: Everything depends on the application. Using sexual and racial information for medical diagnosis is certainly ethical, but using the same information when mining loan payment behavior is not. Even when sensitive information is discarded, there is a risk that models will be built that rely on variables that can be shown to substitute for racial or sexual characteristics. For example, people frequently live in areas that are associated with particular ethnic identities, and so using a zip code in a data mining study runs the risk of building models that are based on race—even though racial information has been explicitly excluded from the data.

Reidentification

Recent work in what are being called *reidentification* techniques has provided sobering insights into the difficulty of anonymizing data. It turns out, for example, that over 85% of Americans can be identified from publicly available records using just three pieces of information: five-digit zip code, birth date (including year), and sex. Don't know the zip code?—over half of Americans can be identified from just city, birth date, and sex. When the Commonwealth of Massachusetts released medical records summarizing every state employee's hospital record in the mid-1990s, the governor gave a public assurance that it had been anonymized by removing all identifying information such as name, address, and social security number. He was surprised to receive his own health records (which included diagnoses and prescriptions) in the mail.

Stories abound of companies releasing allegedly anonymous data in good faith, only to find that many individuals are easily identifiable. In 2006, an Internet services company released to the research community the records of 20 million user searches.

The records were anonymized by removing all personal information—or so the company thought. But pretty soon journalists from *The New York Times* were able to identify the actual person corresponding to user number 4417749 (they sought her permission before exposing her). They did so by analyzing the search terms she used, which included queries for landscapers in her hometown and for several people with the same last name as hers, which reporters correlated with public databases.

Two months later, Netflix, an online movie rental service, released 100 million records of movie ratings (from 1 to 5) with their dates. To their surprise, it turned out to be quite easy to identify people in the database and thus discover all the movies they had rated. For example, if you know approximately when (give or take two weeks) a person in the database rated six movies and you know the ratings, you can identify 99% of the people in the database. By knowing only two movies with their ratings and dates, give or take three days, nearly 70% of people can be identified. From just a little information about your friends (or enemies) you can determine all the movies they have rated on Netflix.

The moral is that if you really do remove all possible identification information from a database, you will probably be left with nothing useful.

Using Personal Information

It is widely accepted that before people make a decision to provide personal information they need to know how it will be used and what it will be used for, what steps will be taken to protect its confidentiality and integrity, what the consequences of supplying or withholding the information are, and any rights of redress they may have. Whenever such information is collected, individuals should be told these things—not in legalistic small print but straightforwardly in plain language they can understand.

The potential use of data mining techniques means that the ways in which a repository of data can be used may stretch far beyond what was conceived when the data was originally collected. This creates a serious problem: It is necessary to determine the conditions under which the data was collected and for what purposes it may be used. Does the ownership of data bestow the right to use it in ways other than those purported when it was originally recorded? Clearly, in the case of explicitly collected personal data, it does not. But in general the situation is complex.

Surprising things emerge from data mining. For example, it has been reported that one of the leading consumer groups in France has found that people with red cars are more likely to default on their car loans. What is the status of such a "discovery"? What information is it based on? Under what conditions was that information collected? In what ways is it ethical to use it? Clearly, insurance companies are in the business of discriminating among people based on stereotypes—young males pay heavily for automobile insurance—but such stereotypes are not based solely on statistical correlations; they also draw on commonsense knowledge about the world as well. Whether the preceding finding says something about the kind of person who chooses a red car, or whether it should be discarded as an irrelevancy, is a matter for human judgment based on knowledge of the world rather than on purely statistical criteria.

When presented with data, you need to ask who is permitted to have access to it, for what purpose it was collected, and what kind of conclusions are legitimate to draw from it. The ethical dimension raises tough questions for those involved in practical data mining. It is necessary to consider the norms of the community that is used to dealing with the kind of data involved, standards that may have evolved over decades or centuries but ones that may not be known to the information specialist. For example, did you know that in the library community it is taken for granted that the privacy of readers is a right that is jealously protected? If you call your university library and ask who has such-and-such a textbook out on loan, they will not tell you. This prevents a student being subjected to pressure from an irate professor to yield access to a book that she desperately needs for her latest grant application. It also prohibits enquiry into the dubious recreational reading tastes of the university ethics committee chairperson. Those who build, say, digital libraries may not be aware of these sensitivities and might incorporate data mining systems that analyze and compare individuals' reading habits to recommend new books—perhaps even selling the results to publishers!

Wider Issues

In addition to various community standards for the use of data, logical and scientific standards must be adhered to when drawing conclusions from it. If you do come up with conclusions (e.g., red car owners being greater credit risks), you need to attach caveats to them and back them up with arguments other than purely statistical ones. The point is that data mining is just a tool in the whole process. It is people who take the results, along with other knowledge, and decide what action to apply.

Data mining prompts another question, which is really a political one concerning the use to which society's resources are being put. We mentioned earlier the application of data mining to basket analysis, where supermarket checkout records are analyzed to detect associations among items that people purchase. What use should be made of the resulting information? Should the supermarket manager place the beer and chips together, to make it easier for shoppers, or farther apart to make it less convenient for them, to maximize their time in the store and therefore their likelihood of being drawn into further purchases? Should the manager move the most expensive, most profitable diapers near the beer, increasing sales to harried fathers of a high-margin item, and add further luxury baby products nearby?

Of course, anyone who uses advanced technologies should consider the wisdom of what they are doing. If *data* is characterized as recorded facts, then *information* is the set of patterns, or expectations, that underlie the data. You could go on to define *knowledge* as the accumulation of your set of expectations and *wisdom* as the value attached to knowledge. Although we will not pursue it further here, this issue is worth pondering.

As we saw at the very beginning of this chapter, the techniques described in this book may be called upon to help make some of the most profound and intimate decisions that life presents. Data mining is a technology that we need to take seriously.

1.7 FURTHER READING

To avoid breaking up the flow of the main text, all references are collected in a section at the end of each chapter. This section describes papers, books, and other resources relevant to the material covered in this chapter. The human in vitro fertilization research mentioned in the opening was undertaken by the Oxford University Computing Laboratory, and the research on cow culling was performed in the Computer Science Department at Waikato University, New Zealand.

The weather problem is from Quinlan (1986) and has been widely used to explain machine learning schemes. The corpus of example problems mentioned in the introduction to Section 1.2 is available from Asuncion and Newman (2007). The contact lens example is from Cendrowska (1987), who introduced the PRISM rule-learning algorithm that we will encounter in Chapter 4. The iris dataset was described in a classic early paper on statistical inference (Fisher, 1936). The labor negotiations data is from the *Collective Bargaining Review*, a publication of Labour Canada issued by the Industrial Relations Information Service (BLI 1988), and the soybean problem was first described by Michalski and Chilausky (1980).

Some of the applications in Section 1.3 are covered in an excellent paper that gives plenty of other applications of machine learning and rule induction (Langley and Simon, 1995); another source of fielded applications is a special issue of the *Machine Learning Journal* (Kohavi and Provost, 1998). Chakrabarti (2003) has written an excellent and comprehensive book on techniques of web mining; another, more recent, book is Liu's *Web data mining* (2009). The loan company application is described in more detail by Michie (1989), the oil slick detector is from Kubat et al. (1998), the electric load forecasting work is by Jabbour et al. (1988), and the application to preventative maintenance of electromechanical devices is from Saitta and Neri (1998). Fuller descriptions of some of the other projects mentioned in Section 1.3 (including the figures of dollar amounts saved and related literature references) appear at the web site of the Alberta Ingenuity Centre for Machine Learning. Luan (2002) describes applications for data mining in higher education. Dasu et al. (2006) have some recommendations for successful data mining. Another special issue of the *Machine Learning Journal* addresses the lessons that have been learned from data mining applications and collaborative problem solving (Lavrac et al., 2004).

The "diapers and beer" story is legendary. According to an article in London's *Financial Times* (February 7, 1996),

> *The oft-quoted example of what data mining can achieve is the case of a large*
> *US supermarket chain which discovered a strong association for many customers*

between a brand of babies' nappies (diapers) and a brand of beer. Most customers who bought the nappies also bought the beer. The best hypothesisers in the world would find it difficult to propose this combination but data mining showed it existed, and the retail outlet was able to exploit it by moving the products closer together on the shelves.

However, it seems that it is just a legend after all; Power (2002) traces its history.

The book *Classification and regression trees*, mentioned in Section 1.4, is by Breiman et al. (1984), and Quinlan's independently derived but similar scheme was described in a series of papers that eventually led to a book (Quinlan, 1993).

The first book on data mining was written by Piatetsky-Shapiro and Frawley (1991)—a collection of papers presented at a workshop on knowledge discovery in databases in the late 1980s. Another book from the same stable has appeared since (Fayyad et al., 1996) from a 1994 workshop. There followed a rash of business-oriented books on data mining, focusing mainly on practical aspects of how it can be put into practice with only rather superficial descriptions of the technology that underlies the methods used. They are valuable sources of applications and inspiration. For example, Adriaans and Zantige (1996) from Syllogic, a European systems and database consultancy, is an early introduction to data mining. Berry and Linoff (1997), from a Pennsylvania-based firm specializing in data warehousing and data mining, give an excellent and example-studded review of data mining techniques for marketing, sales, and customer support. Cabena et al. (1998), written by people from five international IBM laboratories, contains an overview of the data mining process with many examples of real-world applications.

Dhar and Stein (1997) give a business perspective on data mining and include broad-brush, popularized reviews of many of the technologies involved. Groth (1998), working for a provider of data mining software, gives a brief introduction to data mining and then a fairly extensive review of data mining software products; the book includes a CD-ROM containing a demo version of his company's product. Weiss and Indurkhya (1998) look at a wide variety of statistical techniques for making predictions from what they call "big data." Han and Kamber (2006) cover data mining from a database perspective, focusing on the discovery of knowledge in large corporate databases; they also discuss mining complex types of data. Hand et al. (2001) produced an interdisciplinary book on data mining from an international group of authors who are well respected in the field. Finally, Nisbet et al. (2009) have produced a comprehensive handbook of statistical analysis and data mining applications.

Books on machine learning, on the other hand, tend to be academic texts suited for use in university courses rather than as practical guides. Mitchell (1997) wrote an excellent book that covers many techniques of machine learning, including some—notably genetic algorithms and reinforcement learning—that are not covered here. Langley (1996) offers another good text. Although the previously mentioned book by Quinlan (1993) concentrates on a particular learning algorithm, C4.5, which we will cover in detail in Chapters 4 and 6, it is a good introduction to some of the problems and techniques of machine learning. An absolutely excellent book on machine learning from a statistical perspective is Hastie et al. (2009). This is quite a theoretically oriented work, and is beautifully produced with apt and telling figures. Russell and Norvig's *Artificial intelligence: A modern approach* (2009) is the third edition of a classic text that includes a great deal of information on machine learning and data mining.

Pattern recognition is a topic that is closely related to machine learning, and many of the same techniques apply. Duda et al. (2001) is the second edition of a classic and successful book on pattern recognition (Duda and Hart, 1973). Ripley (1996) and Bishop (1995) describe the use of neural networks for pattern recognition; Bishop has a more recent book, *Pattern recognition and machine learning* (2006). Data mining with neural networks is the subject of a 1996 book by Bigus of IBM, which features the IBM Neural Network Utility Product that he developed.

There is a great deal of current interest in support vector machines. Cristianini and Shawe-Taylor (2000) give a nice introduction, and a follow-up work generalizes this to cover additional algorithms, kernels, and solutions with applications to pattern discovery problems in fields such as bioinformatics, text analysis, and image analysis (Shawe-Taylor and Cristianini, 2004). Schölkopf and Smola (2002) provide a comprehensive introduction to support vector machines and related kernel methods by two young researchers who did their Ph.D. research in this rapidly developing area.

The emerging area of reidentification techniques is explored, along with its implications for anonymization, by Ohm (2009).

Input: Concepts, Instances, and Attributes

Before delving into the question of how machine learning schemes operate, we begin by looking at the different forms the input might take and, in Chapter 3, the different kinds of output that might be produced. With any software system, understanding what the inputs and outputs are is far more important than knowing what goes on in between, and machine learning is no exception.

The input takes the form of *concepts*, *instances*, and *attributes*. We call the thing that is to be learned a *concept description*. The idea of a concept, like the very idea of learning in the first place, is hard to pin down precisely, and we won't spend time philosophizing about just what it is and isn't. In a sense, what we are trying to find—the result of the learning process—is a description of the concept that is *intelligible* in that it can be understood, discussed, and disputed, and *operational* in that it can be applied to actual examples. The next section explains some distinctions among different kinds of learning problems—distinctions that are very concrete and very important in practical data mining.

The information that the learner is given takes the form of a set of *instances*. In the examples in Chapter 1, each instance was an individual, independent example of the concept to be learned. Of course, there are many things you might like to learn for which the raw data cannot be expressed as individual, independent instances. Perhaps background knowledge should be taken into account as part of the input. Perhaps the raw data is an agglomerated mass that cannot be fragmented into individual instances. Perhaps it is a single sequence—say a time sequence—that cannot meaningfully be cut into pieces. This book is about simple, practical methods of data mining, and we focus on situations where the information can be supplied in the form of individual examples. However, we do introduce one slightly more complicated scenario where the examples for learning contain multiple instances.

Each instance is characterized by the values of attributes that measure different aspects of the instance. There are many different types of attributes, although typical data mining schemes deal only with numeric and *nominal*, or categorical, ones.

Finally, we examine the question of preparing input for data mining and introduce a simple format—the one that is used by the Weka system that accompanies this book—for representing the input information as a text file.

2.1 WHAT'S A CONCEPT?

Four basically different styles of learning appear in data mining applications. In *classification learning*, the learning scheme is presented with a set of classified examples from which it is expected to learn a way of classifying unseen examples. In *association learning*, any association among features is sought, not just ones that predict a particular *class* value. In *clustering*, groups of examples that belong together are sought. In *numeric prediction*, the outcome to be predicted is not a discrete class but a numeric quantity. Regardless of the type of learning involved, we call the thing to be learned the *concept* and the output produced by a learning scheme the *concept description*.

Most of the examples in Chapter 1 are classification problems. The weather data (Tables 1.2 and 1.3) presents a set of days together with a decision for each as to whether to play the game or not. The problem is to learn how to classify new days as play or don't play. Given the contact lens data (Table 1.1), the problem is to learn how to determine a lens recommendation for a new patient—or more precisely, since every possible combination of attributes is present in the data, the problem is to learn a way of summarizing the given data. For the irises (Table 1.4), the problem is to learn how to determine whether a new iris flower is *setosa*, *versicolor*, or *virginica*, given its sepal length and width and petal length and width. For the labor negotiations data (Table 1.6), the problem is to determine whether a new contract is acceptable or not, on the basis of its duration; wage increase in the first, second, and third years; cost of living adjustment; and so forth.

We assume throughout this book that each example belongs to one, and only one, class. However, there exist classification scenarios in which individual examples may belong to multiple classes. In technical jargon, these are called *multilabeled instances*. One simple way to deal with such situations is to treat them as several different classification problems, one for each possible class, where the problem is to determine whether instances belong to that class or not.

Classification learning is sometimes called *supervised*, because, in a sense, the scheme operates under supervision by being provided with the actual outcome for each of the training examples—the play or don't play judgment, the lens recommendation, the type of iris, the acceptability of the labor contract. This outcome is called the *class* of the example. The success of classification learning can be judged by trying out the concept description that is learned on an independent set of test data for which the true classifications are known but not made available to the machine. The success rate on test data gives an objective measure of how well the concept has been learned. In many practical data mining applications, success is measured more subjectively in terms of how acceptable the learned description—such as the rules or decision tree—is to a human user.

Most of the examples in Chapter 1 can be used equally well for association learning, in which there is no specified class. Here, the problem is to discover any structure in the data that is "interesting." Some association rules for the weather data were given in Section 1.2. Association rules differ from classification rules in two ways: They can "predict" any attribute, not just the class, and they can predict more than one attribute's value at a time. Because of this there are far more association rules than classification rules, and the challenge is to avoid being swamped by them. For this reason, association rules are often limited to those that apply to a certain minimum number of examples—say 80% of the dataset—and have greater than a certain minimum accuracy level—say 95% accurate. Even then, there are usually lots of them, and they have to be examined manually to determine whether they are meaningful or not. Association rules usually involve only nonnumeric attributes; thus, you wouldn't normally look for association rules in the iris dataset.

When there is no specified class, clustering is used to group items that seem to fall naturally together. Imagine a version of the iris data in which the type of iris is omitted, such as in Table 2.1. Then it is likely that the 150 instances fall into natural clusters corresponding to the three iris types. The challenge is to find these clusters and assign the instances to them—and to be able to assign new instances to the clusters as well. It may be that one or more of the iris types splits naturally into subtypes, in which case the data will exhibit more than three natural clusters. The success of clustering is often measured subjectively in terms of how useful the result appears to be to a human user. It may be followed by a second step of classification learning in which rules are learned that give an intelligible description of how new instances should be placed into the clusters.

Table 2.1 Iris Data as a Clustering Problem

	Sepal Length	Sepal Width	Petal Length	Petal Width
1	5.1	3.5	1.4	0.2
2	4.9	3.0	1.4	0.2
3	4.7	3.2	1.3	0.2
4	4.6	3.1	1.5	0.2
5	5.0	3.6	1.4	0.2
...				
51	7.0	3.2	4.7	1.4
52	6.4	3.2	4.5	1.5
53	6.9	3.1	4.9	1.5
54	5.5	2.3	4.0	1.3
55	6.5	2.8	4.6	1.5
...				
101	6.3	3.3	6.0	2.5
102	5.8	2.7	5.1	1.9
103	7.1	3.0	5.9	2.1
104	6.3	2.9	5.6	1.8
105	6.5	3.0	5.8	2.2
...				

Table 2.2 Weather Data with a Numeric Class

Outlook	Temperature	Humidity	Windy	Play Time
Sunny	85	85	false	5
Sunny	80	90	true	0
Overcast	83	86	false	55
Rainy	70	96	false	40
Rainy	68	80	false	65
Rainy	65	70	true	45
Overcast	64	65	true	60
Sunny	72	95	false	0
Sunny	69	70	false	70
Rainy	75	80	false	45
Sunny	75	70	true	50
Overcast	72	90	true	55
Overcast	81	75	false	75
Rainy	71	91	true	10

Numeric prediction is a variant of classification learning in which the outcome is a numeric value rather than a category. The CPU performance problem is one example. Another, shown in Table 2.2, is a version of the weather data in which what is to be predicted is not play or don't play but rather the time (in minutes) to play. With numeric prediction problems, as with other machine learning situations, the predicted value for new instances is often of less interest than the structure of the description that is learned, expressed in terms of what the important attributes are and how they relate to the numeric outcome.

2.2 WHAT'S IN AN EXAMPLE?

The input to a machine learning scheme is a set of instances. These instances are the things that are to be classified or associated or clustered. Although until now we have called them *examples*, henceforth we will generally use the more specific term *instances* to refer to the input. In the standard scenario, each instance is an individual, independent example of the concept to be learned. Instances are characterized by the values of a set of predetermined attributes. This was the case in all of the sample datasets described in Chapter 1 (i.e., the weather, the contact lens, the iris, and the labor negotiations problems). Each dataset is represented as a matrix of instances versus attributes, which in database terms is a single relation, or a *flat file*.

Expressing the input data as a set of independent instances is by far the most common situation for practical data mining. However, it is a rather restrictive way of formulating problems, and it is worth spending some time reviewing why. Problems often involve relationships between objects rather than separate, independent instances. Suppose, to take a specific situation, a family tree is given and we want to learn the concept of *sister*. Imagine your own family tree, with your relatives (and their genders) placed at the nodes. This tree is the input to the learning process, along with a list of pairs of people and an indication of whether they are sisters or not.

Relations

Figure 2.1 shows part of a family tree, below which are two tables that each define sisterhood in a slightly different way. A *yes* in the third column of the individual tables means that the person in the second column is a sister of the person in the first column (that's just an arbitrary decision we've made in setting up this example).

The first thing to notice is that there are a lot of *nos* in the third column of the table on the left, because there are 12 people and $12 \times 12 = 144$ pairs of people in all, and most pairs of people aren't sisters. The table on the right, which gives the same information, records only the positive examples and assumes that all others are negative. The idea of specifying only positive examples and adopting a standing assumption that the rest are negative is called the *closed-world assumption*. It is frequently assumed in theoretical studies; however, it is not of much practical use in real-life problems because they rarely involve "closed" worlds in which you can be certain that all cases are covered.

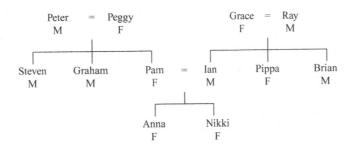

First person	Second person	Sister of?
Peter	Peggy	no
Peter	Steven	no
...	...	...
Steven	Peter	no
Steven	Graham	no
Steven	Pam	yes
Steven	Grace	no
...	...	...
Ian	Pippa	yes
...	...	...
Anna	Nikki	yes
...	...	...
Nikki	Anna	yes

First person	Second person	Sister of?
Steven	Pam	yes
Graham	Pam	yes
Ian	Pippa	yes
Brian	Pippa	yes
Anna	Nikki	yes
Nikki	Anna	yes
all the rest		no

FIGURE 2.1

A family tree and two ways of expressing the sister-of relation.

Table 2.3 Family Tree

Name	Gender	Parent 1	Parent 2
Peter	male	?	?
Peggy	female	?	?
Steven	male	Peter	Peggy
Graham	male	Peter	Peggy
Pam	female	Peter	Peggy
Ian	male	Grace	Ray
...			

Neither table in Figure 2.1 is of any use without the family tree itself. This tree can also be expressed in the form of a table, part of which is shown in Table 2.3. Now the problem is expressed in terms of two relationships, Parent 1 and Parent 2. But these tables do not contain independent sets of instances because values in the Name, Parent 1, and Parent 2 columns of the sister-of relation refer to rows of the family tree relation. We can make them into a single set of instances by collapsing the two tables into a single one, as shown in Table 2.4.

We have at last succeeded in transforming the original relational problem into the form of instances, each of which is an individual, independent example of the concept that is to be learned. Of course, the instances are not really independent—there are plenty of relationships among different rows of the table!—but they are independent as far as the concept of sisterhood is concerned. Most machine learning schemes will still have trouble dealing with this kind of data, as we will see in Section 3.4, but at least the problem has been recast into the right form. A simple rule for the sister-of relation is

```
If second person's gender = female
   and first person's parent 1 = second person's parent 1
   then sister-of = yes
```

This example shows how you can take a relationship between different nodes of a tree and recast it into a set of independent instances. In database terms, you take two relations and join them together to make one, a process of flattening that is technically called *denormalization*. It is always possible to do this with any (finite) set of (finite) relations.

The structure of Table 2.4 can be used to describe any relationship between two people—grandparenthood, second cousins twice removed, and so on. Relationships among more people would require a larger table. Relationships in which the maximum number of people is not specified in advance pose a more serious problem. If we want to learn the concept of *nuclear family* (parents and their children), the number of people involved depends on the size of the largest nuclear family, and although we could guess at a reasonable maximum (10?, 20?), the actual number can only be found by scanning the tree itself. Nevertheless, given a finite set of finite

Table 2.4 Sister-of Relation

First Person				Second Person				Sister of?
Name	Gender	Parent 1	Parent 2	Name	Gender	Parent 1	Parent 2	
Steven	male	Peter	Peggy	Pam	female	Peter	Peggy	yes
Graham	male	Peter	Peggy	Pam	female	Peter	Peggy	yes
Ian	male	Grace	Ray	Pippa	female	Grace	Ray	yes
Brian	male	Grace	Ray	Pippa	female	Grace	Ray	yes
Anna	female	Pam	Ian	Nikki	female	Pam	Ian	yes
Nikki	female	Pam	Ian	Anna	female	Pam	Ian	yes
All the rest								no

relations we could, at least in principle, form a new "superrelation" that contains one row for *every* combination of people, and this would be enough to express any relationship between people no matter how many were involved. The computational and storage costs would, however, be prohibitive.

Another problem with denormalization is that it produces apparent regularities in the data that are completely spurious and are in fact merely reflections of the original database structure. For example, imagine a supermarket database with a relation for customers and the products they buy, one for products and their suppliers, and one for suppliers and their addresses. Denormalizing this will produce a flat file that contains, for each instance, customer, product, supplier, and supplier address. A data mining tool that seeks structure in the database may come up with the fact that customers who buy beer also buy chips, a discovery that could be significant from the supermarket manager's point of view. However, it may also come up with the fact that the supplier address can be predicted exactly from the supplier—a "discovery" that will not impress the supermarket manager at all. This fact masquerades as a significant discovery from the flat file but is present explicitly in the original database structure.

Many abstract computational problems involve relations that are not finite, although clearly any actual set of input examples must be finite. Concepts such as *ancestor-of* involve arbitrarily long paths through a tree, and although the human race, and hence its family tree, may be finite (although prodigiously large), many artificial problems generate data that truly is infinite. Although it may sound abstruse, this situation is the norm in areas such as list processing and logic programming, and it is addressed in a subdiscipline of machine learning called *inductive logic programming*. Computer scientists usually use recursion to deal with situations in which the number of possible examples is infinite. For example,

```
If person 1 is a parent of person 2
   then person 1 is an ancestor of person 2
If person 1 is a parent of person 2
   and person 2 is an ancestor of person 3
   then person 1 is an ancestor of person 3
```

This represents a simple recursive definition of *ancestor* that works no matter how distantly two people are related. Techniques of inductive logic programming can learn recursive rules such as these from a finite set of instances such as those in Table 2.5.

The real drawbacks of such techniques, however, are that they do not cope well with noisy data, and they tend to be so slow as to be unusable on anything but small artificial datasets. They are not covered in this book; see Bergadano and Gunetti (1996) for a comprehensive treatment.

Other Example Types

As we have seen, general relations present substantial challenges, and this book will deal with them no further. Structured examples such as graphs and trees can be

Table 2.5 Another Relation

First Person				Second Person				Ancestor of?
Name	Gender	Parent 1	Parent 2	Name	Gender	Parent 1	Parent 2	
Peter	male	?	?	Steven	male	Peter	Peggy	yes
Peter	male	?	?	Pam	female	Peter	Peggy	yes
Peter	male	?	?	Anna	female	Pam	Ian	yes
Peter	male	?	?	Nikki	female	Pam	Ian	yes
Pam	female	Peter	Peggy	Nikki	female	Pam	Ian	yes
Grace	female	?	?	Ian	male	Grace	Ray	yes
Grace	female	?	?	Nikki	female	Pam	Ian	yes
Other examples here								yes
All the rest								no

47

viewed as special cases of relations that are often mapped into independent instances by extracting local or global features based on their structure and representing them as attributes. Similarly, sequences of items may be treated by describing them, or their individual items, in terms of a fixed set of properties represented by attributes. Fortunately, most practical data mining problems can be expressed quite effectively as a set of instances, each one being an example of the concept to be learned.

In some situations, instead of the individual instances being examples of the concept, each individual example comprises a set of instances that are described by the same attributes. This multi-instance setting covers some important real-world applications. One concerns the inference of characteristics of active drug molecules, where *activity* corresponds to how well a drug molecule bonds to a "bonding site" on a target molecule. The problem is that the drug molecule can assume alternative shapes by rotating its bonds. It is classed as positive if just one of these shapes actually binds to the site and has the desired effect—but it is not known which shape it is. On the other hand, a drug molecule is negative if none of the shapes bind successfully. In this case, a multiple instance is a set of shapes, and the entire set is classified as positive or negative.

Multi-instance problems often also arise naturally when relations from a database are joined—that is, when several rows from a secondary relation are associated with the same row in the target relation. For example, we may want to classify computer users as experts or novices based on descriptions of user sessions that are stored in a secondary table. The target relation just has the classification and the user ID. Joining the two tables creates a flat file. However, the rows pertaining to an individual user are not independent. Classification is performed on a per-user basis, so the set of session instances associated with the same user should be viewed as a single example for learning.

The goal of multi-instance learning is still to produce a concept description, but now the task is more difficult because the learning algorithm has to contend with incomplete information about each training example. Rather than seeing each example in terms of a single definitive attribute vector, the learning algorithm sees each example as a set of attribute vectors. Things would be easy if only the algorithm knew which member of the set was responsible for the example's classification—but it does not.

Several special learning algorithms have been developed to tackle the multi-instance problem; we describe some of them in Chapter 6. It is also possible to apply standard machine learning schemes by recasting the problem as a single table comprising independent instances. Chapter 4 gives some ways of achieving this.

In summary, the input to a data mining scheme is generally expressed as a table of independent instances of the concept to be learned. Because of this it has been suggested, disparagingly, that we should really talk of *file mining* rather than *database mining*. Relational data is more complex than a flat file. A finite set of finite relations can always be recast into a single table, although often at enormous cost in space. Moreover, denormalization can generate spurious regularities in the data, and it is essential to check the data for such artifacts before applying a learning scheme. Potentially infinite concepts can be dealt with by learning rules that are recursive, although that is beyond the scope of this book. Finally, some important real-world problems are most naturally expressed in a multi-instance format, where each example is actually a separate set of instances.

2.3 WHAT'S IN AN ATTRIBUTE?

Each instance that provides the input to machine learning is characterized by its values on a fixed, predefined set of features or *attributes*. The instances are the rows of the tables that we have shown for the weather, the contact lens, the iris, and the CPU performance problems, and the attributes are the columns. (The labor negotiations data was an exception: We presented this with instances in columns and attributes in rows for space reasons.)

The use of a fixed set of features imposes another restriction on the kinds of problems generally considered in practical data mining. What if different instances have different features? If the instances were transportation vehicles, then *number of wheels* is a feature that applies to many vehicles but not to ships, for example, whereas *number of masts* might be a feature that applies to ships but not to land vehicles. The standard workaround is to make each possible feature an attribute and to use a special "irrelevant value" flag to indicate that a particular attribute is not available for a particular case. A similar situation arises when the existence of one feature (say, spouse's name) depends on the value of another (married or single).

The value of an attribute for a particular instance is a measurement of the quantity to which the attribute refers. There is a broad distinction between quantities that are *numeric* and ones that are *nominal*. Numeric attributes, sometimes called *continuous* attributes, measure numbers—either real or integer valued. Note that the term *continuous* is routinely abused in this context; integer-valued attributes are certainly not continuous in the mathematical sense. Nominal attributes take on values in a pre-specified, finite set of possibilities and are sometimes called *categorical*. But there are other possibilities. Statistics texts often introduce "levels of measurement" such as *nominal*, *ordinal*, *interval*, and *ratio*.

Nominal quantities have values that are distinct symbols. The values themselves serve just as labels or names—hence the term *nominal*, which comes from the Latin word for *name*. For example, in the weather data the attribute *outlook* has the values *sunny*, *overcast*, and *rainy*. No relation is implied among these three—no ordering or distance measure. It certainly does not make sense to add the values together, multiply them, or even compare their size. A rule using such an attribute can only test for equality or inequality, as in

```
outlook: sunny      → no
         overcast   → yes
         rainy      → yes
```

Ordinal quantities are ones that make it possible to rank-order the categories. However, although there is a notion of *ordering*, there is no notion of *distance*. For example, in the weather data the attribute *temperature* has values *hot*, *mild*, and *cool*. These are ordered. Whether you say that

$$hot > mild > cool \text{ or } hot < mild < cool$$

is a matter of convention—it does not matter which is used as long as consistency is maintained. What is important is that *mild* lies between the other two. Although it makes sense to compare two values, it does not make sense to add or subtract them— the difference between *hot* and *mild* cannot be compared with the difference between *mild* and *cool*. A rule using such an attribute might involve a comparison, as in

```
temperature = hot → no
temperature < hot → yes
```

Notice that the distinction between nominal and ordinal quantities is not always straightforward and obvious. Indeed, the very example of a nominal quantity that we used before, *outlook*, is not completely clear: You might argue that the three values *do* have an ordering—*overcast* being somehow intermediate between *sunny* and *rainy* as weather turns from good to bad.

Interval quantities have values that are not only ordered but measured in fixed and equal units. A good example is temperature, expressed in degrees (say, degrees Fahrenheit) rather than on the nonnumeric scale implied by cool, mild, and hot. It makes perfect sense to talk about the difference between two temperatures, say 46 and 48 degrees, and compare that with the difference between another two temperatures, say 22 and 24 degrees. Another example is dates. You can talk about the difference between the years 1939 and 1945 (six years) or even the average of the years 1939 and 1945 (1942), but it doesn't make much sense to consider the sum of the years 1939 and 1945 (3884) or three times the year 1939 (5817) because the starting point, year 0, is completely arbitrary—indeed, it has changed many times throughout the course of history. (Children sometimes wonder what the year 300 BCE was called in 300 BCE.)

Ratio quantities are ones for which the measurement scheme inherently defines a zero point. For example, when measuring the distance from one object to another, the distance between the object and itself forms a natural zero. Ratio quantities are treated as real numbers: Any mathematical operations are allowed. It certainly does make sense to talk about three times the distance and even to multiply one distance by another to get an area.

However, the question of whether there is an "inherently" defined zero point depends on what our scientific knowledge is—it's culture relative. For example, Daniel Fahrenheit knew no lower limit to temperature, and his scale is an interval one. Nowadays, however, we view temperature as a ratio scale based on absolute zero. Measurement of time in years since some culturally defined zero, such as AD 0, is not a ratio scale; years since the Big Bang are. Even the zero point of money—where we are usually quite happy to say that something cost twice as much as something else—may not be quite clearly defined for those who constantly max out their credit cards.

Many practical data mining systems accommodate just two of these four levels of measurement: nominal and ordinal. Nominal attributes are sometimes called *categorical, enumerated,* or *discrete. Enumerated* is the standard term used in computer science to denote a categorical data type; however, the strict definition of the term—namely, to put into one-to-one correspondence with the natural numbers—implies an ordering, which is specifically not implied in the machine learning context. *Discrete* also has connotations of ordering because you often discretize a continuous numeric quantity. Ordinal attributes are often coded as *numeric* data, or perhaps *continuous* data, but without the implication of mathematical continuity. A special case of the nominal scale is the *dichotomy*, which has only two members—often designated as *true* and *false* or *yes* and *no* in the weather data. Such attributes are sometimes called *Boolean*.

Machine learning systems can use a wide variety of other information about attributes. For instance, dimensional considerations could be used to restrict the search to expressions or comparisons that are dimensionally correct. Circular ordering could affect the kinds of tests that are considered. For example, in a temporal context, tests on a *day* attribute could involve next day, previous day, next weekday, or same day next week. Partial orderings—that is, generalization or specialization relations—frequently occur in practical situations. Information of this kind is often referred to as *metadata*, data about data. However, the kinds of practical schemes used for data mining are rarely capable of taking metadata into account, although it is likely that these capabilities will develop in the future.

2.4 PREPARING THE INPUT

Preparing input for a data mining investigation usually consumes the bulk of the effort invested in the entire data mining process. While this book is not really about the problems of data preparation, we want to give you a feeling for the issues involved so that you can appreciate the complexities. Following that, we look at a particular input file format, the attribute-relation file format (ARFF), that is used in the Weka system described in Part III. Then we consider issues that arise when converting datasets to such a format, because there are some simple practical points to be aware of. Bitter experience shows that real data is often disappointingly low in quality, and careful checking—a process that has become known as *data cleaning*—pays off many times over.

Gathering the Data Together

When beginning work on a data mining problem, it is first necessary to bring all the data together into a set of instances. We explained the need to denormalize relational data when describing the family tree example. Although it illustrates the basic issue, this self-contained and rather artificial example does not really convey a feeling for what the process will be like in practice. In a real business application, it will be necessary to bring data together from different departments. For example, in a marketing study data will be needed from the sales department, the customer billing department, and the customer service department.

Integrating data from different sources usually presents many challenges—not deep issues of principle but nasty realities of practice. Different departments will use different styles of recordkeeping, different conventions, different time periods, different degrees of data aggregation, and different primary keys, and will have different kinds of error. The data must be assembled, integrated, and cleaned up. The idea of companywide database integration is known as *data warehousing*. Data warehouses provide a single consistent point of access to corporate or organizational data, transcending departmental divisions. They are the place where old data is published in a way that can be used to inform business decisions. The movement toward data warehousing is a recognition of the fact that the fragmented information that an organization uses to support day-to-day operations at a departmental level can have immense strategic value when brought together. Clearly, the presence of a data warehouse is a very useful precursor to data mining, and if it is not available, many of the steps involved in data warehousing will have to be undertaken to prepare the data for mining.

Even a data warehouse may not contain all the necessary data, and you may have to reach outside the organization to bring in data relevant to the problem at hand. For example, weather data had to be obtained in the load forecasting example in Chapter 1, and demographic data is needed for marketing and sales applications. Sometimes called *overlay data*, this is not normally collected by an organization but is clearly relevant to the data mining problem. It, too, must be cleaned up and integrated with the other data that has been collected.

Another practical question when assembling the data is the degree of aggregation that is appropriate. When a dairy farmer decides which cows to sell off, the milk production records, which an automatic milking machine records twice a day, must be aggregated. Similarly, raw telephone call data is not much use when telecommunications firms study their clients' behavior—the data must be aggregated to the customer level. But do you want usage by month or by quarter, and for how many months or quarters back? Selecting the right type and level of aggregation is usually critical for success.

Because so many different issues are involved, you can't expect to get it right the first time. This is why data assembly, integration, cleaning, aggregating, and general preparation take so long.

ARFF Format

We now look at a standard way of representing datasets, called an *ARFF file*. We describe the regular version, but there is also a version called XRFF, which, as the name suggests, gives ARFF header and instance information in the eXstensible Markup Language (XML).

Figure 2.2 shows an ARFF file for the weather data in Table 1.3, the version with some numeric features. Lines beginning with a % sign are comments. Following the comments at the beginning of the file are the name of the relation (*weather*) and a block defining the attributes (*outlook*, *temperature*, *humidity*, *windy*, *play?*). Nominal attributes are followed by the set of values they can take on, enclosed in curly braces. Values can include spaces; if so, they must be placed within quotation marks. Numeric values are followed by the keyword *numeric*.

Although the weather problem is to predict the class value *play?* from the values of the other attributes, the class attribute is not distinguished in any way in the data file. The ARFF format merely gives a dataset; it does not specify which of the attributes is the one that is supposed to be predicted. This means that the same file can be used for investigating how well each attribute can be predicted from the others, or it can be used to find association rules or for clustering.

```
% ARFF file for the weather data with some numeric features
%
@relation weather

@attribute outlook { sunny, overcast, rainy }
@attribute temperature numeric
@attribute humidity numeric
@attribute windy { true, false }
@attribute play? { yes, no }

@data
%
% 14 instances
%
sunny, 85, 85, false, no
sunny, 80, 90, true, no
overcast, 83, 86, false, yes
rainy, 70, 96, false, yes
rainy, 68, 80, false, yes
rainy, 65, 70, true, no
overcast, 64, 65, true, yes
sunny, 72, 95, false, no
sunny, 69, 70, false, yes
rainy, 75, 80, false, yes
sunny, 75, 70, true, yes
overcast, 72, 90, true, yes
overcast, 81, 75, false, yes
rainy, 71, 91, true, no
```

FIGURE 2.2

ARFF file for the weather data.

Following the attribute definitions is an @*data* line that signals the start of the instances in the dataset. Instances are written one per line, with values for each attribute in turn, separated by commas. If a value is missing, it is represented by a single question mark (there are no missing values in this dataset). The attribute specifications in ARFF files allow the dataset to be checked to ensure that it contains legal values for all attributes, and programs that read ARFF files do this checking automatically.

As well as nominal and numeric attributes, exemplified by the weather data, the ARFF format has three further attribute types: string attributes, date attributes, and relation-valued attributes. String attributes have values that are textual. Suppose you have a string attribute that you want to call *description*. In the block defining the attributes it is specified like this:

```
@attribute description string
```

Then, in the instance data, include any character string in quotation marks (to include quotation marks in your string, use the standard convention of preceding each one by a backslash, \). Strings are stored internally in a string table and represented by their address in that table. Thus, two strings that contain the same characters will have the same value.

String attributes can have values that are very long—even a whole document. To be able to use string attributes for text mining, it is necessary to be able to manipulate them. For example, a string attribute might be converted into many numeric attributes, one for each word in the string, whose value is the number of times that word appears. These transformations are described in Section 7.3.

Date attributes are strings with a special format and are introduced like this (for an attribute called *today*):

```
@attribute today date
```

Weka uses the ISO-8601 combined date and time format *yyyy-MM-dd'T'HH:mm:ss* with four digits for the year, two each for the month and day, then the letter *T* followed by the time with two digits for each of hours, minutes, and seconds.[1] In the data section of the file, dates are specified as the corresponding string representation of the date and time—for example, 2004-04-03T12:00:00. Although they are specified as strings, dates are converted to numeric form when the input file is read. Dates can also be converted internally to different formats, so you can have absolute timestamps in the data file and use transformations to forms such as time of day or day of the week to detect periodic behavior.

Relation-valued attributes differ from the other types because they allow multi-instance problems to be represented in ARFF format. The value of a relation attribute is a separate set of instances. The attribute is defined with a name and the type

---

[1]Weka contains a mechanism for defining a date attribute to have a different format by including a special string in the attribute definition.

relational, followed by a nested attribute block that gives the structure of the referenced instances. For example, a relation-valued attribute called *bag*, with a value that is a dataset that has the same structure as the weather data but without the *play* attribute, can be specified like this:

```
@attribute bag relational
    @attribute outlook { sunny, overcast, rainy }
    @attribute temperature numeric
    @attribute humidity numeric
    @attribute windy { true, false }
@end bag
```

The *@end bag* indicates the end of the nested attribute block. Figure 2.3 shows an ARFF file for a multi-instance problem based on the weather data. In this case, each example is made up of an identifier value, two consecutive instances from the original weather data, and a class label.

Each value of the attribute is a string that encapsulates two weather instances separated by the \n character (which represents an embedded new line). This might be appropriate for a game that lasts two days. A similar dataset might be used for games that last for an indeterminate number of days (e.g., first-class cricket takes three to five days). Note, however, that in multi-instance learning the *order* in which

```
% Multiple instance ARFF file for the weather data
%
@relation weather

@attribute bag_ID { 1, 2, 3, 4, 5, 6, 7 }
@attribute bag relational
    @attribute outlook { sunny, overcast, rainy }
    @attribute temperature numeric
    @attribute humidity numeric
    @attribute windy { true, false }
@end bag
@attribute play? { yes, no }

@data
%
% seven "multiple instance" instances
%
1, "sunny, 85, 85, false\nsunny, 80, 90, true", no
2, "overcast, 83, 86, false\nrainy, 70, 96, false", yes
3, "rainy, 68, 80, false\nrainy, 65, 70, true", yes
4, "overcast, 64, 65, true\nsunny, 72, 95, false", yes
5, "sunny, 69, 70, false\nrainy, 75, 80, false", yes
6, "sunny, 75, 70, true\novercast, 72, 90, true", yes
7, "overcast, 81, 75, false\nrainy, 71, 91, true", yes
```

FIGURE 2.3

Multi-instance ARFF file for the weather data.

the instances are given is generally considered unimportant. An algorithm might learn that cricket can be played if none of the days are rainy and at least one is sunny, but not that it can only be played in a certain sequence of weather events.

Sparse Data

Sometimes most attributes have a value of 0 for most of the instances. For example, market basket data records purchases made by supermarket customers. No matter how big the shopping expedition, customers never purchase more than a tiny portion of the items a store offers. The market basket data contains the quantity of each item that the customer purchases, and this is zero for almost all items in stock. The data file can be viewed as a matrix, whose rows and columns represent customers and stock items, and the matrix is "sparse"—nearly all its elements are zero. Another example occurs in text mining, where the instances are documents. Here, the columns and rows represent documents and words, and the numbers indicate how many times a particular word appears in a particular document. Most documents have a rather small vocabulary, so most entries are zero.

It can be impractical to represent each element of a sparse matrix explicitly. Instead of representing each value in order, like this:

```
0, X, 0, 0, 0, 0, Y, 0, 0, 0, "class A"
0, 0, 0, W, 0, 0, 0, 0, 0, 0, "class B"
```

the nonzero attributes can be explicitly identified by the attribute number and their value stated:

```
{1 X, 6 Y, 10 "class A"}
{3 W, 10 "class B"}
```

Each instance is enclosed in braces and contains the index number of each nonzero attribute (indexes start from 0) and its value. Sparse data files have the same *@relation* and *@attribute* tags, followed by an *@data* line, but the data section is different and contains specifications in braces such as those shown previously. Note that the omitted values have a value of 0—they are not "missing" values! If a value is unknown, it must be explicitly represented with a question mark.

Attribute Types

The ARFF format accommodates the two basic data types, nominal and numeric. String attributes and date attributes are effectively nominal and numeric, respectively, although before they are used, strings are often converted into a numeric form such as a word vector. Relation-valued attributes contain separate sets of instances that have basic attributes, such as numeric and nominal ones. How the two basic types are interpreted depends on the learning scheme being used. For example, many schemes treat numeric attributes as ordinal scales and only use less-than and greater-than comparisons between the values. However, some treat them as ratio scales and use distance calculations. You need to understand how machine learning schemes work before using them for data mining.

If a learning scheme treats numeric attributes as though they are measured on ratio scales, the question of normalization arises. Attributes are often normalized to lie in a fixed range—usually from 0 to 1—by dividing all of the values by the maximum value encountered or by subtracting the minimum value and dividing by the range between the maximum and minimum values. Another normalization technique is to calculate the statistical mean and the standard deviation of the attribute values, then subtract the mean from each value and divide the result by the standard deviation. This process is called *standardizing* a statistical variable and results in a set of values whose mean is 0 and the standard deviation is 1.

Some learning schemes—for example, instance-based and regression methods—deal only with ratio scales because they calculate the "distance" between two instances based on the values of their attributes. If the actual scale is ordinal, a numeric distance function must be defined. One way of doing this is to use a two-level distance: 1 if the two values are different and 0 if they are the same. Any nominal quantity can be treated as numeric by using this distance function. However, it is a rather crude technique and conceals the true degree of variation between instances. Another possibility is to generate several synthetic binary attributes for each nominal attribute: We return to this in Section 6.6 when we look at the use of trees for numeric prediction.

Sometimes there is a genuine mapping between nominal quantities and numeric scales. For example, postal zip codes indicate areas that could be represented by geographical coordinates; the leading digits of telephone numbers may do so too, depending on where you live. The first two digits of a student's identification number may be the year in which she first enrolled.

It is very common for practical datasets to contain nominal values that are coded as integers. For example, an integer identifier may be used as a code for an attribute such as *part number*, yet such integers are not intended for use in less-than or greater-than comparisons. If this is the case, it is important to specify that the attribute is nominal rather than numeric.

It is quite possible to treat an ordinal quantity as though it were nominal. Indeed, some machine learning schemes only deal with nominal elements. For example, in the contact lens problem the age attribute is treated as nominal, and the rules generated included these:

```
If age = young and astigmatic = no
   and tear production rate = normal
   then recommendation = soft
If age = pre-presbyopic and astigmatic = no
   and tear production rate = normal
   then recommendation = soft
```

But in fact age, specified in this way, is really an ordinal quantity for which the following is true:

```
young < pre-presbyopic < presbyopic
```

If it were treated as ordinal, the two rules could be collapsed into one:

```
If age ≤ pre-presbyopic and astigmatic = no
   and tear production rate = normal
   then recommendation = soft
```

which is a more compact, and hence more satisfactory, way of saying the same thing.

Missing Values

Most datasets encountered in practice, such as the labor negotiations data in Table 1.6, contain missing values. Missing values are frequently indicated by out-of-range entries; perhaps a negative number (e.g., −1) in a numeric field that is normally only positive, or a 0 in a numeric field that can never normally be 0. For nominal attributes, missing values may be indicated by blanks or dashes. Sometimes different kinds of missing values are distinguished (e.g., unknown versus unrecorded versus irrelevant values) and perhaps represented by different negative integers (e.g., −1, −2, etc.).

You have to think carefully about the significance of missing values. They may occur for a number of reasons, such as malfunctioning measurement equipment, changes in experimental design during data collection, and collation of several similar but not identical datasets. Respondents in a survey may refuse to answer certain questions such as age or income. In an archaeological study, a specimen such as a skull may be damaged so that some variables cannot be measured. In a biological study, plants or animals may die before all variables have been measured. What do these things *mean* about the example under consideration? Might the skull damage have some significance in itself, or is it just because of some random event? Does a plant's early death have some bearing on the case or not?

Most machine learning schemes make the implicit assumption that there is no particular significance in the fact that a certain instance has an attribute value missing: The value is simply not known. However, there may be a good reason why the attribute's value is unknown—perhaps a decision was taken, on the evidence available, not to perform some particular test—and that might convey some information about the instance other than the fact that the value is simply missing. If this is the case, then it would be more appropriate to record *not tested* as another possible value for this attribute or perhaps as another attribute in the dataset. As the preceding examples illustrate, only someone familiar with the data can make an informed judgment about whether a particular value being missing has some extra significance or whether it should simply be coded as an ordinary missing value. Of course, if there seem to be several types of missing values, that is prima facie evidence that something is going on that needs to be investigated.

If missing values mean that an operator has decided not to make a particular measurement, that may convey a great deal more than the mere fact that the value is unknown. For example, people analyzing medical databases have noticed that cases may, in some circumstances, be diagnosable simply from the tests that a doctor decides to make regardless of the outcome of the tests. Then a record of which values are "missing" is all that is needed for a complete diagnosis—the actual values can be ignored completely!

Inaccurate Values

It is important to check data mining files carefully for rogue attributes and attribute values. The data used for mining has almost certainly not been gathered expressly for that purpose. When originally collected, many of the fields probably didn't matter and were left blank or unchecked. Provided it does not affect the original purpose of the data, there is no incentive to correct this situation. However, when the same database is used for mining, the errors and omissions suddenly start to assume great significance. For example, banks do not really need to know the age of their customers, so their databases may contain many missing or incorrect values. But age may be a very significant feature in mined rules.

Typographic errors in a dataset will obviously lead to incorrect values. Often the value of a nominal attribute is misspelled, creating an extra possible value for that attribute. Or perhaps it is not a misspelling but different names for the same thing, such as Pepsi and Pepsi-Cola. Obviously, the point of a defined format such as ARFF is to allow data files to be checked for internal consistency. However, errors that occur in the original data file are often preserved through the conversion process into the file that is used for data mining; thus, the list of possible values that each attribute takes on should be examined carefully.

Typographical or measurement errors in numeric values generally cause outliers that can be detected by graphing one variable at a time. Erroneous values often deviate significantly from the pattern that is apparent in the remaining values. Sometimes, however, inaccurate values are hard to find, particularly without specialist domain knowledge.

Duplicate data presents another source of error. Most machine learning tools will produce different results if some of the instances in the data files are duplicated, because repetition gives them more influence on the result.

People often make deliberate errors when entering personal data into databases. They might make minor changes in the spelling of their street to try to identify whether the information they have provided ends up being sold to advertising agencies that burden them with junk mail. They might adjust the spelling of their name when applying for insurance if they have had insurance refused in the past. Rigid computerized data entry systems often impose restrictions that require imaginative workarounds. One story tells of a foreigner renting a vehicle in the United States. Being from abroad, he had no zip code, yet the computer insisted on one; in desperation the operator suggested that he use the zip code of the rental agency. If this is common practice, future data mining projects may notice a cluster of customers who apparently live in the same district as the agency!

Similarly, a supermarket checkout operator sometimes uses his own frequent buyer card when the customer does not supply one, either so that the customer can get a discount that would otherwise be unavailable or simply to accumulate credit points in the cashier's account. Only a deep semantic knowledge of what is going on will be able to explain systematic data errors like these.

Finally, data goes stale. Many items in a database change as circumstances change. For example, items in mailing lists (e.g., names, addresses, telephone numbers, etc.) change frequently. You need to consider whether the data you are mining is still current.

Getting to Know Your Data

There is no substitute for getting to know your data. Simple tools that show histograms of the distribution of values of nominal attributes, and graphs of the values of numeric attributes (perhaps sorted or simply graphed against instance number), are very helpful. These graphical visualizations of the data make it easy to identify outliers, which may well represent errors in the data file, or arcane conventions for coding unusual situations, such as a missing year as 9999 or a missing weight as −1 kg, that no one has thought to tell you about. Domain experts need to be consulted to explain anomalies, missing values, the significance of integers that represent categories rather than numeric quantities, and so on. Pairwise plots of one attribute against another, or each attribute against the class value, can be extremely revealing.

Data cleaning is a time-consuming and labor-intensive procedure, but one that is absolutely necessary for successful data mining. With a large dataset, people often give up—how can they possibly check it all? Instead, you should sample a few instances and examine them carefully. You'll be surprised at what you find. Time looking at your data is always well spent.

2.5 FURTHER READING

Pyle (1999) provides an extensive guide to data preparation for data mining. There is also a great deal of current interest in data warehousing and the problems it entails. Kimball and Ross (2002) present the best introduction to these that we know of. Cabena et al. (1998) estimate that data preparation accounts for 60% of the effort involved in a data mining application, and they write at some length about the problems involved.

The area of inductive logic programming, which deals with finite and infinite relations, is covered by Bergadano and Gunetti (1996). The different "levels of measurement" for attributes were introduced by Stevens (1946) and are described in detail in the manuals for statistical packages such as SPSS (Nie et al., 1970).

The multi-instance learning setting in its original, quite specific sense, and the drug activity prediction problem that motivated it, was introduced by Dietterich et al. (1997). The multilabeled instance problem, mentioned near the beginning of Section 2.1, is quite a different setting; Read et al. (2009) discuss some approaches for tackling it using standard classification algorithms.

Output: Knowledge Representation

Most of the techniques in this book produce easily comprehensible descriptions of the structural patterns in the data. Before looking at how these techniques work, we have to see how structural patterns can be expressed. There are many different ways for representing the patterns that can be discovered by machine learning, and each one dictates the kind of technique that can be used to infer that output structure from data. Once you understand how the output is represented, you have come a long way toward understanding how it can be generated.

We saw many examples of data mining in Chapter 1. In these cases the output took the form of decision trees and classification rules, which are basic knowledge representation styles that many machine learning methods use. *Knowledge* is really too imposing a word for a decision tree or a collection of rules, and by using it we don't mean to imply that these structures vie with the *real* kind of knowledge that we carry in our heads—it's just that we need some word to refer to the structures that learning methods produce. There are more complex varieties of rules that allow exceptions to be specified, and ones that can express relations among the values of the attributes of different instances. Some problems have a numeric class, and—as mentioned in Chapter 1—the classic way of dealing with these is to use linear models. Linear models can also be adapted to deal with binary classification. Moreover, special forms of trees can be developed for numeric prediction. Instance-based representations focus on the instances themselves rather than rules that govern their attribute values. Finally, some learning schemes generate clusters of instances. These different knowledge representation methods parallel the different kinds of learning problems introduced in Chapter 2.

3.1 TABLES

The simplest, most rudimentary way of representing the output from machine learning is to make it just the same as the input—a *table*. For example, Table 1.2 is a decision table for the weather data: You just look up the appropriate conditions to decide whether or not to play. Exactly the same process can be used for numeric prediction too—in this case, the structure is sometimes referred to as a *regression table*. Less trivially, creating a decision or regression table might involve selecting some of the attributes. If temperature is irrelevant to the decision, for example, a smaller, condensed table with that attribute missing would be a better guide. The problem is, of course, to decide which attributes to leave out without affecting the final decision.

3.2 LINEAR MODELS

Another simple style of representation is a *linear model*, the output of which is just the sum of the attribute values, except that weights are applied to each attribute before adding them together. The trick is to come up with good values for the weights—ones that make the model's output match the desired output. Here, the output and the inputs—attribute values—are all numeric. Statisticians use the word *regression* for the process of predicting a numeric quantity, and *regression model* is another term for this kind of linear model. Unfortunately, this does not really relate to the ordinary use of the word, which means to return to a previous state.

Linear models are easiest to visualize in two dimensions, where they are tantamount to drawing a straight line through a set of data points. Figure 3.1 shows a line fitted to the CPU performance data described in Chapter 1 (Table 1.5), where only the *cache* attribute is used as input. The class attribute *performance* is shown on the vertical axis, with *cache* on the horizontal axis; both are numeric. The straight line represents the "best fit" prediction equation

$$\text{PRP} = 37.06 + 2.47 \text{ CACH}$$

Given a test instance, a prediction can be produced by plugging the observed value of *cache* into this expression to obtain a value for *performance*. Here, the

FIGURE 3.1

A linear regression function for the CPU performance data.

expression comprises a constant "bias" term (37.06) and a weight for the *cache* attribute (2.47). Of course, linear models can be extended beyond a single attribute— the trick is to come up with suitable values for each attribute's weight, and a bias term, that together give a good fit to the training data.

Linear models can also be applied to binary classification problems. In this case, the line produced by the model separates the two classes: It defines where the decision changes from one class value to the other. Such a line is often referred to as the *decision boundary*. Figure 3.2 shows a decision boundary for the iris data that separates the *Iris setosas* from the *Iris versicolors*. In this case, the data is plotted using two of the input attributes—petal length and petal width—and the straight line defining the decision boundary is a function of these two attributes. Points lying on the line are given by the equation

$$2.0 - 0.5 \text{ PETAL-LENGTH} - 0.8 \text{ PETAL-WIDTH} = 0$$

As before, given a test instance, a prediction is produced by plugging the observed values of the attributes in question into the expression. But here we check the result and predict one class if it is greater than or equal to 0 (in this case, *Iris setosa*) and the other if it is less than 0 (*Iris versicolor*). Again, the model can be extended to multiple attributes, in which case the boundary becomes a high-dimensional plane, or "hyperplane," in the instance space. The task is to find values for the weights so that the training data is correctly classified by the hyperplane.

In Figures 3.1 and 3.2, a different fit to the data could be obtained by changing the position and orientation of the line—that is, by changing the weights. The weights for Figure 3.1 were found by a method called *least squares linear regression*; those for Figure 3.2 were found by the perceptron training rule. Both methods are described in Chapter 4.

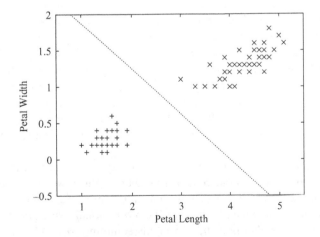

FIGURE 3.2

A linear decision boundary separating *Iris setosas* from *Iris versicolors*.

3.3 TREES

A "divide-and-conquer" approach to the problem of learning from a set of independent instances leads naturally to a style of representation called a *decision tree*. We have seen some examples of decision trees, for the contact lens (Figure 1.2) and labor negotiations (Figure 1.3) datasets. Nodes in a decision tree involve testing a particular attribute. Usually, the test compares an attribute value with a constant. Leaf nodes give a classification that applies to all instances that reach the leaf, or a set of classifications, or a probability distribution over all possible classifications. To classify an unknown instance, it is routed down the tree according to the values of the attributes tested in successive nodes, and when a leaf is reached the instance is classified according to the class assigned to the leaf.

If the attribute that is tested at a node is a nominal one, the number of children is usually the number of possible values of the attribute. In this case, because there is one branch for each possible value, the same attribute will not be retested further down the tree. Sometimes the attribute values are divided into two subsets, and the tree branches just two ways depending on which subset the value lies in; in that case, the attribute might be tested more than once in a path.

If the attribute is numeric, the test at a node usually determines whether its value is greater or less than a predetermined constant, giving a two-way split. Alternatively, a three-way split may be used, in which case there are several different possibilities. If *missing value* is treated as an attribute value in its own right, that will create a third branch. An alternative for an integer-valued attribute would be a three-way split into *less than*, *equal to*, and *greater than*. An alternative for a real-valued attribute, for which *equal to* is not such a meaningful option, would be to test against an interval rather than a single constant, again giving a three-way split: *below*, *within*, and *above*. A numeric attribute is often tested several times in any given path down the tree from root to leaf, each test involving a different constant. We return to this when describing the handling of numeric attributes in Section 6.1.

Missing values pose an obvious problem: It is not clear which branch should be taken when a node tests an attribute whose value is missing. Sometimes, as described in Section 2.4, *missing value* is treated as an attribute value in its own right. If this is not the case, missing values should be treated in a special way rather than being considered as just another possible value that the attribute might take. A simple solution is to record the number of elements in the training set that go down each branch and to use the most popular branch if the value for a test instance is missing.

A more sophisticated solution is to notionally split the instance into pieces and send part of it down each branch, and from there right down to the leaves of the subtrees involved. The split is accomplished using a numeric weight between 0 and 1, and the weight for a branch is chosen to be proportional to the number of training instances going down that branch, all weights summing to 1. A weighted instance may be further split at a lower node. Eventually, the various parts of the instance will each reach a leaf node, and the decisions at these leaf nodes must be recombined using the weights that have percolated down to the leaves. We return to this in Section 6.1.

So far we've described decision trees that divide the data at a node by comparing the value of some attribute with a constant. This is the most common approach. If you visualize this with two input attributes in two dimensions, comparing the value of one attribute with a constant splits the data parallel to that axis. However, there are other possibilities. Some trees compare two attributes with one another, while others compute some function of several attributes. For example, using a hyperplane as described in the previous section results in an *oblique* split that is not parallel to an axis. A *functional tree* can have oblique splits as well as linear models at the leaf nodes, which are used for prediction. It is also possible for some nodes in the tree to specify alternative splits on different attributes, as though the tree designer couldn't make up his or her mind which one to choose. This might be useful if the attributes seem to be equally useful for classifying the data. Such nodes are called *option* nodes, and when classifying an unknown instance, all branches leading from an option node are followed. This means that the instance will end up in more than one leaf, giving various alternative predictions, which are then combined in some fashion—for example, using majority voting.

It is instructive and can even be entertaining to manually build a decision tree for a dataset. To do so effectively, you need a good way of visualizing the data so that you can decide which are likely to be the best attributes to test and what an appropriate test might be. The Weka Explorer, described in Part III, has a User Classifier facility that allows users to construct a decision tree interactively. It presents you with a scatter plot of the data against two selected attributes, which you choose. When you find a pair of attributes that discriminates the classes well, you can create a two-way split by drawing a polygon around the appropriate data points on the scatter plot.

For example, in Figure 3.3(a) the user is operating on a dataset with three classes, the iris dataset, and has found two attributes, *petallength* and *petalwidth*, that do a good job of splitting up the classes. A rectangle has been drawn manually to separate out one of the classes (*Iris versicolor*). Then the user switches to the decision tree view in Figure 3.3(b) to see the tree so far. The left leaf node contains predominantly irises of one type (*Iris versicolor*, contaminated by only one *virginica*); the right one contains predominantly two types (*Iris setosa* and *virginica*, contaminated by only three *versicolors*). The user will probably select the right leaf and work on it next, splitting it further with another rectangle—perhaps based on a different pair of attributes (although, from Figure 3.3(a), these two look pretty good).

Section 11.2 explains how to use Weka's User Classifier facility. Most people enjoy making the first few decisions but rapidly lose interest thereafter, and one very useful option is to select a machine learning scheme and let it take over at any point in the decision tree. Manual construction of decision trees is a good way to get a feel for the tedious business of evaluating different combinations of attributes to split on.

(a)

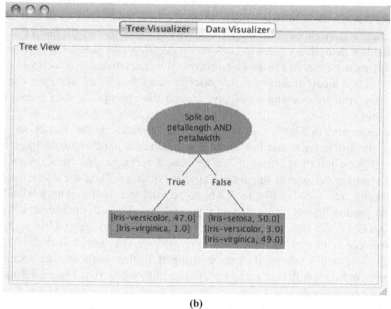

(b)

FIGURE 3.3

Constructing a decision tree interactively: (a) creating a rectangular test involving *petallength* and *petalwidth*, and (b) the resulting (unfinished) decision tree.

The kind of decision trees we've been looking at are designed for predicting categories rather than numeric quantities. When it comes to predicting numeric quantities, as with the CPU performance data in Table 1.5, the same kind of tree can be used, but each leaf would contain a numeric value that is the average of all the training set values to which the leaf applies. Because a numeric quantity is what is predicted, decision trees with averaged numeric values at the leaves are called *regression trees*.

Figure 3.4(a) shows a regression equation for the CPU performance data, and Figure 3.4(b) shows a regression tree. The leaves of the tree are numbers that represent the average outcome for instances that reach the leaf. The tree is much larger and more complex than the regression equation, and if we calculate the average of the absolute values of the errors between the predicted and actual CPU performance measures, it turns out to be significantly less for the tree than for the regression equation. The regression tree is more accurate because a simple linear model poorly represents the data in this problem. However, the tree is cumbersome and difficult to interpret because of its large size.

It is possible to combine regression equations with regression trees. Figure 3.4(c) is a tree whose leaves contain linear expressions—that is, regression equations—rather than single predicted values. This is called a *model tree*. Figure 3.4(c) contains the six linear models that belong at the six leaves, labeled LM1 through LM6. The model tree approximates continuous functions by linear "patches," a more sophisticated representation than either linear regression or regression trees. Although the model tree is smaller and more comprehensible than the regression tree, the average error values on the training data are lower. (However, we will see in Chapter 5 that calculating the average error on the training set is not in general a good way of assessing the performance of models.)

3.4 RULES

Rules are a popular alternative to decision trees, and we have already seen examples in Section 1.2 for the weather (page 9), the contact lens (page 12), the iris (page 13), and the soybean (page 19) datasets. The *antecedent*, or precondition, of a rule is a series of tests just like the tests at nodes in decision trees, while the *consequent*, or conclusion, gives the class or classes that apply to instances covered by that rule, or perhaps gives a probability distribution over the classes. Generally, the preconditions are logically ANDed together, and all the tests must succeed if the rule is to fire. However, in some rule formulations the preconditions are general logical expressions rather than simple conjunctions. We often think of the individual rules as being effectively logically ORed together: If any one applies, the class (or probability distribution) given in its conclusion is applied to the instance. However, conflicts arise when several rules with different conclusions apply; we return to this shortly.

PRP =
   − 56.1
   + 0.049 MYCT
   + 0.015 MMIN
   + 0.006 MMAX
   + 0.630 CACH
   − 0.270 CHMIN
   + 1.46 CHMAX
      (a)

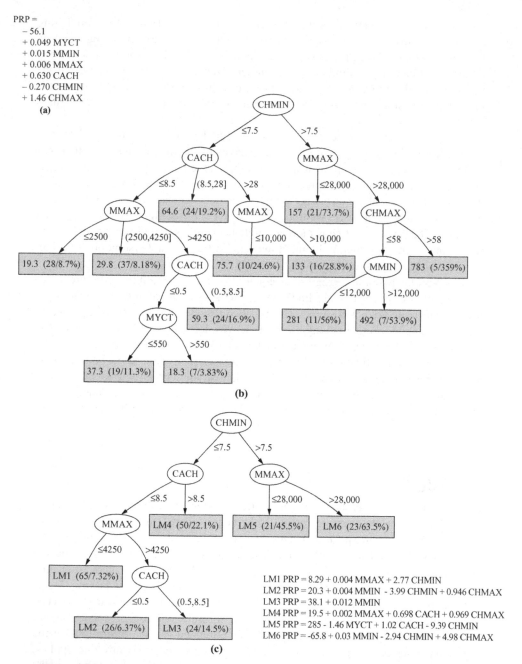

LM1 PRP = 8.29 + 0.004 MMAX + 2.77 CHMIN
LM2 PRP = 20.3 + 0.004 MMIN − 3.99 CHMIN + 0.946 CHMAX
LM3 PRP = 38.1 + 0.012 MMIN
LM4 PRP = 19.5 + 0.002 MMAX + 0.698 CACH + 0.969 CHMAX
LM5 PRP = 285 − 1.46 MYCT + 1.02 CACH − 9.39 CHMIN
LM6 PRP = −65.8 + 0.03 MMIN − 2.94 CHMIN + 4.98 CHMAX

(c)

FIGURE 3.4

Models for the CPU performance data: (a) linear regression, (b) regression tree, and (c) model tree.

Classification Rules

It is easy to read a set of classification rules directly off a decision tree. One rule is generated for each leaf. The antecedent of the rule includes a condition for every node on the path from the root to that leaf, and the consequent of the rule is the class assigned by the leaf. This procedure produces rules that are unambiguous in that the order in which they are executed is irrelevant. However, in general, rules that are read directly off a decision tree are far more complex than necessary, and rules derived from trees are usually pruned to remove redundant tests.

Because decision trees cannot easily express the disjunction implied among the different rules in a set, transforming a general set of rules into a tree is not quite so straightforward. A good illustration of this occurs when the rules have the same structure but different attributes, like

```
If a and b then x
If c and d then x
```

Then it is necessary to break the symmetry and choose a single test for the root node. If, for example, *a* is chosen, the second rule must, in effect, be repeated twice in the tree, as shown in Figure 3.5. This is known as the *replicated subtree problem*.

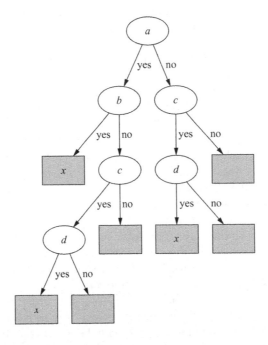

FIGURE 3.5

Decision tree for a simple disjunction.

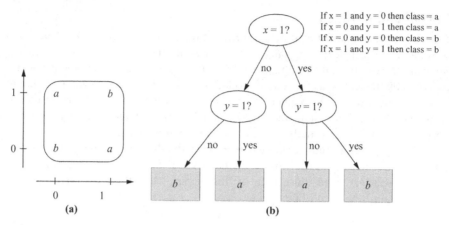

FIGURE 3.6

The exclusive-or problem.

The replicated subtree problem is sufficiently important that it is worth looking at a couple more examples. The left diagram of Figure 3.6 shows an *exclusive-or* function for which the output is *a* if $x = 1$ or $y = 1$ but not both. To make this into a tree, you have to split on one attribute first, leading to a structure like the one shown in the center. In contrast, rules can faithfully reflect the true symmetry of the problem with respect to the attributes, as shown on the right.

In this example the rules are not notably more compact than the tree. In fact, they are just what you would get by reading rules off the tree in the obvious way. But in other situations, rules are much more compact than trees, particularly if it is possible to have a "default" rule that covers cases not specified by the other rules. For example, to capture the effect of the rules in Figure 3.7—in which there are four attributes, *x*, *y*, *z*, and *w*, which can each be 1, 2, or 3—requires the tree shown on the right. Each of the three small gray triangles to the upper right should actually contain the whole three-level subtree that is displayed in gray, a rather extreme example of the replicated subtree problem. This is a distressingly complex description of a rather simple concept.

One reason why rules are popular is that each rule seems to represent an independent "nugget" of knowledge. New rules can be added to an existing rule set without disturbing ones already there, whereas to add to a tree structure may require reshaping the whole tree. However, this independence is something of an illusion because it ignores the question of how the rule set is executed. We explained previously the fact that if rules are meant to be interpreted *in order* as a "decision list," some of them, taken individually and out of context, may be incorrect. On the other hand, if the order of interpretation is supposed to be immaterial, then it is not clear what to do when different rules lead to different conclusions for the same instance. This situation cannot arise for rules that are read directly off a decision tree because

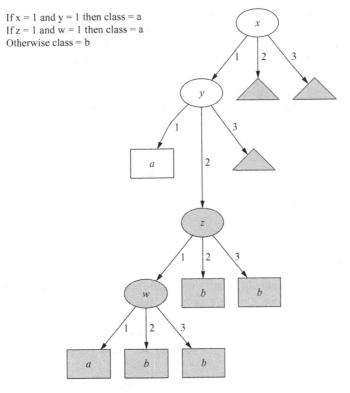

If x = 1 and y = 1 then class = a
If z = 1 and w = 1 then class = a
Otherwise class = b

FIGURE 3.7

Decision tree with a replicated subtree.

the redundancy included in the structure of the rules prevents any ambiguity in interpretation. But it does arise when rules are generated in other ways.

If a rule set gives multiple classifications for a particular example, one solution is to give no conclusion at all. Another is to count how often each rule fires on the training data and go with the most popular one. These strategies can lead to radically different results. A different problem occurs when an instance is encountered that the rules fail to classify at all. Again, this cannot occur with decision trees, or with rules read directly off them, but it can easily happen with general rule sets. One way of dealing with this situation is to decide not to classify such an example; another is to choose the most frequently occurring class as a default. Again, radically different results may be obtained for these strategies. Individual rules are simple, and sets of rules seem deceptively simple—but given just a set of rules with no additional information, it is not clear how it should be interpreted.

A particularly straightforward situation occurs when rules lead to a class that is Boolean (say, *yes* and *no*), and when only rules leading to one outcome (say, *yes*) are expressed. The assumption is that if a particular instance is not in class *yes*, then it must be in class *no*—a form of closed-world assumption. If this is the case, rules cannot conflict and there is no ambiguity in rule interpretation: Any interpretation strategy will give the same result. Such a set of rules can be written as a logic expression in what is called *disjunctive normal form*: that is, as a disjunction (OR) of conjunctive (AND) conditions.

It is this simple special case that seduces people into assuming that rules are very easy to deal with, for here each rule really does operate as a new, independent piece of information that contributes in a straightforward way to the disjunction. Unfortunately, it only applies to Boolean outcomes and requires the closed-world assumption, and both these constraints are unrealistic in most practical situations. Machine learning algorithms that generate rules invariably produce ordered rule sets in multiclass situations, and this sacrifices any possibility of modularity because the order of execution is critical.

Association Rules

Association rules are no different from classification rules except that they can predict any attribute, not just the class, and this gives them the freedom to predict combinations of attributes too. Also, association rules are not intended to be used together as a set, as classification rules are. Different association rules express different regularities that underlie the dataset, and they generally predict different things.

Because so many different association rules can be derived from even a very small dataset, interest is restricted to those that apply to a reasonably large number of instances and have a reasonably high accuracy on the instances to which they apply. The *coverage* of an association rule is the number of instances for which it predicts correctly—this is often called its *support*. Its *accuracy*—often called *confidence*—is the number of instances that it predicts correctly, expressed as a proportion of all instances to which it applies. For example, with the rule

```
If temperature = cool then humidity = normal
```

the coverage is the number of days that are both cool and have normal humidity (4 in the data of Table 1.2), and the accuracy is the proportion of cool days that have normal humidity (100% in this case).

It is usual to specify minimum coverage and accuracy values, and to seek only those rules for which coverage and accuracy are both at least these specified minima. In the weather data, for example, there are 58 rules with coverage and accuracy that are at least 2 and 95%, respectively. (It may also be convenient to specify coverage as a percentage of the total number of instances instead.)

Association rules that predict multiple consequences must be interpreted rather carefully. For example, with the weather data in Table 1.2 we saw this rule:

```
If windy = false and play = no then outlook = sunny
                                and humidity = high
```

This is *not* just a shorthand expression for the two separate rules

```
If windy = false and play = no then outlook = sunny
If windy = false and play = no then humidity = high
```

It does indeed imply that these two rules exceed the minimum coverage and accuracy figures—but it also implies more. The original rule means that the number of examples that are nonwindy, nonplaying, with sunny outlook and high humidity, is at least as great as the specified minimum coverage figure. It also means that the number of such days, expressed as a proportion of nonwindy, nonplaying days, is at least the specified minimum accuracy figure. This implies that the rule

```
If humidity = high and windy = false and play = no then outlook = sunny
```

also holds, because it has the same coverage as the original rule, and its accuracy must be at least as high as the original rule's because the number of high-humidity, nonwindy, nonplaying days is necessarily less than that of nonwindy, nonplaying days—which makes the accuracy greater.

As we have seen, there are relationships between particular association rules: Some rules imply others. To reduce the number of rules that are produced, in cases where several rules are related it makes sense to present only the strongest one to the user. In the previous example, only the first rule should be printed.

Rules with Exceptions

Returning to classification rules, a natural extension is to allow them to have *exceptions*. Then incremental modifications can be made to a rule set by expressing exceptions to existing rules rather than reengineering the entire set. For example, consider the iris problem described earlier. Suppose a new flower was found with the dimensions given in Table 3.1, and an expert declared it to be an instance of *Iris setosa*. If this flower was classified by the rules given in Chapter 1 (see page 14) for this problem, it would be misclassified by two of them:

```
If petal-length ≥ 2.45 and petal-length < 4.45 then Iris-versicolor
If petal-length ≥ 2.45 and petal-length < 4.95 and
    petal-width < 1.55 then Iris-versicolor
```

These rules require modification so that the new instance can be treated correctly. However, simply changing the bounds for the attribute–value tests in these rules may not suffice because the instances used to create the rule set may then be misclassified. Fixing up a rule set is not as simple as it sounds.

Table 3.1 New Iris Flower

Sepal Length	Sepal Width	Petal Length	Petal Width	Type
5.1	3.5	2.6	0.2	?

Instead of changing the tests in the existing rules, an expert might be consulted to explain why the new flower violates them, giving explanations that could be used to extend the relevant rules only. For example, the first of these two rules misclassifies the new *Iris setosa* as an instance of the genus *Iris versicolor*. Instead of altering the bounds on any of the inequalities in the rule, an exception can be made based on some other attribute:

```
If petal-length ≥ 2.45 and petal-length < 4.45
  then Iris-versicolor
  EXCEPT if petal-width < 1.0 then Iris-setosa
```

This rule says that a flower is *Iris versicolor* if its petal length is between 2.45 cm and 4.45 cm *except* when its petal width is less than 1.0 cm, in which case it is *Iris setosa*.

Of course, we might have exceptions to the exceptions, exceptions to these, and so on, giving the rule set something of the character of a tree. As well as being used to make incremental changes to existing rule sets, rules with exceptions can be used to represent the entire concept description in the first place.

Figure 3.8 shows a set of rules that correctly classify all examples in the iris dataset given in Chapter 1. These rules are quite difficult to comprehend at first. Let's follow them through. A default outcome has been chosen, *Iris setosa*, and is shown in the first line. For this dataset, the choice of default is rather arbitrary because there are 50 examples of each type. Normally, the most frequent outcome is chosen as the default.

Subsequent rules give exceptions to this default. The first *if … then*, on lines 2 through 4, gives a condition that leads to the classification *Iris versicolor*. However, there are two exceptions to this rule (lines 5–8), which we will deal with in a moment. If the conditions on lines 2 and 3 fail, the *else* clause on line 9 is reached, which essentially specifies a second exception to the original default. If the condition

```
Default: Iris-setosa                                                    1
except if petal-length >= 2.45 and petal-length < 5.355                 2
           and petal-width < 1.75                                       3
       then Iris-versicolor                                             4
           except if petal-length >= 4.95 and petal-width < 1.55        5
                   then Iris-virginica                                  6
                   else if sepal-length < 4.95 and sepal-width >= 2.45  7
                           then Iris-virginica                          8
       else if petal-length >= 3.35                                     9
           then Iris-virginica                                         10
               except if petal-length < 4.85 and sepal-length < 5.95   11
                       then Iris-versicolor                            12
```

FIGURE 3.8

Rules for the iris data.

on line 9 holds, the classification is *Iris virginica* (line 10). Again, there is an exception to this rule (on lines 11 and 12).

Now return to the exception on lines 5 through 8. This overrides the *Iris versicolor* conclusion on line 4 if either of the tests on lines 5 and 7 holds. As it happens, these two exceptions both lead to the same conclusion, *Iris virginica* (lines 6 and 8). The final exception is the one on lines 11 and 12, which overrides the *Iris virginica* conclusion on line 10 when the condition on line 11 is met, and leads to the classification *Iris versicolor*.

You will probably need to ponder these rules for some minutes before it becomes clear how they are intended to be read. Although it takes some time to get used to reading them, sorting out the *excepts* and *if … then … elses* becomes easier with familiarity. People often think of real problems in terms of rules, exceptions, and exceptions to the exceptions, so it is often a good way to express a complex rule set. But the main point in favor of this way of representing rules is that it scales up well. Although the whole rule set is a little hard to comprehend, each individual conclusion, each individual *then* statement, can be considered just in the context of the rules and exceptions that lead to it, whereas with decision lists, all prior rules need to be reviewed to determine the precise effect of an individual rule. This locality property is crucial when trying to understand large rule sets. Psychologically, people familiar with the data think of a particular set of cases, or kind of case, when looking at any one conclusion in the exception structure, and when one of these cases turns out to be an exception to the conclusion, it is easy to add an *except* clause to cater for it.

It is worth pointing out that the *default … except if … then* structure is logically equivalent to an *if … then … else*, where the *else* is unconditional and specifies exactly what the default did. An unconditional *else* is, of course, a default. (Note that there are no unconditional *elses* in the preceding rules.) Logically, the exception-based rules can be very simply rewritten in terms of regular *if … then … else* clauses. What is gained by the formulation in terms of exceptions is not *logical* but *psychological*. We assume that the defaults and the tests that occur early on apply more widely than the exceptions further down. If this is indeed true for the domain, and the user can see that it is plausible, the expression in terms of (common) rules and (rare) exceptions will be easier to grasp than a different, but logically equivalent, structure.

More Expressive Rules

We have assumed implicitly that the conditions in rules involve testing an attribute value against a constant. But this may not be ideal. Suppose, to take a concrete example, we have the set of eight building blocks of the various shapes and sizes illustrated in Figure 3.9, and we wish to learn the concept of *standing up*. This is a classic two-class problem with classes *standing* and *lying*. The four shaded blocks are positive (*standing*) examples of the concept, and the unshaded blocks are negative (*lying*) examples. The only information the learning algorithm will be given is the *width*, *height*, and *number of sides* of each block. The training data is shown in Table 3.2.

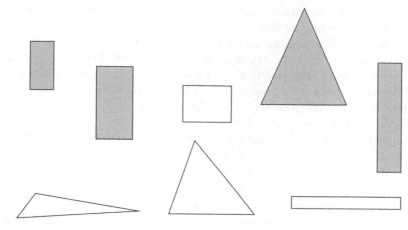

FIGURE 3.9

The shapes problem: shaded = standing; unshaded = lying.

Table 3.2 Training Data for the Shapes Problem			
Width	**Height**	**Sides**	**Class**
2	4	4	standing
3	6	4	standing
4	3	4	lying
7	8	3	standing
7	6	3	lying
2	9	4	standing
9	1	4	lying
10	2	3	lying

A conventional rule set that might be produced for this data is

```
if width ≥ 3.5 and height < 7.0 then lying
if height ≥ 3.5 then standing
```

In case you're wondering, 3.5 is chosen as the breakpoint for *width* because it is halfway between the width of the thinnest lying block, namely 4, and the width of the fattest standing block whose height is less than 7, namely 3. Also, 7.0 is chosen as the breakpoint for *height* because it is halfway between the height of the tallest lying block, namely 6, and the shortest standing block whose width is greater than 3.5, namely 8. It is common to place numeric thresholds halfway between the values that delimit the boundaries of a concept.

Although these two rules work well on the examples given, they are not very good. Many new blocks would not be classified by either rule (e.g., one with width 1 and height 2), and it is easy to devise many legitimate blocks that the rules would not fit.

A person classifying the eight blocks would probably notice that "standing blocks are those that are taller than they are wide." This rule does not compare attribute values with constants; it compares attributes with one another:

```
if width > height then lying
if height > width then standing
```

The actual values of the *height* and *width* attributes are not important, just the result of comparing the two.

Many machine learning schemes do not consider relations between attributes because there is a considerable cost in doing so. One way of rectifying this is to add extra, secondary attributes that say whether two primary attributes are equal or not, or give the difference between them if they are numeric. For example, we might add a binary attribute *is width < height?* to Table 3.2. Such attributes are often added as part of the data engineering process.

With a seemingly rather small further enhancement, the expressive power of the knowledge representation can be extended greatly. The trick is to express rules in a way that makes the role of the instance explicit:

```
if width(block) > height(block) then lying(block)
if height(block) > width(block) then standing(block)
```

Although this may not seem like much of an extension, it is if instances can be decomposed into parts. For example, if a *tower* is a pile of blocks, one on top of the other, the fact that the topmost block of the tower is standing can be expressed by

```
if height(tower.top) > width(tower.top) then standing(tower.top)
```

Here, *tower.top* is used to refer to the topmost block. So far, nothing has been gained. But if *tower.rest* refers to the rest of the tower, then the fact that the tower is composed *entirely* of standing blocks can be expressed by the rules

```
if height(tower.top) > width(tower.top) and standing(tower.rest)
  then standing(tower)
```

The apparently minor addition of the condition *standing(tower.rest)* is a recursive expression that will turn out to be true only if the rest of the tower is composed of standing blocks. That will be tested by a recursive application of the same rule. Of course, it is necessary to ensure that the recursion "bottoms out" properly by adding a further rule, such as

```
if tower=empty then standing(tower.top)
```

Sets of rules like this are called *logic programs*, and this area of machine learning is called *inductive logic programming*. We will not be treating it further in this book.

3.5 INSTANCE-BASED REPRESENTATION

The simplest form of learning is plain memorization, or *rote learning*. Once a set of training instances has been memorized, on encountering a new instance the memory is searched for the training instance that most strongly resembles the new one. The only problem is how to interpret "resembles"—we will explain that shortly. First, however, note that this is a completely different way of representing the "knowledge" extracted from a set of instances: Just store the instances themselves and operate by relating new instances whose class is unknown to existing ones whose class is known. Instead of trying to create rules, work directly from the examples themselves. This is known as *instance-based* learning. In a sense, all the other learning methods are instance-based too, because we always start with a set of instances as the initial training information. But the instance-based knowledge representation uses the instances themselves to represent what is learned, rather than inferring a rule set or decision tree and storing it instead.

In instance-based learning, all the real work is done when the time comes to classify a new instance rather than when the training set is processed. In a sense, then, the difference between this method and the others that we have seen is the time at which the "learning" takes place. Instance-based learning is lazy, deferring the real work as long as possible, whereas other methods are eager, producing a generalization as soon as the data has been seen. In instance-based classification, each new instance is compared with existing ones using a distance metric, and the closest existing instance is used to assign the class to the new one. This is called the *nearest-neighbor* classification method. Sometimes more than one nearest neighbor is used, and the majority class of the closest k neighbors (or the distance-weighted average if the class is numeric) is assigned to the new instance. This is termed the *k-nearest-neighbor* method.

Computing the distance between two examples is trivial when examples have just one numeric attribute: It is just the difference between the two attribute values. It is almost as straightforward when there are several numeric attributes: Generally, the standard Euclidean distance is used. However, this assumes that the attributes are normalized and are of equal importance, and one of the main problems in learning is to determine which are the important features.

When nominal attributes are present, it is necessary to come up with a "distance" between different values of that attribute. What are the distances between, say, the values *red*, *green*, and *blue*? Usually, a distance of zero is assigned if the values are identical; otherwise, the distance is one. Thus, the distance between *red* and *red* is zero but the distance between *red* and *green* is one. However, it may be desirable to use a more sophisticated representation of the attributes. For example, with more colors one could use a numeric measure of hue in color space, making *yellow* closer to *orange* than it is to *green* and *ocher* closer still.

Some attributes will be more important than others, and this is usually reflected in the distance metric by some kind of attribute weighting. Deriving suitable attribute weights from the training set is a key problem in instance-based learning.

It may not be necessary, or desirable, to store *all* the training instances. For one thing, this may make the nearest-neighbor calculation unbearably slow. For another, it may consume unrealistic amounts of storage. Generally, some regions of attribute space are more stable than others with regard to class, and just a few exemplars are needed inside stable regions. For example, you might expect the required density of exemplars that lie well inside class boundaries to be much less than the density that is needed near class boundaries. Deciding which instances to save and which to discard is another key problem in instance-based learning.

An apparent drawback to instance-based representations is that they do not make explicit the structures that are learned. In a sense, this violates the notion of *learning* that we presented at the beginning of this book; instances do not really "describe" the patterns in data. However, the instances combine with the distance metric to carve out boundaries in instance space that distinguish one class from another, and this is a kind of explicit representation of knowledge. For example, given a single instance of each of two classes, the nearest-neighbor rule effectively splits the instance space along the perpendicular bisector of the line joining the instances. Given several instances of each class, the space is divided by a set of lines that represent the perpendicular bisectors of selected lines joining an instance of one class to one of another class. Figure 3.10(a) illustrates a nine-sided polygon that separates the filled-circle class from the open-circle class. This polygon is implicit in the operation of the nearest-neighbor rule.

When training instances are discarded, the result is to save just a few critical examples of each class. Figure 3.10(b) shows only the examples that actually get used in nearest-neighbor decisions: The others (the light-gray ones) can be discarded without affecting the result. These examples serve as a kind of explicit knowledge representation.

Some instance-based representations go further and explicitly generalize the instances. Typically, this is accomplished by creating rectangular regions that enclose examples of the same class. Figure 3.10(c) shows the rectangular regions that might be produced. Unknown examples that fall within one of the rectangles will be assigned the corresponding class; ones that fall outside all rectangles will be subject to the usual nearest-neighbor rule. Of course, this produces different decision boundaries from the straightforward nearest-neighbor rule, as can be seen by superimposing the polygon in Figure 3.10(a) onto the rectangles. Any part of the polygon that lies within a rectangle will be chopped off and replaced by the rectangle's boundary.

Rectangular generalizations in instance space are just like rules with a special form of condition, one that tests a numeric variable against an upper and lower bound and selects the region in between. Different dimensions of the rectangle correspond to tests on different attributes being ANDed together. Choosing snug-fitting rectangular regions as tests leads to more conservative rules than those generally produced by rule-based machine learning schemes, because for each boundary of the region, there is an actual instance that lies on (or just inside) that boundary. Tests such as $x < a$ (where x is an attribute value and a is a constant) encompass an entire half-space—they apply no matter how small x is as long as it is less than a.

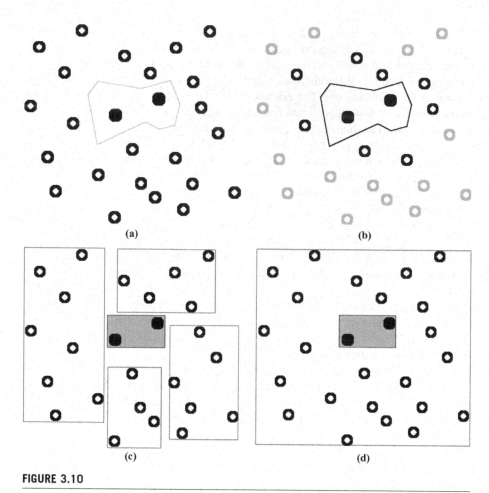

FIGURE 3.10

Different ways of partitioning the instance space.

When doing rectangular generalization in instance space you can afford to be conservative, because if a new example is encountered that lies outside all regions, you can fall back on the nearest-neighbor metric. With rule-based methods the example cannot be classified, or receives just a default classification, if no rules apply to it. The advantage of more conservative rules is that, although incomplete, they may be more perspicuous than a complete set of rules that covers all cases. Finally, ensuring that the regions do not overlap is tantamount to ensuring that at most one rule can apply to an example, eliminating another of the difficulties of rule-based systems—what to do when several rules apply.

A more complex kind of generalization is to permit rectangular regions to nest one within another. Then a region that is basically all one class can contain an inner region with a different class, as illustrated in Figure 3.10(d). It is possible to allow nesting within nesting so that the inner region can itself contain its own inner region of a different class—perhaps the original class of the outer region. This is analogous to allowing rules to have exceptions and exceptions to the exceptions, as in Section 3.4.

It is worth pointing out a slight danger to the technique of visualizing instance-based learning in terms of boundaries in example space: It makes the implicit assumption that attributes are numeric rather than nominal. If the various values that a nominal attribute can take on were laid out along a line, generalizations involving a segment of that line would make no sense: Each test involves either one value for the attribute or all values for it (or perhaps an arbitrary subset of values). Although you can more or less easily imagine extending the examples in Figure 3.10 to several dimensions, it is much harder to imagine how rules involving nominal attributes will look in multidimensional instance space. Many machine learning situations involve numerous attributes, and our intuitions tend to lead us astray when extended to high-dimensional spaces.

3.6 CLUSTERS

When a cluster rather than a classifier is learned, the output takes the form of a diagram that shows how the instances fall into clusters. In the simplest case this involves associating a cluster number with each instance, which might be depicted by laying the instances out in two dimensions and partitioning the space to show each cluster, as illustrated in Figure 3.11(a).

Some clustering algorithms allow one instance to belong to more than one cluster, so the diagram might lay the instances out in two dimensions and draw overlapping subsets representing each cluster—a Venn diagram, as in Figure 3.11(b). Some algorithms associate instances with clusters probabilistically rather than categorically. In this case, for every instance there is a probability or degree of membership with which it belongs to each of the clusters. This is shown in Figure 3.11(c). This particular association is meant to be a probabilistic one, so the numbers for each example sum to 1—although that is not always the case.

Other algorithms produce a hierarchical structure of clusters so that at the top level the instance space divides into just a few clusters, each of which divides into its own subcluster at the next level down, and so on. In this case a diagram such as the one in Figure 3.11(d) is used, in which elements joined together at lower levels are more tightly clustered than ones joined together at higher levels. Such diagrams are called *dendrograms*. This term means just the same thing as *tree diagrams* (the Greek word *dendron* means "tree"), but in clustering the more exotic version seems to be preferred—perhaps because biological species are a prime application area for clustering techniques, and ancient languages are often used for naming in biology.

Clustering is often followed by a stage in which a decision tree or rule set is inferred that allocates each instance to the cluster in which it belongs. Then, the clustering operation is just one step on the way to a structural description.

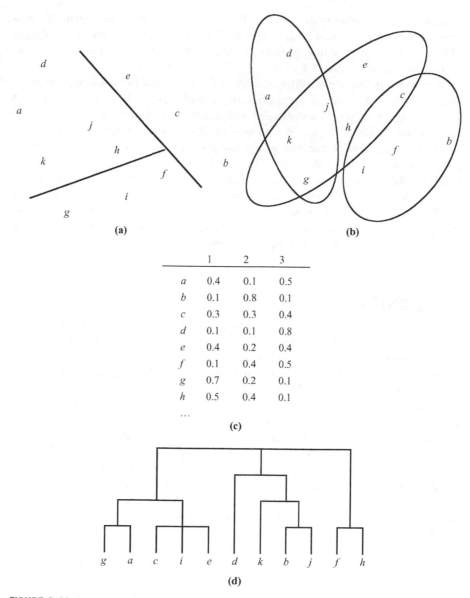

	1	2	3
a	0.4	0.1	0.5
b	0.1	0.8	0.1
c	0.3	0.3	0.4
d	0.1	0.1	0.8
e	0.4	0.2	0.4
f	0.1	0.4	0.5
g	0.7	0.2	0.1
h	0.5	0.4	0.1
...			

(c)

FIGURE 3.11

Different ways of representing clusters.

3.7 **FURTHER READING**

Knowledge representation is a key topic in classical artificial intelligence and early work on it is well represented by a comprehensive series of papers edited by Brachman and Levesque (1985). The area of inductive logic programming and associated topics are covered in detail by de Raedt's book, *Logical and relational learning* (2008).

We mentioned the problem of dealing with conflict among different rules. Various ways of doing this, called *conflict resolution strategies*, have been developed for use with rule-based programming systems. These are described in books on rule-based programming such as Brownstown et al. (1985). Again, however, they are designed for use with handcrafted rule sets rather than ones that have been learned. The use of handcrafted rules with exceptions for a large dataset has been studied by Gaines and Compton (1995), and Richards and Compton (1998) describe their role as an alternative to classic knowledge engineering.

Further information on the various styles of concept representation can be found in the papers that describe machine learning methods for inferring concepts from examples, and these are covered in Section 4.10, Further Reading, and the Discussion sections of Chapter 6.

Algorithms: The Basic Methods

4

Now that we've seen how the inputs and outputs can be represented, it's time to look at the learning algorithms themselves. This chapter explains the basic ideas behind the techniques that are used in practical data mining. We will not delve too deeply into the trickier issues—advanced versions of the algorithms, optimizations that are possible, complications that arise in practice. These topics are deferred to Chapter 6, where we come to grips with real implementations of machine learning schemes such as the ones included in data mining toolkits and used for real-world applications. It is important to understand these more advanced issues so that you know what is really going on when you analyze a particular dataset.

In this chapter we look at the basic ideas. One of the most instructive lessons is that simple ideas often work very well, and we strongly recommend the adoption of a "simplicity-first" methodology when analyzing practical datasets. There are many different kinds of simple structure that datasets can exhibit. In one dataset, there might be a single attribute that does all the work and the others are irrelevant or redundant. In another dataset, the attributes might contribute independently and equally to the final outcome. A third might have a simple logical structure, involving just a few attributes, which can be captured by a decision tree. In a fourth, there may be a few independent rules that govern the assignment of instances to different classes. A fifth might exhibit dependencies among different subsets of attributes. A sixth might involve linear dependence among numeric attributes, where what matters is a weighted sum of attribute values with appropriately chosen weights. In a seventh, classifications appropriate to particular regions of instance space might be governed by the distances between the instances themselves. And in an eighth, it might be that no class values are provided: The learning is unsupervised.

In the infinite variety of possible datasets there are many different kinds of structures that can occur, and a data mining tool—no matter how capable—that is looking for one class of structure may completely miss regularities of a different kind, regardless of how rudimentary those may be. The result is a baroque and opaque classification structure of one kind instead of a simple, elegant, immediately comprehensible structure of another.

Each of the eight examples of different kinds of datasets just sketched leads to a different machine learning scheme that is well suited to discovering the underlying concept. The sections of this chapter look at each of these structures in turn. A final section introduces simple ways of dealing with multi-instance problems, where each example comprises several different instances.

4.1 INFERRING RUDIMENTARY RULES

Here's an easy way to find very simple classification rules from a set of instances. Called *1R* for *1-rule*, it generates a one-level decision tree expressed in the form of a set of rules that all test one particular attribute. 1R is a simple, cheap method that often comes up with quite good rules for characterizing the structure in data. It turns out that simple rules frequently achieve surprisingly high accuracy. Perhaps this is because the structure underlying many real-world datasets is quite rudimentary, and just one attribute is sufficient to determine the class of an instance quite accurately. In any event, it is always a good plan to try the simplest things first.

The idea is this: We make rules that test a single attribute and branch accordingly. Each branch corresponds to a different value of the attribute. It is obvious what is the best classification to give each branch: Use the class that occurs most often in the training data. Then the error rate of the rules can easily be determined. Just count the errors that occur on the training data—that is, the number of instances that do not have the majority class.

Each attribute generates a different set of rules, one rule for every value of the attribute. Evaluate the error rate for each attribute's rule set and choose the best. It's that simple! Figure 4.1 shows the algorithm in the form of pseudocode.

To see the 1R method at work, consider the weather data of Table 1.2 on page 10 (we will encounter it many times again when looking at how learning algorithms work). To classify on the final column, *play*, 1R considers four sets of rules, one for each attribute. These rules are shown in Table 4.1. An asterisk indicates that a random choice has been made between two equally likely outcomes. The number of errors is given for each rule, along with the total number of errors for the rule set as a whole. 1R chooses the attribute that produces rules with the smallest number of

```
For each attribute,
  For each value of that attribute, make a rule as follows:
    count how often each class appears
    find the most frequent class
    make the rule assign that class to this attribute value.
  Calculate the error rate of the rules.
Choose the rules with the smallest error rate.
```

FIGURE 4.1

Pseudocode for 1R.

Table 4.1 Evaluating Attributes in the Weather Data

	Attribute	Rules	Errors	Total Errors
1	outlook	sunny → no	2/5	4/14
		overcast → yes	0/4	
		rainy → yes	2/5	
2	temperature	hot → no*	2/4	5/14
		mild → yes	2/6	
		cool → yes	1/4	
3	humidity	high → no	3/7	4/14
		normal → yes	1/7	
4	windy	false → yes	2/8	5/14
		true → no*	3/6	

A random choice has been made between two equally likely outcomes.

errors—that is, the first and third rule sets. Arbitrarily breaking the tie between these two rule sets gives

```
outlook:  sunny  → no
          overcast → yes
          rainy  → yes
```

We noted at the outset that the game for the weather data is unspecified. Oddly enough, it is apparently played when it is overcast or rainy but not when it is sunny. Perhaps it's an indoor pursuit.

Missing Values and Numeric Attributes

Although a very rudimentary learning scheme, 1R does accommodate both missing values and numeric attributes. It deals with these in simple but effective ways. *Missing* is treated as just another attribute value so that, for example, if the weather data had contained missing values for the *outlook* attribute, a rule set formed on *outlook* would specify four possible class values, one for each of *sunny*, *overcast*, and *rainy*, and a fourth for *missing*.

We can convert numeric attributes into nominal ones using a simple discretization method. First, sort the training examples according to the values of the numeric attribute. This produces a sequence of class values. For example, sorting the numeric version of the weather data (Table 1.3, page 11) according to the values of *temperature* produces the sequence

```
64   65   68   69   70   71   72   72   75   75   80   81   83   85
yes  no   yes  yes  yes  no   no   yes  yes  yes  no   yes  yes  no
```

Discretization involves partitioning this sequence by placing breakpoints in it. One possibility is to place breakpoints wherever the class changes, producing the following eight categories:

```
yes | no | yes yes yes | no no | yes yes yes | no | yes yes | no
```

Choosing breakpoints halfway between the examples on either side places them at 64.5, 66.5, 70.5, 72, 77.5, 80.5, and 84. However, the two instances with value 72 cause a problem because they have the same value of *temperature* but fall into different classes. The simplest fix is to move the breakpoint at 72 up one example, to 73.5, producing a mixed partition in which *no* is the majority class.

A more serious problem is that this procedure tends to form an excessively large number of categories. The 1R method will naturally gravitate toward choosing an attribute that splits into many categories, because this will partition the dataset into many pieces, making it more likely that instances will have the same class as the majority in their partition. In fact, the limiting case is an attribute that has a different value for each instance—that is, an *identification code* attribute that pinpoints instances uniquely—and this will yield a zero error rate on the training set because each partition contains just one instance. Of course, highly branching attributes do not usually perform well on test examples; indeed, the identification code attribute will never get any examples outside the training set correct. This phenomenon is known as *overfitting*; we have already described overfitting-avoidance bias in Chapter 1, and we will encounter this problem repeatedly in subsequent chapters.

For 1R, overfitting is likely to occur whenever an attribute has a large number of possible values. Consequently, when discretizing a numeric attribute, a minimum limit is imposed on the number of examples of the majority class in each partition. Suppose that minimum is set at 3. This eliminates all but two of the preceding partitions. Instead, the partitioning process begins

```
yes   no   yes   yes  |   yes    ...
```

ensuring that there are three occurrences of *yes*, the majority class, in the first partition. However, because the next example is also *yes*, we lose nothing by including that in the first partition, too. This leads to a new division of

```
yes   no   yes   yes   yes  |   no   no   yes   yes   yes  |   no   yes   yes   no
```

where each partition contains at least three instances of the majority class, except the last one, which will usually have less. Partition boundaries always fall between examples of different classes.

Whenever adjacent partitions have the same majority class, as do the first two partitions above, they can be merged together without affecting the meaning of the rule sets. Thus, the final discretization is

```
yes   no   yes   yes   yes   no   no   yes   yes   yes  |   no   yes   yes   no
```

which leads to the rule set

```
temperature:  ≤ 77.5 → yes
              > 77.5 → no
```

The second rule involved an arbitrary choice; as it happens, *no* was chosen. If *yes* had been chosen instead, there would be no need for any breakpoint at all—and as this example illustrates, it might be better to use the adjacent categories to help break ties. In fact, this rule generates five errors on the training set and so is less effective than the preceding rule for *outlook*. However, the same procedure leads to this rule for *humidity*:

```
humidity:  ≤ 82.5 → yes
           > 82.5 and ≤ 95.5 → no
           > 95.5 → yes
```

This generates only three errors on the training set and is the best 1-rule for the data in Table 1.3.

Finally, if a numeric attribute has missing values, an additional category is created for them, and the discretization procedure is applied just to the instances for which the attribute's value is defined.

Discussion

In a seminal paper entitled "Very simple classification rules perform well on most commonly used datasets" (Holte, 1993), a comprehensive study of the performance of the 1R procedure was reported on 16 datasets frequently used by machine learning researchers to evaluate their algorithms. *Cross-validation*, an evaluation technique that we will explain in Chapter 5, was used to ensure that the results were the same as would be obtained on independent test sets. After some experimentation, the minimum number of examples in each partition of a numeric attribute was set at six, not three as used in our illustration.

Surprisingly, despite its simplicity 1R did well in comparison with the state-of-the-art learning schemes, and the rules it produced turned out to be just a few percentage points less accurate, on almost all of the datasets, than the decision trees produced by a state-of-the-art decision tree induction scheme. These trees were, in general, considerably larger than 1R's rules. Rules that test a single attribute are often a viable alternative to more complex structures, and this strongly encourages a simplicity-first methodology in which the baseline performance is established using simple, rudimentary techniques before progressing to more sophisticated learning schemes, which inevitably generate output that is harder for people to interpret.

The 1R procedure learns a one-level decision tree whose leaves represent the various different classes. A slightly more expressive technique is to use a different rule for each class. Each rule is a conjunction of tests, one for each attribute. For numeric attributes the test checks whether the value lies within a given interval; for nominal ones it checks whether it is in a certain subset of that attribute's values. These two types of tests—that is, intervals and subsets—are learned from the training data pertaining to each of the classes. For a numeric attribute, the end points of the interval are the minimum and the maximum values that occur in the training data for that class. For a nominal one, the subset contains just those values that occur for that attribute in the training data for the individual class. Rules representing different classes usually overlap, and at prediction time the one with the most matching tests is predicted. This simple technique often gives a useful first impression of a dataset. It is extremely fast and can be applied to very large quantities of data.

4.2 STATISTICAL MODELING

The 1R method uses a single attribute as the basis for its decisions and chooses the one that works best. Another simple technique is to use all attributes and allow them to make contributions to the decision that are *equally important* and *independent* of one another, given the class. This is unrealistic, of course: What makes real-life datasets interesting is that the attributes are certainly not equally important or independent. But it leads to a simple scheme that, again, works surprisingly well in practice.

Table 4.2 shows a summary of the weather data obtained by counting how many times each attribute–value pair occurs with each value (*yes* and *no*) for *play*. For example, you can see from Table 1.2 (page 10) that *outlook* is *sunny* for five examples, two of which have *play = yes* and three of which have *play = no*. The cells in the first row of the new table simply count these occurrences for all possible values of each attribute, and the *play* figure in the final column counts the total number of occurrences of *yes* and *no*. The lower part of the table contains the same information expressed as fractions, or observed probabilities. For example, of the nine days that *play* is *yes*, *outlook* is *sunny* for two, yielding a fraction of 2/9. For *play* the fractions are different: They are the proportion of days that *play* is *yes* and *no*, respectively.

Now suppose we encounter a new example with the values that are shown in Table 4.3. We treat the five features in Table 4.2—*outlook*, *temperature*, *humidity*, *windy*, and the overall likelihood that *play* is *yes* or *no*—as equally important, independent pieces of evidence and multiply the corresponding fractions. Looking at the outcome *yes* gives

$$\text{Likelihood of } yes = 2/9 \times 3/9 \times 3/9 \times 3/9 \times 9/14 = 0.0053$$

The fractions are taken from the *yes* entries in the table according to the values of the attributes for the new day, and the final 9/14 is the overall fraction representing the proportion of days on which *play* is *yes*. A similar calculation for the outcome *no* leads to

$$\text{Likelihood of } no = 3/5 \times 1/5 \times 4/5 \times 3/5 \times 5/14 = 0.0206$$

Table 4.2 Weather Data with Counts and Probabilities

Outlook	yes	no	Temperature	yes	no	Humidity	yes	no	Windy	yes	no	Play	yes	no
sunny	2	3	hot	2	2	high	3	4	false	6	2		9	5
overcast	4	0	mild	4	2	normal	6	1	true	3	3			
rainy	3	2	cool	3	1									
sunny	2/9	3/5	hot	2/9	2/5	high	3/9	4/5	false	6/9	2/5		9/14	5/14
overcast	4/9	0/5	mild	4/9	2/5	normal	6/9	1/5	true	3/9	3/5			
rainy	3/9	2/5	cool	3/9	1/5									

Table 4.3 A New Day				
Outlook	**Temperature**	**Humidity**	**Windy**	**Play**
Sunny	cool	high	true	?

This indicates that for the new day, *no* is more likely than *yes*—four times more likely. The numbers can be turned into probabilities by normalizing them so that they sum to 1:

$$\text{Probability of } yes = \frac{0.0053}{0.0053 + 0.0206} = 20.5\%$$

$$\text{Probability of } no = \frac{0.0206}{0.0053 + 0.0206} = 79.5\%$$

This simple and intuitive method is based on Bayes' rule of conditional probability. Bayes' rule says that if you have a hypothesis H and evidence E that bears on that hypothesis, then

$$\Pr[H \mid E] = \frac{\Pr[E \mid H]\Pr[H]}{\Pr[E]}$$

We use the notation that $\Pr[A]$ denotes the probability of an event A and $\Pr[A \mid B]$ denotes the probability of A conditional on another event B. The hypothesis H is that *play* will be, say, *yes*, and $\Pr[H \mid E]$ is going to turn out to be 20.5%, just as determined previously. The evidence E is the particular combination of attribute values for the new day—*outlook = sunny, temperature = cool, humidity = high*, and *windy = true*. Let's call these four pieces of evidence E_1, E_2, E_3, and E_4, respectively. Assuming that these pieces of evidence are independent (given the class), their combined probability is obtained by multiplying the probabilities:

$$\Pr[yes \mid E] = \frac{\Pr[E_1 \mid yes] \times \Pr[E_2 \mid yes] \times \Pr[E_3 \mid yes] \times \Pr[E_4 \mid yes] \times \Pr[yes]}{\Pr[E]}$$

Don't worry about the denominator: We will ignore it and eliminate it in the final normalizing step when we make the probabilities for *yes* and *no* sum to 1, just as we did previously. The $\Pr[yes]$ at the end is the probability of a *yes* outcome without knowing any of the evidence E—that is, without knowing anything about the particular day in question—and it's called the *prior probability* of the hypothesis H. In this case, it's just 9/14, because 9 of the 14 training examples had a *yes* value for *play*. Substituting the fractions in Table 4.2 for the appropriate evidence probabilities leads to

$$\Pr[\textit{yes} \mid E] = \frac{2/9 \times 3/9 \times 3/9 \times 3/9 \times 9/14}{\Pr[E]}$$

just as we calculated previously. Again, the $\Pr[E]$ in the denominator will disappear when we normalize.

This method goes by the name of *Naïve Bayes* because it's based on Bayes' rule and "naïvely" assumes independence—it is only valid to multiply probabilities when the events are independent. The assumption that attributes are independent (given the class) in real life certainly is a simplistic one. But despite the disparaging name, Naïve Bayes works very effectively when tested on actual datasets, particularly when combined with some of the attribute selection procedures, which are introduced in Chapter 7, that eliminate redundant, and hence nonindependent, attributes.

Things go badly awry in Naïve Bayes if a particular attribute value does not occur in the training set in conjunction with *every* class value. Suppose that in the training data the attribute value *outlook = sunny* was always associated with the outcome *no*. Then the probability of *outlook = sunny* being given a *yes*—that is, $\Pr[\textit{outlook} = \textit{sunny} \mid \textit{yes}]$—would be zero, and because the other probabilities are multiplied by this, the final probability of *yes* in the previous example would be zero no matter how large they were. Probabilities that are zero hold a veto over the other ones. This is not a good idea. But the bug is easily fixed by minor adjustments to the method of calculating probabilities from frequencies.

For example, the upper part of Table 4.2 shows that for *play = yes*, *outlook* is *sunny* for two examples, *overcast* for four, and *rainy* for three, and the lower part gives these events probabilities of 2/9, 4/9, and 3/9, respectively. Instead, we could add 1 to each numerator, and compensate by adding 3 to the denominator, giving probabilities of 3/12, 5/12, and 4/12, respectively. This will ensure that an attribute value that occurs zero times receives a probability which is nonzero, albeit small. The strategy of adding 1 to each count is a standard technique called the *Laplace estimator* after the great eighteenth-century French mathematician Pierre Laplace. Although it works well in practice, there is no particular reason for adding 1 to the counts: We could instead choose a small constant μ and use

$$\frac{2 + \mu/3}{9 + \mu}, \quad \frac{4 + \mu/3}{9 + \mu}, \quad \text{and} \quad \frac{3 + \mu/3}{9 + \mu}$$

The value of μ, which was set to 3 before, effectively provides a weight that determines how influential the a priori values of 1/3, 1/3, and 1/3 are for each of the three possible attribute values. A large μ says that these priors are very important compared with the new evidence coming in from the training set, whereas a small one gives them less influence. Finally, there is no particular reason for dividing μ into three *equal* parts in the numerators: We could use

$$\frac{2+\mu p_1}{9+\mu}, \quad \frac{4+\mu p_2}{9+\mu}, \quad \text{and } \frac{3+\mu p_3}{9+\mu}$$

instead, where p_1, p_2, and p_3 sum to 1. Effectively, these three numbers are a priori probabilities of the values of the *outlook* attribute being *sunny*, *overcast*, and *rainy*, respectively.

This is now a fully Bayesian formulation where prior probabilities have been assigned to everything in sight. It has the advantage of being completely rigorous, but the disadvantage that it is not usually clear just how these prior probabilities should be assigned. In practice, the prior probabilities make little difference provided that there are a reasonable number of training instances, and people generally just estimate frequencies using the Laplace estimator by initializing all counts to 1 instead of 0.

Missing Values and Numeric Attributes

One of the really nice things about Naïve Bayes is that missing values are no problem at all. For example, if the value of *outlook* were missing in the example of Table 4.3, the calculation would simply omit this attribute, yielding

$$\text{Likelihood of } yes = 3/9 \times 3/9 \times 3/9 \times 9/14 = 0.0238$$

$$\text{Likelihood of } no = 1/5 \times 4/5 \times 3/5 \times 5/14 = 0.0343$$

These two numbers are individually a lot higher than they were before because one of the fractions is missing. But that's not a problem because a fraction is missing in both cases, and these likelihoods are subject to a further normalization process. This yields probabilities for *yes* and *no* of 41% and 59%, respectively.

If a value is missing in a training instance, it is simply not included in the frequency counts, and the probability ratios are based on the number of values that actually occur rather than on the total number of instances.

Numeric values are usually handled by assuming that they have a "normal" or "Gaussian" probability distribution. Table 4.4 gives a summary of the weather data with numeric features from Table 1.3. For nominal attributes, we calculate counts as before, while for numeric ones we simply list the values that occur. Then, instead of normalizing counts into probabilities as we do for nominal attributes, we calculate the mean and the standard deviation for each class and each numeric attribute. The mean value of *temperature* over the *yes* instances is 73, and its standard deviation is 6.2. The mean is simply the average of the values—that is, the sum divided by the number of values. The standard deviation is the square root of the sample variance, which we calculate as follows: Subtract the mean from each value, square the result, sum them together, and then divide by *one less than* the number of values. After we have found this "sample variance," take its square root to yield the standard deviation. This is the standard way of calculating the mean and the standard deviation of a set of numbers. (The "one less than" has to do with the number of degrees of freedom in the sample, a statistical notion that we don't want to get into here.)

Table 4.4 Numeric Weather Data with Summary Statistics

Outlook			Temperature			Humidity			Windy			Play	
	yes	no		yes	no		yes	no		yes	no	yes	no
sunny	2	3		83	85		86	85	false	6	2	9	5
overcast	4	0		70	80		96	90	true	3	3		
rainy	3	2		68	65		80	70					
				64	72		65	95					
				69	71		70	91					
				75			80						
				75			70						
				72			90						
				81			75						
			mean	73	74.6	mean	79.1	86.2					
			std. dev.	6.2	7.9	std. dev.	10.2	9.7					
sunny	2/9	3/5							false	6/9	2/5	9/14	5/14
overcast	4/9	0/5							true	3/9	3/5		
rainy	3/9	2/5											

The probability density function for a normal distribution with mean μ and standard deviation σ is given by the rather formidable expression

$$f(x) = \frac{1}{\sqrt{2\pi}\sigma} e^{-\frac{(x-\mu)^2}{2\sigma^2}}$$

But fear not! All this means is that if we are considering a *yes* outcome when *temperature* has a value of, say, 66, we just need to plug $x = 66$, $\mu = 73$, and $\sigma = 6.2$ into the formula. So the value of the probability density function is

$$f(temperature = 66 \mid yes) = \frac{1}{\sqrt{2\pi} \times 6.2} e^{-\frac{(66-73)^2}{2\times 6.2^2}} = 0.0340$$

And by the same token, the probability density of a *yes* outcome when *humidity* has a value of, say, 90, is calculated in the same way:

$$f(humidity = 90 \mid yes) = 0.0221$$

The probability density function for an event is very closely related to its probability. However, it is not quite the same thing. If temperature is a continuous scale, the probability of the temperature being *exactly* 66—or *exactly* any other value, such as 63.14159262—is zero. The real meaning of the density function $f(x)$ is that the probability that the quantity lies within a small region around x, say between $x - \varepsilon/2$ and $x + \varepsilon/2$, is $\varepsilon \times f(x)$. You might think we ought to factor in the accuracy figure ε when using these density values, but that's not necessary. The same ε would appear in both the *yes* and *no* likelihoods that follow and cancel out when the probabilities were calculated.

Using these probabilities for the new day in Table 4.5 yields

$$\text{Likelihood of } yes = 2/9 \times 0.0340 \times 0.0221 \times 3/9 \times 9/14 = 0.000036$$

$$\text{Likelihood of } no = 3/5 \times 0.0279 \times 0.0381 \times 3/5 \times 5/14 = 0.000137$$

which leads to probabilities

$$\text{Probability of } yes = \frac{0.000036}{0.000036 + 0.000137} = 20.8\%$$

Table 4.5 Another New Day				
Outlook	**Temperature**	**Humidity**	**Windy**	**Play**
Sunny	66	90	true	?

$$\text{Probability of } no = \frac{0.000137}{0.000036 + 0.000137} = 79.2\%$$

These figures are very close to the probabilities calculated earlier for the new day in Table 4.3 because the *temperature* and *humidity* values of 66 and 90 yield similar probabilities to the *cool* and *high* values used before.

The normal-distribution assumption makes it easy to extend the Naïve Bayes classifier to deal with numeric attributes. If the values of any numeric attributes are missing, the mean and standard deviation calculations are based only on the ones that are present.

Naïve Bayes for Document Classification

An important domain for machine learning is document classification, in which each instance represents a document and the instance's class is the document's topic. Documents might be news items and the classes might be domestic news, overseas news, financial news, and sports. Documents are characterized by the words that appear in them, and one way to apply machine learning to document classification is to treat the presence or absence of each word as a Boolean attribute. Naïve Bayes is a popular technique for this application because it is very fast and quite accurate.

However, this does not take into account the number of occurrences of each word, which is potentially useful information when determining the category of a document. Instead, a document can be viewed as a *bag of words*—a set that contains all the words in the document, with multiple occurrences of a word appearing multiple times (technically, a *set* includes each of its members just once, whereas a *bag* can have repeated elements). Word frequencies can be accommodated by applying a modified form of Naïve Bayes called *multinominal* Naïve Bayes.

Suppose $n_1, n_2, ..., n_k$ is the number of times word i occurs in the document, and $P_1, P_2, ..., P_k$ is the probability of obtaining word i when sampling from all the documents in category H. Assume that the probability is independent of the word's context and position in the document. These assumptions lead to a *multinomial distribution* for document probabilities. For this distribution, the probability of a document E given its class H—in other words, the formula for computing the probability $\Pr[E \mid H]$ in Bayes' rule—is

$$\Pr[E \mid H] = N! \times \prod_{i=1}^{k} \frac{P_i^{n_i}}{n_i!}$$

where $N = n_1 + n_2 + ... + n_k$ is the number of words in the document. The reason for the factorials is to account for the fact that the ordering of the occurrences of each word is immaterial according to the bag-of-words model. P_i is estimated by computing the relative frequency of word i in the text of all training documents pertaining to category H. In reality, there could be a further term that gives the probability that the model for category H generates a document whose length is the same as the length of E, but it is common to assume that this is the same for all classes and hence can be dropped.

For example, suppose there are only two words, *yellow* and *blue*, in the vocabulary, and a particular document class H has $\Pr[yellow \mid H] = 75\%$ and $\Pr[blue \mid H] = 25\%$ (you might call H the class of *yellowish green* documents). Suppose E is the document *blue yellow blue* with a length of $N = 3$ words. There are four possible bags of three words. One is {*yellow yellow yellow*}, and its probability according to the preceding formula is

$$\Pr[\{yellow\ yellow\ yellow\} \mid H] = 3! \times \frac{0.75^3}{3!} \times \frac{0.25^0}{0!} = \frac{27}{64}$$

The other three, with their probabilities, are

$$\Pr[\{blue\ blue\ blue\} \mid H] = \frac{1}{64}$$

$$\Pr[\{yellow\ yellow\ blue\} \mid H] = \frac{27}{64}$$

$$\Pr[\{yellow\ blue\ blue\} \mid H] = \frac{9}{64}$$

E corresponds to the last case (recall that in a bag of words the order is immaterial); thus, its probability of being generated by the *yellowish green* document model is 9/64, or 14%. Suppose another class, *very bluish green* documents (call it H'), has $\Pr[yellow \mid H'] = 10\%$ and $\Pr[blue \mid H'] = 90\%$. The probability that E is generated by this model is 24%.

If these are the only two classes, does that mean that E is in the *very bluish green* document class? Not necessarily. Bayes' rule, given earlier, says that you have to take into account the prior probability of each hypothesis. If you know that in fact *very bluish green* documents are twice as rare as *yellowish green* ones, this would be just sufficient to outweigh the 14 to 24% disparity and tip the balance in favor of the *yellowish green* class.

The factorials in the probability formula don't actually need to be computed because, being the same for every class, they drop out in the normalization process anyway. However, the formula still involves multiplying together many small probabilities, which soon yields extremely small numbers that cause underflow on large documents. The problem can be avoided by using logarithms of the probabilities instead of the probabilities themselves.

In the multinomial Naïve Bayes formulation a document's class is determined not just by the words that occur in it but also by the number of times they occur. In general, it performs better than the ordinary Naïve Bayes model for document classification, particularly for large dictionary sizes.

Discussion

Naïve Bayes gives a simple approach, with clear semantics, to representing, using, and learning probabilistic knowledge. It can achieve impressive results. People often find that Naïve Bayes rivals, and indeed outperforms, more sophisticated classifiers on many datasets. The moral is, always try the simple things first. Over and over again people have eventually, after an extended struggle, managed to obtain good results using sophisticated learning schemes, only to discover later that simple methods such as 1R and Naïve Bayes do just as well—or even better.

There are many datasets for which Naïve Bayes does not do well, however, and it is easy to see why. Because attributes are treated as though they were independent given the class, the addition of redundant ones skews the learning process. As an extreme example, if you were to include a new attribute with the same values as *temperature* to the weather data, the effect of the *temperature* attribute would be multiplied: All of its probabilities would be squared, giving it a great deal more influence in the decision. If you were to add 10 such attributes, the decisions would effectively be made on *temperature* alone. Dependencies between attributes inevitably reduce the power of Naïve Bayes to discern what is going on. They can, however, be ameliorated by using a subset of the attributes in the decision procedure, making a careful selection of which ones to use. Chapter 7 shows how.

The normal-distribution assumption for numeric attributes is another restriction on Naïve Bayes as we have formulated it here. Many features simply aren't normally distributed. However, there is nothing to prevent us from using other distributions—there is nothing magic about the normal distribution. If you know that a particular attribute is likely to follow some other distribution, standard estimation procedures for that distribution can be used instead. If you suspect it isn't normal but don't know the actual distribution, there are procedures for "kernel density estimation" that do not assume any particular distribution for the attribute values. Another possibility is simply to discretize the data first.

4.3 DIVIDE-AND-CONQUER: CONSTRUCTING DECISION TREES

The problem of constructing a decision tree can be expressed recursively. First, select an attribute to place at the root node, and make one branch for each possible value. This splits up the example set into subsets, one for every value of the attribute. Now the process can be repeated recursively for each branch, using only those instances that actually reach the branch. If at any time all instances at a node have the same classification, stop developing that part of the tree.

The only thing left is how to determine which attribute to split on, given a set of examples with different classes. Consider (again!) the weather data. There are four possibilities for each split, and at the top level they produce the trees in Figure 4.2.

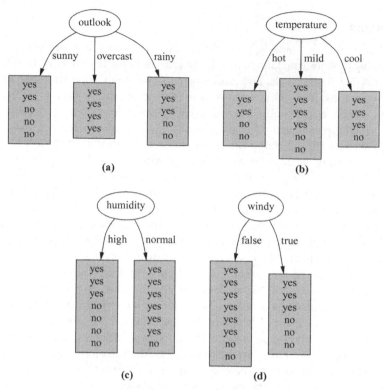

FIGURE 4.2

Tree stumps for the weather data: (a) outlook, (b) temperature, (c) humidity, and (d) windy.

Which is the best choice? The number of *yes* and *no* classes is shown at the leaves. Any leaf with only one class—*yes* or *no*—will not have to be split further, and the recursive process down that branch will terminate. Because we seek small trees, we would like this to happen as soon as possible. If we had a measure of the purity of each node, we could choose the attribute that produces the purest daughter nodes. Take a moment to look at Figure 4.2 and ponder which attribute you think is the best choice.

The measure of purity that we will use is called the *information* and is measured in units called *bits*. Associated with each node of the tree, it represents the expected amount of information that would be needed to specify whether a new instance should be classified *yes* or *no*, given that the example reached that node. Unlike the bits in computer memory, the expected amount of information usually involves fractions of a bit—and is often less than 1! It is calculated based on the number of *yes* and *no* classes at the node. We will look at the details of the calculation shortly, but first let's see how it's used. When evaluating the first tree in Figure 4.2, the number of *yes* and *no* classes at the leaf nodes are [2, 3], [4, 0], and [3, 2], respectively, and the information values of these nodes are

$$\text{info}([2, 3]) = 0.971 \text{ bits}$$

$$\text{info}([4, 0]) = 0.0 \text{ bits}$$

$$\text{info}([3, 2]) = 0.971 \text{ bits}$$

We calculate the average information value of these, taking into account the number of instances that go down each branch—five down the first and third and four down the second:

$$\text{info}([2, 3], [4, 0], [3, 2]) = (5/14) \times 0.971 + (4/14) \times 0 + (5/14) \times 0.971$$
$$= 0.693 \text{ bits}$$

This average represents the amount of information that we expect would be necessary to specify the class of a new instance, given the tree structure in Figure 4.2(a).

Before any of the nascent tree structures in Figure 4.2 were created, the training examples at the root comprised nine *yes* and five *no* nodes, corresponding to an information value of

$$\text{info}([9, 5]) = 0.940 \text{ bits}$$

Thus, the tree in Figure 4.2(a) is responsible for an information gain of

$$\text{gain}(outlook) = \text{info}([9, 5]) - \text{info}([2, 3], [4, 0], [3, 2]) = 0.940 - 0.693$$
$$= 0.247 \text{ bits}$$

which can be interpreted as the informational value of creating a branch on the *outlook* attribute.

The way forward is clear. We calculate the information gain for each attribute and split on the one that gains the most information. In the situation that is shown in Figure 4.2:

- gain(*outlook*) = 0.247 bits
- gain(*temperature*) = 0.029 bits
- gain(*humidity*) = 0.152 bits
- gain(*windy*) = 0.048 bits

Therefore, we select *outlook* as the splitting attribute at the root of the tree. Hopefully this accords with your intuition as the best one to select. It is the only choice for which one daughter node is completely pure, and this gives it a considerable advantage over the other attributes. *Humidity* is the next best choice because it produces a larger daughter node that is almost completely pure.

Then we continue, recursively. Figure 4.3 shows the possibilities for a further branch at the node reached when *outlook* is *sunny*. Clearly, a further split on

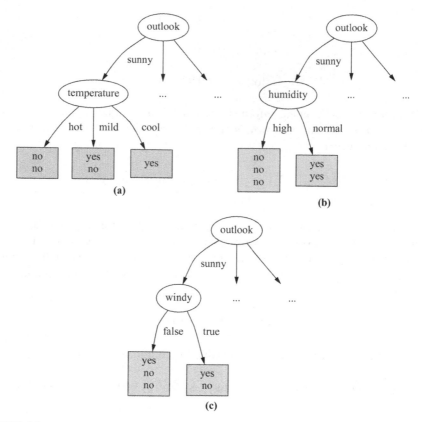

FIGURE 4.3

Expanded tree stumps for the weather data: (a) temperature, (b) humidity, and (c) windy.

outlook will produce nothing new, so we only consider the other three attributes. The information gain for each turns out to be

- gain(*temperature*) = 0.571 bits
- gain(*humidity*) = 0.971 bits
- gain(*windy*) = 0.020 bits

Therefore, we select *humidity* as the splitting attribute at this point. There is no need to split these nodes any further, so this branch is finished.

Continued application of the same idea leads to the decision tree of Figure 4.4 for the weather data. Ideally, the process terminates when all leaf nodes are pure—that is, when they contain instances that all have the same classification. However, it might not be possible to reach this happy situation because there is nothing to stop the training set containing two examples with identical sets of attributes but different classes. Consequently, we stop when the data cannot be split any further. Alternatively, one could stop if the information gain is zero. This is slightly more conservative because

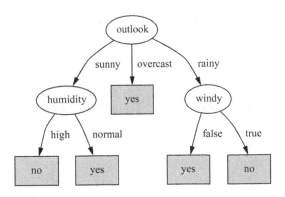

FIGURE 4.4

Decision tree for the weather data.

it is possible to encounter cases where the data can be split into subsets exhibiting identical class distributions, which would make the information gain zero.

Calculating Information

Now it is time to explain how to calculate the information measure that is used as the basis for evaluating different splits. We describe the basic idea in this section, then in the next we examine a correction that is usually made to counter a bias toward selecting splits on attributes with large numbers of possible values.

Before examining the detailed formula for calculating the amount of information required to specify the class of an example given that it reaches a tree node with a certain number of *yes*'s and *no*'s, consider first the kind of properties we would expect this quantity to have

1. When the number of either *yes*'s or *no*'s is zero, the information is zero.
2. When the number of *yes*'s and *no*'s is equal, the information reaches a maximum.

Moreover, the measure should be applicable to multiclass situations, not just to two-class ones.

The information measure relates to the amount of information obtained by making a decision, and a more subtle property of information can be derived by considering the nature of decisions. Decisions can be made in a single stage, or they can be made in several stages, and the amount of information involved is the same in both cases. For example, the decision involved in

$$info([2, 3, 4])$$

can be made in two stages. First decide whether it's the first case or one of the other two cases:

$$info([2, 7])$$

and then decide which of the other two cases it is:

$$\text{info}([3, 4])$$

In some cases the second decision will not need to be made, namely, when the decision turns out to be the first one. Taking this into account leads to the equation

$$\text{info}([2, 3, 4]) = \text{info}([2, 7]) + (7/9) \times \text{info}([3, 4])$$

Of course, there is nothing special about these particular numbers, and a similar relationship should hold regardless of the actual values. Thus, we could add a further criterion to the list above:

3. The information should obey the multistage property that we have illustrated.

Remarkably, it turns out that there is only one function that satisfies all these properties, and it is known as the *information value* or *entropy*:

$$\text{entropy}(p_1, p_2, \ldots, p_n) = -p_1 \log p_1 - p_2 \log p_2 \ldots - p_n \log p_n$$

The reason for the minus signs is that logarithms of the fractions $p_1, p_2, \ldots, p_n$ are negative, so the entropy is actually positive. Usually the logarithms are expressed in base 2, and then the entropy is in units called *bits*—just the usual kind of bits used with computers.

The arguments $p_1, p_2, \ldots$ of the entropy formula are expressed as fractions that add up to 1, so that, for example,

$$\text{info}([2, 3, 4]) = \text{entropy}(2/9, 3/9, 4/9)$$

Thus, the multistage decision property can be written in general as

$$\text{entropy}(p, q, r) = \text{entropy}(p, q+r) + (q+r) \times \text{entropy}\left(\frac{q}{q+r}, \frac{r}{q+r}\right)$$

where $p + q + r = 1$.

Because of the way the log function works, you can calculate the information measure without having to work out the individual fractions:

$$\text{info}([2, 3, 4]) = -2/9 \times \log 2/9 - 3/9 \times \log 3/9 - 4/9 \times \log 4/9$$
$$= [-2\log 2 - 3\log 3 - 4\log 4 + 9\log 9]/9$$

This is the way that the information measure is usually calculated in practice. So the information value for the first node of Figure 4.2(a) is

$$\text{info}([2, 3]) = -2/5 \times \log 2/5 - 3/5 \times \log 3/5 = 0.971 \text{ bits}$$

Highly Branching Attributes

When some attributes have a large number of possible values, giving rise to a multiway branch with many child nodes, a problem arises with the information gain calculation. The problem can best be appreciated in the extreme case when an attribute has a different value for each instance in the dataset—as, for example, an identification code attribute might.

Table 4.6 gives the weather data with this extra attribute. Branching on *ID code* produces the tree stump in Figure 4.5. The information required to specify the class given the value of this attribute is

$$\text{info}([0, 1]) + \text{info}([0, 1]) + \text{info}([1, 0]) + \ldots + \text{info}([1, 0]) + \text{info}([0, 1])$$

which is 0 because each of the 14 terms is 0. This is not surprising: The *ID code* attribute identifies the instance, which determines the class without any ambiguity—just as Table 4.6 shows. Consequently, the information gain of this attribute is just the information at the root, info([9,5]) = 0.940 bits. This is greater than the information gain of any other attribute, and so *ID code* will inevitably be chosen as the splitting attribute. But branching on the identification code is no good for predicting the class of unknown instances and tells nothing about the structure of the decision, which after all are the twin goals of machine learning.

The overall effect is that the information gain measure tends to prefer attributes with large numbers of possible values. To compensate for this, a modification of the measure called the *gain ratio* is widely used. The gain ratio is derived by taking into account the number and size of daughter nodes into which an attribute splits the dataset, disregarding any information about the class. In the situation shown in Figure 4.5, all counts have a value of 1, so the information value of the split is

$$\text{info}([1, 1, \ldots, 1]) = -1/14 \times \log 1/14 \times 14$$

because the same fraction, 1/14, appears 14 times. This amounts to log 14, or 3.807 bits, which is a very high value. This is because the information value of a split is

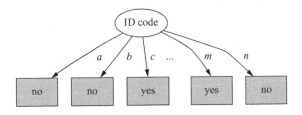

FIGURE 4.5

Tree stump for the *ID code* attribute.

Table 4.6 Weather Data with Identification Codes

ID code	Outlook	Temperature	Humidity	Windy	Play
a	sunny	hot	high	false	no
b	sunny	hot	high	true	no
c	overcast	hot	high	false	yes
d	rainy	mild	high	false	yes
e	rainy	cool	normal	false	yes
f	rainy	cool	normal	true	no
g	overcast	cool	normal	true	yes
h	sunny	mild	high	false	no
i	sunny	cool	normal	false	yes
j	rainy	mild	normal	false	yes
k	sunny	mild	normal	true	yes
l	overcast	mild	high	true	yes
m	overcast	hot	normal	false	yes
n	rainy	mild	high	true	no

the number of bits needed to determine to which branch each instance is assigned, and the more branches there are, the greater this value. The gain ratio is calculated by dividing the original information gain, 0.940 in this case, by the information value of the attribute, 3.807—yielding a gain ratio value of 0.247 for the *ID code* attribute.

Returning to the tree stumps for the weather data in Figure 4.2, *outlook* splits the dataset into three subsets of size 5, 4, and 5, and thus has an intrinsic information value of

$$\text{info}([5, 4, 5]) = 1.577$$

without paying any attention to the classes involved in the subsets. As we have seen, this intrinsic information value is greater for a more highly branching attribute such as the hypothesized *ID code*. Again, we can correct the information gain by dividing by the intrinsic information value to get the gain ratio.

The results of these calculations for the tree stumps of Figure 4.2 are summarized in Table 4.7. *Outlook* still comes out on top, but *humidity* is now a much closer contender because it splits the data into two subsets instead of three. In this particular example, the hypothetical *ID code* attribute, with a gain ratio of 0.247, would still be preferred to any of these four. However, its advantage is greatly reduced. In practical implementations, we can use an ad hoc test to guard against splitting on such a useless attribute.

Unfortunately, in some situations the gain ratio modification overcompensates and can lead to preferring an attribute just because its intrinsic information is much lower than for the other attributes. A standard fix is to choose the attribute that maximizes the gain ratio, provided that the information gain for that attribute is at least as great as the average information gain for all the attributes examined.

Discussion

The divide-and-conquer approach to decision tree induction, sometimes called *top-down induction of decision trees*, was developed and refined over many years by J. Ross Quinlan at the University of Sydney in Australia. Although others have

Table 4.7 Gain Ratio Calculations for Figure 4.2 Tree Stumps

Outlook		Temperature		Humidity		Windy	
info:	0.693	info:	0.911	info:	0.788	info:	0.892
gain: 0.940–0.693	0.247	gain: 0.940–0.911	0.029	gain: 0.940–0.788	0.152	gain: 0.940–0.892	0.048
split info: info([5,4,5])	1.577	split info: info([4,6,4])	1.362	split info: info([7,7])	1.000	split info: info([8,6])	0.985
gain ratio: 0.247/1.577	0.156	gain ratio: 0.029/1.557	0.019	gain ratio: 0.152/1	0.152	gain ratio: 0.048/0.985	0.049

worked on similar methods, Quinlan's research has always been at the very forefront of decision tree induction. The scheme that has been described using the information gain criterion is essentially the same as one known as ID3. The use of the gain ratio was one of many improvements that were made to ID3 over several years; Quinlan described it as robust under a wide variety of circumstances. Although a practical solution, it sacrifices some of the elegance and clean theoretical motivation of the information gain criterion.

A series of improvements to ID3 culminated in a practical and influential system for decision tree induction called C4.5. These improvements include methods for dealing with numeric attributes, missing values, noisy data, and generating rules from trees, and they are described in Section 6.1.

4.4 COVERING ALGORITHMS: CONSTRUCTING RULES

As we have seen, decision tree algorithms are based on a divide-and-conquer approach to the classification problem. They work top-down, seeking at each stage an attribute to split on that best separates the classes, and then recursively processing the subproblems that result from the split. This strategy generates a decision tree, which can if necessary be converted into a set of classification rules—although if it is to produce effective rules, the conversion is not trivial.

An alternative approach is to take each class in turn and seek a way of covering all instances in it, at the same time excluding instances not in the class. This is called a *covering* approach because at each stage you identify a rule that "covers" some of the instances. By its very nature, this covering approach leads to a set of rules rather than to a decision tree.

The covering method can readily be visualized in a two-dimensional space of instances as shown in Figure 4.6(a). We first make a rule covering the *a*'s. For the first test in the rule, split the space vertically as shown in the center picture. This gives the beginnings of a rule:

```
If x > 1.2 then class = a
```

However, the rule covers many *b*'s as well as *a*'s, so a new test is added to it by further splitting the space horizontally as shown in the third diagram:

```
If x > 1.2 and y > 2.6 then class = a
```

This gives a rule covering all but one of the *a*'s. It's probably appropriate to leave it at that, but if it were felt necessary to cover the final *a*, another rule would be needed, perhaps

```
If x > 1.4 and y < 2.4 then class = a
```

The same procedure leads to two rules covering the *b*'s:

```
If x ≤ 1.2 then class = b
If x > 1.2 and y ≤ 2.6 then class = b
```

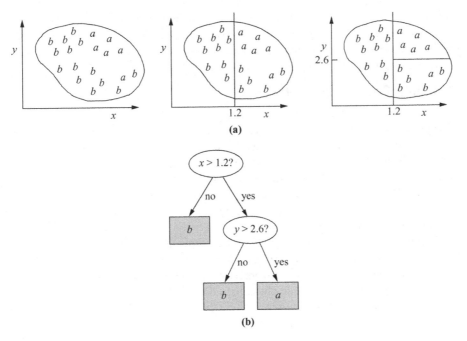

FIGURE 4.6

Covering algorithm: (a) covering the instances, and (b) decision tree for the same problem.

Again, one a is erroneously covered by these rules. If it were necessary to exclude it, more tests would have to be added to the second rule, and additional rules would be needed to cover the b's that these new tests exclude.

Rules versus Trees

A top-down divide-and-conquer algorithm operates on the same data in a manner that is, at least superficially, quite similar to a covering algorithm. It might first split the dataset using the x attribute, and would probably end up splitting it at the same place, $x = 1.2$. However, whereas the covering algorithm is concerned only with covering a single class, the division would take both classes into account because divide-and-conquer algorithms create a single concept description that applies to all classes. The second split might also be at the same place, $y = 2.6$, leading to the decision tree in Figure 4.6(b). This tree corresponds exactly to the set of rules, and in this case there is no difference in effect between the covering and the divide-and-conquer algorithms.

But in many situations there *is* a difference between rules and trees in terms of the perspicuity of the representation. For example, when we described the replicated subtree problem in Section 3.4, we noted that rules can be symmetric whereas trees must select one attribute to split on first, and this can lead to trees that are much larger than an equivalent set of rules. Another difference is that, in the multiclass case, a decision tree split takes all classes into account in trying to maximize the purity of the split, whereas the rule-generating method concentrates on one class at a time, disregarding what happens to the other classes.

A Simple Covering Algorithm

Covering algorithms operate by adding tests to the rule that is under construction, always striving to create a rule with maximum accuracy. In contrast, divide-and-conquer algorithms operate by adding tests to the tree that is under construction, always striving to maximize the separation between the classes. Each of these involves finding an attribute to split on. But the criterion for the best attribute is different in each case. Whereas divide-and-conquer algorithms such as ID3 choose an attribute to maximize the information gain, the covering algorithm we will describe chooses an attribute–value pair to maximize the probability of the desired classification.

Figure 4.7 gives a picture of the situation, showing the space containing all the instances, a partially constructed rule, and the same rule after a new term has been added. The new term restricts the coverage of the rule: The idea is to include as many instances of the desired class as possible and exclude as many instances of other classes as possible. Suppose the new rule will cover a total of t instances, of which p are positive examples of the class and $t - p$ are in other classes—that is, they are errors made by the rule. Then choose the new term to maximize the ratio p/t.

An example will help. For a change, we use the contact lens problem of Table 1.1 (page 6). We will form rules that cover each of the three classes—*hard*, *soft*, and *none*—in turn. To begin, we seek a rule:

```
If ? then recommendation = hard
```

For the unknown term ?, we have nine choices:

```
age = young                              2/8
age = pre-presbyopic                     1/8
age = presbyopic                         1/8
spectacle prescription = myope           3/12
```

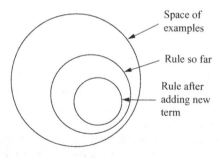

Space of examples

Rule so far

Rule after adding new term

FIGURE 4.7

The instance space during operation of a covering algorithm.

```
spectacle prescription = hypermetrope    1/12
astigmatism = no                         0/12
astigmatism = yes                        4/12
tear production rate = reduced           0/12
tear production rate = normal            4/12
```

The numbers on the right show the fraction of "correct" instances in the set singled out by that choice. In this case, "correct" means that the recommendation is *hard*. For instance, *age = young* selects 8 instances, 2 of which recommend hard contact lenses, so the first fraction is 2/8. (To follow this, you will need to look back at the contact lens data in Table 1.1 (page 6) and count up the entries in the table.)

We select the largest fraction, 4/12, arbitrarily choosing between the seventh and the last choice in the list, and create the rule:

```
If astigmatism = yes then recommendation = hard
```

This rule is quite inaccurate, getting only 4 instances correct out of the 12 that it covers, shown in Table 4.8. So we refine it further:

```
If astigmatism = yes and ? then recommendation = hard
```

Considering the possibilities for the unknown term, ? yields the following seven choices:

```
age = young                              2/4
age = pre-presbyopic                     1/4
age = presbyopic                         1/4
spectacle prescription = myope           3/6
spectacle prescription = hypermetrope    1/6
tear production rate = reduced           0/6
tear production rate = normal            4/6
```

(Again, count the entries in Table 4.8.) The last is a clear winner, getting 4 instances correct out of the 6 that it covers, and it corresponds to the rule

```
If astigmatism = yes and tear production rate = normal
   then recommendation = hard
```

Should we stop here? Perhaps. But let's say we are going for exact rules, no matter how complex they become. Table 4.9 shows the cases that are covered by the rule so far. The possibilities for the next term are now

```
age = young                              2/2
age = pre-presbyopic                     1/2
age = presbyopic                         1/2
spectacle prescription = myope           3/3
spectacle prescription = hypermetrope    1/3
```

It is necessary for us to choose between the first and fourth. So far we have treated the fractions numerically, but although these two are equal (both evaluate to 1), they have different coverage: One selects just two correct instances and the other selects

Table 4.8 Part of Contact Lens Data for Which *Astigmatism = yes*

Age	Spectacle Prescription	Astigmatism	Tear Production Rate	Recommended Lenses
young	myope	yes	reduced	none
young	myope	yes	normal	hard
young	hypermetrope	yes	reduced	none
young	hypermetrope	yes	normal	hard
pre-presbyopic	myope	yes	reduced	none
pre-presbyopic	myope	yes	normal	hard
pre-presbyopic	hypermetrope	yes	reduced	none
pre-presbyopic	hypermetrope	yes	normal	none
presbyopic	myope	yes	reduced	none
presbyopic	myope	yes	normal	hard
presbyopic	hypermetrope	yes	reduced	none
presbyopic	hypermetrope	yes	normal	none

Table 4.9 Part of Contact Lens Data for Which *Astigmatism = yes* and *Tear Production rate = normal*

Age	Spectacle Prescription	Astigmatism	Tear Production Rate	Recommended Lenses
young	myope	yes	normal	hard
young	hypermetrope	yes	normal	hard
pre-presbyopic	myope	yes	normal	hard
pre-presbyopic	hypermetrope	yes	normal	none
presbyopic	myope	yes	normal	hard
presbyopic	hypermetrope	yes	normal	none

three. In the event of a tie, we choose the rule with the greater coverage, giving the final rule:

```
If astigmatism = yes and tear production rate = normal
    and spectacle prescription = myope then recommendation = hard
```

This is indeed one of the rules given for the contact lens problem. But it only covers three out of the four *hard* recommendations. So we delete these three from the set of instances and start again, looking for another rule of the form:

```
If ? then recommendation = hard
```

Following the same process, we will eventually find that *age = young* is the best choice for the first term. Its coverage is one out of 7 the reason for the 7 is that 3 instances have been removed from the original set, leaving 21 instances altogether. The best choice for the second term is *astigmatism = yes*, selecting 1/3 (actually, this is a tie); *tear production rate = normal* is the best for the third, selecting 1/1.

```
If age = young and astigmatism = yes
    and tear production rate = normal
    then recommendation = hard
```

This rule actually covers two of the original set of instances, one of which is covered by the previous rule—but that's all right because the recommendation is the same for each rule.

Now that all the hard-lens cases are covered, the next step is to proceed with the soft-lens ones in just the same way. Finally, rules are generated for the *none* case—unless we are seeking a rule set with a default rule, in which case explicit rules for the final outcome are unnecessary.

What we have just described is the PRISM method for constructing rules. It generates only correct or "perfect" rules. It measures the success of a rule by the accuracy formula p/t. Any rule with accuracy less than 100% is "incorrect" in that

```
For each class C
   Initialize E to the instance set
   While E contains instances in class C
      Create a rule R with an empty left-hand side that predicts class C
      Until R is perfect (or there are no more attributes to use) do
         For each attribute A not mentioned in R, and each value v,
            Consider adding the condition A = v to the LHS of R
            Select A and v to maximize the accuracy p/t
               (break ties by choosing the condition with the largest p)
         Add A = v to R
      Remove the instances covered by R from E
```

FIGURE 4.8

Pseudocode for a basic rule learner.

it assigns cases to the class in question that actually do not have that class. PRISM continues adding clauses to each rule until it is perfect—its accuracy is 100%. Figure 4.8 gives a summary of the algorithm. The outer loop iterates over the classes, generating rules for each class in turn. Note that we reinitialize to the full set of examples each time around. Then we create rules for that class and remove the examples from the set until there are none of that class left. Whenever we create a rule, we start with an empty rule (which covers all the examples), and then restrict it by adding tests until it covers only examples of the desired class. At each stage we choose the most promising test—that is, the one that maximizes the accuracy of the rule. Finally, we break ties by selecting the test with greatest coverage.

Rules versus Decision Lists

Consider the rules produced for a particular class—that is, the algorithm in Figure 4.8 with the outer loop removed. It seems clear from the way that these rules are produced that they are intended to be interpreted in order—that is, as a decision list—testing the rules in turn until one applies and then using that. This is because the instances covered by a new rule are removed from the instance set as soon as the rule is completed (in the last line of the code in Figure 4.8): Thus, subsequent rules are designed for instances that are *not* covered by the rule. However, although it appears that we are supposed to check the rules in turn, we do not have to do so. Consider that any subsequent rules generated for this class will have the same effect—they all predict the same class. This means that it does not matter what order they are executed in: Either a rule will be found that covers this instance, in which case the class in question is predicted, or no such rule is found, in which case the class is not predicted.

Now return to the overall algorithm. Each class is considered in turn, and rules are generated that distinguish instances in that class from the others. No ordering is implied between the rules for one class and those for another. Consequently, the rules that are produced can be executed in any order.

As described in Section 3.4, order-independent rules seem to provide more modularity by acting as independent nuggets of "knowledge," but they suffer from the disadvantage that it is not clear what to do when conflicting rules apply. With rules generated in this way, a test example may receive multiple classifications—that is, it may satisfy rules that apply to different classes. Other test examples may receive no classification at all. A simple strategy to force a decision in ambiguous cases is to choose, from the classifications that are predicted, the one with the most training examples or, if no classification is predicted, to choose the category with the most training examples overall. These difficulties do not occur with decision lists because they are meant to be interpreted in order and execution stops as soon as one rule applies: The addition of a default rule at the end ensures that any test instance receives a classification. It is possible to generate good decision lists for the multiclass case using a slightly different method, as we will see in Section 6.2.

Methods, such as PRISM, can be described as *separate-and-conquer* algorithms: You identify a rule that covers many instances in the class (and excludes ones not in the class), separate out the covered instances because they are already taken care of by the rule, and continue with the process on those that remain. This contrasts with the divide-and-conquer approach of decision trees. The "separate" step results in an efficient method because the instance set continually shrinks as the operation proceeds.

4.5 MINING ASSOCIATION RULES

Association rules are like classification rules. You could find them in the same way, by executing a divide-and-conquer rule-induction procedure for each possible expression that could occur on the right side of the rule. However, not only might any attribute occur on the right side with any possible value, but a single association rule often predicts the value of more than one attribute. To find such rules, you would have to execute the rule-induction procedure once for every possible *combination* of attributes, with every possible combination of values, on the right side. That would result in an enormous number of association rules, which would then have to be pruned down on the basis of their *coverage* (the number of instances that they predict correctly) and their *accuracy* (the same number expressed as a proportion of the number of instances to which the rule applies). This approach is quite infeasible. (Note that, as we mentioned in Section 3.4, what we are calling *coverage* is often called *support* and what we are calling *accuracy* is often called *confidence*.)

Instead, we capitalize on the fact that we are only interested in association rules with high coverage. We ignore, for the moment, the distinction between the left and right sides of a rule and seek combinations of attribute–value pairs that have a prespecified minimum coverage. These are called *item sets*: An attribute–value pair is an *item*. The terminology derives from market basket analysis, in which the items are articles in your shopping cart and the supermarket manager is looking for associations among these purchases.

Item Sets

The first column of Table 4.10 shows the individual items for the weather data in Table 1.2 (page 10), with the number of times each item appears in the dataset given at the right. These are the one-item sets. The next step is to generate the two-item sets by making pairs of the one-item sets. Of course, there is no point in generating a set containing two different values of the same attribute (such as *outlook = sunny* and *outlook = overcast*) because that cannot occur in any actual instance.

Assume that we seek association rules with minimum coverage 2; thus, we discard any item sets that cover fewer than two instances. This leaves 47 two-item sets, some of which are shown in the second column along with the number of times they appear. The next step is to generate the three-item sets, of which 39 have a coverage of 2 or greater. There are six four-item sets, and no five-item sets—for this data, a five-item set with coverage 2 or greater could only correspond to a repeated instance. The first rows of the table, for example, show that there are five days when *outlook = sunny*, two of which have *temperature = hot*, and, in fact, on both of those days *humidity = high* and *play = no* as well.

Table 4.10 Item Sets for Weather Data with Coverage 2 or Greater

	One-Item Sets		Two-Item Sets		Three-Item Sets		Four-Item Sets	
1	outlook = sunny	5	outlook = sunny temperature = mild	2	outlook = sunny temperature = hot humidity = high	2	outlook = sunny temperature = hot humidity = high play = no	2
2	outlook = overcast	4	outlook = sunny temperature = hot	2	outlook = sunny temperature = hot play = no	2	outlook = sunny humidity = high windy = false play = no	2
3	outlook = rainy	5	outlook = sunny humidity = normal	2	outlook = sunny humidity = normal play = yes	2	outlook = overcast temperature = hot windy = false play = yes	2
4	temperature = cool	4	outlook = sunny humidity = high	3	outlook = sunny humidity = high windy = false	2	outlook = rainy temperature = mild windy = false play = yes	2
5	temperature = mild	6	outlook = sunny windy = true	2	outlook = sunny humidity = high play = no	2	outlook = rainy humidity = normal windy = false play = yes	3
6	temperature = hot	4	outlook = sunny windy = false	3	outlook = sunny windy = false play = no	2	temperature = cool humidity = normal windy = false play = yes	2
7	humidity = normal	7	outlook = sunny play = yes	2	outlook = overcast temperature = hot windy = false	2		2
8	humidity = high	7	outlook = sunny play = no	2	outlook = overcast temperature = hot play = yes	3		2

Continued

Table 4.10 Item Sets for Weather Data with Coverage or Greater (*Continued*)

	One-Item Sets	Two-Item Sets	Three-Item Sets	Four-Item Sets
9	windy = true — 6	outlook = overcast temperature = hot — 2	outlook = overcast humidity = normal play = yes — 2	2
10	windy = false — 8	outlook = overcast humidity = normal — 2	outlook = overcast humidity = high play = yes — 2	2
11	play = yes — 9	outlook = overcast humidity = high — 2	outlook = overcast windy = true play = yes — 2	2
12	play = no — 5	outlook = overcast windy = true — 2	outlook = overcast windy = false play = yes — 2	2
13		outlook = overcast windy = false — 2	outlook = rainy temperature = cool humidity = normal — 2	2
...		...	...	
38		humidity = normal windy = false — 4	humidity = normal windy = false play = yes — 4	4
39		humidity = normal play = yes — 6	humidity = high windy = false play = no — 2	2
40		humidity = high windy = true — 3		
...		...		
47		windy = false play = no — 2		

Association Rules

Shortly we will explain how to generate these item sets efficiently. But first let us finish the story. Once all item sets with the required coverage have been generated, the next step is to turn each into a rule, or a set of rules, with at least the specified minimum accuracy. Some item sets will produce more than one rule; others will produce none. For example, there is one three-item set with a coverage of 4 (row 38 of Table 4.10):

```
humidity = normal, windy = false, play = yes
```

This set leads to seven potential rules:

```
If humidity = normal and windy = false then play = yes        4/4
If humidity = normal and play = yes then windy = false        4/6
If windy = false and play = yes then humidity = normal        4/6
If humidity = normal then windy = false and play = yes        4/7
If windy = false then humidity = normal and play = yes        4/8
If play = yes then humidity = normal and windy = false        4/9
If - then humidity = normal and windy = false and play = yes  4/14
```

The figures at the right in this list show the number of instances for which all three conditions are true—that is, the coverage—divided by the number of instances for which the conditions in the antecedent are true. Interpreted as a fraction, they represent the proportion of instances on which the rule is correct—that is, its accuracy. Assuming that the minimum specified accuracy is 100%, only the first of these rules will make it into the final rule set. The denominators of the fractions are readily obtained by looking up the antecedent expression in Table 4.10 (although some are not shown in the table). The final rule above has no conditions in the antecedent, and its denominator is the total number of instances in the dataset.

Table 4.11 shows the final rule set for the weather data, with minimum coverage 2 and minimum accuracy 100%, sorted by coverage. There are 58 rules, 3 with coverage 4, 5 with coverage 3, and 50 with coverage 2. Only 7 have two conditions in the consequent, and none has more than two. The first rule comes from the item set described previously. Sometimes several rules arise from the same item set. For example, rules 9, 10, and 11 all arise from the four-item set in row 6 of Table 4.10:

```
temperature = cool, humidity = normal, windy = false, play = yes
```

which has coverage 2. Three subsets of this item set also have coverage 2:

```
temperature = cool, windy = false
temperature = cool, humidity = normal, windy = false
temperature = cool, windy = false, play = yes
```

and these lead to rules 9, 10, and 11, all of which are 100% accurate (on the training data).

Table 4.11 Association Rules for Weather Data

	Association Rule	Coverage	Accuracy
1	humidity = normal windy = false ⇒ play = yes	4	100%
2	temperature = cool ⇒ humidity = normal	4	100%
3	outlook = overcast ⇒ play = yes	4	100%
4	temperature = cool play = yes ⇒ humidity = normal	3	100%
5	outlook = rainy windy = false ⇒ play = yes	3	100%
6	outlook = rainy play = yes ⇒ windy = false	3	100%
7	outlook = sunny humidity = high ⇒ play = no	3	100%
8	outlook = sunny play = no ⇒ humidity = high	3	100%
9	temperature = cool windy = false ⇒ humidity = normal play = yes	2	100%
10	temperature = cool humidity = normal windy = false ⇒ play = yes	2	100%
11	temperature = cool windy = false play = yes ⇒ humidity = normal	2	100%
12	outlook = rainy humidity = normal windy = false ⇒ play = yes	2	100%
13	outlook = rainy humidity = normal play = yes ⇒ windy = false	2	100%
14	outlook = rainy temperature = mild windy = false ⇒ play = yes	2	100%
15	outlook = rainy temperature = mild play = yes ⇒ windy = false	2	100%
16	temperature = mild windy = false play = yes ⇒ outlook = rainy	2	100%
17	outlook = overcast temperature = hot ⇒ windy = false play = yes	2	100%
18	outlook = overcast windy = false ⇒ temperature = hot play = yes	2	100%

Table 4.11 *Continued*

	Association Rule	Coverage	Accuracy
19	temperature = hot play = yes ⇒ outlook = overcast windy = false	2	100%
20	outlook = overcast temperature = hot windy = false ⇒ play = yes	2	100%
21	outlook = overcast temperature = hot play = yes ⇒ windy = false	2	100%
22	outlook = overcast windy = false play = yes ⇒ temperature = hot	2	100%
23	temperature = hot windy = false play = yes ⇒ outlook = overcast	2	100%
24	windy = false play = no ⇒ outlook = sunny humidity = high	2	100%
25	outlook = sunny humidity = high windy = false ⇒ play = no	2	100%
26	outlook = sunny windy = false play = no ⇒ humidity = high	2	100%
27	humidity = high windy = false play = no ⇒ outlook = sunny	2	100%
28	outlook = sunny temperature = hot ⇒ humidity = high play = no	2	100%
29	temperature = hot play = no ⇒ outlook = sunny humidity = high	2	100%
30	outlook = sunny temperature = hot humidity = high ⇒ play = no	2	100%
31	outlook = sunny temperature = hot play = no ⇒ humidity = high	2	100%
…	…	…	…
58	outlook = sunny temperature = hot ⇒ humidity = high	2	100%

Generating Rules Efficiently

We now consider in more detail an algorithm for producing association rules with specified minimum coverage and accuracy. There are two stages: generating item sets with the specified minimum coverage, and from each item set determining the rules that have the specified minimum accuracy.

The first stage proceeds by generating all one-item sets with the given minimum coverage (the first column of Table 4.10) and then using this to generate the two-item sets (second column), three-item sets (third column), and so on. Each operation involves a pass through the dataset to count the items in each set, and after the pass the surviving item sets are stored in a hash table—a standard data structure that allows elements stored in it to be found very quickly. From the one-item sets, candidate two-item sets are generated, and then a pass is made through the dataset, counting the coverage of each two-item set; at the end the candidate sets with less than minimum coverage are removed from the table. The candidate two-item sets are simply all of the one-item sets taken in pairs, because a two-item set cannot have the minimum coverage unless both its constituent one-item sets have the minimum coverage, too. This applies in general: A three-item set can only have the minimum coverage if all three of its two-item subsets have minimum coverage as well, and similarly for four-item sets.

An example will help to explain how candidate item sets are generated. Suppose there are five three-item sets—(A B C), (A B D), (A C D), (A C E), and (B C D)—where, for example, A is a feature such as *outlook = sunny*. The union of the first two, (A B C D), is a candidate four-item set because its other three-item subsets (A C D) and (B C D) have greater than minimum coverage. If the three-item sets are sorted into lexical order, as they are in this list, then we need only consider pairs with the same first two members. For example, we do not consider (A C D) and (B C D) because (A B C D) can also be generated from (A B C) and (A B D), and if these two are not candidate three-item sets, then (A B C D) cannot be a candidate four-item set. This leaves the pairs (A B C) and (A B D), which we have already explained, and (A C D) and (A C E). This second pair leads to the set (A C D E) whose three-item subsets do not all have the minimum coverage, so it is discarded. The hash table assists with this check: We simply remove each item from the set in turn and check that the remaining three-item set is indeed present in the hash table. Thus, in this example there is only one candidate four-item set, (A B C D). Whether or not it actually has minimum coverage can only be determined by checking the instances in the dataset.

The second stage of the procedure takes each item set and generates rules from it, checking that they have the specified minimum accuracy. If only rules with a single test on the right side were sought, it would be simply a matter of considering each condition in turn as the consequent of the rule, deleting it from the item set, and dividing the coverage of the entire item set by the coverage of the resulting subset—obtained from the hash table—to yield the accuracy of the corresponding rule. Given that we are also interested in association rules with multiple tests in the consequent, it looks like we have to evaluate the effect of placing each *subset* of the item set on the right side, leaving the remainder of the set as the antecedent.

This brute-force method will be excessively computation intensive unless item sets are small, because the number of possible subsets grows exponentially with the size of the item set. However, there is a better way. We observed when describing association rules in Section 3.4 that if the double-consequent rule

```
If windy = false and play = no
    then outlook = sunny and humidity = high
```

holds with a given minimum coverage and accuracy, then both single-consequent rules formed from the same item set must also hold:

```
If humidity = high and windy = false and play = no
    then outlook = sunny
If outlook = sunny and windy = false and play = no
    then humidity = high
```

Conversely, if one or other of the single-consequent rules does not hold, there is no point in considering the double-consequent one. This gives a way of building up from single-consequent rules to candidate double-consequent ones, from double-consequent rules to candidate triple-consequent ones, and so on. Of course, each candidate rule must be checked against the hash table to see if it really does have more than the specified minimum accuracy. But this generally involves checking far fewer rules than the brute-force method. It is interesting that this way of building up candidate ($n + 1$)-consequent rules from actual n-consequent ones is really just the same as building up candidate ($n + 1$)-item sets from actual n-item sets, described earlier.

Discussion

Association rules are often sought for very large datasets, and efficient algorithms are highly valued. The method we have described makes one pass through the dataset for each different size of item set. Sometimes the dataset is too large to read in to main memory and must be kept on disk; then it may be worth reducing the number of passes by checking item sets of two consecutive sizes at the same time. For example, once sets with two items have been generated, all sets of three items could be generated from them before going through the instance set to count the actual number of items in the sets. More three-item sets than necessary would be considered, but the number of passes through the entire dataset would be reduced.

In practice, the amount of computation needed to generate association rules depends critically on the minimum coverage specified. The accuracy has less influence because it does not affect the number of passes that must be made through the dataset. In many situations we would like to obtain a certain number of rules—say 50—with the greatest possible coverage at a prespecified minimum accuracy level. One way to do this is to begin by specifying the coverage to be rather high and to then successively reduce it, reexecuting the entire rule-finding algorithm for each of the coverage values and repeating until the desired number of rules has been generated.

The tabular input format that we use throughout this book, and in particular the standard ARFF format based on it, is very inefficient for many association-rule problems. Association rules are often used in situations where attributes are binary—either present or absent—and most of the attribute values associated with a given instance are absent. This is a case for the sparse data representation described in Section 2.4; the same algorithm for finding association rules applies.

4.6 LINEAR MODELS

The methods we have been looking at for decision trees and rules work most naturally with nominal attributes. They can be extended to numeric attributes either by incorporating numeric-value tests directly into the decision tree or rule-induction scheme, or by prediscretizing numeric attributes into nominal ones. We will see how in Chapters 6 and 7, respectively. However, there are methods that work most naturally with numeric attributes, namely the linear models introduced in Section 3.2; we examine them in more detail here. They can form components of more complex learning methods, which we will investigate later.

Numeric Prediction: Linear Regression

When the outcome, or class, is numeric, and all the attributes are numeric, linear regression is a natural technique to consider. This is a staple method in statistics. The idea is to express the class as a linear combination of the attributes, with predetermined weights:

$$x = w_0 + w_1 a_1 + w_2 a_2 + \ldots + w_k a_k$$

where x is the class; a_1, a_2, ..., a_k are the attribute values; and w_0, w_1, ..., w_k are weights.

The weights are calculated from the training data. Here the notation gets a little heavy, because we need a way of expressing the attribute values for each training instance. The first instance will have a class, say $x^{(1)}$, and attribute values $a_1^{(1)}$, $a_2^{(1)}$, ... , $a_k^{(1)}$, where the superscript denotes that it is the first example. Moreover, it is notationally convenient to assume an extra attribute a_0, with a value that is always 1.

The predicted value for the first instance's class can be written as

$$w_0 a_0^{(1)} + w_1 a_1^{(1)} + w_2 a_2^{(1)} + \ldots + w_k a_k^{(1)} = \sum_{j=0}^{k} w_j a_j^{(1)}$$

This is the predicted, not the actual, value for the class. Of interest is the difference between the predicted and actual values. The method of linear regression is to choose the coefficients w_j—there are $k + 1$ of them—to minimize the sum of the squares of these differences over all the training instances. Suppose there are n training instances; denote the ith one with a superscript (i). Then the sum of the squares of the differences is

$$\sum_{i=1}^{n}\left(x^{(i)} - \sum_{j=0}^{k} w_j a_j^{(i)}\right)^2$$

where the expression inside the parentheses is the difference between the ith instance's actual class and its predicted class. This sum of squares is what we have to minimize by choosing the coefficients appropriately.

This is all starting to look rather formidable. However, the minimization technique is straightforward if you have the appropriate math background. Suffice it to say that given enough examples—roughly speaking, more examples than attributes—choosing weights to minimize the sum of the squared differences is really not difficult. It does involve a matrix inversion operation, but this is readily available as prepackaged software.

Once the math has been accomplished, the result is a set of numeric weights, based on the training data, which can be used to predict the class of new instances. We saw an example of this when looking at the CPU performance data, and the actual numeric weights are given in Figure 3.4(a) (page 68). This formula can be used to predict the CPU performance of new test instances.

Linear regression is an excellent, simple method for numeric prediction, and it has been widely used in statistical applications for decades. Of course, linear models suffer from the disadvantage of, well, linearity. If the data exhibits a nonlinear dependency, the best-fitting straight line will be found, where "best" is interpreted as the least mean-squared difference. This line may not fit very well. However, linear models serve well as building blocks for more complex learning methods.

Linear Classification: Logistic Regression

Linear regression can easily be used for classification in domains with numeric attributes. Indeed, we can use *any* regression technique, whether linear or nonlinear, for classification. The trick is to perform a regression for each class, setting the output equal to 1 for training instances that belong to the class and 0 for those that do not. The result is a linear expression for the class. Then, given a test example of unknown class, calculate the value of each linear expression and choose the one that is largest. This scheme is sometimes called *multiresponse linear regression*.

One way of looking at multiresponse linear regression is to imagine that it approximates a numeric *membership function* for each class. The membership function is 1 for instances that belong to that class and 0 for other instances. Given a new instance, we calculate its membership for each class and select the biggest.

Multiresponse linear regression often yields good results in practice. However, it has two drawbacks. First, the membership values it produces are not proper probabilities because they can fall outside the range 0 to 1. Second, least-squares regression assumes that the errors are not only statistically independent but are also normally distributed with the same standard deviation, an assumption that is blatently violated when the method is applied to classification problems because the observations only ever take on the values 0 and 1.

A related statistical technique called *logistic regression* does not suffer from these problems. Instead of approximating the 0 and 1 values directly, thereby risking illegitimate probability values when the target is overshot, logistic regression builds a linear model based on a transformed target variable.

Suppose first that there are only two classes. Logistic regression replaces the original target variable

$$Pr[1 \mid a_1, a_2, \ldots, a_k]$$

which cannot be approximated accurately using a linear function, by

$$\log[Pr[1 \mid a_1, a_2, \ldots, a_k]/(1 - Pr[1 \mid a_1, a_2, \ldots, a_k])]$$

The resulting values are no longer constrained to the interval from 0 to 1 but can lie anywhere between negative infinity and positive infinity. Figure 4.9(a) plots the transformation function, which is often called the *logit transformation*.

The transformed variable is approximated using a linear function just like the ones generated by linear regression. The resulting model is

$$Pr[1 \mid a_1, a_2, \ldots, a_k] = 1/(1 + \exp(-w_0 - w_1 a_1 - \ldots - w_k a_k))$$

with weights w. Figure 4.9(b) shows an example of this function in one dimension, with two weights $w_0 = -1.25$ and $w_1 = 0.5$.

Just as in linear regression, weights must be found that fit the training data well. Linear regression measures goodness of fit using the squared error. In logistic regression the *log-likelihood* of the model is used instead. This is given by

$$\sum_{i=1}^{n} (1 - x^{(i)}) \log(1 - Pr[1 \mid a_1^{(i)}, a_2^{(i)}, \ldots, a_k^{(i)}]) + x^{(i)} \log(Pr[1 \mid a_1^{(i)}, a_2^{(i)}, \ldots, a_k^{(i)}])$$

where the $x^{(i)}$ are either 0 or 1.

The weights w_i need to be chosen to maximize the log-likelihood. There are several methods for solving this maximization problem. A simple one is to iteratively solve a sequence of weighted least-squares regression problems until the log-likelihood converges to a maximum, which usually happens in a few iterations.

To generalize logistic regression to several classes, one possibility is to proceed in the way described above for multiresponse linear regression by performing logistic regression independently for each class. Unfortunately, the resulting probability estimates will not sum to 1. To obtain proper probabilities it is necessary to couple the individual models for each class. This yields a joint optimization problem, and there are efficient solution methods for this.

The use of linear functions for classification can easily be visualized in instance space. The decision boundary for two-class logistic regression lies where the prediction probability is 0.5—that is:

$$Pr[1 \mid a_1, a_2, \ldots, a_k] = 1/(1 + \exp(-w_0 - w_1 a_1 - \ldots - w_k a_k)) = 0.5$$

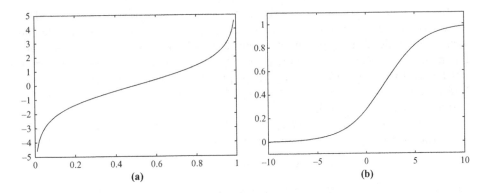

FIGURE 4.9

Logistic regression: (a) the logit transformation and (b) example logistic regression function.

This occurs when

$$-w_0 - w_1 a_1 - \ldots - w_k a_k = 0$$

Because this is a linear equality in the attribute values, the boundary is a plane, or *hyperplane*, in instance space. It is easy to visualize sets of points that cannot be separated by a single hyperplane, and these cannot be discriminated correctly by logistic regression.

Multiresponse linear regression suffers from the same problem. Each class receives a weight vector calculated from the training data. Focus for the moment on a particular pair of classes. Suppose the weight vector for class 1 is

$$w_0^{(1)} + w_1^{(1)} a_1 + w_2^{(1)} a_2 + \ldots + w_k^{(1)} a_k$$

and the same for class 2 with appropriate superscripts. Then an instance will be assigned to class 1 rather than class 2 if

$$w_0^{(1)} + w_1^{(1)} a_1 + \ldots + w_k^{(1)} a_k > w_0^{(2)} + w_1^{(2)} a_1 + \ldots + w_k^{(2)} a_k$$

In other words, it will be assigned to class 1 if

$$(w_0^{(1)} - w_0^{(2)}) + (w_1^{(1)} - w_1^{(2)}) a_1 + \ldots + (w_k^{(1)} - w_k^{(2)}) a_k > 0$$

This is a linear inequality in the attribute values, so the boundary between each pair of classes is a hyperplane.

Linear Classification Using the Perceptron

Logistic regression attempts to produce accurate probability estimates by maximizing the probability of the training data. Of course, accurate probability estimates lead to accurate classifications. However, it is not necessary to perform probability estimation if the sole purpose of the model is to predict class labels. A different approach is to learn a hyperplane that separates the instances pertaining to the different classes—let's assume that there are only two of them. If the data can be separated perfectly into two groups using a hyperplane, it is said to be *linearly separable*. It turns out that if the data is linearly separable, there is a very simple algorithm for finding a separating hyperplane.

The algorithm is called the *perceptron learning rule*. Before looking at it in detail, let's examine the equation for a hyperplane again:

$$w_0 a_0 + w_1 a_1 + w_2 a_2 + \ldots + w_k a_k = 0$$

Here, $a_1, a_2, \ldots, a_k$ are the attribute values, and $w_0, w_1, \ldots, w_k$ are the weights that define the hyperplane. We will assume that each training instance $a_1, a_2, \ldots$ is extended by an additional attribute a_0 that always has the value 1 (as we did in the case of linear regression). This extension, which is called the *bias*, just means that we don't have to include an additional constant element in the sum. If the sum is greater than 0, we will predict the first class; otherwise, we will predict the second class. We want to find values for the weights so that the training data is correctly classified by the hyperplane.

Figure 4.10(a) gives the perceptron learning rule for finding a separating hyperplane. The algorithm iterates until a perfect solution has been found, but it will only work properly if a separating hyperplane exists—that is, if the data is linearly separable. Each iteration goes through all the training instances. If a misclassified instance is encountered, the parameters of the hyperplane are changed so that the misclassified instance moves closer to the hyperplane or maybe even across the hyperplane onto the correct side. If the instance belongs to the first class, this is done by adding its attribute values to the weight vector; otherwise, they are subtracted from it.

To see why this works, consider the situation after an instance a pertaining to the first class has been added:

$$(w_0 + a_0)a_0 + (w_1 + a_1)a_1 + (w_2 + a_2)a_2 + \ldots + (w_k + a_k)a_k$$

This means that the output for a has increased by

$$a_0 \times a_0 + a_1 \times a_1 + a_2 \times a_2 + \ldots + a_k \times a_k$$

This number is always positive. Thus, the hyperplane has moved in the correct direction for classifying instance a as positive. Conversely, if an instance belonging to the second class is misclassified, the output for that instance decreases after the modification, again moving the hyperplane in the correct direction.

These corrections are incremental, and can interfere with earlier updates. However, it can be shown that the algorithm converges in a finite number of iterations if the data is linearly separable. Of course, if the data is not linearly separable, the algorithm will not terminate, so an upper bound needs to be imposed on the number of iterations when this method is applied in practice.

```
Set all weights to zero
Until all instances in the training data are classified correctly
  For each instance I in the training data
    If I is classified incorrectly by the perceptron
      If I belongs to the first class add it to the weight vector
      else subtract it from the weight vector
```

(a)

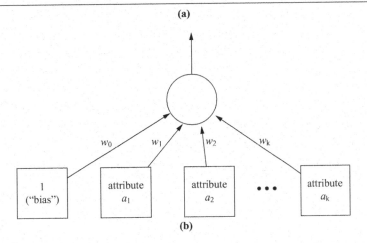

(b)

FIGURE 4.10

The perceptron: (a) learning rule, and (b) representation as a neural network.

The resulting hyperplane is called a *perceptron*, and it's the grandfather of neural networks (we return to neural networks in Section 6.4). Figure 4.10(b) represents the perceptron as a graph with nodes and weighted edges, imaginatively termed a "network" of "neurons." There are two layers of nodes: input and output. The input layer has one node for every attribute, plus an extra node that is always set to 1. The output layer consists of just one node. Every node in the input layer is connected to the output layer. The connections are weighted, and the weights are those numbers found by the perceptron learning rule.

When an instance is presented to the perceptron, its attribute values serve to "activate" the input layer. They are multiplied by the weights and summed up at the output node. If the weighted sum is greater than 0 the output signal is 1, representing the first class; otherwise, it is –1, representing the second.

Linear Classification Using Winnow

The perceptron algorithm is not the only method that is guaranteed to find a separating hyperplane for a linearly separable problem. For datasets with binary attributes there is an alternative known as *Winnow*, which is illustrated in Figure 4.11(a).

```
While some instances are misclassified
   for every instance a
      classify a using the current weights
      if the predicted class is incorrect
         if a belongs to the first class
            for each aᵢ that is 1, multiply wᵢ by α
            (if aᵢ is 0, leave wᵢ unchanged)
         otherwise
            for each aᵢ that is 1, divide wᵢ by α
            (if aᵢ is 0, leave wᵢ unchanged)
```

(a)

```
While some instances are misclassified
   for every instance a
      classify a using the current weights
      if the predicted class is incorrect
         if a belongs to the first class
            for each aᵢ that is 1,
               multiply wᵢ⁺ by α
               divide wᵢ⁻ by α
            (if aᵢ is 0, leave wᵢ⁺ and wᵢ⁻ unchanged)
         otherwise
               multiply wᵢ⁻ by α
               divide wᵢ⁺ by α
            (if aᵢ is 0, leave wᵢ⁺ and wᵢ⁻ unchanged)
```

(b)

FIGURE 4.11

The Winnow algorithm: (a) unbalanced version and (b) balanced version.

The structure of the two algorithms is very similar. Like the perceptron, Winnow only updates the weight vector when a misclassified instance is encountered—it is *mistake driven*.

The two methods differ in how the weights are updated. The perceptron rule employs an additive mechanism that alters the weight vector by adding (or subtracting) the instance's attribute vector. Winnow employs multiplicative updates and alters weights individually by multiplying them by a user-specified parameter α (or its inverse). The attribute values a_i are either 0 or 1 because we are working with binary data. Weights are unchanged if the attribute value is 0, because then they do not participate in the decision. Otherwise, the multiplier is α if that attribute helps to make a correct decision and $1/\alpha$ if it does not.

Another difference is that the threshold in the linear function is also a user-specified parameter. We call this threshold θ and classify an instance as belonging to class 1 if and only if

$$w_0 a_0 + w_1 a_1 + w_2 a_2 + \ldots + w_k a_k > \theta$$

The multiplier α needs to be greater than 1, and the w_i are set to a constant at the start.

The algorithm we have described doesn't allow for negative weights, which—depending on the domain—can be a drawback. However, there is a version, called *Balanced Winnow*, which does allow them. This version maintains two weight vectors, one for each class. An instance is classified as belonging to class 1 if

$$(w_0^+ - w_0^-)a_0 + (w_1^+ - w_1^-)a_1 + \ldots + (w_k^+ - w_k^-)a_k > \theta$$

Figure 4.11(b) shows the balanced algorithm.

Winnow is very effective in homing in on the relevant features in a dataset; therefore, it is called an *attribute-efficient* learner. That means that it may be a good candidate algorithm if a dataset has many (binary) features and most of them are irrelevant. Both Winnow and the perceptron algorithm can be used in an online setting in which new instances arrive continuously, because they can incrementally update their hypotheses as new instances arrive.

4.7 INSTANCE-BASED LEARNING

In instance-based learning the training examples are stored verbatim, and a distance function is used to determine which member of the training set is closest to an unknown test instance. Once the nearest training instance has been located, its class is predicted for the test instance. The only remaining problem is defining the distance function, and that is not very difficult to do, particularly if the attributes are numeric.

Distance Function

Although there are other possible choices, most instance-based learners use Euclidean distance. The distance between an instance with attribute values $a_1^{(1)}, a_2^{(1)}, \ldots, a_k^{(1)}$ (where k is the number of attributes) and one with values $a_1^{(2)}, a_2^{(2)}, \ldots, a_k^{(2)}$ is defined as

$$\sqrt{(a_1^{(1)} - a_1^{(2)})^2 + (a_2^{(1)} - a_2^{(2)})^2 + \ldots + (a_k^{(1)} - a_k^{(2)})^2}$$

When comparing distances it is not necessary to perform the square root operation—the sums of squares can be compared directly. One alternative to the Euclidean distance is the Manhattan, or city-block, metric, where the difference between attribute values is not squared but just added up (after taking the absolute value). Others are obtained by taking powers higher than the square. Higher powers increase the influence of large differences at the expense of small differences. Generally, the Euclidean distance represents a good compromise. Other distance metrics may be more appropriate in special circumstances. The key is to think of actual instances and what it means for them to be separated by a certain distance—what would twice that distance mean, for example?

Different attributes are often measured on different scales, so if the Euclidean distance formula were used directly, the effect of some attributes might be completely dwarfed by others that had larger scales of measurement. Consequently, it is usual to normalize all attribute values to lie between 0 and 1 by calculating

$$a_i = \frac{v_i - \min v_i}{\max v_i - \min v_i}$$

where v_i is the actual value of attribute i, and the maximum and minimum are taken over all instances in the training set.

These formulae implicitly assume numeric attributes. Here the difference between two values is just the numerical difference between them, and it is this difference that is squared and added to yield the distance function. For nominal attributes that take on values that are symbolic rather than numeric, the difference between two values that are not the same is often taken to be 1, whereas if the values are the same the difference is 0. No scaling is required in this case because only the values 0 and 1 are used.

A common policy for handling missing values is as follows. For nominal attributes, assume that a missing feature is maximally different from any other feature value. Thus, if either or both values are missing, or if the values are different, the difference between them is taken as 1; the difference is 0 only if they are not missing and both are the same. For numeric attributes, the difference between two missing values is also taken as 1. However, if just one value is missing, the difference is often taken as either the (normalized) size of the other value or 1 minus that size, whichever is larger. This means that if values are missing, the difference is as large as it can possibly be.

Finding Nearest Neighbors Efficiently

Although instance-based learning is simple and effective, it is often slow. The obvious way to find which member of the training set is closest to an unknown test instance is to calculate the distance from every member of the training set and select the smallest. This procedure is linear in the number of training instances. In other words, the time it takes to make a single prediction is proportional to the number of training instances. Processing an entire test set takes time proportional to the product of the number of instances in the training and test sets.

Nearest neighbors can be found more efficiently by representing the training set as a tree, although it is not quite obvious how. One suitable structure is a *kD-tree*. This is a binary tree that divides the input space with a hyperplane and then splits each partition again, recursively. All splits are made parallel to one of the axes, either vertically or horizontally, in the two-dimensional case. The data structure is called a *kD-tree* because it stores a set of points in k-dimensional space, with k being the number of attributes.

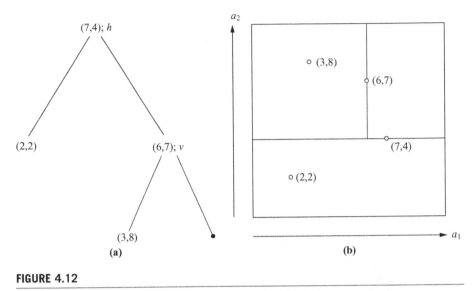

FIGURE 4.12

A *kD*-tree for four training instances: (a) the tree and (b) instances and splits.

Figure 4.12(a) gives a small example with $k = 2$, and Figure 4.12(b) shows the four training instances it represents, along with the hyperplanes that constitute the tree. Note that these hyperplanes are *not* decision boundaries: Decisions are made on a nearest-neighbor basis as explained later. The first split is horizontal (h), through the point (7,4)—this is the tree's root. The left branch is not split further: It contains the single point (2,2), which is a leaf of the tree. The right branch is split vertically (v) at the point (6,7). Its right child is empty, and its left child contains the point (3,8). As this example illustrates, each region contains just one point—or, perhaps, no points. Sibling branches of the tree—for example, the two daughters of the root in Figure 4.12(a)—are not necessarily developed to the same depth. Every point in the training set corresponds to a single node, and up to half are leaf nodes.

How do you build a *kD*-tree from a dataset? Can it be updated efficiently as new training examples are added? And how does it speed up nearest-neighbor calculations? We tackle the last question first.

To locate the nearest neighbor of a given target point, follow the tree down from its root to locate the region containing the target. Figure 4.13 shows a space like that of Figure 4.12(b) but with a few more instances and an extra boundary. The target, which is not one of the instances in the tree, is marked by a star. The leaf node of the region containing the target is colored black. This is not necessarily the target's closest neighbor, as this example illustrates, but it is a good first approximation. In particular, any nearer neighbor must lie closer—within the dashed circle in Figure 4.13. To determine whether one exists, first check whether it is possible for a closer neighbor to lie within the node's sibling. The black node's sibling is shaded in Figure 4.13, and the circle does not intersect it, so the sibling cannot contain a closer

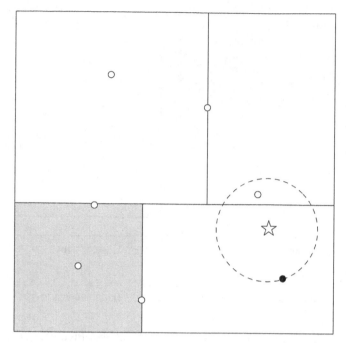

FIGURE 4.13

Using a *kD*-tree to find the nearest neighbor of the star.

neighbor. Then back up to the parent node and check *its* sibling, which here covers everything above the horizontal line. In this case it *must* be explored because the area it covers intersects with the best circle so far. To explore it, find its daughters (the original point's two aunts); check whether they intersect the circle (the left one does not, but the right one does); and descend to see if it contains a closer point (it does).

In a typical case, this algorithm is far faster than examining all points to find the nearest neighbor. The work involved in finding the initial approximate nearest neighbor—the black point in Figure 4.13—depends on the depth of the tree, given by the logarithm of the number of nodes, $\log_2 n$ if the tree is well balanced. The amount of work involved in backtracking to check whether this really is the nearest neighbor depends a bit on the tree, and on how good the initial approximation is. But for a well-constructed tree with nodes that are approximately square rather than long skinny rectangles, it can also be shown to be logarithmic in the number of nodes (if the number of attributes in the dataset is not too large).

How do you build a good tree for a set of training examples? The problem boils down to selecting the first training instance to split at and the direction of the split. Once you can do that, apply the same method recursively to each child of the initial split to construct the entire tree.

To find a good direction for the split, calculate the variance of the data points along each axis individually, select the axis with the greatest variance, and create a splitting hyperplane perpendicular to it. To find a good place for the hyperplane, locate the median value along that axis and select the corresponding point. This makes the split perpendicular to the direction of greatest spread, with half the points lying on either side. This produces a well-balanced tree. To avoid long skinny regions it is best for successive splits to be along different axes, which is likely because the dimension of greatest variance is chosen at each stage. However, if the distribution of points is badly skewed, choosing the median value may generate several successive splits in the same direction, yielding long, skinny hyperrectangles. A better strategy is to calculate the mean rather than the median and use the point closest to that. The tree will not be perfectly balanced, but its regions will tend to be squarish because there is a greater chance that different directions will be chosen for successive splits.

An advantage of instance-based learning over most other machine learning methods is that new examples can be added to the training set at any time. To retain this advantage when using a *kD*-tree, we need to be able to update it incrementally with new data points. To do this, determine which leaf node contains the new point and find its hyperrectangle. If it is empty, simply place the new point there. Otherwise, split the hyperrectangle along its longest dimension to preserve squareness. This simple heuristic does not guarantee that adding a series of points will preserve the tree's balance, nor that the hyperrectangles will be well shaped for a nearest-neighbor search. It is a good idea to rebuild the tree from scratch occasionally—for example, when its depth grows to twice the best possible depth.

As we have seen, *kD*-trees are good data structures for finding nearest neighbors efficiently. However, they are not perfect. Skewed datasets present a basic conflict between the desire for the tree to be perfectly balanced and the desire for regions to be squarish. More important, rectangles—even squares—are not the best shape to use anyway, because of their corners. If the dashed circle in Figure 4.13 were any bigger, which it would be if the black instance were a little further from the target, it would intersect the lower right corner of the rectangle at the top left and then that rectangle would have to be investigated, too—despite the fact that the training instances that define it are a long way from the corner in question. The corners of rectangular regions are awkward.

The solution? Use hyperspheres, not hyperrectangles. Neighboring spheres may overlap, whereas rectangles can abut, but this is not a problem because the nearest-neighbor algorithm for *kD*-trees does not depend on the regions being disjoint. A data structure called a *ball tree* defines *k*-dimensional hyperspheres ("balls") that cover the data points, and arranges them into a tree.

Figure 4.14(a) shows 16 training instances in two-dimensional space, overlaid by a pattern of overlapping circles, and Figure 4.14(b) shows a tree formed from these circles. Circles at different levels of the tree are indicated by different styles of dash, and the smaller circles are drawn in shades of gray. Each node of the tree represents a ball, and the node is dashed or shaded according to the same convention

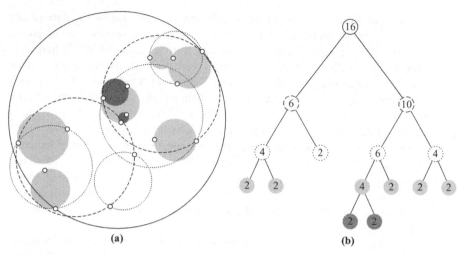

FIGURE 4.14

Ball tree for 16 training instances: (a) instances and balls and (b) the tree.

so that you can identify which level the balls are at. To help you understand the tree, numbers are placed on the nodes to show how many data points are deemed to be inside that ball. But be careful: This is not necessarily the same as the number of points falling within the spatial region that the ball represents. The regions at each level sometimes overlap, but points that fall into the overlap area are assigned to only one of the overlapping balls (the diagram does not show which one). Instead of the occupancy counts in Figure 4.14(b), the nodes of actual ball trees store the center and radius of their ball; leaf nodes record the points they contain as well.

To use a ball tree to find the nearest neighbor to a given target, start by traversing the tree from the top down to locate the leaf that contains the target and find the closest point to the target in that ball. This gives an upper bound for the target's distance from its nearest neighbor. Then, just as for the kD-tree, examine the sibling node. If the distance from the target to the sibling's center exceeds its radius plus the current upper bound, it cannot possibly contain a closer point; otherwise, the sibling must be examined by descending the tree further.

In Figure 4.15 the target is marked with a star and the black dot is its closest currently known neighbor. The entire contents of the gray ball can be ruled out: It cannot contain a closer point because its center is too far away. Proceed recursively back up the tree to its root, examining any ball that may possibly contain a point nearer than the current upper bound.

Ball trees are built from the top down, and as with kD-trees the basic problem is to find a good way of splitting a ball containing a set of data points into two. In practice, you do not have to continue until the leaf balls contain just two points: You can stop earlier, once a predetermined minimum number is reached—and the same goes for kD-trees. Here is one possible splitting method. Choose the point in the ball that

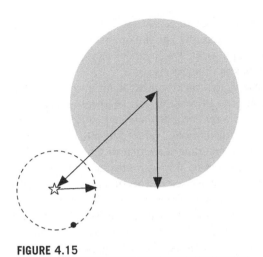

FIGURE 4.15

Ruling out an entire ball (the gray one) based on a target point (star) and its current nearest neighbor.

is farthest from its center, and then a second point that is farthest from the first one. Assign all data points in the ball to the closest one of these two cluster centers; then compute the centroid of each cluster and the minimum radius required for it to enclose all the data points it represents. This method has the merit that the cost of splitting a ball containing n points is only linear in n. There are more elaborate algorithms that produce tighter balls, but they require more computation. We will not describe sophisticated algorithms for constructing ball trees or updating them incrementally as new training instances are encountered.

Discussion

Nearest-neighbor instance-based learning is simple and often works very well. In the scheme we have described, each attribute has exactly the same influence on the decision, just as it does in the Naïve Bayes method. Another problem is that the database can easily become corrupted by noisy exemplars. One solution is to adopt the k-nearest-neighbor strategy, where some fixed, small number k of nearest neighbors—say five—are located and used together to determine the class of the test instance through a simple majority vote. (Note that earlier we used k to denote the number of attributes; this is a different, independent usage.) Another way of proofing the database against noise is to choose the exemplars that are added to it selectively and judiciously. Improved procedures, which are described in Chapter 6, address these shortcomings.

The nearest-neighbor method originated many decades ago, and statisticians analyzed k-nearest-neighbor schemes in the early 1950s. If the number of training instances is large, it makes intuitive sense to use more than one nearest neighbor, but clearly this is dangerous if there are few instances. It can be shown that when k and the number n of instances both become infinite in such a way that $k/n \rightarrow 0$, the probability of error approaches the theoretical minimum for the dataset. The nearest-neighbor method was adopted as a classification scheme in the early 1960s and has been widely used in the field of pattern recognition for almost half a century.

Nearest-neighbor classification was notoriously slow until kD-trees began to be applied in the early 1990s, although the data structure itself was developed much earlier. In practice, these trees become inefficient when the dimension of the space increases and they are only worthwhile when the number of attributes is small—up to 10. Ball trees were developed much more recently and are an instance of a more general structure called a *metric tree*. Sophisticated algorithms can create metric trees that deal successfully with thousands of dimensions.

Instead of storing all training instances, you can compress them into regions. A very simple technique, mentioned at the end of Section 4.1, is to just record the range of values observed in the training data for each attribute and category. Given a test instance, you work out which ranges the attribute values fall into and choose the category with the greatest number of correct ranges for that instance. A slightly more elaborate technique is to construct intervals for each attribute and use the training set to count the number of times each class occurs for each interval on each attribute. Numeric attributes can be discretized into intervals, and "intervals" consisting of a single point can be used for nominal ones. Then, given a test instance, you can determine which intervals the instance resides in and classify it by voting, a method called *voting feature intervals*. These methods are very approximate, but very fast, and can be useful for initial analysis of large datasets.

4.8 CLUSTERING

Clustering techniques apply when there is no class to be predicted but the instances are to be divided into natural groups. These clusters presumably reflect some mechanism that is at work in the domain from which instances are drawn, a mechanism that causes some instances to bear a stronger resemblance to each other than they do to the remaining instances. Clustering naturally requires different techniques to the classification and association learning methods that we have considered so far.

As we saw in Section 3.6, there are different ways in which the result of clustering can be expressed. The groups that are identified may be exclusive: Any instance belongs in only one group. Or they may be overlapping: An instance may fall into several groups. Or they may be probabilistic: An instance belongs to each group with a certain probability. Or they may be hierarchical: A rough division of instances into groups at the top level and each group refined further—perhaps all the way down to individual instances. Really, the choice among these possibilities should be dictated by the nature of the mechanisms that are thought to underlie the particular clustering phenomenon. However, because these mechanisms are rarely known—the very existence of clusters is, after all, something that we're trying to discover—and for pragmatic reasons too, the choice is usually dictated by the clustering tools that are available.

We will examine an algorithm that works in numeric domains, partitioning instances into disjoint clusters. Like the basic nearest-neighbor method of instance-based learning, it is a simple and straightforward technique that has been used for several decades. In Chapter 6 we examine newer clustering methods that perform incremental and probabilistic clustering.

Iterative Distance-Based Clustering

The classic clustering technique is called *k-means*. First, you specify in advance how many clusters are being sought: This is the parameter *k*. Then *k* points are chosen at random as cluster centers. All instances are assigned to their closest cluster center according to the ordinary Euclidean distance metric. Next the *centroid*, or mean, of the instances in each cluster is calculated—this is the "means" part. These centroids are taken to be new center values for their respective clusters. Finally, the whole process is repeated with the new cluster centers. Iteration continues until the same points are assigned to each cluster in consecutive rounds, at which stage the cluster centers have stabilized and will remain the same forever.

This clustering method is simple and effective. It is easy to prove that choosing the cluster center to be the centroid minimizes the total squared distance from each of the cluster's points to its center. Once the iteration has stabilized, each point is assigned to its nearest cluster center, so the overall effect is to minimize the total squared distance from all points to their cluster centers. But the minimum is a local one; there is no guarantee that it is the global minimum. The final clusters are quite sensitive to the initial cluster centers. Completely different arrangements can arise from small changes in the initial random choice. In fact, this is true of all practical clustering techniques: It is almost always infeasible to find globally optimal clusters. To increase the chance of finding a global minimum people often run the algorithm several times with different initial choices and choose the best final result—the one with the smallest total squared distance.

It is easy to imagine situations in which *k*-means fails to find a good clustering. Consider four instances arranged at the vertices of a rectangle in two-dimensional space. There are two natural clusters, formed by grouping together the two vertices at either end of a short side. But suppose the two initial cluster centers happen to fall at the midpoints of the *long* sides. This forms a stable configuration. The two clusters each contain the two instances at either end of a long side—no matter how great the difference between the long and the short sides.

k-means clustering can be dramatically improved by careful choice of the initial cluster centers, often called *seeds*. Instead of beginning with an arbitrary set of seeds, here is a better procedure. Choose the initial seed at random from the entire space, with a uniform probability distribution. Then choose the second seed with a probability that is proportional to the square of the distance from the first. Proceed, at each stage choosing the next seed with a probability proportional to the square of the distance from the closest seed that has already been chosen. This procedure, called *k-means++*, improves both speed and accuracy over the original algorithm with random seeds.

Faster Distance Calculations

The *k*-means clustering algorithm usually requires several iterations, each involving finding the distance of the *k* cluster centers from every instance to determine its cluster. There are simple approximations that speed this up considerably. For example, you can project the dataset and make cuts along selected axes, instead of using the arbitrary hyperplane divisions that are implied by choosing the nearest cluster center. But this inevitably compromises the quality of the resulting clusters.

Here's a better way of speeding things up. Finding the closest cluster center is not so different from finding nearest neighbors in instance-based learning. Can the same efficient solutions—kD-trees and ball trees—be used? Yes! Indeed, they can be applied in an even more efficient way, because in each iteration of k-means all the data points are processed together whereas, in instance-based learning, test instances are processed individually.

First, construct a kD-tree or ball tree for all the data points, which will remain static throughout the clustering procedure. Each iteration of k-means produces a set of cluster centers, and all data points must be examined and assigned to the nearest center. One way of processing the points is to descend the tree from the root until reaching a leaf and check each individual point in the leaf to find its closest cluster center. But it may be that the region represented by a higher interior node falls entirely within the domain of a single cluster center. In that case, all the data points under that node can be processed in one blow!

The aim of the exercise, after all, is to find new positions for the cluster centers by calculating the centroid of the points they contain. The centroid can be calculated by keeping a running vector sum of the points in the cluster, and a count of how many there are so far. At the end, just divide one by the other to find the centroid. Suppose that with each node of the tree we store the vector sum of the points within that node and a count of the number of points. If the whole node falls within the ambit of a single cluster, the running totals for that cluster can be updated immediately. If not, look inside the node by proceeding recursively down the tree.

Figure 4.16 shows the same instances and ball tree as in Figure 4.14, but with two cluster centers marked as black stars. Because all instances are assigned to the closest center, the space is divided in two by the thick line shown in Figure 4.16(a). Begin at the root of the tree in Figure 4.16(b), with initial values for the vector sum and counts for each cluster; all initial values are 0. Proceed recursively down the tree. When node A is reached, all points within it lie in cluster 1, so cluster 1's sum and count can be updated with the sum and count for node A, and we need not descend any further. Recursing back to node B, its ball straddles the boundary between the clusters, so its points must be examined individually. When node C is reached, it falls entirely within cluster 2; again, we can update cluster 2 immediately and we need not descend any further. The tree is only examined down to the frontier marked by the dashed line in Figure 4.16(b), and the advantage is that the nodes below need not be opened—at least not on this particular iteration of k-means. Next time, the cluster centers will have changed and things may be different.

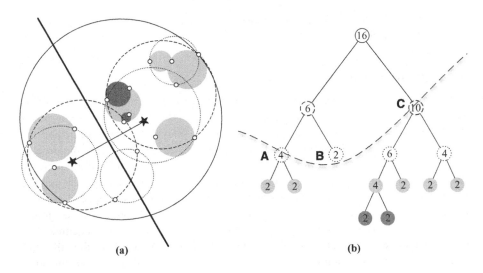

FIGURE 4.16

A ball tree: (a) two cluster centers and their dividing line and (b) the corresponding tree.

Discussion

Many variants of the basic k-means procedure have been developed. Some produce a hierarchical clustering by applying the algorithm with $k = 2$ to the overall dataset and then repeating, recursively, within each cluster.

How do you choose k? Often nothing is known about the likely number of clusters, and the whole point of clustering is to find out. One way is to try different values and choose the best. To do this you need to learn how to evaluate the success of machine learning, which is what Chapter 5 is about. We return to clustering in Section 6.8.

4.9 MULTI-INSTANCE LEARNING

In Chapter 2 we introduced *multi-instance* learning, where each example in the data comprises several different instances. We call these examples *bags* (we noted the difference between bags and sets in Section 4.2). In supervised multi-instance learning, a class label is associated with each bag, and the goal of learning is to determine how the class can be inferred from the instances that make up the bag. While advanced algorithms have been devised to tackle such problems, it turns out that the simplicity-first methodology can be applied here with surprisingly good results. A simple but effective approach is to manipulate the input data to transform it into a single-instance learning problem and then apply standard learning methods, such as the ones described in this chapter. Two such approaches are described in the following sections.

Aggregating the Input

You can convert a multiple-instance problem to a single-instance one by calculating values such as mean, mode, minimum, and maximum that summarize the instances in the bag and adding these as new attributes. Each "summary" instance retains the class label of the bag it was derived from. To classify a new bag the same process is used: A single aggregated instance is created with attributes that summarize the instances in the bag. Surprisingly, for the original drug activity dataset that spurred the development of multi-instance learning, results comparable with special-purpose multi-instance learners can be obtained using just the minimum and maximum values of each attribute for each bag, combined with a support vector machine classifier (see Chapter 6). One potential drawback of this approach is that the best summary statistics to compute depend on the problem at hand. However, the additional computational cost associated with exploring combinations of different summary statistics is offset by the fact that the summarizing process means that fewer instances are processed by the learning algorithm.

Aggregating the Output

Instead of aggregating the instances in each bag, another approach is to learn a classifier directly from the original instances that comprise the bag. To achieve this, the instances in a given bag are all assigned the bag's class label. At classification time, a prediction is produced for each instance in the bag to be predicted, and the predictions are aggregated in some fashion to form a prediction for the bag as a whole. One approach is to treat the predictions as votes for the various class labels. If the classifier is capable of assigning probabilities to the class labels, these could be averaged to yield an overall probability distribution for the bag's class label. This method treats the instances independently and gives them equal influence on the predicted class label.

One problem is that the bags in the training data can contain different numbers of instances. Ideally, each bag should have the same influence on the final model that is learned. If the learning algorithm can accept instance-level weights, this can be achieved by assigning each instance in a given bag a weight inversely proportional to the bag's size. If a bag contains n instances, giving each one a weight of $1/n$ ensures that the instances contribute equally to the bag's class label and each bag receives a total weight of 1.

Discussion

Both methods described previously for tackling multi-instance problems disregard the original multi-instance assumption that a bag is positive if and only if at least one of its instances is positive. Instead, making each instance in a bag contribute equally to its label is the key element that allows standard learning algorithms to be applied. Otherwise, it is necessary to try to identify the "special" instances that are the key to determining the bag's label.

4.10 FURTHER READING

The 1R scheme was proposed and thoroughly investigated by Holte (1993). It was never really intended as a machine learning "method." The point was more to demonstrate that very simple structures underlie most of the practical datasets being used to evaluate machine learning schemes at the time and that putting high-powered inductive inference schemes to work on simple datasets was like using a sledgehammer to crack a nut. Why grapple with a complex decision tree when a simple rule will do? The scheme that generates one simple rule per class is due to Lucio de Souza Coelho of Brazil and Len Trigg of New Zealand, and it has been dubbed *hyperpipes*. A very simple algorithm, it has the advantage of being extremely fast and is quite feasible even with an enormous number of attributes.

Bayes was an eighteenth-century English philosopher who set out his theory of probability in an "Essay towards solving a problem in the doctrine of chances," published in the *Philosophical Transactions of the Royal Society of London* (Bayes, 1763). The rule that bears his name has been a cornerstone of probability theory ever since. The difficulty with the application of Bayes' rule in practice is the assignment of prior probabilities.

Some statisticians, dubbed Bayesians, take the rule as gospel and insist that people make serious attempts to estimate prior probabilities accurately—although such estimates are often subjective. Others, non-Bayesians, prefer the kind of prior-free analysis that typically generates statistical confidence intervals, which we will see in Chapter 5. With a particular dataset, prior probabilities for Naïve Bayes are usually reasonably easy to estimate, which encourages a Bayesian approach to learning. The independence assumption made by the Naïve Bayes method is a great stumbling block, however, and efforts are being made to apply Bayesian analysis without assuming independence. The resulting models are called *Bayesian networks* (Heckerman et al., 1995), and we describe them in Section 6.7.

Bayesian techniques had been used in the field of pattern recognition (Duda and Hart, 1973) for 20 years before they were adopted by machine learning researchers (e.g., Langley et al., 1992) and made to work on datasets with redundant attributes (Langley and Sage 1994) and numeric attributes (John and Langley, 1995). The label *Naïve Bayes* is unfortunate because it is hard to use this method without feeling simpleminded. However, there is nothing naïve about its use in appropriate circumstances. The multinomial Naïve Bayes model, which is particularly useful for text classification, was investigated by McCallum and Nigam (1998).

The classic paper on decision tree induction is Quinlan (1986), who describes the basic ID3 procedure developed in this chapter. A comprehensive description of the method, including the improvements that are embodied in C4.5, appears in a classic book by Quinlan (1993), which gives a listing of the complete C4.5 system, written in the C programming language. PRISM was developed by Cendrowska (1987), who also introduced the contact lens dataset.

Association rules are introduced and described in the database literature rather than in the machine learning literature. Here the emphasis is very much on dealing with huge amounts of data rather than on sensitive ways of testing and evaluating algorithms on limited datasets. The algorithm introduced in this chapter is the Apriori method developed by Agrawal and his associates (Agrawal et al., 1993a, 1993b; Agrawal and Srikant, 1994). A survey of association-rule mining appears in an article by Chen et al. (1996).

Linear regression is described in most standard statistical texts, and a particularly comprehensive treatment can be found in Lawson and Hanson (1995). The use of linear models for classification enjoyed a great deal of popularity in the 1960s; Nilsson (1965) is an excellent reference. He defines a *linear threshold unit* as a binary test of whether a linear function is greater or less than zero and a *linear machine* as a set of linear functions, one for each class, whose value for an unknown example is compared and the largest chosen as its predicted class. In the distant past, perceptrons fell out of favor on publication of an influential book that showed that they had fundamental limitations (Minsky and Papert, 1969); however, more complex systems of linear functions have enjoyed a resurgence in recent years in the form of neural networks, described in Section 6.4. The Winnow algorithms were introduced by Nick Littlestone in his Ph.D. thesis (Littlestone, 1988, 1989). Multiresponse linear classifiers have found application in an operation called *stacking* that combines the output of other learning algorithms, described in Chapter 8 (see Wolpert, 1992).

Fix and Hodges (1951) performed the first analysis of the nearest-neighbor method, and Johns (1961) pioneered its use in classification problems. Cover and Hart (1967) obtained the classic theoretical result that, for large enough datasets, its probability of error never exceeds twice the theoretical minimum. Devroye et al. (1996) showed that k-nearest neighbor is asymptotically optimal for large k and n with $k/n \rightarrow 0$. Nearest-neighbor methods gained popularity in machine learning through the work of Aha (1992), who showed that instance-based learning can be combined with noisy exemplar pruning and attribute weighting and that the resulting methods perform well in comparison with other learning methods. We take this up again in Chapter 6.

The kD-tree data structure was developed by Friedman et al. (1977). Our description closely follows an explanation given by Andrew Moore in his Ph.D. thesis (Moore, 1991). Moore, who, along with Omohundro (1987), pioneered its use in machine learning. Moore (2000) describes sophisticated ways of constructing ball trees that perform well even with thousands of attributes. We took our ball tree example from lecture notes by Alexander Gray of Carnegie-Mellon University. The voting feature interval method mentioned in the Discussion section at the end of Section 4.7 is described by Demiroz and Guvenir (1997).

The k-means algorithm is a classic technique, and many descriptions and variations are available (e.g., Hartigan, 1975). The k-means++ variant, which yields a significant improvement by choosing the initial seeds more carefully, was introduced as recently as 2007 by Arthur and Vassilvitskii (2007). The clever use of kD-trees to speed up k-means clustering, which we have chosen to illustrate using ball trees instead, was pioneered by Moore and Pelleg (2000) in their X-means clustering algorithm. That algorithm contains some other innovations, described in Section 6.8.

The method of dealing with multi-instance learning problems by applying standard single-instance learners to summarized bag-level data was applied in conjunction with support vector machines by Gärtner et al. (2002). The alternative approach of aggregating the output is explained by Frank and Xu (2003).

4.11 WEKA IMPLEMENTATIONS

For classifiers, see Section 11.4 and Table 11.5.

- Inferring rudimentary rules: *OneR, HyperPipes* (learns one rule per class)
- Statistical modeling:
  - *NaïveBayes* and many variants, including *NaiveBayesMultinomial*
- Decision trees: *Id3*
- Decision rules: *Prism*
- Association rules (see Section 11.7 and Table 11.8): *a priori*
- Linear models:
  - SimpleLinearRegression, LinearRegression, Logistic (regression)
  - VotedPerceptron, Winnow
- Instance-based learning: *IB1, VFI* (voting feature intervals)
- Clustering (see Section 11.6 and Table 11.7): *SimpleKMeans*
- Multi-instance learning: *SimpleMI, MIWrapper*

Credibility: Evaluating What's Been Learned

5

Evaluation is the key to making real progress in data mining. There are lots of ways of inferring structure from data: We have encountered many already and will see further refinements, and new methods, in Chapter 6. However, in order to determine which ones to use on a particular problem we need systematic ways to evaluate how different methods work and to compare one with another. But evaluation is not as simple as it might appear at first sight.

What's the problem? We have the training set; surely we can just look at how well different methods do on that. Well, no: As we will see very shortly, performance on the training set is definitely not a good indicator of performance on an independent test set. We need ways of predicting performance bounds in practice, based on experiments with whatever data can be obtained.

When a vast supply of data is available, this is no problem: Just make a model based on a large training set, and try it out on another large test set. But although data mining sometimes involves "big data"—particularly in marketing, sales, and customer support applications—it is often the case that data, quality data, is scarce. The oil slicks mentioned in Chapter 1 (page 23) had to be detected and marked manually—a skilled and labor-intensive process—before being used as training data. Even in the personal loan application data (page 22), there turned out to be only 1000 training examples of the appropriate type. The electricity supply data (page 24) went back 15 years, 5000 days—but only 15 Christmas days and Thanksgivings, and just four February 29s and presidential elections. The electromechanical diagnosis application (page 25) was able to capitalize on 20 years of recorded experience, but this yielded only 300 usable examples of faults. The marketing and sales applications (page 26) certainly involve big data, but many others do not: Training data frequently relies on specialist human expertise—and that is always in short supply.

The question of predicting performance based on limited data is an interesting, and still controversial, one. We will encounter many different techniques, of which one—repeated cross-validation—is probably the method of choice in most practical limited-data situations. Comparing the performance of different machine learning schemes on a given problem is another matter that is not as easy as it sounds: To be sure that apparent differences are not caused by chance effects, statistical tests are needed.

So far we have tacitly assumed that what is being predicted is the ability to classify test instances accurately; however, some situations involve predicting class probabilities rather than the classes themselves, and others involve predicting numeric rather than nominal values. Different methods are needed in each case. Then we look at the question of cost. In most practical data mining situations, the cost of a misclassification error depends on the type of error it is—whether, for example, a positive example was erroneously classified as negative or vice versa. When doing data mining, and evaluating its performance, it is often essential to take these costs into account. Fortunately, there are simple techniques to make most learning schemes cost sensitive without grappling with the algorithm's internals. Finally, the whole notion of evaluation has fascinating philosophical connections. For 2000 years, philosophers have debated the question of how to evaluate scientific theories, and the issues are brought into sharp focus by data mining because what is extracted is essentially a "theory" of the data.

5.1 TRAINING AND TESTING

For classification problems, it is natural to measure a classifier's performance in terms of the *error rate*. The classifier predicts the class of each instance: If it is correct, that is counted as a *success*; if not, it is an *error*. The error rate is just the proportion of errors made over a whole set of instances, and it measures the overall performance of the classifier.

Of course, what we are interested in is the likely future performance on new data, not the past performance on old data. We already know the classifications of each instance in the training set, which after all is why we can use it for training. We are not generally interested in learning about those classifications—although we might be if our purpose is data cleansing rather than prediction. So the question is, is the error rate on old data likely to be a good indicator of the error rate on new data? The answer is a resounding *no*—not if the old data was used during the learning process to train the classifier.

This is a surprising fact, and a very important one. The error rate on the training set is *not* likely to be a good indicator of future performance. Why? Because the classifier has been learned from the very same training data, any estimate of performance based on that data will be optimistic, even hopelessly optimistic.

We have already seen an example of this in the labor relations dataset. Figure 1.3(b) (page 18) was generated directly from the training data, and Figure 1.3(a) was obtained from it by a process of pruning. The former is potentially more accurate on the data that was used to train the classifier, but may perform less well on independent test data because it is overfitted to the training data. The first tree will look good according to the error rate on the training data, better than the second tree. But this does not necessarily reflect how they will perform on independent test data.

The error rate on the training data is called the *resubstitution error* because it is calculated by resubstituting the training instances into a classifier that was constructed from them. Although it is not a reliable predictor of the true error rate on new data, it is nevertheless often useful to know.

To predict the performance of a classifier on new data, we need to assess its error rate on a dataset that played no part in the formation of the classifier. This independent dataset is called the *test set*. We assume that both the training data and the test data are representative samples of the underlying problem.

In some cases the test data might be distinct in nature from the training data. Consider, for example, the credit risk problem from Section 1.3 (page 22). Suppose the bank had training data from branches in New York and Florida and wanted to know how well a classifier trained on one of these datasets would perform in a new branch in Nebraska. It should probably use the Florida data as test data for evaluating the New York–trained classifier and the New York data to evaluate the Florida-trained classifier. If the datasets were amalgamated before training, performance on the test data would probably not be a good indicator of performance on future data in a completely different state.

It is important that the test data is *not used in any way* to create the classifier. For example, some learning schemes involve two stages, one to come up with a basic structure and the second to optimize parameters involved in that structure, and separate sets of data may be needed in the two stages. Or you might try out several learning schemes on the training data and then evaluate them—on a fresh dataset, of course—to see which one works best. But none of this data may be used to determine an estimate of the future error rate.

In such situations people often talk about three datasets: the *training* data, the *validation* data, and the *test* data. The training data is used by one or more learning schemes to come up with classifiers. The validation data is used to optimize parameters of those classifier, or to select a particular one. Then the test data is used to calculate the error rate of the final, optimized, method. Each of the three sets must be chosen independently: The validation set must be different from the training set to obtain good performance in the optimization or selection stage, and the test set must be different from both to obtain a reliable estimate of the true error rate.

It may be that once the error rate has been determined, the test data is bundled back into the training data to produce a new classifier for actual use. There is nothing wrong with this: It is just a way of maximizing the amount of data used to generate the classifier that will actually be employed in practice. With well-behaved learning schemes, this should not decrease predictive performance. Also, once the validation data has been used—maybe to determine the best type of learning scheme to use— then it can be bundled back into the training data to retrain that learning scheme, maximizing the use of data.

If lots of data is available, there is no problem: We take a large sample and use it for training; then another, independent large sample of different data and use it for testing. Provided both samples are representative, the error rate on the test set will give a good indication of future performance. Generally, the larger the training sample, the better the classifier, although the returns begin to diminish once a certain volume of training data is exceeded. And the larger the test sample, the more accurate the error estimate. The accuracy of the error estimate can be quantified statistically, as we will see in Section 5.2.

The real problem occurs when there is not a vast supply of data available. In many situations the training data must be classified manually—and so must the test data, of course, to obtain error estimates. This limits the amount of data that can be used for training, validation, and testing, and the problem becomes how to make the most of a limited dataset. From this dataset, a certain amount is held over for testing—this is called the *holdout* procedure—and the remainder used for training (and, if necessary, part of that is set aside for validation). There's a dilemma here: To find a good classifier, we want to use as much of the data as possible for training; to obtain a good error estimate, we want to use as much of it as possible for testing. Sections 5.3 and 5.4 review widely used methods for dealing with this dilemma.

5.2 PREDICTING PERFORMANCE

Suppose we measure the error of a classifier on a test set and obtain a certain numerical error rate—say 25%. Actually, in this section we talk about success rate rather than error rate, so this corresponds to a success rate of 75%. Now, this is only an estimate. What can you say about the *true* success rate on the target population? Sure, it's expected to be close to 75%. But how close—within 5 or 10%? It must depend on the size of the test set. Naturally, we would be more confident of the 75% figure if it were based on a test set of 10,000 instances rather than a test set of 100 instances. But how much more confident would we be?

To answer these questions, we need some statistical reasoning. In statistics, a succession of independent events that either succeed or fail is called a *Bernoulli process*. The classic example is coin tossing. Each toss is an independent event. Let's say we always predict heads; but rather than "heads" or "tails," each toss is considered a "success" or a "failure." Let's say the coin is biased, but we don't know what the probability of heads is. Then, if we actually toss the coin 100 times and 75 of the tosses are heads, we have a situation very like the one just described for a classifier with an observed 75% success rate on a test set. What can we say about the true success probability? In other words, imagine that there is a Bernoulli process—a biased coin—with a true (but unknown) success rate of p. Suppose that out of N trials, S are successes; thus, the observed success rate is $f = S/N$. The question is, what does this tell you about the true success rate p?

The answer to this question is usually expressed as a confidence interval—that is, p lies within a certain specified interval with a certain specified confidence. For example, if $S = 750$ successes are observed out of $N = 1000$ trials, this indicates that the true success rate must be around 75%. But how close to 75%? It turns out that with 80% confidence, the true success rate p lies between 73.2% and 76.7%. If $S = 75$ successes are observed out of $N = 100$ trials, this also indicates that the true success rate must be around 75%. But the experiment is smaller, and so the 80% confidence interval for p is wider, stretching from 69.1 to 80.1%.

These figures are easy to relate to qualitatively, but how are they derived quantitatively? We reason as follows: The mean and variance of a single Bernoulli trial with success rate p are p and $p(1 - p)$, respectively. If N trials are taken from a Bernoulli process, the expected success rate $f = S/N$ is a random variable with the same mean p; the variance is reduced by a factor of N to $p(1 - p)/N$. For large N, the distribution of this random variable approaches the normal distribution. These are all facts of statistics—we will not go into how they are derived.

The probability that a random variable X, with zero mean, lies within a certain confidence range of width $2z$ is

$$\Pr[-z \le X \le z] = c$$

For a normal distribution, values of c and corresponding values of z are given in tables printed at the back of most statistical texts. However, the tabulations conventionally take a slightly different form: They give the confidence that X will lie outside the range, and they give it for the upper part of the range only:

$$\Pr[X \ge z]$$

This is called a *one-tailed* probability because it refers only to the upper "tail" of the distribution. Normal distributions are symmetric, so the probabilities for the lower tail

$$\Pr[X \le -z]$$

are just the same.

Table 5.1 gives an example. Like other tables for the normal distribution, this assumes that the random variable X has a mean of 0 and a variance of 1. Alternatively, you might say that the z figures are measured in *standard deviations from the mean*. Thus, the figure for $\Pr[X \ge z] = 5\%$ implies that there is a 5% chance that X lies more than 1.65 standard deviations above the mean. Because the distribution is symmetric, the chance that X lies more than 1.65 standard deviations from the mean (above or below) is 10%, or

$$\Pr[-1.65 \le X \le 1.65] = 90\%$$

Now all we need to do is reduce the random variable f to have zero mean and unit variance. We do this by subtracting the mean p and dividing by the standard deviation $\sqrt{p(1 - p)/N}$. This leads to

$$\Pr\left[-z < \frac{f - p}{\sqrt{p(1 - p)/N}} < z\right] = c$$

Here is the procedure for finding confidence limits. Given a particular confidence figure c, consult Table 5.1 for the corresponding z value. To use the table you will first have to subtract c from 1 and then halve the result, so that for $c = 90\%$ you use the table entry for 5%. Linear interpolation can be used for intermediate confidence levels. Then write the inequality in the preceding expression as an equality and invert it to find an expression for p.

The final step involves solving a quadratic equation. Although this is not hard to do, it leads to an unpleasantly formidable expression for the confidence limits:

$$p = \left(f + \frac{z^2}{2N} \pm z\sqrt{\frac{f}{N} - \frac{f^2}{N} + \frac{z^2}{4N^2}}\right) \bigg/ \left(1 + \frac{z^2}{N}\right)$$

The $\pm$ in this expression gives two values for p that represent the upper and lower confidence boundaries. Although the formula looks complicated, it is not hard to work out in particular cases.

This result can be used to obtain the values in the numeric example given earlier. Setting $f = 75\%$, $N = 1000$, and $c = 80\%$ (so that $z = 1.28$) leads to the interval [0.732, 0.767] for p, and $N = 100$ leads to [0.691, 0.801] for the same level of confidence. Note that the normal distribution assumption is only valid for large N (say, $N > 100$). Thus, $f = 75\%$ and $N = 10$ leads to confidence limits [0.549, 0.881], but these should be taken with a grain of salt.

Table 5.1 Confidence Limits for the Normal Distribution

$\Pr[X \geq z]$	z
0.1%	3.09
0.5%	2.58
1%	2.33
5%	1.65
10%	1.28
20%	0.84
40%	0.25

5.3 CROSS-VALIDATION

Now consider what to do when the amount of data for training and testing is limited. The holdout method reserves a certain amount for testing and uses the remainder for training (and sets part of that aside for validation, if required). In practical terms, it is common to hold out one-third of the data for testing and use the remaining two-thirds for training.

Of course, you may be unlucky: The sample used for training (or testing) might not be representative. In general, you cannot tell whether a sample is representative or not. But there is one simple check that might be worthwhile: Each class in the full dataset should be represented in about the right proportion in the training and testing sets. If, by bad luck, all examples with a certain class were omitted from the training set, you could hardly expect a classifier learned from that data to perform well on examples of that class—and the situation would be exacerbated by the fact that the class would necessarily be overrepresented in the test set because none of its instances made it into the training set! Instead, you should ensure that the random sampling is done in a way that guarantees that each class is properly represented in both training and test sets. This procedure is called *stratification*, and we might speak of *stratified holdout*. While it is generally well worth doing, stratification provides only a primitive safeguard against uneven representation in training and test sets.

A more general way to mitigate any bias caused by the particular sample chosen for holdout is to repeat the whole process, training and testing, several times with different random samples. In each iteration a certain proportion, say two-thirds, of the data is randomly selected for training, possibly with stratification, and the remainder is used for testing. The error rates on the different iterations are averaged to yield an overall error rate. This is the *repeated holdout* method of error rate estimation.

In a single holdout procedure, you might consider swapping the roles of the testing and training data—that is, train the system on the test data and test it on the training data—and average the two results, thus reducing the effect of uneven representation in training and test sets. Unfortunately, this is only really plausible with a 50:50 split between training and test data, which is generally not ideal—it is better to use more than half the data for training even at the expense of test data. However, a simple variant forms the basis of an important statistical technique called *cross-validation*. In cross-validation, you decide on a fixed number of *folds*, or partitions, of the data. Suppose we use three. Then the data is split into three approximately equal partitions; each in turn is used for testing and the remainder is used for training. That is, use two-thirds of the data for training and one-third for testing, and repeat the procedure three times so that in the end, every instance has been used exactly once for testing. This is called *threefold cross-validation*, and if stratification is adopted as well—which it often is—it is *stratified threefold cross-validation*.

The standard way of predicting the error rate of a learning technique given a single, fixed sample of data is to use stratified tenfold cross-validation. The data is divided randomly into 10 parts in which the class is represented in approximately the same proportions as in the full dataset. Each part is held out in turn and the learning scheme trained on the remaining nine-tenths; then its error rate is calculated on the holdout set. Thus, the learning procedure is executed a total of 10 times on different training sets (each set has a lot in common with the others). Finally, the 10 error estimates are averaged to yield an overall error estimate.

Why 10? Extensive tests on numerous different datasets, with different learning techniques, have shown that 10 is about the right number of folds to get the best estimate of error, and there is also some theoretical evidence that backs this up. Although these arguments are by no means conclusive, and debate continues to rage in machine learning and data mining circles about what is the best scheme for evaluation, tenfold cross-validation has become the standard method in practical terms. Tests have also shown that the use of stratification improves results slightly. Thus, the standard evaluation technique in situations where only limited data is available is stratified tenfold cross-validation. Note that neither the stratification nor the division into 10 folds has to be exact: It is enough to divide the data into 10 approximately equal sets in which the various class values are represented in approximately the right proportion. Moreover, there is nothing magic about the exact number 10: 5-fold or 20-fold cross-validation is likely to be almost as good.

A single tenfold cross-validation might not be enough to get a reliable error estimate. Different tenfold cross-validation experiments with the same learning scheme and dataset often produce different results because of the effect of random variation in choosing the folds themselves. Stratification reduces the variation, but it certainly does not eliminate it entirely. When seeking an accurate error estimate, it is standard procedure to repeat the cross-validation process 10 times—that is, 10 times tenfold cross-validation—and average the results. This involves invoking the learning algorithm 100 times on datasets that are all nine-tenths the size of the original. Getting a good measure of performance is a computation-intensive undertaking.

5.4 OTHER ESTIMATES

Tenfold cross-validation is the standard way of measuring the error rate of a learning scheme on a particular dataset; for reliable results, 10 times tenfold cross-validation. But many other methods are used instead. Two that are particularly prevalent are *leave-one-out* cross-validation and the *bootstrap*.

Leave-One-Out Cross-Validation

Leave-one-out cross-validation is simply *n*-fold cross-validation, where *n* is the number of instances in the dataset. Each instance in turn is left out, and the learning scheme is trained on all the remaining instances. It is judged by its correctness on the remaining instance—one or zero for success or failure, respectively. The results of all *n* judgments, one for each member of the dataset, are averaged, and that average represents the final error estimate.

This procedure is an attractive one for two reasons. First, the greatest possible amount of data is used for training in each case, which presumably increases the chance that the classifier is an accurate one. Second, the procedure is deterministic: No random sampling is involved. There is no point in repeating it 10 times, or repeating it at all: The same result will be obtained each time. Set against this is the high computational cost, because the entire learning procedure must be executed *n* times and this is usually infeasible for large datasets. Nevertheless, leave-one-out seems to offer a chance of squeezing the maximum out of a small dataset and getting as accurate an estimate as possible.

But there is a disadvantage to leave-one-out cross-validation, apart from the computational expense. By its very nature, it cannot be stratified—worse than that, it *guarantees* a nonstratified sample. Stratification involves getting the correct proportion of examples in each class into the test set, and this is impossible when the test set contains only a single example. A dramatic, although highly artificial, illustration of the problems this might cause is to imagine a completely random dataset that contains exactly the same number of instances of each of two classes. The best that an inducer can do with random data is to predict the majority class, giving a true error rate of 50%. But in each fold of leave-one-out, the opposite class to the test instance is in the majority—and therefore the predictions will always be incorrect, leading to an estimated error rate of 100%!

The Bootstrap

The second estimation method we describe, the bootstrap, is based on the statistical procedure of sampling *with replacement*. Previously, whenever a sample was taken from the dataset to form a training or test set, it was drawn without replacement. That is, the same instance, once selected, could not be selected again. It is like picking teams for football: You cannot choose the same person twice. But dataset instances are not like people. Most learning schemes *can* use the same instance twice, and it makes a difference in the result of learning if it is present in the training set twice. (Mathematical sticklers will notice that we should not really be talking about "sets" at all if the same object can appear more than once.)

The idea of the bootstrap is to sample the dataset with replacement to form a training set. We will describe a particular variant, mysteriously (but for a reason that will soon become apparent) called the *0.632 bootstrap*. For this, a dataset of n instances is sampled n times, with replacement, to give another dataset of n instances. Because some elements in this second dataset will (almost certainly) be repeated, there must be some instances in the original dataset that have not been picked—we will use these as test instances.

What is the chance that a particular instance will not be picked for the training set? It has a $1/n$ probability of being picked each time and so a $1 - 1/n$ probability of *not* being picked. Multiply these probabilities together for a sufficient number of picking opportunities, n, and the result is a figure of

$$\left(1 - \frac{1}{n}\right)^n \approx e^{-1} = 0.368$$

where e is the base of natural logarithms, 2.7183 (not the error rate!) This gives the chance of a particular instance not being picked at all. Thus, for a reasonably large dataset, the test set will contain about 36.8% of the instances and the training set will contain about 63.2% of them (now you can see why it's called the *0.632 bootstrap*). Some instances will be repeated in the training set, bringing it up to a total size of n, the same as in the original dataset.

The figure obtained by training a learning system on the training set and calculating its error over the test set will be a pessimistic estimate of the true error rate because the training set, although its size is n, nevertheless contains only 63% of the instances, which is not a great deal compared, for example, with the 90% used in tenfold cross-validation. To compensate for this, we combine the test-set error rate with the resubstitution error on the instances in the training set. The resubstitution figure, as we warned earlier, gives a very optimistic estimate of the true error and should certainly not be used as an error figure on its own. But the bootstrap procedure combines it with the test error rate to give a final estimate e as follows:

$$e = 0.632 \times e_{\text{test instances}} + 0.368 \times e_{\text{training instances}}$$

Then, the whole bootstrap procedure is repeated several times, with different replacement samples for the training set, and the results are averaged.

The bootstrap procedure may be the best way of estimating the error rate for very small datasets. However, like leave-one-out cross-validation, it has disadvantages that can be illustrated by considering a special, artificial situation. In fact, the very dataset we considered above will do: a completely random dataset with two classes of equal size. The true error rate is 50% for any prediction rule. But a scheme that memorized the training set would give a perfect resubstitution score of 100%, so that $e_{\text{training instances}} = 0$, and the 0.632 bootstrap will mix this in with a weight of 0.368 to give an overall error rate of only 31.6% ($0.632 \times 50\% + 0.368 \times 0\%$), which is misleadingly optimistic.

5.5 COMPARING DATA MINING SCHEMES

We often need to compare two different learning schemes on the same problem to see which is the better one to use. It seems simple: Estimate the error using cross-validation (or any other suitable estimation procedure), perhaps repeated several times, and choose the scheme with the smaller estimate. This is quite sufficient in many practical applications: If one scheme has a lower estimated error than another on a particular dataset, the best we can do is to use the former scheme's model. However, it may be that the difference is simply due to estimation error, and in some circumstances it is important to determine whether one scheme is *really* better than another on a particular problem. This is a standard challenge for machine learning researchers. If a new learning algorithm is proposed, its proponents must show that it improves on the state of the art for the problem at hand and demonstrate that the observed improvement is not just a chance effect in the estimation process.

This is a job for a statistical test based on confidence bounds, the kind we met previously when trying to predict true performance from a given test-set error rate. If there were unlimited data, we could use a large amount for training and evaluate performance on a large independent test set, obtaining confidence bounds just as before. However, if the difference turns out to be significant we must ensure that this is not just because of the particular dataset we happened to base the experiment on. What we want to determine is whether one scheme is better or worse than another on average, across all possible training and test datasets that can be drawn from the domain. Because the amount of training data naturally affects performance, all datasets should be the same size. Indeed, the experiment might be repeated with different sizes to obtain a learning curve.

For the moment, assume that the supply of data is unlimited. For definiteness, suppose that cross-validation is being used to obtain the error estimates (other estimators, such as repeated cross-validation, are equally viable). For each learning scheme we can draw several datasets of the same size, obtain an accuracy estimate for each dataset using cross-validation, and compute the mean of the estimates. Each cross-validation experiment yields a different, independent error estimate. What we are interested in is the mean accuracy across all possible datasets of the same size, and whether this mean is greater for one scheme or the other.

From this point of view, we are trying to determine whether the mean of a set of samples—cross-validation estimates for the various datasets that we sampled from the domain—is significantly greater than, or significantly less than, the mean of another. This is a job for a statistical device known as the *t-test*, or *Student's t-test*. Because the same cross-validation experiment can be used for both learning schemes to obtain a matched pair of results for each dataset, a more sensitive version of the *t*-test known as a *paired t-test* can be used.

We need some notation. There is a set of samples x_1, x_2, ..., x_k obtained by successive tenfold cross-validations using one learning scheme, and a second set of samples y_1, y_2, ..., y_k obtained by successive tenfold cross-validations using the other. Each cross-validation estimate is generated using a different dataset, but all datasets are of the same size and from the same domain. We will get best results if exactly the same cross-validation partitions are used for both schemes, so that x_1 and y_1 are obtained using the same cross-validation split, as are x_2 and y_2, and so on. Denote the mean of the first set of samples by $\bar{x}$ and the mean of the second set by $\bar{y}$. We are trying to determine whether $\bar{x}$ is significantly different from $\bar{y}$.

If there are enough samples, the mean ($\bar{x}$) of a set of independent samples (x_1, x_2, ..., x_k) has a normal (i.e., Gaussian) distribution, regardless of the distribution underlying the samples themselves. Call the true value of the mean μ. If we knew the variance of that normal distribution, so that it could be reduced to have zero mean and unit variance, we could obtain confidence limits on μ given the mean of the samples ($\bar{x}$). However, the variance is unknown, and the only way we can obtain it is to estimate it from the set of samples.

That is not hard to do. The variance of $\bar{x}$ can be estimated by dividing the variance calculated from the samples x_1, x_2, ..., x_k—call it σ_x^2—by k. We can reduce the distribution of $\bar{x}$ to have zero mean and unit variance by using

$$\frac{\bar{x} - \mu}{\sqrt{\sigma_x^2 / k}}$$

The fact that we have to *estimate* the variance changes things somewhat. Because the variance is only an estimate, this does *not* have a normal distribution (although it does become normal for large values of k). Instead, it has what is called a *Student's distribution with $k - 1$ degrees of freedom*. What this means in practice is that we have to use a table of confidence intervals for the Student's distribution rather than the confidence table for the normal distribution given earlier. For 9 degrees of freedom (which is the correct number if we are using the average of 10 cross-validations) the appropriate confidence limits are shown in Table 5.2. If you compare them with Table 5.1 you will see that the Student's figures are slightly more conservative—for a given degree of confidence, the interval is slightly wider—and this reflects the additional uncertainty caused by having to estimate the variance. Different tables are needed for different numbers of degrees of freedom, and if there are more than 100 degrees of freedom the confidence limits are very close to those for the normal distribution. Like Table 5.1, the figures in Table 5.2 are for a "one-sided" confidence interval.

To decide whether the means $\bar{x}$ and $\bar{y}$, each an average of the same number k of samples, are the same or not, we consider the differences d_i between corresponding observations, $d_i = x_i - y_i$. This is legitimate because the observations are paired. The mean of this difference is just the difference between the two means, $\bar{d} = \bar{x} - \bar{y}$, and, like the means themselves, it has a Student's distribution with $k - 1$ degrees of freedom. If the means are the same, the difference is zero (this is called the *null hypothesis*); if they're significantly different, the difference will be significantly different from zero. So for a given confidence level, we will check whether the actual difference exceeds the confidence limit.

First, reduce the difference to a zero-mean, unit-variance variable called the *t-statistic*,

$$t = \frac{\bar{d}}{\sqrt{\sigma_d^2 / k}}$$

where σ_d^2 is the variance of the difference samples. Then, decide on a confidence level—generally, 5% or 1% is used in practice. From this, the confidence limit z is determined using Table 5.2 if k is 10; if it is not, a confidence table of the Student distribution for the k value in question is used. A two-tailed test is appropriate because we do not know in advance whether the mean of the x's is likely to be greater than that of the y's or vice versa; thus, for a 1% test we use the value corresponding to 0.5% in Table 5.2. If the value of t according to the last formula is greater than z, or less than $-z$, we reject the null hypothesis that the means are the same and conclude that there really is a significant difference between the two learning methods on that domain for that dataset size.

Two observations are worth making on this procedure. The first is technical: What if the observations were not paired? That is, what if we were unable, for some reason, to assess the error of each learning scheme on the same datasets? What if the number of datasets for each scheme was not even the same? These conditions could arise if someone else had evaluated one of the schemes and published several different estimates for a particular domain and dataset size—or perhaps just their mean and variance—and we wished to compare this with a different learning scheme. Then it is necessary to use a regular, nonpaired t-test. Instead of taking the mean of the difference, $\bar{d}$, we use the difference of the means, $\bar{x} - \bar{y}$. Of course, that's the same thing: The mean of the difference *is* the difference of the means. But the variance of the difference $\bar{d}$ is *not* the same. If the variance of the samples $x_1, x_2, ..., x_k$ is σ_x^2 and the variance of the samples $y_1, y_2, ..., y_\ell$ is σ_y^2,

$$\frac{\sigma_x^2}{k} + \frac{\sigma_y^2}{\ell}$$

is a good estimate of the variance of the difference of the means. It is this variance (or rather its square root) that should be used as the denominator of the t-statistic given previously. The degrees of freedom, necessary for consulting Student's confidence tables, should be taken conservatively to be the minimum of the degrees of freedom of the two samples. Essentially, knowing that the observations are paired allows the use of a better estimate for the variance, which will produce tighter confidence bounds.

The second observation concerns the assumption that there is essentially unlimited data, so that several independent datasets of the right size can be used. In practice, there is usually only a single dataset of limited size. What can be done? We could split the data into subsets (perhaps 10) and perform a cross-validation on each one. However, the overall result will only tell us whether a learning scheme is preferable for that particular size—one-tenth of the original dataset. Alternatively, the original dataset could be reused—for example, with different randomizations of the dataset for each cross-validation. However, the resulting cross-validation estimates will not be independent because they are not based on independent datasets. In practice, this means that a difference may be judged to be significant when in fact it is not. Indeed, just increasing the number of samples k—that is, the number of cross-validation runs—will eventually yield an apparently significant difference because the value of the t-statistic increases without bound.

Various modifications of the standard t-test have been proposed to circumvent this problem, all of them heuristic and somewhat lacking in theoretical justification. One that appears to work well in practice is the *corrected resampled t-test*. Assume for the moment that the repeated holdout method is used instead of cross-validation, repeated k times on different random splits of the same dataset to obtain accuracy estimates for two learning schemes. Each time, n_1 instances are used for training and n_2 for testing, and differences d_i are computed from performance on the test data. The corrected resampled t-test uses the modified statistic

$$ t = \frac{\bar{d}}{\sqrt{\left(\frac{1}{k} + \frac{n_2}{n_1} \right) \sigma_d^2}} $$

in exactly the same way as the standard t-statistic. A closer look at the formula shows that its value cannot be increased simply by increasing k. The same modified statistic can be used with repeated cross-validation, which is just a special case of repeated holdout in which the individual test sets for *one* cross-validation do not overlap. For tenfold cross-validation repeated 10 times, $k = 100$, $n_2/n_1 = 0.1/0.9$, and σ_d^2 is based on 100 differences.

Table 5.2 Confidence Limits for Student's Distribution with 9 Degrees of Freedom

Pr[X ≥ z]	z
0.1%	4.30
0.5%	3.25
1%	2.82
5%	1.83
10%	1.38
20%	0.88

5.6 PREDICTING PROBABILITIES

Throughout this chapter we have tacitly assumed that the goal is to maximize the success rate of the predictions. The outcome for each test instance is either *correct*, if the prediction agrees with the actual value for that instance, or *incorrect*, if it does not. There are no grays: Everything is black or white, correct or incorrect. In many situations, this is the most appropriate perspective. If the learning scheme, when it is actually applied, results in either a correct or an incorrect prediction, success is the right measure to use. This is sometimes called a *0 – 1 loss function*: The "loss" is either 0 if the prediction is correct or 1 if it is not. The use of *loss* is conventional, although a more optimistic terminology might couch the outcome in terms of profit instead.

Other situations are softer-edged. Most learning schemes can associate a probability with each prediction (as the Naïve Bayes scheme does). It might be more natural to take this probability into account when judging correctness. For example, a correct outcome predicted with a probability of 99% should perhaps weigh more heavily than one predicted with a probability of 51%, and, in a two-class situation, perhaps the latter is not all that much better than an *incorrect* outcome predicted with probability 51%. Whether it is appropriate to take prediction probabilities into account depends on the application. If the ultimate application really is just a prediction of the outcome, and no prizes are awarded for a realistic assessment of the likelihood of the prediction, it does not seem appropriate to use probabilities. If the prediction is subject to further processing, however—perhaps involving assessment by a person, or a cost analysis, or maybe even serving as input to a second-level learning process—then it may well be appropriate to take prediction probabilities into account.

Quadratic Loss Function

Suppose for a single instance there are k possible outcomes, or classes, and for a given instance the learning scheme comes up with a probability vector p_1, p_2, ..., p_k for the classes (where these probabilities sum to 1). The actual outcome for that instance will be one of the possible classes. However, it is convenient to express it as a vector a_1, a_2, ..., a_k whose ith component, where i is the actual class, is 1 and all other components are 0. We can express the penalty associated with this situation as a loss function that depends on both the p vector and the a vector.

One criterion that is frequently used to evaluate probabilistic prediction is the *quadratic loss function*:

$$\sum_j (p_j - a_j)^2$$

Note that this is for a single instance: The summation is over possible outputs, not over different instances. Just one of the a's will be 1 and the rest 0, so the sum contains contributions of p_j^2 for the incorrect predictions and $(1 - p_i)^2$ for the correct one. Consequently, it can be written as

$$1 - 2p_i + \sum_j p_j^2$$

where i is the correct class. When the test set contains several instances, the loss function is summed over them all.

It is an interesting theoretical fact that if you seek to minimize the value of the quadratic loss function in a situation where the actual class is generated probabilistically, the best strategy is to choose for the p vector the actual probabilities of the different outcomes—that is, $p_i = \text{Pr}[\text{class} = i]$. If the true probabilities are known, they will be the best values for p. If they are not, a system that strives to minimize the quadratic loss function will be encouraged to use its best estimate of $\text{Pr}[\text{class} = i]$ as the value for p_i.

This is quite easy to see. Denote the true probabilities by $p_1^*, p_2^*, ..., p_k^*$ so that $p_i^* = \text{Pr}[\text{class} = i]$. The expected value of the quadratic loss function over test instances can be rewritten as

$$E\left[\sum_j (p_j - a_j)^2\right] = \sum_j (E[p_j^2] - 2E[p_j a_j] + E[a_j^2])$$
$$= \sum_j (p_j^2 - 2p_j p_j^* + p_j^*)$$
$$= \sum_j ((p_j - p_j^*)^2 + p_j^*(1 - p_j^*))$$

The first stage involves bringing the expectation inside the sum and expanding the square. For the second, p_j is just a constant and the expected value of a_j is simply p_j^*; moreover, because a_j is either 0 or 1, $a_j^2 = a_j$ and its expected value is p_j^* as well. The third stage is straightforward algebra. To minimize the resulting sum, it is clear that it is best to choose $p_j = p_j^*$, so that the squared term disappears and all that remains is a term that is just the variance of the true distribution governing the actual class.

Minimizing the squared error has a long history in prediction problems. In the present context, the quadratic loss function forces the predictor to be honest about choosing its best estimate of the probabilities—or, rather, it gives preference to predictors that are able to make the best guess at the true probabilities. Moreover, the quadratic loss function has some useful theoretical properties that we will not go into here. For all these reasons, it is frequently used as the criterion of success in probabilistic prediction situations.

Informational Loss Function

Another popular criterion used to evaluate probabilistic prediction is the *informational loss function*,

$$-\log_2 p_i$$

where the ith prediction is the correct one. This is in fact identical to the negative of the log-likelihood function that is optimized by logistic regression, described in Section 4.6 (modulo a constant factor, which is determined by the base of the logarithm). It represents the information (in bits) required to express the actual class i with respect to the probability distribution $p_1, p_2, ..., p_k$. In other words, if you were given the probability distribution and someone had to communicate to you which class was the one that actually occurred, this is the number of bits they would need to encode the information if they did it as effectively as possible. (Of course, it is always possible to use *more* bits.) Because probabilities are always less than 1, their logarithms are negative, and the minus sign makes the outcome positive. For example, in a two-class situation—heads or tails—with an equal probability of each class, the occurrence of a head would take 1 bit to transmit because $-\log_2 1/2$ is 1.

The expected value of the informational loss function, if the true probabilities are $p_1{}^*$, $p_2{}^*$, ..., $p_k{}^*$, is

$$-p_1{}^*\log_2 p_1 - p_2{}^*\log_2 p_2 - ... - p_k{}^*\log_2 p_k$$

Like the quadratic loss function, this expression is minimized by choosing $p_i = p_j{}^*$, in which case the expression becomes the entropy of the true distribution:

$$-p_1{}^*\log_2 p_1{}^* - p_2{}^*\log_2 p_2{}^* - ... - p_k{}^*\log_2 p_k{}^*$$

Thus, the informational loss function also rewards honesty in predictors that know the true probabilities, and encourages predictors that do not to put forward their best guess.

One problem with the informational loss function is that if you assign a probability of 0 to an event that actually occurs, the function's value is infinity. This corresponds to losing your shirt when gambling. Prudent predictors operating under the informational loss function do not assign zero probability to any outcome. This does lead to a problem when no information is available about that outcome on which to base a prediction. This is called the *zero-frequency problem*, and various plausible solutions have been proposed, such as the Laplace estimator discussed for Naïve Bayes in Chapter 4 (page 93).

Discussion

If you are in the business of evaluating predictions of probabilities, which of the two loss functions should you use? That's a good question, and there is no universally agreed-on answer—it's really a matter of taste. They both do the fundamental job expected of a loss function: They give maximum reward to predictors that are capable of predicting the true probabilities accurately. However, there are some objective differences between the two that may help you form an opinion.

The quadratic loss function takes into account not only the probability assigned to the event that actually occurred but also the other probabilities. For example, in a four-class situation, suppose you assigned 40% to the class that actually came up and distributed the remainder among the other three classes. The quadratic loss will depend on how you distributed it because of the sum of the p_j^2 that occurs in the expression given earlier for the quadratic loss function. The loss will be smallest if the 60% was distributed evenly among the three classes: An uneven distribution will increase the sum of the squares. The informational loss function, on the other hand, depends solely on the probability assigned to the class that actually occurred. If you're gambling on a particular event coming up, and it does, who cares about potential winnings from other events?

If you assign a very small probability to the class that actually occurs, the information loss function will penalize you massively. The maximum penalty, for a zero probability, is infinite. The quadratic loss function, on the other hand, is milder, being bounded by

$$1 + \sum_j p_j^2$$

which can never exceed 2.

Finally, proponents of the informational loss function point to a general theory of performance assessment in learning called the *minimum description length (MDL) principle*. They argue that the size of the structures that a scheme learns can be measured in bits of information, and if the same units are used to measure the loss, the two can be combined in useful and powerful ways. We return to this in Section 5.9.

5.7 COUNTING THE COST

The evaluations that have been discussed so far do not take into account the cost of making wrong decisions, wrong classifications. Optimizing the classification rate without considering the cost of the errors often leads to strange results. In one case, machine learning was being used to determine the exact day that each cow in a dairy herd was in estrus, or "in heat." Cows were identified by electronic ear tags, and various attributes were used such as milk volume and chemical composition (recorded automatically by a high-tech milking machine) and milking order—for cows are regular beasts and generally arrive in the milking shed in the same order, except in unusual circumstances such as estrus. In a modern dairy operation it's important to know when a cow is ready: Animals are fertilized by artificial insemination and missing a cycle will delay calving unnecessarily, causing complications down the line. In early experiments, machine learning schemes stubbornly predicted that each cow was *never* in estrus. Like humans, cows have a menstrual cycle of approximately 30 days, so this "null" rule is correct about 97% of the time—an impressive degree of accuracy in any agricultural domain! What was wanted, of course, was rules that predicted the "in estrus" situation more accurately than the "not in estrus" one: The costs of the two kinds of error were different. Evaluation by classification accuracy tacitly assumes equal error costs.

Other examples where errors cost different amounts include loan decisions: The cost of lending to a defaulter is far greater than the lost-business cost of refusing a loan to a nondefaulter. And oil-slick detection: The cost of failing to detect an environment-threatening real slick is far greater than the cost of a false alarm. And load forecasting: The cost of gearing up electricity generators for a storm that doesn't hit is far less than the cost of being caught completely unprepared. And diagnosis:

Table 5.3 Different Outcomes of a Two-Class Prediction

		Predicted Class	
		yes	*no*
Actual Class	*yes*	true positive	false negative
	no	false positive	true negative

The cost of misidentifying problems with a machine that turns out to be free of faults is less than the cost of overlooking problems with one that is about to fail. And promotional mailing: The cost of sending junk mail to a household that doesn't respond is far less than the lost-business cost of not sending it to a household that would have responded. Why—these are all the examples from Chapter 1! In truth, you'd be hard pressed to find an application in which the costs of different kinds of errors were the same.

In the two-class case with classes *yes* and *no*—lend or not lend, mark a suspicious patch as an oil slick or not, and so on—a single prediction has the four different possible outcomes shown in Table 5.3. The *true positives* (TP) and *true negatives* (TN) are correct classifications. A *false positive* (FP) is when the outcome is incorrectly predicted as *yes* (or positive) when it is actually *no* (negative). A *false negative* (FN) is when the outcome is incorrectly predicted as negative when it is actually positive. The *true positive rate* is TP divided by the total number of positives, which is TP + FN; the *false positive rate* is FP divided by the total number of negatives, which is FP + TN. The overall success rate is the number of correct classifications divided by the total number of classifications:

$$\frac{TP + TN}{TP + TN + FP + FN}$$

Finally, the error rate is 1 minus this.

In multiclass prediction, the result on a test set is often displayed as a two-dimensional *confusion matrix* with a row and column for each class. Each matrix element shows the number of test examples for which the actual class is the row and the predicted class is the column. Good results correspond to large numbers down the main diagonal and small, ideally zero, off-diagonal elements. Table 5.4(a) shows a numeric example with three classes. In this case, the test set has 200 instances (the sum of the nine numbers in the matrix), and 88 + 40 + 12 = 140 of them are predicted correctly, so the success rate is 70%.

But is this a fair measure of overall success? How many agreements would you expect *by chance*? This predictor predicts a total of 120 *a*'s, 60 *b*'s, and 20 *c*'s; what if you had a random predictor that predicted the same total numbers of the three classes? The answer is shown in Table 5.4(b). Its first row divides the 100 *a*'s in the test set into these overall proportions, and the second and third rows do the same

Table 5.4 Different Outcomes of a Three-Class Prediction: (a) Actual and (b) Expected

(a)

		Predicted Class			
		a	b	c	Total
Actual Class	a	88	10	2	100
	b	14	40	6	60
	c	18	10	12	40
	Total	120	60	20	

(b)

		Predicted Class			
		a	b	c	Total
Actual Class	a	60	30	10	100
	b	36	18	6	60
	c	24	12	4	40
	Total	120	60	20	

thing for the other two classes. Of course, the row and column totals for this matrix are the same as before—the number of instances hasn't changed, and we have ensured that the random predictor predicts the same number of *a*'s, *b*'s, and *c*'s as the actual predictor.

This random predictor gets $60 + 18 + 4 = 82$ instances correct. A measure called the *Kappa statistic* takes this expected figure into account by deducting it from the predictor's successes and expressing the result as a proportion of the total for a perfect predictor, to yield $140 - 82 = 58$ extra successes out of a possible total of $200 - 82 = 118$, or 49.2%. The maximum value of Kappa is 100%, and the expected value for a random predictor with the same column totals is 0. In summary, the Kappa statistic is used to measure the agreement between predicted and observed categorizations of a dataset, while correcting for an agreement that occurs by chance. However, like the plain success rate, it does not take costs into account.

Cost-Sensitive Classification

If the costs are known, they can be incorporated into a financial analysis of the decision-making process. In the two-class case, in which the confusion matrix is like that of Table 5.3, the two kinds of error—false positives and false negatives—will have different costs; likewise, the two types of correct classification may have different benefits. In the two-class case, costs can be summarized in the form of a 2×2 matrix in which the diagonal elements represent the two types of correct classification and the off-diagonal elements represent the two types of error. In the multiclass case this generalizes to a square matrix whose size is the number of classes, and again the diagonal elements represent the cost of correct classification. Table 5.5(a) and (b) shows default cost matrixes for the two- and three-class cases, whose values simply give the number of errors: Misclassification costs are all 1.

Taking the cost matrix into account replaces the success rate by the average cost (or, thinking more positively, profit) per decision. Although we will not do so here, a complete financial analysis of the decision-making process might also take into account the cost of using the machine learning tool—including the cost of gathering the training data—and the cost of using the model, or decision structure, that it

Table 5.5 Default Cost Matrixes: (a) Two-Class Case and (b) Three-Class Case

		Predicted Class					Predicted Class		
		yes	*no*				*a*	*b*	*c*
Actual Class	*yes*	0	1		Actual Class	*a*	0	1	1
	no	1	0			*b*	1	0	1
						c	1	1	0

(a)	(b)

produces—including the cost of determining the attributes for the test instances. If all costs are known, and the projected number of the four different outcomes in the cost matrix can be estimated, say using cross-validation, it is straightforward to perform this kind of financial analysis.

Given a cost matrix, you can calculate the cost of a particular learned model on a given test set just by summing the relevant elements of the cost matrix for the model's prediction for each test instance. Here, costs are ignored when making predictions, but taken into account when evaluating them.

If the model outputs the probability associated with each prediction, it can be adjusted to minimize the expected cost of the predictions. Given a set of predicted probabilities for each outcome on a certain test instance, one normally selects the most likely outcome. Instead, the model could predict the class with the smallest expected misclassification cost. For example, suppose in a three-class situation the model assigns the classes a, b, and c to a test instance with probabilities p_a, p_b, and p_c, and the cost matrix is that in Table 5.5(b). If it predicts a, the expected cost of the prediction is obtained by multiplying the first column of the matrix, $[0,1,1]$, by the probability vector, $[p_a, p_b, p_c]$, yielding $p_b + p_c$, or $1 - p_a$, because the three probabilities sum to 1. Similarly, the costs for predicting the other two classes are $1 - p_b$ and $1 - p_c$. For this cost matrix, choosing the prediction with the lowest expected cost is the same as choosing the one with the greatest probability. For a different cost matrix it might be different.

We have assumed that the learning scheme outputs probabilities, as Naïve Bayes does. Even if they do not normally output probabilities, most classifiers can easily be adapted to compute them. In a decision tree, for example, the probability distribution for a test instance is just the distribution of classes at the corresponding leaf.

Cost-Sensitive Learning

We have seen how a classifier, built without taking costs into consideration, can be used to make predictions that are sensitive to the cost matrix. In this case, costs are ignored at training time but used at prediction time. An alternative is to do just the opposite: Take the cost matrix into account during the training process and ignore costs at prediction time. In principle, better performance might be obtained if the classifier were tailored by the learning algorithm to the cost matrix.

In the two-class situation, there is a simple and general way to make any learning scheme cost sensitive. The idea is to generate training data with a different proportion of *yes* and *no* instances. Suppose you artificially increase the number of *no* instances by a factor of 10 and use the resulting dataset for training. If the learning scheme is striving to minimize the number of errors, it will come up with a decision structure that is biased toward avoiding errors on the *no* instances because such errors are effectively penalized tenfold. If data with the original proportion of *no* instances is used for testing, fewer errors will be made on these than on *yes* instances—that is, there will be fewer false positives than false negatives—because false positives have been weighted 10 times more heavily than false negatives.

Varying the proportion of instances in the training set is a general technique for building cost-sensitive classifiers.

One way to vary the proportion of training instances is to duplicate instances in the dataset. However, many learning schemes allow instances to be weighted. (As we mentioned in Section 3.2, this is a common technique for handling missing values.) Instance weights are normally initialized to 1. To build cost-sensitive classifiers the weights can be initialized to the relative cost of the two kinds of error, false positives and false negatives.

Lift Charts

In practice, costs are rarely known with any degree of accuracy, and people will want to ponder various different scenarios. Imagine you're in the direct-mailing business and are contemplating a mass mailout of a promotional offer to 1,000,000 households, most of whom won't respond, of course. Let us say that, based on previous experience, the proportion that normally respond is known to be 0.1% (1000 respondents). Suppose a data mining tool is available that, based on known information about the households, identifies a subset of 100,000 for which the response rate is 0.4% (400 respondents). It may well pay off to restrict the mailout to these 100,000 households; this, of course, depends on the mailing cost compared with the return gained for each response to the offer. In marketing terminology, the increase in response rate, a factor of 4 in this case, is known as the *lift* factor yielded by the learning tool. If you knew the costs, you could determine the payoff implied by a particular lift factor.

But you probably want to evaluate other possibilities too. The same data mining scheme, with different parameter settings, may be able to identify 400,000 households for which the response rate will be 0.2% (800 respondents), corresponding to a lift factor of 2. Again, whether this would be a more profitable target for the mailout can be calculated from the costs involved. It may be necessary to factor in the cost of creating and using the model, including collecting the information that is required to come up with the attribute values. After all, if developing the model is very expensive, a mass mailing may be more cost effective than a targeted one.

Given a learning scheme that outputs probabilities for the predicted class of each member of the set of test instances (as Naïve Bayes does), your job is to find subsets of test instances that have a high proportion of positive instances, higher than in the test set as a whole. To do this, the instances should be sorted in descending order of predicted probability of *yes*. Then, to find a sample of a given size with the greatest possible proportion of positive instances, just read the requisite number of instances off the list, starting at the top. If each test instance's class is known, you can calculate the lift factor by simply counting the number of positive instances that the sample includes, dividing by the sample size to obtain a success proportion, and dividing by the success proportion for the complete test set to determine the lift factor.

Table 5.6 Data for a Lift Chart

Rank	Predicted	Actual Class
1	0.95	yes
2	0.93	yes
3	0.93	no
4	0.88	yes
5	0.86	yes
6	0.85	yes
7	0.82	yes
8	0.80	yes
9	0.80	no
10	0.79	yes
11	0.77	no
12	0.76	yes
13	0.73	yes
14	0.65	no
15	0.63	yes
16	0.58	no
17	0.56	yes
18	0.49	no
19	0.48	yes
...	...	...

Table 5.6 shows an example, for a small dataset that has 150 instances, of which 50 are *yes* responses—an overall success proportion of 33%. The instances have been sorted in descending probability order according to the predicted probability of a *yes* response. The first instance is the one that the learning scheme thinks is the most likely to be positive, the second is the next most likely, and so on. The numeric values of the probabilities are unimportant: Rank is the only thing that matters. With each rank is given the actual class of the instance. Thus, the learning scheme was correct about items 1 and 2—they are indeed positives—but wrong about item 3, which turned out to be negative. Now, if you were seeking the most promising sample of size 10, but only knew the predicted probabilities and not the actual classes, your best bet would be the top 10 ranking instances. Eight of these are positive, so the success proportion for this sample is 80%, corresponding to a lift factor of about 2.4.

If you knew the different costs involved, you could work them out for each sample size and choose the most profitable. But a graphical depiction of the various possibilities will often be far more revealing than presenting a single "optimal" decision. Repeating the operation for different-size samples allows you to plot a lift chart like that of Figure 5.1. The horizontal axis shows the sample size as a proportion of the total possible mailout. The vertical axis shows the number of responses obtained. The lower left and upper right points correspond to no mailout at all, with a response of 0, and a full mailout, with a response of 1000. The diagonal line gives the expected result for different-size random samples. But we do not choose random samples; we choose those instances that, according to the data mining tool, are most likely to generate a positive response. These correspond to the upper line, which is derived by summing the actual responses over the corresponding percentage of the instance list sorted in probability order. The two particular scenarios described previously are marked: a 10% mailout that yields 400 respondents and a 40% one that yields 800.

Where you'd like to be in a lift chart is near the upper left corner: At the very best, 1000 responses from a mailout of just 1000, where you send only to those

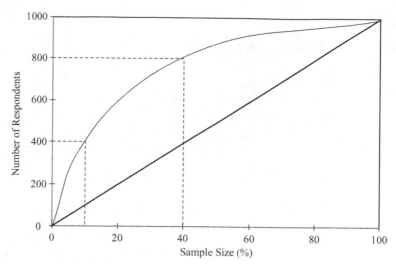

FIGURE 5.1

A hypothetical lift chart.

households that will respond and are rewarded with a 100% success rate. Any selection procedure worthy of the name will keep you above the diagonal—otherwise, you'd be seeing a response that is worse than for random sampling. So the operating part of the diagram is the upper triangle, and the farther to the upper left the better.

Figure 5.2(a) shows a visualization that allows various cost scenarios to be explored in an interactive fashion (called the *cost–benefit analyzer*, it forms part of the Weka workbench described in Part III). Here it is displaying results for predictions generated by the Naïve Bayes classifier on a real-world direct-mail data set. In this example, 47,706 instances were used for training and a further 47,706 for testing. The test instances were ranked according to the predicted probability of a response to the mailout. The graphs show a lift chart on the left and the total cost (or benefit), plotted against the sample size, on the right. At the lower left is a confusion matrix; at the lower right is a cost matrix.

Cost or benefit values associated with incorrect or correct classifications can be entered into the matrix and affect the shape of the curve above. The horizontal slider in the middle allows users to vary the percentage of the population that is selected from the ranked list. Alternatively, one can determine the sample size by adjusting the recall level (the proportion of positives to be included in the sample) or by adjusting a threshold on the probability of the positive class, which here corresponds to a response to the mailout. When the slider is moved, a large cross shows the corresponding point on both graphs. The total cost or benefit associated with the selected sample size is shown at the lower right, along with the expected response to a random mailout of the same size.

FIGURE 5.2

Analyzing the expected benefit of a mailing campaign when the cost of mailing is
(a) $0.50 and (b) $0.80.

In the cost matrix in Figure 5.2(a), a cost of $0.50—the cost of mailing—has been associated with nonrespondents and a benefit of $15.00 with respondents (after deducting the mailing cost). Under these conditions, and using the Naïve Bayes classifier, there is no subset from the ranked list of prospects that yields a greater profit than mailing to the entire population. However, a slightly higher mailing cost changes the situation dramatically, and Figure 5.2(b) shows what happens when it is increased to $0.80. Assuming the same profit of $15.00 per respondent, a maximum profit of $4,560.60 is achieved by mailing to the top 46.7% of the population. In this situation, a random sample of the same size achieves a loss of $99.59.

ROC Curves

Lift charts are a valuable tool, widely used in marketing. They are closely related to a graphical technique for evaluating data mining schemes known as *ROC curves*, which are used in just the same situation, where the learner is trying to select samples of test instances that have a high proportion of positives. The acronym stands for *receiver operating characteristic*, a term used in signal detection to characterize the tradeoff between hit rate and false-alarm rate over a noisy channel. ROC curves depict the performance of a classifier without regard to class distribution or error costs. They plot the true positive rate on the vertical axis against the true negative rate on the horizontal axis. The former is the number of positives included in the sample, expressed as a percentage of the total number of positives (TP Rate = $100 \times$ TP/(TP + FN)); the latter is the number of negatives included in the sample, expressed as a percentage of the total number of negatives (FP Rate = $100 \times$ FP/(FP + TN)). The vertical axis is the same as the lift chart's except that it is expressed as a percentage. The horizontal axis is slightly different—it is the number of negatives rather than the sample size. However, in direct marketing situations where the proportion of positives is very small anyway (like 0.1%), there is negligible difference between the size of a sample and the number of negatives it contains, so the ROC curve and lift chart look very similar. As with lift charts, the upper left corner is the place to be.

Figure 5.3 shows an example ROC curve—the jagged line—for the sample of test data shown earlier in Table 5.6. You can follow it along with the table. From the origin: Go up two (two positives), along one (one negative), up five (five positives), along two (two negatives), up one, along one, up two, and so on. Each point corresponds to drawing a line at a certain position on the ranked list, counting the *yes's* and *no's* above it, and plotting them vertically and horizontally, respectively. As you go farther down the list, corresponding to a larger sample, the number of positives and negatives both increase.

The jagged ROC line in Figure 5.3 depends intimately on the details of the particular sample of test data. This sample dependence can be reduced by applying cross-validation. For each different number of *no's*—that is, each position along the horizontal axis—take just enough of the highest-ranked instances to include that number of *no's*, and count the number of *yes's* they contain. Finally, average that

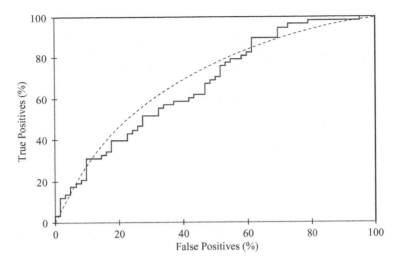

FIGURE 5.3

A sample ROC curve.

number over different folds of the cross-validation. The result is a smooth curve like that in Figure 5.3—although in reality such curves do not generally look quite so smooth.

This is just one way of using cross-validation to generate ROC curves. A simpler approach is to collect the predicted probabilities for all the various test sets (of which there are 10 in a tenfold cross-validation), along with the true class labels of the corresponding instances, and generate a single ranked list based on this data. This assumes that the probability estimates from the classifiers built from the different training sets are all based on equally sized random samples of the data. It is not clear which method is preferable. However, the latter method is easier to implement.

If the learning scheme does not allow the instances to be ordered, you can first make it cost-sensitive as described earlier. For each fold of a tenfold cross-validation, weight the instances for a selection of different cost ratios, train the scheme on each weighted set, count the true positives and false positives in the test set, and plot the resulting point on the ROC axes. (It doesn't matter whether the test set is weighted or not because the axes in the ROC diagram are expressed as the percentage of true and false positives.) However, for probabilistic classifiers such as Naïve Bayes it is far more costly than the method described previously because it involves a separate learning problem for every point on the curve.

It is instructive to look at ROC curves obtained using different learning schemes. For example, in Figure 5.4, method A excels if a small, focused sample is sought— that is, if you are working toward the left side of the graph. Clearly, if you aim to cover just 40% of the true positives you should choose method A, which gives a false positive rate of around 5%, rather than method B, which gives more than 20%

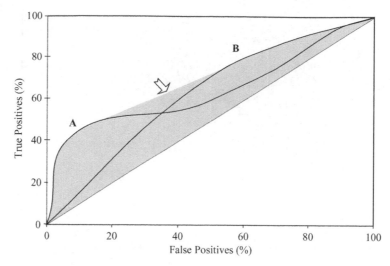

FIGURE 5.4

ROC curves for two learning schemes.

false positives. But method B excels if you are planning a large sample: If you are covering 80% of the true positives, B will give a false positive rate of 60% as compared with method A's 80%. The shaded area is called the *convex hull* of the two curves, and you should always operate at a point that lies on the upper boundary of the convex hull.

What about the region in the middle where neither method A nor method B lies on the convex hull? It is a remarkable fact that you can get anywhere in the shaded region by combining methods A and B and using them at random with appropriate probabilities. To see this, choose a particular probability cutoff for method A that gives true and false positive rates of t_A and f_A, respectively, and another cutoff for method B that gives t_B and f_B. If you use these two schemes at random with probabilities p and q, where $p + q = 1$, then you will get true and false positive rates of $p.t_A + q.t_B$ and $p.f_A + q.f_B$. This represents a point lying on the straight line joining the points (t_A, f_A) and (t_B, f_B), and by varying p and q you can trace out the whole line between these two points. By this device, the entire shaded region can be reached. Only if a particular scheme generates a point that lies on the convex hull should it be used alone. Otherwise, it would always be better to use a combination of classifiers corresponding to a point that lies on the convex hull.

Recall–Precision Curves

People have grappled with the fundamental tradeoff illustrated by lift charts and ROC curves in a wide variety of domains. Information retrieval is a good example. Given a query, a Web search engine produces a list of hits that represent documents supposedly relevant to the query. Compare one system that locates 100 documents, 40 of which are relevant, with another that locates 400 documents, 80 of which are relevant. Which is better? The answer should now be obvious: It depends on the relative cost of false positives, documents returned that aren't relevant, and false negatives, documents that are relevant but aren't returned. Information retrieval researchers define parameters called *recall* and *precision*:

$$\text{Recall} = \frac{\text{number of documents retrieved that are relevant}}{\text{total number of documents that are relevant}}$$

$$\text{Precision} = \frac{\text{number of documents retrieved that are relevant}}{\text{total number of documents that are retrieved}}$$

For example, if the list of *yes*'s and *no*'s in Table 5.6 represented a ranked list of retrieved documents and whether they were relevant or not, and the entire collection contained a total of 40 relevant documents, then "recall at 10" would refer to the recall for the top 10 documents—that is, 8/40 = 20%—while "precision at 10" would be 8/10 = 80%. Information retrieval experts use *recall–precision curves* that plot one against the other, for different numbers of retrieved documents, in just the same way as ROC curves and lift charts—except that, because the axes are different, the curves are hyperbolic in shape and the desired operating point is toward the upper right.

Discussion

Table 5.7 summarizes the three different ways introduced for evaluating the same basic tradeoff; TP, FP, TN, and FN are the numbers of true positives, false positives, true negatives, and false negatives, respectively. You want to choose a set of instances with a high proportion of *yes* instances and a high coverage of the *yes* instances: You can increase the proportion by (conservatively) using a smaller coverage, or (liberally) increase the coverage at the expense of the proportion. Different techniques give different tradeoffs, and can be plotted as different lines on any of these graphical charts.

People also seek single measures that characterize performance. Two that are used in information retrieval are *three-point average recall*, which gives the average precision obtained at recall values of 20%, 50%, and 80%, and *11-point average recall*, which gives the average precision obtained at recall values of 0%, 10%, 20%, 30%, 40%, 50%, 60%, 70%, 80%, 90%, and 100%. Also used in information retrieval is the *F-measure*, which is

$$\frac{2 \times \text{recall} \times \text{precision}}{\text{recall} + \text{precision}} = \frac{2 \times \text{TP}}{2 \times \text{TP} + \text{FP} + \text{FN}}$$

Different terms are used in different domains. Physicians, for example, talk about the *sensitivity* and *specificity* of diagnostic tests. Sensitivity refers to the proportion

Table 5.7 Different Measures Used to Evaluate False Positive versus False Negative Tradeoff

	Domain	Plot	Axes	Explanation of Axes
Lift chart	Marketing	TP vs. subset size	TP	number of true positives
			subset size	$\dfrac{TP+FP}{TP+FP+TN+FN}\times 100\%$
ROC curve	Communications	TP rate vs. FP rate	TP rate	$tp = \dfrac{TP}{TP+FN}\times 100\%$
			FP rate	$fp = \dfrac{FP}{FP+TN}\times 100\%$
Recall–precision curve	Information retrieval	Recall vs. precision	Recall	same as TP rate of tp above
			precision	$\dfrac{TP}{TP+FP}\times 100\%$

of people with disease who have a positive test result—that is, *tp*. Specificity refers to the proportion of people without disease who have a negative test result, which is $1 - fp$. Sometimes the product of these is used as an overall measure:

$$\text{sensitivity} \times \text{specificity} = tp(1 - fp) = \frac{\text{TP} \times \text{TN}}{(\text{TP} + \text{FN}) \times (\text{FP} + \text{TN})}$$

Finally, of course, there is our old friend the success rate:

$$\frac{\text{TP} + \text{TN}}{\text{TP} + \text{FP} + \text{TN} + \text{FN}}$$

To summarize ROC curves in a single quantity, people sometimes use the area under the curve (AUC) because, roughly speaking, the larger area the better the model. The area also has a nice interpretation as the probability that the classifier ranks a randomly chosen positive instance above a randomly chosen negative one. Although such measures may be useful if costs and class distributions are unknown and one scheme must be chosen to handle all situations, no single number is able to capture the tradeoff. That can only be done by two-dimensional depictions such as lift charts, ROC curves, and recall–precision diagrams.

Several methods are commonly employed for computing the area under the ROC curve. One, corresponding to a geometric interpretation, is to approximate it by fitting several trapezoids under the curve and summing up their area. Another is to compute the probability that the classifier ranks a randomly chosen positive instance above a randomly chosen negative one. This can be accomplished by calculating the Mann–Whitney U statistic, or, more specifically, the ρ statistic from the U statistic. This value is easily obtained from a list of test instances sorted in descending order of predicted probability of the positive class. For each positive instance, count how many negative ones are ranked below it (increase the count by $\frac{1}{2}$ if positive and negative instances tie in rank). The U statistic is simply the total of these counts. The ρ statistic is obtained by dividing U by the product of the number of positive and negative instances in the test set—in other words, the U value that would result if all positive instances were ranked above the negative ones.

The area under the precision–recall curve (AUPRC) is an alternative summary statistic that is preferred by some practitioners, particularly in the information retrieval area.

Cost Curves

ROC curves and their relatives are very useful for exploring the tradeoffs among different classifiers over a range of scenarios. However, they are not ideal for evaluating machine learning models in situations with known error costs. For example, it is not easy to read off the expected cost of a classifier for a fixed cost matrix and class distribution. Neither can you easily determine the ranges of applicability of different classifiers. For example, from the crossover point between the two ROC curves in Figure 5.4 it is hard to tell for what cost and class distributions classifier A outperforms classifier B.

Cost curves are a different kind of display on which a single classifier corresponds to a straight line that shows how the performance varies as the class distribution changes. Again, they work best in the two-class case, although you can always make a multiclass problem into a two-class one by singling out one class and evaluating it against the remaining ones.

Figure 5.5(a) plots the expected error against the probability of one of the classes. You could imagine adjusting this probability by resampling the test set in a nonuniform way. We denote the two classes by + and −. The diagonals show the performance of two extreme classifiers: One always predicts +, giving an expected error of 1 if the dataset contains no + instances and 0 if all its instances are +; the other always predicts −, giving the opposite performance. The dashed horizontal line shows the performance of the classifier that is always wrong, and the *x*-axis itself represents the classifier that is always correct. In practice, of course, neither of these is realizable. Good classifiers have low error rates, so where you want to be is as close to the bottom of the diagram as possible.

The line marked A represents the error rate of a particular classifier. If you calculate its performance on a certain test set, its false positive rate, *fp*, is its expected error on a subsample of the test set that contains only examples that are negative ($p[+] = 0$), and its false negative rate, *fn*, is the error on a subsample that contains only positive examples, ($p[+] = 1$). These are the values of the intercepts at the left and right, respectively. You can see immediately from the plot that if $p[+]$ is smaller than about 0.2, predictor A is outperformed by the extreme classifier that always predicts −, while if it is larger than about 0.65, the other extreme classifier is better.

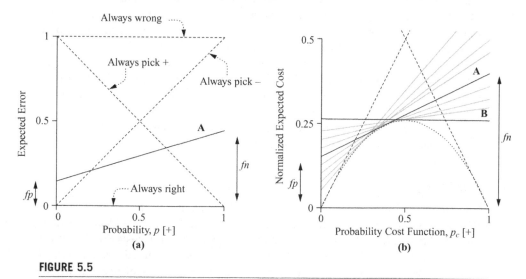

FIGURE 5.5

Effect of varying the probability threshold: (a) error curve and (b) cost curve.

So far we have not taken costs into account, or rather we have used the default cost matrix in which all errors cost the same. Cost curves, which do take cost into account, look very similar—very similar indeed—but the axes are different. Figure 5.5(b) shows a cost curve for the same classifier A (note that the vertical scale has been enlarged, for convenience, and ignore the gray lines for now). It plots the expected cost of using A against the probability cost function, which is a distorted version of $p[+]$ that retains the same extremes: 0 when $p[+] = 0$ and 1 when $p[+] = 1$. Denote by $C[+ \mid -]$ the cost of predicting + when the instance is actually −, and the reverse by $C[- \mid +]$. Then the axes of Figure 5.5(b) are

$$\text{Normalized expected cost} = fn \times p_C[+] + fp \times (1 - p_C[+])$$

$$\text{Probability cost function } p_C[+] = \frac{p[+]C[- \mid +]}{p[+]C[- \mid +] + p[-]C[+ \mid -]}$$

We are assuming here that correct predictions have no cost: $C[+ \mid +] = C[- \mid -] = 0$. If that is not the case, the formulas are a little more complex.

The maximum value that the normalized expected cost can have is 1—that is why it is "normalized." One nice thing about cost curves is that the extreme cost values at the left and right sides of the graph are fp and fn, just as they are for the error curve, so you can draw the cost curve for any classifier very easily.

Figure 5.5(b) also shows classifier B, whose expected cost remains the same across the range—that is, its false positive and false negative rates are equal. As you can see, it outperforms classifier A if the probability cost function exceeds about 0.45, and knowing the costs we could easily work out what this corresponds to in terms of class distribution. In situations that involve different class distributions, cost curves make it easy to tell when one classifier will outperform another.

In what circumstances might this be useful? To return to our example of predicting when cows will be in estrus, their 30-day cycle, or 1/30 prior probability, is unlikely to vary greatly (barring a genetic cataclysm!). But a particular herd may have different proportions of cows that are likely to reach estrus in any given week, perhaps synchronized with—who knows?—the phase of the moon. Then, different classifiers would be appropriate at different times. In the oil spill example, different batches of data may have different spill probabilities. In these situations cost curves can help to show which classifier to use when.

Each point on a lift chart, ROC curve, or recall–precision curve represents a classifier, typically obtained by using different threshold values for a method such as Naïve Bayes. Cost curves represent each classifier by a straight line, and a suite of classifiers will sweep out a curved envelope whose lower limit shows how well that type of classifier can do if the parameter is well chosen. Figure 5.5(b) indicates this with a few gray lines. If the process were continued, it would sweep out the dotted parabolic curve.

The operating region of classifier B ranges from a probability cost value of about 0.25 to a value of about 0.75. Outside this region, classifier B is outperformed by the trivial classifiers represented by dashed lines. Suppose we decide to use classifier

B within this range and the appropriate trivial classifier below and above it. All points on the parabola are certainly better than this scheme. But how much better? It is hard to answer such questions from an ROC curve, but the cost curve makes them easy. The performance difference is negligible if the probability cost value is around 0.5, and below a value of about 0.2 and above 0.8 it is barely perceptible. The greatest difference occurs at probability cost values of 0.25 and 0.75 and is about 0.04, or 4% of the maximum possible cost figure.

5.8 EVALUATING NUMERIC PREDICTION

All the evaluation measures we have described pertain to classification situations rather than numeric prediction situations. The basic principles—using an independent test set rather than the training set for performance evaluation, the holdout method, cross-validation—apply equally well to numeric prediction. But the basic quality measure offered by the error rate is no longer appropriate: Errors are not simply present or absent; they come in different sizes.

Several alternative measures, some of which are summarized in Table 5.8, can be used to evaluate the success of numeric prediction. The predicted values on the test instances are $p_1, p_2, \ldots, p_n$; the actual values are $a_1, a_2, \ldots, a_n$. Notice that p_i means

Table 5.8 Performance Measures for Numeric Prediction

Mean-squared error	$\dfrac{(p_1 - a_1)^2 + \ldots + (p_n - a_n)^2}{n}$
Root mean-squared error	$\sqrt{\dfrac{(p_1 - a_1)^2 + \ldots + (p_n - a_n)^2}{n}}$
Mean-absolute error	$\dfrac{|p_1 - a_1| + \ldots + |p_n - a_n|}{n}$
Relative-squared error*	$\dfrac{(p_1 - a_1)^2 + \ldots + (p_n - a_n)^2}{(a_1 - \bar{a})^2 + \ldots + (a_n - \bar{a})^2}$
Root relative-squared error*	$\sqrt{\dfrac{(p_1 - a_1)^2 + \ldots + (p_n - a_n)^2}{(a_1 - \bar{a})^2 + \ldots + (a_n - \bar{a})^2}}$
Relative-absolute error*	$\dfrac{|p_1 - a_1| + \ldots + |p_n - a_n|}{|a_1 - \bar{a}| + \ldots + |a_n - \bar{a}|}$
Correlation coefficient**	$\dfrac{S_{PA}}{\sqrt{S_P S_A}}$, where $S_{PA} = \dfrac{\sum_i (p_i - \bar{p})(a_i - \bar{a})}{n - 1}$, $S_P = \dfrac{\sum_i (p_i - \bar{p})^2}{n - 1}$, $S_A = \dfrac{\sum_i (a_i - \bar{a})^2}{n - 1}$

*Here, $\bar{a}$ is the mean value over the training data.
**Here, $\bar{a}$ is the mean value over the test data.

something very different here from what it meant in the last section: There it was the probability that a particular prediction was in the ith class; here it refers to the numerical value of the prediction for the ith test instance.

Mean-squared error is the principal and most commonly used measure; sometimes the square root is taken to give it the same dimensions as the predicted value itself. Many mathematical techniques (such as linear regression, explained in Chapter 4) use the mean-squared error because it tends to be the easiest measure to manipulate mathematically: It is, as mathematicians say, "well behaved." However, here we are considering it as a performance measure: All the performance measures are easy to calculate, so mean-squared error has no particular advantage. The question is, is it an appropriate measure for the task at hand?

Mean absolute error is an alternative: Just average the magnitude of the individual errors without taking account of their sign. Mean-squared error tends to exaggerate the effect of outliers—instances when the prediction error is larger than the others—but absolute error does not have this effect: All sizes of error are treated evenly according to their magnitude.

Sometimes it is the *relative* rather than *absolute* error values that are of importance. For example, if a 10% error is equally important whether it is an error of 50 in a prediction of 500 or an error of 0.2 in a prediction of 2, then averages of absolute error will be meaningless—relative errors are appropriate. This effect would be taken into account by using the relative errors in the mean-squared error calculation or the mean absolute error calculation.

Relative squared error in Table 5.8 refers to something quite different. The error is made relative to what it would have been if a simple predictor had been used. The simple predictor in question is just the average of the actual values from the training data, denoted by $\bar{a}$. Thus, relative squared error takes the total squared error and normalizes it by dividing by the total squared error of the default predictor. The root relative squared error is obtained in the obvious way.

The next error measure goes by the glorious name of *relative absolute error* and is just the total absolute error, with the same kind of normalization. In these three relative error measures, the errors are normalized by the error of the simple predictor that predicts average values.

The final measure in Table 5.8 is the correlation coefficient, which measures the statistical correlation between the a's and the p's. The correlation coefficient ranges from 1 for perfectly correlated results, through 0 when there is no correlation, to −1 when the results are perfectly correlated negatively. Of course, negative values should not occur for reasonable prediction methods. Correlation is slightly different from the other measures because it is scale independent in that, if you take a particular set of predictions, the error is unchanged if all the predictions are multiplied by a constant factor and the actual values are left unchanged. This factor appears in every term of S_{PA} in the numerator and in every term of S_P in the denominator, thus canceling out. (This is not true for the relative error figures, despite normalization: If you multiply all the predictions by a large constant, then the difference between the predicted and actual values will change dramatically, as will the percentage errors.) It is also different in that good performance leads to a large value of the correlation coefficient, whereas because the other methods measure error, good performance is indicated by small values.

Which of these measures is appropriate in any given situation is a matter that can only be determined by studying the application itself. What are we trying to minimize? What is the cost of different kinds of error? Often it is not easy to decide. The squared error measures and root-squared error measures weigh large discrepancies much more heavily than small ones, whereas the absolute error measures do not. Taking the square root (root mean-squared error) just reduces the figure to have the same dimensionality as the quantity being predicted. The relative error figures try to compensate for the basic predictability or unpredictability of the output variable: If it tends to lie fairly close to its average value, then you expect prediction to be good and the relative figure compensates for this. Otherwise, if the error figure in one situation is far greater than in another situation, it may be because the quantity in the first situation is inherently more variable and therefore harder to predict, not because the predictor is any worse.

Fortunately, it turns out that in most practical situations the best numerical prediction method is still the best no matter which error measure is used. For example, Table 5.9 shows the result of four different numeric prediction techniques on a given dataset, measured using cross-validation. Method D is the best according to all five metrics: It has the smallest value for each error measure and the largest correlation coefficient. Method C is the second best by all five metrics. The performance of A and B is open to dispute: They have the same correlation coefficient; A is better than B according to mean-squared and relative squared errors, and the reverse is true for absolute and relative absolute error. It is likely that the extra emphasis that the squaring operation gives to outliers accounts for the differences in this case.

When comparing two different learning schemes that involve numeric prediction, the methodology developed in Section 5.5 still applies. The only difference is that success rate is replaced by the appropriate performance measure (e.g., root mean-squared error) when performing the significance test.

Table 5.9 Performance Measures for Four Numeric Prediction Models

	A	B	C	D
Root mean-squared error	67.8	91.7	63.3	57.4
Mean absolute error	41.3	38.5	33.4	29.2
Root relative squared error	42.2%	57.2%	39.4%	35.8%
Relative absolute error	43.1%	40.1%	34.8%	30.4%
Correlation coefficient	0.88	0.88	0.89	0.91

5.9 MINIMUM DESCRIPTION LENGTH PRINCIPLE

What is learned by a machine learning scheme is a kind of "theory" of the domain from which the examples are drawn, a theory that is predictive in that it is capable of generating new facts about the domain—in other words, the class of unseen instances. *Theory* is rather a grandiose term: We are using it here only in the sense of a predictive model. Thus, theories might comprise decision trees or sets of rules—they don't have to be any more "theoretical" than that.

There is a long-standing tradition in science that, other things being equal, simple theories are preferable to complex ones. This is known as *Occam's Razor* after the medieval philosopher William of Occam (or Ockham). Occam's Razor shaves philosophical hairs off a theory. The idea is that the best scientific theory is the smallest one that explains all the facts. As Einstein is reputed to have said, "Everything should be made as simple as possible, but no simpler." Of course, quite a lot is hidden in the phrase "other things being equal," and it can be hard to assess objectively whether a particular theory really does "explain" all the facts on which it is based—that's what controversy in science is all about.

In our case, in machine learning, most theories make errors. And if what is learned is a theory, then the errors it makes are like *exceptions* to the theory. One way to ensure that other things *are* equal is to insist that the information embodied in the exceptions is included as part of the theory when its "simplicity" is judged.

Imagine an imperfect theory for which there are a few exceptions. Not all the data is explained by the theory, but most is. What we do is simply adjoin the exceptions to the theory, specifying them explicitly as exceptions. This new theory is larger: That is a price that, quite justifiably, has to be paid for its inability to explain all the data. However, it may be that the simplicity—is it too much to call it *elegance?*—of the original theory is sufficient to outweigh the fact that it does not quite explain everything compared with a large, baroque theory that is more comprehensive and accurate.

For example, even though Kepler's three laws of planetary motion did not at the time account for the known data quite so well as Copernicus' latest refinement of the Ptolemaic theory of epicycles, they had the advantage of being far less complex, and that would have justified any slight apparent inaccuracy. Kepler was well aware of the benefits of having a theory that was compact, despite the fact that his theory violated his own aesthetic sense because it depended on "ovals" rather than pure circular motion. He expressed this in a forceful metaphor: "I have cleared the Augean stables of astronomy of cycles and spirals, and left behind me only a single cartload of dung."

The *minimum description length*, or MDL, principle takes the stance that the best theory for a body of data is one that minimizes the size of the theory plus the amount of information necessary to specify the exceptions relative to the theory—the smallest "cartload of dung." In statistical estimation theory, this has been applied successfully to various parameter-fitting problems. It applies to machine learning as follows: Given a set of instances, a learning scheme infers a theory—be it ever so simple;

unworthy, perhaps, to be called a "theory"—from them. Using a metaphor of communication, imagine that the instances are to be transmitted through a noiseless channel. Any similarity that is detected among them can be exploited to give a more compact coding. According to the MDL principle, the best theory is the one that minimizes the number of bits required to communicate the theory, along with the labels of the examples from which it was made.

Now the connection with the informational loss function introduced in Section 5.6 should be starting to emerge. That function measures the error in terms of the number of bits required to transmit the instances' class labels, given the probabilistic predictions made by the theory. According to the MDL principle, we need to add to this the "size" of the theory in bits, suitably encoded, to obtain an overall figure for complexity. However, the MDL principle refers to the information required to transmit the examples from which the theory was formed—that is, the *training* instances, not a test set. The overfitting problem is avoided because a complex theory that overfits will be penalized relative to a simple one by virtue of the fact that it takes more bits to encode. At one extreme is a very complex, highly overfitted theory that makes no errors on the training set. At the other is a very simple theory—the null theory—which does not help at all when transmitting the training set. And in between are theories of intermediate complexity, which make probabilistic predictions that are imperfect and need to be corrected by transmitting some information about the training set. The MDL principle provides a means of comparing all these possibilities on an equal footing to see which is the best. We have found the holy grail: an evaluation scheme that works on the training set alone and does not need a separate test set. But the devil is in the details, as we will see.

Suppose a learning scheme comes up with a theory T, based on a training set E of examples, that requires a certain number of bits $L[T]$ to encode, where L is for length. We are only interested in predicting class labels correctly, so we assume that E stands for the collection of class labels in the training set. Given the theory, the training set itself can be encoded in a certain number of bits, $L[E \mid T]$. $L[E \mid T]$ is in fact given by the informational loss function summed over all members of the training set. Then the total description length of theory plus training set is

$$L[T] + L[E|T]$$

and the MDL principle recommends choosing the theory T that minimizes this sum.

There is a remarkable connection between the MDL principle and basic probability theory. Given a training set E, we seek the "most likely" theory T—that is, the theory for which the a posteriori probability $\Pr[T \mid E]$—the probability after the examples have been seen—is maximized. Bayes' rule of conditional probability (the very same rule that we encountered in Section 4.2) dictates that

$$\Pr[T \mid E] = \frac{\Pr[E|T] \Pr[T]}{\Pr[E]}$$

Taking negative logarithms,

$$-\log \Pr[T \mid E] = -\log \Pr[E \mid T] - \log \Pr[T] + \log \Pr[E]$$

Maximizing the probability is the same as minimizing its negative logarithm. Now (as we saw in Section 5.6) the number of bits required to code something is just the negative logarithm of its probability. Furthermore, the final term, $\log \Pr[E]$, depends solely on the training set and not on the learning method. Thus, choosing the theory that maximizes the probability $\Pr[T \mid E]$ is tantamount to choosing the theory that minimizes

$$L[E \mid T] + L[T]$$

In other words, the MDL principle!

This astonishing correspondence with the notion of maximizing the a posteriori probability of a theory after the training set has been taken into account gives credence to the MDL principle. But it also points out where the problems will sprout when the principle is applied in practice. The difficulty with applying Bayes' rule directly is in finding a suitable prior probability distribution $\Pr[T]$ for the theory. In the MDL formulation, that translates into finding how to code the theory T into bits in the most efficient way. There are many ways of coding things, and they all depend on presuppositions that must be shared by encoder and decoder. If you know in advance that the theory is going to take a certain form, you can use that information to encode it more efficiently. How are you going to actually encode T? The devil is in the details.

Encoding E with respect to T to obtain $L[E \mid T]$ seems a little more straightforward: We have already met the informational loss function. But actually, when you encode one member of the training set after another, you are encoding a *sequence* rather than a *set*. It is not necessary to transmit the training set in any particular order, and it ought to be possible to use that fact to reduce the number of bits required. Often, this is simply approximated by subtracting $\log n!$ (where n is the number of elements in E), which is the number of bits needed to specify a particular permutation of the training set (and because this is the same for all theories, it doesn't actually affect the comparison between them). But one can imagine using the frequency of the individual errors to reduce the number of bits needed to code them. Of course, the more sophisticated the method that is used to code the errors, the less the need for a theory in the first place—so whether a theory is justified or not depends to some extent on how the errors are coded. The details, the details.

We end this section as we began, on a philosophical note. It is important to appreciate that Occam's Razor, the preference of simple theories over complex ones, has the status of a philosophical position or "axiom" rather than something that can be proven from first principles. While it may seem self-evident to us, this is a function of our education and the times we live in. A preference for simplicity is—or may be—culture specific rather than absolute.

The Greek philosopher Epicurus (who enjoyed good food and wine and supposedly advocated sensual pleasure—in moderation—as the highest good) expressed almost the opposite sentiment. His *principle of multiple explanations* advises that "If more than one theory is consistent with the data, keep them all" on the basis that if several explanations are equally in agreement, it may be possible to achieve a higher degree of precision by using them together—and, anyway, it would be unscientific to discard some arbitrarily. This brings to mind instance-based learning, in which all the evidence is retained to provide robust predictions, and resonates strongly with decision combination methods such as bagging and boosting (described in Chapter 8) that actually do gain predictive power by using multiple explanations together.

5.10 APPLYING THE MDL PRINCIPLE TO CLUSTERING

One of the nice things about the minimum description length principle is that, unlike other evaluation criteria, it can be applied under widely different circumstances. Although in some sense equivalent to Bayes' rule in that, as we have seen, devising a coding scheme for theories is tantamount to assigning them a prior probability distribution, schemes for coding are somehow far more tangible and easier to think about in concrete terms than intuitive prior probabilities. To illustrate this we will briefly describe—without entering into coding details—how you might go about applying the MDL principle to clustering.

Clustering seems intrinsically difficult to evaluate. Whereas classification or association learning has an objective criterion of success—predictions made on test cases are either right or wrong—this is not so with clustering. It seems that the only realistic evaluation is whether the result of learning—the clustering—proves useful in the application context. (It is worth pointing out that really this is the case for all types of learning, not just clustering.)

Despite this, clustering can be evaluated from a description-length perspective. Suppose a cluster-learning technique divides the training set E into k clusters. If these clusters are natural ones, it should be possible to use them to encode E more efficiently. The best clustering will support the most efficient encoding.

One way of encoding the instances in E with respect to a given clustering is to start by encoding the cluster centers—the average value of each attribute over all instances in the cluster. Then, for each instance in E, transmit which cluster it belongs to (in $\log_2 k$ bits) followed by its attribute values with respect to the cluster center—perhaps as the numeric difference of each attribute value from the center. Couched as it is in terms of averages and differences, this description presupposes numeric attributes and raises thorny questions of how to code numbers efficiently. Nominal attributes can be handled in a similar manner: For each cluster there is a probability distribution for the attribute values, and the distributions are different for different clusters. The coding issue becomes more straightforward: Attribute values are coded with respect to the relevant probability distribution, a standard operation in data compression.

If the data exhibits extremely strong clustering, this technique will result in a smaller description length than simply transmitting the elements of E without any clusters. However, if the clustering effect is not so strong, it will likely increase rather than decrease the description length. The overhead of transmitting cluster-specific distributions for attribute values will more than offset the advantage gained by encoding each training instance relative to the cluster it lies in. This is where more sophisticated coding techniques come in. Once the cluster centers have been communicated, it is possible to transmit cluster-specific probability distributions adaptively, in tandem with the relevant instances: The instances themselves help to define the probability distributions, and the probability distributions help to define the instances. We will not venture further into coding techniques here. The point is that the MDL formulation, properly applied, may be flexible enough to support the evaluation of clustering. But actually doing it satisfactorily in practice is not easy.

5.11 **FURTHER READING**

The statistical basis of confidence tests is well covered in most statistics texts, which also give tables of the normal distribution and Student's distribution. (We use an excellent course text by Wild and Seber (1995) that we recommend very strongly if you can get hold of it.) "Student" is the *nom de plume* of a statistician called William Gosset, who obtained a post as a chemist in the Guinness brewery in Dublin, Ireland, in 1899 and invented the t-test to handle small samples for quality control in brewing. The corrected resampled t-test was proposed by Nadeau and Bengio (2003). Cross-validation is a standard statistical technique, and its application in machine learning has been extensively investigated and compared with the bootstrap by Kohavi (1995a). The bootstrap technique itself is thoroughly covered by Efron and Tibshirani (1993).

The Kappa statistic was introduced by Cohen (1960). Ting (2002) has investigated a heuristic way of generalizing to the multiclass case the algorithm given in Section 5.7 to make two-class learning schemes cost sensitive. Lift charts are described by Berry and Linoff (1997). The use of ROC analysis in signal detection theory is covered by Egan (1975); this work has been extended for visualizing and analyzing the behavior of diagnostic systems (Swets, 1988) and is also used in medicine (Beck and Schultz, 1986). Provost and Fawcett (1997) brought the idea of ROC analysis to the attention of the machine learning and data mining community. Witten et al. (1999b) explain the use of recall and precision in information retrieval systems; the F-measure is described by van Rijsbergen (1979). Drummond and Holte (2000) introduced cost curves and investigated their properties.

The MDL principle was formulated by Rissanen (1985). Kepler's discovery of his economical three laws of planetary motion, and his doubts about them, are recounted by Koestler (1964).

Epicurus' principle of multiple explanations is mentioned by Li and Vityani (1992), quoting from Asmis (1984).

Advanced Data Mining

Implementations: Real Machine Learning Schemes

6

We have seen the basic ideas of several machine learning methods and studied in detail how to assess their performance on practical data mining problems. Now we are well prepared to look at real, industrial-strength, machine learning algorithms. Our aim is to explain these algorithms both at a conceptual level and with a fair amount of technical detail so that you can understand them fully and appreciate the key implementation issues that arise.

In truth, there is a world of difference between the simplistic methods described in Chapter 4 and the actual algorithms that are widely used in practice. The principles are the same. So are the inputs and outputs—methods of knowledge representation. But the algorithms are far more complex, principally because they have to deal robustly and sensibly with real-world problems such as numeric attributes, missing values, and—most challenging of all—noisy data. To understand how the various schemes cope with noise, we will have to draw on some of the statistical knowledge that we learned in Chapter 5.

Chapter 4 opened with an explanation of how to infer rudimentary rules and then examined statistical modeling and decision trees. Then we returned to rule induction and continued with association rules, linear models, the nearest-neighbor method of instance-based learning, and clustering. This chapter develops all these topics.

We begin with decision tree induction and work up to a full description of the C4.5 system, a landmark decision tree program that is probably the machine learning workhorse most widely used in practice to date. Then we describe decision rule induction. Despite the simplicity of the idea, inducing decision rules that perform comparably with state-of-the-art decision trees turns out to be quite difficult in practice. Most high-performance rule inducers find an initial rule set and then refine it using a rather complex optimization stage that discards or adjusts individual rules to make them work better together. We describe the ideas that underlie rule learning in the presence of noise and then go on to cover a scheme that operates by forming partial decision trees, an approach that has been demonstrated to perform well while avoiding complex and ad hoc heuristics. Following this, we take a brief look at how to generate rules with exceptions, which were described in Section 3.4, and examine fast data structures for learning association rules.

There has been a resurgence of interest in linear models with the introduction of *support vector machines*, a blend of linear modeling and instance-based learning.

Support vector machines select a small number of critical boundary instances called *support vectors* from each class and build a linear discriminant function that separates them as widely as possible. This instance-based approach transcends the limitations of linear boundaries by making it practical to include extra nonlinear terms in the function, making it possible to form quadratic, cubic, and higher-order decision boundaries. The same techniques can be applied to the perceptron described in Section 4.6 to implement complex decision boundaries, and also to least squares regression. An older technique for extending the perceptron is to connect units together into multilayer "neural networks." All of these ideas are described in Section 6.4.

Section 6.5 describes classic instance-based learners, developing the simple nearest-neighbor method introduced in Section 4.7 and showing some more powerful alternatives that perform explicit generalization. Following that we extend linear regression for numeric prediction to a more sophisticated procedure that comes up with the tree representation introduced in Section 3.3 and go on to describe locally weighted regression, an instance-based strategy for numeric prediction. Then we examine Bayesian networks, a potentially very powerful way of extending the Naïve Bayes method to make it less "naïve" by dealing with datasets that have internal dependencies. Next we return to clustering and review some methods that are more sophisticated than simple *k*-means, methods that produce hierarchical clusters and probabilistic clusters. We also look at semi-supervised learning, which can be viewed as combining clustering and classification. Finally, we discuss more advanced schemes for multi-instance learning than those covered in Section 4.9.

Because of the nature of the material it contains, this chapter differs from the others in the book. Sections can be read independently, and each is self-contained, including the references to further reading, which are gathered together in Discussion sections.

6.1 DECISION TREES

The first machine learning scheme that we will develop in detail, the C4.5 algorithm, derives from the simple divide-and-conquer algorithm for producing decision trees that was described in Section 4.3. It needs to be extended in several ways before it is ready for use on real-world problems. First, we consider how to deal with numeric attributes and, after that, missing values. Then we look at the all-important problem of pruning decision trees, because although trees constructed by the divide-and-conquer algorithm as described perform well on the training set, they are usually overfitted to the training data and do not generalize well to independent test sets. We then briefly consider how to convert decision trees to classification rules and examine the options provided by the C4.5 algorithm itself. Finally, we look at an alternative pruning strategy that is implemented in the famous CART system for learning classification and regression trees.

Numeric Attributes

The method we described in Section 4.3 only works when all the attributes are nominal, whereas, as we have seen, most real datasets contain some numeric attributes. It is not too difficult to extend the algorithm to deal with these. For a numeric attribute we will restrict the possibilities to a two-way, or binary, split. Suppose we use the version of the weather data that has some numeric features (see Table 1.3). Then, when temperature is being considered for the first split, the temperature values involved are

64	65	68	69	70	71	72	75	80	81	83	85
yes	no	yes	yes	yes	no	no	yes	no	yes	yes	no
						yes	yes				

Repeated values have been collapsed together, and there are only 11 possible positions for the breakpoint—8 if the breakpoint is not allowed to separate items of the same class. The information gain for each can be calculated in the usual way. For example, the test *temperature* < 71.5 produces four *yes*'s and two *no*'s, whereas *temperature* > 71.5 produces five *yes*'s and three *no*'s, and so the information value of this test is

$$\text{info}([4, 2], [5, 3]) = (6/14) \times \text{info}([4, 2]) + (8/14) \times \text{info}([5, 3]) = 0.939 \text{ bits}$$

It is common to place numeric thresholds halfway between the values that delimit the boundaries of a concept, although something might be gained by adopting a more sophisticated policy. For example, we will see in the following that although the simplest form of instance-based learning puts the dividing line between concepts in the middle of the space between them, other methods that involve more than just the two nearest examples have been suggested.

When creating decision trees using the divide-and-conquer method, once the first attribute to split on has been selected, a top-level tree node is created that splits on that attribute, and the algorithm proceeds recursively on each of the child nodes. For each numeric attribute, it appears that the subset of instances at each child node must be re-sorted according to that attribute's values—and, indeed, this is how programs for inducing decision trees are usually written. However, it is not actually necessary to re-sort because the sort order at a parent node can be used to derive the sort order for each child, leading to a speedier implementation. Consider the temperature attribute in the weather data, whose sort order (this time including duplicates) is

64	65	68	69	70	71	72	72	75	75	80	81	83	85
7	*6*	*5*	*9*	*4*	*14*	*8*	*12*	*10*	*11*	*2*	*13*	*3*	*1*

The italicized numbers below each temperature value give the number of the instance that has that value. Thus, instance number 7 has temperature value 64, instance 6 has temperature 65, and so on. Suppose we decide to split at the top level on the attribute *outlook*. Consider the child node for which *outlook* = *sunny*—in fact, the examples with this value of *outlook* are numbers 1, 2, 8, 9, and 11. If the italicized sequence is stored with the example set (and a different sequence must be stored for each numeric attribute)—that is, instance 7 contains a pointer to instance 6, instance 6 points to instance 5, instance 5 points to instance 9, and so on—then it is a simple matter to read off the examples for which *outlook* = *sunny* in order. All that is necessary is to scan through the instances in the indicated order, checking the *outlook* attribute for each and writing down the ones with the appropriate value:

9   8   11   2   1

Thus, repeated sorting can be avoided by storing with each subset of instances the sort order for that subset according to each numeric attribute. The sort order must be determined for each numeric attribute at the beginning; no further sorting is necessary thereafter.

When a decision tree tests a nominal attribute as described in Section 4.3, a branch is made for each possible value of the attribute. However, we have restricted splits on numeric attributes to be binary. This creates an important difference between numeric attributes and nominal ones: Once you have branched on a nominal attribute, you have used all the information that it offers; however, successive splits on a numeric attribute may continue to yield new information. Whereas a nominal attribute can only be tested once on any path from the root of a tree to the leaf, a numeric one can be tested many times. This can yield trees that are messy and difficult to understand because the tests on any single numeric attribute are not located together but can be scattered along the path. An alternative, which is harder to accomplish but produces a more readable tree, is to allow a multiway test on a numeric attribute, testing against several different constants at a single node of the tree. A simpler but less powerful solution is to prediscretize the attribute as described in Section 7.2.

Missing Values

The next enhancement to the decision tree–building algorithm deals with the problems of missing values. Missing values are endemic in real-world datasets. As explained in Chapter 2 (page 58), one way of handling them is to treat them as just another possible value of the attribute; this is appropriate if the fact that the attribute is missing is significant in some way. In that case, no further action need be taken. But if there is no particular significance in the fact that a certain instance has a missing attribute value, a more subtle solution is needed. It is tempting to simply ignore all instances in which some of the values are missing, but this solution is often too draconian to be viable. Instances with missing values often provide a good deal of information. Sometimes the attributes with values that are missing play no part in the decision, in which case these instances are as good as any other.

One question is how to apply a given decision tree to an instance in which some of the attributes to be tested have missing values. We outlined a solution in Section

3.3 that involves notionally splitting the instance into pieces, using a numeric weighting scheme, and sending part of it down each branch in proportion to the number of training instances going down that branch. Eventually, the various parts of the instance will each reach a leaf node, and the decisions at these leaf nodes must be recombined using the weights that have percolated to the leaves. The information gain and gain ratio calculations described in Section 4.3 can also be applied to partial instances. Instead of having integer counts, the weights are used when computing both gain figures.

Another question is how to partition the training set once a splitting attribute has been chosen, to allow recursive application of the decision tree formation procedure on each of the daughter nodes. The same weighting procedure is used. Instances for which the relevant attribute value is missing are notionally split into pieces, one piece for each branch, in the same proportion as the known instances go down the various branches. Pieces of the instance contribute to decisions at lower nodes in the usual way through the information gain calculation, except that they are weighted accordingly. They may be further split at lower nodes, of course, if the values of other attributes are unknown as well.

Pruning

Fully expanded decision trees often contain unnecessary structure, and it is generally advisable to simplify them before they are deployed. Now it is time to learn how to prune decision trees.

By building the complete tree and pruning it afterward we are adopting a strategy of *postpruning* (sometimes called *backward pruning*) rather than *prepruning* (or *forward pruning*). Prepruning would involve trying to decide during the tree-building process when to stop developing subtrees—quite an attractive prospect because that would avoid all the work of developing subtrees only to throw them away afterward. However, postpruning does seem to offer some advantages. For example, situations occur in which two attributes individually seem to have nothing to contribute but are powerful predictors when combined—a sort of combination-lock effect in which the correct combination of the two attribute values is very informative but the attributes taken individually are not. Most decision tree builders postprune; however, prepruning can be a viable alternative when runtime is of particular concern.

Two rather different operations have been considered for postpruning: *subtree replacement* and *subtree raising*. At each node, a learning scheme might decide whether it should perform subtree replacement, subtree raising, or leave the subtree as it is, unpruned. Subtree replacement is the primary pruning operation, and we look at it first. The idea is to select some subtrees and replace them with single leaves. For example, the whole subtree in Figure 1.3(a), involving two internal nodes and four leaf nodes, has been replaced by the single leaf *bad*. This will certainly cause the accuracy on the training set to decrease if the original tree was produced by the decision tree algorithm described previously, because that continued to build the tree until all leaf nodes were pure (or until all attributes had been tested). However, it may increase the accuracy on an independently chosen test set.

When subtree replacement is implemented, it proceeds from the leaves and works back up toward the root. In the Figure 1.3 example, the whole subtree in (a) would not be replaced at once. First, consideration would be given to replacing the three daughter nodes in the *health plan contribution* subtree with a single leaf node. Assume that a decision is made to perform this replacement—we will explain how this decision is made shortly. Then, continuing to work back from the leaves, consideration would be given to replacing the *working hours per week* subtree, which now has just two daughter nodes, by a single leaf node. In the Figure 1.3 example, this replacement was indeed made, which accounts for the entire subtree in (a) being replaced by a single leaf marked *bad*. Finally, consideration would be given to replacing the two daughter nodes in the *wage increase 1st year* subtree with a single leaf node. In this case, that decision was not made, so the tree remains as shown in Figure 1.3(a). Again, we will examine how these decisions are actually made shortly.

The second pruning operation, subtree raising, is more complex, and it is not clear that it is necessarily always worthwhile. However, because it is used in the influential decision tree–building system C4.5, we describe it here. Subtree raising does not occur in the Figure 1.3 example, so we use the artificial example of Figure 6.1 for illustration. Here, consideration is given to pruning the tree in Figure 6.1(a), and the result is shown in Figure 6.1(b). The entire subtree from C downward has been "raised" to replace the B subtree. Note that although the daughters of B and C are shown as leaves, they can be entire subtrees. Of course, if we perform this raising operation, it is necessary to reclassify the examples at the nodes marked 4 and 5 into the new subtree headed by C. This is why the daughters of that node are marked with primes—1′, 2′, and 3′—to indicate that they are not the same as the original

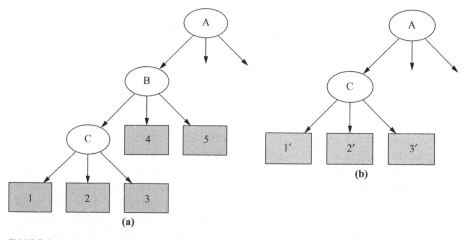

(a)

(b)

FIGURE 6.1

Example of subtree raising, where (a) node C is "raised" to subsume node B (b).

daughters 1, 2, and 3 but differ by the inclusion of the examples originally covered by 4 and 5.

Subtree raising is a potentially time-consuming operation. In actual implementations it is generally restricted to raising the subtree of the most popular branch. That is, we consider doing the raising illustrated in Figure 6.1 provided that the branch from B to C has more training examples than the branches from B to node 4 or from B to node 5. Otherwise, if (for example) node 4 were the majority daughter of B, we would consider raising node 4 to replace B and reclassifying all examples under C, as well as the examples from node 5, into the new node.

Estimating Error Rates

So much for the two pruning operations. Now we must address the question of how to decide whether to replace an internal node by a leaf (for subtree replacement) or whether to replace an internal node by one of the nodes below it (for subtree raising). To make this decision rationally, it is necessary to estimate the error rate that would be expected at a particular node given an independently chosen test set. We need to estimate the error at internal nodes as well as at leaf nodes. If we had such an estimate, it would be clear whether to replace, or raise, a particular subtree simply by comparing the estimated error of the subtree with that of its proposed replacement. Before estimating the error for a subtree proposed for raising, examples that lie under siblings of the current node—the examples at 4 and 5 of Figure 6.1—would have to be temporarily reclassified into the raised tree.

It is no use taking the training set error as the error estimate: That would not lead to any pruning because the tree has been constructed expressly for that particular training set. One way of coming up with an error estimate is the standard verification technique: Hold back some of the data originally given and use it as an independent test set to estimate the error at each node. This is called *reduced-error* pruning. It suffers from the disadvantage that the actual tree is based on less data.

The alternative is to try to make some estimate of error based on the training data itself. That is what C4.5 does, and we will describe its method here. It is a heuristic based on some statistical reasoning, but the statistical underpinning is rather weak. However, it seems to work well in practice. The idea is to consider the set of instances that reach each node and imagine that the majority class is chosen to represent that node. That gives us a certain number of "errors," E, out of the total number of instances, N. Now imagine that the true probability of error at the node is q, and that the N instances are generated by a Bernoulli process with parameter q, of which E turn out to be errors.

This is almost the same situation as we considered when looking at the holdout method in Section 5.2, where we calculated confidence intervals on the true success probability p given a certain observed success rate. There are two differences. One is trivial: Here we are looking at the error rate q rather than the success rate p; these are simply related by $p + q = 1$. The second is more serious: Here the figures E and N are measured from the training data, whereas in Section 5.2 we were considering independent test data. Because of this difference we make a pessimistic estimate of the error rate by using the upper confidence limit rather than stating the estimate as a confidence range.

The mathematics involved is just the same as before. Given a particular confidence c (the default figure used by C4.5 is $c = 25\%$), we find confidence limits z such that

$$\Pr\left[\frac{f - q}{\sqrt{q(1 - q)/N}} > z\right] = c$$

where N is the number of samples, $f = E/N$ is the observed error rate, and q is the true error rate. As before, this leads to an upper confidence limit for q. Now we use that upper confidence limit as a (pessimistic) estimate for the error rate e at the node:

$$e = \frac{f + \frac{z^2}{2N} + z\sqrt{\frac{f}{N} - \frac{f^2}{N} + \frac{z^2}{4N^2}}}{1 + \frac{z^2}{N}}$$

Note the use of the + sign before the square root in the numerator to obtain the upper confidence limit. Here, z is the number of standard deviations corresponding to the confidence c, which for $c = 25\%$ is $z = 0.69$.

To see how all this works in practice, let's look again at the labor negotiations decision tree of Figure 1.3, salient parts of which are reproduced in Figure 6.2 with the number of training examples that reach the leaves added. We use the previous formula with a 25% confidence figure—that is, with $z = 0.69$. Consider the lower left leaf, for which $E = 2$, $N = 6$, and so $f = 0.33$. Plugging these figures into the formula, the upper confidence limit is calculated as $e = 0.47$. That means that instead of using the training set error rate for this leaf, which is 33%, we will use the pessimistic estimate of 47%. This is pessimistic indeed, considering that it would be a bad mistake to let the error rate exceed 50% for a two-class problem. But things are worse for the neighboring leaf, where $E = 1$ and $N = 2$, because the upper confidence limit becomes $e = 0.72$. The third leaf has the same value of e as the first. The next step is to combine the error estimates for these three leaves in the ratio of the number of examples they cover, 6:2:6, which leads to a combined error estimate of 0.51. Now we consider the error estimate for the parent node, *health plan contribution*. This covers nine bad examples and five good ones, so the training set error rate is $f = 5/14$. For these values, the previous formula yields a pessimistic error estimate of $e = 0.46$. Because this is less than the combined error estimate of the three children, they are pruned away.

The next step is to consider the *working hours per week* node, which now has two children that are both leaves. The error estimate for the first, with $E = 1$ and $N = 2$, is $e = 0.72$, while for the second it is $e = 0.46$, as we have just seen. Combining these in the appropriate ratio of 2:14 leads to a value that is higher than the error estimate for the *working hours* node, so the subtree is pruned away and replaced by a leaf node.

The estimated error figures obtained in these examples should be taken with a grain of salt because the estimate is only a heuristic one and is based on a number of shaky assumptions: the use of the upper confidence limit; the assumption of a normal distribution; and the fact that statistics from the training set are used. However, the qualitative behavior of the error formula is correct and the method seems to work reasonably well in practice. If necessary, the underlying confidence level, which we have taken to be 25%, can be tweaked to produce more satisfactory results.

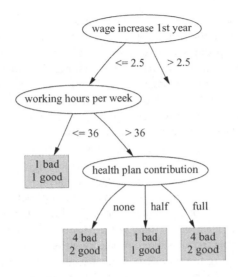

FIGURE 6.2

Pruning the labor negotiations decision tree.

Complexity of Decision Tree Induction

Now that we have learned how to accomplish the pruning operations, we have finally covered all the central aspects of decision tree induction. Let's take stock and examine the computational complexity of inducing decision trees. We will use the standard order notation: O(n) stands for a quantity that grows at most linearly with n, O(n^2) grows at most quadratically with n, and so on.

Suppose the training data contains n instances and m attributes. We need to make some assumption about the size of the tree, and we will assume that its depth is on the order of log n, that is O(log n). This is the standard rate of growth of a tree with n leaves, provided that it remains "bushy" and doesn't degenerate into a few very long, stringy branches. Note that we are tacitly assuming that most of the instances are different from each other and—this is almost the same thing—that the m attributes provide enough tests to allow the instances to be differentiated. For example, if there were only a few binary attributes, they would allow only so many instances to be differentiated and the tree could not grow past a certain point, rendering an "in the limit" analysis meaningless.

The computational cost of building the tree in the first place is O(mnlog n). Consider the amount of work done for one attribute over all nodes of the tree. Not all the examples need to be considered at each node, of course. But at each possible tree depth, the entire set of n instances must be considered in the worst case. And because there are log n different depths in the tree, the amount of work for this one attribute is O(n log n). At each node all attributes are considered, so the total amount of work is O(mn log n).

This reasoning makes some assumptions. If some attributes are numeric, they must be sorted, but once the initial sort has been done there is no need to re-sort at each tree depth if the appropriate algorithm is used (described previously—see page 193). The initial sort takes $O(n \log n)$ operations for each of up to m attributes; thus, the above complexity figure is unchanged. If the attributes are nominal, all attributes do *not* have to be considered at each tree node because attributes that are used further up the tree cannot be reused. However, if attributes are numeric, they can be reused and so they have to be considered at every tree level.

Next, consider pruning by subtree replacement. First an error estimate must be made for every tree node. Provided that counts are maintained appropriately, this is linear in the number of nodes in the tree. Then each node needs to be considered for replacement. The tree has at most n leaves, one for each instance. If it were a binary tree, each attribute being numeric or two-valued, that would give it $2n - 1$ nodes; multiway branches would only serve to decrease the number of internal nodes. Thus, the complexity of subtree replacement is $O(n)$.

Finally, subtree lifting has a basic complexity equal to subtree replacement. But there is an added cost because instances need to be reclassified during the lifting operation. During the whole process, each instance may have to be reclassified at every node between its leaf and the root—that is, as many as $O(\log n)$ times. That makes the total number of reclassifications $O(n \log n)$. And reclassification is not a single operation: One that occurs near the root will take $O(\log n)$ operations, and one of average depth will take half of this. Thus, the total complexity of subtree lifting is as follows: $O(n(\log n)^2)$.

Taking into account all these operations, the full complexity of decision tree induction is

$$O(mn \log n) + O(n(\log n)^2)$$

From Trees to Rules

It is possible to read a set of rules directly off a decision tree, as noted in Section 3.4, by generating a rule for each leaf and making a conjunction of all the tests encountered on the path from the root to that leaf. This produces rules that are unambiguous in that it doesn't matter in what order they are executed. However, the rules are more complex than necessary.

The estimated error rate described previously provides exactly the mechanism necessary to prune the rules. Given a particular rule, each condition in it is considered for deletion by tentatively removing it, working out which of the training examples are now covered by the rule, calculating from this a pessimistic estimate of the error rate of the new rule, and comparing this with the pessimistic estimate for the original rule. If the new rule is better, delete that condition and carry on, looking for other conditions to delete. Leave the rule when there are no remaining conditions that will improve it if they are removed. Once all rules have been pruned in this way, it is necessary to see if there are any duplicates and remove them from the rule set.

This is a greedy approach to detecting redundant conditions in a rule, and there is no guarantee that the best set of conditions will be removed. An improvement would be to consider all subsets of conditions, but this is usually prohibitively expensive. Another solution might be to use an optimization technique such as simulated annealing or a genetic algorithm to select the best version of this rule. However, the simple greedy solution seems to produce quite good rule sets.

The problem, even with the greedy method, is computational cost. For every condition that is a candidate for deletion, the effect of the rule must be reevaluated on all the training instances. This means that rule generation from trees tends to be very slow. The next section describes much faster methods that generate classification rules directly without forming a decision tree first.

C4.5: Choices and Options

The decision tree program C4.5 and its successor C5.0 were devised by Ross Quinlan over a 20-year period beginning in the late 1970s. A complete description of C4.5, the early 1990s version, appears as an excellent and readable book (Quinlan, 1993), along with the full source code. The more recent version, C5.0, is available commercially. Its decision tree induction seems to be essentially the same as that used by C4.5, and tests show some differences but negligible improvements. However, its rule generation is greatly sped up and clearly uses a different technique, although this has not been described in the open literature.

C4.5 works essentially as described in the previous sections. The default confidence value is set at 25% and works reasonably well in most cases; possibly it should be altered to a lower value, which causes more drastic pruning, if the actual error rate of pruned trees on test sets is found to be much higher than the estimated error rate. There is one other important parameter whose effect it is to eliminate tests for which almost all of the training examples have the same outcome. Such tests are often of little use. Consequently, tests are not incorporated into the decision tree unless they have at least two outcomes that have at least a minimum number of instances. The default value for this minimum is 2, but it is controllable and should perhaps be increased for tasks that have a lot of noisy data.

Another heuristic in C4.5 is that candidate splits on numeric attributes are only considered if they cut off a certain minimum number of instances: at least 10% of the average number of instances per class at the current node, or 25 instances—whichever value is smaller (but the minimum just mentioned, 2 by default, is also enforced).

C4.5 Release 8, the last noncommercial version of C4.5, includes an MDL-based adjustment to the information gain for splits on numeric attributes. More specifically, if there are S candidate splits on a certain numeric attribute at the node currently considered for splitting, $\log_2(S)/N$ is subtracted from the information gain, where N is the number of instances at the node. This heuristic, described by Quinlan (1986), is designed to prevent overfitting. The information gain may be negative after subtraction, and tree growing will stop if there are no attributes with positive information gain—a form of prepruning. We mention this here because it can be surprising to obtain a pruned tree even if postpruning has been turned off! This heuristic is also implemented in the software described in Part 3 of this book.

Cost-Complexity Pruning

As mentioned, the postpruning method in C4.5 is based on shaky statistical assumptions, and it turns out that it often does not prune enough. On the other hand, it is very fast and thus popular in practice. However, in many applications it is worthwhile expending more computational effort to obtain a more compact decision tree. Experiments have shown that C4.5's pruning method can yield unnecessary additional structure in the final tree: Tree size continues to grow when more instances are added to the training data even when this does not further increase performance on independent test data. In that case, the more conservative *cost-complexity pruning* method from the Classification and Regression Trees (CART) learning system may be more appropriate.

Cost-complexity pruning is based on the idea of first pruning those subtrees that, relative to their size, lead to the smallest increase in error on the training data. The increase in error is measured by a quantity α that is defined to be the average error increase per leaf of the subtree concerned. By monitoring this quantity as pruning progresses, the algorithm generates a sequence of successively smaller pruned trees. In each iteration it prunes all subtrees that exhibit the smallest value of α among the remaining subtrees in the current version of the tree.

Each candidate tree in the resulting sequence of pruned trees corresponds to one particular threshold value, α_i. The question becomes, which tree should be chosen as the final classification model? To determine the most predictive tree, cost-complexity pruning either uses a holdout set to estimate the error rate of each tree, or, if data is limited, employs cross-validation.

Using a holdout set is straightforward. However, cross-validation poses the problem of relating the α values observed in the sequence of pruned trees for training fold k of the cross-validation to the α values from the sequence of trees for the full dataset: These values are usually different. This problem is solved by first computing the geometric average of α_i and α_{i+1} for tree i from the full dataset. Then, for each fold k of the cross-validation, the tree that exhibits the largest α value smaller than this average is picked. The average of the error estimates for these trees from the k folds, estimated from the corresponding test datasets, is the cross-validation error for tree i from the full dataset.

Discussion

Top-down induction of decision trees is probably the most extensively researched method of machine learning used in data mining. Researchers have investigated a panoply of variations for almost every conceivable aspect of the learning process—for example, different criteria for attribute selection or modified pruning methods. However, they are rarely rewarded by substantial improvements in accuracy over a spectrum of diverse datasets. As discussed, the pruning method used by the CART system for learning decision trees (Breiman et al., 1984) can often produce smaller trees than C4.5's pruning method. This has been investigated empirically by Oates and Jensen (1997).

In our description of decision trees, we have assumed that only one attribute is used to split the data into subsets at each node of the tree. However, it is possible to allow tests that involve several attributes at a time. For example, with numeric attributes each test can be on a linear combination of attribute values. Then the final tree consists of a hierarchy of linear models of the kind we described in Section 4.6, and the splits are no longer restricted to being axis-parallel. Trees with tests involving more than one attribute are called *multivariate* decision trees, in contrast to the simple *univariate* trees that we normally use. The CART system has the option of generating multivariate tests. They are often more accurate and smaller than univariate trees but take much longer to generate and are also more difficult to interpret. We briefly mention one way of generating them in the Principal Components Analysis section in Section 7.3.

6.2 CLASSIFICATION RULES

We call the basic covering algorithm for generating rules that was described in Section 4.4 a separate-and-conquer technique because it identifies a rule that covers instances in a class (and excludes ones not in the class), separates them out, and continues on those that are left. Such algorithms have been used as the basis of many systems that generate rules. There, we described a simple correctness-based measure for choosing what test to add to the rule at each stage. However, there are many other possibilities, and the particular criterion that is used has a significant effect on the rules produced. We examine different criteria for choosing tests in this section. We also look at how the basic rule-generation algorithm can be extended to more practical situations by accommodating missing values and numeric attributes.

But the real problem with all these rule-generation schemes is that they tend to overfit the training data and do not generalize well to independent test sets, particularly on noisy data. To be able to generate good rule sets for noisy data, it is necessary to have some way of measuring the real worth of individual rules. The standard approach to assessing the worth of rules is to evaluate their error rate on an independent set of instances, held back from the training set, and we explain this next. After that, we describe two industrial-strength rule learners: one that combines the simple separate-and-conquer technique with a global optimization step, and another that works by repeatedly building partial decision trees and extracting rules from them. Finally, we consider how to generate rules with exceptions, and exceptions to the exceptions.

Criteria for Choosing Tests

When we introduced the basic rule learner in Section 4.4, we had to figure out a way of deciding which of many possible tests to add to a rule to prevent it from covering any negative examples. For this we used the test that maximizes the ratio p/t, where t is the total number of instances that the new rule will cover, and p is the number of these that are positive—that is, belong to the class in question. This attempts to maximize the "correctness" of the rule on the basis that the higher the proportion of positive examples it covers, the more correct a rule is. One alternative is to calculate an information gain:

$$p\left[\log\frac{p}{t} - \log\frac{P}{T}\right]$$

where p and t are the number of positive instances and the total number of instances covered by the new rule, as before, and P and T are the corresponding number of instances that satisfied the rule *before* the new test was added. The rationale for this is that it represents the total information gained regarding the current positive examples, which is given by the number of them that satisfy the new test, multiplied by the information gained regarding each one.

The basic criterion for choosing a test to add to a rule is to find one that covers as many positive examples as possible while covering as few negative examples as possible. The original correctness-based heuristic, which is just the percentage of positive examples among all examples covered by the rule, attains a maximum when no negative examples are covered regardless of the number of positive examples covered by the rule. Thus, a test that makes the rule exact will be preferred to one that makes it inexact, no matter how few positive examples the former rule covers nor how many positive examples the latter covers. For example, if we consider a test that covers one example that is positive, this criterion will prefer it over a test that covers 1000 positive examples along with one negative one.

The information-based heuristic, on the other hand, places far more emphasis on covering a large number of positive examples regardless of whether the rule so created is exact. Of course, both algorithms continue adding tests until the final rule produced is exact, which means that the rule will be finished earlier using the correctness measure whereas more terms will have to be added if the information-based measure is used. Thus, the correctness-based measure might find special cases and eliminate them completely, saving the larger picture for later (when the more general rule might be simpler because awkward special cases have already been dealt with), whereas the information-based one will try to generate high-coverage rules first and leave the special cases until later. It is by no means obvious that either strategy is superior to the other at producing an exact rule set. Moreover, the whole situation is complicated by the fact that, as described in the following, rules may be pruned and inexact ones tolerated.

Missing Values, Numeric Attributes

As with divide-and-conquer decision tree algorithms, the nasty practical considerations of missing values and numeric attributes need to be addressed. In fact, there is not much more to say. Now that we know how these problems can be solved for decision tree induction, appropriate solutions for rule induction are easily given.

When producing rules using covering algorithms, missing values can be best treated as though they don't match any of the tests. This is particularly suitable when a decision list is being produced, because it encourages the learning algorithm to separate out positive instances using tests that are known to succeed. It has the effect either that instances with missing values are dealt with by rules involving other attributes that are not missing, or that any decisions about them are deferred until most of the other instances have been taken care of, at which time tests will probably emerge that involve other attributes. Covering algorithms for decision lists have a decided advantage over decision tree algorithms in this respect: Tricky examples can be left until late in the process, at which time they will appear less tricky because most of the other examples have already been classified and removed from the instance set.

Numeric attributes can be dealt with in exactly the same way as they are dealt with for trees. For each numeric attribute, instances are sorted according to the attribute's value and, for each possible threshold, a binary less-than/greater-than test is considered and evaluated in exactly the same way that a binary attribute would be.

Generating Good Rules

Suppose you don't want to generate perfect rules that guarantee to give the correct classification on all instances in the training set, but would rather generate "sensible" ones that avoid overfitting the training set and thereby stand a better chance of performing well on new test instances. How do you decide which rules are worthwhile? How do you tell when it becomes counterproductive to continue adding terms to a rule to exclude a few pesky instances of the wrong type, all the while excluding more and more instances of the correct type?

Let's look at a few examples of possible rules—some good and some bad—for the contact lens problem in Table 1.1. Consider first the rule

```
If astigmatism = yes and tear production rate = normal
    then recommendation = hard
```

This gives a correct result for four out of the six cases that it covers; thus, its success fraction is 4/6. Suppose we add a further term to make the rule a "perfect" one:

```
If astigmatism = yes and tear production rate = normal
    and age = young then recommendation = hard
```

This improves accuracy to 2/2. Which rule is better? The second one is more accurate on the training data but covers only two cases, whereas the first one covers six. It may be that the second version is just overfitting the training data. For a practical rule learner we need a principled way of choosing the appropriate version of a rule, preferably one that maximizes accuracy on future test data.

Suppose we split the training data into two parts that we will call a *growing set* and a *pruning set*. The growing set is used to form a rule using the basic covering algorithm. Then a test is deleted from the rule, and the effect is evaluated by trying out the truncated rule on the pruning set and seeing whether it performs better than the original rule. This pruning process repeats until the rule cannot be improved by deleting any further tests. The whole procedure is repeated for each class, obtaining one best rule for each class, and the overall best rule is established by evaluating the rules on the pruning set. This rule is then added to the rule set, the instances it covers are removed from the training data—from both growing and pruning sets—and the process is repeated.

Why not do the pruning as we build up the rule, rather than building up the whole thing and then throwing parts away? That is, why not preprune rather than post-prune? Just as when pruning decision trees it is often best to grow the tree to its maximum size and then prune back, so with rules it is often best to make a perfect rule and then prune it. Who knows?—adding that last term may make a really good rule, a situation that we might never have noticed had we adopted an aggressive prepruning strategy.

It is essential that the growing and pruning sets are separate because it is mis-leading to evaluate a rule on the very data that was used to form it: That would lead to serious errors by preferring rules that were overfitted. Usually the training set is split so that two-thirds of instances are used for growing and one-third for pruning. A disadvantage, of course, is that learning occurs from instances in the growing set only, so the algorithm might miss important rules because some key instances had been assigned to the pruning set. Moreover, the wrong rule might be preferred because the pruning set contains only one-third of the data and may not be com-pletely representative. These effects can be ameliorated by resplitting the training data into growing and pruning sets at each cycle of the algorithm—that is, after each rule is finally chosen.

The idea of using a separate pruning set for pruning—which is applicable to decision trees as well as rule sets—is called *reduced-error pruning*. The variant previously described prunes a rule immediately after it has been grown; it is called *incremental reduced-error pruning*. Another possibility is to build a full, unpruned, rule set first, pruning it afterwards by discarding individual tests. However, this method is much slower.

Of course, there are many different ways to assess the worth of a rule based on the pruning set. A simple measure is to consider how well the rule would do at discriminating the predicted class from other classes if it were the only rule in the theory, operating under the closed-world assumption. Suppose it gets p instances right out of the t instances that it covers, and there are P instances of this class out a total of T instances altogether. The instances that it does not cover include $N - n$ negative ones, where $n = t - p$ is the number of negative instances that the rule covers and $N = T - P$ is the total number of negative instances. Thus, in total the rule makes correct decisions on $p + (N - n)$ instances, and so has an overall success ratio of

$$[p + (N - n)]/T$$

This quantity, evaluated on the test set, has been used to evaluate the success of a rule when using reduced-error pruning.

This measure is open to criticism because it treats noncoverage of negative examples as being as important as coverage of positive ones, which is unrealistic in a situation where what is being evaluated is one rule that will eventually serve alongside many others. For example, a rule that gets $p = 2000$ instances right out of a total coverage of 3000 (i.e., it gets $n = 1000$ wrong) is judged as more successful than one that gets $p = 1000$ out of a total coverage of 1001 (i.e., $n = 1$ wrong), because $[p + (N - n)]/T$ is $[1000 + N]/T$ in the first case but only $[999 + N]/T$ in the second. This is counterintuitive: The first rule is clearly less predictive than the second because it has a 33.3% as opposed to only a 0.1% chance of being incorrect.

Using the success rate p/t as a measure, as was done in the original formulation of the covering algorithm (Figure 4.8), is not the perfect solution either because it would prefer a rule that got a single instance right ($p = 1$) out of a total coverage of 1 (so $n = 0$) to the far more useful rule that got 1000 right out of 1001. Another heuristic that has been used is $(p - n)/t$, but that suffers from exactly the same problem because $(p - n)/t = 2p/t - 1$ and so the result, when comparing one rule with another, is just the same as with the success rate. It seems hard to find a simple measure of the worth of a rule that corresponds with intuition in all cases.

Whatever heuristic is used to measure the worth of a rule, the incremental reduced-error pruning algorithm is the same. A possible rule-learning algorithm based on this idea is given in Figure 6.3. It generates a decision list, creating rules for each class in turn and choosing at each stage the best version of the rule according to its worth on the pruning data. The basic covering algorithm for rule generation (Figure 4.8) is used to come up with good rules for each class, choosing conditions to add to the rule using the accuracy measure p/t that we described earlier.

```
Initialize E to the instance set
Split E into Grow and Prune in the ratio 2:1
  For each class C for which Grow and Prune both contain an instance
    Use the basic covering algorithm to create the best perfect rule
      for class C
    Calculate the worth w(R) for the rule on Prune, and for the rule
      with the final condition omitted w(R-)
    While w(R-) > w(R), remove the final condition from the rule and
      repeat the previous step
  From the rules generated, select the one with the largest w(R)
  Print the rule
  Remove the instances covered by the rule from E
Continue
```

FIGURE 6.3

Algorithm for forming rules by incremental reduced-error pruning.

This method has been used to produce rule-induction schemes that can process vast amounts of data and operate very quickly. It can be accelerated by generating rules for the classes in order rather than generating a rule for each class at every stage and choosing the best. A suitable ordering is the increasing order in which they occur in the training set so that the rarest class is processed first and the most common ones are processed later. Another significant speedup is obtained by stopping the whole process when a rule of sufficiently low accuracy is generated, so as not to spend time generating a lot of rules at the end with very small coverage. However, very simple terminating conditions (such as stopping when the accuracy for a rule is lower than the default accuracy for the class it predicts) do not give the best performance. One criterion that seems to work well is a rather complicated one based on the MDL principle, described later.

Using Global Optimization

In general, rules generated using incremental reduced-error pruning in this manner seem to perform quite well, particularly on large datasets. However, it has been found that a worthwhile performance advantage can be obtained by performing a global optimization step on the set of rules induced. The motivation is to increase the accuracy of the rule set by revising or replacing individual rules. Experiments show that both the size and the performance of rule sets are significantly improved by postinduction optimization. On the other hand, the process itself is rather complex.

To give an idea of how elaborate—and heuristic—industrial-strength rule learners become, Figure 6.4 shows an algorithm called RIPPER, an acronym for *repeated incremental pruning to produce error reduction*. Classes are examined in increasing size and an initial set of rules for a class is generated using incremental reduced-error pruning. An extra stopping condition is introduced that depends on the description length of the examples and rule set. The description-length DL is a complex formula that takes into account the number of bits needed to send a set of examples with respect to a set of rules, the number of bits required to send a rule with k conditions, and the number of bits needed to send the integer k—times an arbitrary factor of 50% to compensate for possible redundancy in the attributes.

Having produced a rule set for the class, each rule is reconsidered and two variants produced, again using reduced-error pruning—but at this stage, instances covered by other rules for the class are removed from the pruning set, and success rate on the remaining instances is used as the pruning criterion. If one of the two variants yields a better description length, it replaces the rule. Next we reactivate the original building phase to mop up any newly uncovered instances of the class. A final check is made, to ensure that each rule contributes to the reduction of description length, before proceeding to generate rules for the next class.

Obtaining Rules from Partial Decision Trees

There is an alternative approach to rule induction that avoids global optimization but nevertheless produces accurate, compact rule sets. The method combines the divide-and-conquer strategy for decision tree learning with the separate-and-conquer

```
Initialize E to the instance set
For each class C, from smallest to largest
    BUILD:
        Split E into Growing and Pruning sets in the ratio 2:1
        Repeat until (a) there are no more uncovered examples of C; or
                (b) the description length (DL) of ruleset and examples is
                64 bits greater than the smallest DL found so far, or (c)
                the error rate exceeds 50%:

            GROW phase: Grow a rule by greedily adding conditions until the
                rule is 100% accurate by testing every possible value of
                each attribute and selecting the condition with greatest
                information gain G
            PRUNE phase: Prune conditions in last-to-first order. Continue
                as long as the worth W of the rule increases
    OPTIMIZE:
        GENERATE VARIANTS:
        For each rule R for class C,
            Split E afresh into Growing and Pruning sets
            Remove all instances from the Pruning set that are covered
             by other rules for C
            Use GROW and PRUNE to generate and prune two competing rules
                from the newly split data:
                    R1 is a new rule, rebuilt from scratch;
                    R2 is generated by greedily adding antecedents to R.
            Prune using the metric A (instead of W) on this reduced data
        SELECT REPRESENTATIVE:
        Replace R by whichever of R, R1 and R2 has the smallest DL.
    MOP UP:
        If there are residual uncovered instances of class C, return to
            the BUILD stage to generate more rules based on these
            instances.
    CLEAN UP:
        Calculate DL for the whole ruleset and for the ruleset with each
            rule in turn omitted; delete any rule that increases the DL
        Remove instances covered by the rules just generated
Continue
```

(a)

$$G = p[\log(p/t) - \log(P/T)]$$
$$W = \frac{p+1}{t+2}$$
$$A = \frac{p+n'}{T} \text{ ; accuracy for this rule}$$

p = number of positive examples covered by this rule (true
    positives)
n = number of negative examples covered by this rule (false
    negatives)
$t = p + n$; total number of examples covered by this rule
$n' = N - n$; number of negative examples not covered by this rule
        (true negatives)
P = number of positive examples of this class
N = number of negative examples of this class
$T = P + N$; total number of examples of this class

(b)

FIGURE 6.4

RIPPER: (a) algorithm for rule learning and (b) meaning of symbols.

one for rule learning. It adopts the separate-and-conquer strategy in that it builds a rule, removes the instances it covers, and continues creating rules recursively for the remaining instances until none are left. However, it differs from the standard approach in the way that each rule is created. In essence, to make a single rule a pruned decision tree is built for the current set of instances, the leaf with the largest coverage is made into a rule, and the tree is discarded.

The prospect of repeatedly building decision trees only to discard most of them is not as bizarre as it first seems. Using a pruned tree to obtain a rule instead of pruning a rule incrementally by adding conjunctions one at a time avoids a tendency to overprune, which is a characteristic problem of the basic separate-and-conquer rule learner. Using the separate-and-conquer methodology in conjunction with decision trees adds flexibility and speed. It is indeed wasteful to build a full decision tree just to obtain a single rule, but the process can be accelerated significantly without sacrificing the advantages.

The key idea is to build a partial decision tree instead of a fully explored one. A partial decision tree is an ordinary decision tree that contains branches to undefined subtrees. To generate such a tree, the construction and pruning operations are integrated in order to find a "stable" subtree that can be simplified no further. Once this subtree has been found, tree building ceases and a single rule is read off.

The tree-building algorithm is summarized in Figure 6.5: It splits a set of instances recursively into a partial tree. The first step chooses a test and divides the instances into subsets accordingly. The choice is made using the same information-gain heuristic that is normally used for building decision trees (Section 4.3). Then the subsets are expanded in increasing order of their average entropy. The reason for this is that the later subsets will most likely not end up being expanded, and a subset with low-average entropy is more likely to result in a small subtree and therefore produce a more general rule. This proceeds recursively until a subset is expanded into a leaf, and then continues further by backtracking. But as soon as an internal node appears that has all its children expanded into leaves, the algorithm checks whether that node is better replaced by a single leaf. This is just the standard subtree replacement

```
Expand-subset (S):
  Choose a test T and use it to split the set of examples into subsets
  Sort subsets into increasing order of average entropy
  while (there is a subset X that has not yet been expanded
         AND all subsets expanded so far are leaves)
    expand-subset(X)
  if (all the subsets expanded are leaves
      AND estimated error for subtree ≥ estimated error for node)
    undo expansion into subsets and make node a leaf
```

FIGURE 6.5

Algorithm for expanding examples into a partial tree.

operation of decision tree pruning (see Section 6.1). If replacement is performed the algorithm backtracks in the standard way, exploring siblings of the newly replaced node. However, if during backtracking a node is encountered all of whose children expanded so far are not leaves—and this will happen as soon as a potential subtree replacement is *not* performed—then the remaining subsets are left unexplored and the corresponding subtrees are left undefined. Due to the recursive structure of the algorithm, this event automatically terminates tree generation.

Figure 6.6 shows a step-by-step example. During the stages in Figure 6.6(a–c), tree building continues recursively in the normal way—except that at each point the lowest-entropy sibling is chosen for expansion: node 3 between stages (a) and (b). Gray elliptical nodes are as yet unexpanded; rectangular ones are leaves. Between stages (b) and (c), the rectangular node will have lower entropy than its sibling, node 5, but cannot be expanded further because it is a leaf. Backtracking occurs and node 5 is chosen for expansion. Once stage of Figure 6.6(c) is reached, there is a node— node 5—that has all its children expanded into leaves, and this triggers pruning. Subtree replacement for node 5 is considered and accepted, leading to stage (d). Next node 3 is considered for subtree replacement, and this operation is again accepted. Backtracking continues, and node 4, having lower entropy than node 2, is expanded into two leaves. Now subtree replacement is considered for node 4, but suppose that node 4 is not replaced. At this point, the process terminates with the three-leaf partial tree of stage (e).

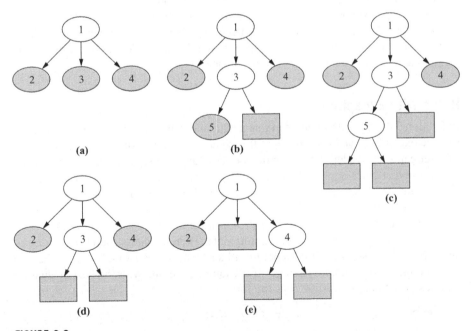

FIGURE 6.6

Example of building a partial tree.

If the data is noise-free and contains enough instances to prevent the algorithm from doing any pruning, just one path of the full decision tree has to be explored. This achieves the greatest possible performance gain over the naïve method that builds a full decision tree each time. The gain decreases as more pruning takes place. For datasets with numeric attributes, the asymptotic time complexity of the algorithm is the same as building the full decision tree because in this case the complexity is dominated by the time required to sort the attribute values in the first place.

Once a partial tree has been built, a single rule is extracted from it. Each leaf corresponds to a possible rule, and we seek the "best" leaf of those subtrees (typically a small minority) that have been expanded into leaves. Experiments show that it is best to aim at the most general rule by choosing the leaf that covers the greatest number of instances.

When a dataset contains missing values, they can be dealt with exactly as they are when building decision trees. If an instance cannot be assigned to any given branch because of a missing attribute value, it is assigned to each of the branches with a weight proportional to the number of training instances going down that branch, normalized by the total number of training instances with known values at the node. During testing, the same procedure is applied separately to each rule, thus associating a weight with the application of each rule to the test instance. That weight is deducted from the instance's total weight before it is passed to the next rule in the list. Once the weight has reduced to 0, the predicted class probabilities are combined into a final classification according to the weights.

This yields a simple but surprisingly effective method for learning decision lists for noisy data. Its main advantage over other comprehensive rule-generation schemes is simplicity, because other methods appear to require a complex global optimization stage to achieve the same level of performance.

Rules with Exceptions

In Section 3.4 (page 73) we learned that a natural extension of rules is to allow them to have exceptions, and exceptions to the exceptions, and so on—indeed, the whole rule set can be considered as exceptions to a default classification rule that is used when no other rules apply. The method of generating a "good" rule, using one of the measures described previously, provides exactly the mechanism needed to generate rules with exceptions.

First, a default class is selected for the top-level rule: It is natural to use the class that occurs most frequently in the training data. Then, a rule is found pertaining to any class other than the default one. Of all such rules it is natural to seek the one with the most discriminatory power—for example, the one with the best evaluation on a test set. Suppose this rule has the form

```
if <condition> then class = <new class>
```

It is used to split the training data into two subsets: one containing instances for which the rule's condition is *true* and the other containing those for which it is *false*.

If either subset contains instances of more than one class, the algorithm is invoked recursively on that subset. For the subset for which the condition is *true*, the "default class" is the new class as specified by the rule; for the subset where the condition is *false*, the default class remains as it was before.

Let's examine how this algorithm would work for the rules with exceptions that were given in Section 3.4 for the iris data of Table 1.4. We will represent the rules in the graphical form shown in Figure 6.7, which is in fact equivalent to the textual rules noted in Figure 3.8. The default of *Iris setosa* is the entry node at the top left. Horizontal, dotted paths show exceptions, so the next box, which contains a rule that concludes *Iris versicolor*, is an exception to the default. Below this is an alternative, a second exception—alternatives are shown by vertical, solid lines—leading to the conclusion *Iris virginica*. Following the upper path horizontally leads to an exception to the *Iris versicolor* rule that overrides it whenever the condition in the top right box holds, with the conclusion *Iris virginica*. Below this is an alternative, leading (as it happens) to the same conclusion. Returning to the box at bottom center, this has its own exception, the lower right box, which gives the conclusion *Iris versicolor*. The numbers at the lower right of each box give the "coverage" of the rule, expressed as the number of examples that satisfy it divided by the number that satisfy its condition but not its conclusion. For example, the condition in the top center box applies to 52 of the examples, and 49 of them are *Iris versicolor*. The strength of this representation is that you can get a very good feeling for the effect of the rules from the boxes toward the left side; the boxes at the right cover just a few exceptional cases.

To create these rules, the default is first set to *Iris setosa* by taking the most frequently occurring class in the dataset. This is an arbitrary choice because, for this

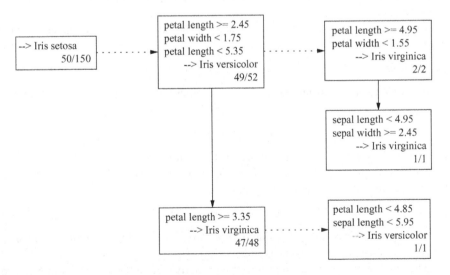

FIGURE 6.7

Rules with exceptions for the iris data.

dataset, all classes occur exactly 50 times; as shown in Figure 6.7 this default "rule" is correct in 50 out of 150 cases. Then the best rule that predicts another class is sought. In this case it is

```
if petal-length ≥ 2.45 and petal-length < 5.355
    and petal-width < 1.75 then Iris-versicolor
```

This rule covers 52 instances, of which 49 are *Iris versicolor*. It divides the dataset into two subsets: the 52 instances that satisfy the condition of the rule and the remaining 98 that do not.

We work on the former subset first. The default class for these instances is *Iris versicolor*. There are only three exceptions, all of which happen to be *Iris virginica*. The best rule for this subset that does not predict *Iris versicolor* is

```
if petal-length ≥ 4.95 and petal-width < 1.55 then Iris-virginica
```

It covers two of the three *Iris virginicas* and nothing else. Again, it divides the subset into two: those instances that satisfy its condition and those that do not. Fortunately, in this case, all those instances that satisfy the condition do indeed have class *Iris virginica*, so there is no need for a further exception. However, the remaining instances still include the third *Iris virginica*, along with 49 *Iris versicolors*, which are the default at this point. Again the best rule is sought:

```
if sepal-length < 4.95 and sepal-width ≥ 2.45 then Iris-virginica
```

This rule covers the remaining *Iris virginica* and nothing else, so it also has no exceptions. Furthermore, all remaining instances in the subset that do not satisfy its condition have the class *Iris versicolor*, which is the default, so no more needs to be done.

Return now to the second subset created by the initial rule, the instances that do not satisfy the condition

```
petal-length ≥ 2.45 and petal-length < 5.355 and petal-width < 1.75
```

Of the rules for these instances that do not predict the default class *Iris setosa*, the best is

```
if petal-length ≥ 3.35 then Iris-virginica
```

It covers all 47 *Iris virginicas* that are in the example set (3 were removed by the first rule, as explained previously). It also covers 1 *Iris versicolor*. This needs to be taken care of as an exception, by the final rule:

```
if petal-length < 4.85 and sepal-length < 5.95 then Iris-versicolor
```

Fortunately, the set of instances that do *not* satisfy its condition are all the default, *Iris setosa*. Thus, the procedure is finished.

The rules that are produced have the property that most of the examples are covered by the high-level rules and the lower-level ones really do represent exceptions. For example, the last exception clause and the deeply nested *else* clause both cover a solitary example, and removing them would have little effect. Even the remaining nested exception rule covers only two examples. Thus, one can get an excellent feeling for what the rules do by ignoring all the deeper structure and looking only at the first level or two. That is the attraction of rules with exceptions.

Discussion

All algorithms for producing classification rules that we have described use the basic covering or separate-and-conquer approach. For the simple, noise-free case this produces PRISM (Cendrowska, 1987), an algorithm that is simple and easy to understand. When applied to two-class problems with the closed-world assumption, it is only necessary to produce rules for one class: Then the rules are in disjunctive normal form and can be executed on test instances without any ambiguity arising. When applied to multiclass problems, a separate rule set is produced for each class; thus, a test instance may be assigned to more than one class, or to no class, and further heuristics are necessary if a unique prediction is sought.

To reduce overfitting in noisy situations, it is necessary to produce rules that are not "perfect" even on the training set. To do this it is necessary to have a measure for the "goodness," or worth, of a rule. With such a measure it is then possible to abandon the class-by-class approach of the basic covering algorithm and start by generating the very best rule, regardless of which class it predicts, and then remove all examples covered by this rule and continue the process. This yields a method for producing a decision list rather than a set of independent classification rules, and decision lists have the important advantage that they do not generate ambiguities when interpreted.

The idea of incremental reduced-error pruning is from Fürnkranz and Widmer (1994) and forms the basis for fast and effective rule induction. The RIPPER rule learner is from Cohen (1995), although the published description appears to differ from the implementation in precisely how the description length (DL) affects the stopping condition. What we have presented here is the basic idea of the algorithm; there are many more details in the implementation.

The whole question of measuring the value of a rule has not yet been satisfactorily resolved. Many different measures have been proposed, some blatantly heuristic and others based on information-theoretical or probabilistic grounds. However, there seems to be no consensus on the best measure to use. An extensive theoretical study of various criteria has been performed by Fürnkranz and Flach (2005).

The rule-learning scheme based on partial decision trees was developed by Frank and Witten (1998). On standard benchmark datasets it produces rule sets that are as accurate as rules generated by C4.5 and more accurate than those of RIPPER; however, it produces larger rule sets than RIPPER. Its main advantage over other schemes is not performance but simplicity: By combining top-down decision tree induction with separate-and-conquer rule learning, it produces good rule sets without any need for global optimization.

The procedure for generating rules with exceptions was developed as an option in the Induct system by Gaines and Compton (1995), who called them *ripple-down* rules. In an experiment with a large medical dataset (22,000 instances, 32 attributes, and 60 classes), they found that people can understand large systems of rules with exceptions more readily than equivalent systems of regular rules because that is the way they think about the complex medical diagnoses that are involved. Richards and Compton (1998) describe their role as an alternative to classic knowledge engineering.

6.3 ASSOCIATION RULES

In Section 4.5 we studied the Apriori algorithm for generating association rules that meet minimum support and confidence thresholds. Apriori follows a generate-and-test methodology for finding frequent item sets, generating successively longer candidate item sets from shorter ones that are known to be frequent. Each different size of candidate item set requires a scan through the dataset to determine whether its frequency exceeds the minimum support threshold. Although some improvements to the algorithm have been suggested to reduce the number of scans of the dataset, the combinatorial nature of this generation process can prove costly, particularly if there are many item sets or item sets are large. Both conditions readily occur even for modest datasets when low support thresholds are used. Moreover, no matter how high the threshold, if the data is too large to fit in main memory, it is undesirable to have to scan it repeatedly—and many association rule applications involve truly massive datasets.

These effects can be ameliorated by using appropriate data structures. We describe a method called FP-growth that uses an extended prefix tree—a frequent-pattern tree, or FP-tree—to store a compressed version of the dataset in main memory. Only two passes are needed to map a dataset into an FP-tree. The algorithm then processes the tree in a recursive fashion to grow large item sets directly, instead of generating candidate item sets and then having to test them against the entire database.

Building a Frequent-Pattern Tree

Like Apriori, the FP-growth algorithm begins by counting the number of times individual items (i.e., attribute–value pairs) occur in the dataset. After this initial pass, a tree structure is created in a second pass. Initially, the tree is empty and the structure emerges as each instance in the dataset is inserted into it.

The key to obtaining a compact tree structure that can be quickly processed to find large item sets is to sort the items in each instance in descending order of their frequency of occurrence in the dataset, which has already been recorded in the first pass, before inserting them into the tree. Individual items in each instance that do not meet the minimum support threshold are not inserted into the tree, effectively removing them from the dataset. The hope is that many instances will share those items that occur most frequently individually, resulting in a high degree of compression close to the tree's root.

We illustrate the process with the weather data, reproduced in Table 6.1(a), using a minimum support threshold of 6. The algorithm is complex, and its complexity far exceeds what would be reasonable for such a trivial example, but a small illustration is the best way of explaining it. Table 6.1(b) shows the individual items, with their frequencies, that are collected in the first pass. They are sorted into descending order and ones whose frequency exceeds the minimum threshold are bolded. Table 6.1(c) shows the original instances, numbered as in Table 6.1(a), with the items in each instance sorted into descending frequency order. Finally, to give

Table 6.1 Preparing Weather Data for Insertion into an FP-Tree

(a)	Outlook	Temperature	Humidity	Windy	Play
1	sunny	hot	high	false	no
2	sunny	hot	high	true	no
3	overcast	hot	high	false	yes
4	rainy	mild	high	false	yes
5	rainy	cool	normal	false	yes
6	rainy	cool	normal	true	no
7	overcast	cool	normal	true	yes
8	sunny	mild	high	false	no
9	sunny	cool	normal	false	yes
10	rainy	mild	normal	false	yes
11	sunny	mild	normal	true	yes
12	overcast	mild	high	true	yes
13	overcast	hot	normal	false	yes
14	rainy	mild	high	true	no

(b)	
play = yes	**9**
windy = false	**8**
humidity = normal	**7**
humidity = high	**7**
windy = true	**6**
temperature = mild	**6**
play = no	5
outlook = sunny	5
outlook = rainy	5
temperature = hot	4
temperature = cool	4
outlook = overcast	4

Continued

Table 6.1 Preparing Weather Data for Insertion into an FP-Tree *Continued*	
(c)	
1	**windy = false, humidity = high,** play = no, outlook = sunny, temperature = hot
2	**humidity = high, windy = true,** play = no, outlook = sunny, temperature = hot
3	**play = yes, windy = false, humidity = high,** temperature = hot, outlook = overcast
4	**play = yes, windy = false, humidity = high, temperature = mild,** outlook = rainy
5	**play = yes, windy = false, humidity = normal,** outlook = rainy, temperature = cool
6	**humidity = normal, windy = true,** play = no, outlook = rainy, temperature = cool
7	**play = yes, humidity = normal, windy = true,** temperature = cool, outlook = overcast
8	**windy = false, humidity = high, temperature = mild,** play = no, outlook = sunny
9	**play = yes, windy = false, humidity = normal,** outlook = sunny, temperature = cool
10	**play = yes, windy = false, humidity = normal, temperature = mild,** outlook = rainy
11	**play = yes, humidity = normal, windy = true, temperature = mild,** outlook = sunny
12	**play = yes, humidity = high, windy = true, temperature = mild,** outlook = overcast
13	**play = yes, windy = false, humidity = normal,** temperature = hot, outlook = overcast
14	**humidity = high, windy = true, temperature = mild,** play = no, outlook = rainy
(d)	
play = yes and windy = false	6
play = yes and humidity = normal	6

(a) The original data, (b) frequency ordering of items with frequent item sets in bold, (c) the data with each instance sorted into frequency order, and (d) the two multiple-item frequent item sets.

an advance peek at the final outcome, Table 6.1(d) shows the only two multiple-item sets whose frequency satisfies the minimum support threshold. Along with the six single-item sets shown in bold in Table 6.1(b), these form the final answer: a total of eight item sets. We are going to have to do a lot of work to find the two multiple-item sets in Table 6.1(d) using the FP-tree method.

Figure 6.8(a) shows the FP-tree structure that results from this data with a minimum support threshold of 6. The tree itself is shown with solid arrows. The numbers at each node show how many times the sorted prefix of items, up to and including the item at that node, occur in the dataset. For example, following the third branch from the left in the tree we can see that, after sorting, two instances begin with the prefix *humidity = high*—that is, the second and last instances of Table 6.1(c). Continuing down that branch, the next node records that the same two instances also have *windy = true* as their next most frequent item. The lowest node in the branch shows that one of these two instances— that is, the last in Table 6.1(c)—contains *temperature = mild* as well. The other instance—that is, the second in Table 6.1(c)—drops out at this stage because its next most frequent item does not meet the minimum support constraint and is therefore omitted from the tree.

On the left side of the diagram a "header table" shows the frequencies of the individual items in the dataset (Table 6.1(b)). These items appear in descending frequency order, and only those with at least minimum support are included. Each item in the header table points to its first occurrence in the tree, and subsequent items in the tree with the same name are linked together to form a list. These lists, emanating from the header table, are shown in Figure 6.8(a) by dashed arrows.

It is apparent from the tree that only two nodes have counts that satisfy the minimum support threshold, corresponding to the item sets *play = yes* (count of 9) and *play = yes* and *windy = false* (count of 6) in the leftmost branch. Each entry in the header table is itself a single-item set that also satisfies the threshold. This identifies as part of the final answer all the bold items in Table 6.1(b) and the first item set in Table 6.1(d). Since we know the outcome in advance we can see that there is only one more item set to go—the second in Table 6.1(d). But there is no hint of it in the data structure of Figure 6.8(a), and we will have to do a lot of work to discover it!

Finding Large Item Sets

The purpose of the links from the header table into the tree structure is to facilitate traversal of the tree to find other large item sets, apart from the two that are already in the tree. This is accomplished by a divide-and-conquer approach that recursively processes the tree to grow large item sets. Each header table list is followed in turn, starting from the bottom of the table and working upward. Actually, the header table can be processed in any order, but it is easier to think about processing the longest paths in the tree first, and these correspond to the lower-frequency items.

Starting from the bottom of the header table, we can immediately add *temperature = mild* to the list of large item sets. Figure 6.8(b) shows the result of the next stage, which is an FP-tree for just those instances in the dataset that include

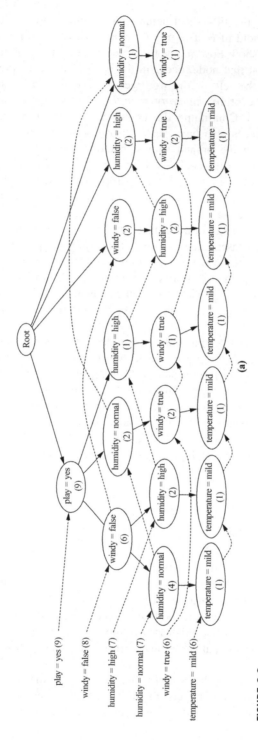

FIGURE 6.8

Extended prefix trees for the weather data: (a) the full data, (b) the data conditional on *temperature = mild*, and (c) the data conditional on *humidity = normal*.

221

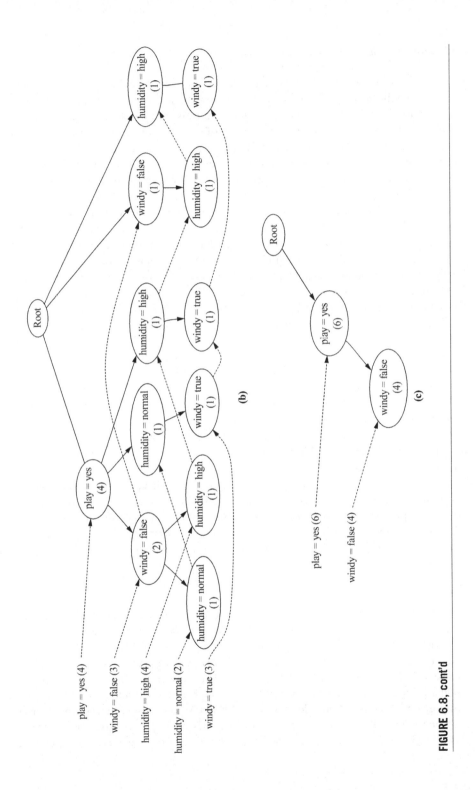

FIGURE 6.8, cont'd

temperature = mild. This tree was not created by rescanning the dataset but by further processing of the tree in Figure 6.8(a), as follows.

To see if a larger item set containing *temperature = mild* can be grown, we follow its link from the header table. This allows us to find all instances that contain *temperature = mild*. From here the new tree in Figure 6.8(b) is created, with counts projected from the original tree corresponding to the set of instances that are conditional on the presence of *temperature = mild*. This is done by propagating the counts from the *temperature = mild* nodes up the tree, each node receiving the sum of its children's counts.

A quick glance at the header table for this new FP-tree shows that the *temperature = mild* pattern cannot be grown any larger because there are no individual items, conditional on *temperature = mild*, that meet the minimum support threshold. Note, however, that it is necessary to create the whole Figure 6.8(b) tree in order to discover this because it is effectively being created bottom up and the counts in the header table to the left are computed from the numbers in the tree. The recursion exits at this point, and processing continues on the remaining header table items in the original FP-tree.

Figure 6.8(c) shows a second example, the FP-tree that results from following the header table link for *humidity = normal*. Here the *windy = false* node has a count of 4, corresponding to the four instances that had *humidity = normal* in the node's left branch in the original tree. Similarly, *play = yes* has a count of 6, corresponding to the four instances from *windy = false* and the two instances that contain *humidity = normal* from the middle branch of the subtree rooted at *play = yes* in Figure 6.8(a).

Processing the header list for this FP-tree shows that the *humidity = normal* item set can be grown to include *play = yes* since these two occur together six times, which meets the minimum support constraint. This corresponds to the second item set in Table 6.1(d), which in fact completes the output. However, in order to be sure that there are no other eligible item sets it is necessary to continue processing the entire header link table in Figure 6.8(a).

Once the recursive tree mining process is complete all large item sets that meet the minimum support threshold have been found. Then association rules are created using the approach explained in Section 4.5. Studies have claimed that the FP-growth algorithm is up to an order of magnitude faster than Apriori at finding large item sets, although this depends on the details of the implementation and the nature of the dataset.

Discussion

The process of recursively creating projected FP-trees can be efficiently implemented within a single prefix tree structure by having a list of frequencies, indexed by recursion depth, at each node in the tree and each element of the header table. The tree structure itself is usually far smaller than the original dataset, and if the dataset is dense it achieves a high level of compression. This outweighs the overhead imposed by the pointers and counters that must be maintained at each node. Only when the support threshold is set very low does the FP-tree's ability to compress the dataset degrade. Under these conditions, the tree becomes bushy, with little node sharing. On massive datasets for which the frequent-pattern tree exceeds main memory, disk-resident trees can be constructed using indexing techniques that have been developed for relational database systems.

The FP-tree data structure and FP-growth algorithm for finding large item sets without candidate generation were introduced by Han et al. (2000) following pioneering work by Zaki et al. (1997); Han et al. (2004) give a more comprehensive description. It has been extended in various ways. Wang et al. (2003) develop an algorithm called CLOSET+ to mine closed item sets—that is, sets for which there is no proper superset that has the same support. Finding large closed item sets provides essentially the same information as finding the complete set of large item sets, but produces few redundant rules and thus eases the task that users face when examining the output of the mining process. GSP (Generalized Sequential Patterns) is a method based on the Apriori algorithm for mining patterns in databases of event sequences (Srikant and Agrawal, 1996). A similar approach to FP-growth is used for event sequences by algorithms called PrefixSpan (Pei et al., 2004) and CloSpan (Yan et al., 2003), and for graph patterns by algorithms called gSpan (Yan and Han, 2002) and CloseGraph (Yan and Han, 2003).

Ceglar and Roddick (2006) provide a comprehensive survey of association rule mining. Some authors have worked on integrating association rule mining with classification. For example, Liu et al. (1998) mine a kind of association rule that they call a "class association rule," and build a classifier on the rules that are found using a technique they call CBA (Classification Based on Associations). Mutter et al. (2004) use classification to evaluate the output of confidence-based association rule mining, and find that standard learners for classification rules are generally preferable to CBA when runtime and size of the rule sets is of concern.

6.4 EXTENDING LINEAR MODELS

Section 4.6 described how simple linear models can be used for classification in situations where all attributes are numeric. Their biggest disadvantage is that they can only represent linear boundaries between classes, which makes them too simple for many practical applications. Support vector machines use linear models to implement nonlinear class boundaries. (Although it is a widely used term, *support vector machines* is something of a misnomer: These are algorithms, not machines.) How can this be possible? The trick is easy: Transform the input using a nonlinear mapping. In other words, transform the instance space into a new space. With a nonlinear mapping, a straight line in the new space doesn't look straight in the original instance space. A linear model constructed in the new space can represent a nonlinear decision boundary in the original space.

Imagine applying this idea directly to the ordinary linear models in Section 4.6. For example, the original set of attributes could be replaced by one giving all products of n factors that can be constructed from these attributes. An example for two attributes, including all products with three factors, is

$$x = w_1 a_1^3 + w_2 a_1^2 a_2 + w_3 a_1 a_2^2 + w_4 a_2^3$$

Here, x is the outcome, a_1 and a_2 are the two attribute values, and there are four weights w_i to be learned. As described in Section 4.6, the result can be used for classification by training one linear system for each class and assigning an unknown instance to the class that gives the greatest output x—the standard technique of multiresponse linear regression. Then, a_1 and a_2 will be the attribute values for the test instance.

To generate a linear model in the space that is spanned by these products, each training instance is mapped into the new space by computing all possible three-factor products of its two attribute values. The learning algorithm is then applied to the transformed instances. To classify an instance, it is processed by the same transformation prior to classification. There is nothing to stop us from adding in more synthetic attributes. For example, if a constant term were included, the original attributes and all two-factor products of them would yield a total of 10 weights to be learned. (Alternatively, adding an additional attribute with a value that was always a constant would have the same effect.) Indeed, polynomials of sufficiently high degree can approximate arbitrary decision boundaries to any required accuracy.

It seems too good to be true—and it is. As you will probably have guessed, problems arise with this procedure due to the large number of coefficients introduced by the transformation in any realistic setting. The first snag is computational complexity. With 10 attributes in the original dataset, suppose we want to include all products with five factors: then the learning algorithm will have to determine more than 2000 coefficients. If its runtime is cubic in the number of attributes, as it is for linear regression, training will be infeasible. That is a problem of practicality. The second problem is one of principle: overfitting. If the number of coefficients is large relative to the number of training instances, the resulting model will be "too nonlinear"—it will overfit the training data. There are just too many parameters in the model.

Maximum-Margin Hyperplane

Support vector machines address both problems. They are based on an algorithm that finds a special kind of linear model: the *maximum-margin hyperplane*. We already know what a hyperplane is—it's just another term for a linear model. To visualize a maximum-margin hyperplane, imagine a two-class dataset whose classes are linearly separable—that is, there is a hyperplane in instance space that classifies all training instances correctly. The maximum-margin hyperplane is the one that gives the greatest separation between the classes—it comes no closer to either than it has to. An example is shown in Figure 6.9, where the classes are represented by open and filled circles, respectively. Technically, the *convex hull* of a set of points is the tightest enclosing convex polygon: Its outline emerges when you connect every point of the set to every other point. Because we have supposed that the two classes are linearly separable, their convex hulls cannot overlap. Among all hyperplanes that separate the classes, the maximum-margin hyperplane is the one that is as far as

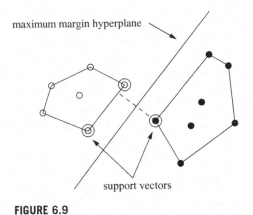

maximum margin hyperplane

support vectors

FIGURE 6.9

A maximum-margin hyperplane.

possible from both convex hulls—it is the perpendicular bisector of the shortest line connecting the hulls (shown dashed in the figure).

The instances that are closest to the maximum-margin hyperplane—the ones with the minimum distance to it—are called *support vectors*. There is always at least one support vector for each class, and often there are more. The important thing is that the set of support vectors uniquely defines the maximum-margin hyperplane for the learning problem. Given the support vectors for the two classes, we can easily construct the maximum-margin hyperplane. All other training instances are irrelevant—they can be deleted without changing the position and orientation of the hyperplane.

A hyperplane separating the two classes might be written as

$$x = w_0 + w_1 a_1 + w_2 a_2$$

in the two-attribute case, where a_1 and a_2 are the attribute values and there are three weights w_i to be learned. However, the equation defining the maximum-margin hyperplane can be written in another form, in terms of the support vectors. Write the class value y of a training instance as either 1 (for *yes*, it is in this class) or –1 (for *no*, it is not). Then the maximum-margin hyperplane can be written as

$$x = b + \sum_{i \text{ is support vector}} \alpha_i y_i \mathbf{a}(i) \bullet \mathbf{a}$$

Here, y_i is the class value of training instance $\mathbf{a}(i)$, while b and α_i are numeric parameters that have to be determined by the learning algorithm. Note that $\mathbf{a}(i)$ and $\mathbf{a}$ are vectors. The vector $\mathbf{a}$ represents a test instance—just as the vector $[a_1, a_2]$ represented a test instance in the earlier formulation. The vectors $\mathbf{a}(i)$ are the support vectors, those circled in Figure 6.9; they are selected members of the training set. The term $\mathbf{a}(i) \bullet \mathbf{a}$ represents the dot product of the test instance with one of the support vectors: $\mathbf{a}(i) \bullet \mathbf{a} = \Sigma_j a(i)_j a_j$. If you are not familiar with dot product notation, you should still be able to understand the gist of what follows: Just think of $\mathbf{a}(i)$ as the whole set of attribute values for the ith support vector. Finally, b and α_i are parameters that determine the hyperplane, just as the weights w_0, w_1, and w_2 are parameters that determine the hyperplane in the earlier formulation.

It turns out that finding the support vectors for the training instances and determining the parameters b and α_i belongs to a standard class of optimization problems known as *constrained quadratic optimization*. There are off-the-shelf software packages for solving these problems (see Fletcher, 1987, for a comprehensive and practical account of solution methods). However, the computational complexity can be reduced, and learning accelerated, if special-purpose algorithms for training support vector machines are applied—but the details of these algorithms lie beyond the scope of this book (see Platt, 1998).

Nonlinear Class Boundaries

We motivated the introduction of support vector machines by claiming that they can be used to model nonlinear class boundaries. However, so far we have only described the linear case. Consider what happens when an attribute transformation, as described before, is applied to the training data before determining the maximum-margin hyperplane. Recall that there are two problems with the straightforward application of such transformations to linear models: computational complexity on the one hand and overfitting on the other.

With support vectors, overfitting is unlikely to occur. The reason is that it is inevitably associated with instability: With an algorithm that overfits, changing one or two instance vectors will make sweeping changes to large sections of the decision boundary. But the maximum-margin hyperplane is relatively stable: It only moves if training instances are added or deleted that are support vectors—and this is true even in the high-dimensional space spanned by the nonlinear transformation. Over-fitting is caused by too much flexibility in the decision boundary. The support vectors are global representatives of the whole set of training points, and there are usually few of them, which gives little flexibility. Thus, overfitting is less likely to occur.

What about computational complexity? This is still a problem. Suppose that the transformed space is a high-dimensional one so that the transformed support vectors and test instance have many components. According to the preceding equation, every time an instance is classified its dot product with all support vectors must be calculated. In the high-dimensional space produced by the nonlinear mapping this is rather expensive. Obtaining the dot product involves one multiplication and one addition for each attribute, and the number of attributes in the new space can be huge. This problem occurs not only during classification but also during training because the optimization algorithms have to calculate the same dot products very frequently. Fortunately, it turns out that it is possible to calculate the dot product *before* the nonlinear mapping is performed, on the original attribute set, using a so-called kernel function based on the dot product.

A high-dimensional version of the preceding equation is simply

$$x = b + \sum \alpha_i y_i (\mathbf{a}(i) \bullet \mathbf{a})^n$$

where n is chosen as the number of factors in the transformation (three in the example we used earlier). If you expand the term $(\mathbf{a}(i) \bullet \mathbf{a})^n$, you will find that it contains all the high-dimensional terms that would have been involved if the test and training vectors were first transformed by including all products of n factors and the dot product of the result was taken. (If you actually do the calculation, you will notice that some constant factors—binomial coefficients—are introduced. However, these do not matter: It is the dimensionality of the space that concerns us; the constants merely scale the axes.)

Because of this mathematical equivalence, the dot products can be computed in the original low-dimensional space, and the problem becomes feasible. In implementation terms, you take a software package for constrained quadratic optimization and every time

a(i) • a is evaluated you evaluate **(a(i) • a)**^{n} instead. It's as simple as that because in both the optimization and the classification algorithms these vectors are only used in this dot product form. The training vectors, including the support vectors, and the test instance all remain in the original low-dimensional space throughout the calculations.

The function $(\mathbf{x} \bullet \mathbf{y})^n$, which computes the dot product of two vectors $\mathbf{x}$ and $\mathbf{y}$ and raises the result to the power n, is called a *polynomial kernel*. A good way of choosing the value of n is to start with 1 (a linear model) and increment it until the estimated error ceases to improve. Usually, quite small values suffice. To include lower-order terms, we can use the kernel $(\mathbf{x} \bullet \mathbf{y} + 1)^n$.

Other kernel functions can be used instead to implement different nonlinear mappings. Two that are often suggested are the *radial basis function (RBF) kernel* and the *sigmoid kernel*. Which one produces the best results depends on the application, although the differences are rarely large in practice. It is interesting to note that a support vector machine with the RBF kernel is simply a type of neural network called an *RBF network* (which we describe later), and one with the sigmoid kernel implements another type of neural network, a multilayer perceptron with one hidden layer (also described later).

Mathematically, any function $K(\mathbf{x}, \mathbf{y})$ is a kernel function if it can be written as $K(\mathbf{x}, \mathbf{y}) = \Phi(\mathbf{x}) \bullet \Phi(\mathbf{y})$, where Φ is a function that maps an instance into a (potentially high-dimensional) feature space. In other words, the kernel function represents a dot product in the feature space created by Φ. Practitioners sometimes apply functions that are not proper kernel functions (the sigmoid kernel with certain parameter settings is an example). Despite the lack of theoretical guarantees, this can nevertheless produce accurate classifiers.

Throughout this section, we have assumed that the training data is linearly separable—either in the instance space or in the new space spanned by the nonlinear mapping. It turns out that support vector machines can be generalized to the case where the training data is not separable. This is accomplished by placing an upper bound on the coefficients α_i. Unfortunately, this parameter must be chosen by the user, and the best setting can only be determined by experimentation. Also, except in trivial cases it is not possible to determine a priori whether the data is linearly separable or not.

Finally, we should mention that compared with other methods such as decision tree learners, even the fastest training algorithms for support vector machines are slow when applied in the nonlinear setting. However, they often produce very accurate classifiers because subtle and complex decision boundaries can be obtained.

Support Vector Regression

The maximum-margin hyperplane concept only applies to classification. However, support vector machine algorithms have been developed for numeric prediction that share many of the properties encountered in the classification case: They produce a model that can usually be expressed in terms of a few support vectors and can be applied to nonlinear problems using kernel functions. As with regular support vector machines, we will describe the concepts involved, but will not attempt to describe the algorithms that actually perform the work.

As with linear regression, covered in Section 4.6, the basic idea is to find a function that approximates the training points well by minimizing the prediction error. The crucial difference is that all deviations up to a user-specified parameter ε are simply discarded. Also, when minimizing the error, the risk of overfitting is reduced by simultaneously trying to maximize the flatness of the function. Another difference is that what is minimized is normally the predictions' absolute error instead of the squared error used in linear regression. (There are, however, versions of the algorithm that use the squared error instead.)

A user-specified parameter ε defines a tube around the regression function in which errors are ignored: For linear support vector regression, the tube is a cylinder. If all training points can fit within a tube of width 2ε, the algorithm outputs the function in the middle of the flattest tube that encloses them. In this case the total perceived error is 0. Figure 6.10(a) shows a regression problem with one attribute,

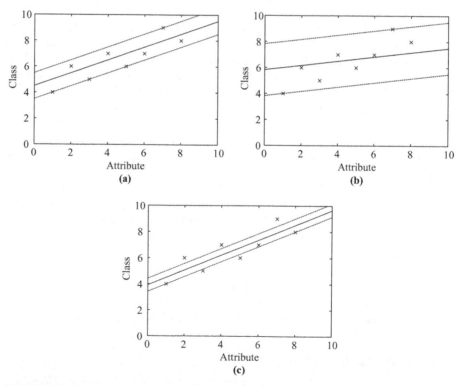

FIGURE 6.10

Support vector regression: (a) $\varepsilon = 1$, (b) $\varepsilon = 2$, and (c) $\varepsilon = 0.5$.

a numeric class, and eight instances. In this case ε was set to 1, so the width of the tube around the regression function (indicated by dotted lines) is 2. Figure 6.10(b) shows the outcome of the learning process when ε is set to 2. As you can see, the wider tube makes it possible to learn a flatter function.

The value of ε controls how closely the function will fit the training data. Too large a value will produce a meaningless predictor—in the extreme case, when 2ε exceeds the range of class values in the training data, the regression line is horizontal and the algorithm just predicts the mean class value. On the other hand, for small values of ε there may be no tube that encloses all the data. In that case, some training points will have nonzero error, and there will be a tradeoff between the prediction error and the tube's flatness. In Figure 6.10(c), ε was set to 0.5 and there is no tube of width 1 that encloses all the data.

For the linear case, the support vector regression function can be written as

$$x = b + \sum_{i \text{ is support vector}} \alpha_i \mathbf{a(i)} \bullet \mathbf{a}$$

As with classification, the dot product can be replaced by a kernel function for nonlinear problems. The support vectors are all those points that do not fall strictly within the tube—that is, the points outside the tube and on its border. As with classification, all other points have coefficient 0 and can be deleted from the training data without changing the outcome of the learning process. In contrast to the classification case, the α_i may be negative.

We have mentioned that as well as minimizing the error, the algorithm simultaneously tries to maximize the flatness of the regression function. In Figures 6.10(a) and (b), where there is a tube that encloses all the training data, the algorithm simply outputs the flattest tube that does so. However, in Figure 6.10(c), there is no tube with error 0, and a tradeoff is struck between the prediction error and the tube's flatness. This tradeoff is controlled by enforcing an upper limit C on the absolute value of the coefficients α_i. The upper limit restricts the influence of the support vectors on the shape of the regression function and is a parameter that the user must specify in addition to ε. The larger C is, the more closely the function can fit the data. In the degenerate case $\varepsilon = 0$, the algorithm simply performs least-absolute-error regression under the coefficient size constraint and all training instances become support vectors. Conversely, if ε is large enough that the tube can enclose all the data, the error becomes 0, there is no tradeoff to make, and the algorithm outputs the flattest tube that encloses the data irrespective of the value of C.

Kernel Ridge Regression

Chapter 4 introduced classic least-squares linear regression as a technique for predicting numeric quantities. In the previous section we saw how the powerful idea of support vector machines can be applied to regression and, furthermore, how nonlinear problems can be tackled by replacing the dot product in the support vector formulation by a kernel function—this is often known as the "kernel trick." For classic linear regression using squared loss, only simple matrix operations are needed to find the model, but this is not the case for support vector regression with the user-specified loss parameter ε. It would be nice to combine the power of the kernel trick with the simplicity of standard least-squares regression. Kernel ridge regression does just that. In contrast to support vector regression, it does not ignore errors smaller than ε, and the squared error is used instead of the absolute error.

Instead of expressing the linear regression model's predicted class value for a given test instance **a** as a weighted sum of the attribute values, as in Chapter 4, it can be expressed as a weighted sum over the dot products of each training instance $\mathbf{a}_j$ and the test instance in question:

$$\sum_{j=0}^{n} \alpha_j \mathbf{a}_j \bullet \mathbf{a}$$

where we assume that the function goes through the origin and an intercept is not required. This involves a coefficient α_j for each training instance, which resembles the situation with support vector machines—except that here j ranges over *all* instances in the training data, not just the support vectors. Again, the dot product can be replaced by a kernel function to yield a nonlinear model.

The sum of the squared errors of the model's predictions on the training data is given by

$$\sum_{i=1}^{n} \left(y_i - \sum_{j=0}^{n} \alpha_j \mathbf{a}_j \bullet \mathbf{a}_i \right)^2$$

This is the squared loss, just as in Chapter 4, and again we seek to minimize it by choosing appropriate α_j's. But now there is a coefficient for each training instance, not just for each attribute, and most data sets have far more instances than attributes. This means that there is a serious risk of overfitting the training data when a kernel function is used instead of the dot product to obtain a nonlinear model.

That is where the *ridge* part of kernel ridge regression comes in. Instead of minimizing the squared loss, we trade closeness of fit against model complexity by introducing a penalty term:

$$\sum_{i=1}^{n} \left(y_i - \sum_{j=0}^{n} \alpha_j \mathbf{a}_j \cdot \mathbf{a}_i \right)^2 + \lambda \sum_{i,j=1}^{n} \alpha_i \alpha_j \mathbf{a}_j \bullet \mathbf{a}_i$$

The second sum penalizes large coefficients. This prevents the model from placing too much emphasis on individual training instances by giving them large coefficients, unless this yields a correspondingly large drop in error. The parameter λ controls the tradeoff between closeness of fit and model complexity. When matrix operations are used to solve for the coefficients of the model, the ridge penalty also has the added benefit of stabilizing degenerate cases. For this reason, it is often applied in standard least-squares linear regression as well.

Although kernel ridge regression has the advantage over support vector machines of computational simplicity, one disadvantage is that there is no sparseness in the vector of coefficients—in other words, no concept of "support vectors." This makes a difference at prediction time because support vector machines have to sum only over the set of support vectors, not the entire training set.

In a typical situation with more instances than attributes, kernel ridge regression is more computationally expensive than standard linear regression, even when using the dot product rather than a kernel. This is because of the complexity of the matrix inversion operation used to find the model's coefficient vector. Standard linear regression requires inverting an $m \times m$ matrix, which has complexity $O(m^3)$, where m is the number of attributes in the data. Kernel ridge regression, on the other hand, involves an $n \times n$ matrix, with complexity $O(n^3)$ where n is the number of instances in the training data. Nevertheless, it is advantageous to use kernel ridge regression in cases where a nonlinear fit is desired, or where there are more attributes than training instances.

Kernel Perceptron

In Section 4.6 we introduced the perceptron algorithm for learning a linear classifier. It turns out that the kernel trick can also be used to upgrade this algorithm to learn nonlinear decision boundaries.

To see this, we first revisit the linear case. The perceptron algorithm repeatedly iterates through the training data instance by instance and updates the weight vector every time one of these instances is misclassified based on the weights learned so far. The weight vector is updated simply by adding or subtracting the instance's attribute values to or from it. This means that the final weight vector is just the sum of the instances that have been misclassified. The perceptron makes its predictions based on whether

$$\sum_i w_i a_i$$

is greater or less than 0, where w_i is the weight for the ith attribute and a_i the corresponding attribute value of the instance that we wish to classify. Instead, we could use

$$\sum_i \sum_j y(j) a'(j)_i a_i$$

Here, $a'(j)$ is the jth misclassified training instance, $a'(j)_i$ its ith attribute value, and $y(j)$ its class value (either +1 or −1). To implement this we no longer keep track of an explicit weight vector: We simply store the instances that have been misclassified so far and use the previous expression to make a prediction.

It looks like we've gained nothing—in fact, the algorithm is much slower because it iterates through all misclassified training instances every time a prediction is made. However, closer inspection of this formula reveals that it can be expressed in terms of dot products between instances. First, swap the summation signs to yield

$$\sum_j y(j) \sum_i a'(j)_i a_i$$

The second sum is just a dot product between two instances and can be written as

$$\sum_j y(j) a'(j) \bullet a$$

This rings a bell! A similar expression for support vector machines enabled the use of kernels. Indeed, we can apply exactly the same trick here and use a kernel function instead of the dot product. Writing this function as $K(...)$ gives

$$\sum_j y(j) K(a'(j), a)$$

In this way the perceptron algorithm can learn a nonlinear classifier simply by keeping track of the instances that have been misclassified during the training process and using this expression to form each prediction.

If a separating hyperplane exists in the high-dimensional space implicitly created by the kernel function, this algorithm will learn one. However, it won't learn the maximum-margin hyperplane found by a support vector machine classifier. This means that classification performance is usually worse. On the plus side, the algorithm is easy to implement and supports incremental learning.

This classifier is called the *kernel perceptron*. It turns out that all sorts of algorithms for learning linear models can be upgraded by applying the kernel trick in a similar fashion. For example, logistic regression can be turned into *kernel logistic regression*. As we saw before, the same applies to regression problems: Linear regression can also be upgraded using kernels. Again, a drawback of these advanced methods for linear and logistic regression (if they are done in a straightforward manner) is that the solution is not "sparse": Every training instance contributes to the solution vector. In support vector machines and the kernel perceptron, only some of the training instances affect the solution, and this can make a big difference in computational efficiency.

The solution vector found by the perceptron algorithm depends greatly on the order in which the instances are encountered. One way to make the algorithm more stable is to use all the weight vectors encountered during learning, not just the final one, letting them vote on a prediction. Each weight vector contributes a certain number of votes. Intuitively, the "correctness" of a weight vector can be measured roughly as the number of successive trials after its inception in which it correctly classified subsequent instances and thus didn't have to be changed. This measure can be used as the number of votes given to the weight vector, giving an algorithm known as the *voted perceptron* that performs almost as well as a support vector machine. (Note that, as mentioned earlier, the various weight vectors in the voted perceptron don't need to be stored explicitly, and the kernel trick can be applied here too.)

Multilayer Perceptrons

Using a kernel is not the only way to create a nonlinear classifier based on the perceptron. In fact, kernel functions are a recent development in machine learning. Previously, neural network proponents used a different approach for nonlinear classification: They connected many simple perceptron-like models in a hierarchical structure. This can represent nonlinear decision boundaries.

Section 4.6 explained that a perceptron represents a hyperplane in instance space. We mentioned there that it is sometimes described as an artificial "neuron." Of course, human and animal brains successfully undertake very complex classification tasks—for example, image recognition. The functionality of each individual neuron that is in a brain is certainly not sufficient to perform these feats. How can they be solved by brainlike structures? The answer must lie in the fact that the neurons in the brain are massively interconnected, allowing a problem to be decomposed into subproblems that can be solved at the neuron level.

This observation inspired the development of artificial networks of neurons—neural nets.

Consider the simple dataset in Figure 6.11. Part (a) shows a two-dimensional instance space with four instances having classes 0 and 1, represented by white and black dots, respectively. No matter how you draw a straight line through this space, you will not be able to find one that separates all the black points from all the white ones. In other words, the problem is not linearly separable, and the simple perceptron algorithm will fail to generate a separating hyperplane (in this two-dimensional instance space a hyperplane is just a straight line). The situation is different in Figure 6.11(b) and Figure 6.11(c): Both these problems are linearly separable. The same holds for Figure 6.11(d), which shows two points in a one-dimensional instance space (in the case of one dimension the separating hyperplane degenerates to a separating point).

If you are familiar with propositional logic, you may have noticed that the four situations in Figure 6.11 correspond to four types of logical connectives. Figure 6.11(a) represents a logical XOR (exclusive-OR), where the class is 1 if and only if exactly one of the attributes has value 1. Figure 6.11(b) represents logical AND, where the class is 1 if and only if both attributes have value 1. Figure 6.11(c) represents OR, where the class is 0 only if both attributes have value 0. Figure 6.11(d) represents NOT, where the class is 0 if and only if the attribute has value 1. Because the last three are linearly separable, a perceptron can represent AND, OR, and NOT. Indeed, perceptrons for the corresponding datasets are shown in Figures 6.11(f–h), respectively. However, a simple perceptron cannot represent XOR because that is not linearly separable. To build a classifier for this type of problem a single perceptron is not sufficient—we need several of them.

Figure 6.11(e) shows a network with three perceptrons, or *units*, labeled A, B, and C. The first two are connected to what is sometimes called the *input layer* of the network, representing the attributes in the data. As in a simple perceptron, the input layer has an additional constant input called the *bias*. However, the third unit does not have any connections to the input layer. Its input consists of the output of units A and B (either 0 or 1) and another constant bias unit. These three units make up the *hidden layer* of the multilayer perceptron. They are called "hidden" because the units have no direct connection to the environment. This layer is what enables the system to represent XOR. You can verify this by trying all four possible combinations of input signals. For example, if attribute a_1 has value 1 and a_2 has value 1, then unit A will output 1 (because $1 \times 1 + 1 \times 1 + -0.5 \times 1 > 0$), unit B will output 0 (because $-1 \times 1 + -1 \times 1 + -1.5 \times 1 < 0$), and unit C will output 0 (because $1 \times 1 + 1 \times 0 + -1.5 \times 1 < 0$). This is the correct answer. Closer inspection of the behavior of the three units reveals that the first one represents OR, the second represents NAND (NOT combined with AND), and the third represents AND. Together they represent the expression $(a_1$ OR $a_2)$ AND $(a_1$ NAND $a_2)$, which is precisely the definition of XOR.

As this example illustrates, any expression from propositional calculus can be converted into a multilayer perceptron, because the three connectives AND, OR, and

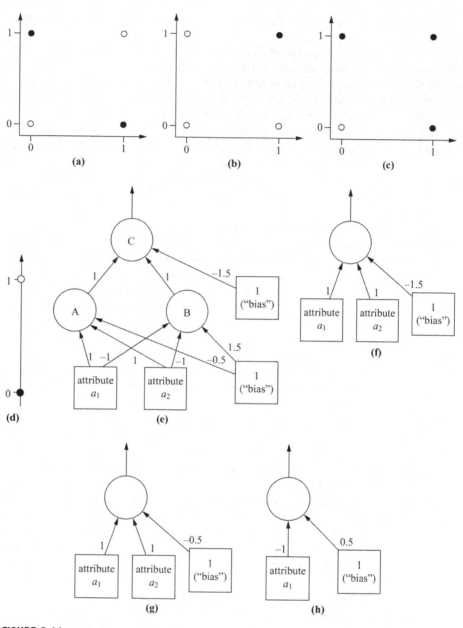

FIGURE 6.11

Example datasets and corresponding perceptrons.

NOT are sufficient for this and we have seen how each can be represented using a perceptron. Individual units can be connected together to form arbitrarily complex expressions. Hence, a multilayer perceptron has the same expressive power as, say, a decision tree. In fact, it turns out that a two-layer perceptron (not counting the input layer) is sufficient. In this case, each unit in the hidden layer corresponds to a variant of AND—because we assume that it may negate some of the inputs before forming the conjunction—joined by an OR that is represented by a single unit in the output layer. In other words, each node in the hidden layer has the same role as a leaf in a decision tree or a single rule in a set of decision rules.

The big question is how to learn a multilayer perceptron. There are two aspects to the problem: learning the structure of the network and learning the connection weights. It turns out that there is a relatively simple algorithm for determining the weights given a fixed network structure. This algorithm is called *backpropagation* and is described in the next section. However, although there are many algorithms that attempt to identify network structure, this aspect of the problem is commonly solved by experimentation—perhaps combined with a healthy dose of expert knowledge. Sometimes the network can be separated into distinct modules that represent identifiable subtasks (e.g., recognizing different components of an object in an image recognition problem), which opens up a way of incorporating domain knowledge into the learning process. Often a single hidden layer is all that is necessary, and an appropriate number of units for that layer is determined by maximizing the estimated accuracy.

Backpropagation

Suppose we have some data and seek a multilayer perceptron that is an accurate predictor for the underlying classification problem. Given a fixed network structure, we must determine appropriate weights for the connections in the network. In the absence of hidden layers, the perceptron learning rule from Section 4.6 can be used to find suitable values. But suppose there are hidden units. We know what the output unit should predict and could adjust the weights of the connections leading to that unit based on the perceptron rule. But the correct outputs for the hidden units are unknown, so the rule cannot be applied there.

It turns out that, roughly speaking, the solution is to modify the weights of the connections leading to the hidden units based on the strength of each unit's contribution to the final prediction. There is a standard mathematical optimization algorithm, called *gradient descent*, which achieves exactly that. Unfortunately, it requires taking derivatives, and the step function that the simple perceptron uses to convert the weighted sum of the inputs into a 0/1 prediction is not differentiable. We need to see whether the step function can be replaced by something else.

Figure 6.12(a) shows the step function: If the input is smaller than 0, it outputs 0; otherwise, it outputs 1. We want a function that is similar in shape but differentiable. A commonly used replacement is shown in Figure 6.12(b). In neural networks terminology it is called the *sigmoid* function, and the version we consider here is defined by

$$f(x) = \frac{1}{1 + e^{-x}}$$

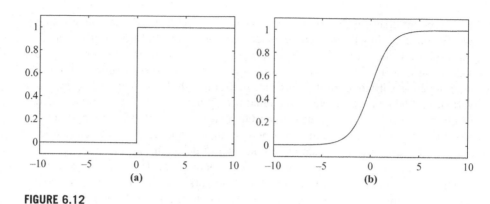

FIGURE 6.12

Step versus sigmoid: (a) step function and (b) sigmoid function.

We encountered it in Section 4.6 when we described the logit transform used in logistic regression. In fact, learning a multilayer perceptron is closely related to logistic regression.

To apply the gradient descent procedure, the error function—the thing that is to be minimized by adjusting the weights—must also be differentiable. The number of misclassifications—measured by the discrete 0 – 1 loss mentioned in Section 5.6—does not fulfill this criterion. Instead, multilayer perceptrons are usually trained by minimizing the squared error of the network's output, essentially treating it as an estimate of the class probability. (Other loss functions are also applicable. For example, if the negative log-likelihood is used instead of the squared error, learning a sigmoid-based perceptron is identical to logistic regression.)

We work with the squared-error loss function because it is most widely used. For a single training instance, it is

$$E = \frac{1}{2}(y - f(x))^2$$

where $f(x)$ is the network's prediction obtained from the output unit and y is the instance's class label (in this case, it is assumed to be either 0 or 1). The factor ½ is included just for convenience and will drop out when we start taking derivatives.

Gradient descent exploits information given by the derivative of the function that is to be minimized—in this case, the error function. As an example, consider a hypothetical error function that happens to be identical to $w^2 + 1$, shown in Figure 6.13. The x-axis represents a hypothetical parameter w that is to be optimized. The derivative of $w^2 + 1$ is simply $2w$. The crucial observation is that, based on the derivative, we can figure out the slope of the function at any particular point. If the derivative is negative, the function slopes downward to the right; if it is positive,

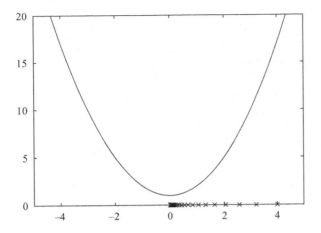

FIGURE 6.13

Gradient descent using the error function $w^2 + 1$.

it slopes downward to the left; and the size of the derivative determines how steep the decline is. Gradient descent is an iterative optimization procedure that uses this information to adjust a function's parameters. It takes the value of the derivative, multiplies it by a small constant called the *learning rate*, and subtracts the result from the current parameter value. This is repeated for the new parameter value, and so on, until a minimum is reached.

Returning to the example, assume that the learning rate is set to 0.1 and the current parameter value w is 4. The derivative is double this—8 at this point. Multiplying by the learning rate yields 0.8, and subtracting this from 4 gives 3.2, which becomes the new parameter value. Repeating the process for 3.2, we get 2.56, then 2.048, and so on. The little crosses in Figure 6.13 show the values encountered in this process. The process stops once the change in parameter value becomes too small. In the example this happens when the value approaches 0, the value corresponding to the location on the x-axis where the minimum of the hypothetical error function is located.

The learning rate determines the step size and hence how quickly the search converges. If it is too large and the error function has several minima, the search may overshoot and miss a minimum entirely, or it may oscillate wildly. If it is too small, progress toward the minimum may be slow. Note that gradient descent can only find a *local* minimum. If the function has several minima—and error functions for multilayer perceptrons usually have many—it may not find the best one. This is a significant drawback of standard multilayer perceptrons compared with, for example, support vector machines.

To use gradient descent to find the weights of a multilayer perceptron, the derivative of the squared error must be determined with respect to each parameter—that is, each weight in the network. Let's start with a simple perceptron without a hidden layer. Differentiating the error function with respect to a particular weight w_i yields

$$\frac{dE}{dw_i} = (f(x) - y)\frac{f(x)}{dw_i}$$

Here, $f(x)$ is the perceptron's output and x is the weighted sum of the inputs.

To compute the second factor on the right side, the derivative of the sigmoid function $f(x)$ is needed. It turns out that this has a particularly simple form that can be written in terms of $f(x)$ itself:

$$\frac{df(x)}{dx} = f(x)(1 - f(x))$$

We use $f'(x)$ to denote this derivative. But we seek the derivative with respect to w_i, not x. Because

$$x = \sum_i w_i a_i$$

the derivative of $f(x)$ with respect to w_i is

$$\frac{df(x)}{dw_i} = f'(x)\,a_i$$

Plugging this back into the derivative of the error function yields

$$\frac{dE}{dw_i} = (f(x) - y)f'(x)\,a_i$$

This expression gives all that is needed to calculate the change of weight w_i caused by a particular example vector **a** (extended by 1 to represent the bias, as explained previously). Having repeated this computation for each training instance, we add up the changes associated with a particular weight w_i, multiply by the learning rate, and subtract the result from w_i's current value.

So far so good. But all this assumes that there is no hidden layer. With a hidden layer, things get a little trickier. Suppose $f(x_i)$ is the output of the ith hidden unit, w_{ij} is the weight of the connection from input j to the ith hidden unit, and w_i is the weight of the ith hidden unit to the output unit. The situation is depicted in Figure 6.14. As before, $f(x)$ is the output of the single unit in the output layer. The update rule for the weights w_i is essentially the same as above, except that a_i is replaced by the output of the ith hidden unit:

$$\frac{dE}{dw_i} = (f(x) - y)f'(x)f(x_i)$$

However, to update the weights w_{ij} the corresponding derivatives must be calculated. Applying the chain rule gives

$$\frac{dE}{dw_{ij}} = \frac{dE}{dx}\frac{dx}{dw_{ij}} = (f(x) - y)f'(x)\frac{dx}{dw_{ij}}$$

The first two factors are the same as in the previous equation. To compute the third factor, differentiate further. Because

$$x = \sum_i w_i f(x_i)$$

then

$$\frac{dx}{dw_{ij}} = w_i\frac{df(x_i)}{dw_{ij}}$$

Furthermore,

$$x_i = \sum_j w_{ij} a_j$$

so

$$\frac{df(x_i)}{dw_{ij}} = f'(x_i)\frac{dx_i}{dw_{ij}} = f'(x_i)a_j$$

This means that we are finished. Putting everything together yields an equation for the derivative of the error function with respect to the weights w_{ij}:

$$\frac{dE}{dw_{ij}} = (f(x) - y)f'(x)w_i f'(x_i)\,a_j$$

As before, we calculate this value for every training instance, add up the changes associated with a particular weight w_{ij}, multiply by the learning rate, and subtract the outcome from the current value of w_{ij}.

   This derivation applies to a perceptron with one hidden layer. If there are two hidden layers, the same strategy can be applied a second time to update the weights pertaining to the input connections of the first hidden layer, propagating the error from the output unit through the second hidden layer to the first one. Because of this error propagation mechanism, this version of the generic gradient descent strategy is called *backpropagation*.

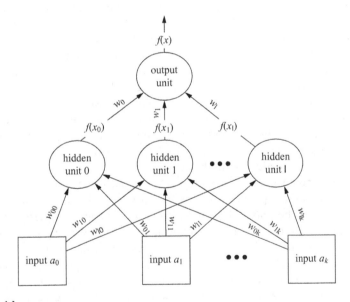

FIGURE 6.14

Multilayer perceptron with a hidden layer.

   We have tacitly assumed that the network's output layer has just one unit, which is appropriate for two-class problems. For more than two classes, a separate network could be learned for each class that distinguishes it from the remaining classes. A more compact classifier can be obtained from a single network by creating an output unit for each class, connecting every unit in the hidden layer to every output unit.

The squared error for a particular training instance is the sum of squared errors taken over all output units. The same technique can be applied to predict several targets, or attribute values, simultaneously by creating a separate output unit for each one. Intuitively, this may give better predictive accuracy than building a separate classifier for each class attribute if the underlying learning tasks are in some way related.

We have assumed that weights are only updated after all training instances have been fed through the network and all the corresponding weight changes have been accumulated. This is *batch* learning because all the training data is processed together. But exactly the same formulas can be used to update the weights incrementally after each training instance has been processed. This is called *stochastic backpropagation* because the overall error does not necessarily decrease after every update. It can be used for online learning, in which new data arrives in a continuous stream and every training instance is processed just once. In both variants of backpropagation, it is often helpful to standardize the attributes to have zero mean and unit standard deviation. Before learning starts, each weight is initialized to a small, randomly chosen value based on a normal distribution with zero mean.

Like any other learning scheme, multilayer perceptrons trained with backpropagation may suffer from overfitting, especially if the network is much larger than what is actually necessary to represent the structure of the underlying learning problem. Many modifications have been proposed to alleviate this. A very simple one, called *early stopping*, works like reduced-error pruning in rule learners: A holdout set is used to decide when to stop performing further iterations of the backpropagation algorithm. The error on the holdout set is measured and the algorithm is terminated once the error begins to increase because that indicates overfitting to the training data. Another method, called *weight decay*, adds to the error function a penalty term that consists of the squared sum of all weights in the network, as in ridge regression. This attempts to limit the influence of irrelevant connections on the network's predictions by penalizing large weights that do not contribute a correspondingly large reduction in the error.

Although standard gradient descent is the simplest technique for learning the weights in a multilayer perceptron, it is by no means the most efficient one. In practice, it tends to be rather slow. A trick that often improves performance is to include a *momentum* term when updating weights: Add to the new weight change a small proportion of the update value from the previous iteration. This smoothes the search process by making changes in direction less abrupt. More sophisticated methods make use of information obtained from the second derivative of the error function as well; they can converge much more quickly. However, even those algorithms can be very slow compared with other methods of classification learning.

A serious disadvantage of multilayer perceptrons that contain hidden units is that they are essentially opaque. There are several techniques that attempt to extract rules from trained neural networks. However, it is unclear whether they offer any advantages over standard rule learners that induce rule sets directly from data, especially considering that this can generally be done much more quickly than learning a multilayer perceptron in the first place.

Although multilayer perceptrons are the most prominent type of neural network, many others have been proposed. Multilayer perceptrons belong to a class of networks called *feed-forward networks* because they do not contain any cycles and the network's output depends only on the current input instance. *Recurrent* neural networks do have cycles. Computations derived from earlier input are fed back into the network, which gives them a kind of memory.

Radial Basis Function Networks

Another popular type of feed-forward network is the *radial basis function* (RBF) network. It has two layers, not counting the input layer, and differs from a multilayer perceptron in the way that the hidden units perform computations. Each hidden unit essentially represents a particular point in input space, and its output, or *activation*, for a given instance depends on the distance between its point and the instance, which is just another point. Intuitively, the closer these two points, the stronger the activation. This is achieved by using a nonlinear transformation function to convert the distance into a similarity measure. A bell-shaped Gaussian *activation function*, of which the width may be different for each hidden unit, is commonly used for this purpose. The hidden units are called RBFs because the points in instance space for which a given hidden unit produces the same activation form a hypersphere or hyperellipsoid. (In a multilayer perceptron, this is a hyperplane.)

The output layer of an RBF network is the same as that of a multilayer perceptron: It takes a linear combination of the outputs of the hidden units and—in classification problems—pipes it through the sigmoid function (or something with a similar shape).

The parameters that such a network learns are (a) the centers and widths of the RBFs and (b) the weights used to form the linear combination of the outputs obtained from the hidden layer. A significant advantage over multilayer perceptrons is that the first set of parameters can be determined independently of the second set and still produce accurate classifiers.

One way to determine the first set of parameters is to use clustering. The simple *k*-means clustering algorithm described in Section 4.8 can be applied, clustering each class independently to obtain *k*-basis functions for each class. Intuitively, the resulting RBFs represent prototype instances. The second set of parameters is then learned by keeping the first parameters fixed. This involves learning a simple linear classifier using one of the techniques we have discussed (e.g., linear or logistic regression). If there are far fewer hidden units than training instances, this can be done very quickly.

A disadvantage of RBF networks is that they give every attribute the same weight because all are treated equally in the distance computation, unless attribute weight parameters are included in the overall optimization process. Thus, they cannot deal effectively with irrelevant attributes, in contrast to multilayer perceptrons. Support vector machines share the same problem. In fact, support vector machines with Gaussian kernels (i.e., "RBF kernels") are a particular type of RBF network, in which one basis function is centered on every training instance, all basis functions have the same width, and the outputs are combined linearly by computing the maximum-margin hyperplane. This has the effect that only some of the RBFs have a nonzero weight—the ones that represent the support vectors.

Stochastic Gradient Descent

We have introduced gradient descent and stochastic backpropagation as optimization methods for learning the weights in a neural network. Gradient descent is, in fact, a general-purpose optimization technique that can be applied whenever the objective function is differentiable. Actually, it turns out that it can even be applied in cases where the objective function is not completely differentiable through use of a device called *subgradients*.

One application is the use of gradient descent to learn linear models such as linear support vector machines or logistic regression. Learning such models using gradient descent is easier than optimizing nonlinear neural networks because the objective function has a global minimum rather than many local minima, which is usually the case for nonlinear networks. For linear problems, a stochastic gradient descent procedure can be designed that is computationally simple and converges very rapidly, allowing models such as linear support vector machines and logistic regression to be learned from large datasets. Moreover, stochastic gradient descent allows models to be learned incrementally, in an online setting.

For support vector machines, the error function—the thing that is to be minimized—is called the *hinge loss*. Illustrated in Figure 6.15, this is so named because it comprises a downwards sloping linear segment joined to a horizontal part at $z = 1$—more formally, $E(z) = \max\{0, 1 - z\}$. For comparison, the figure also shows the $0 - 1$ loss, which is discontinuous, and the squared loss, which is both continuous

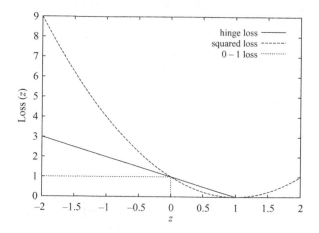

FIGURE 6.15

Hinge, squared, and $0 - 1$ loss functions.

and differentiable. These functions are plotted as a function of the margin $z = y f(x)$, where the class y is either -1 or $+1$ and $f(x)$ is the output of the linear model. Misclassification occurs when $z < 0$, so all loss functions incur their most serious penalties in the negative region. In the linearly separable case, the hinge loss is 0 for a function that successfully separates the data. The maximum-margin hyperplane is given by the smallest weight vector that achieves a zero hinge loss.

The hinge loss is continuous, unlike the $0 - 1$ loss, but is not differentiable at $z = 1$, unlike the squared loss, which is differentiable everywhere. This lack of differentiability presents a problem if gradient descent is used to update the model's weights after a training example has been processed, because the loss function's derivative is needed for this. That is where subgradients come in. The basic idea is that even though the gradient cannot be computed, the minimum will still be found if something resembling a gradient can be substituted. In the case of the hinge loss, the gradient is taken to be 0 at the point of nondifferentiability. In fact, since the hinge loss is 0 for $z \geq 1$, we can focus on that part of the function that is differentiable ($z < 1$) and proceed as usual.

Ignoring the weight decay necessary to find the smallest weight vector, the weight update for a linear support vector machine using the hinge loss is $\Delta w_i = \eta a_i y$, where η is the learning rate. For stochastic gradient descent, all that is needed to compute z for each training instance is to take the dot product between the current weight vector and the instance, multiply the result by the instance's class value, and check to see if the resulting value is less than 1. If so, the weights are updated accordingly. As with perceptrons, a bias term can be included by extending the weight vector by one element and including an additional attribute with each training instance that always has the value 1.

Discussion

Support vector machines originated from research in statistical learning theory (Vapnik, 1999), and a good starting point for exploration is a tutorial by Burges (1998). A general description, including generalization to the case in which the data is not linearly separable, has been published by Cortes and Vapnik (1995). We have introduced the standard version of support vector regression; Schölkopf et al. (1999) present a different version that has one parameter instead of two. Smola and Schölkopf (2004) provide an extensive tutorial on support vector regression.

Ridge regression was introduced in statistics by Hoerl and Kennard (1970) and can now be found in standard statistics texts. Hastie et al. (2009) give a good description of kernel ridge regression. Kernel ridge regression is equivalent to a technique called Gaussian process regression in terms of point estimates produced, but a discussion of Gaussian processes is beyond the scope of this book. The complexity of the most efficient general matrix inversion algorithm is in fact $O(n^{2.807})$ rather than $O(n^3)$.

The (voted) kernel perceptron is due to Freund and Schapire (1999). Cristianini and Shawe-Taylor (2000) provide a nice introduction to support vector machines and other kernel-based methods, including the optimization theory underlying the support vector learning algorithms. We have barely skimmed the surface of these learning schemes, mainly because advanced mathematics lies just beneath. The idea of using kernels to solve nonlinear problems has been applied to many algorithms, for example, principal components analysis (described in Section 7.3). A kernel is essentially a similarity function with certain mathematical properties, and it is possible to define kernel functions over all sorts of structures—for example, sets, strings, trees, and probability distributions. Shawe-Taylor and Cristianini (2004) and Schölkopf and Smola (2002) cover kernel-based learning in detail.

There is extensive literature on neural networks, and Bishop (1995) provides an excellent introduction to both multilayer perceptrons and RBF networks. Interest in neural networks appears to have declined since the arrival of support vector machines, perhaps because the latter generally require fewer parameters to be tuned to achieve the same (or greater) accuracy. However, multilayer perceptrons have the advantage that they can learn to ignore irrelevant attributes, and RBF networks trained using k-means can be viewed as a quick-and-dirty method for finding a nonlinear classifier. Recent studies have shown that multilayer perceptrons achieve performance competitive with more modern learning techniques on many practical datasets.

Recently there has been renewed interest in gradient methods for learning classifiers. In particular, stochastic gradient methods have been explored because they are applicable to large data sets and online learning scenarios. Kivinen et al. (2002), Zhang (2004), and Shalev-Shwartz et al. (2007) explore such methods when applied to learning support vector machines. Kivinen et al. and Shalev-Shwartz et al. provide heuristics for setting the learning rate for gradient descent based on the current iteration, which only require the user to provide a value for a single parameter that determines the closeness of fit to the training data (a so-called regularization parameter). In the vanilla approach, regularization is performed by limiting the number of updates that can be performed.

6.5 INSTANCE-BASED LEARNING

In Section 4.7 we saw how the nearest-neighbor rule can be used to implement a basic form of instance-based learning. There are several practical problems with this simple scheme. First, it tends to be slow for large training sets because the entire set must be searched for each test instance—unless sophisticated data structures such as kD-trees or ball trees are used. Second, it performs badly with noisy data because the class of a test instance is determined by its single nearest neighbor without any "averaging" to help eliminate noise. Third, it performs badly when different attributes affect the outcome to different extents—in the extreme case, when some attributes are completely irrelevant—because all attributes contribute equally to the distance formula. Fourth, it does not perform explicit generalization, although we intimated in Section 3.5 (and illustrated in Figure 3.10) that some instance-based learning systems do indeed perform explicit generalization.

Reducing the Number of Exemplars

The plain nearest-neighbor rule stores a lot of redundant exemplars. Yet it is almost always completely unnecessary to save all the examples seen so far. A simple variant is to classify each example with respect to the examples already seen and to save only ones that are misclassified. We use the term *exemplars* to refer to the already-seen instances that are used for classification. Discarding correctly classified instances reduces the number of exemplars and proves to be an effective way to prune the exemplar database. Ideally, only a single exemplar is stored for each important region of the instance space. However, early in the learning process examples may be discarded that later turn out to be important, possibly leading to some decrease in predictive accuracy. As the number of stored instances increases, the accuracy of the model improves, and so the system makes fewer mistakes.

Unfortunately, the strategy of only storing misclassified instances does not work well in the face of noise. Noisy examples are very likely to be misclassified, and so the set of stored exemplars tends to accumulate those that are least useful. This effect is easily observed experimentally. Thus, this strategy is only a stepping-stone on the way toward more effective instance-based learners.

Pruning Noisy Exemplars

Noisy exemplars inevitably lower the performance of any nearest-neighbor scheme that does not suppress them, because they have the effect of repeatedly misclassifying new instances. There are two ways of dealing with this. One is to locate, instead of the single nearest neighbor, the k-nearest neighbors for some predetermined constant k, and assign the majority class to the unknown instance. The only problem here is determining a suitable value of k. Plain nearest-neighbor learning corresponds to $k = 1$. The more noise, the greater the optimal value of k. One way to proceed is to perform cross-validation tests with several different values and choose the best. Although this is expensive in computation time, it often yields excellent predictive performance.

A second solution is to monitor the performance of each exemplar that is stored and discard ones that do not perform well. This can be done by keeping a record of the number of correct and incorrect classification decisions that each exemplar makes. Two predetermined thresholds are set on the success ratio. When an exemplar's performance drops below the lower one, it is deleted from the exemplar set. If its performance exceeds the upper threshold, it is used for predicting the class of new instances. If its performance lies between the two, it is not used for prediction but, whenever it is the closest exemplar to the new instance (and thus would have been used for prediction if its performance record had been good enough), its success statistics are updated as though it had been used to classify that new instance.

To accomplish this, we use the confidence limits on the success probability of a Bernoulli process that we derived in Section 5.2. Recall that we took a certain number of successes S out of a total number of trials N as evidence on which to base confidence limits on the true underlying success rate p. Given a certain confidence level of, say, 5%, we can calculate upper and lower bounds and be 95% sure that p lies between them.

To apply this to the problem of deciding when to accept a particular exemplar, suppose that it has been used n times to classify other instances and that s of these have been successes. That allows us to estimate bounds, at a particular confidence level, on the true success rate of this exemplar. Now suppose that the exemplar's class has occurred c times out of a total number N of training instances. This allows us to estimate bounds on the default success rate—that is, the probability of successfully classifying an instance of this class without any information about other instances. We insist that the *lower* confidence bound on an exemplar's success rate exceeds the *upper* confidence bound on the default success rate. We use the same method to devise a criterion for rejecting a poorly performing exemplar, requiring that the *upper* confidence bound on its success rate lies below the *lower* confidence bound on the default success rate.

With suitable choices of thresholds, this scheme works well. In a particular implementation, called *IB3* for *Instance-Based Learner version 3*, a confidence level of 5% is used to determine acceptance whereas a level of 12.5% is used for rejection. The lower percentage figure produces a wider confidence interval, which makes for a more stringent criterion because it is harder for the lower bound of one interval to lie above the upper bound of the other. The criterion for acceptance is more stringent than for rejection, making it more difficult for an instance to be accepted. The reason for a less stringent rejection criterion is that there is little to be lost by dropping instances with only moderately poor classification accuracies: They will probably be replaced by similar instances later. Using these thresholds has been found to improve the performance of instance-based learning and, at the same time, dramatically reduce the number of exemplars—particularly noisy exemplars—that are stored.

Weighting Attributes

The Euclidean distance function, modified to scale all attribute values to between 0 and 1, works well in domains in which the attributes are equally relevant to the outcome. Such domains, however, are the exception rather than the rule. In most domains some attributes are irrelevant and some relevant ones are less important than others. The next improvement in instance-based learning is to learn the relevance of each attribute incrementally by dynamically updating feature weights.

In some schemes, the weights are class specific in that an attribute may be more important to one class than to another. To cater for this, a description is produced for each class that distinguishes its members from members of all other classes. This leads to the problem that an unknown test instance may be assigned to several different classes, or no classes at all—a problem that is all too familiar from our description of rule induction. Heuristic solutions are applied to resolve these situations.

The distance metric incorporates the feature weights w_1, w_2, ..., w_m on each dimension:

$$\sqrt{w_1^2(x_1 - y_1)^2 + w_2^2(x_2 - y_2)^2 + \ldots + w_m^2(x_m - y_m)^2}$$

In the case of class-specific feature weights, there will be a separate set of weights for each class.

All attribute weights are updated after each training instance is classified, and the most similar exemplar (or the most similar exemplar of each class) is used as the basis for updating. Call the training instance x and the most similar exemplar y. For each attribute i, the difference $|x_i - y_i|$ is a measure of the contribution of that attribute to the decision. If this difference is small then the attribute contributes positively, whereas if it is large it may contribute negatively. The basic idea is to update the ith weight on the basis of the size of this difference and whether the classification was indeed correct. If the classification is correct the associated weight is increased, and if it is incorrect it is decreased, the amount of increase or decrease being governed by the size of the difference: large if the difference is small and vice versa. The weight change is generally followed by a renormalization step. A simpler strategy, which may be equally effective, is to leave the weights alone if the decision is correct, and if it is incorrect to increase the weights for those attributes that differ most greatly, accentuating the difference. Details of these weight adaptation algorithms are described by Aha (1992).

A good test of whether an attribute weighting scheme works is to add irrelevant attributes to all examples in a dataset. Ideally, the introduction of irrelevant attributes should not affect either the quality of predictions or the number of exemplars stored.

Generalizing Exemplars

Generalized exemplars are rectangular regions of instance space, called *hyperrectangles* because they are high-dimensional. When classifying new instances it is necessary to modify the distance function as described below to allow the distance to a hyperrectangle to be computed. When a new exemplar is classified correctly, it is generalized by simply merging it with the nearest exemplar of the same class. The nearest exemplar may be either a single instance or a hyperrectangle. In the former case, a new hyperrectangle is created that covers the old and the new instance. In the latter, the hyperrectangle is enlarged to encompass the new instance. Finally, if the prediction is incorrect and it was a hyperrectangle that was responsible for the incorrect prediction, the hyperrectangle's boundaries are altered so that it shrinks away from the new instance.

It is necessary to decide at the outset whether overgeneralization caused by nesting or overlapping hyperrectangles is to be permitted or not. If it is to be avoided, a check is made before generalizing a new example to see whether any regions of feature space conflict with the proposed new hyperrectangle. If they do, the generalization is aborted and the example is stored verbatim. Note that overlapping hyperrectangles are precisely analogous to situations in which the same example is covered by two or more rules in a rule set.

In some schemes, generalized exemplars can be nested in that they may be completely contained within one another, in the same way that in some representations rules may have exceptions. To do this, whenever an example is incorrectly classified, a fallback heuristic is tried using the second nearest neighbor if it produces a correct prediction in a further attempt to perform generalization. This second-chance mechanism promotes nesting of hyperrectangles. If an example falls within a rectangle of the wrong class that already contains an exemplar of the same class, the two are generalized into a new "exception" hyperrectangle nested within the original one. For nested generalized exemplars, the learning process frequently begins with a small number of seed instances to prevent all examples of the same class from being generalized into a single rectangle that covers most of the problem space.

Distance Functions for Generalized Exemplars

With generalized exemplars it is necessary to generalize the distance function to compute the distance from an instance to a generalized exemplar, as well as to another instance. The distance from an instance to a hyperrectangle is defined to be zero if the point lies within the hyperrectangle. The simplest way to generalize the distance function to compute the distance from an exterior point to a hyperrectangle is to choose the closest instance within it and to measure the distance to that. However, this reduces the benefit of generalization because it reintroduces dependence on a particular single example. More precisely, whereas new instances that happen to lie within a hyperrectangle continue to benefit from generalizations, ones that lie outside do not. It might be better to use the distance from the nearest part of the hyperrectangle instead.

Figure 6.16 shows the implicit boundaries that are formed between two rectangular classes if the distance metric is adjusted to measure distance to the nearest point of a rectangle. Even in two dimensions the boundary contains a total of nine regions (they are numbered for easy identification); the situation will be more complex for higher-dimensional hyperrectangles.

Proceeding from the lower left, the first region, in which the boundary is linear, lies outside the extent of both rectangles—to the left of both borders of the larger one and below both borders of the smaller one. The second is within the extent of one rectangle—to the right of the leftmost border of the larger rectangle—but outside that of the other—below both borders of the smaller one. In this region the boundary is parabolic because the locus of a point that is the same distance from a given line

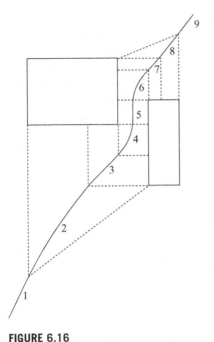

FIGURE 6.16

A boundary between two rectangular classes.

as from a given point is a *parabola*. The third region is where the boundary meets the lower border of the larger rectangle when projected upward and the left border of the smaller one when projected to the right. The boundary is linear in this region because it is equidistant from these two borders. The fourth is where the boundary lies to the right of the larger rectangle but below the bottom of that rectangle. In this case the boundary is parabolic because it is the locus of points equidistant from the lower right corner of the larger rectangle and the left side of the smaller one. The fifth region lies between the two rectangles: Here the boundary is vertical. The pattern is repeated in the upper right part of the diagram: first parabolic, then linear, then parabolic (although this particular parabola is almost indistinguishable from a straight line), and finally linear as the boundary escapes from the scope of both rectangles.

This simple situation certainly defines a complex boundary! Of course, it is not necessary to represent the boundary explicitly; it is generated implicitly by the nearest-neighbor calculation. Nevertheless, the solution is still not a very good one. Whereas taking the distance from the nearest instance within a hyperrectangle is overly dependent on the position of that particular instance, taking the distance to the nearest point of the hyperrectangle is overly dependent on that corner of the rectangle—the nearest example might be far from the corner.

A final problem concerns measuring the distance to hyperrectangles that overlap or are nested. This complicates the situation because an instance may fall within more than one hyperrectangle. A suitable heuristic for use in this case is to choose the class of the most specific hyperrectangle containing the instance—that is, the one covering the smallest area of instance space.

Whether or not overlap or nesting is permitted, the distance function should be modified to take account of both the observed prediction accuracy of exemplars and the relative importance of different features, as described in the sections above on pruning noisy exemplars and attribute weighting.

Generalized Distance Functions

There are many different ways of defining a distance function, and it is hard to find rational grounds for any particular choice. An elegant solution is to consider one instance being transformed into another through a sequence of predefined elementary operations and to calculate the probability of such a sequence occurring if operations are chosen randomly. Robustness is improved if all possible transformation paths are considered, weighted by their probabilities, and the scheme generalizes naturally to the problem of calculating the distance between an instance and a set of other instances by considering transformations to all instances in the set. Through such a technique it is possible to consider each instance as exerting a "sphere of influence," but a sphere with soft boundaries rather than the hard-edged cutoff implied by the k-nearest-neighbor rule, in which any particular example is either "in" or "out" of the decision.

With such a measure, given a test instance that has a class that is unknown, its distance to the set of all training instances in each class in turn is calculated and the closest class is chosen. It turns out that nominal and numeric attributes can be treated in a uniform manner within this transformation-based approach by defining different transformation sets, and it is even possible to take account of unusual attribute types—such as degrees of arc or days of the week, which are measured on a circular scale.

Discussion

Nearest-neighbor methods gained popularity in machine learning through the work of Aha (1992), who showed that, when combined with noisy exemplar pruning and attribute weighting, instance-based learning performs well in comparison with other methods. It is worth noting that although we have described it solely in the context of classification rather than numeric prediction problems, it applies to these equally well: Predictions can be obtained by combining the predicted values of the k-nearest neighbors and weighting them by distance.

Viewed in instance space, the standard rule- and tree-based representations are only capable of representing class boundaries that are parallel to the axes defined by the attributes. This is not a handicap for nominal attributes, but it is for numeric ones. Non-axis-parallel class boundaries can only be approximated by covering the region above or below the boundary with several axis-parallel rectangles, the number of rectangles determining the degree of approximation. In contrast, the instance-based method can easily represent arbitrary linear boundaries. Even with just one example of each of two classes, the boundary implied by the nearest-neighbor rule is a straight line of arbitrary orientation, namely the perpendicular bisector of the line joining the examples.

Plain instance-based learning does not produce explicit knowledge representations except by selecting representative exemplars. However, when combined with exemplar generalization, a set of rules can be obtained that may be compared with those produced by other machine learning schemes. The rules tend to be more conservative because the distance metric, modified to incorporate generalized exemplars, can be used to process examples that do not fall within the rules. This reduces the pressure to produce rules that cover the whole example space or even all of the training examples. On the other hand, the incremental nature of most instance-based learning schemes means that rules are formed eagerly, after only part of the training set has been seen; this inevitably reduces their quality.

We have not given precise algorithms for variants of instance-based learning that involve generalization, because it is not clear what the best way to do generalization is. Salzberg (1991) suggested that generalization with nested exemplars can achieve a high degree of classification of accuracy on a variety of different problems, a conclusion disputed by Wettschereck and Dietterich (1995), who argued that these results were fortuitous and did not hold in other domains. Martin (1995) explored the idea that it is not generalization but the overgeneralization that occurs when hyperrectangles nest or overlap that is responsible for poor performance, and demonstrated that if nesting and overlapping are avoided, excellent results are achieved in a large number of domains. The generalized distance function based on transformations is described by Cleary and Trigg (1995).

Exemplar generalization is a rare example of a learning strategy in which the search proceeds from specific to general rather than from general to specific as in the case of tree or rule induction. There is no particular reason why specific-to-general searching should necessarily be handicapped by forcing the examples to be considered in a strictly incremental fashion, and batch-oriented methods exist that generate rules using a basic instance-based approach. Moreover, it seems that the idea of producing conservative generalizations and coping with instances that are not covered by choosing the "closest" generalization may be generally useful for tree and rule inducers.

6.6 NUMERIC PREDICTION WITH LOCAL LINEAR MODELS

Trees that are used for numeric prediction are just like ordinary decision trees, except that at each leaf they store either a class value that represents the average value of instances that reach the leaf, in which case the tree is called a *regression tree*, or a linear regression model that predicts the class value of instances that reach the leaf, in which case it is called a *model tree*. In what follows we will talk about model trees because regression trees are really a special case.

Regression and model trees are constructed by first using a decision tree induction algorithm to build an initial tree. However, whereas most decision tree algorithms choose the splitting attribute to maximize the information gain, it is appropriate for numeric prediction to instead minimize the intrasubset variation in the class values down each branch. Once the basic tree has been formed, consideration is given to pruning the tree back from each leaf, just as with ordinary decision trees. The only difference between regression tree and model tree induction is that, for the latter, each node is replaced by a regression plane instead of a constant value. The attributes that serve to define that plane are generally those that participate in decisions in the subtree that will be pruned—that is, in nodes beneath the current one and perhaps those that occur on the path to the root node.

Following an extensive description of model trees, we briefly explain how to generate rules from model trees, and then describe another approach to numeric prediction based on generating local linear models: locally weighted linear regression. Whereas model trees derive from the basic divide-and-conquer decision tree methodology, locally weighted regression is inspired by the instance-based methods for classification that we described in the previous section. Like instance-based learning, it performs all "learning" at prediction time. Although locally weighted regression resembles model trees in that it uses linear regression to fit models locally to particular areas of instance space, it does so in quite a different way.

Model Trees

When a model tree is used to predict the value for a test instance, the tree is followed down to a leaf in the normal way, using the instance's attribute values to make routing decisions at each node. The leaf will contain a linear model based on some of the attribute values, and this is evaluated for the test instance to yield a raw predicted value.

Instead of using this raw value directly, however, it turns out to be beneficial to use a smoothing process to reduce the sharp discontinuities that will inevitably occur between adjacent linear models at the leaves of the pruned tree. This is a particular problem for models constructed from a small number of training instances. Smoothing can be accomplished by producing linear models for each internal node, as well as for the leaves, at the time the tree is built. Then, once the leaf model has been used to obtain the raw predicted value for a test instance, that value is filtered along the path back to the root, smoothing it at each node by combining it with the value predicted by the linear model for that node.

An appropriate smoothing calculation is

$$p' = \frac{np + kq}{n + k}$$

where p' is the prediction passed up to the next higher node, p is the prediction passed to this node from below, q is the value predicted by the model at this node, n is the number of training instances that reach the node below, and k is a smoothing constant. Experiments show that smoothing substantially increases the accuracy of predictions.

However, discontinuities remain and the resulting function is not smooth. In fact, exactly the same smoothing process can be accomplished by incorporating the interior models into each leaf model after the tree has been built. Then, during the classification process, only the leaf models are used. The disadvantage is that the leaf models tend to be larger and more difficult to comprehend because many coefficients that were previously zero become nonzero when the interior nodes' models are incorporated.

Building the Tree

The splitting criterion is used to determine which attribute is the best to split that portion T of the training data that reaches a particular node. It is based on treating the standard deviation of the class values in T as a measure of the error at that node, and calculating the expected reduction in error as a result of testing each attribute at that node. The attribute that maximizes the expected error reduction is chosen for splitting at the node.

The expected error reduction, which we call SDR for *standard deviation reduction*, is calculated by

$$\text{SDR} = sd(T) - \sum_i \frac{|T_i|}{|T|} \times sd(T_i)$$

where T_1, T_2, ... are the sets that result from splitting the node according to the chosen attribute, and $sd(T)$ is the standard deviation of the class values.

The splitting process terminates when the class values of the instances that reach a node vary just slightly—that is, when their standard deviation is only a small fraction (say less than 5%) of the standard deviation of the original instance set. Splitting also terminates when just a few instances remain (say four or fewer). Experiments show that the results obtained are not very sensitive to the exact choice of these parameters.

Pruning the Tree

As noted earlier, a linear model is needed for each interior node of the tree, not just at the leaves, for use in the smoothing process. Before pruning, a model is calculated for each node of the unpruned tree. The model takes the form

$$w_0 + w_1 a_1 + w_2 a_2 + \ldots + w_k a_k$$

where a_1, a_2, ..., a_k are attribute values. The weights w_1, w_2, ..., w_k are calculated using standard regression. However, only a subset of the attributes are generally used here—for example, those that are tested in the subtree below this node and perhaps those occurring along the path to the root node. Note that we have tacitly assumed that attributes are numeric; we describe the handling of nominal attributes in the next section.

The pruning procedure makes use of an estimate, at each node, of the expected error for test data. First, the absolute difference between the predicted value and the actual class value is averaged over each of the training instances that reach that node. Because the tree has been built expressly for this dataset, this average will underestimate the expected error for unseen cases. To compensate, it is multiplied by the factor $(n + v)/(n - v)$, where n is the number of training instances that reach the node and v is the number of parameters in the linear model that gives the class value at that node.

The expected error for test data at a node is calculated as described previously, using the linear model for prediction. Because of the compensation factor $(n + v)/(n - v)$, it may be that the linear model can be further simplified by dropping terms to minimize the estimated error. Dropping a term decreases the multiplication factor, which may be enough to offset the inevitable increase in average error over the training instances. Terms are dropped one by one, greedily, as long as the error estimate decreases.

Finally, once a linear model is in place for each interior node, the tree is pruned back from the leaves as long as the expected estimated error decreases. The expected error for the linear model at that node is compared with the expected error from the subtree below. To calculate the latter, the error from each branch is combined into a single, overall value for the node by weighting the branch by the proportion of the training instances that go down it and combining the error estimates linearly using those weights. Alternatively, one can calculate the training error of the subtree and multiply it by the above modification factor based on an ad hoc estimate of the number of parameters in the tree—perhaps adding one for each split point.

Nominal Attributes

Before constructing a model tree, all nominal attributes are transformed into binary variables that are then treated as numeric. For each nominal attribute, the average class value corresponding to each possible value in the set is calculated from the training instances, and the values are sorted according to these averages. Then, if the nominal attribute has k possible values, it is replaced by $k - 1$ synthetic binary attributes, the ith being 0 if the value is one of the first i in the ordering and 1 otherwise. Thus, all splits are binary: They involve either a numeric attribute or a synthetic binary attribute that is treated as numeric.

It is possible to prove analytically that the best split at a node for a nominal variable with k values is one of the $k - 1$ positions obtained by ordering the average class values for each value of the attribute. This sorting operation should really be repeated at each node; however, there is an inevitable increase in noise due to small numbers of instances at lower nodes in the tree (and in some cases nodes may not represent all values for some attributes), and not much is lost by performing the sorting just once before starting to build a model tree.

Missing Values

To take account of missing values, a modification is made to the SDR formula. The final formula, including the missing value compensation, is

$$\text{SDR} = \frac{m}{|T|} \times \left[sd(T) - \sum_{j \in \{L,R\}} \frac{|T_j|}{|T|} \times sd(T_j) \right]$$

where m is the number of instances without missing values for that attribute, and T is the set of instances that reach this node. T_L, T_R are sets that result from splitting on this attribute because all tests on attributes are now binary.

When processing both training and test instances, once an attribute is selected for splitting it is necessary to divide the instances into subsets according to their value for this attribute. An obvious problem arises when the value is missing. An interesting technique called *surrogate splitting* has been developed to handle this situation. It involves finding another attribute to split on in place of the original one and using it instead. The attribute is chosen as the one most highly correlated with the original attribute. However, this technique is both complex to implement and time consuming to execute.

A simpler heuristic is to use the class value as the surrogate attribute, in the belief that, a priori, this is the attribute most likely to be correlated with the one being used for splitting. Of course, this is only possible when processing the training set because for test examples the class is not known. A simple solution for test examples is simply to replace the unknown attribute value by the average value of that attribute for the training examples that reach the node, which has the effect, for a binary attribute, of choosing the most populous subnode. This simple approach seems to work well in practice.

Let's consider in more detail how to use the class value as a surrogate attribute during the training process. We first deal with all instances for which the value of the splitting attribute is known. We determine a threshold for splitting in the usual way, by sorting the instances according to the splitting attribute's value and, for each possible split point, calculating the SDR according to the preceding formula, choosing the split point that yields the greatest reduction in error. Only the instances for which the value of the splitting attribute is known are used to determine the split point.

Next we divide these instances into the two sets L and R according to the test. We determine whether the instances in L or R have the greater average class value, and we calculate the average of these two averages. Then an instance for which this attribute value is unknown is placed into L or R according to whether its class value exceeds this overall average or not. If it does, it goes into whichever of L and R has the greater average class value; otherwise, it goes into the one with the smaller average class value. When the splitting stops, all the missing values will be replaced by the average values of the corresponding attributes of the training instances reaching the leaves.

Pseudocode for Model Tree Induction

Figure 6.17 gives pseudocode for the model tree algorithm we have described. The two main parts are creating a tree by successively splitting nodes, performed by *split*, and pruning it from the leaves upward, performed by *prune*. The *node* data structure contains a type flag indicating whether it is an internal node or a leaf, pointers to the left and right child, the set of instances that reach that node, the attribute that is used for splitting at that node, and a structure representing the linear model for the node.

The sd function called at the beginning of the main program and again at the beginning of *split* calculates the standard deviation of the class values of a set of instances. This is followed by the procedure for obtaining synthetic binary attributes that was described previously. Standard procedures for creating new nodes and printing the final tree are not shown. In *split*, sizeof returns the number of elements in a

```
MakeModelTree (instances)
{
  SD = sd(instances)
  for each k-valued nominal attribute
    convert into k-1 synthetic binary attributes
  root = newNode
  root.instances = instances
  split(root)
  prune(root)
  printTree(root)
}
split(node)
{
  if sizeof(node.instances) < 4 or sd(node.instances) < 0.05*SD
    node.type = LEAF
  else
    node.type = INTERIOR
    for each attribute
      for all possible split positions of the attribute
        calculate the attribute's SDR
    node.attribute = attribute with maximum SDR
    split(node.left)
    split(node.right)
}
prune(node)
{
  if node = INTERIOR then
    prune(node.leftChild)
    prune(node.rightChild)
    node.model = linearRegression(node)
    if subtreeError(node) > error(node) then
      node.type = LEAF
}
subtreeError(node)
{
  l = node.left; r = node.right
  if node = INTERIOR then
    return (sizeof(l.instances)*subtreeError(l)
         + sizeof(r.instances)*subtreeError(r))/sizeof(node.
         instances)
  else return error(node)
}
```

FIGURE 6.17

Pseudocode for model tree induction.

set. Missing attribute values are dealt with as described earlier. The SDR is calculated according to the equation at the beginning of the previous section. Although not shown in the code, it is set to infinity if splitting on the attribute would create a leaf with less than two instances. In *prune*, the `linearRegression` routine recursively descends the subtree collecting attributes, performs a linear regression on the instances at that node as a function of those attributes, and then greedily drops terms if doing so improves the error estimate, as described earlier. Finally, the *error* function returns

$$\frac{n+v}{n-v} \times \sum_{instances} \frac{|\text{deviation from predicted class value}|}{n}$$

where n is the number of instances at the node and v is the number of parameters in the node's linear model.

Figure 6.18 gives an example of a model tree formed by this algorithm for a problem with two numeric and two nominal attributes. What is to be predicted is the rise time of a simulated servo system involving a servo amplifier, motor, lead screw, and sliding carriage. The nominal attributes play important roles. Four synthetic binary attributes have been created for each of the five-valued nominal attributes *motor* and *screw* and are shown in Table 6.2 in terms of the two sets of values to which they correspond. The ordering of these values—D, E, C, B, A for *motor* and coincidentally D, E, C, B, A for *screw* also—is determined from the training data: the rise time averaged over all examples for which *motor* = D is less than that averaged over examples for which *motor* = E, which is less than when *motor* = C, and so on. It is apparent from the magnitude of the coefficients in Table 6.2 that *motor* = D versus E, C, B, A and *screw* = D, E, C, B versus A play leading roles in the LM2, LM3, and LM4 models (among others). Both *motor* and *screw* also play a minor role in several of the models.

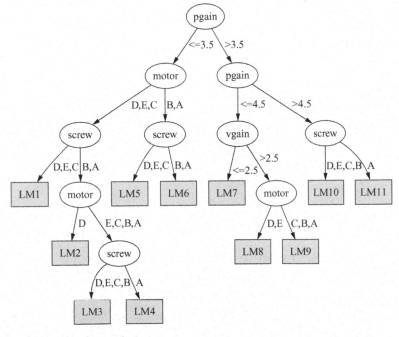

FIGURE 6.18

Model tree for a dataset with nominal attributes.

Table 6.2 Linear Models in the Model Tree

Model	LM1	LM2	LM3	LM4	LM5	LM6	LM7	LM8	LM9	LM10	LM 11
constant term	0.96	1.14	1.43	1.52	2.69	2.91	0.88	0.98	1.11	1.06	0.97
pgain	−0.38	−0.38	−0.38	−0.38	−0.38	−0.38	−0.24	−0.24	−0.24	−0.25	−0.25
vgain	0.71	0.49	0.49	0.49	0.56	0.45	0.13	0.15	0.15	0.10	0.14
motor = D vs. E, C, B, A	0.66	1.14	1.06	1.06	0.50	0.50	0.30	0.40	0.30	0.14	0.14
motor = D, E vs. C, B, A	0.97	0.61	0.65	0.59	0.42	0.42	−0.02	0.06	0.06	0.17	0.22
motor = D, E, C vs. B, A	0.32	0.32	0.32	0.32	0.41	0.41	0.05				
motor = D, E, C, B vs. A					0.08	0.05					
screw = D vs. E, C, B, A	0.13										
screw = D, E vs. C, B, A	0.49	0.54	0.54	0.54	0.39	0.40	0.30	0.20	0.16	0.08	0.08
screw = D, E, C vs. B, A		1.73	1.79	1.79	0.96	1.13	0.22	0.15	0.15	0.16	0.19

Rules from Model Trees

Model trees are essentially decision trees with linear models at the leaves. Like decision trees, they may suffer from the replicated subtree problem explained in Section 3.4, and sometimes the structure can be expressed much more concisely using a set of rules instead of a tree. Can we generate *rules* for numeric prediction? Recall the rule learner described in Section 6.2 that uses separate-and-conquer in conjunction with partial decision trees to extract decision rules from trees. The same strategy can be applied to model trees to generate decision lists for numeric prediction.

First build a partial model tree from all the data. Pick one of the leaves and make it into a rule. Remove the data covered by that leaf, then repeat the process with the remaining data. The question is, how do we build the partial model tree—that is, a tree with unexpanded nodes? This boils down to the question of how to pick which node to expand next. The algorithm of Figure 6.5 (Section 6.2) picks the node of which the entropy for the class attribute is smallest. For model trees, the predictions of which are numeric, simply use the standard deviation instead. This is based on the same rationale: The lower the standard deviation, the shallower the subtree and the shorter the rule. The rest of the algorithm stays the same, with the model tree learner's split selection method and pruning strategy replacing the decision tree learner's. Because the model tree's leaves are linear models, the corresponding rules will have linear models on the right side.

There is one caveat when using model trees in this fashion to generate rule sets. It turns out that using smoothed model trees does not reduce the error in the final rule set's predictions. This may be because smoothing works best for contiguous data, but the separate-and-conquer scheme removes data covered by previous rules, leaving holes in the distribution. Smoothing, if it is done at all, must be performed after the rule set has been generated.

Locally Weighted Linear Regression

An alternative approach to numeric prediction is the method of locally weighted linear regression. With model trees, the tree structure divides the instance space into regions, and a linear model is found for each of them. In effect, the training data determines how the instance space is partitioned. Locally weighted regression, on the other hand, generates local models at prediction time by giving higher weight to instances in the neighborhood of the particular test instance. More specifically, it weights the training instances according to their distance to the test instance and performs a linear regression on the weighted data. Training instances close to the test instance receive a high weight; those far away, a low one. In other words, a linear model is tailor-made for the particular test instance at hand and used to predict the instance's class value.

To use locally weighted regression, you need to decide on a distance-based weighting scheme for the training instances. A common choice is to weight the instances according to the inverse of their Euclidean distance from the test instance. Another possibility is to use the Euclidean distance in conjunction with a Gaussian kernel function. However, there is no clear evidence that the choice of weighting function is critical. More important is the selection of a "smoothing parameter" that is used to scale the distance function—the distance is multiplied by the inverse of this parameter. If it is set to a small value, only instances very close to the test instance will receive significant weight; if it is large, more distant instances will also have a significant impact on the model.

One way of choosing the smoothing parameter is to set it to the distance of the kth-nearest training instance so that its value becomes smaller as the volume of training data increases. If the weighting function is linear, say $1 - distance$, the weight is 0 for all instances further than the kth-nearest one. Then the weighting function has bounded support and only the $(k-1)$th-nearest neighbors need to be considered for building the linear model. The best choice of k depends on the amount of noise in the data. The more noise there is, the more neighbors should be included in the linear model. Generally, an appropriate smoothing parameter is found using cross-validation.

Like model trees, locally weighted linear regression is able to approximate non-linear functions. One of its main advantages is that it is ideally suited for incremental learning: All training is done at prediction time, so new instances can be added to the training data at any time. However, like other instance-based methods, it is slow at deriving a prediction for a test instance. First, the training instances must be scanned to compute their weights; then a weighted linear regression is performed on these instances. Also, like other instance-based methods, locally weighted regression provides little information about the global structure of the training dataset. Note that if the smoothing parameter is based on the kth-nearest neighbor and the weighting function gives zero weight to more distant instances, the kD-trees (page 132) and ball trees described in Section 4.7 can be used to accelerate the process of finding the relevant neighbors.

Locally weighted learning is not restricted to linear regression: It can be applied with any learning technique that can handle weighted instances. In particular, you can use it for classification. Most algorithms can be easily adapted to deal with weights. The trick is to realize that (integer) weights can be simulated by creating several copies of the same instance. Whenever the learning algorithm uses an instance when computing a model, just pretend that it is accompanied by the appropriate number of identical shadow instances. This also works if the weight is not an integer. For example, in the Naïve Bayes algorithm described in Section 4.2, multiply the counts derived from an instance by the instance's weight, and—Voilà!—you have a version of Naïve Bayes that can be used for locally weighted learning.

It turns out that locally weighted Naïve Bayes works quite well in practice, outperforming both Naïve Bayes itself and the k-nearest-neighbor technique. It also compares favorably with more sophisticated ways of enhancing Naïve Bayes by relaxing its intrinsic independence assumption. Locally weighted learning only assumes independence within a neighborhood, not globally in the whole instance space as standard Naïve Bayes does.

In principle, locally weighted learning can also be applied to decision trees and other models that are more complex than linear regression and Naïve Bayes. However, it is less beneficial here because it is primarily a way of allowing simple models to become more flexible by allowing them to approximate arbitrary targets. If the underlying learning algorithm can already do that, there is little point in applying locally weighted learning. Nevertheless, it may improve other simple models—for example, linear support vector machines and logistic regression.

Discussion

Regression trees were introduced in the CART system of Breiman et al. (1984). CART, for *classification and regression trees*, incorporated a decision tree inducer for discrete classes like that of C4.5, as well as a scheme for inducing regression trees. Many of the techniques described in this section, such as the method of handling nominal attributes and the surrogate device for dealing with missing values, were included in CART. However, model trees did not appear until much more recently, being first described by Quinlan (1992). Using model trees for generating rule sets (although not partial trees) has been explored by Hall et al. (1999).

A comprehensive description (and implementation) of model tree induction is given by Wang and Witten (1997). Neural nets are also commonly used for predicting numeric quantities, although they suffer from the disadvantage that the structures they produce are opaque and cannot be used to help understand the nature of the solution. There are techniques for producing understandable insights from the structure of neural networks, but the arbitrary nature of the internal representation means that there may be dramatic variations between networks of identical architecture trained on the same data. By dividing the function being induced into linear patches, model trees provide a representation that is reproducible and at least somewhat comprehensible.

There are many variations of locally weighted learning. For example, statisticians have considered using locally quadratic models instead of linear ones and have applied locally weighted logistic regression to classification problems. Also, many different potential weighting and distance functions can be found in the literature. Atkeson et al. (1997) have written an excellent survey on locally weighted learning, primarily in the context of regression problems. Frank et al. (2003) evaluated the use of locally weighted learning in conjunction with Naïve Bayes.

6.7 BAYESIAN NETWORKS

The Naïve Bayes classifier of Section 4.2 and the logistic regression models of Section 4.6 both produce probability estimates rather than hard classifications. For each class value, they estimate the probability that a given instance belongs to that class. Most other types of classifiers can be coerced into yielding this kind of information if necessary. For example, probabilities can be obtained from a decision tree by computing the relative frequency of each class in a leaf and from a decision list by examining the instances that a particular rule covers.

Probability estimates are often more useful than plain predictions. They allow predictions to be ranked and their expected cost to be minimized (see Section 5.7). In fact, there is a strong argument for treating classification learning as the task of learning class probability estimates from data. What is being estimated is the conditional probability distribution of the values of the class attribute given the values of the other attributes. Ideally, the classification model represents this conditional distribution in a concise and easily comprehensible form.

Viewed in this way, Naïve Bayes classifiers, logistic regression models, decision trees, and so on, are just alternative ways of representing a conditional probability distribution. Of course, they differ in representational power. Naïve Bayes classifiers and logistic regression models can only represent simple distributions, whereas decision trees can represent—or at least approximate—arbitrary distributions. However, decision trees have their drawbacks: They fragment the training set into smaller and smaller pieces, which inevitably yields less reliable probability estimates, and they suffer from the replicated subtree problem described in Section 3.4. Rule sets go some way toward addressing these shortcomings, but the design of a good rule learner is guided by heuristics with scant theoretical justification.

Does this mean that we have to accept our fate and live with these shortcomings? No! There is a statistically based alternative: a theoretically well-founded way of representing probability distributions concisely and comprehensibly in a graphical manner; the structures are called *Bayesian networks*. They are drawn as a network of nodes, one for each attribute, connected by directed edges in such a way that there are no cycles—a *directed acyclic graph*.

In our explanation of how to interpret Bayesian networks and how to learn them from data, we will make some simplifying assumptions. We assume that all attributes are nominal and that there are no missing values. Some advanced learning algorithms can create new attributes in addition to the ones present in the data—so-called hidden attributes with values that cannot be observed. These can support better models if they represent salient features of the underlying problem, and Bayesian networks provide a good way of using them at prediction time. However, they make both learning and prediction far more complex and time consuming, so we will not consider them here.

Making Predictions

Figure 6.19 shows a simple Bayesian network for the weather data. It has a node for each of the four attributes *outlook*, *temperature*, *humidity*, and *windy* and one for the class attribute *play*. An edge leads from the *play* node to each of the other nodes. However, in Bayesian networks the structure of the graph is only half the story. Figure 6.19 shows a table inside each node. The information in the tables defines a probability distribution that is used to predict the class probabilities for any given instance.

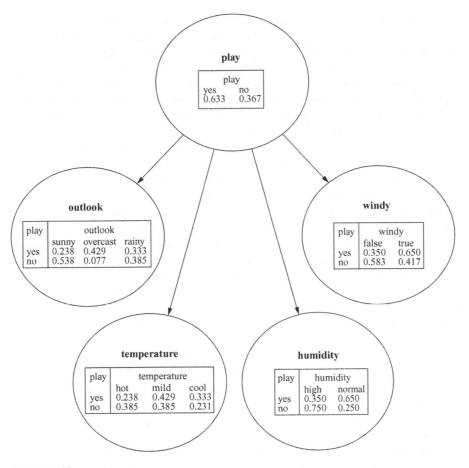

FIGURE 6.19

A simple Bayesian network for the weather data.

Before looking at how to compute this probability distribution, consider the information in the tables. The lower four tables (for *outlook*, *temperature*, *humidity*, and *windy*) have two parts separated by a vertical line. On the left are the values of *play*, and on the right are the corresponding probabilities for each value of the attribute represented by the node. In general, the left side contains a column for every edge pointing to the node, in this case just the *play* attribute. That is why the table associated with *play* itself does not have a left side: It has no parents. Each row of probabilities corresponds to one combination of values of the parent attributes, and the entries in the row show the probability of each value of the node's attribute given this combination. In effect, each row defines a probability distribution over the values of the node's attribute. The entries in a row always sum to 1.

Figure 6.20 shows a more complex network for the same problem, where three nodes (*windy*, *temperature*, and *humidity*) have two parents. Again, there is one column on the left for each parent and as many columns on the right as the attribute has values. Consider the first row of the table associated with the *temperature* node. The left side gives a value for each parent attribute, *play* and *outlook*; the right gives a probability for each value of *temperature*. For example, the first number (0.143) is the probability of *temperature* taking on the value *hot*, given that *play* and *outlook* have values *yes* and *sunny*, respectively.

How are the tables used to predict the probability of each class value for a given instance? This turns out to be very easy because we are assuming that there are no missing values. The instance specifies a value for each attribute. For each node in the network, look up the probability of the node's attribute value based on the row determined by its parents' attribute values. Then just multiply all these probabilities together.

For example, consider an instance with values *outlook = rainy*, *temperature = cool*, *humidity = high*, and *windy = true*. To calculate the probability for *play = no*, observe that the network in Figure 6.20 gives probability 0.367 from node *play*, 0.385 from *outlook*, 0.429 from *temperature*, 0.250 from *humidity*, and 0.167 from *windy*. The product is 0.0025. The same calculation for *play = yes* yields 0.0077. However, these are clearly not the final answers: The final probabilities must sum to 1, whereas 0.0025 and 0.0077 don't. They are actually the joint probabilities $\Pr[play = no, E]$ and $\Pr[play = yes, E]$, where E denotes all the evidence given by the instance's attribute values. Joint probabilities measure the likelihood of observing an instance that exhibits the attribute values in E as well as the respective class value. They only sum to 1 if they exhaust the space of all possible attribute–value combinations, including the class attribute. This is certainly not the case in our example.

The solution is quite simple (we already encountered it in Section 4.2). To obtain the conditional probabilities $\Pr[play = no \mid E]$ and $\Pr[play = yes \mid E]$, normalize the joint probabilities by dividing them by their sum. This gives probability 0.245 for *play = no* and 0.755 for *play = yes*.

Just one mystery remains: Why multiply all those probabilities together? It turns out that the validity of the multiplication step hinges on a single assumption—namely that, given values for each of a node's parents, knowing the values for any other set of nondescendants does not change the probability associated with each of the node's possible values. In other words, other sets of nondescendants do not provide any information about the likelihood of the node's values over and above the information provided by the parents. This can be written as

$$\Pr[\text{node} \mid \text{parents plus any other nondescendants}] = \Pr[\text{node} \mid \text{parents}]$$

which must hold for all values of the nodes and attributes involved. In statistics this property is called *conditional independence*. Multiplication is valid provided that each node is conditionally independent of its grandparents, great-grandparents, and

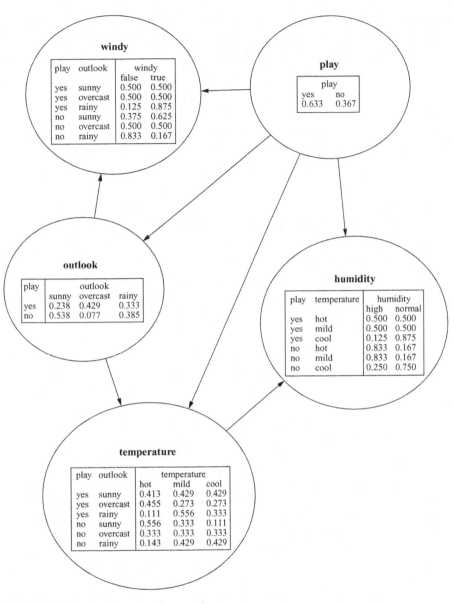

FIGURE 6.20

Another Bayesian network for the weather data.

indeed any other set of nondescendants, given its parents. The multiplication step follows as a direct result of the chain rule in probability theory, which states that the joint probability of m attributes a_i can be decomposed into this product:

$$\Pr[a_1, a_2, \ldots, a_n] = \prod_{i=1}^{m} \Pr[a_i | a_{i-1}, \ldots, a_1]$$

The decomposition holds for any order of the attributes. Because our Bayesian network is an acyclic graph, its nodes can be ordered to give all ancestors of a node a_i indices smaller than i. Then, because of the conditional independence assumption,

$$\Pr[a_1, a_2, \ldots, a_m] = \prod_{i=1}^{m} \Pr[a_i | a_{i-1}, \ldots, a_1] = \prod_{i=1}^{m} \Pr[a_i | a_i\text{'s parents}]$$

which is exactly the multiplication rule that we applied earlier.

The two Bayesian networks in Figures 6.19 and 6.20 are fundamentally different. The first (Figure 6.19) makes stronger independence assumptions because for each of its nodes the set of parents is a subset of the corresponding set of parents in the second (Figure 6.20). In fact, Figure 6.19 is almost identical to the simple Naïve Bayes classifier of Section 4.2. (The probabilities are slightly different but only because each count has been initialized to 0.5 to avoid the zero-frequency problem.) The network in Figure 6.20 has more rows in the conditional probability tables and hence more parameters; it may be a more accurate representation of the underlying domain.

It is tempting to assume that the directed edges in a Bayesian network represent causal effects. But be careful! In our case, a particular value of *play* may enhance the prospects of a particular value of *outlook*, but it certainly doesn't cause it—it is more likely to be the other way around. Different Bayesian networks can be constructed for the same problem, representing exactly the same probability distribution. This is done by altering the way in which the joint probability distribution is factorized to exploit conditional independencies. The network that has directed edges model causal effects is often the simplest one with the fewest parameters. Thus, human experts who construct Bayesian networks for a particular domain often benefit by representing causal effects by directed edges. However, when machine learning techniques are applied to induce models from data whose causal structure is unknown, all they can do is construct a network based on the correlations that are observed in the data. Inferring causality from correlation is always a dangerous business.

Learning Bayesian Networks

The main way to construct a learning algorithm for Bayesian networks is to define two components: a function for evaluating a given network based on the data and a method for searching through the space of possible networks. The quality of a given network is measured by the probability of the data given the network. We calculate the probability that the network accords to each instance and multiply these probabilities together over all instances. In practice, this quickly yields numbers too small to be represented properly (called *arithmetic underflow*), so we use the sum of the logarithms of the probabilities rather than their product. The resulting quantity is the log-likelihood of the network given the data.

Assume that the structure of the network—the set of edges—is given. It's easy to estimate the numbers in the conditional probability tables: Just compute the relative frequencies of the associated combinations of attribute values in the training data. To avoid the zero-frequency problem each count is initialized with a constant as described in Section 4.2. For example, to find the probability that *humidity = normal* given that *play = yes* and *temperature = cool* (the last number of the third row of the *humidity* node's table in Figure 6.20), observe from Table 1.2 (page 10) that there are three instances with this combination of attribute values in the weather data and no instances with *humidity = high* and the same values for *play* and *temperature*. Initializing the counts for the two values of *humidity* to 0.5 yields the probability $(3 + 0.5)/(3 + 0 + 1) = 0.875$ for *humidity = normal*.

The nodes in the network are predetermined, one for each attribute (including the class). Learning the network structure amounts to searching through the space of possible sets of edges, estimating the conditional probability tables for each set, and computing the log-likelihood of the resulting network based on the data as a measure of the network's quality. Bayesian network learning algorithms differ mainly in the way in which they search through the space of network structures. Some algorithms are introduced below.

There is one caveat. If the log-likelihood is maximized based on the training data, it will always be better to add more edges: The resulting network will simply overfit. Various methods can be employed to combat this problem. One possibility is to use cross-validation to estimate the goodness of fit. A second is to add a penalty for the complexity of the network based on the number of parameters—that is, the total number of independent estimates in all the probability tables. For each table, the number of independent probabilities is the total number of entries minus the number of entries in the last column, which can be determined from the other columns because all rows must sum to 1. Let K be the number of parameters, LL the log-likelihood, and N the number of instances in the data. Two popular measures for evaluating the quality of a network are the *Akaike Information Criterion* (AIC):

$$\text{AIC score} = -LL + K$$

and the following *MDL metric* based on the MDL principle:

$$\text{MDL score} = -LL + \frac{K}{2}\log N$$

In both cases the log-likelihood is negated, so the aim is to minimize these scores.

A third possibility is to assign a prior distribution over network structures and find the most likely network by combining its prior probability with the probability accorded to the network by the data. This is the "Bayesian" approach to network scoring. Depending on the prior distribution used, it can take various forms. However, true Bayesians would average over all possible network structures rather than singling out one particular network for prediction. Unfortunately, this generally requires a great deal of computation. A simplified approach is to average over all network structures that are substructures of a given network. It turns out that this can be implemented very efficiently by changing the method for calculating the conditional probability tables so that the resulting probability estimates implicitly contain information from all subnetworks. The details of this approach are rather complex and will not be described here.

The task of searching for a good network structure can be greatly simplified if the right metric is used for scoring. Recall that the probability of a single instance based on a network is the product of all the individual probabilities from the various conditional probability tables. The overall probability of the dataset is the product of these products for all instances. Because terms in a product are interchangable, the product can be rewritten to group together all factors relating to the same table. The same holds for the log-likelihood, using sums instead of products. This means that the likelihood can be optimized separately for each node of the network. This can be done by adding, or removing, edges from other nodes to the node that is being optimized—the only constraint is that cycles must not be introduced. The same trick also works if a local scoring metric such as AIC or MDL is used instead of plain log-likelihood, because the penalty term splits into several components, one for each node, and each node can be optimized independently.

Specific Algorithms

Now we move on to actual algorithms for learning Bayesian networks. One simple and very fast learning algorithm, called *K2*, starts with a given ordering of the attributes (i.e., nodes). Then it processes each node in turn and greedily considers adding edges from previously processed nodes to the current one. In each step it adds the edge that maximizes the network's score. When there is no further improvement, attention turns to the next node. As an additional mechanism for overfitting avoidance, the number of parents for each node can be restricted to a predefined maximum. Because only edges from previously processed nodes are considered and there is a fixed ordering, this procedure cannot introduce cycles. However, the result depends on the initial ordering, so it makes sense to run the algorithm several times with different random orderings.

The Naïve Bayes classifier is a network with an edge leading from the class attribute to each of the other attributes. When building networks for classification, it sometimes helps to use this network as a starting point for the search. This can be done in K2 by forcing the class variable to be the first one in the ordering and initializing the set of edges appropriately.

Another potentially helpful trick is to ensure that every attribute in the data is in the *Markov blanket* of the node that represents the class attribute. A node's Markov blanket includes all its parents, children, and children's parents. It can be shown that a node is conditionally independent of all other nodes given values for the nodes in its Markov blanket. Thus, if a node is absent from the class attribute's Markov blanket, its value is completely irrelevant to the classification. Conversely, if K2 finds a network that does not include a relevant attribute in the class node's Markov blanket, it might help to add an edge that rectifies this shortcoming. A simple way of doing this is to add an edge from the attribute's node to the class node or from the class node to the attribute's node, depending on which option avoids a cycle.

A more sophisticated but slower version of K2 is not to order the nodes but to greedily consider adding or deleting edges between arbitrary pairs of nodes (all the while ensuring acyclicity, of course). A further step is to consider inverting the direction of existing edges as well. As with any greedy algorithm, the resulting network only represents a *local* maximum of the scoring function: It is always advisable to run such algorithms several times with different random initial configurations. More sophisticated optimization strategies such as simulated annealing, tabu search, or genetic algorithms can also be used.

Another good learning algorithm for Bayesian network classifiers is called *tree-augmented Naïve Bayes* (TAN). As the name implies, it takes the Naïve Bayes classifier and adds edges to it. The class attribute is the single parent of each node of a Naïve Bayes network. TAN considers adding a second parent to each node. If the class node and all corresponding edges are excluded from consideration, and assuming that there is exactly one node to which a second parent is not added, the resulting classifier has a tree structure rooted at the parentless node—this is where the name comes from. For this restricted type of network there is an efficient algorithm for finding the set of edges that maximizes the network's likelihood based on computing the network's maximum weighted spanning tree. This algorithm is linear in the number of instances and quadratic in the number of attributes.

The type of network learned by the TAN algorithm is called a *one-dependence estimator*. An even simpler type of network is the *superparent one-dependence estimator*. Here, exactly one other node, apart from the class node, is elevated to parent status and becomes the parent of every other nonclass node. It turns out that a simple ensemble of these one-dependence estimators yields very accurate classifiers: In each of these estimators, a different attribute becomes the extra parent node. Then, at prediction time, class probability estimates from the different one-dependence estimators are simply averaged. This scheme is known as *AODE*, for *averaged one-dependence estimator*. Normally, only estimators with certain supports in the data are used in the ensemble, but more sophisticated selection schemes are possible. Because no structure learning is involved for each superparent one-dependence estimator, AODE is a very efficient classifier.

All the scoring metrics that we have described so far are likelihood-based in the sense that they are designed to maximize the joint probability $\Pr[a_1, a_2, \ldots, a_n]$ for each instance. However, in classification, what we really want to maximize is the conditional probability of the class given the values of the other attributes—in other words, the conditional likelihood. Unfortunately, there is no closed-form solution for the maximum conditional-likelihood probability estimates that are needed for the tables in a Bayesian network. On the other hand, computing the conditional likelihood for a given network and dataset is straightforward—after all, this is what logistic regression does. Thus, it has been proposed to use standard maximum-likelihood probability estimates in the network, but to use the conditional likelihood to evaluate a particular network structure.

Another way of using Bayesian networks for classification is to build a separate network for each class value, based on the data pertaining to that class, and combine their predictions using Bayes' rule. The set of networks is called a *Bayesian multinet*. To obtain a prediction for a particular class value, take the corresponding network's probability and multiply it by the class's prior probability. Do this for each class and normalize the result as we did previously. In this case we would not use the conditional likelihood to learn the network for each class value.

All the network learning algorithms we have introduced are score-based. A different strategy, which we will not explain here, is to piece a network together by testing individual conditional independence assertions based on subsets of the attributes. This is known as *structure learning by conditional independence tests*.

Data Structures for Fast Learning

Learning Bayesian networks involves a lot of counting. For each network structure considered in the search, the data must be scanned afresh to obtain the counts needed to fill out the conditional probability tables. Instead, could they be stored in a data structure that eliminated the need for scanning the data over and over again? An obvious way is to precompute the counts and store the nonzero ones in a table—say, the hash table mentioned in Section 4.5. Even so, any nontrivial dataset will have a huge number of nonzero counts.

Again, consider the weather data from Table 1.2. There are five attributes, two with three values and three with two values. This gives $4 \times 4 \times 3 \times 3 \times 3 = 432$ possible counts. Each component of the product corresponds to an attribute, and its contribution to the product is one more than the number of its values because the attribute may be missing from the count. All these counts can be calculated by treating them as item sets, as explained in Section 4.5, and setting the minimum coverage to 1. But even without storing counts that are 0, this simple scheme runs into memory problems very quickly. The FP-growth data structure described in Section 6.3 was designed for efficient representation of data in the case of item set mining. In the following, we describe a structure that has been used for Bayesian networks.

It turns out that the counts can be stored effectively in a structure called an *all-dimensions (AD) tree*, which is analogous to the *k*D-trees used for the nearest-neighbor search described in Section 4.7. For simplicity, we illustrate this using a reduced version of the weather data that only has the attributes *humidity*, *windy*, and *play*. Figure 6.21(a) summarizes the data. The number of possible counts is $3 \times 3 \times$

Humidity	Windy	Play	Count
high	true	yes	1
high	true	no	2
high	false	yes	2
high	false	no	2
normal	true	yes	2
normal	true	no	1
normal	false	yes	4
normal	false	no	0

(a)

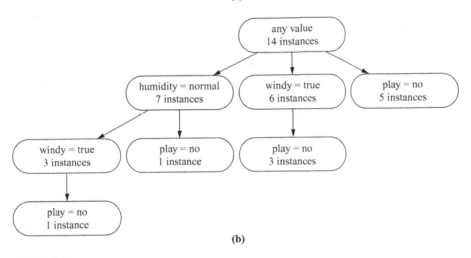

(b)

FIGURE 6.21

The weather data: (a) reduced version and (b) corresponding AD-tree.

3 = 27, although only eight of them are shown. For example, the count for *play = no* is 5 (count them!).

Figure 6.21(b) shows an AD-tree for this data. Each node says how many instances exhibit the attribute values that are tested along the path from the root to that node. For example, the leftmost leaf says that there is one instance with values *humidity = normal, windy = true,* and *play = no,* and the rightmost leaf says that there are five instances with *play = no.*

It would be trivial to construct a tree that enumerates all 27 counts explicitly. However, that would gain nothing over a plain table and is obviously not what the tree in Figure 6.21(b) does because it contains only 8 counts. There is, for example, no branch that tests *humidity = high.* How was the tree constructed, and how can all counts be obtained from it?

Assume that each attribute in the data has been assigned an index. In the reduced version of the weather data we give *humidity* index 1, *windy* index 2, and *play* index 3. An AD-tree is generated by expanding each node corresponding to an attribute *i* with the values of all attributes that have indices *j > i,* with two important restrictions: The most populous expansion for each attribute is omitted (breaking ties arbitrarily) as are expansions with counts that are zero. The root node is given index 0, so for this node all attributes are expanded, subject to the same restrictions.

For example, Figure 6.21(b) contains no expansion for *windy = false* from the root node because with eight instances it is the most populous expansion: The value *false* occurs more often in the data than the value *true*. Similarly, from the node labeled *humidity = normal* there is no expansion for *windy = false* because *false* is the most common value for *windy* among all instances with *humidity = normal*. In fact, in our example the second restriction—namely that expansions with zero counts are omitted—never kicks in because the first restriction precludes any path that starts with the tests *humidity = normal* and *windy = false*, which is the only way to reach the solitary 0 in Figure 6.21(a).

Each node of the tree represents the occurrence of a particular combination of attribute values. It is straightforward to retrieve the count for a combination that occurs in the tree. However, the tree does not explicitly represent many nonzero counts because the most populous expansion for each attribute is omitted. For example, the combination *humidity = high* and *play = yes* occurs three times in the data but has no node in the tree. Nevertheless, it turns out that any count can be calculated from those that the tree stores explicitly.

Here's a simple example. Figure 6.21(b) contains no node for *humidity = normal*, *windy = true*, and *play = yes*. However, it shows three instances with *humidity = normal* and *windy = true*, and one of them has a value for *play* that is different from *yes*. It follows that there must be two instances for *play = yes*. Now for a trickier case: How many times does *humidity = high*, *windy = true*, and *play = no* occur? At first glance it seems impossible to tell because there is no branch for *humidity = high*. However, we can deduce the number by calculating the count for *windy = true* and *play = no* (3) and subtracting the count for *humidity = normal*, *windy = true*, and *play = no* (1). This gives 2, the correct value.

This idea works for any subset of attributes and any combination of attribute values, but it may have to be applied recursively. For example, to obtain the count for *humidity = high*, *windy = false*, and *play = no*, we need the count for *windy = false* and *play = no* and the count for *humidity = normal*, *windy = false*, and *play = no*. We obtain the former by subtracting the count for *windy = true* and *play = no* (3) from the count for *play = no* (5), giving 2, and we obtain the latter by subtracting the count for *humidity = normal*, *windy = true*, and *play = no* (1) from the count for *humidity = normal* and *play = no* (1), giving 0. Thus, there must be 2 − 0 = 2 instances with *humidity = high*, *windy = false*, and *play = no*, which is correct.

AD-trees only pay off if the data contains many thousands of instances. It is pretty obvious that they do not help on the weather data. The fact that they yield no benefit on small datasets means that, in practice, it makes little sense to expand the tree all the way down to the leaf nodes. Usually, a cutoff parameter k is employed, and nodes covering fewer than k instances hold a list of pointers to these instances rather than a list of pointers to other nodes. This makes the trees smaller and more efficient to use.

Discussion

The K2 algorithm for learning Bayesian networks was introduced by Cooper and Herskovits (1992). Bayesian scoring metrics are covered by Heckerman et al. (1995). The TAN algorithm was introduced by Friedman et al. (1997), who also describe multinets. Grossman and Domingos (2004) show how to use the conditional likelihood for scoring networks. Guo and Greiner (2004) present an extensive comparison of scoring metrics for Bayesian network classifiers. Bouckaert (1995) describes averaging over subnetworks. Averaged one-dependence estimators are described by Webb et al. (2005). AD-trees were introduced and analyzed by Moore and Lee (1998)—the same Andrew Moore whose work on kD-trees and ball trees was mentioned in Section 4.7. In a more recent paper, Komarek and Moore (2000) introduce AD-trees for incremental learning that are also more efficient for datasets with many attributes.

We have only skimmed the surface of the subject of learning Bayesian networks. We left open questions of missing values, numeric attributes, and hidden attributes. We did not describe how to use Bayesian networks for regression tasks. Bayesian networks are a special case of a wider class of statistical models called *graphical models*, which include networks with undirected edges called *Markov networks*. Graphical models are attracting great attention in the machine learning community today.

6.8 CLUSTERING

In Section 4.8 we examined the k-means clustering algorithm in which k initial points are chosen to represent initial cluster centers, all data points are assigned to the nearest one, the mean value of the points in each cluster is computed to form its new cluster center, and iteration continues until there are no changes in the clusters. This procedure only works when the number of clusters is known in advance, and this section begins by describing what you can do if it is not.

Next we take a look at techniques for creating a hierarchical clustering structure by "agglomeration"—that is, starting with individual instances and successively joining them up into clusters. Then we look at a method that works incrementally; that is, process each new instance as it appears. This method was developed in the late 1980s and embodied in a pair of systems called Cobweb (for nominal attributes) and Classit (for numeric attributes). Both come up with a hierarchical grouping of instances and use a measure of cluster "quality" called *category utility*. Finally, we examine a statistical clustering method based on a mixture model of different probability distributions, one for each cluster. It does not partition instances into disjoint clusters as k-means does but instead assigns instances to classes probabilistically, not deterministically. We explain the basic technique and sketch the working of a comprehensive clustering scheme called AutoClass.

Choosing the Number of Clusters

Suppose you are using k-means but do not know the number of clusters in advance. One solution is to try out different possibilities and see which is best. A simple strategy is to start from a given minimum, perhaps $k = 1$, and work up to a small fixed maximum. Note that on the training data the "best" clustering according to the total squared distance criterion will always be to choose as many clusters as there are data points! To penalize solutions with many clusters you will have to apply something like the MDL criterion of Section 5.9.

Another possibility is to begin by finding a few clusters and determining whether it is worth splitting them. You could choose $k = 2$, perform k-means clustering until it terminates, and then consider splitting each cluster. Computation time will be reduced considerably if the initial two-way clustering is considered irrevocable and splitting is investigated for each component independently. One way to split a cluster is to make a new seed one standard deviation away from the cluster's center in the direction of its greatest variation, and to make a second seed the same distance in the opposite direction. (Alternatively, if this is too slow, choose a distance proportional to the cluster's bounding box and a random direction.) Then apply k-means to the points in the cluster with these two new seeds.

Having tentatively split a cluster, is it worthwhile retaining the split or is the original cluster equally plausible by itself? It's no good looking at the total squared distance of all points to their cluster center—this is bound to be smaller for two subclusters. A penalty should be incurred for inventing an extra cluster, and this is a job for the MDL criterion. That principle can be applied to see whether the information required to specify the two new cluster centers, along with the information required to specify each point with respect to them, exceeds the information required to specify the original center and all the points with respect to it. If so, the new clustering is unproductive and should be abandoned. If the split is retained, try splitting each new cluster further. Continue the process until no worthwhile splits remain.

Additional implementation efficiency can be achieved by combining this iterative clustering process with the kD-tree or ball tree data structure advocated in Section 4.8. Then the data points are reached by working down the tree from the root. When considering splitting a cluster, there is no need to consider the whole tree; just look at those parts of it that are needed to cover the cluster. For example, when deciding whether to split the lower left cluster in Figure 4.16(a) (below the thick line), it is only necessary to consider nodes A and B of the tree in Figure 4.16(b) because node C is irrelevant to that cluster.

Hierarchical Clustering

Forming an initial pair of clusters and then recursively considering whether it is worth splitting each one further produces a hierarchy that can be represented as a binary tree called a *dendrogram*. In fact, we illustrated a dendrogram in Figure

3.11(d) (there some of the branches were three-way). The same information could be represented as a Venn diagram of sets and subsets: The constraint that the structure is hierarchical corresponds to the fact that, although subsets can include one another, they cannot intersect. In some cases there exists a measure of the degree of dissimilarity between the clusters in each set; then the height of each node in the dendrogram can be made proportional to the dissimilarity between its children. This provides an easily interpretable diagram of a hierarchical clustering.

An alternative to the top-down method for forming a hierarchical structure of clusters is to use a bottom-up approach, which is called *agglomerative* clustering. This idea was proposed many years ago and has recently enjoyed a resurgence in popularity. The basic algorithm is simple. All you need is a measure of distance (or a similarity measure) between any two clusters. (If you have a similarity measure instead, it is easy to convert that into a distance.) You begin by regarding each instance as a cluster in its own right; then find the two closest clusters, merge them, and keep on doing this until only one cluster is left. The record of mergings forms a hierarchical clustering structure—a binary dendrogram.

There are numerous possibilities for the distance measure. One is the minimum distance between the clusters—the distance between their two closest members. This yields what is called the *single-linkage* clustering algorithm. Since this measure takes into account only the two closest members of a pair of clusters, the procedure is sensitive to outliers: The addition of just a single new instance can radically alter the entire clustering structure. Also, if we define the diameter of a cluster to be the greatest distance between its members, single-linkage clustering can produce clusters with very large diameters. Another measure is the maximum distance between the clusters, instead of the minimum. Two clusters are considered close only if all instances in their union are relatively similar—sometimes called the *complete-linkage* method. This measure, which is also sensitive to outliers, seeks compact clusters with small diameters. However, some instances may end up much closer to other clusters than they are to the rest of their own cluster.

There are other measures that represent a compromise between the extremes of minimum and maximum distance between cluster members. One is to represent clusters by the centroid of their members, as the *k*-means algorithm does, and use the distance between centroids—the *centroid-linkage* method. This works well when the instances are positioned in multidimensional Euclidean space and the notion of centroid is clear, but not when all we have is a pairwise similarity measure between instances, because centroids are not instances and the similarity between them may be impossible to define.

Another measure, which avoids this problem, is to calculate the average distance between each pair of members of the two clusters—the *average-linkage* method. Although this seems like a lot of work, you would have to calculate all pairwise distances in order to find the maximum or minimum anyway, and averaging them isn't much additional burden. Both these measures have a technical deficiency: Their results depend on the numerical scale on which distances are measured. The minimum and maximum distance measures produce a result that depends only on the *ordering* between the distances involved. In contrast, the result of both centroid-based and average-distance clustering can be altered by a monotonic transformation of all distances, even though it preserves their relative ordering.

Another method, called *group-average* clustering, uses the average distance between all members of the merged cluster. This differs from the "average" method just described because it includes in the average pairs from the same original cluster. Finally, *Ward's* clustering method calculates the increase in the sum of squares of the distances of the instances from the centroid before and after fusing two clusters. The idea is to minimize the increase in this squared distance at each clustering step.

All these measures will produce the same hierarchical clustering result if the clusters are compact and well separated. However, in other cases they can yield quite different structures.

Example of Hierarchical Clustering

Figure 6.22 shows the result of agglomerative hierarchical clustering. (These visualizations have been generated using the FigTree program.[1]) In this case the dataset contained 50 examples of different kinds of creatures, from dolphin to mongoose, from giraffe to lobster. There was 1 numeric attribute (number of legs, ranging from 0 to 6, but scaled to the range [0, 1]) and 15 Boolean attributes such as *has feathers*, *lays eggs*, and *venomous*, which are treated as binary attributes with values 0 and 1 in the distance calculation.

Two kinds of display are shown: a standard dendrogram and a polar plot. Figures 6.22(a) and (b) show the output from an agglomerative clusterer plotted in two different ways, and Figures 6.22(c) and (d) show the result of a different agglomerative clusterer plotted in the same two ways. The difference is that the pair in Figures 6.22(a) and (b) was produced using the complete-linkage measure and the pair in Figures 6.22(c) and (d) was produced using the single-linkage measure. You can see that the complete-linkage method tends to produce compact clusters while the single-linkage method produces clusters with large diameters at fairly low levels of the tree.

In all four visualizations the height of each node in the dendrogram is proportional to the dissimilarity between its children, measured as the Euclidean distance between instances. A numeric scale is provided beneath Figures 6.22(a) and (c). The total dissimilarity from root to leaf is far greater for the complete-linkage method in Figures 6.22(a) and (b) than for the single-linkage method in Figures 6.22(c) and (d) since the former involves the maximum distance and the latter the minimum distance between instances in each cluster. In the first case the total dissimilarity is a little less than 3.75, which is almost the maximum possible distance between instances—the distance between two instances that differ in 14 of the 15 attributes is $\sqrt{14} \approx 3.74$. In the second it is a little greater than 2 (that is, $\sqrt{4}$), which is what a difference in four Boolean attributes would produce.

---

[1] See *http://tree.bio.ed.ac.uk/software/figtree/* for more information.

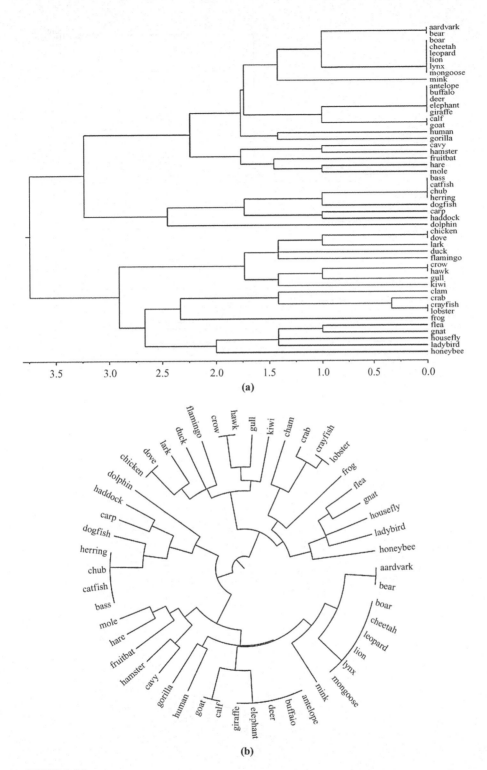

FIGURE 6.22

Hierarchical clustering displays.

Continued

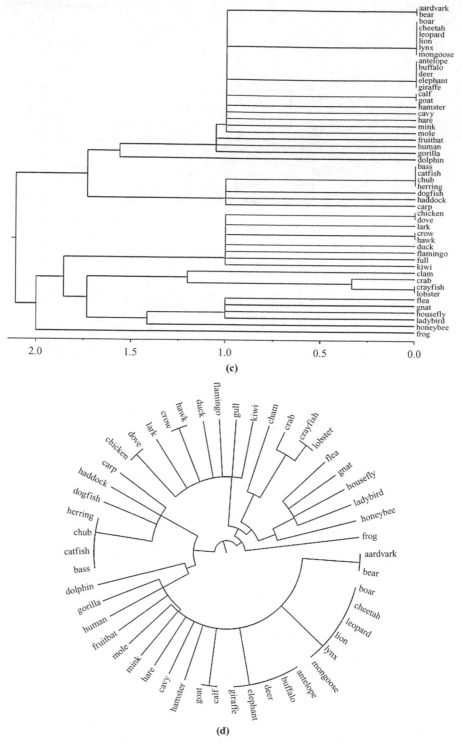

(c)

(d)

FIGURE 6.22, cont'd

For the complete-linkage method (Figure 6.22(a)), many elements join together at a dissimilarity of 1, which corresponds to a difference in a single Boolean attribute. Only one pair has a smaller dissimilarity: *crab* and *crayfish*, which differ only in the number of legs (4/6 and 6/6, respectively, after scaling). Other popular dissimilarities are $\sqrt{2}$, $\sqrt{3}$, $\sqrt{4}$, and so on, corresponding to differences in two, three, and four Boolean attributes. For the single-linkage method (Figure 6.22(c)) that uses the minimum distance between clusters, even more elements join together at a dissimilarity of 1.

Which of the two display methods—the standard dendogram and the polar plot—is more useful is a matter of taste. Although more unfamiliar at first, the polar plot spreads the visualization more evenly over the space available.

Incremental Clustering

Whereas the *k*-means algorithm iterates over the whole dataset until convergence is reached and the hierarchical method examines all the clusters present so far at each stage of merging, the clustering methods we examine next work incrementally, instance by instance. At any stage the clustering forms a tree with instances at the leaves and a root node that represents the entire dataset. In the beginning the tree consists of the root alone. Instances are added one by one, and the tree is updated appropriately at each stage. Updating may be merely a case of finding the right place to put a leaf representing the new instance, or it may involve a radical restructuring of the part of the tree that is affected by the new instance. The key to deciding how and where to update is a quantity called *category utility* that measures the overall quality of a partition of instances into clusters. We defer detailed consideration of how this is defined until the next section and look first at how the clustering algorithm works.

The procedure is best illustrated by an example. We will use the familiar weather data again, but without the *play* attribute. To track progress, the 14 instances are labeled *a*, *b*, *c*, …, *n* (as in Table 4.6), and for interest we include the classes *yes* or *no* in the label—although it should be emphasized that for this artificial dataset there is little reason to suppose that the two classes of instance should fall into separate categories. Figure 6.23 shows the situation at salient points throughout the clustering procedure.

At the beginning, when new instances are absorbed into the structure, they each form their own subcluster under the overall top-level cluster. Each new instance is processed by tentatively placing it in each of the existing leaves and evaluating the category utility of the resulting set of the top-level node's children to see if the leaf is a good "host" for the new instance. For each of the first five instances, there is no such host: It is better, in terms of category utility, to form a new leaf for each instance. With the sixth it finally becomes beneficial to form a cluster, joining the new instance *f* with the old one—the host—*e*. If you look back at Table 4.6 you will see that the fifth and sixth instances are indeed very similar, differing only in the *windy* attribute (and *play*, which is being ignored here). The next example, *g*, is

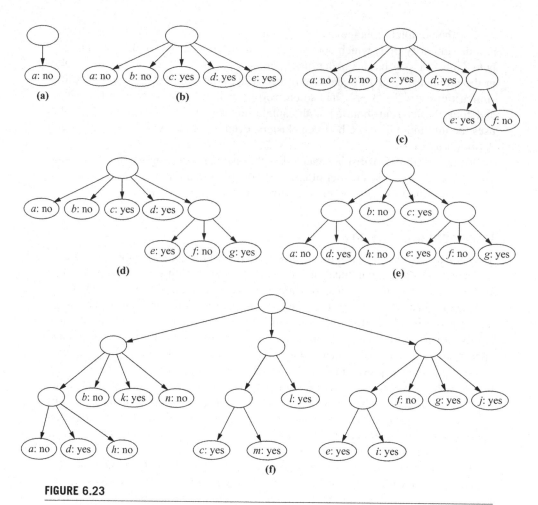

FIGURE 6.23

Clustering the weather data.

placed in the same cluster (it differs from *f* only in *outlook*). This involves another call to the clustering procedure. First, *g* is evaluated to see which of the five children of the root makes the best host; it turns out to be the rightmost, the one that is already a cluster. Then the clustering algorithm is invoked with this as the root, and its two children are evaluated to see which would make the better host. In this case it proves best, according to the category utility measure, to add the new instance as a subcluster in its own right.

If we were to continue in this vein, there would be no possibility of any radical restructuring of the tree, and the final clustering would be excessively dependent on the ordering of examples. To avoid this, there is provision for restructuring, and you can see it come into play when instance *h* is added in the next step shown in Figure 6.23(e). In this case two existing nodes are *merged* into a single cluster: Nodes *a* and *d* are merged before the new instance *h* is added. One way of accomplishing this would be to consider all pairs of nodes for merging and evaluate the category utility of each pair. However, that would be computationally expensive, and would involve a lot of repeated work if it were undertaken whenever a new instance was added.

Instead, whenever the nodes at a particular level are scanned for a suitable host, both the best-matching node—the one that produces the greatest category utility for the split at that level—and the runner-up are noted. The best one will form the host for the new instance (unless that new instance is better off in a cluster of its own). However, before setting to work on putting the new instance in with the host, consideration is given to merging the host and the runner-up. In this case, *a* is the preferred host and *d* is the runner-up. When a merge of *a* and *d* is evaluated, it turns out that it would improve the category utility measure. Consequently, these two nodes are merged, yielding a version of the fifth hierarchy before *h* is added. Then consideration is given to the placement of *h* in the new, merged node; it turns out to be best to make it a subcluster in its own right, as shown.

An operation converse to merging is also implemented, called *splitting*. Whenever the best host is identified, and merging has not proved beneficial, consideration is given to splitting the host node. Splitting has exactly the opposite effect of merging, taking a node and replacing it with its children. For example, splitting the rightmost node in Figure 6.23(d) would raise the *e*, *f*, and *g* leaves up a level, making them siblings of *a*, *b*, *c*, and *d*. Merging and splitting provide an incremental way of restructuring the tree to compensate for incorrect choices caused by infelicitous ordering of examples.

The final hierarchy for all 14 examples is shown in Figure 6.23(f). There are three major clusters, each of which subdivides further into its own subclusters. If the *play/don't play* distinction really represented an inherent feature of the data, a single cluster would be expected for each outcome. No such clean structure is observed, although a (very) generous eye might discern a slight tendency at lower levels for *yes* instances to group together, and likewise for *no* instances.

Exactly the same scheme works for numeric attributes. Category utility is defined for these as well, based on an estimate of the mean and standard deviation of the value of that attribute. Details are deferred to the next subsection. However, there is just one problem that we must attend to here: When estimating the standard deviation of an attribute for a particular node, the result will be zero if the node contains only one instance, as it does more often than not. Unfortunately, zero variances produce infinite values in the category utility formula. A simple heuristic solution is to impose a minimum variance on each attribute. It can be argued that because no measurement is completely precise, it is reasonable to impose such a minimum: It represents the measurement error in a single sample. This parameter is called *acuity*.

Figure 6.24(a) shows a hierarchical clustering produced by the incremental algorithm for part of the iris dataset (30 instances, 10 from each class). At the top level there are two clusters (i.e., subclusters of the single node representing the whole dataset). The first contains both *Iris virginicas* and *Iris versicolors*, and the second contains only *Iris setosas*. The *Iris setosas* themselves split into two subclusters, one

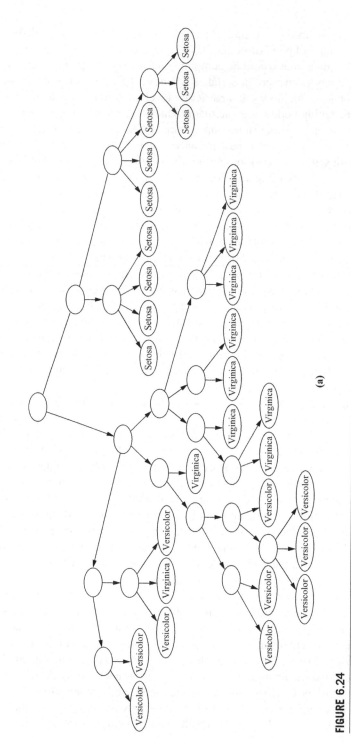

FIGURE 6.24

Hierarchical clusterings of the iris data.

(a)

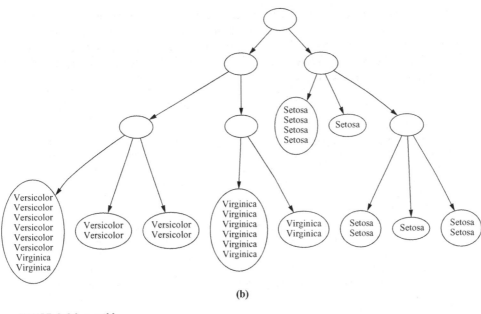

(b)

FIGURE 6.24, cont'd

with four cultivars and the other with six. The other top-level cluster splits into three subclusters, each with a fairly complex structure. Both the first and second contain only *Iris versicolors*, with one exception, a stray *Iris virginica*, in each case; the third contains only *Iris virginicas*. This represents a fairly satisfactory clustering of the iris data: It shows that the three genera are not artificial at all but reflect genuine differences in the data. This is, however, a slightly overoptimistic conclusion because quite a bit of experimentation with the acuity parameter was necessary to obtain such a nice division.

The clusterings produced by this scheme contain one leaf for every instance. This produces an overwhelmingly large hierarchy for datasets of any reasonable size, corresponding, in a sense, to overfitting the particular dataset. Consequently, a second numerical parameter called *cutoff* is used to suppress growth. Some instances are deemed to be sufficiently similar to others not to warrant formation of their own child node, and this parameter governs the similarity threshold. Cutoff is specified in terms of category utility: When the increase in category utility from adding a new node is sufficiently small, that node is cut off.

Figure 6.24(b) shows the same iris data, clustered with cutoff in effect. Many leaf nodes contain several instances: These are children of the parent node that have been cut off. The division into the three types of iris is a little easier to see from this hierarchy because some of the detail is suppressed. Again, however, some experimentation with the cutoff parameter was necessary to get this result, and in fact a sharper cutoff leads to much less satisfactory clusters.

Similar clusterings are obtained if the full iris dataset of 150 instances is used. However, the results depend on the ordering of examples: Figure 6.24 was obtained by alternating the three varieties of iris in the input file. If all *Iris setosas* are presented first, followed by all *Iris versicolors* and then all *Iris virginicas*, the resulting clusters are quite unsatisfactory.

Category Utility

Now we look at how the category utility, which measures the overall quality of a partition of instances into clusters, is calculated. In Section 5.9 we learned how the MDL measure could, in principle, be used to evaluate the quality of clustering. Category utility is not MDL-based but rather resembles a kind of quadratic loss function defined on conditional probabilities.

The definition of category utility is rather formidable:

$$CU(C_1, C_2, \ldots, C_k) = \frac{\sum_\ell \Pr[C_\ell] \sum_i \sum_j (\Pr[a_i = v_{ij} \mid C_\ell]^2 - \Pr[a_i = v_{ij}]^2)}{k}$$

where $C_1, C_2, \ldots, C_k$ are the k clusters; the outer summation is over these clusters; the next inner one sums over the attributes; a_i is the ith attribute, and it takes on values v_{i1}, $v_{i2}, \ldots$, which are dealt with by the sum over j. Note that the probabilities themselves are obtained by summing over all instances; thus, there is a further implied level of summation.

This expression makes a great deal of sense if you take the time to examine it. The point of having a cluster is that it will give some advantage in predicting the values of attributes of instances in that cluster—that is, $\Pr[a_i = v_{ij} \mid C_\ell]$ is a better estimate of the probability that attribute a_i has value v_{ij}, for an instance in cluster C_ℓ, than $\Pr[a_i = v_{ij}]$ because it takes account of the cluster the instance is in. If that information doesn't help, the clusters aren't doing much good! So what the measure calculates, inside the multiple summation, is the amount by which that information *does* help in terms of the differences between squares of probabilities. This is not quite the standard squared-difference metric because that sums the squares of the differences (which produces a symmetric result) and the present measure sums the difference of the squares (which, appropriately, does not produce a symmetric result). The differences between squares of probabilities are summed over all attributes, and all their possible values, in the inner double summation. Then it is summed over all clusters, weighted by their probabilities, in the outer summation.

The overall division by k is a little hard to justify because the squared differences have already been summed over the categories. It essentially provides a "per cluster" figure for the category utility that discourages overfitting. Otherwise, because the probabilities are derived by summing over the appropriate instances, the very best category utility would be obtained by placing each instance in its own cluster. Then $\Pr[a_i = v_{ij} \mid C_\ell]$ would be 1 for the value that attribute a_i actually has for the single instance in category C_ℓ and 0 for all other values; the numerator of the category utility formula will end up as

$$m - \sum_i \sum_j \Pr[a_i = v_{ij}]^2$$

where m is the total number of attributes. This is the greatest value that the numerator can have; thus, if it were not for the additional division by k in the category utility formula, there would never be any incentive to form clusters containing more than one member. This extra factor is best viewed as a rudimentary overfitting-avoidance heuristic.

This category utility formula applies only to nominal attributes. However, it can be easily extended to numeric attributes by assuming that their distribution is normal with a given (observed) mean μ and standard deviation σ. The probability density function for an attribute a is

$$f(a) = \frac{1}{\sqrt{2\pi}\sigma} \exp\left(-\frac{(a-\mu)^2}{2\sigma^2}\right)$$

The analog of summing the squares of attribute–value probabilities is

$$\sum_j \Pr[a_i = v_{ij}]^2 \Leftrightarrow \int f(a_i)^2 da_i = \frac{1}{2\sqrt{\pi}\sigma_i}$$

where σ_i is the standard deviation of the attribute a_i. Thus, for a numeric attribute we estimate the standard deviation from the data, both within the cluster (σ_{il}) and for the data over all clusters (σ_i), and use these in the category utility formula:

$$CU(C_1, C_2, \ldots, C_k) = \frac{1}{k}\sum_l \Pr[C_l] \frac{1}{2\sqrt{\pi}} \sum_i \left(\frac{1}{\sigma_{il}} - \frac{1}{\sigma_i}\right)$$

Now the problem mentioned that occurs when the standard deviation estimate is zero becomes apparent: A zero standard deviation produces an infinite value of the category utility formula. Imposing a prespecified minimum variance on each attribute, the acuity, is a rough-and-ready solution to the problem.

Probability-Based Clustering

Some of the shortcomings of the heuristic clustering method have already become apparent: the arbitrary division by k in the category utility formula that is necessary to prevent overfitting, the need to supply an artificial minimum value for the standard deviation of clusters, and the ad hoc cutoff value to prevent every single instance from becoming a cluster in its own right. On top of this is the uncertainty inherent in incremental algorithms. To what extent is the result dependent on the order of examples? Are the local restructuring operations of merging and splitting really enough to reverse the effect of bad initial decisions caused by unlucky ordering? Does the final result represent even a *local* maximum of category utility? Add to this the problem that one never knows how far the final configuration is to a *global* maximum—and, of course, the standard trick of repeating the clustering procedure several times and choosing the best will destroy the incremental nature of the algorithm. Finally, doesn't the hierarchical nature of the result really beg the question of which are the *best* clusters? There are so many clusters in Figure 6.24 that it is difficult to separate the wheat from the chaff.

A more principled statistical approach to the clustering problem can overcome some of these shortcomings. From a probabilistic perspective, the goal of clustering is to find the most likely set of clusters available given the data (and, inevitably, prior expectations). Because no finite amount of evidence is enough to make a completely firm decision on the matter, instances—even training instances—should not be placed categorically in one cluster or the other: Instead, they have a certain probability of belonging to each cluster. This helps to eliminate the brittleness that is often associated with schemes that make hard and fast judgments.

The foundation for statistical clustering is a statistical model called *finite mixtures*. A *mixture* is a set of k probability distributions, representing k clusters, that govern the attribute values for members of that cluster. In other words, each distribution gives the probability that a particular instance would have a certain set of attribute values if it were *known* to be a member of that cluster. Each cluster has a different distribution. Any particular instance "really" belongs to one and only one of the clusters, but it is not known which one. Finally, the clusters are not equally likely: There is some probability distribution that reflects their relative populations.

The simplest finite-mixture situation is when there is only one numeric attribute, which has a Gaussian or normal distribution for each cluster—but with different means and variances. The clustering problem is to take a set of instances—in this case each instance is just a number—and a prespecified number of clusters, and work out each cluster's mean and variance and the population distribution between the clusters. The mixture model combines several normal distributions, and its probability density function looks like a mountain range with a peak for each component.

Figure 6.25 shows a simple example. There are two clusters, A and B, and each has a normal distribution with means and standard deviations μ_A and σ_A for cluster A and μ_B and σ_B for cluster B. Samples are taken from these distributions, using cluster A with probability p_A and cluster B with probability p_B (where $p_A + p_B = 1$), resulting in a dataset like that shown. Now, imagine being given the dataset without the classes—just the numbers—and being asked to determine the five parameters that characterize the model: μ_A, σ_A, μ_B, σ_B, and p_A (the parameter p_B can be calculated directly from p_A). That is the finite-mixture problem.

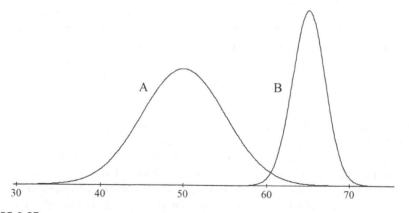

FIGURE 6.25

A two-class mixture model.

If you knew which of the two distributions each instance came from, finding the five parameters would be easy—just estimate the mean and standard deviation for the cluster A samples and the cluster B samples separately, using the formulas

$$\mu = \frac{x_1 + x_2 + \ldots + x_n}{n}$$

and

$$\sigma^2 = \frac{(x_1 - \mu)^2 + (x_2 - \mu)^2 + \ldots + (x_n - \mu)^2}{n-1}$$

(The use of $n-1$ rather than n as the denominator in the second formula is a technicality of sampling: It makes little difference in practice if n is used instead.) Here, $x_1, x_2, \ldots, x_n$ are the samples from the distribution A or B. To estimate the fifth parameter p_A, just take the proportion of the instances that are in the A cluster.

If you knew the five parameters, finding the probabilities that a given instance comes from each distribution would be easy. Given an instance x, the probability that it belongs to cluster A is

$$\Pr[A \mid x] = \frac{\Pr[x \mid A] \times \Pr[A]}{\Pr[x]} = \frac{f(x; \mu_A, \sigma_A) p_A}{\Pr[x]}$$

where $f(x; \mu_A, \sigma_A)$ is the normal distribution function for cluster A—that is,

$$f(x; \mu, \sigma) = \frac{1}{\sqrt{2\pi}\sigma} e^{-\frac{(x-\mu)^2}{2\sigma^2}}$$

The denominator $\Pr[x]$ will disappear: We calculate the numerators for both $\Pr[A \mid x]$ and $\Pr[B \mid x]$ and normalize them by dividing by their sum. This whole procedure is just the same as the way numeric attributes are treated in the Naïve Bayes learning scheme of Section 4.2. And the caveat explained there applies here too: Strictly speaking, $f(x; \mu_A, \sigma_A)$ is not the probability $\Pr[x \mid A]$ because the probability of x being any particular real number is zero, but the normalization process makes the final result correct. Note that the final outcome is not a particular cluster but rather the *probabilities* with which x belongs to cluster A and cluster B.

The EM Algorithm

The problem is that we know neither of these things: not the distribution that each training instance came from nor the five mixture model parameters. So we adopt the procedure used for the k-means clustering algorithm and iterate. Start with initial guesses for the five parameters, use them to calculate the cluster probabilities for each instance, use these probabilities to reestimate the parameters, and repeat. (If you prefer, you can start with guesses for the classes of the instances instead.) This is called the *EM algorithm*, for *expectation maximization*. The first step—calculation of the cluster probabilities, which are the "expected" class values—is "expectation"; the second, calculation of the distribution parameters, is "maximization" of the likelihood of the distributions given the data available.

A slight adjustment must be made to the parameter estimation equations to account for the fact that it is only cluster probabilities, not the clusters themselves, that are known for each instance. These probabilities just act like weights. If w_i is the probability that instance i belongs to cluster A, the mean and standard deviation for cluster A are

$$\mu_A = \frac{w_1 x_1 + w_2 x_2 + \ldots + w_n x_n}{w_1 + w_2 + \ldots + w_n}$$

and

$$\sigma_A^2 = \frac{w_1(x_1 - \mu)^2 + w_2(x_2 - \mu)^2 + \ldots + w_n(x_n - \mu)^2}{w_1 + w_2 + \ldots + w_n}$$

where now the x_i are *all* the instances, not just those belonging to cluster A. (This differs in a small detail from the estimate for the standard deviation given later: If all weights are equal, the denominator is n rather than $n - 1$. Technically speaking, this is a "maximum-likelihood" estimator for the variance whereas the previous formula is for an "unbiased" estimator. The difference is not important in practice.)

Now consider how to terminate the iteration. The k-means algorithm stops when the classes of the instances don't change from one iteration to the next—a "fixed point" has been reached. In the EM algorithm things are not quite so easy: The algorithm converges toward a fixed point but never actually gets there. We can see how close it is getting by calculating the overall likelihood that the data came from this dataset, given the values for the five parameters. This overall likelihood is obtained by multiplying the probabilities of the individual instances i:

$$\prod_i (p_A \Pr[x_i \mid A] + p_B \Pr[x_i \mid B])$$

where the probabilities given the clusters A and B are determined from the normal distribution function $f(x; \mu, \sigma)$. This overall likelihood is a measure of the "goodness" of the clustering and increases at each iteration of the EM algorithm.

Again, there is a technical difficulty with equating the probability of a particular value of x with $f(x; \mu, \sigma)$, and in this case the effect does not disappear because no probability normalization operation is applied. The upshot is that the likelihood expression is not a probability and does not necessarily lie between 0 and 1; nevertheless, its magnitude still reflects the quality of the clustering. In practical implementations its logarithm is calculated instead: This is done by summing the logarithms of the individual components, avoiding multiplications. But the overall conclusion still holds: You should iterate until the increase in log-likelihood becomes negligible. For example, a practical implementation might iterate until the difference between successive values of log-likelihood is less than 10^{-10} for 10 successive iterations. Typically, the log-likelihood will increase very sharply over the first few iterations and then converge rather quickly to a point that is virtually stationary.

Although the EM algorithm is guaranteed to converge to a maximum, this is a *local* maximum and may not necessarily be the same as the global maximum. For a better chance of obtaining the global maximum, the whole procedure should be repeated several times, with different initial guesses for the parameter values. The overall log-likelihood figure can be used to compare the different final configurations obtained: Just choose the largest of the local maxima.

Extending the Mixture Model

Now that we have seen the Gaussian mixture model for two distributions, let's consider how to extend it to more realistic situations. The basic method is just the same, but because the mathematical notation becomes formidable we will not develop it in full detail.

Changing the algorithm from two-class problems to multiclass problems is completely straightforward as long as the number k of normal distributions is given in advance. The model can easily be extended from a single numeric attribute per instance to multiple attributes as long as independence between attributes is assumed. The probabilities for each attribute are multiplied together to obtain the joint probability for the instance, just as in the Naïve Bayes method.

When the dataset is known in advance to contain correlated attributes, the independence assumption no longer holds. Instead, two attributes can be modeled jointly by a bivariate normal distribution, in which each has its own mean value but the two standard deviations are replaced by a "covariance matrix" with four numeric parameters. There are standard statistical techniques for estimating the class probabilities of instances and for estimating the means and covariance matrix given the instances and their class probabilities. Several correlated attributes can be handled using a multivariate distribution. The number of parameters increases with the square of the number of jointly varying attributes. With n independent attributes, there are $2n$ parameters, a mean and a standard deviation for each. With n covariant attributes, there are $n + n(n + 1)/2$ parameters, a mean for each, and an $n \times n$ covariance matrix that is symmetric and therefore involves $n(n + 1)/2$ different quantities. This escalation in the number of parameters has serious consequences for overfitting, as we will explain later.

To cater for nominal attributes, the normal distribution must be abandoned. Instead, a nominal attribute with v possible values is characterized by v numbers representing the probability of each one. A different set of numbers is needed for every class; kv parameters in all. The situation is very similar to the Naïve Bayes method. The two steps of expectation and maximization correspond exactly to operations we have studied before. Expectation—estimating the cluster to which each instance belongs given the distribution parameters—is just like determining the class of an unknown instance. Maximization—estimating the parameters from the classified instances—is just like determining the attribute–value probabilities from the training instances, with the small difference that in the EM algorithm instances are assigned to classes probabilistically rather than categorically. In Section 4.2 we encountered the problem that probability estimates can turn out to be zero, and the same problem occurs here too. Fortunately, the solution is just as simple—use the Laplace estimator.

Naïve Bayes assumes that attributes are independent—that is the reason why it is called "naïve." A pair of correlated nominal attributes with v_1 and v_2 possible values, respectively, can be replaced by a single covariant attribute with $v_1 v_2$ possible values. Again, the number of parameters escalates as the number of dependent attributes increases, and this has implications for probability estimates and overfitting.

The presence of both numeric and nominal attributes in the data to be clustered presents no particular problem. Covariant numeric and nominal attributes are more difficult to handle, and we will not describe them here.

Missing values can be accommodated in various different ways. In principle, they should be treated as unknown and the EM process adapted to estimate them as well as the cluster means and variances. A simple way is to replace them by means or modes in a preprocessing step.

With all these enhancements, probabilistic clustering becomes quite sophisticated. The EM algorithm is used throughout to do the basic work. The user must specify the number of clusters to be sought, the type of each attribute (numeric or nominal), which attributes are to be modeled as covarying, and what to do about missing values. Moreover, different distributions can be used. Although the normal distribution is usually a good choice for numeric attributes, it is not suitable for attributes (such as weight) that have a predetermined minimum (0 in the case of weight) but no upper bound; in this case a "log-normal" distribution is more appropriate. Numeric attributes that are bounded above and below can be modeled by a "log-odds" distribution. Attributes that are integer counts rather than real values are best modeled by the "Poisson" distribution. A comprehensive system might allow these distributions to be specified individually for each attribute. In each case, the distribution involves numeric parameters—probabilities of all possible values for discrete attributes and mean and standard deviation for continuous ones.

In this section we have been talking about clustering. But you may be thinking that these enhancements could be applied just as well to the Naïve Bayes algorithm too—and you'd be right. A comprehensive probabilistic modeler could accommodate both clustering and classification learning, nominal and numeric attributes with a variety of distributions, various possibilities of covariation, and different ways of dealing with missing values. The user would specify, as part of the domain knowledge, which distributions to use for which attributes.

Bayesian Clustering

However, there is a snag: overfitting. You might say that if we are not sure which attributes are dependent on each other, why not be on the safe side and specify that *all* the attributes are covariant? The answer is that the more parameters there are, the greater the chance that the resulting structure is overfitted to the training data—and covariance increases the number of parameters dramatically. The problem of overfitting occurs throughout machine learning, and probabilistic clustering is no exception. There are two ways that it can occur: through specifying too large a number of clusters and through specifying distributions with too many parameters.

The extreme case of too many clusters occurs when there is one for every data point: Clearly, that will be overfitted to the training data. In fact, in the mixture model, problems will occur whenever any of the normal distributions becomes so narrow that the cluster is centered on just one data point. Consequently, implementations generally insist that clusters contain at least two different data values.

Whenever there are a large number of parameters, the problem of overfitting arises. If you were unsure of which attributes were covariant, you might try out different possibilities and choose the one that maximized the overall probability of the data given the clustering that was found. Unfortunately, the more parameters there are, the larger the overall data probability will tend to be—not necessarily because of better clustering but because of overfitting. The more parameters there are to play with, the easier it is to find a clustering that seems good.

It would be nice if somehow you could penalize the model for introducing new parameters. One principled way of doing this is to adopt a Bayesian approach in which every parameter has a prior probability distribution. Then, whenever a new parameter is introduced, its prior probability must be incorporated into the overall likelihood figure. Because this will involve multiplying the overall likelihood by a number less than 1—the prior probability—it will automatically penalize the addition of new parameters. To improve the overall likelihood, the new parameters will have to yield a benefit that outweighs the penalty.

In a sense, the Laplace estimator that was introduced in Section 4.2, and whose use we advocated earlier to counter the problem of zero probability estimates for nominal values, is just such a device. Whenever observed probabilities are small, the Laplace estimator exacts a penalty because it makes probabilities that are zero, or close to zero, greater, and this will decrease the overall likelihood of the data. Making two nominal attributes covariant will exacerbate the problem of small probabilities. Instead of $v_1 + v_2$ parameters, where v_1 and v_2 are the number of possible values, there are now $v_1 v_2$, greatly increasing the chance of a large number of small estimated probabilities. In fact, the Laplace estimator is tantamount to using a particular prior distribution for the introduction of new parameters.

The same technique can be used to penalize the introduction of large numbers of clusters, just by using a prespecified prior distribution that decays sharply as the number of clusters increases. AutoClass is a comprehensive Bayesian clustering scheme that uses the finite-mixture model with prior distributions on all the parameters. It allows both numeric and nominal attributes and uses the EM algorithm to estimate the parameters of the probability distributions to best fit the data. Because there is no guarantee that the EM algorithm converges to the global optimum, the procedure is repeated for several different sets of initial values. But that is not all. AutoClass considers different numbers of clusters and can consider different amounts of covariance and different underlying probability distribution types for the numeric attributes. This involves an additional, outer level of search. For example, it initially evaluates the log-likelihood for 2, 3, 5, 7, 10, 15, and 25 clusters: After that, it fits a log-normal distribution to the resulting data and randomly selects from it more values to try. As you might imagine, the overall algorithm is extremely computation intensive. In fact, the actual implementation starts with a prespecified time bound and continues to iterate as long as time allows. Give it longer and the results may be better!

FIGURE 6.26

DensiTree showing possible hierarchical clusterings of a given dataset.

Rather than showing just the most likely clustering to the user, it may be best to present all of them, weighted by probability. Recently, fully Bayesian techniques for *hierarchical* clustering have been developed that produce as output a probability distribution over possible hierarchical structures representing a dataset. Figure 6.26 is a visualization, known as a *DensiTree*, that shows the set of all trees for a particular dataset in a triangular shape. The tree is best described in terms of its "clades," a biological term from the Greek *klados* meaning *branch*, for a group of the same species that includes all ancestors. Here, there are five clearly distinguishable clades. The first and fourth correspond to a single leaf, while the fifth has two leaves that are so distinct they might be considered clades in their own right. The second and third clades each have five leaves, and there is large uncertainty in their topology. Such visualizations make it easy for people to grasp the possible hierarchical clusterings of their data, at least in terms of the big picture.

Discussion

The clustering methods that have been described produce different kinds of output. All are capable of taking new data in the form of a test set and classifying it according to clusters that were discovered by analyzing a training set. However, the hierarchical and incremental clustering methods are the only ones that generate an explicit knowledge structure that describes the clustering in a way that can be visualized and reasoned about. The other algorithms produce clusters that could be visualized in instance space if the dimensionality were not too high.

If a clustering method were used to label the instances of the training set with cluster numbers, that labeled set could then be used to train a rule or decision tree learner. The resulting rules or tree would form an explicit description of the classes. A probabilistic clustering scheme could be used for the same purpose, except that each instance would have multiple weighted labels and the rule or decision tree learner would have to be able to cope with weighted instances—as many can.

Another application of clustering is to fill in any values of the attributes that may be missing. For example, it is possible to make a statistical estimate of the value of unknown attributes of a particular instance, based on the class distribution for the instance itself and the values of the unknown attributes for other examples.

All the clustering methods we have examined make, at some level, a basic assumption of independence among the attributes. AutoClass does allow the user to specify in advance that two or more attributes are dependent and should be modeled with a joint probability distribution. (There are restrictions, however: Nominal attributes may vary jointly, as may numeric attributes, but not both together. Moreover, missing values for jointly varying attributes are not catered for.) It may be advantageous to preprocess a dataset to make the attributes more independent, using statistical techniques such as the principal components transform described in Section 7.3. Note that joint variation that is specific to particular classes will not be removed by such techniques; they only remove overall joint variation that runs across all classes.

Our description of how to modify k-means to find a good value of k by repeatedly splitting clusters and seeing whether the split is worthwhile follows the X-means algorithm of Moore and Pelleg (2000). However, instead of the MDL principle, they use a probabilistic scheme called the Bayes Information Criterion (Kass and Wasserman, 1995). Efficient agglomerative methods for hierarchical clustering were developed by Day and Edelsbrünner (1984), and the ideas are described in recent books (Duda et al., 2001; Hastie et al., 2009). The incremental clustering procedure, based on the merging and splitting operations, was introduced in systems called Cobweb for nominal attributes (Fisher, 1987) and Classit for numeric attributes (Gennari et al., 1990). Both are based on a measure of category utility that had been defined previously (Gluck and Corter, 1985). The AutoClass program is described by Cheeseman and Stutz (1995). Two implementations have been produced: the original research implementation, written in LISP, and a follow-up public implementation in C that is 10 or 20 times faster but somewhat more restricted—for example, only the normal-distribution model is implemented for numeric attributes. DensiTrees were developed by Bouckaert (2010).

A hierarchical clustering method called BIRCH (balanced iterative reducing and clustering using hierarchies) has been developed specifically for large multidimensional datasets, where it is necessary for efficient operation to minimize input–output costs (Zhang et al., 1996). It incrementally and dynamically clusters multidimensional metric data points, seeking the best clustering within given memory and time constraints. It typically finds a good clustering with a single scan of the data, which can then be improved by further scans.

6.9 SEMISUPERVISED LEARNING

When introducing the machine learning process in Chapter 2 (page 40), we drew a sharp distinction between supervised and unsupervised learning—classification and clustering. In this chapter we have studied a lot of techniques for both. Recently, researchers have begun to explore territory between the two, sometimes called *semisupervised learning*, in which the goal is classification but the input contains both unlabeled and labeled data. You can't do classification without labeled data, of course, because only the labels tell what the classes are. But it is sometimes attractive to augment a small amount of labeled data with a large pool of unlabeled data. It turns out that the unlabeled data can help you learn the classes. How can this be?

First, why would you want it? Many situations present huge volumes of raw data, but assigning classes is expensive because it requires human insight. Text mining provides some classic examples. Suppose you want to classify web pages into predefined groups. In an academic setting you might be interested in faculty pages, graduate student pages, course information pages, research group pages, and department pages. You can easily download thousands, or millions, of relevant pages from university web sites. But labeling the training data is a laborious manual process. Or suppose your job is to use machine learning to spot names in text, differentiating between personal names, company names, and place names. You can easily download megabytes, or gigabytes, of text, but making this into training data by picking out the names and categorizing them can only be done manually. Cataloging news articles, sorting electronic mail, learning users' reading interests—the applications are legion. Leaving text aside, suppose you want to learn to recognize certain famous people in television broadcast news. You can easily record hundreds or thousands of hours of newscasts, but again labeling is manual. In any of these scenarios it would be enormously attractive to be able to leverage a large pool of unlabeled data to obtain excellent performance from just a few labeled examples, particularly if you were the graduate student who had to do the labeling!

Clustering for Classification

How can unlabeled data be used to improve classification? Here's a simple idea. Use Naïve Bayes to learn classes from a small labeled dataset and then extend it to a large unlabeled dataset using the EM iterative clustering algorithm from the previous section. The procedure is this. First, train a classifier using the labeled data. Second, apply it to the unlabeled data to label it with class probabilities (the "expectation" step). Third, train a new classifier using the labels for all the data (the "maximization" step). Fourth, iterate until convergence. You could think of this as iterative clustering, where starting points and cluster labels are gleaned from the labeled data. The EM procedure guarantees finding model parameters that have equal or greater likelihood at each iteration. The key question, which can only be answered empirically, is whether these higher likelihood parameter estimates will improve classification accuracy.

Intuitively, this might work well. Consider document classification. Certain phrases are indicative of the classes. Some of them occur in labeled documents, whereas others occur only in unlabeled ones. There are, however, probably some documents that contain both, and the EM procedure uses these to generalize the learned model to use phrases that do not appear in the labeled dataset. For example, both *supervisor* and *Ph.D. topic* might indicate a graduate student's home page. Suppose only the former phrase occurs in the labeled documents. EM iteratively generalizes the model to correctly classify documents that contain just the latter.

This might work with any classifier and any iterative clustering algorithm. But it is basically a bootstrapping procedure, and you must take care to ensure that the feedback loop is a positive one. Using probabilities rather than hard decisions seems beneficial because it allows the procedure to converge slowly instead of jumping to conclusions that may be wrong. Naïve Bayes, together with the basic probabilistic EM procedure, is a particularly apt choice because the two share the same fundamental assumption: independence between attributes or, more precisely, conditional independence between attributes given the class.

Of course, the independence assumption is universally violated. Even our little example used the two-word phrase *Ph.D. topic*, whereas actual implementations would likely use individual words as attributes—and the example would have been far less compelling if we had substituted either of the single terms *Ph.D.* or *topic*. The phrase *Ph.D. students* is probably more indicative of faculty rather than graduate student home pages; the phrase *research topic* is probably less discriminating. It is the very fact that *Ph.D.* and *topic* are *not* conditionally independent given the class that makes the example work: It is their combination that characterizes graduate student pages.

Nevertheless, coupling Naïve Bayes and EM in this manner works well in the domain of document classification. In a particular classification task it attained the performance of a traditional learner using fewer than one-third of the labeled training instances, as well as five times as many unlabeled ones. This is a good tradeoff when labeled instances are expensive but unlabeled ones are virtually free. With a small number of labeled documents, classification accuracy can be improved dramatically by incorporating many unlabeled ones.

Two refinements to the procedure have been shown to improve performance. The first is motivated by experimental evidence showing that when there are many labeled documents the incorporation of unlabeled data may reduce rather than increase accuracy. Hand-labeled data is (or should be) inherently less noisy than automatically labeled data. The solution is to introduce a weighting parameter that reduces the contribution of the unlabeled data. This can be incorporated into the maximization step of EM by maximizing the weighted likelihood of the labeled and unlabeled instances. When the parameter is close to 0, unlabeled documents have little influence on the shape of EM's hill-climbing surface; when it is close to 1, the algorithm reverts to the original version in which the surface is equally affected by both kinds of document.

The second refinement is to allow each class to have several clusters. As explained in the previous section, the EM clustering algorithm assumes that the data is generated randomly from a mixture of different probability distributions, one per cluster. Until now, a one-to-one correspondence between mixture components and classes has been assumed. In many circumstances, including document classification, this is unrealistic because most documents address multiple topics. With several clusters per class, each labeled document is initially assigned randomly to each of its components in a probabilistic fashion. The maximization step of the EM algorithm remains as before, but the expectation step is modified not only to probabilistically label each example with the classes but to probabilistically assign it to the components within the class. The number of clusters per class is a parameter that depends on the domain and can be set by cross-validation.

Co-training

Another situation in which unlabeled data can improve classification performance is when there are two different and independent perspectives on the classification task. The classic example again involves documents, this time web documents, where the two perspectives are the *content* of a web page and the *links* to it from other pages. These two perspectives are well known to be both useful and different: Successful web search engines capitalize on them both using secret recipes. The text that labels a link to another web page gives a revealing clue as to what that page is about—perhaps even more revealing than the page's own content, particularly if the link is an independent one. Intuitively, a link labeled *my advisor* is strong evidence that the target page is a faculty member's home page.

The idea, called *co-training*, is this. Given a few labeled examples, first learn a different model for each perspective—in this case a content-based and a hyperlink-based model. Then use each one separately to label the unlabeled examples. For each model, select the example that it most confidently labels as positive and the one it most confidently labels as negative, and add these to the pool of labeled examples. Better yet, maintain the ratio of positive and negative examples in the labeled pool by choosing more of one kind than the other. In either case, repeat the whole procedure, training both models on the augmented pool of labeled examples, until the unlabeled pool is exhausted.

There is some experimental evidence, using Naïve Bayes throughout as the learner, that this bootstrapping procedure outperforms one that employs all the features from both perspectives to learn a single model from the labeled data. It relies on having two different views of an instance that are redundant but not completely correlated. Various domains have been proposed, from spotting celebrities in televised newscasts using video and audio separately to mobile robots with vision, sonar, and range sensors. The independence of the views reduces the likelihood of both hypotheses agreeing on an erroneous label.

EM and Co-training

On datasets with two feature sets that are truly independent, experiments have shown that co-training gives better results than using EM as described previously. Even better performance, however, can be achieved by combining the two into a modified version of co-training called *co-EM*. Co-training trains two classifiers representing different perspectives, A and B, and uses both to add new examples to the training pool by choosing whichever unlabeled examples they classify most positively or negatively. The new examples are few in number and deterministically labeled. Co-EM, on the other hand, trains classifier A on the labeled data and uses it to *probabilistically* label *all* the unlabeled data. Next it trains classifier B on both the labeled data and the unlabeled data with classifier A's tentative labels, and then it probabilistically relabels all the data for use by classifier A. The process iterates until the classifiers converge. This procedure seems to perform consistently better than co-training because it does not commit to the class labels that are generated by classifiers A and B but rather reestimates their probabilities at each iteration.

The range of applicability of co-EM, like co-training, is still limited by the requirement for multiple independent perspectives. But there is some experimental evidence to suggest that even when there is no natural split of features into independent perspectives, benefits can be achieved by manufacturing such a split and using co-training—or, better yet, co-EM—on the split data. This seems to work even when the split is made randomly; performance could surely be improved by engineering the split so that the feature sets are maximally independent. Why does this work? Researchers have hypothesized that these algorithms succeed in part because the split makes them more robust to the assumptions that their underlying classifiers make.

There is no particular reason to restrict the base classifier to Naïve Bayes. Support vector machines probably represent the most successful technology for text categorization today. However, for the EM iteration to work it is necessary that the classifier labels the data probabilistically; it must also be able to use probabilistically weighted examples for training. Support vector machines can easily be adapted to do both. We explained how to adapt learning algorithms to deal with weighted instances in Section 6.6, under Locally Weighted Linear Regression (page 258). One way of obtaining probability estimates from support vector machines is to fit a one-dimensional logistic model to the output, effectively performing logistic regression as described in Section 4.6 on the output. Excellent results have been reported for text classification using co-EM with the support vector machine (SVM) classifier. It outperforms other variants of SVM and seems quite robust to varying proportions of labeled and unlabeled data.

Discussion

Nigam et al. (2000) thoroughly explored the idea of clustering for classification, showing how the EM clustering algorithm can use unlabeled data to improve an initial classifier built by Naïve Bayes. The idea of co-training is older: Blum and Mitchell (1998) pioneered it and developed a theoretical model for the use of labeled and unlabeled data from different independent perspectives. Nigam and Ghani (2000) analyzed the effectiveness and applicability of co-training, relating it to the traditional use of standard expectation maximization to fill in missing values; they also introduced the co-EM algorithm. Up to this point, co-training and co-EM have been applied mainly to small two-class problems. Ghani (2002) used error-correcting output codes to address multiclass situations with many classes. Brefeld and Scheffer (2004) extended co-EM to use a support vector machine rather than Naïve Bayes.

6.10 MULTI-INSTANCE LEARNING

All the techniques described in this chapter so far are for the standard machine learning scenario where each example consists of a single instance. Before moving on to methods for transforming the input data in Chapter 7, we revisit the more complex setting of multi-instance learning, in which each example consists of a bag of instances instead. We describe approaches that are more advanced than the simple techniques discussed in Section 4.9. First, we consider how to convert multi-instance learning to single-instance learning by transforming the data. Then we discuss how to upgrade single-instance learning algorithms to the multi-instance case. Finally, we take a look at some methods that have no direct equivalent in single-instance learning.

Converting to Single-Instance Learning

Section 4.9 (page 142) presented some ways of applying standard single-instance learning algorithms to multi-instance data by aggregating the input or the output. Despite their simplicity, these techniques often work surprisingly well in practice. Nevertheless, there are clearly situations in which they will fail. Consider the method of aggregating the input by computing the minimum and maximum values of numeric attributes present in the bag and treating the result as a single instance. This will yield a huge loss of information because attributes are condensed to summary statistics individually and independently. Can a bag be converted to a single instance without discarding quite so much information?

The answer is yes, although the number of attributes that are present in the so-called "condensed" representation may increase substantially. The basic idea is to partition the instance space into regions and create one attribute per region in the single-instance representation. In the simplest case, attributes can be Boolean: If a bag has at least one instance in the region corresponding to a particular attribute the value of the attribute is set to true; otherwise, it is set to false. However, to preserve more information the condensed representation could instead contain numeric attributes, the values of which are counts that indicate how many instances of the bag lie in the corresponding region.

Regardless of the exact types of attributes that are generated, the main problem is to come up with a partitioning of the input space. A simple approach is to partition it into hypercubes of equal size. Unfortunately, this only works when the space has very few dimensions (i.e., attributes): The number of cubes required to achieve a given granularity grows exponentially with the dimension of the space. One way to make this approach more practical is to use unsupervised learning. Simply take all the instances from all the bags in the training data, discard their class labels, and form a big single-instance dataset; then process it with a clustering technique such as k-means. This will create regions corresponding to the different clusters (k regions, in the case of k-means). Then, for each bag, create one attribute per region in the condensed representation and use it as described previously.

Clustering is a rather heavy-handed way to infer a set of regions from the training data because it ignores information about class membership. An alternative approach that often yields better results is to partition the instance space using decision tree learning. Each leaf of a tree corresponds to one region of instance space. But how can a decision tree be learned when the class labels apply to entire bags of instances rather than to individual instances? The approach described under Aggregating the Output in Section 4.9 can be used: Take the bag's class label and attach it to each of its instances. This yields a single-instance dataset, ready for decision tree learning. Many of the class labels will be incorrect—the whole point of multi-instance learning is that it is not clear how bag-level labels relate to instance-level ones. However, these class labels are only being used to obtain a partition of instance space. The next step is to transform the multi-instance dataset into a single-instance one that represents how instances from each bag are distributed throughout the space. Then another single-instance learning method is applied—perhaps, again, decision tree learning—that determines the importance of individual attributes in the condensed representation which correspond to regions in the original space.

Using decision trees and clustering yields "hard" partition boundaries, where an instance either does or does not belong to a region. Such partitions can also be obtained using a distance function, combined with some reference points, by assigning instances to their closest reference point. This implicitly divides the space into regions, each corresponding to one reference point. (In fact, this is exactly what happens in k-means clustering: The cluster centers are the reference points.) But there is no fundamental reason to restrict attention to hard boundaries: We can make the region membership function "soft" by using distance—transformed into a similarity score—to compute attribute values in the condensed representation of a bag. All that is needed is some way of aggregating the similarity scores between each bag and reference point into a single value—for example, by taking the maximum similarity between each instance in that bag and the reference point.

In the simplest case, each instance in the training data can be used as a reference point. That creates a large number of attributes in the condensed representation, but it preserves much of the information from a bag of instances in its corresponding single-instance representation. This method has been successfully applied to multi-instance problems.

Regardless of how the approach is implemented, the basic idea is to convert a bag of instances into a single one by describing the distribution of instances from this bag in instance space. Alternatively, ordinary learning methods can be applied to multi-instance data by aggregating the output rather than the input. Section 4.9 described a simple way: Join instances of bags in the training data into a single dataset by attaching bag-level class labels to them, perhaps weighting instances to give each bag the same total weight. A single-instance classification model can then be built. At classification time, predictions for individual instances are combined—for example, by averaging predicted class probabilities.

Although this approach often works well in practice, attaching bag-level class labels to instances is simplistic. Generally, the assumption in multi-instance learning is that only some of the instances—perhaps just one—are responsible for the class label of the associated bag. How can the class labels be corrected to yield a more accurate representation of the true underlying situation? This is obviously a difficult problem; if it were solved, it would make little sense to investigate other approaches to multi-instance learning. One method that has been applied is iterative: Start by assigning each instance its bag's class label and learn a single-instance classification model; then replace the instances' class labels by the predicted labels of this single-instance classification model for these instances. Repeat the whole procedure until the class labels remain unchanged from one iteration to the next.

Some care is needed to obtain sensible results. For example, suppose every instance in a bag were to receive a class label that differs from the bag's label. Such a situation should be prevented by forcing the bag's label on at least one instance— for example, the one with the largest predicted probability for this class.

This iterative approach has been investigated for the original multi-instance scenario with two class values, where a bag is positive if and only if one of its instances is positive. In that case it makes sense to assume that all instances from negative bags are truly negative and modify only the class labels of instances from positive bags. At prediction time, bags are classified as positive if one of their instances is classified as positive.

Upgrading Learning Algorithms

Tackling multi-instance learning by modifying the input or output so that single-instance schemes can be applied is appealing because there is a large battery of such techniques that can then be used directly, without any modification. However, it may not be the most efficient approach. An alternative is to adapt the internals of a single-instance algorithm to the multi-instance setting. This can be done in a particularly elegant fashion if the algorithm in question only considers the data through application of a distance (or similarity) function, as with nearest-neighbor classifiers or support vector machines. These can be adapted by providing a distance (or similarity) function for multi-instance data that computes a score between two bags of instances.

In the case of kernel-based methods such as support vector machines, the similarity must be a proper kernel function that satisfies certain mathematical properties. One that has been used for multi-instance data is the so-called *set kernel*. Given a kernel function for pairs of instances that support vector machines can apply to single-instance data—for example, one of the kernel functions considered in Section 6.4—the set kernel sums it over all pairs of instances from the two bags being compared. This idea is generic and can be applied with any single-instance kernel function.

Nearest-neighbor learning has been adapted to multi-instance data by applying variants of the Hausdorff distance, which is defined for sets of points. Given two bags and a distance function between pairs of instances—for example, the Euclidean distance—the Hausdorff distance between the bags is the largest distance from any instance in one bag to its closest instance in the other bag. It can be made more robust to outliers by using the *n*th-largest distance rather than the maximum.

For learning algorithms that are not based on similarity scores, more work is required to upgrade them to multi-instance data. There are multi-instance algorithms for rule learning and for decision tree learning, but we will not describe them here. Adapting algorithms to the multi-instance case is more straightforward if the algorithm concerned is essentially a numerical optimization strategy that is applied to the parameters of some function by minimizing a loss function on the training data. Logistic regression (Section 4.6) and multilayer perceptrons (Section 6.4) fall into this category; both have been adapted to multi-instance learning by augmenting them with a function that aggregates instance-level predictions. The so-called "soft maximum" is a differentiable function that is suitable for this purpose: It aggregates instance-level predictions by taking their (soft) maximum as the bag-level prediction.

Dedicated Multi-Instance Methods

Some multi-instance learning schemes are not based directly on single-instance algorithms. Here is an early technique that was specifically developed for the drug activity prediction problem mentioned in Section 2.2 (page 49), in which instances are conformations of a molecule and a molecule (i.e., a bag) is considered positive if and only if it has at least one active conformation. The basic idea is to learn a single hyperrectangle that contains at least one instance from each positive bag in the training data and no instances from any negative bags. Such a rectangle encloses an area of instance space where all positive bags overlap, but it contains no negative instances—an area that is common to all active molecules but not represented in any inactive ones. The particular drug activity data originally considered was high-dimensional, with 166 attributes describing each instance. In such a case it is computationally difficult to find a suitable hyperrectangle. Consequently, a heuristic approach was developed that is tuned to this particular problem.

Other geometric shapes can be used instead of hyperrectangles. Indeed, the same basic idea has been applied using hyperspheres (balls). Training instances are treated as potential ball centers. For each one, a radius is found that yields the smallest number of errors for the bags in the training data. The original multi-instance assumption is used to make predictions: A bag is classified as positive if and only if it has at least one instance inside the ball. A single ball is generally not powerful enough to yield good classification performance. However, this method is not intended as a standalone algorithm. Rather, it is advocated as a "weak" learner to be used in conjunction with boosting algorithms (see Section 8.4) to obtain a powerful ensemble classifier—an ensemble of balls.

The dedicated multi-instance methods discussed so far have hard decision boundaries: An instance either falls inside or outside a ball or hyperrectangle. Other multi-instance algorithms use soft concept descriptions couched in terms of probability theory. The so-called *diverse-density* method is a classic example, again designed with the original multi-instance assumption in mind. Its basic and most commonly used form learns a single reference point in instance space. The probability that an instance is positive is computed from its distance to this point: It is 1 if the instance coincides with the reference point and decreases with increasing distance from this point, usually based on a bell-shaped function.

The probability that a bag is positive is obtained by combining the individual probabilities of the instances it contains, generally using the "noisy-OR" function. This is a probabilistic version of the logical OR. If all instance-level probabilities are 0, the noisy-OR value—and thus the bag-level probability—is 0; if at least one instance-level probability is 1, the value is 1; otherwise, the value falls somewhere in between.

The diverse density is defined as the probability of the class labels of the bags in the training data, computed based on this probabilistic model. It is maximized when the reference point is located in an area where positive bags overlap and no negative bags are present, just as for the two geometric methods discussed previously. A numerical optimization routine such as gradient ascent can be used to find the reference point that maximizes the diverse-density measure. In addition to the location of the reference point, implementations of diverse density also optimize the scale of the distance function in each dimension because generally not all attributes are equally important. This can improve predictive performance significantly.

Discussion

Condensing the input data by aggregating information into simple summary statistics is a well-known technique in multirelational learning, used in the RELAGGS system by Krogel and Wrobel (2002); multi-instance learning can be viewed as a special case of this more general setting (de Raedt, 2008). The idea of replacing simple summary statistics by region-based attributes, derived from partitioning the instance space, was explored by Weidmann et al. (2003) and Zhou and Zhang (2007). Using reference points to condense bags was investigated by Chen et al. (2006) and evaluated in a broader context by Foulds and Frank (2008). Andrews et al. (2003) proposed manipulating the class labels of individual instances using an iterative learning process for learning support vector machine classifiers based on the original multi-instance assumption.

Nearest-neighbor learning based on variants of the Hausdorff distance was investigated by Wang and Zucker (2000). Gärtner et al. (2002) experimented with the set kernel to learn support vector machine classifiers for multi-instance data. Multi-instance algorithms for rule and decision tree learning, which are not covered here, have been described by Chevaleyre and Zucker (2001) and Blockeel et al. (2005). Logistic regression has been adapted for multi-instance learning by Xu and Frank (2004) and Ray and Craven (2005); multilayer perceptrons have been adapted by Ramon and de Raedt (2000).

Hyperrectangles and spheres were considered as concept descriptions for multi-instance learning by Dietterich et al. (1997) and Auer and Ortner (2004), respectively. The diverse-density method is the subject of Maron's (1998) Ph.D. thesis, and is also described in Maron and Lozano-Peréz (1997).

The multi-instance literature makes many different assumptions regarding the type of concept to be learned, defining, for example, how the bag-level and instance-level class labels are connected, starting with the original assumption that a bag is labeled positive if and only if one of its instances is positive. A review of assumptions in multi-instance learning can be found in Foulds and Frank (2010).

6.11 WEKA IMPLEMENTATIONS

For classifiers, see Section 11.4 and Table 11.5. For clustering methods, see Section 11.6 and Table 11.7.

- Decision trees:
    - *J48* (implementation of C4.5)
    - *SimpleCart* (minimum cost-complexity pruning à la CART)
    - *REPTree* (reduced-error pruning)
- Classification rules:
    - *JRip* (RIPPER rule learner)
    - *Part* (rules from partial decision trees)
    - *Ridor* (ripple-down rule learner)
- Association rules (see Section 11.7 and Table 11.8):
    - *FPGrowth* (frequent-pattern trees)
    - *GeneralizedSequentialPatterns* (find large item trees in sequential data)
- Linear models and extensions:
    - *SMO* and variants for learning support vector machines
    - *LibSVM* (uses third-party *libsvm* library)
    - *MultilayerPerceptron*
    - *RBFNetwork* (radial-basis function network)
    - *SPegasos* (SVM using stochastic gradient descent)

- Instance-based learning:
  - *IBk* (k-nearest neighbour classifier)
  - *KStar* (generalized distance functions)
  - *NNge* (rectangular generalizations)
- Numeric prediction:
  - *M5P* (model trees)
  - *M5Rules* (rules from model trees)
  - *LWL* (locally weighted learning)
- Bayesian networks:
  - *BayesNet*
  - *AODE, WAODE* (averaged one-dependence estimator)
- Clustering:
  - *XMeans*
  - *Cobweb* (includes Classit)
  - *EM*
- Multi-instance learning:
  - *MISVM* (iterative method for learning SVM by relabeling instances)
  - *MISMO* (SVM with multi-instance kernel)
  - *CitationKNN* (nearest-neighbor method with Hausdorff distance)
  - *MILR* (logistic regression for multi-instance data)
  - *MIOptimalBall* (learning balls for multi-instance classification)
  - *MIDD* (the diverse-density method using the noisy-OR function)

Data Transformations

In Chapter 6 we examined a vast array of machine learning methods: decision trees, classification and association rules, linear models, instance-based schemes, numeric prediction techniques, Bayesian networks, clustering algorithms, and semisupervised and multi-instance learning. All are sound, robust techniques that are eminently applicable to practical data mining problems.

But successful data mining involves far more than selecting a learning algorithm and running it over your data. For one thing, many learning schemes have various parameters, and suitable values must be chosen for these. In most cases, results can be improved markedly by a suitable choice of parameter values, and the appropriate choice depends on the data at hand. For example, decision trees can be pruned or unpruned, and in the former case a pruning parameter may have to be chosen. In the k-nearest-neighbor method of instance-based learning, a value for k will have to be chosen. More generally, the learning scheme itself will have to be chosen from the range of schemes that are available. In all cases, the right choices depend on the data itself.

It is tempting to try out several learning schemes and several parameter values on your data, and see which works best. But be careful! The best choice is not necessarily the one that performs best on the training data. We have repeatedly cautioned about the problem of overfitting, where a learned model is too closely tied to the particular training data from which it was built. It is incorrect to assume that performance on the training data faithfully represents the level of performance that can be expected on the fresh data to which the learned model will be applied in practice.

Fortunately, we have already encountered the solution to this problem in Chapter 5. There are two good methods for estimating the expected true performance of a learning scheme: the use of a large dataset that is quite separate from the training data, in the case of plentiful data, and cross-validation (see Section 5.3), if data is scarce. In the latter case, a single tenfold cross-validation is typically used in practice, although to obtain a more reliable estimate the entire procedure should be repeated 10 times. Once suitable parameters have been chosen for the learning scheme, use the whole training set—all the available training instances—to produce the final learned model that is to be applied to fresh data.

Note that the performance obtained with the chosen parameter value during the tuning process is *not* a reliable estimate of the final model's performance, because the final model potentially overfits the data that was used for tuning. To ascertain how well it will perform, you need yet another large dataset that is quite separate from any data used during learning and tuning. The same is true for cross-validation: You need an "inner" cross-validation for parameter tuning and an "outer" cross-validation for error estimation. With tenfold cross-validation, this involves running the learning scheme 100 times. To summarize: When assessing the performance of a learning scheme, any parameter tuning that goes on should be treated as though it were an integral part of the training process.

There are other important processes that can materially improve success when applying machine learning techniques to practical data mining problems, and these are the subject of this chapter. They constitute a kind of data engineering—engineering the input data into a form suitable for the learning scheme chosen and engineering the output to make it more effective. You can look on them as a bag of tricks that you can apply to practical data mining problems to enhance the chance of success. Sometimes they work; other times they don't—and at the present state of the art, it's hard to say in advance whether they will or not. In an area such as this, where trial and error is the most reliable guide, it is particularly important to be resourceful and have an understanding of what the tricks are.

In this chapter we examine six different ways in which the input can be massaged to make it more amenable for learning methods: attribute selection, attribute discretization, data projections, sampling, data cleansing, and converting multiclass problems to two-class ones. Consider the first, attribute selection. In many practical situations there are far too many attributes for learning schemes to handle, and some of them—perhaps the overwhelming majority—are clearly irrelevant or redundant. Consequently, the data must be preprocessed to select a subset of the attributes to use in learning. Of course, many learning schemes themselves try to select attributes appropriately and ignore irrelevant or redundant ones, but in practice their performance can frequently be improved by preselection. For example, experiments show that adding useless attributes causes the performance of learning schemes such as decision trees and rules, linear regression, instance-based learners, and clustering methods to deteriorate.

Discretization of numeric attributes is absolutely essential if the task involves numeric attributes but the chosen learning scheme can only handle categorical ones. Even schemes that can handle numeric attributes often produce better results, or work faster, if the attributes are prediscretized. The converse situation, in which categorical attributes must be represented numerically, also occurs (although less often), and we describe techniques for this case, too.

Data projection covers a variety of techniques. One transformation, which we have encountered before when looking at relational data in Chapter 2 and support vector machines in Chapter 6, is to add new, synthetic attributes whose purpose is to present existing information in a form that is suitable for the machine learning scheme to pick up on. More general techniques that do not depend so intimately on the semantics of the particular data mining problem at hand include principal components analysis and random projections. We also cover partial least-squares regression as a data projection technique for regression problems.

Sampling the input is an important step in many practical data mining applications, and is often the only way in which really large-scale problems can be handled. Although it is fairly simple, we include a brief section on techniques of sampling, including a way of incrementally producing a random sample of a given size when the total size of the dataset is not known in advance.

Unclean data plagues data mining. We emphasized in Chapter 2 the necessity of getting to know your data: understanding the meaning of all the different attributes, the conventions used in coding them, the significance of missing values and duplicate data, measurement noise, typographical errors, and the presence of systematic errors—even deliberate ones. Various simple visualizations often help with this task. There are also automatic methods of cleansing data, of detecting outliers, and of spotting anomalies, which we describe, including a class of techniques referred to as *one-class learning* in which only a single class of instances is available at training time.

Finally, we examine techniques for refining the output of learning schemes that estimate class probabilities by recalibrating the estimates that they make. This is primarily of importance when accurate probabilities are required, as in cost-sensitive classification, though it can also improve classification performance.

7.1 ATTRIBUTE SELECTION

Most machine learning algorithms are designed to learn which are the most appropriate attributes to use for making their decisions. For example, decision tree methods choose the most promising attribute to split on at each point and should—in theory—never select irrelevant or unhelpful attributes. Having more features should surely—in theory—result in more discriminating power, never less. "What's the difference between theory and practice?" an old question asks. The answer goes, "There is no difference between theory and practice—in theory. But in practice, there is." Here there is too: In practice, adding irrelevant or distracting attributes to a dataset often confuses machine learning systems.

Experiments with a decision tree learner (C4.5) have shown that adding to standard datasets a random binary attribute generated by tossing an unbiased coin impacts classification performance, causing it to deteriorate (typically by 5 to 10% in the situations tested). This happens because at some point in the trees that are learned, the irrelevant attribute is invariably chosen to branch on, causing random errors when test data is processed. How can this be when decision tree learners are cleverly designed to choose the best attribute for splitting at each node? The reason is subtle. As you proceed further down the tree, less and less data is available to help make the selection decision. At some point, with little data, the random attribute will look good just by chance. Because the number of nodes at each level increases exponentially with depth, the chance of the rogue attribute looking good somewhere along the frontier multiplies up as the tree deepens. The real problem is that you inevitably reach depths at which only a small amount of data is available for attribute selection. If the dataset were bigger it wouldn't necessarily help—you'd probably just go deeper.

Divide-and-conquer tree learners and separate-and-conquer rule learners both suffer from this effect because they inexorably reduce the amount of data on which they base judgments. Instance-based learners are very susceptible to irrelevant attributes because they always work in local neighborhoods, taking just a few training instances into account for each decision. Indeed, it has been shown that the number of training instances needed to produce a predetermined level of performance for instance-based learning increases exponentially with the number of irrelevant attributes present. Naïve Bayes, by contrast, does not fragment the instance space and robustly ignores irrelevant attributes. It assumes by design that all attributes are conditionally independent of one another, an assumption that is just right for random "distracter" attributes. But through this very same assumption, Naïve Bayes pays a heavy price in other ways because its operation is damaged by adding redundant attributes.

The fact that irrelevant distracters degrade the performance of state-of-the-art decision tree and rule learners is, at first, surprising. Even more surprising is that *relevant* attributes can also be harmful. For example, suppose that in a two-class dataset a new attribute was added that had the same value as the class to be predicted most of the time (65%) and the opposite value the rest of the time, randomly distributed among the instances. Experiments with standard datasets have shown that this can cause classification accuracy to deteriorate (by 1 to 5% in the situations tested). The problem is that the new attribute is (naturally) chosen for splitting high up in the tree. This has the effect of fragmenting the set of instances available at the nodes below so that other choices are based on sparser data.

Because of the negative effect of irrelevant attributes on most machine learning schemes, it is common to precede learning with an attribute selection stage that strives to eliminate all but the most relevant attributes. The best way to select relevant attributes is manually, based on a deep understanding of the learning problem and what the attributes actually mean. However, automatic methods can also be useful. Reducing the dimensionality of the data by deleting unsuitable attributes improves the performance of learning algorithms. It also speeds them up, although this may be outweighed by the computation involved in attribute selection. More important, dimensionality reduction yields a more compact, more easily interpretable representation of the target concept, focusing the user's attention on the most relevant variables.

Scheme-Independent Selection

When selecting a good attribute subset, there are two fundamentally different approaches. One is to make an independent assessment based on general characteristics of the data; the other is to evaluate the subset using the machine learning algorithm that will ultimately be employed for learning. The first is called the *filter* method because the attribute set is filtered to produce the most promising subset before learning commences. The second is called the *wrapper* method because the learning algorithm is wrapped into the selection procedure. Making an independent assessment of an attribute subset would be easy if there were a good way of determining when an attribute was relevant to choosing the class. However, there is no universally accepted measure of relevance, although several different ones have been proposed.

One simple scheme-independent method of attribute selection is to use just enough attributes to divide up the instance space in a way that separates all the training instances. For example, if just one or two attributes are used, there will generally be several instances that have the same combination of attribute values. At the other extreme, the full set of attributes will likely distinguish the instances uniquely so that no two instances have the same values for all attributes. (This will not necessarily be the case, however; datasets sometimes contain instances with the same attribute values but different classes.) It makes intuitive sense to select the smallest attribute subset that serves to distinguish all instances uniquely. This can easily be found using an exhaustive search, although at considerable computational expense. Unfortunately, this strong bias toward consistency of the attribute set on the training data is statistically unwarranted and can lead to overfitting—the algorithm may go to unnecessary lengths to repair an inconsistency that was in fact merely caused by noise.

Machine learning algorithms can be used for attribute selection. For instance, you might first apply a decision tree algorithm to the full dataset and then select only those attributes that are actually used in the tree. While this selection would have no effect at all if the second stage merely built another tree, it will have an effect on a different learning algorithm. For example, the nearest-neighbor algorithm is notoriously susceptible to irrelevant attributes, and its performance can be improved by using a decision tree builder as a filter for attribute selection first. The resulting nearest-neighbor scheme can also perform better than the decision tree algorithm used for filtering.

As another example, the simple 1R scheme described in Chapter 4 has been used to select the attributes for a decision tree learner by evaluating the effect of branching on different attributes (although an error-based method such as 1R may not be the optimal choice for ranking attributes, as we will see later when covering the related problem of supervised discretization). Often the decision tree performs just as well when only the two or three top attributes are used for its construction—and it is much easier to understand. In this approach, the user determines how many attributes to use for building the decision tree.

Another possibility is to use an algorithm that builds a linear model—for example, a linear support vector machine—and ranks the attributes based on the size of the coefficients. A more sophisticated variant applies the learning algorithm repeatedly. It builds a model, ranks the attributes based on the coefficients, removes the lowest-ranked one, and repeats the process until all attributes have been removed. This method of *recursive feature elimination* has been found to yield better results on certain datasets (e.g., when identifying important genes for cancer classification) than simply ranking attributes based on a single model. With both methods it is important to ensure that the attributes are measured on the same scale; otherwise, the coefficients are not comparable. Note that these techniques just produce a ranking; another method must be used to determine the appropriate number of attributes to use.

Attributes can be selected using instance-based learning methods too. You could sample instances randomly from the training set and check neighboring records of the same and different classes—"near hits" and "near misses." If a near hit has a different value for a certain attribute, that attribute appears to be irrelevant and its weight should be decreased. On the other hand, if a near miss has a different value, the attribute appears to be relevant and its weight should be increased. Of course, this is the standard kind of procedure used for attribute weighting for instance-based learning, described in Section 6.5. After repeating this operation many times, selection takes place: Only attributes with positive weights are chosen. As in the standard incremental formulation of instance-based learning, different results will be obtained each time the process is repeated, because of the different ordering of examples. This can be avoided by using all training instances and taking into account all near hits and near misses of each.

A more serious disadvantage is that the method will not detect an attribute that is redundant because it is correlated with another attribute. In the extreme case, two identical attributes would be treated in the same way, either both selected or both rejected. A modification has been suggested that appears to go some way toward addressing this issue by taking the current attribute weights into account when computing the nearest hits and misses.

Another way of eliminating redundant attributes as well as irrelevant ones is to select a subset of attributes that individually correlate well with the class but have little intercorrelation. The correlation between two nominal attributes A and B can be measured using the *symmetric uncertainty*:

$$U(A, B) = 2\frac{H(A) + H(B) - H(A, B)}{H(A) + H(B)}$$

where H is the entropy function described in Section 4.3. The entropies are based on the probability associated with each attribute value; $H(A, B)$, the joint entropy of A and B, is calculated from the joint probabilities of all combinations of values of A and B.

The symmetric uncertainty always lies between 0 and 1. Correlation-based feature selection determines the goodness of a set of attributes using

$$\sum_{j} U(A_j, C) \Big/ \sqrt{\sum_{i} \sum_{j} U(A_i, A_j)}$$

where C is the class attribute and the indices i and j range over all attributes in the set. If all m attributes in the subset correlate perfectly with the class and with one another, the numerator becomes m and the denominator $\sqrt{m^2}$, which is also m. Thus, the measure is 1, which turns out to be the maximum value it can attain (the minimum is 0). Clearly, this is not ideal, because we want to avoid redundant attributes. However, any subset of this set will also have value 1. When using this criterion to search for a good subset of attributes, it makes sense to break ties in favor of the smallest subset.

Searching the Attribute Space

Most methods for attribute selection involve searching the space of attributes for the subset that is most likely to predict the class best. Figure 7.1 illustrates the attribute space for the—by now all-too-familiar—weather dataset. The number of possible attribute subsets increases exponentially with the number of attributes, making an exhaustive search impractical on all but the simplest problems.

Typically, the space is searched greedily in one of two directions: top to bottom and bottom to top in the figure. At each stage, a local change is made to the current attribute subset by either adding or deleting a single attribute. The downward direction, where you start with no attributes and add them one at a time, is called *forward selection*. The upward one, where you start with the full set and delete attributes one at a time, is *backward elimination*.

In forward selection, each attribute that is not already in the current subset is tentatively added to it, and the resulting set of attributes is evaluated—using, for example, cross-validation, as described in the following section. This evaluation produces a numeric measure of the expected performance of the subset. The effect of adding each attribute in turn is quantified by this measure, the best one is chosen,

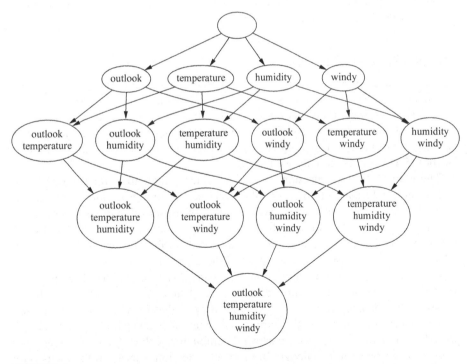

FIGURE 7.1

Attribute space for the weather dataset.

and the procedure continues. However, if no attribute produces an improvement when added to the current subset, the search ends. This is a standard greedy search procedure and guarantees to find a locally—but not necessarily globally—optimal set of attributes.

Backward elimination operates in an entirely analogous fashion. In both cases a slight bias is often introduced toward smaller attribute sets. This can be done for forward selection by insisting that if the search is to continue, the evaluation measure must not only increase, but must increase by at least a small predetermined quantity. A similar modification works for backward elimination.

More sophisticated search schemes exist. Forward selection and backward elimination can be combined into a bidirectional search; again, one can begin either with all the attributes or with none of them. Best-first search is a method that does not just terminate when the performance starts to drop but keeps a list of all attribute subsets evaluated so far, sorted in order of the performance measure, so that it can revisit an earlier configuration instead. Given enough time it will explore the entire space, unless this is prevented by some kind of stopping criterion. Beam search is similar but truncates its list of attribute subsets at each stage so that it only contains a fixed number—the beam width—of most promising candidates. Genetic algorithm search procedures are loosely based on the principle of natural selection: They "evolve" good feature subsets by using random perturbations of a current list of candidate subsets and combining them based on performance.

Scheme-Specific Selection

The performance of an attribute subset with scheme-specific selection is measured in terms of the learning scheme's classification performance using just those attributes. Given a subset of attributes, accuracy is estimated using the normal procedure of cross-validation described in Section 5.3. Of course, other evaluation methods such as performance on a holdout set (Section 5.3) or the bootstrap estimator (Section 5.4) could be equally well used.

The entire attribute selection process is rather computation intensive. If each evaluation involves a tenfold cross-validation, the learning procedure must be executed 10 times. With m attributes, the heuristic forward selection or backward elimination multiplies evaluation time by a factor proportional to m^2 in the worst case. For more sophisticated searches, the penalty will be far greater, up to 2^m for an exhaustive algorithm that examines each of the 2^m possible subsets.

Good results have been demonstrated on many datasets. In general terms, backward elimination produces larger attribute sets than forward selection but better classification accuracy in some cases. The reason is that the performance measure is only an estimate, and a single optimistic estimate will cause both of these search procedures to halt prematurely—backward elimination with too many attributes and forward selection with not enough. But forward selection is useful if the focus is on understanding the decision structures involved, because it often reduces the number of attributes with only a small effect on classification accuracy. Experience seems to show that more sophisticated search techniques are not generally justified, although they can produce much better results in certain cases.

One way to accelerate the search process is to stop evaluating a subset of attributes as soon as it becomes apparent that it is unlikely to lead to higher accuracy than another candidate subset. This is a job for a paired statistical significance test, performed between the classifier based on this subset and all the other candidate classifiers based on other subsets. The performance difference between two classifiers on a particular test instance can be −1, 0, or 1 depending on, respectively, whether the first classifier is worse than, the same as, or better than the second on that instance. A paired t-test (described in Section 5.5) can be applied to these figures over the entire test set, effectively treating the results for each instance as an independent estimate of the difference in performance. Then the cross-validation for a classifier can be prematurely terminated as soon as it turns out to be significantly worse than another, which, of course, may never happen. We might want to discard classifiers more aggressively by modifying the t-test to compute the probability that one classifier is better than another classifier by at least a small user-specified threshold. If this probability becomes very small, we can discard the former classifier on the basis that it is very unlikely to perform substantially better than the latter.

This methodology is called *race search* and can be implemented with different underlying search strategies. When it is used with forward selection, we race all possible single-attribute additions simultaneously and drop those that do not perform well enough. In backward elimination, we race all single-attribute deletions. *Schemata search* is a more complicated method specifically designed for racing; it runs an iterative series of races that each determine whether or not a particular attribute should be included. The other attributes for this race are included or excluded randomly at each point in the evaluation. As soon as one race has a clear winner, the next iteration of races begins, using the winner as the starting point. Another search strategy is to rank the attributes first using, for example, their information gain (assuming they are discrete), and then race the ranking. In this case the race includes no attributes, the top-ranked attribute, the top two attributes, the top three, and so on.

A simple method for accelerating a scheme-specific search is to preselect a given number of attributes by ranking them first using a criterion like the information gain and discarding the rest before applying scheme-specific selection. This has been found to work surprisingly well on high-dimensional datasets such as gene expression and text categorization data, where only a couple of hundred of attributes are used instead of several thousands. In the case of forward selection, a slightly more sophisticated variant is to restrict the number of attributes available for expanding the current attribute subset to a fixed-sized subset chosen from the ranked list of attributes—creating a sliding window of attribute choices—rather than making all (unused) attributes available for consideration in each step of the search process.

Whatever way you do it, scheme-specific attribute selection by no means yields a uniform improvement in performance. Because of the complexity of the process, which is greatly increased by the feedback effect of including a target machine learning algorithm in the attribution selection loop, it is quite hard to predict the conditions under which it will turn out to be worthwhile. As in many machine learning situations, trial and error using your own particular source of data is the final arbiter.

There is one type of classifier for which scheme-specific attribute selection is an essential part of the learning process: the decision table. As mentioned in Section 3.1, the entire problem of learning decision tables consists of selecting the right attributes to be included. Usually this is done by measuring the table's cross-validation performance for different subsets of attributes and choosing the best-performing subset. Fortunately, leave-one-out cross-validation is very cheap for this kind of classifier. Obtaining the cross-validation error from a decision table derived from the training data is just a matter of manipulating the class counts associated with each of the table's entries, because the table's structure doesn't change when instances are added or deleted. The attribute space is generally searched by best-first search because this strategy is less likely to get stuck in a local maximum than others, such as forward selection.

Let's end our discussion with a success story. Naïve Bayes is a learning method for which a simple scheme-specific attribute selection approach has shown good results. Although this method deals well with random attributes, it has the potential to be misled when there are dependencies among attributes, and particularly when redundant ones are added. However, good results have been reported using the forward selection algorithm—which is better able to detect when a redundant attribute is about to be added than the backward elimination approach—in conjunction with a very simple, almost "naïve," metric that determines the quality of an attribute subset to be simply the performance of the learned algorithm on the *training* set. As was emphasized in Chapter 5, training set performance is certainly not a reliable indicator of test set performance. Nevertheless, experiments show that this simple modification to Naïve Bayes markedly improves its performance on those standard datasets for which it does not do so well as tree- or rule-based classifiers, and does not have any negative effect on results on datasets on which Naïve Bayes already does well. *Selective Naïve Bayes*, as this learning method is called, is a viable machine learning technique that performs reliably and well in practice.

7.2 DISCRETIZING NUMERIC ATTRIBUTES

Some classification and clustering algorithms deal with nominal attributes only and cannot handle ones measured on a numeric scale. To use them on general datasets, numeric attributes must first be "discretized" into a small number of distinct ranges. Even learning algorithms that handle numeric attributes sometimes process them in ways that are not altogether satisfactory. Statistical clustering methods often assume that numeric attributes have a normal distribution—often not a very plausible assumption in practice—and the standard extension of the Naïve Bayes classifier for numeric attributes adopts the same assumption. Although most decision tree and decision rule learners can handle numeric attributes, some implementations work much more slowly when numeric attributes are present because they repeatedly sort the attribute values. For all these reasons the question arises, what is a good way to discretize numeric attributes into ranges before any learning takes place?

We have already encountered some methods for discretizing numeric attributes. The 1R learning scheme described in Chapter 4 uses a simple but effective technique: Sort the instances by the attribute's value and assign the value into ranges at the points that the class value changes—except that a certain minimum number of instances in the majority class (six) must lie in each of the ranges, which means that any given range may include a mixture of class values. This is a "global" method of discretization that is applied to all continuous attributes before learning starts.

Decision tree learners, on the other hand, deal with numeric attributes on a local basis, examining attributes at each node of the tree when it is being constructed to see whether they are worth branching on, and only at that point deciding on the best place to split continuous attributes. Although the tree-building method we examined in Chapter 6 only considers binary splits of continuous attributes, one can imagine a full discretization taking place at that point, yielding a multiway split on a numeric attribute. The pros and cons of the local versus global approach are clear. Local discretization is tailored to the actual context provided by each tree node, and will produce different discretizations of the same attribute at different places in the tree if that seems appropriate. However, its decisions are based on less data as tree depth increases, which compromises their reliability. If trees are developed all the way out to single-class leaves before being pruned back, as with the normal technique of backward pruning, it is clear that many discretization decisions will be based on data that is grossly inadequate.

When using global discretization before applying a learning scheme, there are two possible ways of presenting the discretized data to the learner. The most obvious is to treat discretized attributes like nominal ones: Each discretization interval is represented by one value of the nominal attribute. However, because a discretized attribute is derived from a numeric one, its values are ordered, and treating it as nominal discards this potentially valuable ordering information. Of course, if a learning scheme can handle ordered attributes directly, the solution is obvious: Each discretized attribute is declared to be of type "ordered."

If the learning scheme cannot handle ordered attributes, there is still a simple way of enabling it to exploit the ordering information: Transform each discretized attribute into a set of binary attributes before the learning scheme is applied. If the discretized attribute has k values, it is transformed into $k - 1$ binary attributes. If the original attribute's value is i for a particular instance, the first $i - 1$ of these new attributes are set to *false* and the remainder are set to *true*. In other words, the $(i - 1)$th binary attribute represents whether the discretized attribute is less than i. If a decision tree learner splits on this attribute, it implicitly utilizes the ordering information it encodes. Note that this transformation is independent of the particular discretization method being applied: It is simply a way of coding an ordered attribute using a set of binary attributes.

Unsupervised Discretization

There are two basic approaches to the problem of discretization. One is to quantize each attribute in the absence of any knowledge of the classes of the instances in the training set—so-called *unsupervised* discretization. The other is to take the classes into account when discretizing—*supervised* discretization. The former is the only possibility when dealing with clustering problems where the classes are unknown or nonexistent.

The obvious way of discretizing a numeric attribute is to divide its range into a predetermined number of equal intervals: a fixed, data-independent yardstick. This is frequently done at the time when data is collected. But, like any unsupervised discretization method, it runs the risk of destroying distinctions that would have turned out to be useful in the learning process by using gradations that are too coarse or, that by unfortunate choices of boundary, needlessly lump together many instances of different classes.

Equal-width binning often distributes instances very unevenly: Some bins contain many instances while others contain none. This can seriously impair the ability of the attribute to help build good decision structures. It is often better to allow the intervals to be of different sizes, choosing them so that the same number of training examples fall into each one. This method, called *equal-frequency binning*, divides the attribute's range into a predetermined number of bins based on the distribution of examples along that axis—sometimes called *histogram equalization* because if you take a histogram of the contents of the resulting bins it will be completely flat. If you view the number of bins as a resource, this method makes the best use of it.

However, equal-frequency binning is still oblivious to the instances' classes, and this can cause bad boundaries. For example, if all instances in a bin have one class, and all instances in the next higher bin have another except for the first, which has the original class, surely it makes sense to respect the class divisions and include that first instance in the previous bin, sacrificing the equal-frequency property for the sake of homogeneity. Supervised discretization—taking classes into account during the process—certainly has advantages. Nevertheless, it has been found that equal-frequency binning can yield excellent results, at least in conjunction with the Naïve Bayes learning scheme, when the number of bins is chosen in a data-dependent fashion by setting it to the square root of the number of instances. This method is called *proportional k-interval discretization*.

Entropy-Based Discretization

Because the criterion used for splitting a numeric attribute during the formation of a decision tree works well in practice, it seems a good idea to extend it to more general discretization by recursively splitting intervals until it is time to stop. In Chapter 6 we saw how to sort the instances by the attribute's value and consider, for each possible splitting point, the information gain of the resulting split. To discretize the attribute, once the first split is determined, the splitting process can be repeated in the upper and lower parts of the range, and so on, recursively.

To see this working in practice, we revisit the example given in Section 6.1 for discretizing the temperature attribute of the weather data, of which the values are as follows:

64	65	68	69	70	71	72	75	80	81	83	85
yes	no	yes	yes	yes	no	no	yes	no	yes	yes	no
						yes	yes				

(Repeated values have been collapsed together.) The information gain for each of the 11 possible positions for the breakpoint is calculated in the usual way. For example, the information value of the test *temperature* < 71.5, which splits the range into four *yes* and two *no* versus five *yes* and three *no*, is

$$\text{info}([4, 2], [5, 3]) = (6/14) \times \text{info}([4, 2]) + (8/14) \times \text{info}([5, 3]) = 0.939 \text{ bits}$$

This represents the amount of information required to specify the individual values of *yes* and *no* given the split. We seek a discretization that makes the subintervals as pure as possible; thus, we choose to split at the point where the information value is smallest. (This is the same as splitting where the information *gain*, defined as the difference between the information value without the split and that with the split, is largest.) As before, we place numeric thresholds halfway between the values that delimit the boundaries of a concept.

The graph labeled A in Figure 7.2 shows the information values at each possible cut point at this first stage. The cleanest division—the smallest information value—is at a temperature of 84 (0.827 bits), which separates off just the very final value, a *no* instance, from the preceding list. The instance classes are written below the horizontal axis to make interpretation easier. Invoking the algorithm again on the lower range of temperatures, from 64 to 83, yields the graph labeled B. This has a minimum at 80.5 (0.800 bits), which splits off the next two values, both *yes* instances. Again invoking the algorithm on the lower range, now from 64 to 80, produces the graph labeled C (shown dotted to help distinguish it from the others). The minimum is at 77.5 (0.801 bits), splitting off another *no* instance. Graph D has a minimum at 73.5 (0.764 bits), splitting off two *yes* instances. Graph E (again dashed, purely to make it more easily visible), for the temperature range 64 to 72, has a minimum at 70.5 (0.796 bits), which splits off two *no* and one *yes*. Finally, graph F, for the range 64 to 70, has a minimum at 66.5 (0.4 bits).

The final discretization of the *temperature* attribute is shown in Figure 7.3. The fact that recursion only ever occurs in the first interval of each split is an artifact of this example: In general, both the upper and lower intervals will have to be split further. Underneath each division is the label of the graph in Figure 7.2 that is responsible for it, and below that the actual value of the split point.

It can be shown theoretically that a cut point that minimizes the information value will never occur between two instances of the same class. This leads to a useful

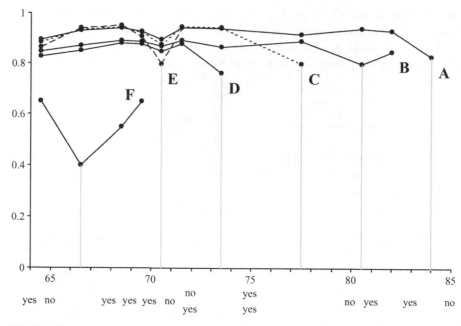

FIGURE 7.2

Discretizing the *temperature* attribute using the entropy method.

	64	65	68	69	70	71	72	75	80	81	83	85
	yes	no	yes	yes	yes	no	no yes	yes yes	no	yes	yes	no
		F				E		D	C	B		A
		66.5				70.5		73.5	77.5	80.5		84

FIGURE 7.3

The result of discretizing the *temperature* attribute.

optimization: It is only necessary to consider potential divisions that separate instances of different classes. Notice that if class labels were assigned to the intervals based on the majority class in the interval, there would be no guarantee that adjacent intervals would receive different labels. You might be tempted to consider merging intervals with the same majority class (e.g., the first two intervals of Figure 7.3), but as we will see later this is not a good thing to do in general.

The only problem left to consider is the stopping criterion. In the temperature example most of the intervals that were identified were "pure" in that all their instances had the same class, and there is clearly no point in trying to split such an interval. (Exceptions were the final interval, which we tacitly decided not to split, and the interval from 70.5 to 73.5.) In general, however, things are not so straightforward.

A good way to stop the entropy-based splitting discretization procedure turns out to be the MDL principle that we encountered in Chapter 5 (page 183). In accordance with that principle, we want to minimize the size of the "theory" plus the size of the information necessary to specify all the data given that theory. In this case, if we do split, the "theory" is the splitting point, and we are comparing the situation in which we split with that in which we do not. In both cases we assume that the instances are known but their class labels are not. If we do not split, the classes can be transmitted by encoding each instance's label. If we do, we first encode the split point (in $\log_2[N - 1]$ bits, where N is the number of instances), then the classes of the instances below that point, and then the classes of those above it.

You can imagine that if the split is a good one—say, all the classes below it are *yes* and all those above are *no*—then there is much to be gained by splitting. If there is an equal number of *yes* and *no* instances, each instance costs 1 bit without splitting but hardly more than 0 bits with splitting—it is not quite 0 because the class values associated with the split itself must be encoded, but this penalty is amortized across all the instances. In this case, if there are many examples, the penalty of having to encode the split point will be far outweighed by the information that is saved by splitting.

We emphasized in Section 5.9 that when applying the MDL principle, the devil is in the details. In the relatively straightforward case of discretization, the situation is tractable although not simple. The amounts of information can be obtained exactly under certain reasonable assumptions. We will not go into the details, but the upshot is that the split dictated by a particular cut point is worthwhile if the information gain for that split exceeds a certain value that depends on the number of instances N, the number of classes k, the entropy of the instances E, the entropy of the instances in each subinterval E_1 and E_2, and the number of classes represented in each subinterval k_1 and k_2:

$$gain > \frac{\log_2(N - 1)}{N} + \frac{\log_2(3^k - 2) - kE + k_1E_1 + k_2E_2}{N}$$

The first component is the information needed to specify the splitting point; the second is a correction due to the need to transmit the classes that correspond to the upper and lower subintervals.

When applied to the temperature example, this criterion prevents any splitting at all. The first split removes just the final example, and, as you can imagine, very little actual information is gained by this when transmitting the classes—in fact, the MDL criterion will never create an interval containing just one example. Failure to discretize *temperature* effectively disbars it from playing any role in the final decision structure because the same discretized value will be given to all instances. In this situation, this is perfectly appropriate: *Temperature* does not occur in good decision trees or rules for the weather data. In effect, failure to discretize is tantamount to attribute selection.

Other Discretization Methods

The entropy-based method with the MDL stopping criterion is one of the best general techniques for supervised discretization. However, many other methods have been investigated. For example, instead of proceeding top-down by recursively splitting intervals until some stopping criterion is satisfied, you could work bottom-up, first placing each instance into its own interval and then considering whether to merge adjacent intervals. You could apply a statistical criterion to see which would be the best two intervals to merge, and merge them if the statistic exceeds a certain preset confidence level, repeating the operation until no potential merge passes the test. The χ^2 test is a suitable one and has been used for this purpose. Instead of specifying a preset significance threshold, more complex techniques are available to determine an appropriate level automatically.

A rather different approach is to count the number of errors that a discretization makes when predicting each training instance's class, assuming that each interval receives the majority class. For example, the 1R method described earlier is error-based—it focuses on errors rather than the entropy. However, the best possible discretization in terms of error count is obtained by using the largest possible number of intervals, and this degenerate case should be avoided by restricting the number of intervals in advance.

Let's consider the best way to discretize an attribute into k intervals in a way that minimizes the number of errors. The brute-force method of finding this is exponential in k and therefore infeasible. However, there are much more efficient schemes that are based on the idea of dynamic programming. Dynamic programming applies not just to the error count measure but to any given additive impurity function, and it can find the partitioning of N instances into k intervals in a way that minimizes the impurity in time proportional to kN^2. This gives a way of finding the best entropy-based discretization, yielding a potential improvement in the quality of the discretization (in practice a negligible one) over the recursive entropy-based method described previously. The news for error-based discretization is even better because there is an algorithm that can be used to minimize the error count in time linear in N.

Entropy-Based versus Error-Based Discretization

Why not use error-based discretization, since the optimal discretization can be found very quickly? The answer is that there is a serious drawback to error-based discretization: It cannot produce adjacent intervals with the same label (such as the first two of Figure 7.3). The reason is that merging two such intervals will not affect the error count, but it will free up an interval that can be used elsewhere to reduce the error count.

Why would anyone want to generate adjacent intervals with the same label? The reason is best illustrated with an example. Figure 7.4 shows the instance space for a simple two-class problem with two numeric attributes ranging from 0 to 1. Instances

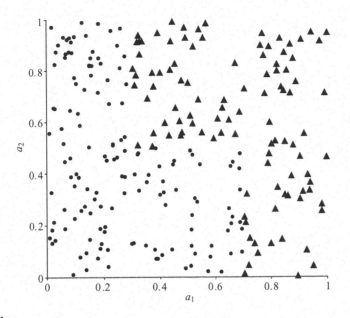

FIGURE 7.4

Class distribution for a two-class, two-attribute problem.

belong to one class (the dots) if their first attribute ($a1$) is less than 0.3, or if the first attribute is less than 0.7 *and* their second attribute ($a2$) is less than 0.5. Otherwise, they belong to the other class (triangles). The data in Figure 7.4 has been artificially generated according to this rule.

Now suppose we are trying to discretize both attributes with a view to learning the classes from the discretized attributes. The very best discretization splits $a1$ into three intervals (0–0.3, 0.3–0.7, and 0.7–1) and $a2$ into two intervals (0–0.5 and 0.5–1). Given these nominal attributes, it will be easy to learn how to tell the classes apart with a simple decision tree or rule algorithm. Discretizing $a2$ is no problem. For $a1$, however, the first and last intervals will have opposite labels (*dot* and *triangle*, respectively). The second will have whichever label happens to occur most in the region from 0.3 to 0.7 (it is in fact *dot* for the data in Figure 7.4). Either way, this label must inevitably be the same as one of the adjacent labels—of course, this is true whatever the class probability happens to be in the middle region. Thus, this discretization will not be achieved by any method that minimizes the error counts because such a method cannot produce adjacent intervals with the same label.

The point is that what changes as the value of $a1$ crosses the boundary at 0.3 is not the majority class but the class *distribution*. The majority class remains *dot*. The distribution, however, changes markedly, from 100% before the boundary to just over 50% after it. And the distribution changes again as the boundary at 0.7 is crossed, from 50 to 0%. Entropy-based discretization methods are sensitive to changes in the distribution even though the majority class does not change. Error-based methods are not sensitive.

Converting Discrete Attributes to Numeric Attributes

There is a converse problem to discretization. Some learning algorithms—notably the nearest-neighbor instance-based method and numeric prediction techniques involving regression—naturally handle only attributes that are numeric. How can they be extended to nominal attributes?

In instance-based learning, as described in Section 4.7 (page 132), discrete attributes can be treated as numeric by defining as 0 the "distance" between two nominal values that are the same and as 1 the distance between two values that are different, regardless of the actual values involved. Rather than modifying the distance function, this can be achieved by an attribute transformation: Replace a k-valued nominal attribute by k synthetic binary attributes, one for each value indicating whether the attribute has that value or not. If the attributes have equal weight, this achieves the same effect on the distance function. The distance is insensitive to the attribute values because only "same" or "different" information is encoded, not the shades of difference that may be associated with the various possible values of the attribute. More subtle distinctions can be made if the attributes have weights reflecting their relative importance.

If the values of the attribute can be ordered, more possibilities arise. For a numeric prediction problem, the average class value corresponding to each value of a nominal attribute can be calculated from the training instances and used to determine an ordering—this technique was introduced for model trees in Section 6.6 (page 253). (It is hard to come up with an analogous way of ordering attribute values for a classification problem.) An ordered nominal attribute can be replaced by an integer in the obvious way, but this implies not just an ordering but also a metric on the attribute's values. The implication of a metric can be avoided by creating $k - 1$ synthetic binary attributes for a k-valued nominal attribute, in the manner described on page 315. This encoding still implies an ordering among different values of the attribute—adjacent values differ in just one of the synthetic attributes whereas distant ones differ in several—but does not imply an equal distance between the attribute values.

7.3 PROJECTIONS

Resourceful data miners have a toolbox full of techniques, such as discretization, for transforming data. As we emphasized in Section 2.4, data mining is hardly ever a matter of simply taking a dataset and applying a learning algorithm to it. Every problem is different. You need to think about the data and what it means, and (creatively) examine it from diverse points of view to arrive at a suitable perspective. Transforming it in different ways can help you get started. In mathematics, a *projection* is a kind of function or mapping that transforms data in some way.

You don't have to make your own toolbox by implementing the projections yourself. Comprehensive environments for data mining, such as the one described in Part III of this book, contain a wide range of suitable tools for you to use. You do not necessarily need a detailed understanding of how they are implemented. What you do need to understand is what the tools do and how they can be applied. In Part III we list, and briefly describe, all the transformations in the Weka data mining workbench.

Data often calls for general mathematical transformations of a set of attributes. It might be useful to define new attributes by applying specified mathematical functions to existing ones. Two *date* attributes might be subtracted to give a third attribute representing *age*—an example of a semantic transformation driven by the meaning of the original attributes. Other transformations might be suggested by known properties of the learning algorithm. If a linear relationship involving two attributes, A and B, is suspected, and the algorithm is only capable of axis-parallel splits (as most decision tree and rule learners are), the ratio A:B might be defined as a new attribute. The transformations are not necessarily mathematical ones, but may involve real-world knowledge such as days of the week, civic holidays, or chemical atomic numbers. They could be expressed as operations in a spreadsheet or as functions that are implemented by arbitrary computer programs.

Or you can reduce several nominal attributes to one by concatenating their values, producing a single $k_1 \times k_2$-valued attribute from attributes with k_1 and k_2 values, respectively. Discretization converts a numeric attribute to nominal, and we saw earlier how to convert in the other direction too.

As another kind of transformation, you might apply a clustering procedure to the dataset and then define a new attribute with a value for any given instance that is the cluster that contains it using an arbitrary labeling for the clusters. Alternatively, with probabilistic clustering, you could augment each instance with its membership probabilities for each cluster, including as many new attributes as there are clusters.

Sometimes it is useful to add noise to data, perhaps to test the robustness of a learning algorithm; to take a nominal attribute and change a given percentage of its values; to obfuscate data by renaming the relation, attribute names, and nominal and string attribute values (because it is often necessary to anonymize sensitive datasets); to randomize the order of instances or produce a random sample of the dataset by resampling it; to reduce a dataset by removing a given percentage of instances, or all instances that have certain values for nominal attributes, or numeric values above or below a certain threshold; or to remove outliers by applying a classification method to the dataset and deleting misclassified instances.

Different types of input call for their own transformations. If you can input sparse data files (see Section 2.4), you may need to be able to convert datasets to nonsparse form and vice versa. Textual input and time series input call for their own specialized conversions, described in the following sections. But first we look at two general techniques for transforming data with numeric attributes into a lower-dimensional form that may be more useful for mining.

Principal Components Analysis

In a dataset with m numeric attributes, you can visualize the data as a cloud of points in m-dimensional space—the stars in the sky, a swarm of flies frozen in time, a two-dimensional scatter plot on paper. The attributes represent the coordinates of the space. But the axes you use, the coordinate system itself, is arbitrary. You can place horizontal and vertical axes on the paper and represent the points of the scatter plot using those coordinates, or you could draw an arbitrary straight line to represent the x-axis and one perpendicular to it to represent the y-axis. To record the positions of the flies you could use a conventional coordinate system with a north–south axis, an east–west axis, and an up–down axis. But other coordinate systems would do equally well. Creatures like flies don't know about north, south, east, and west, although, being subject to gravity, they may perceive up–down as something special. And as for the stars in the sky, who's to say what the "right" coordinate system is? Over the centuries our ancestors moved from a geocentric perspective to a heliocentric one to a purely relativistic one, each shift of perspective being accompanied by turbulent religious–scientific upheavals and painful reexamination of humankind's role in God's universe.

Back to the dataset. Just as in these examples, there is nothing to stop you from transforming all the data points into a different coordinate system. But unlike these examples, in data mining there often *is* a preferred coordinate system, defined not by some external convention but by the very data itself. Whatever coordinates you use, the cloud of points has a certain variance in each direction, indicating the degree of spread around the mean value in that direction. It is a curious fact that if you add up the variances along each axis and then transform the points into a different coordinate system and do the same there, you get the same total variance in both cases. This is always true provided the coordinate systems are *orthogonal*—that is, each axis is at right angles to the others.

The idea of principal components analysis is to use a special coordinate system that depends on the cloud of points as follows: Place the first axis in the direction of greatest variance of the points to maximize the variance along that axis. The second axis is perpendicular to it. In two dimensions there is no choice—its direction is determined by the first axis—but in three dimensions it can lie anywhere in the plane perpendicular to the first axis, and in higher dimensions there is even more choice, though it is always constrained to be perpendicular to the first axis. Subject to this constraint, choose the second axis in the way that maximizes the variance along it. And so on, choosing each axis to maximize its share of the remaining variance.

How do you do this? It's not hard, given an appropriate computer program, and it's not hard to understand, given the appropriate mathematical tools. Technically—for those who understand the italicized terms—you calculate the *covariance matrix* of the mean-centered coordinates of the points and *diagonalize* it to find the *eigenvectors*. These are the axes of the transformed space, sorted in order of *eigenvalue*—because each eigenvalue gives the variance along its axis.

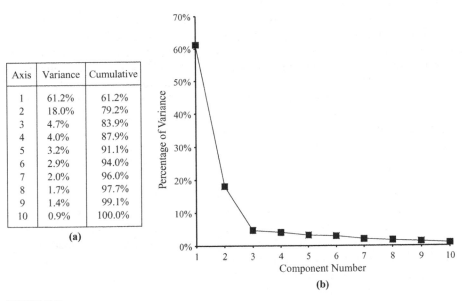

Axis	Variance	Cumulative
1	61.2%	61.2%
2	18.0%	79.2%
3	4.7%	83.9%
4	4.0%	87.9%
5	3.2%	91.1%
6	2.9%	94.0%
7	2.0%	96.0%
8	1.7%	97.7%
9	1.4%	99.1%
10	0.9%	100.0%

(a)

(b)

FIGURE 7.5

Principal components transform of a dataset: (a) variance of each component and (b) variance plot.

Figure 7.5 shows the result of transforming a particular dataset with 10 numeric attributes, corresponding to points in 10-dimensional space. Imagine the original dataset as a cloud of points in 10 dimensions—we can't draw it! Choose the first axis along the direction of greatest variance, the second perpendicular to it along the direction of next greatest variance, and so on. The table in the figure gives the variance along each new coordinate axis in the order in which the axes were chosen. Because the sum of the variances is constant regardless of the coordinate system, they are expressed as percentages of that total. We call axes *components* and say that each one "accounts for" its share of the variance. Figure 7.5(b) plots the variance that each component accounts for against the component's number. You can use all the components as new attributes for data mining, or you might want to choose just the first few, the *principal components*, and discard the rest. In this case, three principal components account for 84% of the variance in the dataset; seven account for more than 95%.

On numeric datasets it is common to use principal components analysis prior to data mining as a form of data cleanup and attribute selection. For example, you might want to replace the numeric attributes with the principal component axes or with a subset of them that accounts for a given proportion—say, 95%—of the variance. Note that the scale of the attributes affects the outcome of principal components analysis, and it is common practice to standardize all attributes to zero mean and unit variance first.

Another possibility is to apply principal components analysis recursively in a decision tree learner. At each stage an ordinary decision tree learner chooses to split in a direction that is parallel to one of the axes. However, suppose a principal components transform is performed first, and the learner chooses an axis in the transformed space. This equates to a split along an oblique line in the original space. If the transform is performed afresh before each split, the result will be a multivariate decision tree with splits that are in directions that are not parallel with the axes or with one another.

Random Projections

Principal components analysis transforms the data linearly into a lower-dimensional space—but it's expensive. The time taken to find the transformation (which is a matrix comprising the eigenvectors of the covariance matrix) is cubic in the number of dimensions. This makes it infeasible for datasets with a large number of attributes. A far simpler alternative is to use a random projection of the data into a subspace with a predetermined number of dimensions. It's very easy to find a random projection matrix. But will it be any good?

In fact, theory shows that random projections preserve distance relationships quite well on average. This means that they could be used in conjunction with kD-trees or ball trees to do approximate nearest-neighbor search in spaces with a huge number of dimensions. First transform the data to reduce the number of attributes; then build a tree for the transformed space. In the case of nearest-neighbor classification you could make the result more stable, and less dependent on the choice of random projection, by building an ensemble classifier that uses multiple random matrices.

Not surprisingly, random projections perform worse than projections carefully chosen by principal components analysis when used to preprocess data for a range of standard classifiers. However, experimental results have shown that the difference is not too great—and it tends to decrease as the number of dimensions increases. And, of course, random projections are far cheaper computationally.

Partial Least-Squares Regression

As mentioned earlier, principal components analysis is often performed as a preprocessing step before applying a learning algorithm. When the learning algorithm is linear regression, the resulting model is known as *principal components regression*. Since principal components are themselves linear combinations of the original attributes, the output of principal components regression can be reexpressed in terms of the original attributes. In fact, if all the components are used—not just the "principal" ones—the result is the same as that obtained by applying least-squares regression to the original input data. Using fewer than the full set of components results in a reduced regression.

Partial least-squares differs from principal components analysis in that it takes the class attribute into account, as well as the predictor attributes, when constructing a coordinate system. The idea is to calculate derived directions that, as well as having high variance, are strongly correlated with the class. This can be advantageous when seeking as small a set of transformed attributes as possible to use for supervised learning.

There is a simple iterative method for computing the partial least-squares directions that involves only dot product operations. Starting with input attributes that have been standardized to have zero mean and unit variance, the attribute coefficients for the first partial least-squares direction are found by taking the dot product between each attribute vector and the class vector in turn. To find the second direction the same approach is used, but the original attribute values are replaced by the difference between the attribute's value and the prediction from a simple univariate regression that uses the first direction as the single predictor of that attribute. These differences are called *residuals*. The process continues in the same fashion for each remaining direction, with residuals for the attributes from the previous iteration forming the input for finding the current partial least-squares direction.

Here is a simple worked example that should help make the procedure clear. For the first five instances from the CPU performance data in Table 1.5 (page 15), Table 7.1(a) shows the values of CHMIN and CHMAX (after standardization to zero mean and unit variance) and PRP (not standardized). The task is to find an expression for the target attribute PRP in terms of the other two. The attribute coefficients for the first partial least-squares direction are found by taking the dot product between the class and each attribute in turn. The dot product between the PRP and CHMIN columns is −0.4472, and that between PRP and CHMAX is 22.981. Thus, the first partial least-squares direction is

$$\text{PLS } 1 = -0.4472 \text{ CHMIN} + 22.981 \text{ CHMAX}$$

Table 7.1(b) shows the values for PLS 1 obtained from this formula.

The next step is to prepare the input data for finding the second partial least-squares direction. To this end, PLS 1 is regressed onto CHMIN and CHMAX in

Table 7.1 First Five Instances from the CPU Performance Data

	(a)			(b)	(c)		
	chmin	chmax	prp	pls 1	chmin	chmax	prp
1	1.7889	1.7678	198	39.825	0.0436	0.0008	198
2	−0.4472	−0.3536	269	−7.925	−0.0999	−0.0019	269
3	−0.4472	−0.3536	220	−7.925	−0.0999	−0.0019	220
4	−0.4472	−0.3536	172	−7.925	−0.0999	−0.0019	172
5	−0.4472	−0.7071	132	−16.05	0.2562	0.005	132

(a) original values, (b) first partial least-squares direction, and (c) residuals from the first direction.

turn, resulting in linear equations that predict each of these attributes individually from PLS 1. The coefficients are found by taking the dot product between PLS 1 and the attribute in question, and dividing the result by the dot product between PLS 1 and itself. The resulting univariate regression equations are

$$\text{CHMIN} = 0.0438 \text{ PLS } 1$$

$$\text{CHMAX} = 0.0444 \text{ PLS } 1$$

Table 7.1(c) shows the CPU data in preparation for finding the second partial least-squares direction. The original values of CHMIN and CHMAX have been replaced by residuals—that is, the difference between the original value and the output of the corresponding univariate regression equation given before (the target value PRP remains the same). The entire procedure is repeated using this data as input to yield the second partial least-squares direction, which is

$$\text{PLS } 2 = -23.6002 \text{ CHMIN} + -0.4593 \text{ CHMAX}$$

After this last partial least-squares direction has been found, the attribute residuals are all zero. This reflects the fact that, as with principal components analysis, the full set of directions account for all of the variance in the original data.

When the partial least-squares directions are used as input to linear regression, the resulting model is known as a *partial least-squares regression model*. As with principal components regression, if all the directions are used, the solution is the same as that obtained by applying linear regression to the original data.

Text to Attribute Vectors

In Section 2.4 we introduced string attributes that contain pieces of text, and there remarked that the value of a string attribute is often an entire document. String attributes are basically nominal, with an unspecified number of values. If they are treated simply as nominal attributes, models can be built that depend on whether the values of two string attributes are equal or not. But that does not capture any internal structure of the string or bring out any interesting aspects of the text it represents.

You could imagine decomposing the text in a string attribute into paragraphs, sentences, or phrases. Generally, however, the word is the most useful unit. The text in a string attribute is usually a sequence of words, and it is often best represented in terms of the words it contains. For example, you might transform the string attribute into a set of numeric attributes, one for each word, that represents how often each word appears. The set of words—that is, the set of new attributes—is determined from the dataset and is typically quite large. If there are several string attributes with properties that should be treated separately, the new attribute names must be distinguished, perhaps by a user-determined prefix.

Conversion into words—*tokenization*—is not as simple an operation as it sounds. Tokens may be formed from contiguous alphabetic sequences with nonalphabetic characters discarded. If numbers are present, numeric sequences may be retained too. Numbers may involve + or − signs, may contain decimal points, and may have exponential notation—in other words, they must be parsed according to a defined number syntax. An alphanumeric sequence may be regarded as a single token. Perhaps the space character is the token delimiter; perhaps whitespace (including the tab and new-line characters) and punctuation are too. Periods can be difficult: Sometimes they should be considered part of the word (e.g., with initials, titles, abbreviations, and numbers), but sometimes they should not (e.g., if they are sentence delimiters). Hyphens and apostrophes are similarly problematic.

All words may be converted to lowercase before being added to the dictionary. Words on a fixed, predetermined list of function words, or *stopwords*—such as *the*, *and*, and *but*—could be ignored. Note that stopword lists are language dependent. In fact, so are capitalization conventions (German capitalizes all nouns), number syntax (Europeans use the comma for a decimal point), punctuation conventions (Spanish has an initial question mark), and, of course, character sets. Text is complicated!

Low-frequency words such as *hapax legomena*[1] are often discarded. Sometimes it is found beneficial to keep the most frequent k words after stopwords have been removed—or perhaps the top k words for each class.

Along with all these tokenization options, there is the question of what the value of each word attribute should be. The value may be the word count—the number of times the word appears in the string—or it may simply indicate the word's presence or absence. Word frequencies could be normalized to give each document's attribute vector the same Euclidean length. Alternatively, the frequencies f_{ij} for word i in document j can be transformed in various standard ways. One standard logarithmic term-frequency measure is $\log(1 + f_{ij})$. A measure that is widely used in information retrieval is TF × IDF, or "term frequency times inverse document frequency."

Here, the term frequency is modulated by a factor that depends on how commonly the word is used in other documents. The TF × IDF metric is typically defined as

$$f_{ij} \log \frac{\text{number of documents}}{\text{number of documents that include word } i}$$

The idea is that a document is basically characterized by the words that appear often in it, which accounts for the first factor, except that words used in every document or almost every document are useless as discriminators, which accounts for the second. TF × IDF is used to refer not just to this particular formula but to a general class of measures of the same type. For example, the frequency factor f_{ij} may be replaced by a logarithmic term such as $\log(1 + f_{ij})$.

---

[1] A *hapax legomena* is a word that only occurs once in a given corpus of text.

Time Series

In time series data, each instance represents a different time step and the attributes give values associated with that time, such as in weather forecasting or stock market prediction. You sometimes need to be able to replace an attribute's value in the current instance by the corresponding value in some other instance in the past or the future. Even more common is to replace an attribute's value by the *difference* between the current value and the value in some previous instance. For example, the difference—often called the *Delta*—between the current value and the preceding one is often more informative than the value itself. The first instance, for which the time-shifted value is unknown, may be removed or replaced with a missing value. The Delta value is essentially the first derivative scaled by some constant that depends on the size of the time step. Successive Delta transformations take higher derivatives.

In some time series, instances do not represent regular samples; instead, the time of each instance is given by a *timestamp* attribute. The difference between time-stamps is the step size for that instance, and if successive differences are taken for other attributes they should be divided by the step size to normalize the derivative. In other cases, each attribute may represent a different time, rather than each instance, so that the time series is from one attribute to the next rather than one instance to the next. Then, if differences are needed, they must be taken between one attribute's value and the next attribute's value for each instance.

7.4 SAMPLING

In many applications involving a large volume of data it is necessary to come up with a random sample of much smaller size for processing. A random sample is one in which each instance in the original dataset has an equal chance of being included. Given a batch of N instances, a sample of any desired size is easily created: Just generate uniform random integers between 1 and N and retrieve the corresponding instances until the appropriate number has been collected. This is sampling *with replacement*, because the same instance might be selected more than once. (In fact, we used sampling with replacement for the bootstrap algorithm in Section 5.4—page 155.) For sampling *without replacement*, simply note, when selecting each instance, whether it has already been chosen and, if so, discard the second copy. If the sample size is much smaller than the full dataset, there is little difference between sampling with and without replacement.

Reservoir Sampling

Sampling is such a simple procedure that it merits little discussion or explanation. But there is a situation in which producing a random sample of a given size becomes a little more challenging. What if the training instances arrive one by one but the total number of them—the value of *N*—is not known in advance? Or suppose we need to be able to run a learning algorithm on a sample of a given size from a continuous stream of instances at any time, without repeatedly performing an entire sampling operation? Or perhaps the number of training instances is so vast that it is impractical to store them all before taking a sample?

All these situations call for a way of generating a random sample of an input stream without storing up all the instances and waiting for the last one to arrive before beginning the sampling procedure. Is it possible to generate a random sample of a given size and still guarantee that each instance has an equal chance of being selected? The answer is yes. Furthermore, there is a simple algorithm to do so.

The idea is to use a "reservoir" of size *r*, the size of the sample that is to be generated. To begin, place successive instances from the input stream in the reservoir until it is full. If the stream were to stop there, we would have the trivial case of a random sample of size *r* from an input stream of the same size. But most likely more instances will come in. The next one should be included in the sample with probability $r/(r+1)$—in fact, if the input stream were to stop there, $(N = r + 1)$, *any* instance should be in the sample with this probability. Consequently, with probability $r/(r+1)$ we replace a random instance in the reservoir with this new instance. And we carry on in the same vein, replacing a random reservoir element with the next instance with probability $r/(r+2)$ and so on. In general, the *i*th instance in the input stream is placed into the reservoir at a random location with probability r/i. It is easy to show by induction that once this instance has been processed the probability of any particular instance being in the reservoir is just the same, namely r/i. Thus, at any point in the procedure, the reservoir contains a random sample of size *r* from the input stream. You can stop at any time, secure in the knowledge that the reservoir contains the desired random sample.

This method samples without replacement. Sampling with replacement is a little harder, although for large datasets and small reservoirs there is little difference between the two. But if you really want a sample of size *r* with replacement, you could set up *r* independent reservoirs, each with size 1. Run the algorithm concurrently for all of these, and at any time their union is a random sample with replacement.

7.5 CLEANSING

A problem that plagues practical data mining is poor quality of the data. Errors in large databases are extremely common. Attribute values, and class values too, are frequently unreliable and corrupted. Although one way of addressing this problem is to painstakingly check through the data, data mining techniques themselves can sometimes help to solve the problem.

Improving Decision Trees

It is a surprising fact that decision trees induced from training data can often be simplified, without loss of accuracy, by discarding misclassified instances from the training set, relearning, and then repeating until there are no misclassified instances. Experiments on standard datasets have shown that this hardly affects the classification accuracy of C4.5, a standard decision tree–induction scheme. In some cases it improves slightly; in others it deteriorates slightly. The difference is rarely statistically significant—and even when it is, the advantage can go either way. What the technique does affect is decision tree size. The resulting trees are invariably much smaller than the original ones, even though they perform about the same.

What is the reason for this? When a decision tree–induction method prunes away a subtree, it applies a statistical test that decides whether that subtree is "justified" by the data. The decision to prune accepts a small sacrifice in classification accuracy on the training set in the belief that this will improve test-set performance. Some training instances that were classified correctly by the unpruned tree will now be misclassified by the pruned one. In effect, the decision has been taken to ignore these training instances.

But that decision has only been applied locally, in the pruned subtree. Its effect has not been allowed to percolate further up the tree, perhaps resulting in different choices being made of attributes to branch on. Removing the misclassified instances from the training set and relearning the decision tree is just taking the pruning decisions to their logical conclusion. If the pruning strategy is a good one, this should not harm performance. And it may improve it by allowing better attribute choices to be made.

It would no doubt be even better to consult a human expert. Misclassified training instances could be presented for verification, and those that were found to be wrong could be deleted—or, better still, corrected.

Notice that we are assuming that the instances are not misclassified in any systematic way. If instances are systematically corrupted in both training and test sets—for example, one class value might be substituted for another—it is only to be expected that training on the erroneous training set would yield better performance on the (also erroneous) test set.

Interestingly enough, it has been shown that when artificial noise is added to attributes (rather than added to classes), test-set performance is improved if the same noise is added in the same way to the training set. In other words, when attribute noise is the problem, it is not a good idea to train on a "clean" set if performance is to be assessed on a "dirty" one. A learning scheme can learn to compensate for attribute noise, in some measure, if given a chance. In essence, it can learn which attributes are unreliable and, if they are all unreliable, how best to use them together to yield a more reliable result. To remove noise from attributes for the training set denies the opportunity to learn how best to combat that noise. But with class noise (rather than attribute noise), it is best to train on noise-free instances if possible, if accurate classification is the goal.

Robust Regression

The problems caused by noisy data have been known in linear regression for years. Statisticians often check data for outliers and remove them manually. In the case of linear regression, outliers can be identified visually, although it is never completely clear whether an outlier is an error or just a surprising, but correct, value. Outliers dramatically affect the usual least-squares regression because the squared distance measure accentuates the influence of points far away from the regression line.

Statistical methods that address the problem of outliers are called *robust*. One way of making regression more robust is to use an absolute-value distance measure instead of the usual squared one. This weakens the effect of outliers. Another possibility is to try to identify outliers automatically and remove them from consideration. For example, one could form a regression line and then remove from consideration those 10% of points that lie furthest from the line. A third possibility is to minimize the *median* (rather than the mean) of the squares of the divergences from the regression line. It turns out that this estimator is very robust and actually copes with outliers in the *x*-direction as well as outliers in the *y*-direction, which is the normal direction one thinks for outliers.

A dataset that is often used to illustrate robust regression is a graph of international telephone calls made from Belgium during the years 1950 through 1973, shown in Figure 7.6. This data is taken from the Belgian Statistical Survey published by the Ministry of Economy. The plot seems to show an upward trend over the years, but there is an anomalous group of points from 1964 to 1969. It turns out that during this period, results were mistakenly recorded as the total number of *minutes* of the calls. The years 1963 and 1970 are also partially affected. This error causes a large fraction of outliers in the *y*-direction.

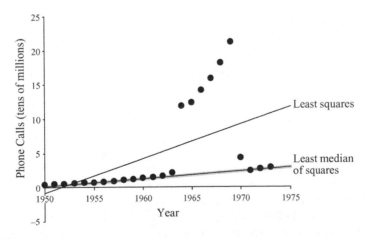

FIGURE 7.6

Number of international phone calls from Belgium, 1950–1973.

Not surprisingly, the usual least-squares regression line is seriously affected by this anomalous data. However, the least *median* of squares line remains remarkably unperturbed. This line has a simple and natural interpretation. Geometrically, it corresponds to finding the narrowest strip covering half of the observations, where the thickness of the strip is measured in the vertical direction—this strip is marked gray in Figure 7.6. The least median of squares line lies at the exact center of this band. Note that this notion is often easier to explain and visualize than the normal least-squares definition of regression. Unfortunately, there is a serious disadvantage to median-based regression techniques: They incur high computational cost, which often makes them infeasible for practical problems.

Detecting Anomalies

A serious problem with any form of automatic detection of apparently incorrect data is that the baby may be thrown out with the bathwater. Short of consulting a human expert, there is no way of telling whether a particular instance really is an error or whether it just does not fit the type of model that is being applied. In statistical regression, visualizations help. It will usually be visually apparent, even to the non-expert, if the wrong kind of curve is being fitted—a straight line is being fitted to data that lies on a parabola, for example. The outliers in Figure 7.6 certainly stand out to the eye. But most classification problems cannot be so easily visualized: The notion of "model type" is more subtle than a regression line. And although it is known that good results are obtained on most standard datasets by discarding instances that do not fit a decision tree model, this is not necessarily of great comfort when dealing with a particular new dataset. The suspicion will remain that perhaps the new dataset is simply unsuited to decision tree modeling.

One solution that has been tried is to use several different learning schemes (e.g., a decision tree, a nearest-neighbor learner, and a linear discriminant function) to filter the data. A conservative approach is to ask that all three schemes fail to classify an instance correctly before it is deemed erroneous and removed from the data. In some cases, filtering the data in this way and using the filtered data as input to a final learning scheme gives better performance than simply using the three learning schemes and letting them vote on the outcome. Training all three schemes on the *filtered* data and letting them vote can yield even better results. However, there is a danger to voting techniques: Some learning algorithms are better suited to certain types of data than others, and the most appropriate scheme may simply get outvoted! We will examine a more subtle method of combining the output from different classifiers, called *stacking*, in Section 8.7 (page 369). The lesson, as usual, is to get to know your data and look at it in many different ways.

One possible danger with filtering approaches is that they might conceivably just be sacrificing instances of a particular class (or group of classes) to improve accuracy on the remaining classes. Although there are no general ways to guard against this, it has not been found to be a common problem in practice.

Finally, it is worth noting once again that automatic filtering is a poor substitute for getting the data right in the first place. And if this is too time-consuming and expensive to be practical, human inspection could be limited to those instances that are identified by the filter as suspect.

One-Class Learning

In most classification problems, training data is available for all classes that can occur at prediction time, and the learning algorithm uses the data for the different classes to determine decision boundaries that discriminate between them. However, some problems exhibit only a single class of instances at training time, while at prediction time new instances with unknown class labels can belong either to this target class or to a new class that was not available during training. Then, two different predictions are possible: *target*, meaning that an instance belongs to the class experienced during training, and *unknown*, where the instance does not appear to belong to that class. This type of learning problem is known as *one-class classification*.

In many cases, one-class problems can be reformulated into two-class ones because there is data from other classes that can be used for training. However, there are genuine one-class applications where it is impossible or inappropriate to make use of negative data during training. For example, consider password hardening, a biometric system that strengthens a computer login process by not only requiring the correct password to be typed, but also requiring that it be typed with the correct rhythm. This is a one-class problem; a single user must be verified and during training time only data from that user is available—we cannot ask anyone else to provide data without supplying them with the password!

Even in applications where instances from several classes are available at training time, it may be best to focus solely on the target class under consideration—if, for example, new classes may occur at prediction time that differ from all those available during training. Continuing with the typing-rhythm scenario, suppose we are to recognize typists in a situation where the text is not fixed—the current typist is to be verified as who he or she claims to be from his or her rhythmic patterns on a block of free text. This task is fundamentally different from distinguishing one user from a group of other users because we must be prepared to refuse attackers that the system has never seen before.

Outlier Detection

One-class classification is often called *outlier* (or novelty) detection because the learning algorithm is being used to differentiate between data that appears normal and abnormal with respect to the distribution of the training data. Earlier in this section we talked about making regression more robust against outliers by replacing the usual squared distance measure with the absolute-value one, and about trying to detect anomalies by using several different learning schemes.

A generic statistical approach to one-class classification is to identify outliers as instances that lie beyond a distance d from a given percentage p of the training data. Alternatively, a probability density can be estimated for the target class by fitting a statistical distribution, such as a Gaussian, to the training data; any test instances with a low probability value can be marked as outliers. The challenge is to identify an appropriate distribution for the data at hand. If this cannot be done, one can adopt a nonparametric approach such as kernel density estimation (mentioned at the end of Section 4.2, page 99). An advantage of the density estimation approach is that the threshold can be adjusted at prediction time to obtain a suitable rate of outliers.

Multiclass classifiers can be tailored to the one-class situation by fitting a boundary around the target data and deeming instances that fall outside it to be outliers. The boundary can be generated by adapting the inner workings of existing multiclass classifiers such as support vector machines. These methods rely heavily on a parameter that determines how much of the target data is likely to be classified as outliers. If it is chosen too conservatively, data in the target class will erroneously be rejected. If it is chosen too liberally, the model will overfit and reject too much legitimate data. The rejection rate usually cannot be adjusted during testing, because an appropriate parameter value needs to be chosen at training time.

Generating Artificial Data

Rather than modify the internal workings of a multiclass classifier to form a one-class decision boundary directly, another possibility is to generate artificial data for the outlier class and apply any off-the-shelf classifier. Not only does this allow any classifier to be used, but if the classifier produces class probability estimates the rejection rate can be tuned by altering the threshold.

The most straightforward approach is to generate uniformly distributed data and learn a classifier that can discriminate this from the target. However, different decision boundaries will be obtained for different amounts of artificial data: If too much is generated it will overwhelm the target class and the learning algorithm will always predict the artificial class. This problem can be avoided if the objective of learning is viewed as accurate class probability estimation rather than minimizing the classification error. For example, bagged decision trees (described in Section 8.2 (page 352), which have been shown to yield good class probability estimators, can be used.

Once a class probability estimation model has been obtained in this fashion, different thresholds on the probability estimates for the target class correspond to different decision boundaries surrounding the target class. This means that, as in the density estimation approach to one-class classification, the rate of outliers can be adjusted at prediction time to yield an outcome appropriate for the application at hand.

There is one significant problem. As the number of attributes increases, it quickly becomes infeasible to generate enough artificial data to obtain adequate coverage of the instance space, and the probability that a particular artificial instance occurs inside or close to the target class diminishes to a point that makes any kind of discrimination impossible.

The solution is to generate artificial data that is as close as possible to the target class. In this case, because it is no longer uniformly distributed, the distribution of this artificial data—call this the "reference" distribution—must be taken into account when computing the membership scores for the resulting one-class model. In other words, the class probability estimates of the two-class classifier must be combined with the reference distribution to obtain membership scores for the target class.

To elaborate a little further, let T denote the target class for which we have training data and seek a one-class model, and A the artificial class, for which we generate data using a known reference distribution. What we would like to obtain is $\Pr[X \mid T]$, the density function of the target class, for any instance X—of course, we know $\Pr[X \mid A]$, the density function of the reference distribution. Assume for the moment that we know the true class probability function $\Pr[T \mid X]$. In practice, we need to estimate this function using a class probability estimator learned from the training data. A simple application of Bayes' rule can be used to express $\Pr[X \mid T]$ in terms of $\Pr[T]$, $\Pr[T \mid X]$, and $\Pr[X \mid A]$:

$$\Pr[X \mid T] = \frac{(1 - \Pr[T])\Pr[T \mid X]}{\Pr[T](1 - \Pr[T \mid X])}\Pr[X \mid A]$$

To use this equation in practice, choose $\Pr[X \mid A]$, generate a user-specified amount of artificial data from it, label it A, and combine it with instances in the training set for the target class, labeled T. The proportion of target instances is an estimate of $\Pr[T]$, and a standard learning algorithm can be applied to this two-class dataset to obtain a class probability estimator $\Pr[T \mid X]$. Given that the value for $\Pr[X \mid A]$ can be computed for any particular instance X, everything is at hand to compute an estimate of the target density function $\Pr[X \mid T]$ for any instance X. To perform classification we choose an appropriate threshold, adjusted to tune the rejection rate to any desired value.

One question remains, namely, how to choose the reference density $\Pr[X \mid A]$. We need to be able to generate artificial data from it and to compute its value for any instance X. Another requirement is that the data it generates should be close to the target class. In fact, ideally the reference density is identical to the target density, in which case $\Pr[T \mid X]$ becomes a constant function that any learning algorithm should be able to induce—the resulting two-class learning problem becomes trivial. This is unrealistic because it would require us to know the density of the target class. However, this observation gives a clue as to how to proceed: Apply any density estimation technique to the target data and use the resulting function to model the artificial class. The better the match between $\Pr[X \mid A]$ and $\Pr[X \mid T]$, the easier the resulting two-class class probability estimation task becomes.

In practice, given the availability of powerful methods for class probability estimation and the relative lack of such techniques for density estimation, it makes sense to apply a simple density estimation technique to the target data first to obtain $\Pr[X \mid A]$ and then employ a state-of-the-art class probability estimation method to the two-class problem that is obtained by combining the artificial data with the data from the target class.

7.6 TRANSFORMING MULTIPLE CLASSES TO BINARY ONES

Recall from Chapter 6 that some learning algorithms—for example, standard support vector machines—only work with two-class problems. In most cases, sophisticated multiclass variants have been developed, but they may be very slow or difficult to implement. As an alternative, it is common practice to transform multiclass problems into multiple two-class ones: The dataset is decomposed into several two-class problems, the algorithm is run on each one, and the outputs of the resulting classifiers are combined. Several popular techniques can implement this idea. We begin with a very simple one that was touched on when we were discussing how to use linear regression for classification; we then move on to pairwise classification and more advanced techniques—error-correcting output codes and ensembles of nested dichotomies—that can often be profitably applied even when the underlying learning algorithm is able to deal with multiclass problems directly.

Simple Methods

At the beginning of the Linear Classification section in Chapter 4 (page 125) we learned how to transform a multiclass dataset for multiresponse linear regression to perform a two-class regression for each class. The idea essentially produces several two-class datasets by discriminating each class against the union of all the other classes. This technique is commonly called *one-vs.-rest* (or somewhat misleadingly, *one-vs.-all*). For each class, a dataset is generated containing a copy of each instance in the original data, but with a modified class value. If the instance has the class associated with the corresponding dataset, it is tagged *yes*; otherwise, *no*. Then classifiers are built for each of these binary datasets—classifiers that output a confidence figure with their predictions; for example, the estimated probability that the class is *yes*. During classification, a test instance is fed into each binary classifier, and the final class is the one associated with the classifier that predicts *yes* most confidently.

Of course, this method is sensitive to the accuracy of the confidence figures produced by the classifiers: If some classifiers have an exaggerated opinion of their own predictions, the overall result will suffer. That is why it can be important to carefully tune parameter settings in the underlying learning algorithm. For example, in standard support vector machines for classification, it is generally necessary to tune the parameter C, which provides an upper bound to the influence of each support vector and controls the closeness of fit to the training data, and the value of the kernel parameter—for example, the degree of the exponent in a polynomial kernel. This can be done based on internal cross-validation. It has been found empirically that the one-vs.-rest method can be very competitive, at least in the case of kernel-based classifiers, when appropriate parameter tuning is done. Note that it may also be useful to apply techniques for calibrating confidence scores, discussed in the next section, to the individual two-class models.

Another simple and general method for multiclass problems is *pairwise classification*. Here, a classifier is built for every pair of classes, using only the instances from these two classes. The output on an unknown test example is based on which class receives the most votes. This scheme generally yields accurate results in terms of classification error. It can also be used to produce probability estimates by applying a method called *pairwise coupling*, which calibrates the individual probability estimates from the different classifiers.

If there are k classes, pairwise classification builds a total of $k(k-1)/2$ classifiers. Although this sounds unnecessarily computation intensive, it is not. In fact, if the classes are evenly populated, a pairwise classifier is at least as quick to train as any other multiclass method. The reason is that each of the pairwise learning problems only involves instances pertaining to the two classes under consideration. If n instances are divided evenly among k classes, this amounts to $2n/k$ instances per problem. Suppose the learning algorithm for a two-class problem with n instances takes time proportional to n seconds to execute. Then the runtime for pairwise classification is proportional to $k(k-1)/2 \times 2n/k$ seconds, which is $(k-1)n$. In other words, the method scales linearly with the number of classes. If the learning algorithm takes more time—say proportional to n^2—the advantage of the pairwise approach becomes even more pronounced.

Error-Correcting Output Codes

The simple methods discussed above are often very effective. Pairwise classification in particular can be a very useful technique. It has been found that it can in some cases improve accuracy even when the underlying learning algorithm, such as a decision tree learner, can deal with multiclass problems directly. This may be due to the fact that pairwise classification actually generates an ensemble of many classifiers. Ensemble learning is a well-known strategy for obtaining accurate classifiers, and we will discuss several ensemble learning methods in Chapter 8. It turns out that there are methods other than pairwise classification that can be used to generate an ensemble classifier by decomposing a multiclass problem into several two-class subtasks. The one we discuss next is based on error-correcting output codes.

Two-class decompositions of multiclass problems can be viewed in terms of the so-called "output codes" they correspond to. Let us revisit the simple one-vs.-rest method to see what such codes look like. Consider a multiclass problem with four classes a, b, c, and d. The transformation can be visualized as illustrated in Table 7.2(a), where *yes* and *no* are mapped to 1 and 0, respectively. Each of the original class values is converted into a 4-bit code word, 1 bit per class, and the four classifiers predict the bits independently. Interpreting the classification process in terms of these code words, errors occur when the wrong binary bit receives the highest confidence.

However, we do not have to use the particular code words shown. Indeed, there is no reason why each class must be represented by 4 bits. Look instead at the code of Table 7.2(b), where classes are represented by 7 bits. When applied to a dataset,

Table 7.2 Transforming a Multiclass Problem into a Two-Class One

(a)		(b)	
Class	Class Vector	Class	Class Vector
a	1 0 0 0	a	1 1 1 1 1 1 1
b	0 1 0 0	b	0 0 0 0 1 1 1
c	0 0 1 0	c	0 0 1 1 0 0 1
d	0 0 0 1	d	0 1 0 1 0 1 0

(a) standard method and (b) error-correcting code.

seven classifiers must be built instead of four. To see what that might buy, consider the classification of a particular instance. Suppose it belongs to class a, and that the predictions of the individual classifiers are 1 0 1 1 1 1 1, respectively. Obviously, comparing this code word with those in Table 7.2(b), the second classifier has made a mistake: It predicted 0 instead of 1, *no* instead of *yes*.

Comparing the predicted bits with the code word associated with each class, the instance is clearly closer to a than to any other class. This can be quantified by the number of bits that must be changed to convert the predicted code word into those of Table 7.2(b): The *Hamming distance*, or the discrepancy between the bit strings, is 1, 3, 3, and 5 for the classes a, b, c, and d, respectively. We can safely conclude that the second classifier made a mistake and correctly identify a as the instance's true class.

The same kind of error correction is not possible with the code words shown in Table 7.2(a) because any predicted string of 4 bits, other than these four 4-bit words, has the same distance to at least two of them. Thus, the output codes are not "error correcting."

What determines whether a code is error correcting or not? Consider the Hamming distance between the code words representing different classes. The number of errors that can be possibly corrected depends on the minimum distance between any pair of code words, say d. The code can guarantee to correct up to $(d - 1)/2$ 1-bit errors because if this number of bits of the correct code word are flipped, it will still be the closest and will therefore be identified correctly. In Table 7.2(a) the Hamming distance for each pair of code words is 2. Thus, the minimum distance d is also 2, and we can correct no more than 0 errors! However, in the code of Table 7.2(b) the minimum distance is 4 (in fact, the distance is 4 for all pairs). That means it is guaranteed to correct 1-bit errors.

We have identified one property of a good error-correcting code: The code words must be well separated in terms of their Hamming distance. Because they comprise the rows of the code table, this property is called *row separation*. There is a second requirement that a good error-correcting code should fulfill: *column separation*. The Hamming distance between every pair of columns must be large, as must the distance between each column and the complement of every other column. The seven columns in Table 7.2(b) are separated from one another (and their complements) by at least 1 bit.

Column separation is necessary because if two columns are identical (or if one is the complement of another), the corresponding classifiers will make the same errors. Error correction is weakened if the errors are correlated—in other words, if many bit positions are simultaneously incorrect. The greater the distance between columns, the more errors are likely to be corrected.

With fewer than four classes it is impossible to construct an effective error-correcting code because good row separation and good column separation cannot be achieved simultaneously. For example, with three classes there are only eight possible columns (2^3), four of which are complements of the other four. Moreover, columns with all 0s or all 1s provide no discrimination. This leaves just three possible columns, and the resulting code is not error correcting at all. (In fact, it is the standard "one-vs.-rest" encoding.)

If there are few classes, an exhaustive error-correcting code, such as the one in Table 7.2(b), can be built. In an exhaustive code for the k classes, the columns comprise every possible k-bit string, except for complements and the trivial all-0 or all-1 strings. Each of the code words contains $2^{k-1} - 1$ bits. The code is constructed as follows: The code word for the first class consists of all 1s; that for the second class has 2^{k-2} 0s followed by $2^{k-2} - 1$ 1s; the third has 2^{k-3} 0s followed by 2^{k-3} 1s followed by 2^{k-3} 0s followed by $2^{k-3} - 1$ 1s; and so on. The ith code word consists of alternating runs of 2^{k-i} 0s and 1s, the last run being one short.

With more classes, exhaustive codes are infeasible because the number of columns increases exponentially and too many classifiers have to be built. In that case, more sophisticated methods are employed, which can build a code with good error-correcting properties from a smaller number of columns.

Error-correcting output codes do not work for local learning algorithms such as instance-based learners, which predict the class of an instance by looking at nearby training instances. In the case of a nearest-neighbor classifier, all output bits would be predicted using the same training instance. The problem can be circumvented by using different attribute subsets to predict each output bit, decorrelating the predictions.

Ensembles of Nested Dichotomies

Error-correcting output codes often produce accurate classifiers for multiclass problems. However, the basic algorithm produces classifications, whereas often we would like class probability estimates as well—for example, to perform cost-sensitive classification using the minimum expected cost approach discussed in Section 5.7 (page 167). Fortunately, there is a method for decomposing multiclass problems into two-class ones that provides a natural way of computing class probability estimates, so long as the underlying two-class models are able to produce probabilities for the corresponding two-class subtasks.

The idea is to recursively split the full set of classes from the original multiclass problem into smaller and smaller subsets, while splitting the full dataset of instances into subsets corresponding to these subsets of classes. This yields a binary tree of classes. Consider the hypothetical four-class problem discussed earlier. At the root node is the full set of classes $\{a, b, c, d\}$, which is split into disjoint subsets, say $\{a, c\}$ and $\{b, d\}$, along with the instances pertaining to these two subsets of classes. The two subsets form the two successor nodes in the binary tree. These subsets are then split further into one-element sets, yielding successors $\{a\}$ and $\{c\}$ for the node $\{a, c\}$ and successors $\{b\}$ and $\{d\}$ for the node $\{b, d\}$. Once we reach one-element subsets, the splitting process stops.

The resulting binary tree of classes is called a *nested dichotomy* because each internal node and its two successors define a dichotomy—for example, discriminating between classes $\{a, c\}$ and $\{b, d\}$ at the root node—and the dichotomies are nested in a hierarchy. We can view a nested dichotomy as a particular type of sparse output code. Table 7.3 shows the output code matrix for the example just discussed. There is one dichotomy for each internal node of the tree structure. Thus, given that the example involves three internal nodes, there are three columns in the code matrix. In contrast to the class vectors considered before, the matrix contains elements marked X that indicate that instances of the corresponding classes are simply omitted from the associated two-class learning problems.

What is the advantage of this kind of output code? It turns out that, because the decomposition is hierarchical and yields disjoint subsets, there is a simple method for computing class probability estimates for each element in the original set of multiple classes, assuming two-class estimates for each dichotomy in the hierarchy. The reason is the chain rule from probability theory, which we already encountered when discussing Bayesian networks in Section 6.7 (page 265).

Suppose we want to compute the probability for class a given a particular instance x—that is, the conditional probability $\Pr[a \mid x]$. This class corresponds to one of the four leaf nodes in the hierarchy of classes in the previous example. First, we learn two-class models that yield class probability estimates for the three two-class datasets at the internal nodes of the hierarchy. Then, from the two-class model at the root node, an estimate of the conditional probability $\Pr[\{a, b\} \mid x]$—namely, that x belongs to either a or b—can be obtained. Moreover, we can obtain an estimate of $\Pr[\{a\} \mid x, \{a, b\}]$—the probability that x belongs to a given that we already know

Table 7.3 Nested Dichotomy in the Form of a Code Matrix	
Class	**Class Vector**
a	0 0 X
b	1 X 0
c	0 1 X
d	1 X 1

that it belongs to either a or b—from the model that discriminates between the one-element sets $\{a\}$ and $\{b\}$. Now, based on the chain rule, $\Pr[\{a\} \mid x] = \Pr[\{a\} \mid \{a, b\}, x] \times \Pr[\{a, b\} \mid x]$. Thus, to compute the probability for any individual class of the original multiclass problem—any leaf node in the tree of classes—we simply multiply together the probability estimates collected from the internal nodes encountered when proceeding from the root node to this leaf node: the probability estimates for all subsets of classes that contain the target class.

Assuming that the individual two-class models at the internal nodes produce accurate probability estimates, there is reason to believe that the multiclass probability estimates obtained using the chain rule will generally be accurate. However, it is clear that estimation errors will accumulate, causing problems for very deep hierarchies. A more basic issue is that in the previous example we arbitrarily decided on a particular hierarchical decomposition of the classes. Perhaps there is some background knowledge regarding the domain concerned, in which case one particular hierarchy may be preferable because certain classes are known to be related, but this is generally not the case.

What can be done? If there is no reason a priori to prefer any particular decomposition, perhaps all of them should be considered, yielding an *ensemble* of nested dichotomies. Unfortunately, for any nontrivial number of classes there are too many potential dichotomies, making an exhaustive approach infeasible. But we could consider a subset, taking a random sample of possible tree structures, building two-class models for each internal node of each tree structure (with caching of models, given that the same two-class problem may occur in multiple trees), and then averaging the probability estimates for each individual class to obtain the final estimates.

Empirical experiments show that this approach yields accurate multiclass classifiers and is able to improve predictive performance even in the case of classifiers, such as decision trees, that can deal with multiclass problems directly. In contrast to standard error-correcting output codes, the technique often works well even when the base learner is unable to model complex decision boundaries. The reason is that, generally speaking, learning is easier with fewer classes so results become more successful the closer we get to the leaf nodes in the tree. This also explains why the pairwise classification technique described earlier works particularly well for simple models such as ones corresponding to hyperplanes: It creates the simplest possible dichotomies! Nested dichotomies appear to strike a useful balance between the simplicity of the learning problems that occur in pairwise classification—after all, the lowest-level dichotomies involve pairs of individual classes—and the power of the redundancy embodied in standard error-correcting output codes.

7.7 CALIBRATING CLASS PROBABILITIES

Class probability estimation is obviously more difficult than classification. Given a way of generating class probabilities, classification error is minimized as long as the correct class is predicted with maximum probability. However, a method for accurate classification does not imply a method of generating accurate probability estimates: The estimates that yield the correct classification may be quite poor when assessed according to the quadratic (page 160) or informational (page 161) loss discussed in Section 5.6. Yet—as we have stressed several times—it is often more important to obtain accurate conditional class probabilities for a given instance than to simply place the instance into one of the classes. Cost-sensitive prediction based on the minimum expected cost approach is one example where accurate class probability estimates are very useful.

Consider the case of probability estimation for a dataset with two classes. If the predicted probabilities are on the correct side of the 0.5 threshold commonly used for classification, no classification errors will be made. However, this does not mean that the probability estimates themselves are accurate. They may be systematically too optimistic—too close to either 0 or 1—or too pessimistic—not close enough to the extremes. This type of bias will increase the measured quadratic or informational loss, and will cause problems when attempting to minimize the expected cost of classifications based on a given cost matrix.

Figure 7.7 demonstrates the effect of overoptimistic probability estimation for a two-class problem. The x-axis shows the predicted probability of the multinomial Naïve Bayes model from Section 4.2 (page 97) for one of two classes in a text classification problem with about 1000 attributes representing word frequencies. The y-axis shows the observed relative frequency of the target class. The predicted probabilities and relative frequencies were collected by running a tenfold cross-validation. To estimate relative frequencies, the predicted probabilities were first discretized into 20 ranges using equal-frequency discretization. Observations corresponding to one interval were then pooled—predicted probabilities on the one hand and corresponding 0/1 values on the other—and the pooled values are shown as the 20 points in the plot.

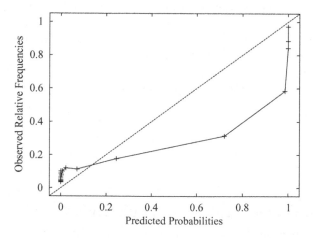

FIGURE 7.7

Overoptimistic probability estimation for a two-class problem.

This kind of plot, known as a *reliability diagram*, shows how reliable the estimated probabilities are. For a well-calibrated class probability estimator, the observed curve will coincide with the diagonal. This is clearly not the case here. The Naïve Bayes model is too optimistic, generating probabilities that are too close to 0 and 1. This is not the only problem: The curve is quite far from the line that corresponds to the 0.5 threshold that is used for classification. This means that classification performance will be affected by the poor probability estimates that the model generates.

The fact that we seek a curve that lies close to the diagonal makes the remedy clear: Systematic misestimation should be corrected by using post hoc calibration of the probability estimates to map the empirically observed curve into a diagonal. A coarse way of doing this is to use the data from the reliability diagram directly for calibration, and map the predicted probabilities to the observed relative frequencies in the corresponding discretization intervals. Data for this can be obtained using internal cross-validation or a holdout set so that the actual test data remains untouched.

Discretization-based calibration is very fast. However, determining appropriate discretization intervals is not easy. With too few, the mapping is too coarse; with too many, each interval contains insufficient data for a reliable estimate of relative frequencies. However, other ways of calibrating can be devised. The key is to realize that calibrating probability estimates for two-class problems is a function estimation problem with one input—the estimated class probability—and one output—the calibrated probability. In principle, complex functions could be used to estimate the mapping—perhaps arbitrary polynomials. However, it makes sense to assume that the observed relationship is at least monotonically increasing, in which case increasing functions should be used.

Assuming that the calibration function is piecewise constant and monotonically increasing, there is an efficient algorithm that minimizes the squared error between the observed class "probabilities" (which are either 0 or 1 when no binning is applied) and the resulting calibrated class probabilities. Estimating a piecewise constant monotonically increasing function is an instance of *isotonic regression*, for which there is a fast algorithm based on the pair-adjacent violators (PAV) approach. The data consists of estimated probabilities and 0/1 values; assume it has been sorted according to the estimated probabilities. The basic PAV algorithm iteratively merges pairs of neighboring data points that violate the monotonicity constraint by computing their weighted mean—initially this will be the mean of 0/1 values—and using it to replace the original data points. This is repeated until all conflicts have been resolved. It can be shown that the order in which data points are merged does not affect the outcome of the process. The result is a function that increases monotonically in a stepwise fashion. This naïve algorithm is quadratic in the number of data points, but there is a clever variant that operates in linear time.

Another popular calibration method, which also presupposes a monotonic relationship, is to assume a linear relation between the log-odds of the estimated class probabilities and the target class probabilities. The logistic function is appropriate here, and logistic regression can be used to estimate the calibration function, with the caveat that it is important to use log-odds of the estimated class probabilities rather than the raw values as the input for logistic regression.

Given that logistic regression, with only two parameters, uses a simpler model than the PAV approach, it can be more appropriate when little data is available for calibration. However, with a large volume of data, PAV-based calibration is generally preferable. Logistic regression has the advantage that it can be easily applied to calibrate probabilities for multiclass problems because multiclass versions of logistic regression exist. In the case of isotonic regression it is common to use the one-vs.-rest method for problems with more than two classes, but pairwise coupling or ensembles of nested dichotomies—discussed in Section 7.6—offer an alternative.

Note that situations exist in which the relationship between the estimated and true probabilities is not monotonic. However, rather than switching to a more complex calibration method—or using discretization-based calibration, which does not assume monotonicity—this should perhaps be taken as an indication that the underlying class probability estimation method is not powerful enough for the problem at hand.

7.8 FURTHER READING

Attribute selection, under the term *feature selection*, has been investigated in the field of pattern recognition for decades. Backward elimination, for example, was introduced in the early 1960s (Marill and Green, 1963). Kittler (1978) surveys the feature-selection algorithms that have been developed for pattern recognition. Best-first search and genetic algorithms are standard artificial intelligence techniques (Winston, 1992; Goldberg, 1989).

The experiments that show the performance of decision tree learners deteriorating when new attributes are added are reported by John (1997), who gives a nice explanation of attribute selection. The idea of finding the smallest attribute set that carves up the instances uniquely is from Almuallin and Dietterich (1991, 1992) and was further developed by Liu and Setiono (1996). Kibler and Aha (1987) and Cardie (1993) both investigated the use of decision tree algorithms to identify features for nearest-neighbor learning; Holmes and Nevill-Manning (1995) used OneR to order features for selection. Kira and Rendell (1992) used instance-based methods to select features, leading to a scheme called Relief for *Recursive Elimination of Features*. Gilad-Bachrach et al. (2004) show how this scheme can be modified to work better with redundant attributes. The correlation-based feature-selection method was developed by Hall (2000).

The use of wrapper methods for feature selection is from John et al. (1994) and Kohavi and John (1997), and genetic algorithms have been applied within a wrapper framework by Vafaie and DeJong (1992) and Cherkauer and Shavlik (1996). The selective Naïve Bayes learning scheme is from Langley and Sage (1994). Guyon et al. (2002) present and evaluate the recursive feature-elimination scheme in conjunction with support vector machines. The method of raced search was developed by Moore and Lee (1994). Gütlein et al. (2009) investigate how to speed up scheme-specific selection for datasets with many attributes using simple ranking-based methods.

Dougherty et al. (1995) give a brief account of supervised and unsupervised discretization, along with experimental results comparing the entropy-based method with equal-width binning and the OneR method. Frank and Witten (1999) describe the effect of using the ordering information in discretized attributes. Proportional k-interval discretization for Naïve Bayes was proposed by Yang and Webb (2001). The entropy-based method for discretization, including the use of the MDL stopping criterion, was developed by Fayyad and Irani (1993). The bottom-up statistical method using the χ^2 test is from Kerber (1992), and its extension to an automatically determined significance level is described by Liu and Setiono (1997). Fulton et al. (1995) investigate the use of dynamic programming for discretization and derive the quadratic time bound for a general impurity function (e.g., entropy) and the linear one for error-based discretization. The example used for showing the weakness of error-based discretization is adapted from Kohavi and Sahami (1996), who were the first to clearly identify this phenomenon.

Principal components analysis is a standard technique that can be found in most statistics textbooks. Fradkin and Madigan (2003) analyze the performance of random projections. The algorithm for partial least-squares regression is from Hastie et al. (2009). The TF × IDF metric is described by Witten et al. (1999b).

The experiments on using C4.5 to filter its own training data were reported by John (1995). The more conservative approach of a consensus filter involving several different learning algorithms has been investigated by Brodley and Friedl (1996). Rousseeuw and Leroy (1987) describe the detection of outliers in statistical regression, including the least median of squares method; they also present the telephone data of Figure 7.6. It was Quinlan (1986) who noticed that removing noise from the training instance's attributes can decrease a classifier's performance on similarly noisy test instances, particularly at higher noise levels.

Barnett and Lewis (1994) address the general topic of outliers in statistical data, while Pearson (2005) describes the statistical approach of fitting a distribution to the target data. Schölkopf et al. (2000) describe the use of support vector machines for novelty detection, while Abe et al. (2006), among others, use artificial data as a second class. Combining density estimation and class probability estimation using artificial data is suggested as a generic approach to unsupervised learning by Hastie et al. (2009), and Hempstalk et al. (2008) describe it in the context of one-class classification. Hempstalk and Frank (2008) discuss the fair comparison of one-class and multiclass classification when several classes are available at training time and we want to discriminate against an entirely new class at prediction time.

Vitter (1985) explored the idea of reservoir sampling; he called the method we described algorithm R. Its computational complexity is O(N), where N is the number of instances in the stream, because a random number must be generated for every instance in order to determine whether, and where, to place it in the reservoir. Vitter describes several other algorithms that improve on R by reducing the number of random numbers that must be generated in order to produce the sample.

Rifkin and Klautau (2004) show that the one-vs.-rest method for multiclass classification can work well if appropriate parameter tuning is applied. Friedman (1996) describes the technique of pairwise classification, Fürnkranz (2002) further analyzes it, and Hastie and Tibshirani (1998) extend it to estimate probabilities using pairwise coupling. Fürnkranz (2003) evaluates pairwise classification as a technique for ensemble learning. The idea of using error-correcting output codes for classification gained wide acceptance after a paper by Dieterich and Bakiri (1995); Ricci and Aha (1998) showed how to apply such codes to nearest-neighbor classifiers. Frank and Kramer (2004) introduce ensembles of nested dichotomies for multiclass problems. Dong et al. (2005) considered using balanced nested dichotomies rather than unrestricted random hierarchies to reduce training time.

The importance of methods for calibrating class probability estimates is now well-established. Zadrozny and Elkan (2002) applied the PAV approach and logistic regression to calibration, and also investigated how to deal with multiclass problems. Niculescu-Mizil and Caruana (2005) compared a variant of logistic regression and the PAV-based method in conjunction with a large set of underlying class probability estimators, and found that the latter is preferable for sufficiently large calibration sets. They also found that multilayer perceptrons and bagged decision trees produce well-calibrated probabilities and do not require an extra calibration step. Stout (2008) describes a linear-time algorithm for isotonic regression based on minimizing the squared error.

7.9 WEKA IMPLEMENTATIONS

Attribute selection (see Section 11.8 and Tables 11.9 and 11.10):

- *CfsSubsetEval* (correlation-based attribute subset evaluator)
- *ConsistencySubsetEval* (measures class consistency for a given set of attributes)
- *ClassifierSubsetEval* (uses a classifier for evaluating subsets of attributes)
- *SVMAttributeEval* (ranks attributes according to the magnitude of the coefficients learned by a support vector machine)
- *ReliefF* (instance-based approach for ranking attributes)
- *WrapperSubsetEval* (uses a classifier plus cross-validation)
- *GreedyStepwise* (forward selection and backward elimination search)
- *LinearForwardSelection* (forward selection with a sliding window of attribute choices at each step of the search)
- *BestFirst* (search method that uses greedy hill-climbing with backtracking)
- *RaceSearch* (uses the race search methodology)
- *Ranker* (ranks individual attributes according to their evaluation)

Learning decision tables—*DecisionTable* (see Section 11.4 and Table 11.5)

Discretization (see Section 11.3):
- *Discretize* in Table 11.1 (provides a variety of options for unsupervised discretization)
- *PKIDiscretize* in Table 11.1 (proportional k-interval discretization)
- *Discretize* in Table 11.3 (provides a variety of options for supervised discretization)

Other data transformation operations (see Section 11.3):
- *PrincipalComponents* and *RandomProjection* in Table 11.1 (principal components analysis and random projections)
- Operations in Table 11.1 include arithmetic operations; time-series operations; obfuscation; generating cluster membership values; adding noise; various conversions between numeric, binary, and nominal attributes; and various data-cleansing operations.
- Operations in Table 11.2 include resampling and reservoir sampling.
- Operations in Table 11.3 include partial least-squares transformation.
- *MultiClassClassifier* (see Table 11.6; includes many ways of handling multiclass problems with two-class classifiers, including error-correcting output codes)
- *END* (see Table 11.6; ensembles of nested dichotomies)

Ensemble Learning

Having studied how to massage the input and calibrate the output, we now turn to techniques for combining different models learned from the data. There are some surprises in store. For example, it is often advantageous to take the training data and derive several different training sets from it, learn a model from each, and combine them to produce an ensemble of learned models. Indeed, techniques for doing this can be very powerful. It is, for example, possible to transform a relatively weak learning scheme into an extremely strong one (in a precise sense that we will explain). Loss of interpretability is a drawback when applying ensemble learning, but there are ways to derive intelligible structured descriptions based on what these methods learn. Finally, if several learning schemes are available, it may be advantageous not to choose the best-performing one for your dataset (using cross-validation) but to use them all and combine the results.

Many of these results are quite counterintuitive, at least at first blush. How can it be a good idea to use many different models together? How can you possibly do better than choose the model that performs best? Surely, all this runs counter to Occam's razor, which advocates simplicity? How can you possibly obtain first-class performance by combining indifferent models, as one of these techniques appears to do? But consider committees of humans, which often come up with wiser decisions than individual experts. Recall Epicurus' view that, faced with alternative explanations, one should retain them all. Imagine a group of specialists each of whom excels in a limited domain even though none is competent across the board. In struggling to understand how these methods work, researchers have exposed all sorts of connections and links that have led to even greater improvements.

8.1 COMBINING MULTIPLE MODELS

When wise people make critical decisions, they usually take into account the opinions of several experts rather than relying on their own judgment or that of a solitary trusted advisor. For example, before choosing an important new policy direction, a benign dictator consults widely: He or she would be ill advised to follow just one expert's opinion blindly. In a democratic setting, discussion of different viewpoints may produce a consensus; if not, a vote may be called for. In either case, different expert opinions are being combined.

In data mining, a model generated by machine learning can be regarded as an expert. *Expert* is probably too strong a word!—depending on the amount and quality of the training data, and whether the learning algorithm is appropriate to the problem at hand, the expert may in truth be regrettably ignorant—but we use the term nevertheless. An obvious approach to making decisions more reliable is to combine the output of several different models. Several machine learning techniques do this by learning an ensemble of models and using them in combination: Prominent among these are schemes called *bagging*, *boosting*, and *stacking*. They can all, more often than not, increase predictive performance over a single model. And they are general techniques that are able to be applied to classification tasks and numeric prediction problems.

Bagging, boosting, and stacking have been developed over the last couple of decades, and their performance is often astonishingly good. Machine learning researchers have struggled to understand why. And during that struggle, new methods have emerged that are sometimes even better. For example, whereas human committees rarely benefit from noisy distractions, shaking up bagging by adding random variants of classifiers can improve performance. Closer analysis reveals that boosting—perhaps the most powerful of the three methods—is closely related to the established statistical technique of additive models, and this realization has led to improved procedures.

These combined models share the disadvantage of being rather hard to analyze: They can comprise dozens or even hundreds of individual models, and although they perform well it is not easy to understand in intuitive terms what factors are contributing to the improved decisions. In the last few years methods have been developed that combine the performance benefits of committees with comprehensible models. Some produce standard decision tree models; others introduce new variants of trees that provide optional paths.

8.2 BAGGING

Combining the decisions of different models means amalgamating the various outputs into a single prediction. The simplest way to do this in the case of classification is to take a vote (perhaps a weighted vote); in the case of numeric prediction it is to calculate the average (perhaps a weighted average). Bagging and boosting both adopt this approach, but they derive the individual models in different ways. In bagging the models receive equal weight, whereas in boosting weighting is used to give more influence to the more successful ones—just as an executive might place different values on the advice of different experts depending on how successful their predictions were in the past.

To introduce bagging, suppose that several training datasets of the same size are chosen at random from the problem domain. Imagine using a particular machine learning technique to build a decision tree for each dataset. You might expect these trees to be practically identical and to make the same prediction for each new test instance. But, surprisingly, this assumption is usually quite wrong, particularly if the training datasets are fairly small. This is a rather disturbing fact and seems to cast a shadow over the whole enterprise! The reason for it is that decision tree induction (at least the standard top-down method described in Chapter 4) is an unstable process: Slight changes to the training data may easily result in a different attribute being chosen at a particular node, with significant ramifications for the structure of the subtree beneath that node. This automatically implies that there are test instances for which some of the decision trees produce correct predictions and others do not.

Returning to the preceding experts analogy, consider the experts to be the individual decision trees. We can combine the trees by having them vote on each test instance. If one class receives more votes than any other, it is taken as the correct one. Generally, the more the merrier: Predictions made by voting become more reliable as more votes are taken into account. Decisions rarely deteriorate if new training sets are discovered, trees are built for them, and their predictions participate in the vote as well. In particular, the combined classifier will seldom be less accurate than a decision tree constructed from just one of the datasets. (Improvement is not guaranteed, however. It can be shown theoretically that pathological situations exist in which the combined decisions are worse.)

Bias–Variance Decomposition

The effect of combining multiple hypotheses can be viewed through a theoretical device known as the *bias–variance decomposition*. Suppose we could have an infinite number of independent training sets of the same size and use them to make an infinite number of classifiers. A test instance is processed by all classifiers, and a single answer is determined by majority vote. In this idealized situation, errors will still occur because no learning scheme is perfect: The error rate will depend on how well the machine learning method matches the problem at hand, and there is also the effect of noise in the data, which cannot possibly be learned.

Suppose the expected error rate were evaluated by averaging the error of the combined classifier over an infinite number of independently chosen test examples. The error rate for a particular learning algorithm is called its *bias* for the learning problem and measures how well the learning method matches the problem. (We include the "noise" component in the bias term because it is generally unknown in practice anyway.) This technical definition is a way of quantifying the vaguer notion of bias that was introduced in Section 1.5 (page 31): It measures the "persistent" error of a learning algorithm that can't be eliminated even by taking an infinite number of training sets into account. Of course, it cannot be calculated exactly in practical situations; it can only be approximated.

A second source of error in a learned model, in a practical situation, stems from the particular training set used, which is inevitably finite and therefore not fully representative of the actual population of instances. The expected value of this component of the error, over all possible training sets of the given size and all possible test sets, is called the *variance* of the learning method for that problem. The total expected error of a classifier is made up of the sum of bias and variance—this is the *bias–variance decomposition*.

Note that we are glossing over the details here. The bias–variance decomposition was introduced in the context of numeric prediction based on squared error, where there is a widely accepted way of performing it. However, the situation is not so clear for classification, and several competing decompositions have been proposed. Regardless of the specific decomposition used to analyze the error, combining multiple classifiers in this manner generally decreases the expected error by reducing the variance component. The more classifiers that are included, the greater the reduction in variance. Of course, a difficulty arises when putting this voting scheme into practice: Usually there's only one training set, and obtaining more data is either impossible or expensive.

Bagging attempts to neutralize the instability of learning methods by simulating the process described previously using a given training set. Instead of sampling a fresh, independent training dataset each time, the original training data is altered by deleting some instances and replicating others. Instances are randomly sampled, with replacement, from the original dataset to create a new one of the same size. This sampling procedure inevitably replicates some of the instances and deletes others. If this idea strikes a chord, it is because we encountered it in Section 5.4 (page 155) when explaining the bootstrap method for estimating the generalization error of a learning method; indeed, the term *bagging* stands for *bootstrap aggregating*. Bagging applies the learning scheme—for example, a decision tree inducer—to each one of these artificially derived datasets, and the classifiers generated from them vote for the class to be predicted. The algorithm is summarized in Figure 8.1.

The difference between bagging and the idealized procedure described before is the way in which the training datasets are derived. Instead of obtaining independent datasets from the domain, bagging just resamples the original training data. The datasets generated by resampling are different from one another but are certainly not independent because they are all based on one dataset. However, it turns out that bagging produces a combined model that often performs significantly better than the single model built from the original training data, and is never substantially worse.

Bagging can also be applied to learning schemes for numeric prediction—for example, model trees. The only difference is that, instead of voting on the outcome, the individual predictions, being real numbers, are averaged. The bias–variance decomposition is applied to numeric prediction by decomposing the expected value

Model Generation

```
Let n be the number of instances in the training data.
For each of t iterations:
  Sample n instances with replacement from training data.
  Apply the learning algorithm to the sample.
  Store the resulting model.
```

Classification

```
For each of the t models:
  Predict class of instance using model.
Return class that has been predicted most often.
```

FIGURE 8.1

Algorithm for bagging.

of the mean-squared error of the predictions on fresh data. Bias is defined as the mean-squared error expected when averaging over models built from all possible training datasets of the same size, and variance is the component of the expected error of a single model that is due to the particular training data it was built from. It can be shown theoretically that averaging over infinitely many models built from independent training sets always reduces the expected value of the mean-squared error. (As we mentioned earlier, the analogous result is not true for classification.)

Bagging with Costs

Bagging helps most if the underlying learning scheme is unstable in that small changes in the input data can lead to quite different classifiers. Indeed, results can be improved by increasing the diversity in the ensemble of classifiers by making the learning scheme as unstable as possible. For example, when bagging decision trees, which are already unstable, better performance is often achieved by switching pruning off, which makes them even more unstable. Another improvement can be obtained by changing the way that predictions are combined for classification. As originally formulated, bagging uses voting. But when the models can output probability estimates and not just plain classifications, it makes intuitive sense to average these probabilities instead. Not only does this often improve classification slightly, but the bagged classifier also generates probability estimates—ones that are often more accurate than those produced by the individual models. Implementations of bagging commonly use this method of combining predictions.

In Section 5.7 (page 166), we showed how to make a classifier cost sensitive by minimizing the expected cost of predictions. Accurate probability estimates are necessary because they are used to obtain the expected cost of each prediction. Bagging is a prime candidate for cost-sensitive classification because it produces very accurate probability estimates from decision trees and other powerful, yet unstable, classifiers. However, a disadvantage is that bagged classifiers are hard to analyze.

A method called *MetaCost* combines the predictive benefits of bagging with a comprehensible model for cost-sensitive prediction. It builds an ensemble classifier using bagging and deploys it to relabel the training data by giving every training instance the prediction that minimizes the expected cost, based on the probability estimates obtained from bagging. MetaCost then discards the original class labels and learns a single new classifier—for example, a single pruned decision tree—from the relabeled data. This new model automatically takes costs into account because they have been built into the class labels! The result is a single cost-sensitive classifier that can be analyzed to see how predictions are made.

In addition to the cost-sensitive *classification* technique just mentioned, Section 5.7 (page 167) also described a cost-sensitive *learning* method that learns a cost-sensitive classifier by changing the proportion of each class in the training data to reflect the cost matrix. MetaCost seems to produce more accurate results than this method, but it requires more computation. If there is no need for a comprehensible model, MetaCost's postprocessing step is superfluous: It is better to use the bagged classifier directly in conjunction with the minimum expected cost method.

8.3 RANDOMIZATION

Bagging generates a diverse ensemble of classifiers by introducing randomness into the learning algorithm's input, often with excellent results. But there are other ways of creating diversity by introducing randomization. Some learning algorithms already have a built-in random component. For example, when learning multilayer perceptrons using the backpropagation algorithm (as described in Section 6.4—page 235), the initial network weights are set to small randomly chosen values. The learned classifier depends on the random numbers because the algorithm may find a different local minimum of the error function. One way to make the outcome of classification more stable is to run the learner several times with different random number seeds and combine the classifiers' predictions by voting or averaging.

Almost every learning method is amenable to some kind of randomization. Consider an algorithm that greedily picks the best option at every step, such as a decision tree learner that picks the best attribute to split on at each node. It could be randomized by picking one of the N best options at random instead of a single winner, or by choosing a random subset of options and picking the best from that. Of course, there is a tradeoff: More randomness generates more variety in the learner but makes less use of the data, probably decreasing the accuracy of each individual model. The best dose of randomness can only be prescribed by experiment.

Although bagging and randomization yield similar results, it sometimes pays to combine them because they introduce randomness in different, perhaps complementary, ways. A popular algorithm for learning random forests builds a randomized decision tree in each iteration of the bagging algorithm, and often produces excellent predictors.

Randomization versus Bagging

Randomization demands more work than bagging because the learning algorithm must be modified, but it can profitably be applied to a greater variety of learners. Bagging fails with stable learning algorithms whose output is insensitive to small changes in the input. For example, it is pointless to bag nearest-neighbor classifiers because their output changes very little if the training data is perturbed by sampling. But randomization can be applied even to stable learners: The trick is to randomize in a way that makes the classifiers diverse without sacrificing too much performance. A nearest-neighbor classifier's predictions depend on the distances between instances, which in turn depend heavily on which attributes are used to compute them, so nearest-neighbor classifiers can be randomized by using different, randomly chosen subsets of attributes. In fact, this approach is called the *random subspaces* method for constructing an ensemble of classifiers and was proposed as a method for learning a random forest. As with bagging, it does not require any modification to the learning algorithm. Of course, random subspaces can be used in conjunction with bagging in order to introduce randomness to the learning process in terms of both instances and attributes.

Returning to plain bagging, the idea is to exploit instability in the learning algorithm in order to create diversity among the ensemble members—but the degree of diversity achieved is less than that of other ensemble learning methods such as random forests because of randomization built into the learning algorithm, or boosting (discussed in Section 8.4). This is because bootstrap sampling creates training data sets with a distribution that resembles the original data. Consequently, the classifiers learned by bagging are individually quite accurate, but their low diversity can detract from the overall accuracy of the ensemble. Introducing randomness in the learning algorithm increases diversity but sacrifices accuracy of the individual classifiers. If it were possible for ensemble members to be both diverse and individually accurate, smaller ensembles could be used. Of course, this would have computational benefits.

Rotation Forests

An ensemble learning method called *rotation forests* has the specific goal of creating diverse yet accurate classifiers. It combines the random subspace and bagging approaches with principal components feature generation to construct an ensemble of decision trees. In each iteration, the input attributes are randomly divided into k disjoint subsets. Principal components analysis is applied to each subset in turn in order to create linear combinations of the attributes in the subset that are rotations of the original axes. The k sets of principal components are used to compute values for the derived attributes; these comprise the input to the tree learner at each iteration. Because all the components obtained on each subset are retained, there are as many derived attributes as there are original ones. To discourage the generation of identical coefficients if the same feature subset is chosen in different iterations, principal component analysis is applied to training instances from a randomly chosen subset of the class values (however, the values of the derived attributes that are input to the tree learner are computed from all the instances in the training data). To further increase diversity, a bootstrap sample of the data can be created in each iteration before the principal components transformations are applied.

Experiments indicate that rotation forests can give similar performance to random forests, with far fewer trees. An analysis of diversity (measured by the Kappa statistic, introduced in Section 5.7 (page 166), which can be used to measure agreement between classifiers) versus error for pairs of ensemble members shows a minimal increase in diversity and reduction in error for rotation forests when compared to bagging. However, this appears to translate into significantly better performance for the ensemble as a whole.

8.4 BOOSTING

We have explained that bagging exploits the instability inherent in learning algorithms. Intuitively, combining multiple models only helps when these models are significantly different from one another and each one treats a reasonable percentage of the data correctly. Ideally, the models complement one another, each being a specialist in a part of the domain where the other models don't perform very well—just as human executives seek advisors whose skills and experience complement, rather than duplicate, one another.

The boosting method for combining multiple models exploits this insight by explicitly seeking models that complement one another. First, the similarities: Like bagging, boosting uses voting (for classification) or averaging (for numeric prediction) to combine the output of individual models. Again like bagging, it combines models of the same type—for example, decision trees. However, boosting is iterative. Whereas in bagging individual models are built separately, in boosting each new model is influenced by the performance of those built previously. Boosting encourages new models to become experts for instances handled incorrectly by earlier ones by assigning greater weight to those instances. A final difference is that boosting weights a model's contribution by its confidence rather than giving equal weight to all models.

AdaBoost

There are many variants on the idea of boosting. We describe a widely used method called *AdaBoost.M1* that is designed specifically for classification. Like bagging, it can be applied to any classification learning algorithm. To simplify matters we assume that the learning algorithm can handle weighted instances, where the weight of an instance is a positive number (we revisit this asumption later). The presence of instance weights changes the way in which a classifier's error is calculated: It is the sum of the weights of the misclassified instances divided by the total weight of all instances, instead of the fraction of instances that are misclassified. By weighting instances, the learning algorithm can be forced to concentrate on a particular set of instances, namely those with high weight. Such instances become particularly important because there is a greater incentive to classify them correctly. The C4.5 algorithm, described in Section 6.1, is an example of a learning method that can accommodate weighted instances without modification because it already uses the notion of fractional instances to handle missing values.

The boosting algorithm, summarized in Figure 8.2, begins by assigning equal weight to all instances in the training data. It then calls the learning algorithm to form a classifier for this data and reweights each instance according to the classifier's output. The weight of correctly classified instances is decreased, and that of misclassified ones is increased. This produces a set of "easy" instances with low weight and a set of "hard" ones with high weight. In the next iteration—and all subsequent ones—a classifier is built for the reweighted data, which consequently focuses on classifying the hard instances correctly. Then the instances' weights are increased or decreased according to the output of this new classifier. As a result, some hard instances might become even harder and easier ones even easier; on the other hand, other hard instances might become easier, and easier ones harder—all possibilities can occur in practice. After each iteration, the weights reflect how often the instances have been misclassified by the classifiers produced so far. By maintaining a measure

Model Generation

```
Assign equal weight to each training instance.
For each of t iterations:
  Apply learning algorithm to weighted dataset and store resulting
    model.
  Compute error e of model on weighted dataset and store error.
  If e equal to zero, or e greater or equal to 0.5:
    Terminate model generation.
  For each instance in dataset:
    If instance classified correctly by model:
      Multiply weight of instance by e / (1 - e).
  Normalize weight of all instances.
```

Classification

```
Assign weight of zero to all classes.
For each of the t (or less) models:
  Add -log(e / (1 - e)) to weight of class predicted by model.
Return class with highest weight.
```

FIGURE 8.2

Algorithm for boosting.

of "hardness" with each instance, this procedure provides an elegant way of generating a series of experts that complement one another.

How much should the weights be altered after each iteration? The answer depends on the current classifier's overall error. More specifically, if e denotes the classifier's error on the weighted data (a fraction between 0 and 1), then weights are updated by

$$weight \leftarrow weight \times e/(1 - e)$$

for correctly classified instances, and the weights remain unchanged for misclassified ones. Of course, this does not increase the weight of misclassified instances as claimed earlier. However, after all weights have been updated they are renormalized so that their sum remains the same as it was before. Each instance's weight is divided by the sum of the new weights and multiplied by the sum of the old ones. This automatically increases the weight of each misclassified instance and reduces that of each correctly classified one.

Whenever the error on the weighted training data exceeds or equals 0.5, the boosting procedure deletes the current classifier and does not perform any more iterations. The same thing happens when the error is 0 because then all instance weights become 0.

We have explained how the boosting method generates a series of classifiers. To form a prediction, their output is combined using a weighted vote. To determine the weights, note that a classifier that performs well on the weighted training data from which it was built (e close to 0) should receive a high weight, and a classifier that performs badly (e close to 0.5) should receive a low one. The AdaBoost.M1 algorithm uses

$$weight = -\log \frac{e}{1 - e}$$

which is a positive number between 0 and infinity. Incidentally, this formula explains why classifiers that perform perfectly on the training data must be deleted: When e is 0 the weight is undefined. To make a prediction, the weights of all classifiers that vote for a particular class are summed, and the class with the greatest total is chosen.

We began by assuming that the learning algorithm can cope with weighted instances. Any algorithm can be adapted to deal with weighted instances; we explained how at the end of Section 6.6, Locally Weighted Linear Regression (page 258). Instead of changing the learning algorithm, it is possible to generate an unweighted dataset from the weighted data by resampling—the same technique that bagging uses. Whereas for bagging, each instance is chosen with equal probability, for boosting, instances are chosen with probability proportional to their weight. As a result, instances with high weight are replicated frequently, and ones with low weight may never be selected. Once the new dataset becomes as large as the original one, it is fed into the learning scheme instead of the weighted data. It's as simple as that.

A disadvantage of this procedure is that some instances with low weight don't make it into the resampled dataset, so information is lost before the learning scheme is applied. However, this can be turned into an advantage. If the learning scheme produces a classifier with an error that exceeds 0.5, boosting must terminate if the weighted data is used directly, whereas with resampling it might be possible to produce a classifier with an error below 0.5 by discarding the resampled dataset and generating a new one from a different random seed. Sometimes more boosting iterations can be performed by resampling than when using the original weighted version of the algorithm.

The Power of Boosting

The idea of boosting originated in a branch of machine learning research known as *computational learning theory*. Theoreticians are interested in boosting because it is possible to derive performance guarantees. For example, it can be shown that the error of the combined classifier on the training data approaches 0 very quickly as more iterations are performed (exponentially quickly in the number of iterations). Unfortunately, as explained in Section 5.1, guarantees for the training error are not very interesting because they do not necessarily indicate good performance on fresh data. However, it can be shown theoretically that boosting only fails on fresh data if the individual classifiers are too "complex" for the amount of training data present or if their training errors become too large too quickly (in a precise sense explained by Schapire et al., 1997). As usual, the problem lies in finding the right balance between the individual models' complexity and their fit to the data.

If boosting does succeed in reducing the error on fresh test data, it often does so in a spectacular way. One very surprising finding is that performing more boosting iterations can reduce the error on new data long after the error of the combined classifier on the training data has dropped to 0. Researchers were puzzled by this result because it seems to contradict Occam's razor, which declares that, of two hypotheses that explain the empirical evidence equally well, the simpler one is to be preferred. Performing more boosting iterations without reducing the training error does not explain the training data any better, and it certainly adds complexity to the combined classifier. The contradiction can be resolved by considering the classifier's confidence in its predictions. More specifically, we measure confidence by the difference between the estimated confidence for the true class and that of the most likely predicted class other than the true class—a quantity known as the *margin*. The larger the margin, the more confident the classifier is in predicting the true class. It turns out that boosting can increase the margin long after the training error has dropped to 0. The effect can be visualized by plotting the cumulative distribution of the margin values of all the training instances for different numbers of boosting iterations, giving a graph known as the *margin curve*. Thus, if the explanation of empirical evidence takes the margin into account, Occam's razor remains as sharp as ever.

The beautiful thing about boosting is that a powerful combined classifier can be built from very simple ones as long as they achieve less than 50% error on the reweighted data. Usually, this is easy—certainly for learning problems with two classes! Simple learning schemes are called *weak* learners, and boosting converts weak learners into strong ones. For example, good results for two-class problems can often be obtained by boosting extremely simple decision trees that have only one level, called *decision stumps*. Another possibility is to apply boosting to an algorithm that learns a single conjunctive rule—such as a single path in a decision tree—and classifies instances based on whether or not the rule covers them. Of course, multiclass datasets make it more difficult to achieve error rates below 0.5. Decision trees can still be boosted, but they usually need to be more complex than decision stumps. More sophisticated algorithms have been developed that allow very simple models to be boosted successfully in multiclass situations.

Boosting often produces classifiers that are significantly more accurate on fresh data than ones generated by bagging. However, unlike bagging, boosting sometimes fails in practical situations: It can generate a classifier that is significantly less accurate than a single classifier built from the same data. This indicates that the combined classifier overfits the data.

8.5 ADDITIVE REGRESSION

When boosting was first investigated it sparked intense interest among researchers because it could coax first-class performance from indifferent learners. Statisticians soon discovered that it could be recast as a greedy algorithm for fitting an additive model. Additive models have a long history in statistics. Broadly, the term refers to any way of generating predictions by summing up contributions obtained from other models. Most learning algorithms for additive models do not build the base models independently but ensure that they complement one another and try to form an ensemble of base models that optimizes predictive performance according to some specified criterion.

Boosting implements *forward stagewise additive modeling*. This class of algorithms starts with an empty ensemble and incorporates new members sequentially. At each stage the model that maximizes the predictive performance of the ensemble as a whole is added, without altering those already in the ensemble. Optimizing the ensemble's performance implies that the next model should focus on those training instances on which the ensemble performs poorly. This is exactly what boosting does by giving those instances larger weights.

Numeric Prediction

Here's a well-known forward stagewise additive modeling method for numeric prediction. First, build a standard regression model—for example, a regression tree. The errors it exhibits on the training data—the differences between predicted and observed values—are called *residuals*. Then correct for these errors by learning a second model—perhaps another regression tree—that tries to predict the observed residuals. To do this, simply replace the original class values by their residuals before learning the second model. Adding the predictions made by the second model to those of the first one automatically yields lower error on the training data. Usually some residuals still remain because the second model is not a perfect one, so we continue with a third model that learns to predict the residuals of the residuals, and so on. The procedure is reminiscent of the use of rules with exceptions for classification that we discussed in Section 3.4 (page 73).

If the individual models minimize the squared error of the predictions, as linear regression models do, this algorithm minimizes the squared error of the ensemble as a whole. In practice, it also works well when the base learner uses a heuristic approximation instead, such as the regression and model tree learners described in Section 6.6. In fact, there is no point in using standard linear regression as the base learner for additive regression because the sum of linear regression models is again a linear regression model and the regression algorithm itself minimizes the squared error. However, it is a different story if the base learner is a regression model based on a single attribute, the one that minimizes the squared error. Statisticians call this *simple* linear regression, in contrast to the standard multi-attribute method, properly called *multiple* linear regression. In fact, using additive regression in conjunction with simple linear regression and iterating until the squared error of the ensemble decreases no further yields an additive model identical to the least-squares multiple linear regression function.

Forward stagewise additive regression is prone to overfitting because each model added fits the training data closer and closer. To decide when to stop, use cross-validation. For example, perform a cross-validation for every number of iterations up to a user-specified maximum and choose the one that minimizes the cross-validated estimate of squared error. This is a good stopping criterion because cross-validation yields a fairly reliable estimate of the error on future data. Incidentally, using this method in conjunction with simple linear regression as the base learner effectively combines multiple linear regression with built-in attribute selection. The reason is that the next most important attribute's contribution is only included if it decreases the cross-validated error.

For implementation convenience, forward stagewise additive regression usually begins with a level-0 model that simply predicts the mean of the class on the training data so that every subsequent model fits residuals. This suggests another possibility for preventing overfitting: Instead of subtracting a model's entire prediction to generate target values for the next model, shrink the predictions by multiplying them by a user-specified constant factor between 0 and 1 before subtracting. This reduces the model's fit to the residuals and consequently reduces the chance of overfitting. Of course, it may increase the number of iterations needed to arrive at a good additive model. Reducing the multiplier effectively damps down the learning process, increasing the chance of stopping at just the right moment but also increasing runtime.

Additive Logistic Regression

Additive regression can also be applied to classification just as linear regression can. But we know from Section 4.6 that logistic regression is more suitable than linear regression for classification. It turns out that a similar adaptation can be made to additive models by modifying the forward stagewise modeling method to perform additive *logistic* regression. Use the logit transform to translate the probability estimation problem into a regression problem, as we did in Section 4.6 (page 126), and solve the regression task using an ensemble of models—for example, regression trees—just as for additive regression. At each stage, add the model that maximizes the probability of the data given the ensemble classifier.

Suppose f_j is the jth regression model in the ensemble and $f_j(\mathbf{a})$ is its prediction for instance $\mathbf{a}$. Assuming a two-class problem, use the additive model $\Sigma f_j(\mathbf{a})$ to obtain a probability estimate for the first class:

$$p(1 \mid \mathbf{a}) = \frac{1}{1 + e^{-\Sigma f_j(\mathbf{a})}}$$

This closely resembles the expression used in Section 4.6 (page 126), except that here it is abbreviated by using vector notation for the instance $\mathbf{a}$ and the original weighted sum of the attributes' values is replaced by a sum of arbitrarily complex regression models f.

Figure 8.3 shows the two-class version of the so-called *LogitBoost* algorithm, which performs additive logistic regression and generates the individual models f_j. Here, y_i is 1 for an instance in the first class and 0 for an instance in the second. In each iteration this algorithm fits a regression model f_j to a weighted version of the original dataset based on dummy class values z_i and weights w_i. We assume that $p(1 \mid \mathbf{a})$ is computed using the f_j that were built in previous iterations.

The derivation of this algorithm is beyond the scope of this book, but it can be shown that the algorithm maximizes the probability of the data with respect to the ensemble if each model f_j is determined by minimizing the squared error on the corresponding regression problem. In fact, if multiple linear regression is used to form the f_j, the algorithm converges to the maximum-likelihood, linear-logistic regression model: It is an incarnation of the iteratively reweighted least-squares method mentioned in Section 4.6 (page 126).

Superficially, LogitBoost looks quite different from AdaBoost, but the predictors they produce differ mainly in that the former optimizes the likelihood directly whereas the latter optimizes an exponential loss function that can be regarded as an approximation to it. From a practical perspective, the difference is that LogitBoost uses a regression scheme as the base learner whereas AdaBoost works with classification algorithms.

We have only shown the two-class version of LogitBoost, but the algorithm can be generalized to multiclass problems. As with additive regression, the danger of overfitting can be reduced by shrinking the predictions of the individual f_j by a

Model generation

```
for j = 1 to t iterations:
  for each instance a[i]:
    set the target value for the regression to
      z[i] = (y[i] - p(1|a[i])) / [p(1|a[i]) * (1 - p(1|a[i]))]
    set the weight w[i] of instance a[i] to p(1|a[i]) * (1 - p(1|a[i]))
  fit a regression model f[j] to the data with class values z[i] and
    weights w[i]
```

Classification

```
predict class 1 if p(1 | a) > 0.5, otherwise predict class 0
```

FIGURE 8.3

Algorithm for additive logistic regression.

predetermined multiplier and using cross-validation to determine an appropriate number of iterations.

8.6 INTERPRETABLE ENSEMBLES

Bagging, boosting, and randomization all produce ensembles of classifiers. This makes it very difficult to analyze what kind of information has been extracted from the data. It would be nice to have a single model with the same predictive performance. One possibility is to generate an artificial dataset, by randomly sampling points from the instance space and assigning them the class labels predicted by the ensemble classifier, and then learn a decision tree or rule set from this new dataset. To obtain similar predictive performance from the tree as from the ensemble, a huge dataset may be required, but in the limit this strategy should be able to replicate the performance of the ensemble classifier—and it certainly will if the ensemble itself consists of decision trees.

Option Trees

Another approach is to derive a single structure that can represent an ensemble of classifiers compactly. This can be done if the ensemble consists of decision trees; the result is called an *option tree*. Option trees differ from decision trees in that they contain two types of node: decision nodes and option nodes. Figure 8.4 shows a simple example for the weather data, with only one option node. To classify an instance, filter it down through the tree. At a decision node take just one of the

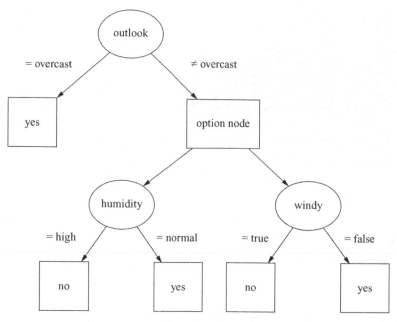

FIGURE 8.4

Simple option tree for the weather data.

branches, as usual, but at an option node take *all* of the branches. This means that the instance ends up in more than one leaf, and the classifications obtained from those leaves must somehow be combined into an overall classification. This can be done simply by voting, taking the majority vote at an option node to be the prediction of the node. In that case it makes little sense to have option nodes with only two options (as in Figure 8.4) because there will only be a majority if both branches agree. Another possibility is to average the probability estimates obtained from the different paths, using either an unweighted average or a more sophisticated Bayesian approach.

Option trees can be generated by modifying an existing decision tree learner to create an option node if there are several splits that look similarly useful according to their information gain. All choices within a certain user-specified tolerance of the best one can be made into options. During pruning, the error of an option node is the average error of its options.

Another possibility is to grow an option tree by incrementally adding nodes to it. This is commonly done using a boosting algorithm, and the resulting trees are usually called *alternating decision trees* instead of option trees. In this context, the decision nodes are called *splitter nodes* and the option nodes are called *prediction nodes*. Prediction nodes are leaves if no splitter nodes have been added to them yet. The standard alternating decision tree applies to two-class problems, and with each prediction node a positive or negative numeric value is associated. To obtain a

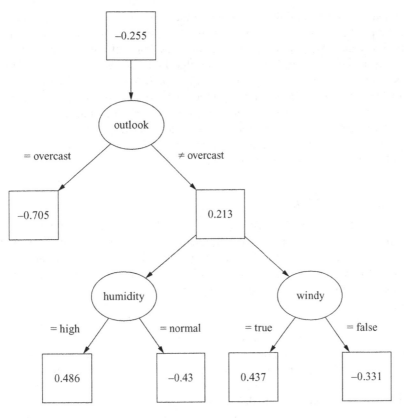

FIGURE 8.5

Alternating decision tree for the weather data.

prediction for an instance, filter it down all applicable branches and sum up the values from any prediction nodes that are encountered; predict one class or the other depending on whether the sum is positive or negative.

A simple example tree for the weather data is shown in Figure 8.5, where a positive value corresponds to class *play = no* and a negative one to *play = yes*. To classify an instance with *outlook = sunny*, *temperature = hot*, *humidity = normal*, and *windy = false*, filter it down to the corresponding leaves, obtaining values −0.255, 0.213, −0.430, and −0.331. The sum of these values is negative; thus, predict *play = yes*. Alternating decision trees always have a prediction node at the root, as in this example.

The alternating tree is grown using a boosting algorithm—for example, a boosting algorithm that employs a base learner for numeric prediction, such as the Logit-Boost method described previously. Assume that the base learner produces a single conjunctive rule in each boosting iteration. Then an alternating decision tree can be generated by simply adding each rule into the tree. The numeric scores associated with the prediction nodes are obtained from the rules. However, the resulting tree would grow large very quickly because the rules from different boosting iterations are likely to be different. Thus, learning algorithms for alternating decision trees consider only those rules that extend one of the *existing* paths in the tree by adding a splitter node and two corresponding prediction nodes (assuming binary splits). In the standard version of the algorithm, every possible location in the tree is considered for addition and a node is added according to a performance measure that depends on the particular boosting algorithm employed. However, heuristics can be used instead of an exhaustive search to speed up the learning process.

Logistic Model Trees

Option trees and alternating trees yield very good classification performance based on a single structure, but they may still be difficult to interpret when there are many option nodes because it becomes difficult to see how a particular prediction is derived. However, it turns out that boosting can also be used to build very effective decision trees that do not include any options at all. For example, the LogitBoost algorithm has been used to induce trees with linear-logistic regression models at the leaves. These are called *logistic model trees* and are interpreted in the same way as the model trees for regression described in Section 6.6.

LogitBoost performs additive logistic regression. Suppose that each iteration of the boosting algorithm fits a simple regression function by going through all the attributes, finding the simple regression function with the smallest error, and adding it into the additive model. If the LogitBoost algorithm is run until convergence, the result is a maximum-likelihood, multiple-logistic regression model. However, for optimum performance on future data it is usually unnecessary to wait for convergence—and to do so is often detrimental. An appropriate number of boosting iterations can be determined by estimating the expected performance for a given number of iterations using cross-validation and stopping the process when performance ceases to increase.

A simple extension of this algorithm leads to logistic model trees. The boosting process terminates when there is no further structure in the data that can be modeled using a linear-logistic regression function. However, there may still be structure that linear models can fit if attention is restricted to subsets of the data, obtained, for example, by splitting the data using a standard decision tree criterion such as information gain. Then, once no further improvement can be obtained by adding more simple linear models, the data is split and boosting is resumed separately in each subset. This process takes the logistic model generated so far and refines it separately for the data in each subset. Again, cross-validation is run in each subset to determine an appropriate number of iterations to perform in that subset.

The process is applied recursively until the subsets become too small. The resulting tree will surely overfit the training data, and one of the standard methods of decision tree learning can be used to prune it. Experiments indicate that the pruning operation is very important. Using the cost-complexity pruning method discussed in Section 6.1 (page 202), which chooses the right tree size using cross-validation, the algorithm produces small but very accurate trees with linear logistic models at the leaves.

8.7 STACKING

Stacked generalization, or *stacking* for short, is a different way of combining multiple models. Although developed some years ago, it is less widely used than bagging and boosting partly because it is difficult to analyze theoretically and partly because there is no generally accepted best way of doing it—the basic idea can be applied in many different variations.

Unlike bagging and boosting, stacking is not normally used to combine models of the same type—for example, a set of decision trees. Instead, it is applied to models built by different learning algorithms. Suppose you have a decision tree inducer, a Naïve Bayes learner, and an instance-based learning scheme and you want to form a classifier for a given dataset. The usual procedure would be to estimate the expected error of each algorithm by cross-validation and to choose the best one to form a model for prediction on future data. But isn't there a better way? With three learning algorithms available, can't we use all three for prediction and combine the outputs?

One way to combine outputs is by voting—the same mechanism used in bagging. However, (unweighted) voting only makes sense if the learning schemes perform comparably well. If two of the three classifiers make predictions that are grossly incorrect, we will be in trouble! Instead, stacking introduces the concept of a *metalearner*, which replaces the voting procedure. The problem with voting is that it's not clear which classifier to trust. Stacking tries to *learn* which classifiers are the reliable ones, using another learning algorithm—the metalearner—to discover how best to combine the output of the base learners.

The input to the metamodel—also called the *level-1 model*—are the predictions of the base models, or *level-0 models*. A level-1 instance has as many attributes as there are level-0 learners, and the attribute values give the predictions of these learners on the corresponding level-0 instance. When the stacked learner is used for classification, an instance is first fed into the level-0 models, and each one guesses a class value. These guesses are fed into the level-1 model, which combines them into the final prediction.

There remains the problem of training the level-1 learner. To do this, we need to find a way of transforming the level-0 training data (used for training the level-0 learners) into level-1 training data (used for training the level-1 learner). This seems straightforward: Let each level-0 model classify a training instance, and attach to their predictions the instance's actual class value to yield a level-1 training instance. Unfortunately, this doesn't work well. It allows simplistic rules to be learned, such as *always believe the output of classifier A, and ignore B and C.* This rule may well be appropriate for particular base classifiers A, B, and C; and if so it will probably be learned. But just because it seems appropriate on the training data doesn't necessarily mean that it will work well on the test data—because it will inevitably learn to prefer classifiers that overfit the training data over ones that make decisions more realistically.

Consequently, stacking does not simply transform the level-0 training data into level-1 data in this manner. Recall from Chapter 5 that there are better methods of estimating a classifier's performance than using the error on the training set. One is to hold out some instances and use them for an independent evaluation. Applying this to stacking, we reserve some instances to form the training data for the level-1 learner and build level-0 classifiers from the remaining data. Once the level-0 classifiers have been built they are used to classify the instances in the holdout set, forming the level-1 training data. Because the level-0 classifiers haven't been trained on these instances, their predictions are unbiased; therefore, the level-1 training data accurately reflects the true performance of the level-0 learning algorithms. Once the level-1 data has been generated by this holdout procedure, the level-0 learners can be reapplied to generate classifiers from the full training set, making slightly better use of the data and leading to better predictions.

The holdout method inevitably deprives the level-1 model of some of the training data. In Chapter 5, cross-validation was introduced as a means of circumventing this problem for error estimation. This can be applied in conjunction with stacking by performing a cross-validation for every level-0 learner. Each instance in the training data occurs in exactly one of the test folds of the cross-validation, and the predictions of the level-0 inducers built from the corresponding training fold are used to build a level-1 training instance from it. This generates a level-1 training instance for each level-0 training instance. Of course, it is slow because a level-0 classifier has to be trained for each fold of the cross-validation, but it does allow the level-1 classifier to make full use of the training data.

Given a test instance, most learning schemes are able to output probabilities for every class label instead of making a single categorical prediction. This can be exploited to improve the performance of stacking by using the probabilities to form the level-1 data. The only difference from the standard procedure is that each nominal level-1 attribute—representing the class predicted by a level-0 learner—is replaced by several numeric attributes, each representing a class probability output by the level-0 learner. In other words, the number of attributes in the level-1 data is multiplied by the number of classes. This procedure has the advantage that the level-1 learner is privy to the confidence that each level-0 learner associates with its predictions, thereby amplifying communication between the two levels of learning.

An outstanding question remains: What algorithms are suitable for the level-1 learner? In principle, any learning scheme can be applied. However, because most of the work is already done by the level-0 learners, the level-1 classifier is basically just an arbiter and it makes sense to choose a rather simple algorithm for this purpose. In the words of David Wolpert, the inventor of stacking, it is reasonable that "relatively global, smooth" level-1 generalizers should perform well. Simple linear models or trees with linear models at the leaves usually work well.

Stacking can also be applied to numeric prediction. In that case, the level-0 models and the level-1 model all predict numeric values. The basic mechanism remains the same; the only difference lies in the nature of the level-1 data. In the numeric case, each level-1 attribute represents the numeric prediction made by one of the level-0 models, and instead of a class value the numeric target value is attached to level-1 training instances.

8.8 FURTHER READING

Ensemble learning is a popular research topic in machine learning research, with many related publications. The term *bagging* (for "bootstrap aggregating") was coined by Breiman (1996b), who investigated the properties of bagging theoretically and empirically for both classification and numeric prediction.

The bias–variance decomposition for classification presented in Section 8.2 is due to Dietterich and Kong (1995). We chose this version because it is both accessible and elegant. However, the variance can turn out to be negative because, as we mentioned, aggregating models from independent training sets by voting may in pathological situations actually *increase* the overall error compared to a model from a single training set. This is a serious disadvantage because variances are normally squared quantities—the square of the standard deviation—and therefore cannot become negative. In his technical report, Breiman (1996c) proposed a different bias–variance decomposition for classification. This has caused some confusion in the literature because three different versions of this report can be located on the Web. The official version, entitled "Arcing classifiers," describes a more complex decomposition that cannot, by construction, produce negative variance. However, the original version, entitled "Bias, variance, and arcing classifiers," follows Dietterich and Kong's formulation (except that Breiman splits the bias term into bias plus noise). There is also an intermediate version with the original title but the new decomposition; it includes an appendix in which Breiman explains that he abandoned the old definition because it can produce negative variance. (Authors sometimes mistakenly refer to the earlier drafts, which have been superseded, or use an earlier title for the latest, official, report.) However, in the new version (and in decompositions proposed by other authors) the bias of the aggregated classifier can exceed the bias of a classifier built from a single training set, which also seems counterintuitive.

The MetaCost algorithm was introduced by Domingos (1999).

The random subspace method was suggested as an approach for learning ensemble classifiers by Ho (1998) and applied as a method for learning ensembles of nearest-neighbor classifiers by Bay (1999). Randomization was evaluated by Dietterich (2000) and compared with bagging and boosting. Random forests were introduced by Breiman (2001). Rotation forests are a relatively new ensemble learning method introduced by Rodriguez et al. (2006). Subsequent studies by Kuncheva and

Rodriguez (2007) show that the main factors responsible for its performance are the use of principal components transformations (as opposed to other feature-extraction methods such as random projections) and the application of principal components analysis to random subspaces of the original input attributes.

Freund and Schapire (1996) developed the AdaBoost.M1 boosting algorithm and derived theoretical bounds for its performance. Later they improved these bounds using the concept of margins (Freund and Schapire, 1999). Drucker (1997) adapted AdaBoost.M1 for numeric prediction. The LogitBoost algorithm was developed by Friedman et al. (2000). Friedman (2001) describes how to make boosting more resilient in the presence of noisy data.

Domingos (1997) describes how to derive a single interpretable model from an ensemble using artificial training examples. Bayesian option trees were introduced by Buntine (1992), and majority voting was incorporated into option trees by Kohavi and Kunz (1997). Freund and Mason (1999) introduced alternating decision trees; experiments with multiclass alternating decision trees were reported by Holmes et al. (2002). Landwehr et al. (2005) developed logistic model trees using the LogitBoost algorithm.

Stacked generalization originated with Wolpert (1992), who presented the idea in the neural-network literature; it was applied to numeric prediction by Breiman (1996a). Ting and Witten (1997a) compared different level-1 models empirically and found that a simple linear model performs best; they also demonstrated the advantage of using probabilities as level-1 data. A combination of stacking and bagging has also been investigated (Ting and Witten, 1997b).

8.9 WEKA IMPLEMENTATIONS

In Weka, ensemble learning is done using the mechanism of "metalearners," described near the end of Section 11.2. They are covered in Section 11.5 and listed in Table 11.6, excluding the *RandomForest* classifier, which is located in Weka's *trees* package (Section 11.4 and Table 11.5), and the interpretable ensembles, which are also located there:

- Bagging:
  - *Bagging* (bag a classifier; works for regression too)
  - *MetaCost* (make a classifier cost-sensitive)
- Randomization:
  - *RandomCommittee* (ensembles using different random number seeds)
  - *RandomSubSpace* (ensembles using random subsets of attributes)
  - *RandomForest* (bag ensembles of random trees)
  - *RotationForest* (ensembles using rotated random subspaces)
- Boosting: *AdaBoostM1*
- Additive regression:
  - *AdditiveRegression*
  - *LogitBoost* (additive logistic regression)

- Interpretable ensembles:
  - *ADTree* (alternating decision trees)
  - *LADTree* (learns alternating decision trees using LogitBoost)
  - *LMT* (logistic model trees)
- Selecting or combining algorithms:
  - *MultiScheme* (selection using cross-validation)
  - *Vote* (simple combination of predictions)
  - *Stacking* (learns how to combine predictions)

Moving on: Applications and Beyond

9

Machine learning is a burgeoning new technology for mining knowledge from data, a technology that a lot of people are beginning to take seriously. We don't want to oversell it. The kind of machine learning we know is not about the big problems: futuristic visions of autonomous robot servants, philosophical conundrums of consciousness, metaphysical issues of free will, evolutionary (or theological) questions of where intelligence comes from, linguistic debates over language learning, psychological theories of child development, or cognitive explanations of what intelligence is and how it works. For us, it's far more prosaic: Machine learning is about algorithms for inferring structure from data and ways of validating that structure. These algorithms are not abstruse and complicated, but they're not completely obvious and trivial either.

Looking forward, the main challenge ahead is applications. Opportunities abound. Wherever there is data, things can be learned from it. Whenever there is too much data for people to pore over themselves, the mechanics of learning will have to be automatic. But the inspiration will certainly not be automatic! Applications will come not from computer programs, nor from machine learning experts, nor from the data itself, but from the people who work with the data and the problems from which it arises. That is why we have written this book, and that is what the Weka system described in Part III is for—to empower those who are not machine learning experts to apply these techniques to problems that arise in daily working life. The ideas are simple. The algorithms are here. The rest is really up to you!

Of course, development of the technology is certainly not finished. Machine learning is a hot research topic, and new ideas and techniques continually emerge. To give a flavor of the scope and variety of research fronts, we close Part II by looking at some topical areas in the world of data mining.

9.1 APPLYING DATA MINING

In 2006 a poll was taken by the organizers of the International Data Mining Conference to identify the top 10 data mining algorithms. Table 9.1 shows the results, in order. It is good to see that they are all covered in this book! The conference organizers divided the algorithms into rough categories, which are also shown. Many of

Table 9.1 Top 10 Algorithms in Data Mining

	Algorithm	Category	Book Section
1	C4.5	Classification	4.3, 6.2
2	*k*-means	Clustering	4.8
3	SVM	Statistical learning	6.4
4	Apriori	Association analysis	4.5, 6.3
5	EM	Statistical learning	6.8
6	PageRank	Link mining	9.6
7	Adaboost	Ensemble learning	8.4
8	kNN	Classification	4.7, 6.5
9	Naïve Bayes	Classification	4.2
10	CART	Classification	6.1

Note: *The information here was obtained during a 2006 poll conducted by the International Data Mining Conference.*

the assignments are rather arbitrary—Naïve Bayes, for example, is certainly a statistical learning method, and we have introduced EM as a statistically based clustering algorithm. Nevertheless, the emphasis on classification over other forms of learning, which reflects the emphasis in this book, is evident in the table, as is the dominance of C4.5, which we have also noted. One algorithm in Table 9.1 that has not been mentioned so far is the PageRank algorithm for link mining, which we were a little surprised to see in this list. Section 9.6 contains a brief description.

We have repeatedly stressed that productive use of data mining is not just a matter of finding some data and then blindly applying learning algorithms to it. Of course, the existence of the Weka workbench makes that easy to do—and therein lies a danger. We have seen many publications that seem to follow this methodology: The authors run a plethora of learning algorithms on a particular dataset and then write an article claiming that such-and-such a machine learning method is best for such-and-such a problem—with little apparent understanding of what those algorithms do, the nature of the data, or consideration of statistical significance. The usefulness of such studies is questionable.

A related but rather different issue concerns the improvements in machine learning methods that have been reported over the years. In a 2006 paper provocatively entitled "Classifier technology and the illusion of progress," David Hand, a prominent statistician and machine learning researcher, points out that a great many algorithms have been devised for supervised classification, and a great many comparative studies have been conducted that apparently establish the superiority of new methods over their predecessors. Yet he contends that the continued steady progress that publication of these studies seems to document is, in fact, to a large extent illusory. This message brings to mind the 1R machine learning scheme some 15 years earlier with which we began Chapter 4. As pointed out there, 1R was never really intended as a machine learning "method" but was devised to demonstrate that putting high-powered inductive inference methods to work on simple datasets is like using a sledgehammer to crack a nut. That insight underlies the simplicity-first methodology that pervades this book, of which Hand's recent paper is a salutary reminder.

How can progress be largely illusory, given documented improvements in measured classification success? The claim is basically that the differences in performance are very small and, in practical applications, are likely to be swamped by other sources of uncertainty. There are many reasons for this. Simple methods may not perform as well as complex ones, but they often perform nearly as well. An extremely simple model—always choose the majority class—sets a baseline upon which any learning method should be able to improve. Consider the improvement over the baseline achieved by a simple method as a proportion of the improvement over the baseline achieved by a sophisticated method. For a variety of randomly chosen datasets, it turns out that a very simple method achieved more than 90% of the improvement yielded by the most sophisticated scheme. This is not so surprising. In standard classification schemes such as decision trees and rules, a huge proportional gain in predictive accuracy is achieved at the beginning of the process when the first branch or rule is determined, and subsequent gains are small—usually very small indeed.

Small improvements are easily swamped by other factors. A fundamental assumption of machine learning is that the training data is representative of the distribution from which future data will be chosen—the assumption is generally that the data is independent and identically distributed (often abbreviated to IID). But in real life, things drift. Yet training data is always retrospective. And it might be quite old. Consider the loan scenario introduced in Section 1.3 (page 22). To collect a substantial volume of training data (and thorough training needs a substantial volume), we must wait until many loans have been issued. And then we must wait until the end of the loan period (two years? five years?) for the outcome to be known. By the time we use it for training, the data is quite old. And what has changed in the meantime? There are new ways of doing things. The bank has changed the way it defines measurements on which the features are based. New features have become available. Policies have altered. Is that ancient data really representative of today's problem?

Another fundamental problem is the reliability of the class labels in the training data. There may be small errors—random or even systematic ones—in which case, perhaps, we should stick to simpler models because the higher-order terms of more complex models may be very inaccurate. In determining class labels, someone, somewhere, may be mapping a gray world onto a black-and-white one, which requires judgment and invites inconsistency. And things may change: The notion of a "defaulter" on a loan—say, unpaid bills for three months—may be subtly different today than it was before—perhaps, in today's economic climate, hard-pressed customers will be given another couple of month's leeway before calling in the bailiffs. The point is not that learning will necessarily fail. The changes may be fairly subtle, and the learned models may still work well. The point is that the extra few percent gained by a sophisticated model over a simple one may be swamped by other factors.

Another issue, when looking at comparative experiments with machine learning methods, is who is doing the driving. It's not just a matter of firing up the various different methods and recording the results. Many machine learning schemes benefit from tweaking—optimization to fit the problem at hand. Hopefully the data used for tweaking is kept entirely separate from that used for training and testing (otherwise the results are dishonest). But it is natural that an expert in some particular method—maybe the person who developed it—can squeeze more performance out of it than someone else. If they are trying to get their work published, they will certainly want to present the new method in the best possible light. They may not be so experienced at squeezing good performance out of existing, competitive methods—or so diligent. New methods always look better than old ones; also, more complicated schemes are harder to criticize than simpler ones!

The upshot is that small gains in laboratory performance, even though real, may be swamped by other factors when machine learning is applied to a practical data mining problem. If you want to do something worthwhile on a practical dataset, you need to take the entire problem context into account.

9.2 LEARNING FROM MASSIVE DATASETS

The enormous proliferation of very large databases in today's companies and scientific institutions makes it necessary for machine learning algorithms to operate on massive datasets. Two separate dimensions become critical when any algorithm is applied to very large datasets: space and time.

Suppose the data is so large that it cannot be held in main memory. This causes no difficulty if the learning scheme works in an incremental fashion, processing one instance at a time when generating the model. An instance can be read from the input file, the model can be updated, the next instance can be read, and so on—without ever holding more than one training instance in main memory. This is "data stream learning," and we discuss it in the next section. Other methods, such as basic instance-based schemes and locally weighted regression, need access to all the training instances at prediction time. In that case, sophisticated caching and indexing mechanisms have to be employed to keep only the most frequently used parts of a dataset in memory and to provide rapid access to relevant instances in the file.

The other critical dimension when applying learning algorithms to massive datasets is time. If the learning time does not scale linearly (or almost linearly) with the number of training instances, it will eventually become infeasible to process very large datasets. In some applications the number of attributes is a critical factor, and only methods that scale linearly in the number of attributes are acceptable. Alternatively, prediction time might be the crucial issue. Fortunately, there are many learning algorithms that scale gracefully during both training and testing. For example, the training time for Naïve Bayes is linear in both the number of instances and the number of attributes. For top-down decision tree inducers, we saw in Section 6.1 (page 199) that training time is linear in the number of attributes and, if the tree is uniformly bushy, log-linear in the number of instances (if subtree raising is not used).

When a dataset is too large for a particular learning algorithm to be applied, there are three ways to make learning feasible. The first is trivial: Instead of applying the scheme to the full dataset, use just a small subset for training. Of course, information is lost when subsampling is employed. However, the loss may be negligible because the predictive performance of a learned model often flattens out long before all the training data is incorporated into it. If this is the case, it can easily be verified by observing the model's performance on a holdout test set for training sets of different sizes.

This kind of behavior, called the *law of diminishing returns*, may arise because the learning problem is a simple one, so that a small volume of training data is sufficient to learn an accurate model. Alternatively, the learning algorithm might be incapable of grasping the detailed structure of the underlying domain. This is often observed when Naïve Bayes is employed in a complex domain: Additional training data may not improve the performance of the model, whereas a decision tree's accuracy may continue to climb. In this case, of course, if predictive performance is the main objective, you should switch to the more complex learning algorithm. But beware of overfitting! Take care not to assess performance on the training data.

Parallelization is another way of reducing the time complexity of learning. The idea is to split the problem into smaller parts, solve each using a separate processor, and combine the results together. To do this, a parallelized version of the learning algorithm must be created. Some algorithms lend themselves naturally to parallelization. Nearest-neighbor methods, for example, can be easily distributed among several processors by splitting the data into parts and letting each processor find the nearest neighbor in its part of the training set. Decision tree learners can be parallelized by letting each processor build a subtree of the complete tree. Bagging and stacking (although not boosting) are naturally parallel algorithms. However, parallelization is only a partial remedy because with a fixed number of processors, the algorithm's asymptotic time complexity cannot be improved.

A simple way to apply any algorithm to a large dataset is to split the data into chunks of limited size and learn models separately for each one, combining the results using voting or averaging. Either a parallel bagging-like scheme or a sequential boosting-like scheme can be employed for this purpose. Boosting has the advantage that new chunks can be weighted based on the classifiers learned from previous chunks, thus transferring knowledge between chunks. In both cases, memory consumption increases linearly with dataset size; thus, some form of pruning is necessary for very large datasets. This can be done by setting aside some validation data and only adding a model from a new chunk to the committee classifier if it increases the committee's performance on the validation set. The validation set can also be used to identify an appropriate chunk size by running the method with several different chunk sizes in parallel and monitoring performance on the validation set.

The best but most challenging way to enable a learning paradigm to deal with very large datasets would be to develop new algorithms with lower computational complexity. In some cases, it is provably impossible to derive exact algorithms with lower complexity. Decision tree learners that deal with numeric attributes fall into this category. Their asymptotic time complexity is dominated by the sorting process for the numeric attribute values, a procedure that must be performed at least once for any given dataset. However, stochastic algorithms can sometimes be derived that approximate the true solution but require a much smaller amount of time.

Background knowledge can make it possible to vastly reduce the amount of data that needs to be processed by a learning algorithm. Depending on which attribute is the class, most of the attributes in a huge dataset might turn out to be irrelevant when background knowledge is taken into account. As usual, it pays to carefully engineer the data that is passed to the learning scheme and make the greatest possible use of any prior information about the learning problem at hand. If insufficient background knowledge is available, the attribute filtering algorithms described in Section 7.1 (page 308) can often drastically reduce the amount of data—possibly at the expense of a minor loss in predictive performance. Some of these—for example, attribute selection using decision trees or the 1R learning scheme—are linear in the number of attributes.

To give a feeling for the volume of data that can be handled by straightforward implementations of machine learning algorithms on ordinary microcomputers, we ran Weka's decision tree learner J4.8 on a dataset with 4.9 M instances, 40 attributes (almost all numeric), and a class with 25 values.[1] We used a reasonably modern Linux machine running Sun's 64-bit Java Virtual Machine (Java 1.6) in server mode with 6 Gb of heap space (half of this was required just to load the data). The resulting tree, which had 1388 nodes, took two hours to build. (A method that presorts the attributes and uses reduced-error pruning took only 30 minutes.) In general, Java is a little slower than equivalent C/C++ code—but less than twice as slow.

There are datasets today that truly deserve the adjective *massive*. Scientific datasets from astrophysics, nuclear physics, earth science, and molecular biology are measured in terabytes. So are datasets containing records of financial transactions. Application of standard programs for machine learning to such datasets in their entirety is a very challenging proposition.

9.3 DATA STREAM LEARNING

One way of addressing massive datasets is to develop learning algorithms that treat the input as a continuous data stream. In the new paradigm of data stream mining, which has developed during the last decade, algorithms are developed that cope

---

[1]We used the 1999 KDD Cup data at *http://kdd.ics.uci.edu/databases/kddcup99/kddcup99.html*. (See also *http://iscx.ca/NSL-KDD*.)

naturally with datasets that are many times the size of main memory—perhaps even indefinitely large. The core assumption is that each instance can be inspected once only (or at most once) and must then be discarded to make room for subsequent instances. The learning algorithm has no control over the order in which instances are processed and must update its model incrementally as each one arrives. Most models also satisfy the "anytime" property—they are ready to be applied at any point during the learning process. Such algorithms are ideal for real-time learning from data streams, making predictions in real time while adapting the model to changes in the evolving input stream. They are typically applied to online learning from data produced by physical sensors.

For such applications, the algorithm must operate indefinitely yet use a limited amount of memory. Even though we have stipulated that instances are discarded as soon as they have been processed, it is obviously necessary to remember at least something about at least some of the instances; otherwise, the model would be static. And as time progresses, the model grows—inexorably. But it must not be allowed to grow without bound. When processing big data, memory is quickly exhausted unless limits are enforced on every aspect of its use. Moving from space to time, algorithms intended for real-time application must process instances faster than they arrive, dealing with each one within a fixed, constant, preferably small, time bound. This does not allow, for example, for occasional complex reorganizations of a tree model—unless the cost can be amortized over several instances, which introduces a further level of complexity.

Naïve Bayes is a rare example of an algorithm that needs no adaptation to deal with data streams. Training is incremental: It merely involves updating a fixed set of numeric parameters. Memory usage is small because no structure is added to the model. Other classifiers with the same properties include 1R and the basic percep-tron. Multilayer neural nets usually have a fixed structure as well, and as we saw in Section 6.4 (page 238), stochastic backpropagation updates weights incrementally after each training instance has been processed, rather than in a batch operation, and thus is suitable for online learning. Rules with exceptions make modifications incre-mentally by expressing exceptions to existing rules rather than reengineering the entire set, and thus could be rendered suitable for data stream learning—although care would need to be taken to ensure that memory usage did not increase inexorably as the number of exceptions increased. Instance-based algorithms and related methods such as locally weighted linear regression are also incremental, but do not usually operate within a fixed memory bound.

To convey the flavor of how a standard algorithm might be adapted for stream processing, we will examine the case of decision trees, which have the advantage of evolving structure in a form that is interpretable. Early work on incremental induction of decision trees devised methods for creating a tree and allowing it to be restructured when sufficient evidence had accumulated that an alternative version would be better. However, a large amount of information needs to be retained to support the restructuring operation—in some cases, all of the training data. Further-more, restructuring tends to be slow—sometimes slower than recreating the entire tree from scratch. Although interesting, these methods do not support indefinite processing of data streams in real time.

Their problem is that they adopt the usual paradigm of squeezing as much information as possible out of the available instances. With data streams, this is not necessarily appropriate—it is perfectly acceptable to discard some information about the instances because if it is important it will always reappear. A new paradigm of "Hoeffding trees" was introduced in 2000, which builds models that can be proven equivalent to standard decision trees if the data is static and the number of examples is large enough.

Hoeffding trees are based on a simple idea known as the *Hoeffding bound*. It makes intuitive sense that, given enough independent observations, the true mean of a random variable will not differ from the estimated mean by more than a certain amount. In fact, the Hoeffding bound states that with probability $1 - \delta$, a random variable of range R will not differ from the estimated mean after n observations by more than

$$\varepsilon = \sqrt{\frac{\ln(1/\delta)}{2n}} \times R$$

This bound holds regardless of the probability distribution that underlies the values. Being general, it is more conservative than distribution-dependent bounds. Although tighter bounds are known for particular distributions, the Hoeffding formulation works well empirically.

The basic issue in decision tree induction is to choose an attribute to branch on at each stage. To apply the Hoeffding bound, first set a small value of δ (say 10^{-7}), which is the probability that the choice of attribute will be incorrect. The random variable being estimated is the difference in information gain between the best two attributes, and R is the base two logarithms of the number of possible class labels. For example, if the difference in gain between the best two attributes is estimated to be 0.3, and the preceding formula yields a value for ε of 0.1, the bound guarantees that the actual difference in gain exceeds 0.2 with high probability, which represents positive separation for the best attribute. Thus, it is safe to split.

If the difference in information gain between the best two attributes is less than ε, it is not safe to split. However, ε will decrease as n continues to increase, so it is simply a matter of waiting until more examples have been seen—although, of course, this may alter the estimate of which are the two best attributes and how far apart they are.

This simple test is the core principle of Hoeffding trees: to decide, with probability $1 - \delta$, that a particular attribute exhibits greater information gain than all the others. That is, the gap between it and its closest competitor exceeds ε. The bound decays rapidly as more examples are seen—for example, for a two-class problem ($R = 1$) with $\delta = 10^{-7}$, it falls below 0.1 after the first 1000 examples and below 0.01 after the first 100,000. One might object that as the number of leaves grows indefinitely, the probability of making incorrect decisions will continually increase even though the probability of error at each one falls below δ. This is true—except that, working within finite memory, the number of leaves cannot grow indefinitely. Given a maximum tree size, keeping the overall probability of error within a given bound is just a matter of choosing an appropriate value for δ. The basic principle can be applied to measures other than the information gain and to learning methods other than decision trees.

There are many other issues. A tie-breaking strategy is advisable to permit further development of the tree in situations where the top two attributes exhibit very similar information gains. Indeed, the presence of two identical attributes could block any development of the tree at all. To prevent this, nodes should be split whenever the Hoeffding bound falls below a small prespecified tie-breaking parameter, no matter how close the next best option. To increase efficiency the Hoeffding test may be performed periodically for each leaf, after k new instances have reached it, and only when a mix of classes have reached the leaf; otherwise, there is no need to split. Prepruning is another simple possibility. The algorithm can incorporate this by also evaluating the merit of not splitting at all—that is, by splitting only if the best attribute's information gain at the node exceeds zero. Unlike prepruning in the batch learning setting, this is not a permanent decision: Nodes are only prevented from splitting until it appears that a split will be useful.

Now consider memory usage. What must be stored within a leaf is simply counts of the number of times each class label reaches that leaf, for each attribute value. This causes problems for numeric attributes, which require separate treatment. Unsupervised discretization is easy, but supervised prediscretization is infeasible because it is inconsistent with stream-based processing. A Gaussian approximation can be made for numeric attributes on a per-class basis and updated using simple incremental update algorithms for mean and variance. To prevent indefinite growth in memory requirements, a strategy must be devised to limit the total number of nodes in the tree. This can be done by deactivating leaves that look insufficiently promising in terms of the accuracy gain that further development might yield. The potential gain is bounded by the expected number of mistakes a leaf might make, so this is an obvious candidate for measuring its promise. Leaves can periodically be ordered from most to least promising and deactivated accordingly. A further possibility for saving space is to abandon attributes that seem to be poor predictors and discard their statistics from the model.

Although this section has focused on decision trees for classification, researchers have studied stream-based versions of all the classical data mining problems: regression, clustering, ensemble methods, association rules, and so on. An open-source system called Moa, for Massive Online Analysis, is closely related to Weka and contains a collection of online learning algorithms, as well as tools for evaluation.[2]

---

[2] See *http://moa.cs.waikato.ac.nz*. The moa, like the weka, is a flightless New Zealand bird, but it is very large—and also, unfortunately, extinct.

9.4 INCORPORATING DOMAIN KNOWLEDGE

Throughout this book we have emphasized the importance of getting to know your data when undertaking practical data mining. Knowledge of the domain is absolutely essential for success. Data about data is often called *metadata*, and one of the frontiers in machine learning is the development of ways to allow learning methods to take metadata into account in a useful way.

You don't have to look far for examples of how metadata might be applied. In Chapter 2 (page 52), we divided attributes into nominal and numeric. But we also noted that many finer distinctions are possible. If an attribute is numeric an ordering is implied, but sometimes there is a zero point and sometimes not (for time intervals there is, but for dates there is not). Even the ordering may be nonstandard: Angular degrees have a different ordering from integers because $360°$ is the same as $0°$ and $180°$ is the same as $-180°$ or indeed $900°$. Discretization schemes assume ordinary linear ordering, as do learning schemes that accommodate numeric attributes, but it would be a routine matter to extend them to circular orderings. Categorical data may also be ordered. Imagine how much more difficult our lives would be if there were no conventional ordering for letters of the alphabet. (Looking up a listing in the Hong Kong telephone directory presents an interesting and nontrivial problem!) And the rhythms of everyday life are reflected in circular orderings: days of the week, months of the year. To further complicate matters there are many other kinds of ordering, such as partial orderings on subsets: subset A may include subset B, or subset B may include subset A, or neither may include the other. Extending ordinary learning schemes to take account of this kind of information in a satisfactory and general way is an open research problem.

Metadata often involves relations among attributes. Three kinds of relation can be distinguished: semantic, causal, and functional. A *semantic* relation between two attributes indicates that if the first is included in a rule, the second should be, too. In this case, it is known a priori that the attributes only make sense together. For example, in the agricultural data that we have analyzed, an attribute called *milk production* measures how much milk an individual cow produces, and the purpose of our investigation meant that this attribute had a semantic relationship with three other attributes: *cow-identifier*, *herd-identifier*, and *farmer-identifier*. In other words, a milk production value can only be understood in the context of the cow that produced the milk, and the cow is further linked to a specific herd owned by a given farmer. Semantic relations are, of course, problem dependent: They depend not just on the dataset but also on what you are trying to do with it.

Causal relations occur when one attribute causes another. In a system that is trying to predict an attribute caused by another, we know that the other attribute should be included to make the prediction more meaningful. For example, in the agricultural data mentioned previously there is a chain from the farmer, herd, and cow identifiers, through measured attributes such as milk production, down to the attribute that records whether a particular cow was retained or sold by the farmer. Learned rules should recognize this chain of dependence.

Functional dependencies occur in many databases, and the people who create databases strive to identify them for the purpose of normalizing the relations in the database. When learning from the data, the significance of a functional dependency of one attribute on another is that if the latter is used in a rule there is no need to consider the former. Learning schemes often rediscover functional dependencies that are already known. Not only does this generate meaningless or, more accurately, tautological rules, but also other, more interesting patterns may be obscured by the functional relationships. However, there has been much work in automatic database design on the problem of inferring functional dependencies from example queries, and the methods developed should prove useful in weeding out tautological rules generated by learning schemes.

Taking these kinds of metadata, or prior domain knowledge, into account when doing induction using any of the algorithms we have met does not seem to present any deep or difficult technical challenges. The only real problem—and it is a big one—is how to express the metadata in a general and easily understandable way so that it can be generated by a person and used by the algorithm.

It seems attractive to couch the metadata knowledge in just the same representation as the machine learning scheme generates. We focus on rules, which are the norm for much of this work. The rules that specify metadata correspond to prior knowledge of the domain. Given training examples, additional rules can be derived by one of the rule-induction schemes we have already met. In this way, the system might be able to combine "experience" (from examples) with "theory" (from domain knowledge). It would be capable of confirming and modifying its programmed-in knowledge based on empirical evidence. Loosely put, the user tells the system what he or she knows and gives it some examples, and the system figures the rest out for itself!

To make use of prior knowledge expressed as rules in a sufficiently flexible way, it is necessary for the system to be able to perform logical deduction. Otherwise, the knowledge has to be expressed in precisely the right form for the learning algorithm to take advantage of it, which is likely to be too demanding for practical use. Consider causal metadata: If attribute A causes B and B causes C, we would like the system to deduce that A causes C rather than having to state that fact explicitly. Although in this simple example explicitly stating the new fact presents little problem, in practice, with extensive metadata, it will be unrealistic to expect users to express all logical consequences of their prior knowledge.

A combination of deduction from prespecified domain knowledge and induction from training examples seems like a flexible way of accommodating metadata. At one extreme, when examples are scarce (or nonexistent), deduction is the prime (or only) means of generating new rules. At the other, when examples are abundant but metadata is scarce (or nonexistent), the standard machine learning techniques described in this book suffice. Practical situations span the territory between.

This is a compelling vision, and methods of inductive logic programming, mentioned in Section 3.4 (page 75), offer a general way of specifying domain knowledge explicitly through statements in a formal logic language. However, current logic programming solutions suffer serious shortcomings in real-world environments. They tend to be brittle and to lack robustness, and they may be so computation intensive as to be completely infeasible on datasets of any practical size. Perhaps this stems from the fact that they use first-order logic—that is, they allow variables to be introduced into the rules. The machine learning schemes we have seen, the input and output of which are represented in terms of attributes and constant values, perform their machinations in propositional logic, without variables, greatly reducing the search space and avoiding all sorts of difficult problems of circularity and termination.

Some aspire to realize the vision without the accompanying brittleness and computational infeasibility of full logic programming solutions by adopting simplified reasoning systems. Others place their faith in the general mechanism of Bayesian networks, introduced in Section 6.7, in which causal constraints can be expressed in the initial network structure and hidden variables can be postulated and evaluated automatically. Probabilistic logic learning offers a way to cope with both the complexity and the uncertainty of the real world by combining logic programming with statistical reasoning. It will be interesting to see whether systems that allow flexible specification of different types of domain knowledge will become widely deployed.

9.5 TEXT MINING

Data mining is about looking for patterns in data. Likewise, text mining is about looking for patterns in text: It is the process of analyzing text to extract information that is useful for particular purposes. Compared with the kind of data we have been talking about in this book, text is unstructured, amorphous, and difficult to deal with. Nevertheless, in modern Western culture, text is the most common vehicle for the formal exchange of information. The motivation for trying to extract information from it is compelling—even if success is only partial.

The superficial similarity between text and data mining conceals real differences. In the Preface (page xxi), we characterized data mining as the extraction of implicit, previously unknown, and potentially useful information from data. With text mining, however, the information to be extracted is clearly and explicitly stated in the text. It is not hidden at all—most authors go to great pains to make sure that they express themselves clearly and unambiguously. From a human point of view, the only sense in which it is "previously unknown" is that time restrictions make it infeasible for people to read the text themselves. The problem, of course, is that the information is not couched in a manner that is amenable to automatic processing. Text mining strives to bring it out in a form that is suitable for consumption by computers or by people who do not have time to read the full text.

A requirement common to both data and text mining is that the information extracted should be potentially useful. In one sense, this means *actionable*—capable of providing a basis for actions to be taken automatically. In the case of data mining, this notion can be expressed in a relatively domain-independent way: Actionable patterns are ones that allow nontrivial predictions to be made on new data from the same source. Performance can be measured by counting successes and failures, statistical techniques can be applied to compare different data mining methods on the same problem, and so on. However, in many text mining situations it is hard to characterize what "actionable" means in a way that is independent of the particular domain at hand. This makes it difficult to find fair and objective measures of success.

As we have emphasized throughout this book, "potentially useful" is often given another interpretation in practical data mining: The key to success is that the information extracted must be *comprehensible* in that it helps to explain the data. This is necessary whenever the result is intended for human consumption rather than (or as well as) a basis for automatic action. This criterion is less applicable to text mining because, unlike data mining, the input itself is comprehensible. Text mining with comprehensible output is tantamount to summarizing salient features from a large body of text, which is a subfield in its own right: *text summarization*.

We have already encountered one important text mining problem: *document classification*, in which each instance represents a document and the instance's class is the document's topic. Documents are characterized by the words that appear in them. The presence or absence of each word can be treated as a Boolean attribute, or documents can be treated as bags of words, rather than sets, by taking word frequencies into account. We encountered this distinction in Section 4.2 (page 97), where we learned how to extend Naïve Bayes to the bag-of-words representation, yielding the multinomial version of the algorithm.

There is, of course, an immense number of different words, and most of them are not very useful for document classification. This presents a classic feature-selection problem. Some words—for example function words, often called *stopwords*—can usually be eliminated a priori, but although these occur very frequently there are not all that many of them. Other words occur so rarely that they are unlikely to be useful for classification. Paradoxically, infrequent words are common—nearly half the words in a document or corpus of documents occur just once. Nevertheless, such an overwhelming number of words remain after these word classes are removed that further feature selection may be necessary using the methods described in Section 7.1 (page 307). Another issue is that the bag-of-words (or set-of-words) model neglects word order and contextual effects. There is a strong case for detecting common phrases and treating them as single units.

Document classification is supervised learning: The categories are known beforehand and given in advance for each training document. The unsupervised version of the problem is called *document clustering*. Here there is no predefined class, but groups of cognate documents are sought. Document clustering can assist information retrieval by creating links between similar documents, which in turn allows related documents to be retrieved once one of the documents has been deemed relevant to a query.

There are many applications of document classification. A relatively easy categorization task, *language identification*, provides an important piece of metadata for documents in international collections. A simple representation that works well for language identification is to characterize each document by a profile that consists of the *n-grams*, or sequences of *n* consecutive letters (for some small value such as

$n = 3$), that appear in it. The most frequent 300 or so n-grams are highly correlated with the language. A more challenging application is *authorship ascription*, where a document's author is uncertain and must be guessed from the text. Here, the stopwords, not the content words, are the giveaway because their distribution is author dependent but topic independent. A third problem is the *assignment of key phrases* to documents from a controlled vocabulary of possible phrases, given a large number of training documents that are tagged from this vocabulary.

Another general class of text mining problems is *metadata extraction*. Metadata was mentioned earlier as data about data: In the realm of text the term generally refers to salient features of a work, such as author, title, subject classification, subject headings, and keywords. Metadata is a kind of highly structured (and therefore actionable) document summary. The idea of metadata is often expanded to encompass words or phrases that stand for objects or "entities" in the world, leading to the notion of *entity extraction*. Ordinary documents are full of such terms: phone numbers, fax numbers, street addresses, email addresses, email signatures, abstracts, tables of contents, lists of references, tables, figures, captions, meeting announcements, web addresses, and more. In addition, there are countless domain-specific entities, such as International Standard Book Numbers (ISBNs), stock symbols, chemical structures, and mathematical equations. These terms act as single vocabulary items, and many document-processing tasks can be significantly improved if they are identified as such. They can aid searching, interlinking, and cross-referencing between documents.

How can textual entities be identified? Rote learning—that is, dictionary lookup—is one idea, particularly when coupled with existing resources—lists of personal names and organizations, information about locations from gazetteers, or abbreviation and acronym dictionaries. Another is to use capitalization and punctuation patterns for names and acronyms; titles (e.g., Ms.), suffixes (e.g., Jr.), and baronial prefixes (e.g., von); or unusual language statistics for foreign names. Regular expressions suffice for artificial constructs such as uniform resource locators (URLs); explicit grammars can be written to recognize dates and sums of money. Even the simplest task opens up opportunities for learning to cope with the huge variation that real-life documents present. As just one example, what could be simpler than looking up a name in a table? But the name of Libyan leader Muammar Qaddafi is represented in 47 different ways in documents that have been received by the Library of Congress!

Many short documents describe a particular kind of object or event, combining entities into a higher-level composite that represents the document's entire content. The task of identifying the composite structure, which can often be represented as a template with slots that are filled by individual pieces of structured information, is called *information extraction*. Once the entities have been found, the text is parsed to determine relationships among them. Typical extraction problems require finding the predicate structure of a small set of predetermined propositions. These are usually simple enough to be captured by shallow parsing techniques such as small finite-state grammars, although matters may be complicated by ambiguous pronoun references and attached prepositional phrases and other modifiers. Machine learning has been applied to information extraction by seeking rules that extract fillers for slots in the template. These rules may be couched in pattern-action form, the patterns expressing constraints on the slot-filler and words in its local context. These constraints may involve the words themselves, their part-of-speech tags, and their semantic classes.

Taking information extraction a step further, the extracted information can be used in a subsequent step to learn rules—not rules about how to extract information but rules that characterize the content of the text itself. These rules might predict the values for certain slot-fillers from the rest of the text. In certain tightly constrained situations, such as Internet job postings for computing-related jobs, information extraction based on a few manually constructed training examples can compete with an entire manually constructed database in terms of the quality of the rules inferred.

Text mining is a burgeoning technology that is still, because of its newness and intrinsic difficulty, in a fluid state—akin, perhaps, to the state of machine learning in the mid-1980s. There is no real consensus about what it covers: Broadly interpreted, all natural language processing comes under the ambit of text mining. It is usually difficult to provide general and meaningful evaluations because the mining task is highly sensitive to the particular text under consideration. Automatic text mining techniques have a long way to go before they rival the ability of people, even without any special domain knowledge, to glean information from large document collections.

9.6 WEB MINING

The World Wide Web is a massive repository of text. Almost all of it differs from ordinary "plain" text because it contains explicit structural markup. Some markup is internal and indicates document structure or format; other markup is external and defines explicit hypertext links between documents. Both these information sources give additional leverage for mining web documents. *Web mining* is like text mining but takes advantage of this extra information and often improves results by capitalizing on the existence of topic directories and other information on the Web.

Consider internal markup. Internet resources that contain relational data—telephone directories, product catalogs, and so on—use HyperText Markup Language (HTML) formatting commands to clearly present the information they contain to Web users. However, it is quite difficult to extract data from such resources in an automatic way. To do so, software systems use simple parsing modules called *wrappers* to analyze the page structure and extract the requisite information. If wrappers are coded by hand, which they often are, this is a trivial kind of text mining because it relies on the pages having a fixed, predetermined structure from which information can be extracted algorithmically. But pages rarely obey the rules. Their structures vary; web sites evolve. Errors that are insignificant to human readers throw automatic extraction procedures completely awry. When change occurs, adjusting a wrapper manually can be a nightmare that involves getting your head around the existing code and patching it up in a way that does not cause breakage elsewhere.

Enter *wrapper induction*—learning wrappers automatically from examples. The input is a training set of pages along with tuples representing the information derived from each page. The output is a set of rules that extracts the tuples by parsing the page. For example, it might look for certain HTML delimiters—paragraph boundaries (*<p>*), list entries (*<li>*), or boldface (*<b>*)—that the web page designer has used to set off key items of information, and learn the sequence in which entities are presented. This could be accomplished by iterating over all choices of delimiters, stopping when a consistent wrapper is encountered. Then recognition will depend only on a minimal set of cues, providing some defense against extraneous text and markers in the input. Alternatively, one might follow Epicurus' advice at the end of Section 5.9 (page 186) and seek a robust wrapper that uses multiple cues to guard against accidental variation. The great advantage of automatic wrapper induction is that when errors are caused by stylistic variants it is a simple matter to add these to the training data and reinduce a new wrapper that takes them into account. Wrapper induction reduces recognition problems when small changes occur and makes it far easier to produce new sets of extraction rules when structures change radically.

One of the problems with the Web is that a lot of it is rubbish. In order to separate the wheat from the chaff, a metric called PageRank was introduced by the founders of Google; it is used in various guises by other search engines too, and in many other web mining applications. It attempts to measure the prestige of a web page or site, where *prestige* is, according to a dictionary definition, "high standing achieved through success or influence." The hope is that this is a good way to determine authority, defined as "an accepted source of expert information or advice." Recall that the PageRank algorithm was identified earlier in Table 9.1 as one of the top 10 data mining algorithms, the only one that we have not encountered so far. It is perhaps questionable whether it should be classed as a data mining algorithm, but it is worth describing all the same.

The key is external markup in the form of hyperlinks. In a networked community, people reward success with links. If you link to my page, it's probably because you find it useful and informative—it's a successful web page. If a host of people link to it, that indicates prestige: My page is successful and influential. Look at Figure 9.1, which shows a tiny fraction of the Web, including links between pages. Which ones do you think are most authoritative? Page **F** has five incoming links, which indicates that five people found it worth linking to, so there's a good chance that this page is more authoritative than the others. **B** is second best, with four links.

Merely counting links is a crude measure. Some web pages have thousands of outgoing links, whereas others have just one or two. Rarer links are more discriminating and should count more than others. A link from your page to mine bestows more prestige if your page has few outlinks. In Figure 9.1 the many links emanating from page **A** mean that each one carries less weight simply because **A** is a prolific linker. From **F**'s point of view, the links from **D** and **E** may be more valuable than

FIGURE 9.1

A tangled "web."

the one from **A**. There is another factor: A link is more valuable if it comes from a prestigious page. The link from **B** to **F** may be better than the others into **F** because **B** is more prestigious. Admittedly, this factor involves a certain circularity, and without further analysis it's not clear that it can be made to work. But indeed it can.

Here are the details. We define the PageRank of a page to be a number between 0 and 1 that measures its prestige. Each link into the page contributes to its Page-Rank. The amount it contributes is the PageRank of the linking page divided by the number of outlinks from it. The PageRank of any page is calculated by summing that quantity over all links into it. The value for **D** in Figure 9.1 is calculated by adding one-fifth of the value for **A** (because it has five outlinks) to one-half the value for **C**.

A simple iterative method is used to resolve the apparently circular nature of the calculation. Start by randomly assigning an initial value to each page. Then recompute each page's PageRank by summing the appropriate quantities, described earlier, over its inlinks. If the initial values are thought of as an approximation to the true value of PageRank, the new values are a better approximation. Keep going, generating a third approximation, a fourth, and so on. At each stage, recompute the Page-Rank for every page in the Web. Stop when, for every page, the next iteration turns out to give almost exactly the same PageRank as the previous one.

Subject to two modifications discussed later, this iteration is guaranteed to converge, and fairly quickly too. Although the precise details are shrouded in secrecy, today's search engines probably seek an accuracy for the final values of between

10^{-9} and 10^{-12}. An early experiment reported 50 iterations for a much smaller version of the Web than the one that exists today, before the details became commercial; several times as many iterations are needed now. Google is thought to run programs for several days to perform the PageRank calculation for the entire Web, and the operation is—or at any rate, used to be—performed every few weeks.

There are two problems with the calculation we have described. You probably have a mental picture of PageRank flowing through the tangled "web" of Figure 9.1, coming into a page through its inlinks and leaving it through its outlinks. What if there are no inlinks (page **H**)? Or no outlinks (page **G**)?

To operationalize this picture, imagine a web surfer who clicks links at random. He takes the current page, chooses an outlink at random, and goes to that link's target page. The probability of taking any particular link is smaller if there are many outlinks, which is exactly the behavior we want from PageRank. It turns out that the PageRank of a given page is proportional to the probability that the surfer randomly searching lands on that page.

Now the problem raised by a page with no outlinks becomes apparent: It's a PageRank sink because when surfers come in they cannot get out. More generally, a set of pages might link to each other but not to anywhere else. This incestuous group is also a PageRank sink: The random surfer gets stuck in a trap. And a page with no inlinks? Random surfers never reach it. In fact, they never reach any group of pages that has no inlinks from the rest of the Web, even though it may have internal links and outlinks to the Web at large.

These two problems mean that the iterative calculation described above does not converge, as we earlier claimed it would. But the solution is simple: *teleportation*. With a certain small probability, just make the surfer arrive at a randomly chosen page instead of following a link from the one she is on. That solves both problems. If surfers are stuck at **G** they will eventually teleport out of it. And if they can't reach **H** by surfing, they will eventually teleport into it.

The teleport probability has a strong influence on the rate of convergence of the iterative algorithm—and on the accuracy of its results. At the extreme, if it were equal to 1, meaning that the surfer always teleported, the link structure would have no effect on PageRank, and no iteration would be necessary. If it were 0 and the surfer never teleported, the calculation would not converge at all. Early published experiments used a teleportation probability of 0.15; some speculate that search engines increase it a little to hasten convergence.

Instead of teleporting to a randomly chosen page, you could choose a predetermined probability for each page, and—once you had decided to teleport—use that probability to determine where to land. This does not affect the calculation. But it does affect the result. If a page was discriminated against by receiving a smaller probability than the others, it would end up with a smaller PageRank than it deserves. This gives search engine operators an opportunity to influence the results of the calculation—an opportunity that they probably use to discriminate against certain sites (e.g., ones they believe are trying to gain an unfair advantage by exploiting the PageRank system). This is the stuff of which lawsuits are made.

9.7 ADVERSARIAL SITUATIONS

A prime application of machine learning is junk email filtering. When we wrote the second edition of this book (2005), the scourge of unwanted email was a burning issue; now, as we write the third edition (2011), the problem seems to have abated despite the continual growth of spam (by some estimates it accounts for 95% of all emails). This is largely due to the widespread use of spam filtering, which often uses learning techniques. At first blush, junk email filtering appears to present a standard problem of document classification: Divide documents into "ham" and "spam" on the basis of the text they contain, guided by training data, of which there are copious amounts. But it differs from ordinary document classification because it involves an adversarial aspect. The documents that are being classified are not chosen at random from an unimaginably huge set of all possible documents; they contain emails that are carefully crafted to evade the filtering process, designed specifically to beat the system.

Early spam filters simply discarded messages containing "spammy" words that connote such things as sex, lucre, and quackery. Of course, much legitimate correspondence concerns gender, money, and medicine: A balance must be struck. So filter designers recruited Bayesian text classification schemes that learned to strike an appropriate balance during the training process. Spammers quickly adjusted with techniques that concealed the spammy words by misspelling them; overwhelmed them with legitimate text, perhaps printed in white on a white background so that only the filter saw it; or simply put the spam text elsewhere, in an image or a URL that most mail readers download automatically.

The problem is complicated by the fact that it is hard to compare spam detection algorithms objectively. Although training data abounds, privacy issues preclude publishing large public corpora of representative email. And there are strong temporal effects. Spam changes character rapidly, invalidating sensitive statistical tests such as cross-validation. Finally, the bad guys can also use machine learning. For example, if they could get hold of examples of what your filter blocks and what it lets through, they could use this as training data to learn how to evade filtering.

There are, unfortunately, many other examples of adversarial learning situations in our world today. Closely related to junk email is search engine spam: sites that attempt to deceive Internet search engines into placing them prominently in lists of search results. Highly ranked pages yield direct financial benefits to their owners because they present opportunities for advertising, providing strong motivation for profit seekers. Then there are the computer virus wars, in which designers of viruses and virus protection software react to one another's innovations. Here the motivation tends to be general disruption and denial of service rather than monetary gain.

Computer network security is a continually escalating battle. Protectors harden networks, operating systems, and applications, and attackers find vulnerabilities in all three areas. Intrusion detection systems sniff out unusual patterns of activity that might be caused by a hacker's reconnaissance activity. Attackers realize this and try to obfuscate their trails, perhaps by working indirectly or by spreading their activities over a long time—or, conversely, by striking very quickly. Data mining is being applied to this problem in an attempt to discover semantic connections among attacker traces in computer network data that intrusion detection systems miss. This is a large-scale problem: Audit logs used to monitor computer network security can amount to gigabytes a day even in medium-size organizations.

Many automated threat detection systems are based on matching current data to known attack types. The U.S. Federal Aviation Administration developed the Computer-Assisted Passenger Prescreening System (CAPPS), which screens airline passengers on the basis of their flight records and flags individuals for additional checked baggage screening. Although the exact details are unpublished, CAPPS is, for example, thought to assign higher threat scores to cash payments. However, this approach can only spot known or anticipated threats. Researchers are using unsupervised approaches such as anomaly and outlier detection in an attempt to detect suspicious activity. As well as flagging potential threats, anomaly detection systems can be applied to the detection of illegal activities such as financial fraud and money laundering.

Data mining is being used today to sift through huge volumes of data in the name of homeland defense. Heterogeneous information such as financial transactions, healthcare records, and network traffic is being mined to create profiles, construct social network models, and detect terrorist communications. This activity raises serious privacy concerns and has resulted in the development of privacy-preserving data mining techniques. These algorithms try to discern patterns in the data without accessing the original data directly, typically by distorting it with random values. To preserve privacy, they must guarantee that the mining process does not receive enough information to reconstruct the original data. This is easier said than done.

On a lighter note, not all adversarial data mining is aimed at combating nefarious activity. Multi-agent systems in complex, noisy, real-time domains involve autonomous agents that must both collaborate as a team and compete against antagonists. If you are having trouble visualizing this, think soccer. Robo-soccer is a rich and popular domain for exploring how machine learning can be applied to such difficult problems. Players must not only hone low-level skills but must also learn to work together and adapt to the behavior patterns of different opponents.

Finally, machine learning has been used to solve an actual historical literary mystery by unmasking a prolific author who had attempted to conceal his identity. As Koppel and Schler (2004) relate, Ben Ish Chai was the leading rabbinic scholar in Baghdad in the late nineteenth century. Among his vast literary legacy are two separate collections of about 500 Hebrew–Aramaic letters written in response to legal queries. He is known to have written one collection. Although Chai claims to have found the other in an archive, historians suspect that he wrote it, too but attempted to disguise his authorship by deliberately altering his style. The problem this case presents to machine learning is that there is no corpus of work to ascribe to the mystery author. There were a few known candidates, but the letters could equally well have been written by anyone. A new technique appropriately called *unmasking* was developed that creates a model to distinguish the known author's work A from the unknown author's work X, iteratively removes those features that are most useful for distinguishing the two, and examines the speed with which cross-validation accuracy degrades as more features are removed.

The hypothesis is that if work X is written by work A's author, who is trying to conceal his identity, whatever differences there are between work X and work A will be reflected in only a relatively small number of features compared with the differences between work X and the works of a completely different author, say the author of work B. In other words, when work X is compared with works A and B, the accuracy curve as features are removed will decline much faster for work A than it does for work B. Koppel and Schler concluded that Ben Ish Chai did indeed write the mystery letters, and their technique is a striking example of original and creative use of machine learning in an adversarial situation.

9.8 UBIQUITOUS DATA MINING

We began this book by pointing out that we are overwhelmed with data. Nowhere does this impact the lives of ordinary people more than on the World Wide Web. At present, the Web contains around 10 to 20 billion documents, totaling perhaps 50 Tb—and it continues to grow. No one can keep pace with the information explosion. Whereas data mining originated in the corporate world because that's where the databases are, text mining is moving machine learning technology out of the companies and into the home. Whenever we are overwhelmed by data on the Web, text mining promises tools to tame it. Applications are legion. Finding friends and contacting them, maintaining financial portfolios, shopping for bargains in an electronic world, using data detectors of any kind—all of these could be accomplished automatically without explicit programming. Already, text mining techniques are being used to predict what link you're going to click next, to organize documents for you, sort your mail, and prioritize your search results. In a world where information is overwhelming, disorganized, and anarchic, text mining may be the solution we so desperately need.

Many believe that the Web is but the harbinger of an even greater paradigm shift known as *ubiquitous computing*. Small portable devices are everywhere—mobile telephones, personal digital assistants, personal stereo and video players, digital cameras, mobile Web access. Already some devices integrate all these functions. They know our location in physical time and space, help us communicate in social space, organize our personal planning space, recall our past, and envelop us in global information space. It is easy to find dozens of processors in a American middle-class home today. They do not communicate with one another or with the global information infrastructure—yet. But they will, and when they do the potential for data mining will soar.

Take consumer music. Popular music leads the vanguard of technological advance. Sony's original Walkman paved the way to today's ubiquitous portable electronics. Apple's iPOD pioneered large-scale portable storage. Napster's network technology spurred the development of peer-to-peer protocols. Recommender systems such as Firefly brought computing to social networks. Content-aware music services are migrating to portable devices. Applications for data mining in networked communities of people will be legion: discovering musical trends, tracking preferences and tastes, and analyzing listening behaviors.

Ubiquitous computing will weave digital space closely into real-world activities. To many—extrapolating their own computer experiences of extreme frustration, arcane technology, perceived personal inadequacy, and machine failure—this sounds like a nightmare. But proponents point out that it can't be like that because, if it is, it won't work. Today's visionaries foresee a world of "calm" computing in which hidden machines silently cooperate behind the scenes to make our lives richer and easier. They'll reach beyond the big problems of corporate finance and school homework to the little annoyances such as where are the car keys, can I get a parking place, and is that shirt I saw last week at Macy's still on the rack? Clocks will find the correct time after a power failure, the microwave will download new recipes from the Internet, kid's toys will refresh themselves with new games and new vocabularies. Clothes labels will track washing, coffee cups will alert cleaning staff to mold, light switches will save energy if no one is in the room, and pencils will digitize everything we draw. Where will data mining be in this new world? Everywhere!

It's difficult to point to examples of a future that does not yet exist. But the advances in user interface technology are suggestive. Many repetitive tasks in direct-manipulation computer interfaces cannot be automated with standard application tools, forcing users to perform the same interface actions over and over again. This typifies the frustrations alluded to previously: Who's in charge—me or it? Experienced programmers might write a script to carry out such tasks on their behalf, but as operating systems accrue layer upon layer of complexity, the power of programmers to command the machine is eroded; it vanishes altogether when complex functionality is embedded in appliances rather than in general-purpose computers.

Research in *programming by demonstration* enables ordinary users to automate predictable tasks without requiring any programming knowledge at all. The user need only know how to perform the task in the usual way to be able to communicate it to the computer. One system, called *Familiar*, helps users automate iterative tasks involving existing applications on Macintosh computers. It works across applications and can work with completely new ones never before encountered. It does this by using Apple's scripting language to glean information from each application and exploiting that information to make predictions. The agent tolerates noise. It generates explanations to inform the user about its predictions, and it incorporates feedback. It's adaptive: It learns specialized tasks for individual users. Furthermore, it is sensitive to each user's style. If two people were teaching a task and happened to give identical demonstrations, Familiar would not necessarily infer identical programs—it's tuned to users' habits because it learns from their interaction history.

Familiar employs standard machine learning techniques to infer the user's intent. Rules are used to evaluate predictions so that the best one can be presented to the user at each point. These rules are conditional so that users can teach classification tasks such as sorting files based on their type and assigning labels based on their size. They are learned incrementally: The agent adapts to individual users by recording their interaction history.

Many difficulties arise. One is scarcity of data. Users are loath to demonstrate several iterations of a task—they think the agent should immediately catch on to what they are doing. Whereas a data miner would consider a 100-instance dataset miniscule, users bridle at the prospect of demonstrating a task even half a dozen times. A second difficulty is the plethora of attributes. The computer desktop environment has hundreds of features that any given action might depend on. This means that small datasets are overwhelmingly likely to contain attributes that are apparently highly predictive but nevertheless irrelevant, and specialized statistical tests are needed to compare alternative hypotheses. A third difficulty is that the iterative, improvement-driven development style that characterizes data mining applications fails. It is impossible *in principle* to create a fixed training and testing corpus for an interactive problem, such as programming by demonstration, because each improvement in the agent alters the test data by affecting how users react to it. A fourth difficulty is that existing application programs provide limited access to application and user data: Often, the raw material on which successful operation depends is inaccessible, buried deep within the application program.

Data mining is already widely used at work. Text and web mining is bringing the techniques in this book into our own lives as we read our email and surf the Web. As for the future, it will be stranger than we can imagine. The spreading computing infrastructure will offer untold opportunities for learning. Data mining will be in there, behind the scenes, playing a role that will turn out to be foundational.

9.9 FURTHER READING

Wu et al. (2008) describe the process of identifying the top 10 algorithms in data mining for presentation at the International Conference on Data Mining in 2006 in Hong Kong; they have followed this up with a book that describes all the algorithms (Wu and Kumar, 2009). The paper on the "illusion of progress" in classification is by Hand (2006), and it was he who found that a very simple method achieves more than 90 percent of the classification improvement yielded by the most sophisticated scheme.

There is a substantial volume of literature that treats the topic of massive datasets, and we can only point to a few references here. Fayyad and Smyth (1995) describe the application of data mining to voluminous data from scientific experiments. Shafer et al. (1996) describe a parallel version of a top-down decision tree inducer. A sequential decision tree algorithm for massive disk-resident datasets has been developed by Mehta et al. (1996). The technique of applying any algorithm to a large dataset by splitting it into smaller chunks and bagging or boosting the result is described by Breiman (1999); Frank et al. (2002) explain the related pruning and selection scheme.

Early work on incremental decision trees is reported by Utgoff (1989) and Utgoff et al. (1997). The Hoeffding tree was introduced by Domingos and Hulten (2000). Our description of it, including extensions and improvement, closely follows Kirkby's Ph.D. thesis (2007). The Moa system is described by Bifet et al. (2010).

Despite its importance, comparatively little seems to have been written about the general problem of incorporating metadata into practical data mining. A scheme for encoding domain knowledge into propositional rules and its use for both deduction and induction has been investigated by Giraud-Carrier (1996). The related area of inductive logic programming, which deals with knowledge represented by first-order logic rules, is covered by Bergadano and Gunetti (1996). Probabilistic logic learning is covered by de Raedt (2008).

Text mining is an emerging area, and there are few comprehensive surveys of the area as a whole: Witten (2004) provides one. A large number of feature-selection and machine learning techniques have been applied to text categorization (Sebastiani, 2002). Martin (1995) describes applications of document clustering to information retrieval. Cavnar and Trenkle (1994) show how to use n-gram profiles to ascertain with high accuracy the language in which a document is written. The use of support vector machines for authorship ascription is described by Diederich et al. (2003); the same technology was used by Dumais et al. (1998) to assign key phrases from a controlled vocabulary to documents on the basis of a large number of training documents. The use of machine learning to extract key phrases from document text has been investigated by Turney (1999), Frank et al. (1999), and Medelyan and Witten (2008).

Appelt (1996) describes many problems of information extraction. Many authors have applied machine learning to seek rules that extract slot-fillers for templates, for example, Soderland et al. (1995), Huffman (1996), and Freitag (2002). Califf and Mooney (1999) and Nahm and Mooney (2000) investigated the problem of extracting information from job ads posted by Internet newsgroups. An approach to finding information in running text based on compression techniques has been reported by Witten et al. (1999a). Mann (1993) notes the plethora of variations of Muammar Qaddafi in documents received by the U.S. Library of Congress.

Chakrabarti (2003) has written an excellent and comprehensive book on techniques of web mining. Kushmerick et al. (1997) developed techniques of wrapper induction. The founders of Google wrote an early paper that introduced the Page-Rank algorithm (Brin and Page, 1998). At the same time, Kleinberg (1998) described a system called HITS (hypertext-induced topic selection) that has some superficial similarities with PageRank but produces strikingly different results.

The first paper on junk email filtering was written by Sahami et al. (1998). Our material on computer network security is culled from Yurcik et al. (2003). The information on the CAPPS system comes from the U.S. House of Representatives Subcommittee on Aviation (2002), and the use of unsupervised learning for threat detection is described by Bay and Schwabacher (2003). Problems with current privacy-preserving data mining techniques have been identified by Datta et al. (2003). Stone and Veloso (2000) surveyed multi-agent systems of the kind that are used for playing robo-soccer from a machine learning perspective. The fascinating story of Ben Ish Chai and the technique used to unmask him is from Koppel and Schler (2004).

The vision of calm computing, as well as the examples we have mentioned, is from Weiser and Brown (1997). More information on different methods of programming by demonstration can be found in compendia by Cypher (1993) and Lieberman (2001). Mitchell et al. (1994) report some experience with learning apprentices. Familiar is described by Paynter (2000). Permutation tests (Good, 1994) are statistical tests that are suitable for small sample problems: Frank (2000) describes their application in machine learning.

The Weka Data Mining Workbench

Introduction to Weka

Experience shows that no single machine learning scheme is appropriate to all data mining problems. The universal learner is an idealistic fantasy. As we have emphasized throughout this book, real datasets vary, and to obtain accurate models the bias of the learning algorithm must match the structure of the domain. Data mining is an experimental science.

The Weka workbench is a collection of state-of-the-art machine learning algorithms and data preprocessing tools. It includes virtually all the algorithms described in this book. It is designed so that you can quickly try out existing methods on new datasets in flexible ways. It provides extensive support for the whole process of experimental data mining, including preparing the input data, evaluating learning schemes statistically, and visualizing the input data and the result of learning. As well as a variety of learning algorithms, it includes a wide range of preprocessing tools. This diverse and comprehensive toolkit is accessed through a common interface so that its users can compare different methods and identify those that are most appropriate for the problem at hand.

Weka was developed at the University of Waikato in New Zealand; the name stands for *Waikato Environment for Knowledge Analysis*. (Outside the university, the weka, pronounced to rhyme with *Mecca*, is a flightless bird with an inquisitive nature found only on the islands of New Zealand.) The system is written in Java and distributed under the terms of the GNU General Public License. It runs on almost any platform and has been tested under Linux, Windows, and Macintosh operating systems—and even on a personal digital assistant. It provides a uniform interface to many different learning algorithms, along with methods for pre- and postprocessing and for evaluating the result of learning schemes on any given dataset.

10.1 WHAT'S IN WEKA?

Weka provides implementations of learning algorithms that you can easily apply to your dataset. It also includes a variety of tools for transforming datasets, such as the algorithms for discretization described in Chapter 7. You can preprocess a dataset, feed it into a learning scheme, and analyze the resulting classifier and its performance—all without writing any program code at all.

The workbench includes methods for the main data mining problems: regression, classification, clustering, association rule mining, and attribute selection. Getting to know the data is an integral part of the work, and many data visualization facilities and data preprocessing tools are provided. All algorithms take their input in the form of a single relational table in the ARFF format described in Section 2.4, which can be read from a file or generated by a database query.

One way of using Weka is to apply a learning method to a dataset and analyze its output to learn more about the data. Another is to use learned models to generate predictions on new instances. A third is to apply several different learners and compare their performance in order to choose one for prediction. In the interactive Weka interface, you select the learning method you want from a menu. Many methods have tunable parameters, which you access through a property sheet or *object editor*. A common evaluation module is used to measure the performance of all classifiers.

Implementations of actual learning schemes are the most valuable resource that Weka provides. But tools for preprocessing the data, called *filters*, come a close second. Like classifiers, you select filters from a menu and tailor them to your requirements. We will show how different filters can be used, list the filtering algorithms, and describe their parameters. Weka also includes implementations of algorithms for learning association rules, clustering data for which no class value is specified, and selecting relevant attributes in the data, which we describe briefly.

10.2 HOW DO YOU USE IT?

The easiest way to use Weka is through a graphical user interface called *Explorer*. This gives access to all of its facilities using menu selection and form filling. For example, you can quickly read in a dataset from an ARFF file (or spreadsheet) and build a decision tree from it. But learning decision trees is just the beginning: There are many other algorithms to explore. The Explorer interface helps you do just that. It guides you by presenting choices as menus, by forcing you to work in an appropriate order by graying out options until they are applicable, and by presenting options as forms to be filled out. Helpful *tool tips* pop up as the mouse passes over items on the screen to explain what they do. Sensible default values ensure that you can get results with a minimum of effort—but you will have to think about what you are doing to understand what the results mean.

There are two other graphical user interfaces to Weka. The *Knowledge Flow* interface allows you to design configurations for streamed data processing. A fundamental disadvantage of the Explorer interface is that it holds everything in main memory—when you open a dataset, it immediately loads it all in. This means that the Explorer can only be applied to small- to medium-size problems. However, Weka contains some incremental algorithms that can be used to process very large datasets. The Knowledge Flow interface lets you drag boxes representing learning algorithms and data sources around the screen and join them together into the configuration you want. It enables you to specify a data stream by connecting components representing data sources, preprocessing tools, learning algorithms, evaluation methods, and visualization modules. If the filters and learning algorithms are capable of incremental learning, data will be loaded and processed incrementally.

Weka's third interface, *Experimenter*, is designed to help you answer a basic practical question when applying classification and regression techniques: Which methods and parameter values work best for the given problem? There is usually no way to answer this question a priori, and one reason we developed the workbench was to provide an environment that enables Weka users to compare a variety of learning techniques. This can be done interactively using the Explorer interface. However, the Experimenter interface allows you to automate the process by making it easy to run classifiers and filters with different parameter settings on a corpus of datasets, to collect performance statistics, and to perform significance tests. Advanced users can employ Experimenter to distribute the computing load across multiple machines using Java remote method invocation (RMI). In this way, you can set up large-scale statistical experiments and leave them to run.

Behind these interactive interfaces lies the basic functionality of Weka. This can be accessed in raw form by entering textual commands, which gives access to all features of the system. When you fire up Weka, you have to choose among four different user interfaces: the Explorer, the Knowledge Flow, the Experimenter, and command-line interfaces. We describe them in turn in the next chapters. Most people choose Explorer, at least initially.

10.3 WHAT ELSE CAN YOU DO?

An important resource when working with Weka is the online documentation, which has been automatically generated from the source code and concisely reflects its structure. We will explain how to use this documentation. We will also identify Weka's major building blocks, highlighting which parts contain supervised learning methods, which contain tools for data preprocessing, and which contain methods for other learning schemes. The online documentation gives the only complete list of available algorithms because Weka is continually growing and—being generated automatically from the source code—the online documentation is always up to date. Moreover, it becomes essential if you want to proceed to the next level and access the library from your own Java programs or write and test learning schemes of your own.

In most data mining applications, the machine learning component is just a small part of a far larger software system. If you intend to write a data mining application, you will want to access the programs in Weka from inside your own code. By doing so, you can solve the machine learning subproblem of your application with a minimum of additional programming. We show how to do that by presenting an example of a simple data mining application in Java. This will enable you to become familiar with the basic data structures in Weka, representing instances, classifiers, and filters.

If you intend to become an expert in machine learning algorithms (or, indeed, if you already are one), you'll probably want to implement your own algorithms without having to address such mundane details as reading the data from a file, implementing filtering algorithms, or providing code to evaluate the results. If so, we have good news for you: Weka already includes all this. To make full use of it, you must become acquainted with the basic data structures. To help you reach this point, we will describe these structures in more detail and explain an illustrative implementation of a classifier in Chapter 16.

10.4 HOW DO YOU GET IT?

Weka is available from *www.cs.waikato.ac.nz/ml/weka*. You can download either a platform-specific installer or an executable Java jar file that you run in the usual way if Java is installed. We recommend that you download and install it now, and follow through the examples in the upcoming chapters.

The Explorer

Weka's main graphical user interface, the Explorer, gives access to all its facilities using menu selection and form filling. It is illustrated in Figure 11.1. There are six different panels, selected by the tabs at the top, corresponding to the various data mining tasks that Weka supports.

11.1 GETTING STARTED

Suppose you have some data and you want to build a decision tree from it. First, you need to prepare the data, then fire up the Explorer and load it in. Next, you select a decision tree construction method, build a tree, and interpret the output. It's easy to do it again with a different tree construction algorithm or a different evaluation method. In the Explorer you can flip back and forth between the results you have obtained, evaluate the models that have been built on different datasets, and visualize graphically both the models and the datasets themselves, including any classification errors the models make.

Preparing the Data

The data is often presented in a spreadsheet or database. However, Weka's native data storage method is the ARFF format (see Section 2.4, page 52). You can easily convert from a spreadsheet to ARFF. The bulk of an ARFF file consists of a list of the instances, and the attribute values for each instance are separated by commas (see Figure 2.2). Most spreadsheet and database programs allow you to export data into a file in comma-separated value (CSV) format as a list of records with commas between items. Having done this, you need only load the file into a text editor or word processor; add the dataset's name using the @*relation* tag, the attribute information using @*attribute*, and an @*data* line; then save the file as raw text. For example, Figure 11.2 shows an Excel spreadsheet containing the weather data from Section 1.2 (page 9), the data in CSV form loaded into Microsoft Word, and the result of converting it manually into an ARFF file. However, you don't actually have to go through these steps to create the ARFF file yourself because the Explorer can read CSV spreadsheet files directly, as described later.

FIGURE 11.1

The Explorer interface.

Loading the Data into the Explorer

Let's load this data into the Explorer and start analyzing it. Fire up Weka to get the *GUI Chooser* panel in Figure 11.3(a). Select *Explorer* from the four choices on the right side. (The others were mentioned earlier: *Simple CLI* is the old-fashioned command-line interface.)

What you see next is the main Explorer screen, shown in Figure 11.3(b). Actually, the figure shows what it will look like *after* you have loaded in the weather data. The six tabs along the top are the basic operations that the Explorer supports: Right now we are on *Preprocess*. Click the *Open file* button to bring up a standard dialog through which you can select a file. Choose the *weather.arff* file. If you have it in CSV format, change from *ARFF data files* to *CSV data files*. When you specify a .csv file it is automatically converted into ARFF format.

Figure 11.3(b) shows the screen once you have loaded the file. This tells you about the dataset: It has 14 instances and 5 attributes (center left); the attributes are called *outlook*, *temperature*, *humidity*, *windy*, and *play* (lower left). The first attribute, *outlook*, is selected by default (you can choose others by clicking them) and has no missing values, three distinct values, and no unique values; the actual

FIGURE 11.2

Weather data: (a) spreadsheet, (b) CSV format, and (c) ARFF.

values are *sunny*, *overcast*, and *rainy* and they occur five, four, and five times, respectively (center right). A histogram at the lower right shows how often each of the two values of the *play* class occurs for each value of the *outlook* attribute. The *outlook* attribute is used because it appears in the box above the histogram, but you can draw a histogram of any other attribute instead. Here, *play* is selected as the class attribute; it is used to color the histogram, and any filters that require a class value use it too.

The *outlook* attribute in Figure 11.3(b) is nominal. If you select a numeric attribute, you see its minimum and maximum values, mean, and standard deviation. In

FIGURE 11.3

The Weka Explorer: (a) choosing the Explorer interface and (b) reading in the weather data.

this case the histogram will show the distribution of the class as a function of this attribute (an example appears later in Figure 11.10).

You can delete an attribute by clicking its checkbox and using the *Remove* button. *All* selects all the attributes, *None* selects none, *Invert* inverts the current selection, and *Pattern* selects those attributes of which the names match a user-supplied regular expression. You can undo a change by clicking the *Undo* button. The *Edit* button brings up an editor that allows you to inspect the data, search for particular values and edit them, and delete instances and attributes. Right-clicking on values and column headers brings up corresponding context menus.

Building a Decision Tree

To see what the C4.5 decision tree learner described in Section 6.1 (page 201) does with this dataset, use the *J4.8* algorithm, which is Weka's implementation of this decision tree learner. (*J4.8* actually implements a later and slightly improved version called C4.5 revision 8, which was the last public version of this family of algorithms before the commercial implementation C5.0 was released.) Click the *Classify* tab to get a screen that looks like Figure 11.4(b). Actually, the figure shows what it will look like *after* you have analyzed the weather data.

First select the classifier by clicking the *Choose* button at the top left, opening up the *trees* section of the hierarchical menu in Figure 11.4(a), and finding *J48*. The menu structure represents the organization of the Weka code into modules, which is described in Chapter 14 (page 519). For now, just open up the hierarchy as

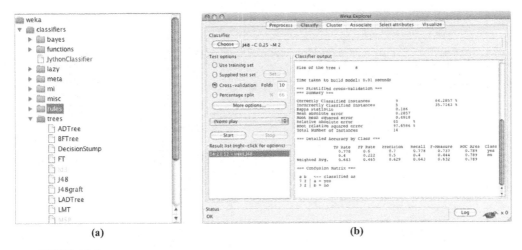

FIGURE 11.4

Using *J4.8*: (a) finding it in the classifiers list and (b) the *Classify* tab.

necessary—the items you need to select are always at the lowest level. Once selected, *J48* appears in the line beside the *Choose* button as shown in Figure 11.4(b), along with its default parameter values. If you click that line, the *J4.8* classifier's object editor opens up and you can see what the parameters mean and alter their values if you wish. The Explorer generally chooses sensible defaults.

Having chosen the classifier, invoke it by clicking the *Start* button. Weka works for a brief period—when it is working, the little bird at the lower right of Figure 11.4(b) jumps up and dances—and then produces the output shown in the main panel of Figure 11.4(b).

Examining the Output

Figure 11.5 shows the full output (Figure 11.4(b) only gives the lower half). At the beginning is a summary of the dataset and the fact that tenfold cross-validation was used to evaluate it. That is the default, and if you look closely at Figure 11.4(b) you will see that the *Cross-validation* box on the left is checked. Then comes a pruned decision tree in textual form. The model that is shown here is always one generated from the full dataset available from the *Preprocess* panel. The first split is on the *outlook* attribute, and then, at the second level, the splits are on *humidity* and *windy*, respectively.

In the tree structure, a colon introduces the class label that has been assigned to a particular leaf, followed by the number of instances that reach that leaf, expressed as a decimal number because of the way the algorithm uses fractional instances to handle missing values. If there were incorrectly classified instances (there aren't in

```
=== Run information ===

Scheme:        weka.classifiers.trees.J48 -C 0.25 -M 2
Relation:      weather
Instances:     14
Attributes:    5
               outlook
               temperature
               humidity
               windy
               play
Test mode:     10-fold cross-validation

=== Classifier model (full training set) ===

J48 pruned tree
------------------

outlook = sunny
|   humidity <= 75: yes (2.0)
|   humidity > 75: no (3.0)
outlook = overcast: yes (4.0)
outlook = rainy
|   windy = TRUE: no (2.0)
|   windy = FALSE: yes (3.0)

Number of Leaves  :   5

Size of the tree :    8

Time taken to build model: 0.27 seconds

=== Stratified cross-validation ===
=== Summary ===

Correctly Classified Instances         9                 64.2857 %
Incorrectly Classified Instances       5                 35.7143 %
Kappa statistic                        0.186
Mean absolute error                    0.2857
Root mean squared error                0.4818
Relative absolute error               60        %
Root relative squared error           97.6586 %
Total Number of Instances             14

=== Detailed Accuracy By Class ===

              TP Rate  FP Rate Precision Recall  F-Measure  ROC Area Class

              0.778    0.6      0.7       0.778    0.737      0.789    yes
              0.4      0.222    0.5       0.4      0.444      0.789    no
Weighted      0.643    0.465    0.629     0.643    0.632      0.789
Avg.

=== Confusion Matrix ===

 a b   <-- classified as
 7 2 | a = yes
 3 2 | b = no
```

FIGURE 11.5

Output from the *J4.8* decision tree learner.

this example) their number would appear too; thus, *2.0/1.0* means that two instances reached that leaf, of which one is classified incorrectly. Beneath the tree structure the number of leaves is printed; then the total number of nodes (*Size of the tree*). There is a way to view decision trees more graphically, which will be shown later in this chapter.

The next part of the output gives estimates of the tree's predictive performance. In this case they are obtained using stratified cross-validation with 10 folds, the default in Figure 11.4(b). As you can see, more than 30% of the instances (5 out of 14) have been misclassified in the cross-validation. This indicates that the results obtained from the training data are optimistic compared with what might be obtained from an independent test set from the same source. From the confusion matrix at the end (described in Section 5.7, page 164) observe that 2 instances of class *yes* have been assigned to class *no* and 3 of class *no* are assigned to class *yes*.

As well as the classification error, the evaluation module also outputs the Kappa statistic (see Section 5.7, page 166), the mean absolute error, and the root mean-squared error of the class probability estimates assigned by the tree. The root mean-squared error is the square root of the average squared loss (see Section 5.6, page 160). The mean absolute error is calculated in a similar way using the absolute instead of the squared difference. It also outputs relative errors, which are based on the prior probabilities (i.e., those obtained by the *ZeroR* learning scheme described later). Finally, for each class it also outputs some statistics described in Section 5.7. Also reported is the per-class average of each statistic, weighted by the number of instances from each class.

Doing It Again

You can easily run *J4.8* again with a different evaluation method. Select *Use training set* (near the top left in Figure 11.4(b)) and click *Start*. The classifier output is quickly replaced to show how well the derived model performs on the training set, instead of showing the cross-validation results. This evaluation is highly optimistic (see Section 5.1, page 148). It may still be useful because it generally represents an upper bound to the model's performance on fresh data. In this case, all 14 training instances are classified correctly. In some cases a classifier may decide to leave some instances unclassified, in which case these will be listed as *Unclassified Instances*. This does not happen for most learning schemes in Weka.

The panel in Figure 11.4(b) has further test options: *Supplied test set*, in which you specify a separate file containing the test set, and *Percentage split*, with which you can hold out a certain percentage of the data for testing. You can output the predictions for each instance by clicking the *More options* button and checking the appropriate entry. There are other useful options, such as suppressing some output and including other statistics such as entropy evaluation measures and cost-sensitive evaluation. For the latter, you must enter a cost matrix: Type the number of classes into the *Classes* box (and terminate it with the *Enter* or *Return* key) to get a default cost matrix (see Section 5.7, page 166), then edit the values as required.

The small pane at the lower left of Figure 11.4(b), which contains one highlighted line, is a history list of the results. The Explorer adds a new line whenever you run a classifier. Because you have now run the classifier twice, the list will contain two items. To return to a previous result set, click the corresponding line and the output for that run will appear in the *Classifier Output* pane. This makes it easy to explore different classifiers or evaluation schemes and revisit the results to compare them.

Working with Models

The result history list is the entry point to some powerful features of the Explorer. When you right-click an entry, a menu appears that allows you to view the results in a separate window or to save the result buffer. More important, you can save the model that Weka has generated in the form of a Java object file. You can reload a model that was saved previously, which generates a new entry in the result list. If you now supply a test set, you can reevaluate the old model on that new set.

Several items on the right-click menu allow you to visualize the results in various ways. At the top of the Explorer interface is a separate *Visualize* tab, but that is different: It shows the dataset, not the results for a particular model. By right-clicking an entry in the history list you can see the classifier errors. If the model is a tree or a Bayesian network you can see its structure. You can also view the margin curve and various cost and threshold curves, including the cost–benefit analyzer tool (see Section 5.7, page 170). For all of these you must choose a class value from a submenu. The *Visualize threshold curve* menu item allows you to see the effect of varying the probability threshold above which an instance is assigned to that class. You can select from a wide variety of curves that include the ROC and recall–precision curves (see Table 5.7). To see these, choose the x-axis and y-axis appropriately from the menus given. For example, set X to *False Positive Rate* and Y to *True Positive Rate* for an ROC curve or X to *Recall* and Y to *Precision* for a recall–precision curve.

Figure 11.6 shows two ways of looking at the result of using *J4.8* to classify the iris dataset (see Section 1.2, page 13)—we use this rather than the weather data because it produces more interesting pictures. Figure 11.6(a) shows the tree; right-click a blank space in this window to bring up a menu enabling you to automatically scale the view or force the tree into the window. Drag the mouse to pan around the space. It's also possible to visualize the instance data at any node if it has been saved by the learning algorithm.

Figure 11.6(b) shows the classifier errors on a two-dimensional plot. You can choose which attributes to use for X and Y using the selection boxes at the top. Alternatively, click one of the speckled horizontal strips to the right of the plot: Left-click for X and right-click for Y. Each strip shows the spread of instances along that attribute. X and Y appear beside the ones you have chosen for the axes.

The data points are colored according to their class: blue, red, and green for *Iris setosa*, *Iris versicolor*, and *Iris virginica*, respectively (there is a key at the bottom of the screen). Correctly classified instances are shown as crosses; incorrectly classified ones appear as boxes (of which there are three in Figure 11.6(b)). You can

(a)

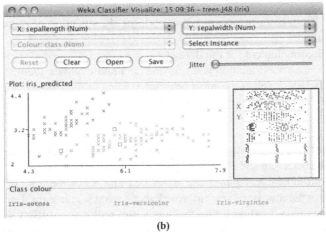

(b)

FIGURE 11.6

Visualizing the result of *J4.8* on the iris dataset: (a) the tree and (b) the classifier errors.

click on an instance to bring up relevant details: its instance number, the values of the attributes, its class, and the predicted class.

When Things Go Wrong

Beneath the result history list, at the bottom of Figure 11.4(b), is a status line that says, simply, *OK*. Occasionally this changes to *See error log*, an indication that something has gone wrong. For example, there may be constraints among the various selections you can make in a panel. Most of the time the interface grays out inappropriate selections and refuses to let you choose them. But, occasionally, the interactions are more complex, and you can end up selecting an incompatible set of options. In this case, the status line changes when Weka discovers the incompatibility—typically when you press *Start*. To see the error, click the *Log* button to the left of the bird in the lower right corner of the interface. Weka also writes a detailed log to a file in the user's home directory called *weka.log*, which often contains more information about the causes of problems than the Explorer's Log window because it captures debugging output directed to the standard out and error channels (see Section 11.2).

11.2 EXPLORING THE EXPLORER

We have briefly investigated two of the six tabs at the top of the Explorer window in Figure 11.3(b) and Figure 11.4(b). In summary, here's what all of the tabs do:

1. *Preprocess:* Choose the dataset and modify it in various ways.
2. *Classify:* Train learning schemes that perform classification or regression and evaluate them.
3. *Cluster:* Learn clusters for the dataset.
4. *Associate:* Learn association rules for the data and evaluate them.
5. *Select attributes:* Select the most relevant aspects in the dataset.
6. *Visualize:* View different two-dimensional plots of the data and interact with them.

Each tab gives access to a whole range of facilities. In our tour so far, we have barely scratched the surface of the *Preprocess* and *Classify* panels.

At the bottom of every panel is a *status* box and a *Log* button. The status box displays messages that keep you informed about what's going on. For example, if the Explorer is busy loading a file, the status box will say so. Right-clicking anywhere inside this box brings up a menu with two options: display the amount of memory available to Weka and run the Java garbage collector. Note that the garbage collector runs constantly as a background task anyway.

Clicking the *Log* button opens a textual log of the actions that Weka has performed in this session, with timestamps.

As noted earlier, the little bird at the lower right of the window jumps up and dances when Weka is active. The number beside the × shows how many concurrent processes are running. If the bird is standing but stops moving, it's sick! Something has gone wrong, and you may have to restart the Explorer.

Loading and Filtering Files

Along the top of the *Preprocess* panel in Figure 11.3(b) are buttons for opening files, URLs, and databases. Initially, only files of which the names end in .arff appear in the file browser; to see others, change the *Format* item in the file selection box.

Converting Files to ARFF

Weka has converters for the following file formats:

- Spreadsheet files with extension .csv.
- C4.5's native file format with extensions .names and .data.
- Serialized instances with extension .bsi.
- LIBSVM format files with extension .libsvm.
- SVM-Light format files with extension .dat.
- XML-based ARFF format files with extension .xrff.

The appropriate converter is used based on the file extension. If Weka cannot load the data, it tries to interpret it as ARFF. If that fails, it pops up the box shown in Figure 11.7(a).

This is a generic object editor, used throughout Weka for selecting and configuring an object. For example, when you set parameters for a classifier, you use the

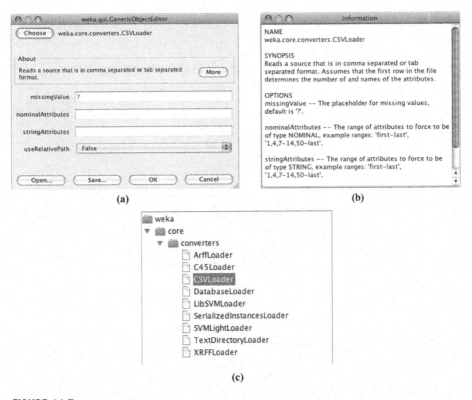

(a)   (b)

(c)

FIGURE 11.7

Generic Object Editor: (a) the editor, (b) more information (click *More*), and (c) choosing a converter (click *Choose*).

FIGURE 11.8

The SQLViewer tool.

same kind of box. The *CSVLoader* for .csv files is selected by default, and the *More* button gives you more information about it, shown in Figure 11.7(b). It is always worth looking at the documentation! In this case, it explains that the spreadsheet's first row determines the attribute names and gives a brief description of the *CSV-Loader*'s options. Click *OK* to use this converter. For a different one, click *Choose* to select from the list in Figure 11.7(c).

The *ArffLoader* is the first option, and we reached this point only because it failed. The second option is for the C4.5 format, in which there are two files for a dataset, one giving field names and the other giving the actual data. The third option, *CSVLoader*, is the default, and we clicked *Choose* because we want a different one. The fourth option is for reading from a database rather than a file; however, the *SQLViewer* tool, shown in Figure 11.8 and accessible by pressing the *Open DB* button on the *Preprocess* panel, is a more user-friendly route for accessing a database. The *serialized instances* option is for reloading datasets that have been saved as a Java-serialized object. Any Java object can be saved in this format and reloaded. As a native Java format, it is quicker to load than an ARFF file, which must be parsed and checked. When repeatedly reloading a large dataset it may be worth saving it in this form.

The eighth menu item is for importing a directory containing plaintext files for the purposes of text mining. The imported directory is expected to have a specific structure—namely, a set of subdirectories, each containing one or more text files with the extension .txt. Each text file becomes one instance in the dataset, with a string attribute holding the contents of the file and a nominal class attribute holding the name of the subdirectory that it came from. This dataset can then be further processed into word frequencies (see Section 7.3, page 328) using the *StringTo-WordVector* filter (covered in the next section). The last option is for loading data files in XRFF, the XML Attribute Relation File format. As the name suggests, this gives ARFF header and instance information in the XML markup language.

Further features of the generic object editor in Figure 11.7(a) are *Save*, which saves a configured object, and *Open*, which opens a previously saved one. These are not useful for this particular kind of object. However, other generic object editor panels have many editable properties, and having gone to some trouble to set them up you may want to save the configured object to reuse later.

Files on your computer are not the only source of datasets for Weka. You can open a URL, and Weka will use the hypertext transfer protocol (HTTP) to download an ARFF file from the Web. Or you can open a database (*Open DB*)—any database that has a Java database connectivity (JDBC) driver—and retrieve instances using the SQL *Select* statement. This returns a relation that Weka reads in as an ARFF file. To make this work with your database, you may need to modify the file *weka/experiment/DatabaseUtils.props* in the Weka distribution by adding your database driver to it. (To access this file, expand the *weka.jar* file in the Weka distribution.) Figure 11.8 shows the *SQLViewer* tool that appears when *Open DB* is clicked. In this example, the iris dataset has been extracted from a single database table.

Data can be saved in all these formats (with the exception of the directory containing text files) using the *Save* button in the *Preprocess* panel (Figure 11.3(b)). It is also possible to generate artificial data using the *Generate* button. Artificial data suitable for classification can be generated from decision lists, radial-basis function networks, and Bayesian networks, as well as from the classic LED24 domain. Artificial regression data can be generated according to mathematical expressions. There are also several generators for producing artificial data for clustering purposes. Apart from loading and saving datasets, the *Preprocess* panel also allows you to filter them. Filters are an important component of Weka.

Using Filters

Clicking *Choose* (near the top left) in Figure 11.3(b) gives a list of filters like that in Figure 11.9(a). Actually, you get a collapsed version—click on an arrow to open up its contents. We will describe how to use a simple filter to delete specified attributes from a dataset—in other words, to perform manual attribute selection. The same effect can be achieved more easily by selecting the relevant attributes using

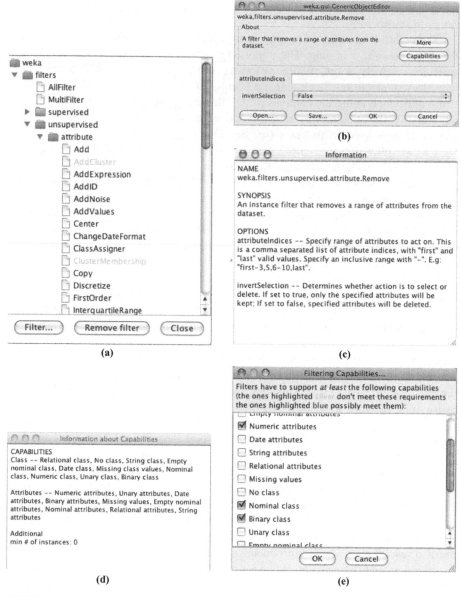

FIGURE 11.9

Choosing a filter: (a) the *filters* menu, (b) an object editor, (c) more information (click *More*), (d) information about the filter's capabilities (click *Capabilities*), and (e) constraints on capabilities.

the tick boxes and pressing the *Remove* button. Nevertheless, we describe the equivalent filtering operation explicitly, as an example.

Remove is an unsupervised attribute filter, and to see it you must scroll further down the list. When selected, it appears in the line beside the *Choose* button, along with its parameter values—in this case, the line reads simply "Remove." Click that line to bring up a generic object editor with which you can examine and alter the filter's properties. (You did the same thing earlier by clicking the *J48* line in Figure 11.4(b) to open the *J4.8* classifier's object editor.) The object editor for the *Remove* filter is shown in Figure 11.9(b).

To learn about it, click *More* to show the information in Figure 11.9(c). This explains that the filter removes a range of attributes from the dataset. It has an option, *attributeIndices*, that specifies the range to act on and another called *invertSelection* that determines whether the filter selects attributes or deletes them. There are boxes for both of these in the object editor shown in Figure 11.9(b), and in fact we have already set them to *1,2* (to affect attributes 1 and 2, namely *outlook* and *temperature*) and *False* (to remove rather than retain them). Click *OK* to set these properties and close the box. Notice that the line beside the *Choose* button now reads *Remove –R 1,2*. In the command-line version of the *Remove* filter, the option *–R* is used to specify which attributes to remove. After configuring an object it's often worth glancing at the resulting command-line formulation that the Explorer sets up.

Figure 11.9 demonstrates a further feature of the generic object editor, namely capabilities. Algorithms in Weka may provide information about what data characteristics they can handle and, if they do, a *Capabilities* button appears underneath *More* in the generic object editor (Figure 11.9(b)). Clicking it brings up Figure 11.9(d), which gives information about what the method can do. Here, it states that *Remove* can handle many attribute characteristics, such as different types (nominal, numeric, relational, etc.) and missing values. It shows the minimum number of instances that are required for *Remove* to operate on.

Figure 11.9(e) shows a list of selected constraints on the capabilities which is obtained by clicking the *Filter* button at the bottom of Figure 11.9(a). If the current dataset exhibits some characteristic that is ticked in Figure 11.9(e) but missing from the capabilities for the *Remove* filter (Figure 11.9(d)), the *Apply* button to the right of *Choose* in Figure 11.3(b) will be grayed out, as will the entry in the list in Figure 11.9(a). Although you cannot apply it, you can nevertheless select a grayed-out entry to inspect its options, documentation, and capabilities using the generic object editor. You can release individual constraints by deselecting them in Figure 11.9(e), or click the *Remove filter* button to clear all the constraints.

Apply the filter by clicking *Apply* (at the right side of Figure 11.3(b)). Immediately, the screen in Figure 11.10 appears—just like the one in Figure 11.3(b) but with only three attributes, *humidity*, *windy*, and *play*. At this point the fifth button in the row near the top becomes active. *Undo* reverses the filtering operation and restores the original dataset, which is useful when you experiment with different filters.

FIGURE 11.10

The weather data with two attributes removed.

The first attribute, *humidity*, is selected and a summary of its values appears on the right. As a numeric attribute, the minimum and maximum values, mean, and standard deviation are shown. In Figure 11.10 is a histogram that shows the distribution of the *play* attribute. Unfortunately, this display is impoverished because the attribute has so few different values that they fall into two equal-size bins. More realistic datasets yield more informative histograms.

Training and Testing Learning Schemes

The *Classify* panel lets you train and test learning schemes that perform classification or regression. Section 11.1 explained how to interpret the output of a decision tree learner and showed the performance figures that are automatically generated by the evaluation module. The interpretation of these is the same for all models that predict a categorical class. However, when evaluating models for numeric prediction, Weka produces a different set of performance measures.

As an example, in Figure 11.11(a) the CPU performance dataset from Table 1.5 has been loaded into Weka. You can see the histogram of values of the first attribute, *MYCT*, at the lower right. In Figure 11.11(b) the model tree inducer M5′ has been

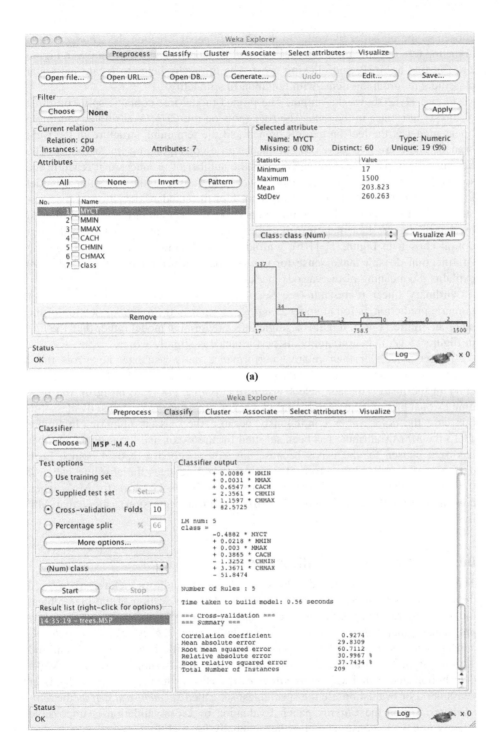

FIGURE 11.11

Processing the CPU performance data with M5′.

chosen as the classifier by going to the *Classify* panel, clicking the *Choose* button at the top left, opening up the *trees* section of the hierarchical menu shown in Figure 11.4(a), finding *M5P*, and clicking *Start*. The hierarchy helps to locate particular classifiers by grouping items with common functionality.

Figure 11.12 shows the output. The pruned model tree contains splits on three of the six attributes in the data. The root splits on the *CHMIN* attribute, yielding a linear model at the leaf on the left branch and the remaining structure in the right branch. There are five leaves in all, each with a corresponding linear model. The first number in parentheses at each leaf is the number of instances that reach it; the second is the root mean-squared error of the predictions from the leaf's linear model for those instances, expressed as a percentage of the standard deviation of the class attribute computed over all the training data. The description of the tree is followed by several figures that measure its performance. These are derived from the test option chosen in Figure 11.11(b), tenfold cross-validation (not stratified because stratification doesn't make sense for numeric prediction). Section 5.8 (Table 5.8) explains the meaning of the various measures.

Ordinary linear regression (see Section 4.6, page 124), another scheme for numeric prediction, is found under *LinearRegression* in the *functions* section of the menu in Figure 11.4(a). It builds a single linear regression model rather than the five in Figure 11.12; not surprisingly, its performance is slightly worse.

To get a feel for their relative performance, let's visualize the errors these schemes make, as we did for the iris dataset in Figure 11.6(b). Right-click the entry in the history list and select *Visualize classifier errors* to bring up the two-dimensional plot of the data in Figure 11.13. The points are color-coded by class—in this case the color varies continuously because the class is numeric. In Figure 11.13 the *MMAX* attribute has been selected for the x-axis and the instance number has been chosen for the y-axis because this gives a good spread of points. Each data point is marked by a cross of which the size indicates the absolute value of the error for that instance. The smaller crosses in Figure 11.13(a) (for M5′), when compared with those in Figure 11.13(b) (for linear regression), show that M5′ is superior.

Do It Yourself: The User Classifier

The User Classifier (mentioned in Section 3.2, page 65) allows Weka users to build their own classifiers interactively. It resides in the *trees* section of the hierarchical menu in Figure 11.4(a) under *UserClassifier*. We illustrate its operation on a new problem, segmenting visual image data into classes such as *grass*, *sky*, *foliage*, *brick*, and *cement* based on attributes giving average intensity, hue, size, position, and various simple textural features. The training data file is supplied with the Weka distribution and called *segment-challenge.arff*. Having loaded it, select the User Classifier. For evaluation use the special test set called *segment-test.arff* as the *Supplied test set* on the *Classify* panel. Evaluation by cross-validation is impossible when you have to construct a classifier manually for each fold.

```
=== Run information ===

Scheme:        weka.classifiers.trees.M5P -M 4.0
Relation:      cpu
Instances:     209
Attributes:    7
               MYCT
               MMIN
               MMAX
               CACH
               CHMIN
               CHMAX
               class
Test mode:     10-fold cross-validation

=== Classifier model (full training set) ===

M5 pruned model tree:
(using smoothed linear models)

CHMIN <= 7.5 : LM1 (165/12.903%)
CHMIN >  7.5 :
|   MMAX <= 28000 :
|   |   MMAX <= 13240 :
|   |   |   CACH <= 81.5 : LM2 (6/18.551%)
|   |   |   CACH >  81.5 : LM3 (4/30.824%)
|   |   MMAX >  13240 : LM4 (11/24.185%)
|   MMAX >  28000 : LM5 (23/48.302%)

LM num: 1
class = -0.0055 * MYCT + 0.0013 * MMIN + 0.0029 * MMAX + 0.8007 * CACH
        + 0.4015 * CHMAX   + 11.0971

LM num: 2
class = -1.0307 * MYCT + 0.0086 * MMIN + 0.0031 * MMAX + 0.7866 * CACH
        - 2.4503 * CHMIN + 1.1597 * CHMAX + 70.8672

LM num: 3
class = -1.1057 * MYCT + 0.0086 * MMIN + 0.0031 * MMAX + 0.7995 * CACH
        - 2.4503 * CHMIN + 1.1597 * CHMAX + 83.0016

LM num: 4
class = -0.8813 * MYCT + 0.0086 * MMIN + 0.0031 * MMAX + 0.6547 * CACH
        - 2.3561 * CHMIN + 1.1597 * CHMAX + 82.5725

LM num: 5
class = -0.4882 * MYCT + 0.0218 * MMIN + 0.003 * MMAX + 0.3865 * CACH
        - 1.3252 * CHMIN + 3.3671 * CHMAX - 51.8474

Number of Rules : 5

Time taken to build model: 0.56 seconds

=== Cross-validation ===
=== Summary ===

Correlation coefficient                0.9274
Mean absolute error                   29.8309
Root mean squared error               60.7112
Relative absolute error               30.9967 %
Root relative squared error           37.7434 %
Total Number of Instances            209
```

FIGURE 11.12

Output from the M5′ program for numeric prediction.

FIGURE 11.13

Visualizing the errors: (a) from M5′ and (b) from linear regression.

Following *Start*, a new window appears and Weka waits for you to build the classifier. The *Tree Visualizer* and *Data Visualizer* tabs switch between different views. The former shows the current state of the classification tree, and each node gives the number of instances of each class at that node. The aim is to come up with a tree in which the leaf nodes are as pure as possible. Initially, there is only one node, the root, which contains all the data. Switch to the *Data Visualizer* to create a split. This shows the same two-dimensional plot that we saw in Figure 11.6(b) for the iris dataset and in Figure 11.13 for the CPU performance data. The attributes to use for X and Y are selected as before, and the goal here is to find a combination that separates the classes as cleanly as possible. Figure 11.14(a) shows a good choice: *region-centroid-row* for X and *intensity-mean* for Y.

Having found a good separation, you must specify a region in the graph. Four tools for this appear in the pull-down menu below the *y*-axis selector. *Select Instance* identifies a particular instance. *Rectangle* (shown in Figure 11.14(a)) allows you to drag out a rectangle on the graph. With *Polygon* and *Polyline* you build a free-form polygon or draw a free-form polyline (left-click to add a vertex and right-click to complete the operation). Once an area has been selected, it turns gray. In Figure 11.14(a) the user has defined a rectangle. The *Submit* button creates two new nodes in the tree, one holding the selected instances and the other holding all the rest. *Clear* clears the selection; *Save* saves the instances in the current tree node as an ARFF file.

At this point, the *Tree Visualizer* shows the tree in Figure 11.14(b). There is a pure node for the *sky* class, but the other node is mixed and should be split further. Clicking on different nodes determines which subset of data is shown by the *Data Visualizer*. Continue adding nodes until you are satisfied with the result—that is, until the leaf nodes are mostly pure. Then right-click on any blank space in the *Tree Visualizer* and choose *Accept the Tree*. Weka evaluates your tree on the test set and outputs performance statistics (90% is a good score on this problem).

Building trees manually is very tedious. But Weka can complete the task for you by building a subtree under any node: Just right-click the node.

Using a Metalearner

Metalearners (see Chapter 8) take simple classifiers and turn them into more powerful learners. For example, to boost decision stumps in the Explorer, go to the *Classify* panel and choose the classifier *AdaboostM1* from the *meta* section of the hierarchical menu. When you configure this classifier by clicking it, the object editor shown in Figure 11.15 appears. This has its own classifier field, which we set to *DecisionStump* (as shown). This method could itself be configured by clicking (except that *DecisionStump* happens to have no editable properties). Click *OK* to return to the main *Classify* panel and *Start* to try out boosting decision stumps up to 10 times. It turns out that this mislabels only 7 of the 150 instances in the iris data—good performance considering the rudimentary nature of decision stumps and the rather small number of boosting iterations.

(a)

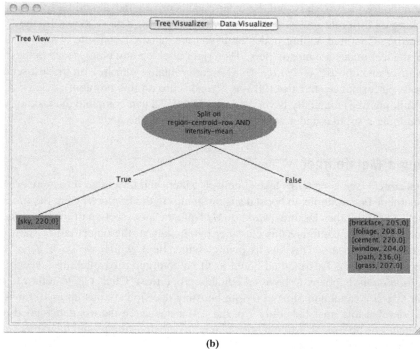

(b)

FIGURE 11.14

Working on segment-challenge data with the User Classifier: (a) data and (b) tree visualizers.

FIGURE 11.15

Configuring a metalearner for boosting decision stumps.

Clustering and Association Rules

Use the *Cluster* and *Associate* panels to invoke clustering algorithms (see Section 6.8, page 272) and methods for finding association rules (see Section 4.5, page 116). When clustering, Weka shows the number of clusters and how many instances each cluster contains. For some algorithms the number of clusters can be specified by setting a parameter in the object editor. For probabilistic clustering methods, Weka measures the log-likelihood of the clusters on the training data: The larger this quantity, the better the model fits the data. Increasing the number of clusters normally increases the likelihood, but may overfit.

The controls on the *Cluster* panel are similar to those for *Classify*. You can specify some of the same evaluation methods—use training set, supplied test set, and percentage split (the last two are used with the log-likelihood). A further method, classes to clusters evaluation, compares how well the chosen clusters match a pre-assigned class in the data. You select an attribute (which must be nominal) that represents the "true" class. Having clustered the data, Weka determines the majority class in each cluster and prints a confusion matrix showing how many errors there would be if the clusters were used instead of the true class. If your dataset has a class attribute, you can ignore it during clustering by selecting it from a pull-down list of attributes and see how well the clusters correspond to actual class values. Finally, you can choose whether or not to store the clusters for visualization. The only reason not to do so is to conserve space. As with classifiers, you visualize the results by right-clicking on the result list, which allows you to view two-dimensional scatter plots like the one in Figure 11.6(b). If you have chosen classes to clusters evaluation, the class assignment errors are shown. For the *Cobweb* clustering scheme, you can also visualize the tree.

```
1.  outlook=overcast 4 ==> play=yes 4       conf:(1)
2.  temperature=cool 4 ==> humidity=normal 4       conf:(1)
3.  humidity=normal windy=FALSE 4 ==> play=yes 4       conf:(1)
4.  outlook=sunny play=no 3 ==> humidity=high 3       conf:(1)
5.  outlook=sunny humidity=high 3 ==> play=no 3       conf:(1)
6.  outlook=rainy play=yes 3 ==> windy=FALSE 3       conf:(1)
7.  outlook=rainy windy=FALSE 3 ==> play=yes 3       conf:(1)
8.  temperature=cool play=yes 3 ==> humidity=normal 3       conf:(1)
9.  outlook=sunny temperature=hot 2 ==> humidity=high 2       conf:(1)
10. temperature=hot play=no 2 ==> outlook=sunny 2       conf:(1)
```

FIGURE 11.16

Output from the *Apriori* program for association rules.

The *Associate* panel is simpler than *Classify* or *Cluster*. Weka contains six algorithms for determining association rules and no methods for evaluating such rules. Figure 11.16 shows the output from the *Apriori* program for association rules (described in Section 4.5) on the nominal version of the weather data. Despite the simplicity of the data, several rules are found. The number before the arrow is the number of instances for which the antecedent is true; that after the arrow is the number of instances for which the consequent is true also; the confidence (in parentheses) is the ratio between the two. Ten rules are found by default: You can ask for more by using the object editor to change *numRules*.

Attribute Selection

The *Select attributes* panel gives access to several methods for attribute selection. As explained in Section 7.1 (page 307), this involves an attribute evaluator and a search method. Both are chosen in the usual way and configured with the object editor. You must also decide which attribute to use as the class. Attribute selection can be performed using the full training set or using cross-validation. In the latter case it is done separately for each fold, and the output shows how many times—that is, in how many of the folds—each attribute was selected. The results are stored in the history list. When you right-click an entry here you can visualize the dataset in terms of the selected attributes (choose *Visualize reduced data*).

Visualization

The *Visualize* panel helps you visualize a dataset—not the result of a classification or clustering model, but the dataset itself. It displays a matrix of two-dimensional scatter plots of every pair of attributes. Figure 11.17(a) shows the iris dataset. You can select an attribute—normally the class—for coloring the data points using the controls at the bottom. If it is nominal, the coloring is discrete; if it is numeric, the color spectrum ranges continuously from blue (low values) to orange (high values).

(a)

(b)

FIGURE 11.17

Visualizing the iris dataset.

Data points with no class value are shown in black. You can change the size of each plot, the size of the points, and the amount of jitter, which is a random displacement applied to X and Y values to separate points that lie on top of one another. Without jitter, a thousand instances at the same data point would look just the same as one instance. You can reduce the size of the matrix of plots by selecting certain attributes, and you can subsample the data for efficiency. Changes in the controls do not take effect until the *Update* button is clicked.

Click one of the plots in the matrix to enlarge it. For example, clicking on the top left plot brings up the panel in Figure 11.17(b). You can zoom in on any area of this panel by choosing *Rectangle* from the menu near the top right and dragging out a rectangle on the viewing area like that shown. The *Submit* button near the top left rescales the rectangle into the viewing area.

11.3 FILTERING ALGORITHMS

Now we take a detailed look at the filtering algorithms implemented within Weka. These are accessible from the Explorer and from the Knowledge Flow and Experimenter interfaces described in Chapters 12 and 13. All filters transform the input dataset in some way. When a filter is selected using the *Choose* button, its name appears in the line beside that button. Click that line to get a generic object editor to specify its properties. What appears in the line is the command-line version of the filter, and the parameters are specified with minus signs. This is a good way of learning how to use the Weka commands directly.

There are two kinds of filter: unsupervised and supervised (see Section 7.2, page 316). This seemingly innocuous distinction masks an issue that is rather fundamental. Filters are often applied to a training dataset and then also applied to the test file. If the filter is supervised—for example, if it uses class values to derive good intervals for discretization—applying it to the test data will bias the results. It is the discretization intervals derived from the *training* data that must be applied to the test data. When using supervised filters, you must to be careful to ensure that the results are evaluated fairly, which is an issue that does not arise with unsupervised filters.

We treat Weka's unsupervised and supervised filtering methods separately. Within each type there is a further distinction between *attribute filters*, which work on the attributes in the datasets, and *instance filters*, which work on the instances. To learn more about a particular filter, select it in the Weka Explorer and look at its associated object editor, which defines what the filter does and the parameters it takes.

Unsupervised Attribute Filters

Table 11.1 lists Weka's unsupervised attribute filters. Many of the operations were introduced in Chapter 7.

Table 11.1 Unsupervised Attribute Filters

Name	Function
Add	Add a new attribute, the values of which are all marked as missing
AddCluster	Add a new nominal attribute representing the cluster assigned to each instance by a given clustering algorithm
AddExpression	Create a new attribute by applying a specified mathematical function to existing attributes
AddID	Add an attribute that contains a unique ID for each instance in the dataset
AddNoise	Change a percentage of a given nominal attribute's values
AddValues	Add the labels from a user-supplied list to an attribute if they are missing. The labels can be optionally sorted.
Center	Center all numeric attributes in the given dataset to have zero mean (apart from the class attribute, if set)
ChangeDateFormat	Change the string used to format a date attribute
ClassAssigner	Set or unset the class attribute
ClusterMembership	Use a cluster to generate cluster membership values, which then form new attributes
Copy	Copy a range of attributes in the dataset
Discretize	Convert numeric attributes to nominal: Specify which attributes, number of bins, whether to optimize the number of bins, output binary attributes, use equal-width (default) or equal-frequency binning
FirstOrder	Apply a first-order differencing operator to a range of numeric attributes
InterquartileRange	Create new attributes to indicate outliers and extreme values. Interquartile ranges are used to define what constitutes an outlier or an extreme value.
KernelFilter	Produce a kernel matrix for a dataset. The new dataset contains one attribute and one instance for every instance in the source dataset. Attribute values for a particular instance in the new dataset hold the result of evaluating a kernel function on the instance in question and the original instance corresponding to each attribute.

Continued

Table 11.1 Unsupervised Attribute Filters *Continued*

Name	Function
MakeIndicator	Replace a nominal attribute by a Boolean attribute. Assign value 1 to instances with a particular range of attribute values, else 0. By default, the Boolean attribute is coded as numeric.
MathExpression	Similar to *AddExpression*, but modifies existing attributes in situ rather than creating a new attribute
MergeTwoValues	Merge two values of a given attribute: Specify the index of the two values to be merged
MultiInstanceToPropositional	Convert a multi-instance dataset into a single-instance one by giving each instance its bag's class value and optionally setting its weight
NominalToBinary	Change a nominal attribute to several binary ones, one for each value
NominalToString	Convert nominal attributes into string attributes
Normalize	Scale all numeric values in the dataset to lie within the interval [0,1]
NumericCleaner	Replace values of numeric attributes that are too small, too large, or too close to a particular value with user-supplied default values
NumericToBinary	Convert all numeric attributes into binary ones: Nonzero values become 1
NumericToNominal	Convert numeric attributes to nominal by simply adding all observed values for a numeric attribute into the list of nominal values
NumericTransform	Transform a numeric attribute using any Java function
Obfuscate	Obfuscate the dataset by renaming the relation, all attribute names, and nominal and string attribute values
PartitionedMultiFilter	A meta filter that applies a set of filters to a corresponding set of attribute ranges and assembles the output into a new dataset
PKIDiscretize	Discretize numeric attributes using equal-frequency binning, where the number of bins is equal to the square root of the number of values (excluding missing values)

Table 11.1 *Continued*

Name	Function
PrincipalComponents	Perform a principal components analysis and transformation of the input data
PropositionalToMultiInstance	Convert a single-instance dataset (with a bag ID attribute) to multi-instance format using relational attributes
RandomProjection	Project the data onto a lower-dimensional subspace using a random matrix
RandomSubset	Create a new dataset that includes a percentage of the original number of attributes chosen at random
RELAGGS	Use the RELAGGS algorithm to convert multi-instance data to single-instance format
Remove	Remove attributes
RemoveType	Remove attributes of a given type (nominal, numeric, string, or date)
RemoveUseless	Remove constant attributes, along with nominal attributes that vary too much
Reorder	Change the order of the attributes
ReplaceMissingValues	Replace all missing values for nominal and numeric attributes with the modes and means of the training data
Standardize	Standardize all numeric attributes to have zero mean and unit variance
StringToNominal	Convert a string attribute to nominal
StringToWordVector	Convert a string attribute to a vector that represents word occurrence frequencies; you can choose the delimiter(s)—and there are many more options
SwapValues	Swap two values of an attribute
TimeSeriesDelta	Replace attribute values in the current instance with the difference between the current value and the value in some previous (or future) instance
TimeSeriesTranslate	Replace attribute values in the current instance with the equivalent value in some previous (or future) instance
Wavelet	Perform a Haar wavelet transformation

Adding and Removing Attributes

Add inserts an attribute at a given position, the value of which is declared to be missing for all instances. Use the generic object editor to specify the attribute's name, where it will appear in the list of attributes, and its possible values (for nominal attributes); for data attributes you can also specify the date format. *Copy* copies existing attributes so that you can preserve them when experimenting with filters that overwrite attribute values. Several attributes can be copied together using an expression such as *1–3* for the first three attributes, or *first-3,5,9-last* for attributes 1, 2, 3, 5, 9, 10, 11, 12, ... The selection can be inverted, affecting all attributes *except* those specified. These features are shared by many filters.

AddID inserts a numeric identifier attribute at the user-specified index in the list of attributes. An identifier attribute is useful for keeping track of individual instances after a dataset has been processed in various ways, such as being transformed by other filters or having the order of the instances randomized.

Remove has already been described. Similar filters are *RemoveType*, which deletes all attributes of a given type (nominal, numeric, string, date, or relational), and *RemoveUseless*, which deletes constant attributes and nominal attributes of which the values are different for almost all instances. You can decide how much variation is tolerated before an attribute is deleted by specifying the number of distinct values as a percentage of the total number of values. Note that some unsupervised attribute filters behave differently if the menu in the *Preprocess* panel has been used to set a class attribute (by default, the last attribute is the class attribute). For example, *RemoveType* and *RemoveUseless* both skip the class attribute.

InterquartileRange adds new attributes that indicate whether the values of instances can be considered outliers or extreme values. The definitions of outlier and extreme value are based on the difference between the 25th and 75th quartile of an attribute's values. Values are flagged as extreme if they exceed the 75th quartile (or fall below the 25th quartile) by the product of the user-specified extreme value factor and the interquartile range. Values that are not extreme values but exceed the 75th quartile (or fall below the 25th quartile) by the product of the outlier factor and the interquartile range are flagged as outliers. The filter can be configured to flag an instance as an outlier or extreme if any of its attribute values are deemed outliers or extreme, or to generate an outlier–extreme indicator pair for each attribute. It is also possible to flag all extreme values as outliers and to output attributes that indicate by how many interquartile ranges an attribute's value deviates from the median.

AddCluster applies a clustering algorithm to the data before filtering it. You use the object editor to choose the clustering algorithm. Clusterers are configured just as filters are (see Section 11.6). The *AddCluster* object editor contains its own *Choose* button for the clusterer, and you configure the clusterer by clicking its line and getting *another* object editor panel, which must be filled in before returning to the *AddCluster* object editor. This is probably easier to understand when you do it in practice than when you read about it in a book! At any rate, once you have chosen a clusterer, *AddCluster* uses it to assign a cluster number to each instance, as a new attribute. The object editor also allows you to ignore certain attributes when clustering, specified as described previously for *Copy*. *ClusterMembership* uses a clusterer, again specified in the filter's object editor, to generate membership values. A new version of each instance is created of which the attributes are these values. The class attribute, if set, is ignored during clustering.

AddExpression creates a new attribute by applying a mathematical function to numeric attributes. The expression can contain attribute references and constants; arithmetic operators $+$, $-$, $*$, $/$, and $\wedge$; the functions *log* and *exp*, *abs* and *sqrt*, *floor*, *ceil* and *rint*,[1] *sin*, *cos*, and *tan*; and parentheses. Attributes are specified by the prefix *a*—for example, *a7* is the seventh attribute. An example expression is

$$a1 \wedge 2 * a5 / \log(a7 * 4.0)$$

There is a debug option that replaces the new attribute's value with a postfix parse of the supplied expression.

MathExpression is similar to *AddExpression* but can be applied to multiple attributes. Rather than creating a new attribute, it replaces the original values with the result of the expression *in situ*; because of this, the expression cannot reference the value of other attributes. All the operators that apply to *AddExpression* can be used, as well as the minimum, maximum, mean, sum, sum-squared, and standard deviation of the attribute being processed. Furthermore, simple if–then–else expressions involving the operators and functions can be applied as well.

Whereas *AddExpression* and *MathExpression* apply mathematical functions specified in textual form, *NumericTransform* performs an arbitrary transformation by applying a given Java function to selected numeric attributes. The function can be anything that takes a *double* as its argument and returns another *double*—for example, *sqrt()* in *java.lang.Math*. One parameter is the name of the Java class that implements the function (which must be a fully qualified name); another is the name of the transformation method itself.

Normalize scales all numeric values in the dataset to lie between 0 and 1. The normalized values can be further scaled and translated with user-supplied constants. *Center* and *Standardize* transform them to have zero mean; *Standardize* gives them unit variance too. All three skip the class attribute, if set. *RandomSubset* randomly selects a subset of the attributes to include in the output; the user specifies how many (as a percentage of the number of attributes). The class attribute, if set, is always included.

PartitionedMultiFilter is a special filter that applies a set of filters to a corresponding set of attribute ranges in the input dataset. The user supplies and configures each filter, and defines the range of attributes for them to work with. There is an option to delete attributes that are not covered by any of the ranges. Only filters that operate on attributes are allowed. The output of the individual filters is assembled

---

[1]The *rint* function rounds to the closest integer.

into a new dataset. *Reorder* alters the order of the attributes in the data; the new order is specified by supplying a list of attribute indices. By omitting or duplicating indices it is possible to delete attributes or make several copies of them.

Changing Values

SwapValues swaps the positions of two values of a nominal attribute. The order of values is entirely cosmetic—it does not affect learning at all—but if the class is selected, changing the order affects the layout of the confusion matrix. *Merge-TwoValues* merges values of a nominal attribute into a single category. The new value's name is a concatenation of the two original ones, and every occurrence of either of the original values is replaced by the new one. The index of the new value is the smaller of the original indices. For example, if you merge the first two values of the *outlook* attribute in the weather data—in which there are five *sunny*, four *overcast*, and five *rainy* instances—the new *outlook* attribute will have values *sunny_overcast* and *rainy*; there will be nine *sunny_overcast* instances and the original five *rainy* ones.

One way of dealing with missing values is to replace them globally before applying a learning scheme. *ReplaceMissingValues* replaces each missing value by the mean for numeric attributes and the mode for nominal ones. If a class is set, missing values of that attribute are not replaced by default, but this can be changed.

NumericCleaner replaces the values of numeric attributes that are too small, too large, or too close to a particular value with default values. A different default can be specified for each case, along with thresholds for what is considered to be too large or small and a tolerance value for defining too close.

AddValues adds any values that are not already present in a nominal attribute from a user-supplied list. The labels can optionally be sorted. *ClassAssigner* can be used to set or unset a dataset's class attribute. The user supplies the index of the new class attribute; a value of 0 unsets the existing class attribute.

Conversions

Many filters convert attributes from one form to another. *Discretize* uses equal-width or equal-frequency binning (see Section 7.2, page 316) to discretize a range of numeric attributes, specified in the usual way. For the former method the number of bins can be specified or chosen automatically by maximizing the likelihood using leave-one-out cross-validation. It is also possible to create several binary attributes instead of one multivalued one. For equal-frequency discretization, the desired number of instances per interval can be changed. *PKIDiscretize* discretizes numeric attributes using equal-frequency binning; the number of bins is the square root of the number of values (excluding missing values). Both these filters skip the class attribute by default.

MakeIndicator converts a nominal attribute into a binary indicator attribute and can be used to transform a multiclass dataset into several two-class ones. It substitutes a binary attribute for the chosen nominal one, of which the values for each instance are 1 if a particular original value was present and 0 otherwise. The new attribute is declared to be numeric by default, but it can be made nominal if desired.

For some learning schemes, such as support vector machines, multivalued nominal attributes must be converted to binary ones. The *NominalToBinary* filter transforms all specified multivalued nominal attributes in a dataset into binary ones, replacing each attribute with k values by k binary attributes using a simple one-per-value encoding. The new attributes will be numeric by default. Attributes that are already binary are left untouched. *NumericToBinary* converts all numeric attributes into nominal binary ones (except the class, if set). If the value of the numeric attribute is exactly 0, the new attribute will be 0, and if it is missing, the new attribute will be missing; otherwise, the value of the new attribute will be 1. These filters also skip the class attribute. *NumericToNominal* converts numeric attributes to nominal ones by simply adding every distinct numeric value to the list of nominal values. This can be a useful filter to apply after importing a .csv file—Weka's csv import facility creates a numeric attribute for any data column with values that can all be parsed as numbers, but it might make sense to interpret the values of an integer attribute as discrete instead.

FirstOrder takes a range of N numeric attributes and replaces them with $N - 1$ numeric attributes with values that are the differences between consecutive attribute values from the original instances. For example, if the original attribute values were 3, 2, and 1, the new ones will be -1 and -1.

KernelFilter converts the data to a kernel matrix: It outputs a new dataset, containing the same number of instances as before, in which each value is the result of evaluating a kernel function on a pair of original instances. By default, all values are transformed to center them around 0, although they are not rescaled to unit variance. However, different filters can be specified.

PrincipalComponents performs a principal components transformation on the dataset. First, any multivalued nominal attributes are converted to binary, and missing values are replaced by means. The data is standardized (by default). The number of components is normally determined based on the user-specified proportion of variance to be covered, but it is also possible to specify the number of components explicitly.

The *Wavelet* filter applies a Haar wavelet transformation to the data. A *MultiFilter* are used to replace missing values with means and modes, and to normalize the data. The user can adjust the configuration of *MultiFilter* in order to modify the preprocessing that is done.

String Conversion

A string attribute has an unspecified number of values. *StringToNominal* converts it to nominal with a set number of values. You should ensure that all string values that will appear in potential test data are represented in the dataset. *NominalToString* converts the other way.

StringToWordVector produces numeric attributes that represent the frequency of words in the value of a string attribute. The set of words—that is, the new attribute set—is determined from the full set of values in the string attribute. The new attributes can be named with a user-determined prefix to keep attributes derived from different string attributes distinct.

There are many options that affect tokenization. Words can be formed from contiguous alphabetic sequences or separated by a given set of delimiter characters. In the latter case, they can be further split into n-grams (with user-supplied minimum and maximum length), or they can be processed by a stemming algorithm. They can be converted to lowercase before being added to the dictionary, or all words on a supplied list of stopwords can be ignored. Words that are not among the top k words ranked by frequency can be discarded (slightly more than k words will be retained if there are ties at the kth position). If a class attribute has been assigned, the top k words for each class will be kept (this can be turned off by the user). The value of each word attribute reflects its presence or absence in the string, but this can be changed. A count of the number of times the word appears in the string can be used instead. Word frequencies can be normalized to give each document's attribute vector the same Euclidean length—the length chosen is not 1 to avoid the very small numbers that would entail, but is the average length of all documents that appear as values of the original string attribute. Alternatively, the frequencies f_{ij} for word i in document j can be transformed using $\log(1 + f_{ij})$ or the TF $\times$ IDF measure (see Section 7.3, page 329).

ChangeDateFormat alters the formatting string that is used to parse date attributes. Any format supported by Java's *SimpleDateFormat* class can be specified.

Multi-Instance Data

There are two filters that convert multi-instance data into single-instance format. *MultiInstanceToPropositional* takes the "aggregating the output" approach (see Section 4.9, page 142), converting multi-instance data involving a single relational attribute to single-instance format by assigning to each instance in a bag the bag's class value. There are several options for setting the weight of the new instances in order to adjust for bags of different sizes. *RELAGGS* implements the "aggregating the input" approach by computing summary statistics (e.g., mean, minimum, and maximum) for the attribute values in each bag. It has an option to avoid computing statistics for nominal attributes with more than a user-specified maximum number of values, effectively removing them from the data.

PropositionalToMultiInstance is a simple filter for converting in the other direction—that is, from single- to multi-instance format involving a single relational attribute. It assumes that the first attribute in the data is an ID that indicates the bag to which the instance belongs.

Time Series

Two filters work with time series data. *TimeSeriesTranslate* replaces the values of an attribute (or attributes) in the current instance with the equivalent value in some other (previous or future) instance. *TimeSeriesDelta* replaces attribute values in the current instance with the difference between the current value and the value in some other instance. In both cases, instances in which the time-shifted value is unknown may be removed or missing values used.

Randomizing

Other attribute filters degrade the data. *AddNoise* takes a nominal attribute and changes a given percentage of its values. Missing values can be retained or changed along with the rest. *Obfuscate* anonymizes data by renaming the relation, the attribute names, and the nominal and string attribute values. *RandomProjection* projects the dataset onto a lower-dimensional subspace using a random matrix with columns of unit length (see Section 7.3, page 326). The class attribute is not included in the projection.

Unsupervised Instance Filters

Weka's instance filters, listed in Table 11.2, affect all instances in a dataset rather than all values of a particular attribute or attributes.

Table 11.2 Unsupervised Instance Filters

Name	Function
NonSparseToSparse	Convert all incoming instances to sparse format (see Section 2.4, page 56)
Normalize	Treat numeric attributes as a vector and normalize the vector to a given length
Randomize	Randomize the order of instances in a dataset
RemoveFolds	Output a specified cross-validation fold for the dataset
RemoveFrequentValues	Remove instances containing the n most frequent or infrequent values of a nominal attribute
RemoveMisclassified	Remove instances that are incorrectly classified according to a specified classifier—useful for removing outliers
RemovePercentage	Remove a given percentage of a dataset
RemoveRange	Remove a given range of instances from a dataset
RemoveWithValues	Filter out instances with certain attribute values
Resample	Produce a random subsample of a dataset, sampling with replacement
ReservoirSample	Uniformly sample n instances from a dataset read incrementally
SparseToNonSparse	Convert all incoming sparse instances into nonsparse format
SubsetByExpression	Retain instances according to the evaluation of a logical expression involving mathematical and logical operators applied to attribute values

Randomizing and Subsampling

You can *Randomize* the order of instances in the dataset. *Normalize* treats all numeric attributes (excluding the class) as a vector and normalizes it to a given length. You can specify the vector length and the norm to be used.

There are various ways of generating subsets of the data. Use *Resample* to produce a random sample by sampling with or without replacement, or *RemoveFolds* to split it into a given number of cross-validation folds and reduce it to just one of them. If a random number seed is provided, the dataset will be shuffled before the subset is extracted. *ReservoirSample* uses the reservoir sampling algorithm described in Section 7.4 (page 330) to produce a random sample (without replacement) from a dataset. When used from the Knowledge Flow interface (see Chapter 12) or from the command-line interface (see Chapter 14), the dataset is read incrementally so that datasets that exceed main memory can be sampled.

RemovePercentage removes a given percentage of instances, and *RemoveRange* removes a certain range of instance numbers. To remove all instances that have certain values for nominal attributes, or numeric values above or below a certain threshold, use *RemoveWithValues*. By default, all instances are deleted that exhibit one of a given set of nominal attribute values (if the specified attribute is nominal) or a numeric value below a given threshold (if it is numeric). However, the matching criterion can be inverted. The attribute information is normally left unchanged, but this can be altered so that corresponding values of a nominal attribute are deleted from its definition.

RemoveFrequentValues can be used to remove those instances containing the most- or least-frequent values of a particular nominal attribute; the user can specify how many frequent or infrequent values to remove.

SubsetByExpression selects all instances that satisfy a user-supplied logical expression. The expression can involve mathematical operators and functions, such as those used by *AddExpression* and *MathExpression*, and logical operators (e.g., *and*, *or*, and *not*) applied to attribute values. For example, the expression

$$(\text{CLASS is 'mammal'}) \text{ and } (\text{ATT14} > 2)$$

selects only those instances of which the class attribute has the value *mammal* and the 14th attribute exceeds 2.

You can remove outliers by applying a classification method to the dataset (specifying it just as the clustering method was specified previously for *AddCluster*) and use *RemoveMisclassified* to delete the instances that it misclassifies. The process is normally repeated until the data is fully cleansed, but a maximum number of iterations can be specified instead. Cross-validation can be used rather than evaluation on the training data, and for numeric classes an error threshold can be specified.

Sparse Instances

The *NonSparseToSparse* and *SparseToNonSparse* filters convert between the regular representation of a dataset and its sparse representation (see Section 2.4, page 56).

Supervised Filters

Supervised filters are available from the Explorer's *Preprocess* panel, just as unsupervised ones are. You need to be careful with them because, despite appearances, they are not really preprocessing operations. We noted this earlier with regard to discretization—the test data splits must not use the test data's class values because these are supposed to be unknown—and it is true for supervised filters in general.

Because of popular demand, Weka allows you to invoke supervised filters as a preprocessing operation, just like unsupervised filters. However, if you intend to use them for classification, you should adopt a different methodology. A metalearner is provided that invokes a filter in a way that wraps the learning algorithm into the filtering mechanism. This filters the test data using the filter that has been created by the training data. It is also useful for some unsupervised filters. For example, in *StringToWordVector* the dictionary will be created from the training data alone: Words that are novel in the test data will be discarded. To use a supervised filter in this way, invoke the *FilteredClassifier* metalearning scheme from the *meta* section of the menu displayed by the *Classify* panel's *Choose* button. Figure 11.18(a) shows the object editor for this metalearning scheme. With it, you choose a classifier and a filter. Figure 11.18(b) shows the menu of filters.

Supervised filters, like unsupervised ones, are divided into attribute and instance filters, listed in Tables 11.3 and 11.4.

Supervised Attribute Filters

Discretize, highlighted in Figure 11.18, uses the MDL method of supervised discretization (see Section 7.2). You can specify a range of attributes or force the

(a)   (b)

FIGURE 11.18

Using Weka's metalearner for discretization: (a) configuring *FilteredClassifier* and (b) the menu of filters.

Table 11.3 Supervised Attribute Filters

Name	Function
AddClassification	Add predictions from a classifier (class labels or probability distributions) as new attributes
AttributeSelection	Provides access to the same attribute selection methods as the Select attributes panel
ClassOrder	Randomize, or otherwise alter, the ordering of class values
Discretize	Convert numeric attributes to nominal
NominalToBinary	Convert nominal attributes to binary, using a supervised method if the class is numeric
PLSFilter	Compute partial least-squares directions from the input data and transform it into partial least-squares space

Table 11.4 Supervised Instance Filters

Name	Function
Resample	Produce a random subsample of a dataset, sampling with replacement
SMOTE	Resample a dataset by applying the Synthetic Minority Oversampling Technique
SpreadSubsample	Produce a random subsample with a given spread between class frequencies, sampling with replacement
StratifiedRemoveFolds	Output a specified stratified cross-validation fold for the dataset

discretized attribute to be binary. The class must be nominal. By default Fayyad and Irani's (1993) criterion is used, but Kononenko's method (1995) is an option.

There is a supervised version of the *NominalToBinary* filter that transforms all multivalued nominal attributes to binary ones. In this version, the transformation depends on whether the class is nominal or numeric. If nominal, the same method as before is used: An attribute with k values is transformed into k binary attributes. If the class is numeric, however, the method described in Section 6.6 (page 253) is applied. In either case the class itself is not transformed.

ClassOrder changes the ordering of the class values. The user determines whether the new ordering is random or in ascending or descending class frequency. This filter must not be used with the *FilteredClassifier* metalearning scheme! *AttributeSelection* can be used for automatic attribute selection and provides the same functionality as the Explorer's *Select attributes* panel (described later).

AddClassification adds to the data the predictions of a given classifier, which can be either trained on the input dataset or loaded from a file as a serialized object. New attributes can be added that hold the predicted class value, the predicted probability distribution (if the class is nominal), or a flag that indicates misclassified instances (or, for numeric classes, the difference between the predicted and actual class values).

PLSFilter computes the partial least-squares directions for the input data and uses them to transform it into partial least-squares space. The result is the same as that produced by the method described in Section 7.3 (page 326). (Two different algorithms are implemented; they yield the same result modulo a constant factor.) The number of directions to compute can be specified, and it is possible to retain the original class attribute in the new dataset or to replace it with predictions. Missing values are replaced by defaults, and the input data can be either centered or standardized before computing the partial least squares. The dataset must be entirely numeric: If it contains nominal attributes, the user must remove them or transform them to numeric ones.

Supervised Instance Filters

There are four supervised instance filters. *Resample* is like the eponymous unsupervised instance filter except that it maintains the class distribution in the subsample. Alternatively, it can be configured to bias the class distribution toward a uniform one. Sampling can be performed with (default) or without replacement. *SpreadSubsample* also produces a random subsample, but the frequency difference between the rarest and the most common class can be controlled—for example, you can specify at most a 2:1 difference in class frequencies. You can also limit the number of instances in any class by specifying an explicit maximum count.

SMOTE is another filter that samples the data and alters the class distribution (Chawla et al., 2002). Like *SpreadSubsample*, it can be used to adjust the relative frequency between minority and majority classes in the data—but it takes care not to undersample majority classes and it oversamples the minority class by creating synthetic instances using a *k*-nearest-neighbor approach. The user can specify the oversampling percentage and the number of neighbors to use when creating synthetic instances.

Like the unsupervised instance filter *RemoveFolds*, *StratifiedRemoveFolds* outputs a specified cross-validation fold for the dataset, except that this time the fold is stratified.

11.4 LEARNING ALGORITHMS

On the *Classify* panel, when you select a learning algorithm using the *Choose* button the command-line version of the classifier appears in the line beside the button, including the parameters specified with minus signs. To change the parameters, click that line to get an appropriate object editor. Table 11.5 lists Weka's classifiers. They are

Table 11.5 Classifier Algorithms in Weka

	Name	Function
Bayes	AODE	Averaged one-dependence estimators
	AODEsr	Averaged one-dependence estimators with subsumption resolution
	BayesianLogisticRegression	Bayesian approach to learning a linear logistic regression model
	BayesNet	Learns Bayesian nets
	ComplementNaiveBayes	Builds a Complement Naïve Bayes classifier
	DMNBText	Discriminative multinomial Naïve Bayes classifier
	HNB	Hidden Naïve Bayes classifier
	NaiveBayes	Standard probabilistic Naïve Bayes classifier
	NaiveBayesMultinomial	Multinomial version of Naïve Bayes
	NaiveBayesMultinomial-Updateable	Incremental multinomial Naïve Bayes classifier that learns one instance at a time
	NaiveBayesSimple	Simple implementation of Naïve Bayes
	NaiveBayesUpdateable	Incremental Naïve Bayes classifier that learns one instance at a time
	WAODE	Weightily averaged one-dependence estimators

Trees		
	ADTree	Builds alternating decision trees
	BFTree	Builds a decision tree using a best-first search
	DecisionStump	Builds one-level decision trees
	FT	Builds a functional tree with oblique splits and linear functions at the leaves
	Id3	Basic divide-and-conquer decision tree algorithm
	J48	C4.5 decision tree learner (implements C4.5 revision 8)
	J48graft	C4.5 with grafting
	LADTree	Builds multiclass alternating decision trees using LogitBoost
	LMT	Builds logistic model trees
	M5P	M5′ model tree learner
	NBTree	Builds a decision tree with Naïve Bayes classifiers at the leaves
	RandomForest	Constructs random forests
	RandomTree	Constructs a tree that considers a given number of random features at each node
	REPTree	Fast tree learner that uses reduced-error pruning
	SimpleCart	Decision tree learner using CART's minimal cost complexity pruning
	UserClassifier	Allows users to build their own decision tree

Continued

Table 11.5 Classifier Algorithms in Weka *Continued*

	Name	Function
Rules	ConjunctiveRule	Simple conjunctive rule learner
	DecisionTable	Builds a simple decision table majority classifier
	DTNB	Hybrid classifier combining decision tables and Naïve Bayes
	JRip	Ripper algorithm for fast, effective rule induction
	M5Rules	Obtains rules from model trees built using M5'
	Nnge	Nearest-neighbor method of generating rules using nonnested generalized exemplars
	OneR	1R classifier
	PART	Obtains rules from partial decision trees built using J4.8
	Prism	Simple covering algorithm for rules
	Ridor	Ripple-down rule learner
	ZeroR	Predicts the majority class (if nominal) or the average value (if numeric).
Functions	GaussianProcesses	Gaussian processes for regression
	IsotonicRegression	Builds an isotonic regression model
	LeastMedSq	Robust regression using the median rather than the mean
	LibLINEAR	Wrapper classifier for using the third-party *LIBLINEAR* library for regression

LibSVM	Wrapper classifier for using the third-party *LIBSVM* library for support vector machines
LinearRegression	Standard multiple linear regression
Logistic	Builds linear logistic regression models
MultilayerPerceptron	Backpropagation neural network
PaceRegression	Builds linear regression models using Pace regression
PLSClassifier	Builds partial least-squares directions and uses them for prediction
RBFNetwork	Implements a radial basis function network
SimpleLinearRegression	Learns a linear regression model based on a single attribute
SimpleLogistic	Builds linear logistic regression models with built-in attribute selection
SMO	Sequential minimal optimization algorithm for support vector classification
SMOreg	Sequential minimal optimization algorithm for support vector regression
SPegasos	Binary class linear support vector machine or logistic regression learned via stochastic gradient descent
VotedPerceptron	Voted Perceptron algorithm
Winnow	Mistake-driven perceptron with multiplicative updates
Lazy	
IB1	Basic nearest-neighbor instance-based learner
IBk	k-nearest-neighbors classifier
KStar	Nearest neighbor with generalized distance function
LBR	Lazy Bayesian Rules classifier
LWL	General algorithm for locally weighted learning

Continued

Table 11.5 Classifier Algorithms in Weka *Continued*

	Name	Function
MI	*CitationKNN*	Citation KNN distance-based method
	MDD	Diverse density using the collective assumption
	MIBoost	Boosting for multi-instance data using the collective assumption
	MIDD	Standard diverse density algorithm
	MIEMDD	EM-based diverse density algorithm
	MILR	Multi-instance logistic regression
	MINND	Nearest-neighbor method using Kullback-Leibler distance
	MIOptimalBall	Classifies multi-instance data using distance to a reference point
	MISMO	SMO using multi-instance kernels
	MISVM	Iteratively applies a single-instance SVM learner to multi-instance data
	MIWrapper	Applies single-instance learner using the aggregating-the-output approach
	SimpleMI	Applies single-instance learner using the aggregating-the-input approach
Misc	*HyperPipes*	Extremely simple, fast learner based on hypervolumes in instance space
	VFI	Voting feature intervals method, simple and fast

divided into Bayesian classifiers, trees, rules, functions, lazy classifiers, multi-instance classifiers, and a final miscellaneous category. We describe them briefly here, along with their parameters. To learn more, choose one in the Weka Explorer interface and examine its object editor. A further kind of classifier, the Metalearner, is described in the next section.

Bayesian Classifiers

NaiveBayes implements the probabilistic Naïve Bayes classifier (see Section 4.2, page 93). *NaiveBayesSimple* uses the normal distribution to model numeric attributes. *NaiveBayes* can use kernel density estimators, which improve performance if the normality assumption is grossly incorrect; it can also handle numeric attributes using supervised discretization.

Figure 11.19 shows the output of *NaiveBayes* on the weather data. The salient difference between this and the output in Figure 11.5 of *J48* on the same data is that instead of a tree in textual form, here the parameters of the Naïve Bayes model are presented in a table. The first column shows attributes and the other two show class values; entries are either frequency counts of nominal values or parameters of normal distributions for numeric attributes. For example, Figure 11.19 shows that the mean temperature value for instances of class *yes* is 72.9697, while for instances for which *windy* = *yes* the values *true* and *false* occur 4 and 7 times, respectively. The grand total of the *yes* and *no* counts for *windy* is, surprisingly, 18—more than the 14 instances in the weather data (the situation for *outlook* is even worse, totaling 20). The reason is that *NaiveBayes* avoids zero frequencies by applying the Laplace correction, which involves initializing each count to 1 rather than to 0.

NaiveBayesUpdateable is an incremental version that processes one instance at a time; it can use a kernel estimator but not discretization. *NaiveBayesMultinomial* implements the multinomial Bayes' classifier (see Section 4.2, page 97); *NaiveBayesMultinomialUpdateable* is an incremental version. *ComplementNaiveBayes* builds a Complement Naïve Bayes classifier as described by Rennie et al. (2003) (the TF × IDF and length normalization transforms used in this paper can be performed using the *StringToWordVector* filter).

AODE is the averaged one-dependence estimator discussed in Section 6.7 (page 268). *WAODE* is a version of AODE that creates a weighted ensemble of one-dependence estimators rather than a simple average (Jiang and Zhang, 2006). The weight for each ensemble member is proportional to the mutual information between its superparent and the class attribute. *AODEsr* is a version of AODE that incorporates the lazy elimination of highly related attribute values at classification time (Zheng and Webb, 2006). *HNB* learns a hidden Naïve Bayes model—a kind of simple Bayesian network where each attribute has the class as a parent node and another special "hidden" parent node that combines the influences of all the other attributes (Zhang et al., 2005). Each attribute's hidden node is constructed from the average of weighted one-dependence estimators, the weights of which are computed using conditional mutual information.

```
=== Run information ===

Scheme:        weka.classifiers.bayes.NaiveBayes
Relation:      weather
Instances:     14
Attributes:    5
               outlook
               temperature
               humidity
               windy
               play
Test mode:     10-fold cross-validation

=== Classifier model (full training set) ===

Naive Bayes Classifier

                    Class
Attribute           yes      no
                   (0.63)  (0.38)
==================================
outlook
  sunny             3.0      4.0
  overcast          5.0      1.0
  rainy             4.0      3.0
  [total]          12.0      8.0

temperature
  mean            72.9697  74.8364
  std. dev.        5.2304    7.384
  weight sum            9        5
  precision        1.9091   1.9091

humidity
  mean            78.8395  86.1111
  std. dev.        9.8023   9.2424
  weight sum            9        5
  precision        3.4444   3.4444

windy
  TRUE              4.0      4.0
  FALSE             7.0      3.0
  [total]          11.0      7.0

Time taken to build model: 0 seconds

=== Stratified cross-validation ===
=== Summary ===

Correctly Classified Instances         9             64.2857 %
Incorrectly Classified Instances       5             35.7143 %
Kappa statistic                        0.1026
Mean absolute error                    0.4649
Root mean squared error                0.543
Relative absolute error               97.6254 %
Root relative squared error          110.051  %
Total Number of Instances             14

=== Detailed Accuracy By Class ===

          TP Rate  FP Rate  Precision  Recall  F-Measure  ROC Area  Class

          0.889    0.8      0.667      0.889   0.762      0.444     yes
          0.2      0.111    0.5        0.2     0.286      0.444     no
Weighted  0.643    0.554    0.607      0.643   0.592      0.444
Avg.

=== Confusion Matrix ===

 a b   <-- classified as
 8 1 |  a = yes
 4 1 |  b = no
```

452 **FIGURE 11.19**

Output of *NaiveBayes* on the weather data.

Another Naïve Bayes scheme for text classification is *DMNBtext* (Su et al., 2008). This learns a multinomial Naïve Bayes classifier in a combined generative and discriminative fashion. The parameters of a Bayesian network are traditionally learned in generative fashion, calculating frequency counts for the conditional probability tables from the training data—thereby maximizing the likelihood of the data given the model. In contrast, parameter values that maximize the generalization accuracy (or conditional likelihood) are desirable in classification settings. *DMNBText* injects a discriminative element into parameter learning by considering the current classifier's prediction for a training instance before updating frequency counts. When processing a given training instance, the counts are incremented by one minus the predicted probability for the instance's class value. *DMNBText* allows users to specify how many iterations over the training data the algorithm will make, and whether word frequency information should be ignored—in which case, the method learns a standard Naïve Bayes model rather than a multinomial one.

BayesianLogisticRegression takes a Bayesian approach to learning a binomial logistic regression function by allowing the user to place a prior distribution on the values for the model's coefficients. Zero-mean Gaussian and Laplace distributions can be used for the prior. Both favor sparseness in the coefficients, Laplace more so than Gaussian, which makes this approach suitable for learning logistic regression models for high-dimensional problems—for example, text classification (Genkin et al., 2007). The user can opt to set the variance of the prior to a specific value or have it chosen, within a specified range, through the use of cross-validation.

BayesNet learns Bayesian nets under the assumptions made in Section 6.7: nominal attributes (numeric ones are prediscretized) and no missing values (any such values are replaced globally). There are four different algorithms for estimating the conditional probability tables of the network. Search is done using K2 or the TAN algorithm (see Section 6.7, page 267) or more sophisticated methods based on hill-climbing, simulated annealing, tabu search, and genetic algorithms. Optionally, search speed can be improved using AD-trees (see Section 6.7, page 269). There are also two algorithms that use conditional independence tests to learn the structure of the network; alternatively, the network structure can be loaded from an XML (eXtensible Markup Language) file. More details on the implementation of Bayesian networks in Weka can be found in Bouckaert (2004).

You can observe the network structure by right-clicking the history item and selecting *Visualize graph*. Figure 11.20(a) shows the graph for the nominal version of the weather data, which in fact corresponds to the Naïve Bayes result with all probabilities conditioned on the class value. This is because the search algorithm defaults to K2 with the maximum number of parents of a node set to one. Reconfiguring this to three by clicking on *K2* in the configuration panel yields the more interesting network in Figure 11.20(b). Clicking on a node shows its probability distribution—Figure 11.20(c) is obtained by clicking on the *windy* node in Figure 11.20(b).

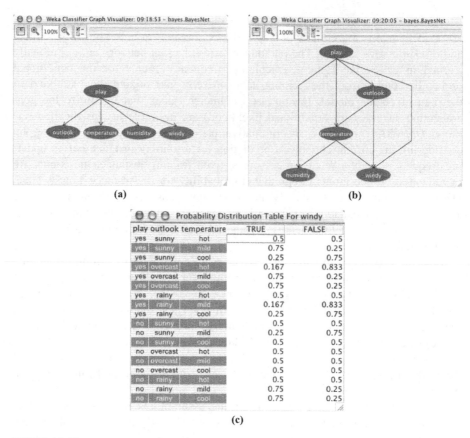

(a)   **(b)**

(c)

FIGURE 11.20

Visualizing a Bayesian network for the weather data (nominal version): (a) default output, (b) with the maximum number of parents set to three in the search algorithm, and (c) the probability distribution table for the *windy* node in (b).

Trees

Of the tree classifiers in Table 11.5 we have already encountered the *UserClassifier* (see Section 11.2). We have also seen how to use *J4.8*, which reimplements C4.5 (see Section 6.1, page 201). To see the options, click the line beside the *Choose* button in Figure 11.4(b) to bring up the object editor in Figure 11.21. You can build a binary tree instead of one with multiway branches. You can set the confidence threshold for pruning (default 0.25) and the minimum number of instances permissible at a leaf (default 2). Instead of standard C4.5 pruning you can choose reduced-error pruning (see Section 6.2, page 206). The *numFolds* parameter (default 3) determines the size of the pruning set: The data is divided equally into that number of parts and the last one used for pruning. When visualizing the tree it is nice to be

FIGURE 11.21

Changing the parameters for *J4.8*.

able to consult the original data points, which you can do if *saveInstanceData* has been turned on (it is off, or *False*, by default to reduce memory requirements). You can suppress subtree raising, yielding a more efficient algorithm; force the algorithm to use the unpruned tree instead of the pruned one; or use Laplace smoothing for predicted probabilities (see Section 4.2, page 93).

Table 11.5 shows many other decision tree methods. *Id3* implements the basic algorithm explained in Chapter 4. *DecisionStump*, designed for use with the boosting methods described later, builds one-level binary decision trees for datasets with a categorical or numeric class, dealing with missing values by treating them as a separate value and extending a third branch from the stump. Trees built by *RandomTree* test a given number of random features at each node, performing no pruning. *RandomForest* constructs random forests by bagging ensembles of random trees (see Section 8.3, page 356).

J48graft is an extended version of *J48* that considers grafting additional branches onto the tree in a postprocessing phase (Webb, 1999). The grafting process attempts to achieve some of the power of ensemble methods such as bagged and boosted trees while maintaining a single interpretable structure. It identifies regions of the instance space that are either empty or contain only misclassified examples and explores alternative classifications by considering different tests that could have been selected at nodes above the leaf containing the region in question.

REPTree builds a decision or regression tree using information gain/variance reduction and prunes it using reduced-error pruning (see Section 6.2, page 206). Optimized for speed, it only sorts values for numeric attributes once (see Section 6.1, page 192). It deals with missing values by splitting instances into pieces, as C4.5 does. You can set the minimum number of instances per leaf, maximum tree depth (useful when boosting trees), minimum proportion of training set variance for a split (numeric classes only), and number of folds for pruning.

BFTree constructs a decision tree using a best-first expansion of nodes rather than the depth-first expansion used by standard decision tree learners (such as C4.5). Pre- and postpruning options are available that are based on finding the best number of expansions to use via cross-validation on the training data. While fully grown trees are the same for best-first and depth-first algorithms, the pruning mechanism used by *BFTree* will yield a different pruned tree structure than that produced by depth-first methods.

SimpleCart is a decision tree learner for classification that employs the minimal cost-complexity pruning strategy (see Section 6.1, page 202). Though named after the CART (classification and regression tree) learner that pioneered this strategy (Breiman et al., 1984), the similarity ends here: It provides none of CART's other features. You can set the minimum number of instances per leaf, the percentage of training data used to construct the tree, and the number of cross-validation folds used in the pruning procedure.

NBTree is a hybrid between decision trees and Naïve Bayes. It creates trees with leaves that are Naïve Bayes classifiers for the instances that reach the leaf. When constructing the tree, cross-validation is used to decide whether a node should be split further or a Naïve Bayes model used instead (Kohavi, 1996).

M5P is the model tree learner described in Section 6.6 (page 251).

LMT builds logistic model trees (see Section 8.6, page 368). It can deal with binary and multiclass target variables, numeric and nominal attributes, and missing values. When fitting the logistic regression functions at a node using the LogitBoost algorithm, it uses cross-validation to determine how many iterations to run just once, and employs the same number throughout the tree instead of cross-validating at every node. This heuristic (which you can switch off) improves the runtime considerably, with little effect on accuracy. Alternatively, you can set the number of boosting iterations to be used throughout the tree manually, or use a fast heuristic based on the Akaike Information Criterion instead of cross-validation. Weight trimming can be used to further improve runtime. Normally, it is the misclassification error that cross-validation minimizes, but the root mean-squared error of the probabilities can be chosen instead. The splitting criterion can be based on C4.5's information gain (the default) or on the LogitBoost residuals, striving to improve the purity of the residuals. *LMT* employs the minimal cost-complexity pruning mechanism (see Section 6.1, page 202) to produce a compact tree structure.

FT builds functional trees (Gama, 2004)—that is, trees for classification with linear functions at the leaves and, optionally, at interior nodes as well. It builds on the *LMT* implementation and expands the choice of attributes to split on at interior nodes by creating synthetic attributes that hold the class probabilities predicted by that node's logistic regression model. Like *LMT*, C4.5's splitting criterion is used to select an attribute to split on. If a synthetic attribute is chosen, the split is oblique, not axis-parallel. Unlike *LMT*, *FT* uses standard C4.5 pruning rather than minimal cost-complexity pruning. The user has the option of having the algorithm build trees with functions only at the leaves (in which case, *FT* behaves like *LMT*, but with C4.5 pruning), only at the interior nodes, or at both.

ADTree builds an alternating decision tree for two-class problems using boosting (see Section 8.6, page 270). The number of boosting iterations is a parameter that can be tuned to suit the dataset and the desired complexity–accuracy tradeoff. Each iteration adds three nodes to the tree (one split node and two prediction nodes) unless nodes can be merged. The default search method is the exhaustive search (*Expand all paths*); the others are heuristics and are much faster. You can determine whether to save instance data for visualization. *LADTree* is an alternating decision tree algorithm that can handle multiclass problems based on the LogitBoost algorithm (Holmes et al., 2002). Like *ADTree*, the number of boosting iterations is a parameter that can be tuned for the data at hand and determines the size of the tree constructed.

Rules

Table 11.5 earlier in the chapter shows many methods for generating rules.

DecisionTable builds a decision table majority classifier (see Section 7.1, page 314). It evaluates feature subsets using best-first search and can use cross-validation for evaluation (Kohavi, 1995b). An option uses the nearest-neighbor method to determine the class for each instance that is not covered by a decision table entry, instead of the table's global majority, based on the same set of features.

DTNB is a hybrid classifier that combines a decision table with Naïve Bayes (Hall and Frank, 2008). The algorithm divides the attributes into two distinct subsets, one modeled by Naïve Bayes and the other by the decision table. A greedy search, guided by leave-one-out cross-validation and starting with all attributes modeled by the decision table, is used to decide which attributes should be modeled by Naïve Bayes; consideration is also given to dropping an attribute entirely from the model. The predictions produced by the two methods are combined into an overall prediction using Bayes' rule. Users can select the evaluation measure used for cross-validation: Options for classification problems include accuracy, root mean-squared error on the class probabilities, mean absolute error on the class probabilities, and area under the ROC curve. For numeric classes root mean-squared error is used.

OneR is the 1R classifier (see Section 4.1, page 86) with one parameter—the minimum bucket size for discretization. Figure 11.22 shows its output for the labor negotiations data. The *Classifier model* part shows that *wage-increase-first-year* has been identified as the basis of the rule produced, with a split at the value 2.9 dividing *bad* outcomes from *good* ones (the class is also *good* if the value of that attribute is missing). Beneath the rule the fraction of training instances correctly classified by the rule is given in parentheses.

```
=== Run information ===

Scheme:       weka.classifiers.rules.OneR -B 6
Relation:     labor-neg-data
Instances:    57
Attributes:   17
              duration
              wage-increase-first-year
              wage-increase-second-year
              wage-increase-third-year
              cost-of-living-adjustment
              working-hours
              pension
              standby-pay
              shift-differential
              education-allowance
              statutory-holidays
              vacation
              longterm-disability-assistance
              contribution-to-dental-plan
              bereavement-assistance
              contribution-to-health-plan
              class
Test mode:    10-fold cross-validation

=== Classifier model (full training set) ===

wage-increase-first-year:
        < 2.9    -> bad
        >= 2.9   -> good
        ?        -> good
(48/57 instances correct)

Time taken to build model: 0.01 seconds

=== Stratified cross-validation ===
=== Summary ===

Correctly Classified Instances          43              75.4386 %
Incorrectly Classified Instances        14              24.5614 %
Kappa statistic                          0.4063
Mean absolute error                      0.2456
Root mean squared error                  0.4956
Relative absolute error                 53.6925 %
Root relative squared error            103.7961 %
Total Number of Instances               57

=== Detailed Accuracy By Class ===

             TP Rate  FP Rate  Precision  Recall  F-Measure  ROC Area  Class
               0.45    0.081     0.75      0.45     0.563      0.684    bad
               0.919   0.55      0.756     0.919    0.829      0.684    good
Weighted Avg.  0.754   0.385     0.754     0.754    0.736      0.684

=== Confusion Matrix ===

  a  b    <-- classified as
  9 11  |  a = bad
  3 34  |  b = good
```

FIGURE 11.22

Output of *OneR* on the labor negotiations data.

ConjunctiveRule learns a single rule that predicts either a numeric or a nominal class value. Uncovered test instances are assigned the default class value (or distribution) of the uncovered training instances. The information gain (nominal class) or variance reduction (numeric class) of each antecedent is computed, and rules are pruned using reduced-error pruning. *ZeroR* is even simpler: It predicts the test data's majority class (if nominal) or average value (if numeric). *Prism* implements the elementary covering algorithm for rules (see Section 4.4, page 108).

PART obtains rules from partial decision trees (see Section 6.2, page 208). It builds the tree using C4.5's heuristics with the same user-defined parameters as *J4.8.* Figure 11.23 shows the output of *PART* for the labor negotiations data. Three rules are found and are intended to be processed in order, the prediction generated for any test instance being the outcome of the first rule that fires. The last, "catch-all" rule will always fire. As with *J48*, the numbers in parentheses that follow each rule give the number of instances that are covered by the rule followed by the number that are misclassified (if any).

M5Rules obtains regression rules from model trees built using M5′ (see Section 6.2). *Ridor* learns rules with exceptions (see Section 6.2, page 212) by generating the default rule, using incremental reduced-error pruning to find exceptions with the smallest error rate, finding the best exceptions for each exception, and iterating.

JRip implements RIPPER (see Section 6.2, page 208), including heuristic global optimization of the rule set (Cohen, 1995). *NNge* is a nearest-neighbor method for generating rules using non-nested generalized exemplars (see Section 6.5, page 246).

Functions

The *functions* category of Table 11.5 includes an assorted group of classifiers that can be written down as mathematical equations in a reasonably natural way. Other methods, such as decision trees and rules, cannot (there are exceptions: Naïve Bayes has a simple mathematical formulation). Four of them implement linear regression (see Section 4.6, page 124). *SimpleLinearRegression* learns a linear regression model based on a single attribute—it chooses the one that yields the smallest squared error. Missing values and nonnumeric attributes are not allowed. Figure 11.24 shows the output of *SimpleLinearRegression* for the CPU performance data. The attribute that has the smallest squared error in this case is *MMAX*.

LinearRegression performs standard least-squares multiple linear regression and can optionally perform attribute selection, either greedily using backward elimination (see Section 7.1, page 311) or by building a full model from all attributes and dropping the terms one by one, in decreasing order of their standardized coefficients, until a stopping criteria is reached (this method was described in a slightly different context in Section 6.6 under Pruning the Tree). Both methods use a version of the AIC termination criterion discussed in Section 6.7 (page 266). The implementation has two further refinements: a heuristic mechanism for detecting collinear attributes (which can be turned off) and a *ridge* parameter that stabilizes degenerate cases and can reduce overfitting by penalizing large coefficients. Technically,

```
=== Run information ===

Scheme:        weka.classifiers.rules.PART -M 2 -C 0.25 -Q 1
Relation:      labor-neg-data
Instances:     57
Attributes:    17
               duration
               wage-increase-first-year
               wage-increase-second-year
               wage-increase-third-year
               cost-of-living-adjustment
               working-hours
               pension
               standby-pay
               shift-differential
               education-allowance
               statutory-holidays
               vacation
               longterm-disability-assistance
               contribution-to-dental-plan
               bereavement-assistance
               contribution-to-health-plan
               class
Test mode:     10-fold cross-validation

=== Classifier model (full training set) ===

PART decision list
------------------

wage-increase-first-year > 2.5 AND
longterm-disability-assistance = yes AND
statutory-holidays > 10: good (25.67)

wage-increase-first-year <= 4 AND
working-hours > 36: bad (19.4/1.58)

: good (11.93/2.18)

Number of Rules  :        3

Time taken to build model: 0.07 seconds

=== Stratified cross-validation ===
=== Summary ===

Correctly Classified Instances          45              78.9474 %
Incorrectly Classified Instances        12              21.0526 %
Kappa statistic                          0.5378
Mean absolute error                      0.2884
Root mean squared error                  0.4339
Relative absolute error                 63.0507 %
Root relative squared error             90.8836 %
Total Number of Instances               57
```

FIGURE 11.23

Output of *PART* for the labor negotiations data.

```
=== Detailed Accuracy By Class ===

              TP Rate  FP Rate  Precision  Recall  F-Measure  ROC Area  Class
              0.7      0.162    0.7        0.7     0.7        0.726     bad
              0.838    0.3      0.838      0.838   0.838      0.726     good
Weighted Avg. 0.789    0.252    0.789      0.789   0.789      0.726

=== Confusion Matrix ===

  a   b    <-- classified as
 14   6  |  a = bad
  6  31  |  b = good
```

FIGURE 11.23, cont'd

```
=== Run information ===

Scheme:        weka.classifiers.functions.SimpleLinearRegression
Relation:      cpu
Instances:     209
Attributes:    7
               MYCT
               MMIN
               MMAX
               CACH
               CHMIN
               CHMAX
               class
Test mode:     10-fold cross-validation

=== Classifier model (full training set) ===

Linear regression on MMAX

0.01 * MMAX - 34

Time taken to build model: 0 seconds

=== Cross-validation ===
=== Summary ===

Correlation coefficient                  0.7844
Mean absolute error                     53.8054
Root mean squared error                 99.5674
Relative absolute error                 55.908  %
Root relative squared error             61.8997 %
Total Number of Instances              209
```

FIGURE 11.24

Output of *SimpleLinearRegression* for the CPU performance data.

LinearRegression implements ridge regression, which is described in standard statistics texts.

LeastMedSq is a robust linear regression method that minimizes the median (rather than the mean) of the squares of divergences from the regression line (see Section 7.5, page 333) (Rousseeuw and Leroy, 1987). It repeatedly applies standard linear regression to subsamples of the data and outputs the solution that has the smallest median-squared error.

PaceRegression builds linear regression models using the technique of Pace regression (Wang and Witten, 2002). When there are many attributes, Pace regression is particularly good at determining which ones to discard—indeed, under certain regularity conditions it is provably optimal as the number of attributes tends to infinity.

IsotonicRegression implements the method for learning an isotonic regression function based on the pair-adjacent violators approach (see Section 7.7, page 345). *PLSClassifier* learns a partial least-squares regression model (see Section 7.3, page 328). It uses the *PLSFilter* to transform the training data into partial least-squares space and then learns a linear regression from the transformed data. All the options of the *PLSFilter* are available to the user in the object editor for the *PLSClassifier*.

SMO implements the sequential minimal-optimization algorithm for training a support vector classifier (see Section 6.4), using kernel functions such as polynomial or Gaussian kernels (Platt, 1998; Keerthi et al., 2001). Missing values are replaced globally, nominal attributes are transformed into binary ones, and attributes are normalized by default—note that the coefficients in the output are based on the normalized data. Normalization can be turned off, or the input standardized to zero mean and unit variance. Pairwise classification is used for multiclass problems. Logistic regression models can be fitted to the support vector machine output to obtain probability estimates. In the multiclass case, the predicted probabilities will be coupled pairwise (Hastie and Tibshirani, 1998). When working with sparse instances, turn normalization off for faster operation.

Figure 11.25 shows the output of *SMO* on the iris data. A polynomial kernel with an exponent of 1 has been used, making the model a linear support vector machine. Since the iris data contains three class values, three binary *SMO* models have been output—one hyperplane to separate each of the possible pair of class values. Furthermore, since the machine is linear, the hyperplanes are expressed as functions of the attribute values in the original (albeit normalized) space. Figure 11.26 shows the result when the exponent of the polynomial kernel is set to 2, making the support vector machine nonlinear. There are three binary *SMO* models as before, but this time the hyperplanes are expressed as functions of the support vectors (see Section 6.4, page 225). Each of the support vectors is shown enclosed in angle brackets, along with the value of its coefficient α. The value of the offset parameter, β (which is the same as α_0), is shown as the last component of each function.

SMOreg implements the sequential minimal-optimization algorithm for learning a support vector regression model (Smola and Schölkopf, 2004).

```
=== Run information ===

Scheme:  weka.classifiers.functions.SMO -C 1.0 -L 0.0010 -P 1.0E-12 -N
    0 -V -1 -W 1 -K "weka.classifiers.functions.supportVector.PolyKernel -C
    250007 -E 1.0" efd
Relation:     iris
Instances:    150
Attributes:   5
              sepallength
              sepalwidth
              petallength
              petalwidth
              class
Test mode:    10-fold cross-validation

=== Classifier model (full training set) ===

SMO

Kernel used:  Linear Kernel: K(x,y) = <x,y>

Classifier for classes: Iris-setosa, Iris-versicolor

BinarySMO

Machine linear: showing attribute weights, not support vectors.

        0.6829 * (normalized) sepallength +  -1.523  * (normalized)
                sepalwidth
+       2.2034 * (normalized) petallength +  1.9272 * (normalized)
                petalwidth
-       0.7091

Number of kernel evaluations: 352 (70.32% cached)

Classifier for classes: Iris-setosa, Iris-virginica

BinarySMO

Machine linear: showing attribute weights, not support vectors.

        0.5886 * (normalized) sepallength +  -0.5782 * (normalized)
                sepalwidth
+       1.6429 * (normalized) petallength +  1.4777 * (normalized)
                petalwidth
-       1.1668

Number of kernel evaluations: 284 (68.996% cached)

Classifier for classes: Iris-versicolor, Iris-virginica

BinarySMO

Machine linear: showing attribute weights, not support vectors.

        0.3176 * (normalized) sepallength +  -0.863  * (normalized)
                sepalwidth
+       3.0543 * (normalized) petallength +  4.0815 * (normalized)
                petalwidth
-       4.5924

Number of kernel evaluations: 453 (61.381% cached)

Time taken to build model: 0.13 seconds
```

Continued

FIGURE 11.25

Output of *SMO* on the iris data.

```
=== Stratified cross-validation ===
=== Summary ===
Correctly Classified Instances        144              96      %
Incorrectly Classified Instances      6                4       %
Kappa statistic                       0.94
Mean absolute error                   0.2311
Root mean squared error               0.288
Relative absolute error               52       %
Root relative squared error           61.101   %
Total Number of Instances             150

=== Detailed Accuracy By Class ===

         TP Rate  FP Rate Precision Recall F-Measure ROC Area  Class
         1        0       1         1      1         1         Iris-setosa
         0.98     0.05    0.907     0.98   0.942     0.965     Iris-versicolor
         0.9      0.01    0.978     0.9    0.938     0.97      Iris-virginica
Weighted 0.96     0.02    0.962     0.96   0.96      0.978
Avg.

=== Confusion Matrix ===

  a  b  c   <-- classified as
 50  0  0 |  a = Iris-setosa
  0 49  1 |  b = Iris-versicolor
  0  5 45 |  c = Iris-virginica
```

FIGURE 11.25, cont'd

SPegasos (Shalev-Shwartz et al., 2007) learns a linear support vector machine for two-class problems using stochastic gradient descent (see Section 6.4, page 240). Nominal attributes are converted to binary ones automatically. By default, missing values are replaced with means/modes and attributes are normalized. The user can specify the number of epochs (iterations over the training data) to perform and the value of "lambda," the regularization constant for controlling the closeness of fit. Two loss functions are provided: the hinge loss (the default setting) for learning a support vector machine, and the log loss, which results in a logistic regression rather than a support vector machine. *SPegasos* can be trained in batch mode or incrementally, one instance at a time. If trained incrementally, the epochs' parameter has no effect because each instance is processed just once.

VotedPerceptron is the voted perceptron algorithm (see Section 6.4, page 232). *Winnow* (see Section 4.6, page 129) modifies the basic perceptron to use multiplicative updates. The implementation allows for a second multiplier β—different from $1/\alpha$—to be used in place of the divisions in Figure 4.11, and also provides the balanced version of the algorithm.

GaussianProcesses implements the Bayesian Gaussian process technique for nonlinear regression. Users can specify the kernel function, along with a "noise" regularization parameter for controlling the closeness of fit. They can choose to have the training data normalized or standardized before learning the regression. For point estimates, this method is equivalent to kernel ridge regression (see Section 6.4, page 229).

```
=== Run information ===

Scheme:  weka.classifiers.functions.SMO -C 1.0 -L 0.0010 -P 1.0E-12 -N
    0 -V -1 -W 1 -K "weka.classifiers.functions.supportVector.PolyKernel
    -C 250007 -E 2.0"
Relation:     iris
Instances:    150
Attributes:   5
              sepallength
              sepalwidth
              petallength
              petalwidth
              class
Test mode:    10-fold cross-validation

=== Classifier model (full training set) ===

SMO

Kernel used:
  Poly Kernel: K(x,y) = <x,y>^2.0

Classifier for classes: Iris-setosa, Iris-versicolor
BinarySMO

      1       * <0.333333 0.166667 0.457627 0.375 > * X]
  -       1   * <0.222222 0.541667 0.118644 0.166667 > * X]
  -       1   * <0.138889 0.416667 0.067797 0.083333 > * X]
  -       1   * <0.166667 0.416667 0.067797 0.041667 > * X]
  +       1   * <0.222222 0.208333 0.338983 0.416667 > * X]
  -       1   * <0.055556 0.125 0.050847 0.083333 > * X]
  -       1   * <0.027778 0.375 0.067797 0.041667 > * X]
  +       1   * <0.166667 0.166667 0.389831 0.375 > * X]
  +       1   * <0.361111 0.208333 0.491525 0.416667 > * X]
  +       1   * <0.194444 0 0.423729 0.375 > * X]
  -       1   * <0.194444 0.416667 0.101695 0.041667 > * X]
  -       1   * <0.138889 0.458333 0.101695 0.041667 > * X]
  +       1   * <0.194444 0.125 0.389831 0.375 > * X]
  +   0.3697 * <0.361111 0.375 0.440678 0.5 > * X]
  -   0.4599 * <0.138889 0.416667 0.067797 0 > * X]
  -   0.9098 * <0.194444 0.625 0.101695 0.208333 > * X]
  +       1   * <0.333333 0.166667 0.474576 0.416667 > * X]
  +       1   * <0.388889 0.25 0.423729 0.375 > * X]
  -   0.8085

Number of support vectors: 18

Number of kernel evaluations: 2416 (72.564% cached)

Classifier for classes: Iris-setosa, Iris-virginica

BinarySMO

      1       * <0.166667 0.208333 0.59322 0.666667 > * X]
  -   0.856   * <0.055556 0.125 0.050847 0.083333 > * X]
  +   0.1315 * <0.555556 0.333333 0.694915 0.583333 > * X]
  -       1   * <0.222222 0.541667 0.118644 0.166667 > * X]
  +       1   * <0.472222 0.083333 0.677966 0.583333 > * X]
  -   0.2756 * <0.194444 0.625 0.101695 0.208333 > * X]
  -   1.0183

Number of support vectors: 6

Number of kernel evaluations: 1364 (60.726% cached)
Classifier for classes: Iris-versicolor, Iris-virginica
```

FIGURE 11.26

Continued

Output of *SMO* with a nonlinear kernel on the iris data.

```
BinarySMO

      1       *  <0.555556 0.208333 0.677966 0.75 > * X]
  -       1        *  <0.305556 0.416667 0.59322 0.583333 > * X]
  -       1        *  <0.666667 0.458333 0.627119 0.583333 > * X]
  -       1        *  <0.472222 0.583333 0.59322 0.625 > * X]
  +       1        *  <0.444444 0.416667 0.694915 0.708333 > * X]
  -       1        *  <0.527778 0.083333 0.59322 0.583333 > * X]
  +       1        *  <0.416667 0.291667 0.694915 0.75 > * X]
  -       1        *  <0.472222 0.291667 0.694915 0.625 > * X]
  +     0.4559 *  <0.555556 0.375 0.779661 0.708333 > * X]
  -       1        *  <0.666667 0.416667 0.677966 0.666667 > * X]
  +       1        *  <0.611111 0.416667 0.762712 0.708333 > * X]
  -       1        *  <0.5 0.375 0.627119 0.541667 > * X]
  -       1        *  <0.722222 0.458333 0.661017 0.583333 > * X]
  +       1        *  <0.472222 0.083333 0.677966 0.583333 > * X]
  +       1        *  <0.583333 0.458333 0.762712 0.708333 > * X]
  +       1        *  <0.611111 0.5 0.694915 0.791667 > * X]
  +       1        *  <0.5 0.416667 0.661017 0.708333 > * X]
  -       1        *  <0.694444 0.333333 0.644068 0.541667 > * X]
  -       1        *  <0.5 0.416667 0.610169 0.541667 > * X]
  +       1        *  <0.416667 0.291667 0.694915 0.75 > * X]
  +       1        *  <0.527778 0.333333 0.644068 0.708333 > * X]
  -       1        *  <0.444444 0.5 0.644068 0.708333 > * X]
  +       1        *  <0.5 0.25 0.779661 0.541667 > * X]
  +       1        *  <0.555556 0.291667 0.661017 0.708333 > * X]
  +       1        *  <0.361111 0.333333 0.661017 0.791667 > * X]
  -       1        *  <0.555556 0.208333 0.661017 0.583333 > * X]
  -     0.4559 *  <0.555556 0.125 0.576271 0.5 > * X]
  +       1        *  <0.555556 0.333333 0.694915 0.583333 > * X]
  +       1        *  <0.166667 0.208333 0.59322 0.666667 > * X]
  +       1        *  <0.805556 0.416667 0.813559 0.625 > * X]
  -       1        *  <0.555556 0.541667 0.627119 0.625 > * X]
  +       1        *  <0.472222 0.416667 0.644068 0.708333 > * X]
  -       1        *  <0.361111 0.416667 0.59322 0.583333 > * X]
  -       1        *  <0.583333 0.5 0.59322 0.583333 > * X]
  -       1        *  <0.472222 0.375 0.59322 0.583333 > * X]
  -       1        *  <0.611111 0.333333 0.610169 0.583333 > * X]
  -     3.5378

Number of support vectors: 36

Number of kernel evaluations: 3524 (66.711% cached)

Time taken to build model: 0.06 seconds

=== Stratified cross-validation ===
=== Summary ===

Correctly Classified Instances          144              96      %
Incorrectly Classified Instances          6               4      %
Kappa statistic                          0.94
Mean absolute error                      0.2311
Root mean squared error                  0.288
Relative absolute error                  52        %
Root relative squared error              61.101    %
Total Number of Instances               150
```

FIGURE 11.26, cont'd

```
=== Detailed Accuracy By Class ===

          TP Rate  FP Rate  Precision  Recall  F-Measure  ROC Area  Class
          1        0        1          1       1          1         Iris-setosa
          0.94     0.03     0.94       0.94    0.94       0.955     Iris-versicolor
          0.94     0.03     0.94       0.94    0.94       0.972     Iris-virginica
Weighted  0.96     0.02     0.96       0.96    0.96       0.976
Avg.

=== Confusion Matrix ===

  a   b   c   <-- classified as
 50   0   0  |  a = Iris-setosa
  0  47   3  |  b = Iris-versicolor
  0   3  47  |  c = Iris-virginica
```

FIGURE 11.26, cont'd

SimpleLogistic builds logistic regression models (see Section 4.6, page 126), fitting them using LogitBoost with simple regression functions as base learners and determining how many iterations to perform using cross-validation, which supports automatic attribute selection (Landwehr et al., 2005). *SimpleLogistic* generates a degenerate logistic model tree comprising a single node, and supports the options given earlier for *LMT*.

Logistic is an alternative implementation for building and using a multinomial logistic regression model with a ridge estimator to guard against overfitting by penalizing large coefficients, based on work by le Cessie and van Houwelingen (1992). Figure 11.27 shows its output on the iris data. The coefficients of the regression functions are shown in tabular form, one for each class value except for the last class. Given m input attributes and k classes, the probability predicted for class j (with the exception of the last class) is given by

$$\Pr[j \mid a_1, a_2, \ldots, a_m] = \frac{\exp(w_0^j + w_1^j a_1 + w_2^j a_2 + \ldots + w_m^j a_m)}{1 + \sum_{j=1}^{k-1} \exp(w_0^j + w_1^j a_1 + w_2^j a_2 + \ldots + w_m^j a_m)}$$

where w_0^j is the intercept term for class j. The probability of the last class k is given by

$$1 - \sum_{j=1}^{k-1} \Pr[j \mid a_1, a_2, \ldots, a_m]$$

Beneath the table of regression coefficients is a second table giving an estimate of the odds ratio for each input attribute and class value. For a given attribute, this value gives an indication of its influence on the class when the values of the other attributes are held fixed.

RBFNetwork implements a Gaussian radial basis function network (see Section 6.4, page 239), deriving the centers and widths of hidden units using k-means and

```
Scheme:        weka.classifiers.functions.Logistic -R 1.0E-8 -M -1
Relation:      iris
Instances:     150
Attributes:    5
               sepallength
               sepalwidth
               petallength
               petalwidth
               class
Test mode:     10-fold cross-validation

=== Classifier model (full training set) ===

Logistic Regression with ridge parameter of 1.0E-8
Coefficients...
                         Class
Variable           Iris-setosa  Iris-versicolor
===================================================
sepallength            21.8065           2.4652
sepalwidth              4.5648           6.6809
petallength           -26.3083          -9.4293
petalwidth            -43.887          -18.2859
Intercept               8.1743          42.637

Odds Ratios...
                         Class
Variable           Iris-setosa  Iris-versicolor
===================================================
sepallength     2954196662.0161        11.7653
sepalwidth           96.0426          797.0304
petallength               0             0.0001
petalwidth                0                  0

Time taken to build model: 0.02 seconds

=== Stratified cross-validation ===
=== Summary ===

Correctly Classified Instances        144            96       %
Incorrectly Classified Instances        6             4       %
Kappa statistic                         0.94
Mean absolute error                     0.0287
Root mean squared error                 0.1424
Relative absolute error                 6.456   %
Root relative squared error            30.2139 %
Total Number of Instances             150

=== Detailed Accuracy By Class ===

        TP Rate  FP Rate  Precision  Recall  F-Measure  ROC Area  Class
          1        0        1          1       1          1        Iris-setosa
          0.92     0.02     0.958      0.92    0.939      0.97     Iris-versicolor
          0.96     0.04     0.923      0.96    0.941      0.975    Iris-virginica
Weighted  0.96     0.02     0.96       0.96    0.96       0.982
Avg.

=== Confusion Matrix ===

  a   b   c    <-- classified as
 50   0   0  |  a = Iris-setosa
  0  46   4  |  b = Iris-versicolor
  0   2  48  |  c = Iris-virginica
```

FIGURE 11.27

Output of *Logistic* on the iris data.

combining the outputs obtained from the hidden layer using logistic regression if the class is nominal and linear regression if it is numeric. The activations of the basis functions are normalized to sum to 1 before they are fed into the linear models. You can specify k, the number of clusters; the maximum number of logistic regression iterations for nominal-class problems; the minimum standard deviation for the clusters; and the ridge value for regression. If the class is nominal, k-means is applied separately to each class to derive k clusters for each class.

LibSVM and *LibLINEAR* are both wrapper classifiers that allow third-party implementations of support vector machines and logistic regression to be used in Weka. To use them, the jar file for the library in question must be in the class path for the Java virtual machine. The former gives access to the LIBSVM library of support vector classification and regression algorithms (Chang and Lin, 2001), which provides several types of support vector machines for multiclass classification, regression, and one-class problems, and gives a choice of linear, polynomial, radial-basis, and sigmoid kernels. The latter gives access to the LIBLINEAR library (Fan et al., 2008), which includes fast implementations of linear support vector machines for classification and logistic regression.

Neural Networks

MultilayerPerceptron is a neural network that trains using backpropagation (see Section 6.4, page 235). Although listed under *functions* in Table 11.5, it differs from the other schemes because it has its own user interface. If you load up the numeric version of the weather data, invoke *MultilayerPerceptron*, set *GUI* to *True* in its object editor, and run the network by clicking *Start* on the *Classify* panel, the diagram in Figure 11.28 appears in a separate window. This network has three layers: an input layer on the left with one rectangular box for each attribute (colored green); a hidden layer next to it (red) to which all the input nodes are connected; and an output layer at the right (orange). The labels at the far right show the classes that the output nodes represent. Output nodes for numeric classes are automatically converted to unthresholded linear units.

Before clicking *Start* to run the network, you can alter its structure by adding nodes and connections. Nodes can be selected or deselected. All six nodes in the hidden and output layers in Figure 11.28(a) are deselected, indicated by the gray color of their center. To select a node, simply click on it. This changes the color of its center from gray to bright yellow. To deselect a node, right-click in an empty space. To add a node, ensure that none is selected and left-click anywhere in the panel; the new node will be selected automatically. In Figure 11.28(a), new node has been added at the lower center. To connect two nodes, select the start node and then click on the end one. If several start nodes are selected, they are all connected to the end node. If you click in empty space instead, a new node is created as the end node. Notice that connections are directional (although the directions are not shown). The start nodes remain selected; thus, you can add an entire hidden layer with just a few clicks, as shown in Figure 11.28(b). To remove a node, ensure that no nodes are

(a)

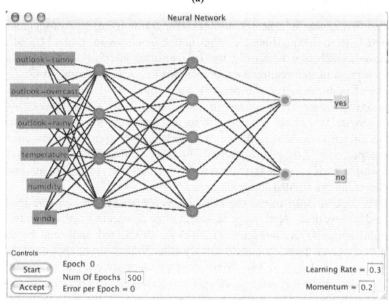

(b)

FIGURE 11.28

Using Weka's neural-network graphical user interface: (a) beginning the process of editing the network to add a second hidden layer and (b) the finished network with two hidden layers.

selected and right-click it; this also removes all connections to it. To remove a single connection, select one node and right-click the node at the other end.

As well as configuring the structure of the network, you can control the learning rate, the momentum (see Section 6.4, page 238), and the number of passes that will be taken through the data, called *epochs*. The network begins to train when you click *Start*, and a running indication of the epoch and the error for that epoch is shown at the lower left of the panels in Figure 11.28. Note that the error is based on a network that changes as the value is computed. For numeric classes the error value depends on whether the class is normalized. The network stops when the specified number of epochs is reached, at which point you can accept the result or increase the desired number of epochs and press *Start* again to continue training.

MultilayerPerceptron need not be run through the graphical interface. Several parameters can be set from the object editor to control its operation. If you are using the graphical interface, they govern the initial network structure, which you can override interactively. With *autoBuild* set, hidden layers are added and connected up. The default is to have the one hidden layer shown in Figure 11.28(a); however, without *autoBuild* this would not appear and there would be no connections. The *hiddenLayers* parameter defines what hidden layers are present and how many nodes each one contains. Figure 11.28(a) is generated by a value of *4* (one hidden layer with four nodes), and although Figure 11.28(b) was created by adding nodes interactively, it could have been generated by setting *hiddenLayers* to *4,5* (one hidden layer with four nodes and another with five). The value is a comma-separated list of integers; *0* gives no hidden layers. Furthermore, there are predefined values that can be used instead of integers: *i* is the number of attributes, *o* the number of class values, *a* the average of the two, and *t* their sum. The default, *a*, was used to generate Figure 11.28(a).

The parameters *learningRate* and *momentum* set values for these variables, which can be overridden in the graphical interface. A *decay* parameter causes the learning rate to decrease with time: It divides the starting value by the epoch number to obtain the current rate. This sometimes improves performance and may stop the network from diverging. The *reset* parameter automatically resets the network with a lower learning rate and begins training again if it is diverging from the answer (this option is only available if the graphical interface is *not* used).

The *trainingTime* parameter sets the number of training epochs. Alternatively, a percentage of the data can be set aside for validation (using *validationSetSize*): Then training continues until performance on the validation set starts to deteriorate consistently, or until the specified number of epochs is reached. If the percentage is set to *0*, no validation set is used. The *validationThreshold* parameter determines how many consecutive times the validation set error can deteriorate before training is stopped.

The *NominalToBinaryFilter* filter is specified in the *MultilayerPerceptron* object editor by default; turning it off may improve performance on data in which the nominal attributes are actually ordinal. The attributes can be normalized (with *normalizeAttributes*); in addition, a numeric class can be normalized (with *normalizeNumericClass*). Both may improve performance; these options are turned on by default.

Lazy Classifiers

Lazy learners store the training instances and do no real work until classification time. *IB1* is a basic instance-based learner (see Section 4.7, page 131) that finds the training instance closest in Euclidean distance to the given test instance and predicts the same class as this training instance. If several instances qualify as the closest, the first one found is used.

IBk is a *k*-nearest-neighbor classifier. A variety of different search algorithms can be used to speed up the task of finding the nearest neighbors. A linear search is the default, but other options include *k*D-trees, ball trees, and so-called "cover trees" (Beygelzimer et al., 2006). The distance function used is a parameter of the search method. The default is the same as for *IB1*—that is, the Euclidean distance; other options include Chebyshev, Manhattan, and Minkowski distances. The number of nearest neighbors (default $k = 1$) can be specified explicitly in the object editor or determined automatically using leave-one-out cross-validation, subject to an upper limit given by the specified value. Predictions from more than one neighbor can be weighted according to their distance from the test instance, and two different formulas are implemented for converting the distance into a weight. The number of training instances kept by the classifier can be restricted by setting the window size option. As new training instances are added, the oldest ones are removed to maintain the number of training instances at this size.

KStar is a nearest-neighbor method with a generalized distance function based on transformations (see Section 6.5, page 248).

LBR (for *Lazy Bayesian Rules*) is a Bayesian classifier that defers all processing to classification time. For each test instance it selects a set of attributes for which the independence assumption should not be made; the others are treated as independent of one another given the class and the selected set of attributes. It works well, but is computationally quite expensive (Zheng and Webb, 2000). Attributes need to be discretized before applying this classifier.

LWL is a general algorithm for locally weighted learning. It assigns weights using an instance-based method and builds a classifier from the weighted instances. The classifier is selected in *LWL*'s object editor: A good choice is Naïve Bayes for classification problems and linear regression for regression problems (see Section 6.6, page 258). You can set the number of neighbors used, which determines the kernel bandwidth, and the kernel shape to use for weighting—linear, inverse, or Gaussian. Attribute normalization is turned on by default.

Multi-Instance Classifiers

Classifiers in the MI category handle multi-instance data. *MIDD*, *MIEMDD*, and *MDD* are all variants of the diverse-density algorithm described in Section 6.10

(page 301). *MIDD* is the standard version; it maximizes the bag-level likelihood using the noisy-or model. The data can be normalized or standardized first. *MIEMDD* combines the diverse-density algorithm with an EM-style iterative approach. As well as the option to normalize or standardize the data, the user can specify a random seed to initialize the iterative process. *MIDD* and *MIEMDD* operate on the standard multi-instance assumption that a bag is positive if and only if it contains at least one positive instance. *MDD*, on the other hand, makes the "collective" assumption that all individual instances in a bag contribute equally and independently to its class label.

MILR is an adaptation of standard single-instance logistic regression to the multi-instance setting (see Section 6.10, page 299). It has one mode of operation based on the standard multi-instance assumption and two based on the collective assumption. As in single-instance logistic regression, a ridge parameter can be used to guard against overfitting.

MISMO and *MISVM* both upgrade support vector machines to the multi-instance setting (see Section 6.10). The former uses the SMO algorithm in conjunction with a kernel function designed for multi-instance data. The user can select between a multi-instance polynomial or radial-basis function kernel. Alternatively, the bag-level data can be summarized by the maximum and minimum attribute values—in which case the multi-instance kernels degenerate to their single-instance equivalents and the standard SMO options apply. *MISVM* implements an alternative support vector machine method using a single-instance classifier in the iterative fashion described in Section 6.10 (page 300).

Three multi-instance classifiers use distance-based approaches. Given a target bag to be classified, *CitationKNN* (see Section 6.10) considers not only its nearest neighbors—the "references"—but also those bags in the training set for which the target bag is the nearest one—the "citers." There is an option for setting how many of each to use, and also an option for setting the rank of the Hausdorff distance—that is, use the nth largest distance instead of the largest. *MINND* represents each bag by a normal distribution with a diagonal covariance matrix and finds nearest neighbors using the Kullback-Leibler distance. *MIOptimalBall* classifies unknown bags based on the distance of their instances to a reference point (see Section 6.10, page 300). Because of its simplicity, this is a good base classifier for use with a boosting algorithm such as *AdaBoostM1* (Section 11.5).

SimpleMI and *MIWrapper* apply standard single-instance learners to multi-instance data using the methods of aggregating the input and output, respectively (see Section 4.9, page 142). The former can aggregate bag-level data using the coordinate-wise geometric average, arithmetic average, or minimum and maximum values. The latter allows users to specify whether to aggregate the instance-level probability estimates from the single-instance model using the average, geometric average, or maximum. Users can also specify whether each instance in a bag receives a weight of 1, or whether weights are normalized to give each bag the same weight. *MIBoost* is a boosting algorithm inspired by AdaBoost that builds a series of weak classifiers using a single-instance learner (Xu and Frank, 2004). Probability estimates for individual instances are combined using the geometric mean to form bag-level probability estimates. The single-instance base learner and the number of iterations to perform are configurable options.

Miscellaneous Classifiers

The "Misc." category in Table 11.5 includes three classifiers, two of which were mentioned at the end of Section 4.7 (page 138). *HyperPipes*, for discrete classification problems, records the range of values observed in the training data for each attribute and category and works out which ranges contain the attribute values of a test instance, choosing the category with the largest number of correct ranges. *VFI* (*voting feature intervals*) constructs intervals around each class by discretizing numeric attributes and using point intervals for nominal ones, records class counts for each interval on each attribute, and classifies test instances by voting (Demiroz and Guvenir, 1997). A simple attribute weighting scheme assigns higher weight to more confident intervals, where confidence is a function of entropy. *VFI* is faster than Naïve Bayes but slower than *HyperPipes*. Neither method can handle missing values. *SerializedClassifier* loads a model that has been serialized to a file and uses it for prediction. Providing a new training dataset has no effect because it encapsulates a static model. Similarly, performing cross-validation using *SerializedClassifier* makes little sense.

11.5 METALEARNING ALGORITHMS

Metalearning algorithms, listed in Table 11.6, take classifiers and turn them into more powerful learners. One parameter specifies the base classifier; others specify the number of iterations for iterative schemes such as bagging and boosting and an initial seed for the random-number generator. We already met *FilteredClassifier* in Section 11.3: It runs a classifier on data that has been passed through a filter, which is a parameter. The filter's own parameters are based exclusively on the training data, which is the appropriate way to apply a supervised filter to test data.

Bagging and Randomization

Bagging bags a classifier to reduce variance (see Section 8.2, page 352). This implementation works for both classification and regression, depending on the base learner. In the case of classification, predictions are generated by averaging probability estimates, not by voting. One parameter is the size of the bags as a percentage of the training set. Another is whether to calculate the out-of-bag error, which gives the average error of the ensemble members (Breiman, 2001).

   Dagging is similar to *Bagging*, but as input to each member of the ensemble it uses disjoint stratified folds of the training data instead of bootstrap samples (Ting and Witten, 1997b). This can be useful when building an ensemble of classifiers that have poor time complexity in terms of the number of instances. The number of folds

Table 11.6 Metalearning Algorithms in Weka

	Name	Function
Meta	AdaBoostM1	Boost using the AdaBoostM1 method
	AdditiveRegression	Enhance the performance of a regression method by iteratively fitting the residuals
	AttributeSelectedClassifier	Reduce dimensionality of data by attribute selection
	Bagging	Bag a classifier; works for regression too
	ClassificationViaClustering	Perform classification using a clusterer
	ClassificationViaRegression	Perform classification using a regression method
	CostSensitiveClassifier	Make a base classifier cost sensitive
	CVParameterSelection	Perform parameter selection by cross-validation
	Dagging	Similar to Bagging, but using disjoint training sets
	Decorate	Build ensembles of classifiers by using specially constructed artificial training examples
	END	Ensembles of nested dichotomies
	FilteredClassifier	Run a classifier on filtered data
	Grading	Metalearners of which the inputs are base-level predictions that have been marked as correct or incorrect
	GridSearch	Perform a grid search over a pair of classifier options
	LogitBoost	Perform additive logistic regression
	MetaCost	Make a classifier cost sensitive
	MultiBoostAB	Combine boosting and bagging using the MultiBoosting method
	MultiClassClassifier	Use two-class classifier for multiclass datasets
	MultiScheme	Use cross-validation to select a classifier from several candidates
	OrdinalClassClassifier	Apply standard classification algorithms to problems with an ordinal class value
	RacedIncrementalLogitBoost	Batch-based incremental learning by racing logit-boosted committees
	RandomCommittee	Build an ensemble of randomizable base classifiers
	RandomSubSpace	Build an ensemble of base classifiers, each trained using a different randomly chosen attribute subset
	RegressionByDiscretization	Discretize the class attribute and employ a classifier
	RotationForest	Build an ensemble of base classifiers, each trained using a random subspace that has been transformed using principal components analysis
	Stacking	Combine several classifiers using the stacking method
	StackingC	More efficient version of stacking
	ThresholdSelector	Optimize the F-measure for a probabilistic classifier
	Vote	Combine classifiers using average of probability estimates or numeric predictions

is a parameter that controls not only the size of the training set presented to each base classifier but also the number of classifiers in the ensemble.

RandomCommittee is even simpler: It builds an ensemble of base classifiers and averages their predictions. Each one is based on the same data but uses a different random-number seed (see Section 8.3, page 356). This only makes sense if the base classifier is randomized; otherwise, all classifiers would be the same.

RandomSubSpace builds an ensemble of classifiers, each trained using a randomly selected subset of the input attributes (see Section 8.3). Aside from the number of iterations and random seed to use, it provides a parameter to control the size of the attribute subsets. *RotationForest* implements the rotation forest ensemble learner described in Section 8.3 (page 357). Although the classic paper on rotation forests (Rodriguez et al., 2006) uses random subspaces and principal components to create an ensemble of decision trees, Weka's implementation allows the base classifier to be any classification or regression scheme. The principal components transformation is performed by Weka's filter of the same name. *RotationForest* can be configured to use other projections such as random projections or partial least squares. Other parameters control the size of the subspaces and the number of instances that are input to the projection filter.

Boosting

AdaBoostM1 implements the algorithm described in Section 8.4 (Figure 8.2). It can be accelerated by specifying a threshold for weight pruning. *AdaBoostM1* resamples if the base classifier cannot handle weighted instances (you can force resampling anyway). *MultiBoostAB* combines boosting with a variant of bagging to prevent overfitting (Webb, 2000).

Whereas boosting only applies to nominal classes, *AdditiveRegression* enhances the performance of a regression learner (see Section 8.5, page 362). There are two parameters: shrinkage, which governs the learning rate, and the maximum number of models to generate. If the latter is infinite, work continues until the error stops decreasing.

Decorate builds ensembles of diverse classifiers by using specially constructed artificial training examples (Melville and Mooney, 2005).[2] One parameter is the number of artificial examples to use as a proportion of the training data. Another is the desired number of classifiers in the ensemble, although execution may terminate prematurely because the number of iterations can also be capped. Larger ensembles usually produce more accurate models but have greater training time and model complexity.

LogitBoost performs additive logistic regression (see Section 8.5, page 364). Like *AdaBoostM1*, it can be accelerated by specifying a threshold for weight pruning. The

---

[2]The random forest scheme was mentioned on page 357, 455. It is really a metalearner, but Weka includes it among the decision tree methods because it is hardwired to a particular classifier, *RandomTree*.

appropriate number of iterations can be determined using internal cross-validation; there is a shrinkage parameter that can be tuned to prevent overfitting; also, you can choose resampling instead of reweighting. *RacedIncrementalLogitBoost* learns by racing LogitBoosted committees, and operates incrementally by processing the data in batches, making it useful for large datasets (Frank et al., 2002). Each committee member is learned from a different batch. The batch size starts at a given minimum and repeatedly doubles until it reaches a preset maximum. Resampling is used if the base classifier cannot handle weighted instances (you can force resampling anyway). Log-likelihood pruning can be used within each committee: This discards new committee members if they decrease the log-likelihood based on the validation data. It is up to you to determine how many instances to hold out for validation. The validation data is also used to determine which committee to retain when training terminates.

Combining Classifiers

Vote provides a baseline method for combining classifiers. The default scheme is to average their probability estimates or numeric predictions, for classification and regression, respectively. Other combination schemes are available—for example, using majority voting for classification. *MultiScheme* selects the best classifier from a set of candidates using cross-validation of percentage accuracy or mean-squared error for classification and regression, respectively. The number of folds is a parameter. Performance on training data can be used instead.

Stacking combines classifiers using stacking (see Section 8.7, page 369) for both classification and regression problems. You specify the base classifiers, the metalearner, and the number of cross-validation folds. *StackingC* implements a more efficient variant for which the metalearner must be a numeric prediction scheme (Seewald, 2002). In *Grading*, the inputs to the metalearner are base-level predictions that have been marked (i.e., "graded") as correct or incorrect. For each base classifier, a metalearner is learned that predicts when the base classifier will err. Just as stacking may be viewed as a generalization of voting, grading generalizes selection by cross-validation (Seewald and Fürnkranz, 2001).

Cost-Sensitive Learning

There are two metalearners for cost-sensitive learning (see Section 5.7, page 167). The cost matrix can be supplied as a parameter or loaded from a file in the directory set by the *onDemandDirectory* property, named by the relation name and with the extension *cost*. *CostSensitiveClassifier* either reweights training instances according to the total cost assigned to each class (cost-sensitive learning, page 167) or predicts the class with the least expected misclassification cost rather than the most likely one (cost-sensitive classification, page 166). *MetaCost* generates a single cost-sensitive classifier from the base learner (see Section 8.2, page 356). This implementation uses all bagging iterations when reclassifying training data (Domingos, 1999, reports a marginal improvement when using only those iterations containing each training instance to reclassify it). You can specify each bag's size and the number of bagging iterations.

Optimizing Performance

Four metalearners use the wrapper technique to optimize the base classifier's performance. *AttributeSelectedClassifier* selects attributes, reducing the data's dimensionality before passing it to the classifier (see Section 7.1, page 308). You can choose the attribute evaluator and the search method as in the *Select attributes* panel described in Section 11.2. *CVParameterSelection* optimizes performance by using cross-validation to select parameters. For each parameter you give a string containing its lower and upper bounds and the desired number of increments. For example, to vary parameter –P from 1 to 10 in increments of 1, use

P 1 10 10

The number of cross-validation folds can be specified.

GridSearch is similar to *CVParameterSelection*, but is limited to optimizing two parameters by searching a two-dimensional grid. However, it offers the ability to optimize parameters of a classifier, a preprocessing filter, or one parameter from each. The user can choose to optimize accuracy, root mean-squared error, root relative-squared error, mean absolute error, relative absolute error, correlation coefficient, kappa or a linear combination of correlation coefficient, root relative-squared error, and relative absolute error (whereas *CVParameterSelection* can only optimize accuracy or root mean-squared error for classification and regression, respectively).

Like *CVParameterSelection*, *GridSearch* allows users to specify the lower and upper bounds for each parameter, and the desired number of increments. It also allows the value of each target parameter to be set using a mathematical expression involving the same operators and functions as for the *MathExpressionFilter*, and parameters that include arbitrary constants, the value of one of the bounds, the step size, or the current iteration number. It performs a quick initial evaluation of the grid using twofold cross-validation on the training data. Following this, the best grid point—according to the chosen evaluation metric—is explored more closely using a hill-climbing search that considers adjacent parameter pairs in the grid. For this phase, tenfold cross-validation is used. If one of the adjacent points proves to be superior, it becomes the new center and another tenfold cross-validation is performed. This process continues until no better point is found, or the best point is on the boundary of the grid. In the latter case the user has the option of allowing *GridSearch* to automatically extend the grid and continue the search. The maximum number of times the grid can be extended in this fashion is another user-definable option.

The fourth metalearner, *ThresholdSelector*, optimizes one of a number of different evaluation metrics, including *F*-measure, precision, recall, accuracy, and true positive rate (see Section 5.7, page 163), by selecting a probability threshold on the classifier's output. Performance can measured on the training data, on a holdout set, or by cross-validation. The probabilities returned by the base learner can be rescaled into the full range [0,1], which is useful if the scheme's probabilities are restricted to a narrow subrange. The metalearner can be applied to multiclass problems by specifying the class value for which the optimization is performed as

1. The first class value.
2. The second class value.
3. Whichever value is least frequent.
4. Whichever value is most frequent.
5. The first class named *yes*, *pos(itive)*, or *1*.

Retargeting Classifiers for Different Tasks

Six metalearners adapt learners designed for one kind of task to another. *ClassificationViaRegression* performs classification using a regression method by binarizing the class and building a regression model for each value. *RegressionByDiscretization* is a regression scheme that discretizes the class attribute into a specified number of bins using equal-width discretization and then employs a classifier. The predictions are the weighted average of the mean class value for each discretized interval, with weights based on the predicted probabilities for the intervals. *ClassificationViaClustering* performs classification using a clustering algorithm; the majority class in each cluster is used for making predictions. *OrdinalClassClassifier* applies standard classification algorithms to ordinal-class problems (Frank and Hall, 2001).

MultiClassClassifier handles multiclass problems with two-class classifiers using any of these methods:

1. One versus all the rest.
2. Pairwise classification using voting to predict.
3. Exhaustive error-correcting codes (see Section 7.6, page 341).
4. Randomly selected error-correcting codes.

Random code vectors are known to have good error-correcting properties: A parameter specifies the length of the code vector (in bits). For pairwise classification, pairwise coupling of probability estimates can be turned on. *END* implements the ensembles of nested dichotomies method (see Section 7.6) for handling multiclass problems with two-class classifiers. Several types of nested dichotomies can be used, including two that are balanced with respect to the data or to classes in the data.

11.6 CLUSTERING ALGORITHMS

Table 11.7 lists Weka's clustering algorithms. *Cobweb*, *EM*, *SimpleKMeans*, and *HierarchicalClusterer* were described in Section 6.8 (page 272). For the *EM* implementation you can specify how many clusters to generate, or the algorithm can decide using cross-validation—in which case, the number of folds is fixed at 10 (unless there are fewer than 10 training instances). You can specify the maximum number of iterations and set the minimum allowable standard deviation for the normal-density calculation. Clusters are Gaussian distributions with diagonal covariance matrices. *SimpleKMeans* clusters data using k-means; the number of clusters is specified by a parameter. The user can choose between the Euclidean and Manhattan distance metrics. In the latter case the algorithm is actually k-medians instead of k-means, and the centroids are based on medians rather than means in order to minimize the within-cluster distance function.

Figure 11.29 shows the output of *SimpleKMeans* for the weather data, with default options: two clusters and Euclidean distance. The result of clustering is shown as a table with rows that are attribute names and columns that correspond to the cluster centroids; an additional cluster at the beginning shows the entire dataset. The number of instances in each cluster appears in parentheses at the top of its column. Each table entry is either the mean (numeric attribute) or mode (nominal

Table 11.7 Clustering Algorithms

Name	Function
CLOPE	Fast clustering of transactional data
Cobweb	Implements the Cobweb and Classit clustering algorithms
DBScan	Nearest-neighbor-based clustering that automatically determines the number of clusters
EM	Cluster using expectation maximization
FarthestFirst	Cluster using the farthest first traversal algorithm
FilteredClusterer	Runs a clusterer on filtered data
HierarchicalClusterer	Agglomerative hierarchical clustering
MakeDensityBasedCluster	Wrap a clusterer to make it return distribution and density
OPTICS	Extension of DBScan to hierarchical clustering
sIB	Cluster using the sequential information bottleneck algorithm
SimpleKMeans	Cluster using the k-means method
XMeans	Extension of k-means

```
=== Run information ===

Scheme:        weka.clusterers.SimpleKMeans -N 2 -A "weka.core.
    EuclideanDistance - R first-last" -I 500 -S 10
Relation:      weather
Instances:     14
Attributes:    5
               outlook
               temperature
               humidity
               windy
               play
Test mode:     evaluate on training data

=== Model and evaluation on training set ===

kMeans
======

Number of iterations: 3
Within cluster sum of squared errors: 16.237456311387238
Missing values globally replaced with mean/mode

Cluster centroids:
                              Cluster#
Attribute       Full Data          0           1
                    (14)          (9)         (5)
==================================================
outlook           sunny        sunny    overcast
temperature      73.5714      75.8889        69.4
humidity         81.6429      84.1111        77.2
windy              FALSE        FALSE        TRUE
play                 yes          yes         yes

Clustered Instances

0        9 ( 64%)
1        5 ( 36%)
```

FIGURE 11.29

Output of *SimpleKMeans* on the weather data.

attribute) of the corresponding attribute for the cluster in that column; users can choose to show standard deviations (numeric attributes) and frequency counts (nominal attributes) as well. The bottom of the output shows the result of applying the learned clustering model. In this case, it assigned each training instance to one of the clusters, showing the same result as the parenthetical numbers at the top of each column. An alternative is to use a separate test set or a percentage split of the training data, in which case the figures would be different.

Figure 11.30 shows the output of *EM* for the same data, with the number of clusters set to two. Although there is no notion of the number of instances in each cluster, the columns are again headed by its prior probability in parentheses. The table entries show the parameters of normal distributions for numeric attributes or frequency counts for the values of nominal attributes—and here the fractional count

```
=== Run information ===

Scheme:       weka.clusterers.EM -I 100 -N 2 -M 1.0E-6 -S 100
Relation:     weather
Instances:    14
Attributes:   5
              outlook
              temperature
              humidity
              windy
              play
Test mode:    evaluate on training data

=== Model and evaluation on training set ===

EM
==

Number of clusters: 2

                Cluster
Attribute          0        1
                (0.36)   (0.64)
==============================
outlook
  sunny          3.8801   3.1199
  overcast       1.8886   4.1114
  rainy          2.1706   4.8294
  [total]        7.9392  12.0608
temperature
  mean          76.9298  71.7407
  std. dev.      5.8179   5.8319
humidity
  mean          90.0868  77.0398
  std. dev.      3.7298   9.1727
windy
  TRUE           3.2249   4.7751
  FALSE          3.7144   6.2856
  [total]        6.9392  11.0608
play
  yes            2.2053   8.7947
  no             4.7339   2.2661
  [total]        6.9392  11.0608
Clustered Instances

0        5 ( 36%)
1        9 ( 64%)

Log likelihood: -9.13099
```

FIGURE 11.30

Output of *EM* on the weather data.

values reveal the "soft" nature of the clusters produced by the EM algorithm, in that any instance can be split between several clusters. At the bottom, the log-likelihood of the model (again with respect to the training data) is shown, as well as the number of instances assigned to each cluster when the learned model is applied to the data as a classifier.

XMeans implements an extended version of *k*-means by Moore and Pelleg (2000). It uses a Bayesian information criterion for selecting the number of clusters (see Section 6.8, page 292), and can use *k*D-trees for speed (see Section 4.7, page 132). The user can specify the distance function to use, the minimum and maximum number of clusters to consider, and the maximum number of iterations to perform.

Cobweb implements both the Cobweb algorithm for nominal attributes and the Classit algorithm for numeric attributes. The ordering and priority of the merging and splitting operators differ between the original Cobweb and Classit papers (where they are somewhat ambiguous). This implementation always compares four different ways of treating a new instance and chooses the best: adding it to the best host, making it into a new leaf, merging the two best hosts and adding it to the merged node, and splitting the best host and adding it to one of the splits. *Acuity* and *cutoff* are parameters.

HierarchicalClusterer implements agglomerative (bottom-up) generation of hierarchical clusters (see Section 6.8, page 273). Several different link types, which are ways of measuring the distance between clusters, are available as options.

FilteredClusterer allows the data to be passed through a filter before it reaches a clusterer. Both the filter and the base clusterer are options that the user can configure.

FarthestFirst implements the farthest-first traversal algorithm of Hochbaum and Shmoys (1985), cited by Sanjoy Dasgupta (2002); it is a fast, simple, approximate clusterer modeled on *k*-means. *MakeDensityBasedClusterer* is a metaclusterer that wraps a clustering algorithm to make it return a probability distribution and density. To each cluster and attribute it fits a discrete distribution or a symmetric normal distribution (of which the minimum standard deviation is a parameter).

CLOPE implements a fast clustering technique for market basket–type data (Yang et al., 2002). It uses a cluster-quality heuristic based on histograms—that is, the number of distinct items and the count of each item computed from the item sets in a cluster. A good cluster is one where the number of items shared among the item sets in a cluster is high compared to the number of distinct items. The overall goodness of a set of clusters is the sum of the goodness of the individual clusters. The degree of intracluster similarity (i.e., the preference for common items between item sets in a cluster) can be controlled with a "repulsion" parameter.

DBScan uses the Euclidean distance metric to determine which instances belong together in a cluster (Ester et al., 1996), but, unlike *k*-means, it can determine the number of clusters automatically, find arbitrarily shaped clusters, and incorporate a notion of outlier. A cluster is defined as containing at least a minimum number of points, every pair of points of which either lies within a user-specified distance (ε) of each other or is connected by a series of points in the cluster that each lie within

FIGURE 11.31

Clusters formed by *DBScan* on the iris data.

a distance ε of the next point in the chain. Smaller values of ε yield denser clusters because instances must be closer to one another to belong to the same cluster. Depending on the value of ε and the minimum cluster size, it is possible that some instances will not belong to any cluster. These are considered outliers.

Figure 11.31 shows the clusters formed by *DBScan* on the iris data (without the class attribute) using $\varepsilon = 0.2$ and a minimum cluster size of 5. Two clusters have been found—the *Iris setosas* in one and the *Iris viginicas* and *versicolors* in the other. Three instances are deemed outliers (denoted by *M* in the plot), one *setosa* (lower left) and two *virginicas* (upper right). In the two-dimensional space that is being used to visualize the results (sepal width versus petal width), they do indeed appear to lie outside both clusters. If the minimum cluster size were reduced to 2, then the two outlying *virginicas* would form a third cluster because they lie within $\varepsilon = 0.2$ of each other.

OPTICS is an extension of *DBScan* to hierarchical clustering (Ankerst et al., 1999). It imposes an ordering on the instances, which, along with two-dimensional visualization, exposes the hierarchical structure of the clusters. The ordering process places instances that are closest to one another, according to the distance metric, beside one another in the list. Furthermore, it annotates each adjacent pair of instances with the "reachability distance," which is the minimum value of ε that allows the pair to belong to the same cluster. The clusters become apparent when ordering is plotted against reachability distance. Because instances in a cluster have

FIGURE 11.32

OPTICS visualization for the iris data.

low reachability distance to their nearest neighbors, the clusters appear as valleys in the visualization. The deeper the valley, the denser the cluster.

Figure 11.32 shows an *OPTICS* visualization for the iris data, using the same values for ε and minimum cluster size as for *DBScan*. The two clusters found by *DBScan* using these parameter settings correspond to the two main valleys between the three high peaks in the plot. Various clusterings can be obtained by setting a threshold on the reachability value—that is, by drawing a horizontal line at a given reachability value through the plot. The valley on either side of a peak intersected by the line is a cluster of its own.

sIB is an algorithm designed for document clustering that uses an information-theoretic distance metric (Slonim et al., 2002). The number of clusters to find and the maximum number of iterations to perform can be specified by the user.

11.7 ASSOCIATION-RULE LEARNERS

Weka has six association-rule learners, listed in Table 11.8. *Apriori* implements the Apriori algorithm (see Section 4.5). It starts with a minimum support of 100% of the data items and decreases this in steps of 5% until there are at least 10 rules with

Table 11.8 Association-Rule Learners

Name	Function
Apriori	Find association rules using the Apriori algorithm
FilteredAssociator	Run an associator on filtered data
FPGrowth	Association rule mining using frequent pattern trees
GeneralizedSequentialPatterns	Find large item sets in sequential data
PredictiveApriori	Find association rules sorted by predictive accuracy
Tertius	Confirmation-guided discovery of association or classification rules

the required minimum confidence of 0.9 or until the support has reached a lower bound of 10%, whichever occurs first. (These default values can be changed.) There are four alternative metrics for ranking rules: *Confidence*, which is the proportion of the examples covered by the premise that are also covered by the consequent (called *accuracy* in Section 4.5); *Lift*, which is determined by dividing the confidence by the support (called *coverage* in Section 4.5, page 116); *Leverage*, which is the proportion of additional examples covered by both the premise and the consequent beyond those expected if the premise and consequent were statistically independent; and *Conviction*, a measure defined by Brin et al. (1997). You can also specify a significance level, and rules will be tested for significance at this level. *Apriori* has an option to limit the rules found to those that contain just the value of a single attribute in the consequence of the rule. Such rules are called "class" association rules—that is, classification rules.

In order to process market basket data with *Apriori*, where we are interested in knowing (from the items present in shoppers' baskets) which items are purchased together, it is necessary to encode the input ARFF data in a specific way. In particular, since we are not interested in co-occurrence of items not present in shopping baskets, the attributes corresponding to items should be declared as single-valued nominal ones in the ARFF file. Missing values can be used to indicate the absence of an item from a shopping basket.

FPGrowth implements the frequent-pattern tree mining algorithm described in Section 6.3 (page 216). Being designed for market basket data, *Apriori*'s special encoding for this type of data is not implemented here. All attributes are expected to be binary nominal ones, and the user can specify which of the two values is to be treated as positive—that is, which one indicates presence in the basket (the default is to use the second value). *FPGrowth* can operate on either standard or sparse instances. Most of its options are the same as for *Apriori*. It finds the requested number of rules in the same way—by iteratively decreasing the minimum support. Optionally, the user can have *FPGrowth* find all the rules that meet the lower bound for the minimum support and the minimum value set for the ranking metric (confidence, lift, leverage, or conviction).

FilteredAssociator allows the data to be passed through a filter before it reaches an associator. Both the filter and the base associator are options that the user can configure.

GeneralizedSequentialPatterns implements a version of Srikant and Agrawal's (1996) GSP algorithm for finding large item sets that occur sequentially over time. The input data must contain a special nominal attribute that groups transactions (instances) together in time. All instances with the same nominal sequence identifier are grouped together, defining a time window from which sequential patterns can be extracted—for example, the identifier might group transactions according to the day on which they occur. The instances within each group are treated as occurring sequentially, in the order in which they appear in the data. Sequential large item sets, consisting of item combinations that occur across transactions sequentially within a group, are found that meet a user-supplied minimum-support threshold. The output can be optionally filtered to show only those sequential patterns that contain specific items the user is interested in.

PredictiveApriori combines confidence and support into a single measure of *predictive accuracy* (Scheffer, 2001) and finds the best *n* association rules in order. Internally, the algorithm successively increases the support threshold because the value of predictive accuracy depends on it. *Tertius* finds rules according to a confirmation measure (Flach and Lachiche, 1999), seeking rules with multiple conditions in the consequent, like Apriori—but differing in that these conditions are ORed together, not ANDed. It can be set to find rules that predict a single condition or a predetermined attribute (i.e., classification rules). One parameter determines whether negation is allowed in the antecedent, the consequent, or both; others give the number of rules sought, minimum degree of confirmation, minimum coverage, maximum proportion of counterinstances, and maximum rule size. Missing values can match any value, never match, or be significant and possibly appear in rules.

11.8 ATTRIBUTE SELECTION

Figure 11.33 shows that part of Weka's attribute selection panel where you specify the attribute evaluator and search method; Tables 11.9 and 11.10 list the choices. Attribute selection is normally done by searching the space of attribute subsets, evaluating each one (see Section 7.1, page 307). This is achieved by combining 1 of the 6 attribute subset evaluators in Table 11.9 with 1 of the 10 search methods in Table 11.10. A potentially faster but less accurate approach is to evaluate the attributes individually and sort them, discarding attributes that fall below a chosen cutoff point. This is achieved by selecting one of the 11 single-attribute evaluators in Table 11.9 and using the ranking method in Table 11.10. The Weka interface allows both possibilities by letting the user choose a selection method from Table 11.9 and a search method from Table 11.10, producing an error message if you select an inappropriate

FIGURE 11.33

Attribute selection: specifying an evaluator and a search method.

combination. The status line refers you to the error log for the message (see the end of Section 11.1).

Attribute Subset Evaluators

Subset evaluators take a subset of attributes and return a numerical measure that guides the search. They are configured like any other Weka object. *CfsSubsetEval* assesses the predictive ability of each attribute individually and the degree of redundancy among them, preferring sets of attributes that are highly correlated with the class but with low intercorrelation (see Section 7.1, page 310). An option iteratively adds attributes that have the highest correlation with the class, provided that the set does not already contain an attribute whose correlation with the attribute in question is even higher. *Missing* can be treated as a separate value, or its counts can be distributed among other values in proportion to their frequency. *ConsistencySubsetEval* evaluates attribute sets by the degree of consistency in class values when the training instances are projected onto the set. The consistency of any subset of attributes can never improve on that of the full set, so this evaluator is usually used in conjunction with a random or exhaustive search that seeks the smallest subset with a consistency that is the same as that of the full attribute set.

Whereas the previously mentioned subset evaluators are filter methods of attribute selection (see Section 7.1, page 309), *ClassifierSubsetEval* and *WrapperSubsetEval* are wrapper methods. *ClassifierSubsetEval* uses a classifier, specified in the object editor as a parameter, to evaluate sets of attributes on the training data or on a separate holdout set. *WrapperSubsetEval* also uses a classifier to evaluate attribute sets, but it employs cross-validation to estimate the accuracy of the learning scheme for each set.

The remaining two subset evaluators are meta-evaluators—that is, they augment a base subset evaluator with preprocessing options. *CostSensitiveSubsetEval* takes a base subset evaluator and makes it cost sensitive by weighting or resampling the training data according to a supplied cost matrix. *FilteredSubsetEval* applies a filter to the training data before attribute selection is performed. Selecting a filter that alters the number or ordering of the original attributes generates an error message.

Table 11.9 Attribute Evaluation Methods for Attribute Selection

	Name	Function
Attribute Subset Evaluator	*CfsSubsetEval*	Consider predictive value of each attribute individually, along with the degree of redundancy among them
	ClassifierSubsetEval	Use a classifier to evaluate the attribute set
	ConsistencySubsetEval	Project training set onto attribute set and measure consistency in class values
	CostSensitiveSubsetEval	Makes its base subset evaluator cost sensitive
	FilteredSubsetEval	Apply a subset evaluator to filtered data
	WrapperSubsetEval	Use a classifier plus cross-validation
Single-Attribute Evaluator	*ChiSquaredAttributeEval*	Compute the chi-squared statistic of each attribute with respect to the class
	CostSensitiveAttributeEval	Make its base attribute evaluator cost sensitive
	FilteredAttributeEval	Apply an attribute evaluator to filtered data
	GainRatioAttributeEval	Evaluate attribute based on gain ratio
	InfoGainAttributeEval	Evaluate attribute based on information gain
	LatentSemanticAnalysis	Perform a latent semantic analysis and transformation
	OneRAttributeEval	Use *OneR*'s methodology to evaluate attributes
	PrincipalComponents	Perform principal components analysis and transformation
	ReliefFAttributeEval	Instance-based attribute evaluator
	SVMAttributeEval	Use a linear support vector machine to determine the value of attributes
	SymmetricalUncertAttributeEval	Evaluate attribute based on symmetrical uncertainty

	Name	Function
Table 11.10 Search Methods for Attribute Selection		
Search Method	BestFirst	Greedy hill climbing with backtracking
	ExhaustiveSearch	Search exhaustively
	GeneticSearch	Search using a simple genetic algorithm
	GreedyStepwise	Greedy hill climbing without backtracking; optionally generate ranked list of attributes
	LinearForwardSelection	Extension of BestFirst that considers a restricted number of the remaining attributes when expanding the current point in the search
	RaceSearch	Use race search methodology
	RandomSearch	Search randomly
	RankSearch	Sort the attributes and rank promising subsets using an attribute subset evaluator
	ScatterSearchV1	Search using an evolutionary scatter search algorithm
	SubsetSizeForwardSelection	Extension of LinearForwardSelection that performs an internal cross-validation in order to determine the optimal subset size
Ranking Method	Ranker	Rank individual attributes (not subsets) according to their evaluation

Single-Attribute Evaluators

Single-attribute evaluators are used with the *Ranker* search method to generate a ranked list from which *Ranker* discards a given number (explained in the next section). They can also be used in the *RankSearch* method. *ReliefFAttributeEval* is instance-based: It samples instances randomly and checks neighboring instances of the same and different classes (see Section 7.1, page 310). It operates on discrete and continuous class data. Parameters specify the number of instances to sample, the number of neighbors to check, whether to weight neighbors by distance, and an exponential function that governs how rapidly weights decay with distance.

InfoGainAttributeEval evaluates attributes by measuring their information gain with respect to the class. It discretizes numeric attributes first using the MDL-based discretization method (it can be set to binarize them instead). This method, along with the next three, can treat *missing* as a separate value or distribute the counts among other values in proportion to their frequency. *ChiSquaredAttributeEval* evaluates attributes by computing the chi-squared statistic with respect to the class. *GainRatioAttributeEval* evaluates attributes by measuring their gain ratio with respect to the class. *SymmetricalUncertAttributeEval* evaluates an attribute by measuring its symmetrical uncertainty with respect to the class (see Section 7.1, page 310).

OneRAttributeEval uses the simple accuracy measure adopted by the *OneR* classifier. It can use the training data for evaluation, as *OneR* does, or it can apply internal cross-validation: The number of folds is a parameter. It adopts *OneR*'s simple discretization method: The minimum bucket size is a parameter.

SVMAttributeEval evaluates attributes using recursive feature elimination with a linear support vector machine (see Section 7.1, page 309). Attributes are selected one by one based on the size of their coefficients, relearning after each one. To speed things up a fixed number (or proportion) of attributes can be removed at each stage. Indeed, a proportion can be used until a certain number of attributes remain, thereupon switching to the fixed-number method—rapidly eliminating many attributes and then considering each remaining one more intensively. Various parameters are passed on to the support vector machine: complexity, epsilon, tolerance, and the filtering method used.

Unlike other single-attribute evaluators, *PrincipalComponents* and *LatentSemanticAnalysis* transform the set of attributes. In the case of *PrincipalComponents*, the new attributes are ranked in order of their eigenvalues (see Section 7.3, page 324). Optionally, a subset is selected by choosing sufficient eigenvectors to account for a given proportion of the variance (95% by default). Finally, the reduced data can be transformed back to the original space.

LatentSemanticAnalysis applies a singular value decomposition to the training data. Singular value decomposition is related to principal components analysis—both produce directions that are linear combinations of the original attribute values—but differs in that it is computed from a matrix containing the original data values rather than the attribute correlation or covariance matrix. Selecting the k directions with the highest singular values gives a rank k approximation to the original data matrix. Latent semantic analysis is so named because of its application to text mining, where instances represent documents and attributes represent the terms that occur in them. In some sense, the directions that the technique produces can be thought of as merging terms with similar meaning. *LatentSemanticAnalysis* allows the user to specify the number of directions to extract (i.e., the rank) and whether or not the data is normalized before the analysis is performed.

The remaining two attribute evaluators, *CostSensitiveAttributeEval* and *FilteredAttributeEval*, are meta-evaluators: They are the single-attribute versions of their subset-based counterparts described earlier. The former augments a base evaluator by weighting or resampling the training data according to a cost matrix; the latter applies a filter to the training data before the base evaluator is applied.

Search methods

Search methods traverse the attribute space to find a good subset. Quality is measured by the chosen attribute subset evaluator. Each search method can be configured with Weka's object editor. *BestFirst* performs greedy hill climbing with backtracking; you can specify how many consecutive nonimproving nodes must be encountered before the system backtracks. It can search forward from the empty set of attributes, backward from the full set, or start at an intermediate point (specified by a list of attribute indexes) and search in both directions by considering all possible single-attribute additions and deletions. Subsets that have been evaluated are cached for efficiency; the cache size is a parameter.

GreedyStepwise searches greedily through the space of attribute subsets. Like *BestFirst*, it may progress forward from the empty set or backward from the full set. Unlike *BestFirst*, it does not backtrack but terminates as soon as adding or deleting the best remaining attribute decreases the evaluation metric. In an alternative mode, it ranks attributes by traversing the space from empty to full (or vice versa) and recording the order in which attributes are selected. You can specify the number of attributes to retain or set a threshold below which attributes are discarded.

LinearForwardSelection and *SubsetSizeForwardSelection* are extensions of *BestFirst* aimed at, respectively, reducing the number of evaluations performed during the search and producing a compact final subset (Gutlein et al., 2009). *LinearForwardSelection* limits the number of attribute expansions in each forward selection step. There are two modes of operation; both begin by ranking the attributes individually using a specified subset evaluator. In the first mode, called *fixed set*, a forward best-first search is performed on just the k top-ranked attributes. In the second mode, called *fixed width*, the search considers expanding the best subset at each step by selecting an attribute from the k top-ranked attributes. However, rather than shrinking the available pool of attributes after every expansion, it is held at a constant size k by adding further attributes from the initial ranked list (so long as any remain). The mode of operation and the value of k are parameters. Like *BestFirst*, you can set the degree of backtracking, the size of the lookup cache, and a list of attributes to begin the search. As well as the standard forward search, *LinearForwardSelection* offers an option to perform a floating forward search, which considers a number of consecutive single-attribute elimination steps after each forward step—so long as this results in an improvement.

SubsetSizeForwardSelection extends *LinearForwardSelection* with a process to determine the optimal subset size. This is achieved by performing an m-fold cross-validation on the training data. *LinearForwardSelection* is applied m times—once for each training set in the cross-validation. A given test fold is used to evaluate each size of subset explored by *LinearForwardSelection* in its corresponding training set. The performance for each size of subset is then averaged over the folds. Finally, *LinearForwardSelection* is performed on all the data to find a subset of that optimal size. As well as the options provided by *LinearForwardSelection*, the evaluator to use in determining the optimal subset size can be specified, along with the number of folds.

When paired with wrapper-based evaluation, both *LinearForwardSelection* and *SubsetSizeForwardSelection* have been shown to combat the overfitting that can occur when standard forward selection or best-first searches are used with wrappers. Moreover, both select smaller final subsets than standard forward selection and best-first, while maintaining comparable accuracy (provided k is chosen to be sufficiently large). *LinearForwardSelection* is faster than standard forward selection and best-first selection.

RaceSearch, used with *ClassifierSubsetEval*, calculates the cross-validation error of competing attribute subsets using race search (see Section 7.1). The four different searches described on page 313 are implemented: forward selection, backward elimination, schemata search, and rank racing. In the last case, a separate attribute evaluator (which can also be specified) is used to generate an initial ranking. Using forward selection, it is also possible to generate a ranked list of attributes by continuing racing until all attributes have been selected: The ranking is set to the order in which they are added. As with *GreedyStepwise*, you can specify the number of attributes to retain or set a threshold below which attributes are discarded.

GeneticSearch uses a simple genetic algorithm (Goldberg, 1989). Parameters include population size, number of generations, and probabilities of crossover and mutation. You can specify a list of attribute indexes as the starting point, which becomes a member of the initial population. Progress reports can be generated every so many generations. *RandomSearch* randomly searches the space of attribute subsets. If an initial set is supplied, it searches for subsets that improve on (or equal) the starting point and have fewer (or the same number of) attributes. Otherwise, it starts from a random point and reports the best subset found. Placing all attributes in the initial set yields Liu and Setiono's (1996) probabilistic feature-selection algorithm. You can determine the fraction of the search space to explore. *ExhaustiveSearch* searches through the space of attribute subsets, starting from the empty set, and reports the best subset found. If an initial set is supplied, it searches backward from this starting point and reports the smallest subset with a better (or equal) evaluation.

RankSearch sorts attributes using a single-attribute evaluator and then ranks promising subsets using an attribute subset evaluator. The latter was specified earlier in the top box of Figure 11.33, as usual; the attribute evaluator is specified as a property in *RankSearch*'s object editor. It starts by sorting the attributes with the single-attribute evaluator and then evaluates subsets of increasing size using the subset evaluator—the best attribute, the best attribute plus the next best one, and so on—reporting the best subset. This procedure has low computational complexity: The number of times both evaluators are called is linear in the number of attributes.

Using a simple single-attribute evaluator (e.g., *GainRatioAttributeEval*), the selection procedure is very fast.

ScatterSearchV1 uses an evolution-based scatter search algorithm (Laguna and Marti, 2003). Parameters include the population, size, random number seed, and strategy used to generate new population members from existing ones.

Finally, we describe *Ranker*, which as noted earlier is not a search method for attribute subsets but a ranking scheme for individual attributes. It sorts attributes by their individual evaluations and must be used in conjunction with one of the single-attribute evaluators in the lower part of Table 11.9—not an attribute subset evaluator. *Ranker* not only ranks attributes but also performs attribute selection by removing the lower-ranking ones. You can set a cutoff threshold below which attributes are discarded, or specify how many attributes to retain. You can specify certain attributes that must be retained regardless of their rank.

The Knowledge Flow Interface

12

With the Knowledge Flow interface, users select Weka components from a tool bar, place them on a layout canvas, and connect them into a directed graph that processes and analyzes data. It provides an alternative to the Explorer for those who like thinking in terms of how data flows through the system. It also allows the design and execution of configurations for streamed data processing, which the Explorer cannot do. You invoke the Knowledge Flow interface by selecting *KnowledgeFlow* from the choices in the right panel shown in Figure 11.3(a).

12.1 GETTING STARTED

Here is a step-by-step example that loads an ARFF file and performs a cross-validation using *J4.8*. We describe how to build up the final configuration shown in Figure 12.1. First, create a source of data by clicking on the *DataSources* tab (leftmost entry in the bar at the top) and selecting *ARFFLoader* from the toolbar. The mouse cursor changes to crosshairs to signal that you should next place the component. Do this by clicking anywhere on the canvas, whereupon a copy of the ARFF loader icon appears there. To connect it to an ARFF file, right-click it to bring up the pop-up menu shown in Figure 12.2(a). Click *Configure* to get the file browser in Figure 12.2(b), from which you select the desired ARFF file (alternatively, double-clicking on a component's icon is a short-cut for selecting *Configure* from the pop-up menu).

Now we specify which attribute is the class using a *ClassAssigner* object. This is on the *Evaluation* panel, so click the *Evaluation* tab, select the *ClassAssigner*, and place it on the canvas. To connect the data source to the class assigner, right-click the data source icon and select *dataSet* from the menu, as shown in Figure 12.2(a). A rubber-band line appears. Move the mouse over the class assigner component and left-click. A red line labeled *dataSet* appears, joining the two components. Having connected the class assigner, choose the class by right-clicking it, selecting *Configure*, and entering the location of the class attribute.

We will perform cross-validation on the *J48* classifier. In the data flow model, we first connect the *CrossValidationFoldMaker* to create the folds on which the classifier will run, and then pass its output to an object representing *J48*.

FIGURE 12.1

The Knowledge Flow interface.

CrossValidationFoldMaker is on the *Evaluation* panel. Select it, place it on the canvas, and connect it to the class assigner by right-clicking the latter and selecting *dataSet* from the menu (which is similar to that in Figure 12.2(a)). Next, select *J48* from the *Classifiers* panel and place a *J48* component on the canvas; there are so many different classifiers that you have to scroll along the toolbar to find it. Connect *J48* to the cross-validation fold maker in the usual way, but make the connection *twice* by first choosing *trainingSet* and then *testSet* from the pop-up menu for the cross-validation fold maker. The next step is to select a *ClassifierPerformanceEvaluator* from the *Evaluation* panel and connect *J48* to it by selecting the *batchClassifier* entry from the pop-up menu for *J48*. Finally, from the *Visualization* toolbar place a *TextViewer* component on the canvas. Connect the classifier performance evaluator to it by selecting the *text* entry from the pop-up menu for the performance evaluator.

At this stage the configuration is as shown in Figure 12.1 except that there is as yet no graph viewer. Start the flow of execution by selecting *Start loading* from the pop-up menu for the ARFF loader, shown in Figure 12.2(a). For a small dataset

Edit:
Delete
Set name
Configure...
Connections:
instance
dataSet
Actions:
Start loading

(a)   (b)

FIGURE 12.2

Configuring a data source: (a) right-click menu and (b) file browser obtained from the *Configure* menu item.

Component	Parameters	Time	Status
[KnowledgeFlow]		0:0:20	Flow loaded.
ArffLoader		–	Finished.
CrossValidationFoldMaker		–	Finished.
J48	–C 0.25 –M 2	–	Finished.
ClassifierPerformanceEvaluator		–	Finished.

FIGURE 12.3

Status area after executing the configuration shown in Figure 12.1.

things happen quickly. Progress information appears in the status area at the bottom of the interface. The entries in the status area show the progress of each step in the flow, along with their parameter settings (for learning schemes) and elapsed time. Any errors that occur in a processing step are shown in the status area by highlighting the corresponding row in red. Figure 12.3 shows the status area after executing the configuration shown in Figure 12.1. Choosing *Show results* from the text viewer's pop-up menu brings up the results of cross-validation in a separate window, in the same form as for the Explorer.

To complete the example, add a *GraphViewer* and connect it to *J48*'s *graph* output to see a graphical representation of the trees produced for each fold of the cross-validation. Once you have redone the cross-validation with this extra component in place, selecting *Show results* from its pop-up menu produces a list of trees, one for each cross-validation fold. By creating cross-validation folds and passing them to the classifier, the Knowledge Flow model provides a way to hook into the results for each fold. The Explorer cannot do this: It treats cross-validation as an evaluation method that is applied to the output of a classifier.

12.2 COMPONENTS

Most of the Knowledge Flow components will be familiar from the Explorer. The *Classifiers* panel contains all of Weka's classifiers, the *Filters* panel contains the filters, the *Clusterers* panel holds the clusterers, and the *Associations* panel holds the association rule learners. Classifiers in the Knowledge Flow have the option of processing cross-validation training sets in parallel. In fact, since dual-core processors are the norm these days, the default is to process two cross-validation training folds in parallel. The option that controls this is called *Execution slots* and is available from the object editor that appears when *Configure* is selected after right-clicking on a *Classifiers* component.

Possible data sources are ARFF files, XML ARFF files, CSV files exported from spreadsheets, the C4.5 file format, databases, serialized instances, LibSVM and SVMLight data formats, and a special loader (*TextDirectoryLoader*) to load a directory of plaintext files into a single set of instances. There is a data sink that corresponds to each data source, with the exception of the *TextDirectoryLoader*.

The components for visualization and evaluation, which are listed in Table 12.1, have not all been encountered yet. Under *Visualization*, the *DataVisualizer* pops up a panel for visualizing data in a two-dimensional scatter plot, as in Figure 11.6(b), in which you can select the attributes you would like to see. *ScatterPlot-Matrix* pops up a matrix of two-dimensional scatter plots for every pair of attributes, shown in Figure 11.17(a). *AttributeSummarizer* gives a matrix of histograms, one for each attribute, like that in the lower right corner of Figure 11.3(b). *Model PerformanceChart* draws ROC curves and other threshold curves. *CostBenefit-Analysis* allows interactive exploration of the tradeoffs in cost or benefit arising from different cost matrices (see Section 5.7, page 166). *GraphViewer*, used earlier, pops up a panel for visualizing tree-based models, as in Figure 11.6(a). As before, you can zoom, pan, and visualize the instance data at a node (if it has been saved by the learning algorithm).

StripChart is a new visualization component designed for use with incremental learning. In conjunction with the *IncrementalClassifierEvaluator* described next, it displays a learning curve that plots accuracy—both the percentage accuracy and the root mean-squared probability error—against time. It shows a fixed-size time window that scrolls horizontally to reveal the latest results.

Table 12.1 Visualization and Evaluation Components

	Name	Function
Visualization	*DataVisualizer*	Visualize data in a two-dimensional scatter plot
	ScatterPlotMatrix	Matrix of scatter plots
	AttributeSummarizer	Set of histograms, one for each attribute
	ModelPerformanceChart	Draw ROC and other threshold curves
	CostBenefitAnalysis	Visualize cost or benefit tradeoffs
	TextViewer	Visualize data or models as text
	GraphViewer	Visualize tree-based models
	StripChart	Display a scrolling plot of data
Evaluation	*TrainingSetMaker*	Make dataset into a training set
	TestSetMaker	Make dataset into a test set
	CrossValidationFoldMaker	Split dataset into folds
	TrainTestSplitMaker	Split dataset into training and test sets
	InstanceStreamToBatchMaker	Collect instances from a stream and assemble them into a batch dataset
	ClassAssigner	Assign one of the attributes to be the class
	ClassValuePicker	Choose a value for the *positive* class
	ClassifierPerformanceEvaluator	Collect evaluation statistics for batch evaluation
	IncrementalClassifierEvaluator	Collect evaluation statistics for incremental evaluation
	ClustererPerformanceEvaluator	Collect evaluation statistics for clusterers
	PredictionAppender	Append a classifier's predictions to a dataset
	SerializedModelSaver	Save trained models as serialized Java objects

The *Evaluation* panel has the components listed in the lower part of Table 12.1. *TrainingSetMaker* and *TestSetMaker* make a dataset into the corresponding kind of set. *CrossValidationFoldMaker* constructs cross-validation folds from a dataset; *TrainTestSplitMaker* splits it into training and test sets by holding part of the data out for the test set. *InstanceStreamToBatchMaker* collects instances arriving in a stream from an incoming "instance" connection and produces a batch dataset when the last instance has arrived. *ClassAssigner* allows you to decide which attribute is the class. With *ClassValuePicker* you choose a value that is treated as the *positive* class when generating ROC and other threshold curves. *ClassifierPerformanceEvaluator* collects evaluation statistics: It can send the textual evaluation to a text viewer and the threshold curves to a performance chart. *IncrementalClassifierEvaluator* performs the same function for incremental classifiers: It computes running squared errors and so on. There is also *ClustererPerformanceEvaluator*, which is similar to *ClassifierPerformanceEvaluator*. *PredictionAppender* takes a classifier and a dataset and appends the classifier's predictions to the dataset. *SerializedModelSaver* takes a classifier or clusterer and saves the model out to a file as a serialized Java object.

12.3 CONFIGURING AND CONNECTING THE COMPONENTS

You establish the knowledge flow by configuring individual components and connecting them. Figure 12.4 shows typical operations that are available by right-clicking the various component types. These menus shown have up to three sections: *Edit*, *Connections*, and *Actions*. The *Edit* operations delete components and open up their configuration panel. You can give a component a name by choosing *Set name* from the pop-up menu. Classifiers and filters are configured just as in the Explorer. Data sources are configured by opening a file (as we

FIGURE 12.4

Operations on the Knowledge Flow components.

saw previously) or by setting a database connection, and evaluation components are configured by setting parameters such as the number of folds for cross-validation. The *Actions* operations are specific to the type of component, such as starting to load data from a data source or opening a window to show the results of visualization. The *Connections* operations are used to connect components together by selecting the type of connection from the source component and then clicking on the target object. Not all of the targets are suitable; applicable ones are highlighted. Items on the *Connections* menu are disabled (grayed out) until the component receives other connections that render them applicable.

There are two kinds of connections from data sources: *dataSet* connections and *instance* connections. The former are for batch operations such as classifiers like *J48*; the latter are for stream operations such as *NaiveBayesUpdateable*. A data source component cannot provide both types of connection: Once one is selected, the other is disabled. When a *dataSet* connection is made to a batch classifier, the classifier needs to know whether it is intended to serve as a training set or a test set. To do this, you first make the data source into a test or training set using the *TestSetMaker* or *TrainingSetMaker* components from the *Evaluation* panel.

On the other hand, an *instance* connection to an incremental classifier is made directly: There is no distinction between training and testing because the instances that flow update the classifier incrementally. In this case a prediction is made for each incoming instance and incorporated into the test results; then the classifier is trained on that instance. If you make an *instance* connection to a batch classifier, it will be used as a test instance because training cannot possibly be incremental whereas testing always can be. Conversely, it is quite possible to test an incremental classifier in batch mode using a *dataSet* connection.

Connections from a filter component are enabled when the component receives input from a data source, whereupon follow-on *dataSet* or *instance* connections can be made. *Instance* connections cannot be made to supervised filters or to unsupervised filters that cannot handle data incrementally (e.g., *Discretize*). To get a test or training set out of a filter, you need to put the appropriate kind in.

The classifier menu has two types of connection. The first type, namely *graph* and *text* connections, provides graphical and textual representations of the classifier's learned state, and it is only activated when it receives a training set input. The other type, *batchClassifier* and *incrementalClassifier*, makes data available to a performance evaluator, and it is activated only when a test set input is present too. Which one is activated depends on the type of the classifier.

Evaluation components are a mixed bag. *TrainingSetMaker* and *TestSetMaker* turn a dataset into a training or test set. *CrossValidationFoldMaker* turns a dataset into *both* a training set and a test set. *ClassifierPerformanceEvaluator* (used in the example in Section 12.1) generates textual and graphical output for visualization components. Other evaluation components operate like filters: They enable follow-on *dataSet*, *instance*, *trainingSet*, or *testSet* connections depending on the input (e.g., *ClassAssigner* assigns a class to a dataset). *InstanceStreamToBatchMaker* takes an incoming stream of instances and assembles them into a batch dataset. This is particularly useful when placed after a reservoir sampling filter—it allows the instances output by reservoir sampling to be used to train batch learning schemes.

Visualization components do not have connections, although some have actions such as *Show results* and *Clear results*.

12.4 INCREMENTAL LEARNING

In most respects the Knowledge Flow interface is functionally similar to the Explorer: You can do similar things with both. It does provide some additional flexibility—for example, you can see the tree that *J48* makes for each cross-validation fold. But its real strength is the potential for incremental operation.

Weka has several classifiers that can handle data incrementally: *AODE*, a version of Naïve Bayes (*NaiveBayesUpdateable*), *Winnow*, instance-based learners (*IB1*, *IBk*, *KStar*, *LWL*), *DMNBText*, *NaiveBayesMultinomialUpdateable*, and *NNge*. The meta-learner *RacedIncrementalLogitBoost* operates incrementally (see Section 11.1, page 477). All filters that work instance by instance are incremental: *Add*, *AddExpression*, *AddValues*, *ChangeDateFormat*, *ClassAssigner*, *Copy*, *FirstOrder*, *MakeIndicator*, *MergeTwoValues*, *NonSparseToSparse*, *NumericToBinary*, *NumericTransform*, *NumericCleaner*, *Obfuscate*, *RandomSubset*, *Remove*, *RemoveType*, *RemoveWith-Values*, *Reorder*, *ReservoirSample*, *SparseToNonSparse*, and *SwapValues*.

If all components connected up in the Knowledge Flow interface operate incrementally, so does the resulting learning system. It does not read in the dataset before learning starts, as the Explorer does. Instead, the data source component reads the input instance by instance and passes it through the Knowledge Flow chain.

Figure 12.5(a) shows a configuration that works incrementally. An *instance* connection is made from the loader to a class assigner component, which, in turn, is connected to the updatable Naïve Bayes classifier. The classifier's text output is taken to a viewer that gives a textual description of the model. Also, an *incrementalClassifier* connection is made to the corresponding performance evaluator. This produces an output of type *chart*, which is piped to a strip chart visualization component to generate a scrolling data plot.

Figure 12.5(b) shows the strip chart output. It plots both accuracy and the root mean-squared probability error against time. As time passes, the whole plot (including the axes) moves leftward to make room for new data at the right. When the vertical axis representing time 0 can move left no farther, it stops and the time origin starts to increase from 0 to keep pace with the data coming in at the right. Thus, when the chart is full it shows a window of the most recent time units.

(a)

(b)

FIGURE 12.5

A Knowledge Flow that operates incrementally: (a) the configuration and (b) strip chart output.

The strip chart can be configured to alter the number of instances shown on the *x*-axis.

This particular Knowledge Flow configuration can process input files of any size, even ones that do not fit into the computer's main memory. However, it all depends on how the classifier operates internally. For example, although they are incremental, many instance-based learners store the entire dataset internally.

The Experimenter

The Explorer and Knowledge Flow environments help you determine how well machine learning schemes perform on given datasets. But serious investigative work involves substantial experiments—typically running several learning schemes on different datasets, often with various parameter settings—and these interfaces are not really suitable for this. The Experimenter enables you to set up large-scale experiments, start them running, leave them and come back when they have finished, and then analyze the performance statistics that have been collected. They automate the experimental process. The statistics can be stored in ARFF format, and can themselves be the subject of further data mining. You invoke this interface by selecting *Experimenter* from the choices in the right panel in Figure 11.3(a).

Whereas the Knowledge Flow transcends limitations of space by allowing machine learning runs that do not load in the whole dataset at once, the Experimenter transcends limitations of time. It contains facilities for advanced users to distribute the computing load across multiple machines using Java RMI. You can set up big experiments and just leave them to run.

13.1 GETTING STARTED

As an example, we will compare the *J48* decision tree method with the baseline methods *OneR* and *ZeroR* on the iris dataset. The Experimenter has three panels: *Setup*, *Run*, and *Analyze*. Figure 13.1(a) shows the first: You select the others from the tabs at the top. Here, the experiment has already been set up. To do this, first click *New* (toward the right at the top) to start a new experiment (the other two buttons in that row save an experiment and open a previously saved one). Then, on the line below, select the destination for the results—in this case the file *Experiment1*— and choose *CSV file*. Underneath, select the datasets—we have only one, the iris data. To the right of the datasets, select the algorithms to be tested—we have three. Click *Add new* to get a standard Weka object editor from which you can choose and configure a classifier. Repeat this operation to add the three classifiers. Now the experiment is ready.

The other settings in Figure 13.1(a) are all default values. If you want to reconfigure a classifier that is already in the list, you can use the *Edit selected* button. You can also save the options for a particular classifier in XML format for later reuse. You can right-click on an entry to copy the configuration to the clipboard, and add or enter a configuration from the clipboard.

Running an Experiment

To run the experiment, click the *Run* tab, which brings up a panel that contains a *Start* button (and little else); click it. A brief report is displayed when the operation is finished. The file *Experiment1.csv* contains the results. The first two lines are shown in Figure 13.1(b): They are in CSV format and can be read directly into a spreadsheet, the first part of which appears in Figure 13.1(c). Each row represents one fold of a tenfold cross-validation (see the *Fold* column). The cross-validation is run 10 times (the *Run* column) for each classifier (the *Scheme* column). Thus, the file contains 100 rows for each classifier, which makes 300 rows in all (plus the header row). Each row contains plenty of information, including the options supplied to the machine learning scheme; the number of training and test instances; the number (and percentage) of correct, incorrect, and unclassified instances; the mean absolute error and the root mean-squared error; and much more.

There is a great deal of information in the spreadsheet, but it is hard to digest. In particular, it is not easy to answer the question posed previously: How does *J48*

(a)

FIGURE 13.1

An experiment: (a) setting it up, (b) results file, and (c) spreadsheet with results.

Dataset,Run,Fold,Scheme,Scheme_options,Scheme_version_ID,Date_time,Number_of_training_instances,Number_of_testing_instances,Number_correct,Number_incorrect,Number_unclassified,Percent_correct,Percent_incorrect,Percent_unclassified,Kappa_statistic,Mean_absolute_error,Root_mean_squared_error,Relative_absolute_error,Root_relative_squared_error,SF_prior_entropy,SF_scheme_entropy,SF_entropy_gain,SF_mean_prior_entropy,SF_mean_scheme_entropy,SF_mean_entropy_gain,KB_information,KB_mean_information,KB_relative_information,True_positive_rate,Num_true_positives,False_positive_rate,Num_false_positives,True_negative_rate,Num_true_negatives,False_negative_rate,Num_false_negatives,IR_precision,IR_recall,F_measure,Area_under_ROC,Weighted_avg_true_positive_rate,Weighted_avg_false_positive_rate,Weighted_avg_true_negative_rate,Weighted_avg_false_negative_rate,Weighted_avg_IR_precision,Weighted_avg_IR_recall,Weighted_avg_F_measure,Weighted_avg_area_under_ROC,Elapsed_Time_training,Elapsed_Time_testing,UserCPU_Time_training,UserCPU_Time_testing,Serialized_Model_Size,Serialized_Train_Set_Size,Serialized_Test_Set_Size,Summary,measureTreeSize,measureNumLeaves,measureNumRules

iris,1,1,weka.classifiers.trees.J48,'-C 0.25 -M 2',-217731683936444444,2.0103030223E7,135,0,15,0,14.0,1.0,0,0,93.333333333333333,6.666666666666667,0.0,0.9,2177316839364444,2.0103030223E7,135,0,15.0,14.0,1.0,0,0,93.333333333333333,6.666666666666667,0.0,0.9,0.0450160137965016,0.1693176548766098,10.1286030104212857,35.9176985813562284,23.7744375108173 5,2.6327150 99281766,21.1417224115535582,1.5849625007211567,0.1755143399521177 4,1.4094481607690388,21.6156535998679 9 4,1.4410435733245328,1363.795899990507,1.0,5.0,0.0,0.0,0.10.0,0.0,0.0,1.0,1.0,1.0,0.9333333333333333 33,0.0333333333333333,0.9666666666666667,0.0666666666666667,0.9444444444444445,0.9333333333333333,0.9 3265993265599326,1.0,0.059,0.0050,0.024114,0.001788,4449.0,11071.0,2791.0,'Number of leaves: 4\nSize of the tree: 7\n',7.0,4.0,4.0

FIGURE 13.1, cont'd

(b)

Continued

Experiment1.txt

	A	B	C	D	E	H	I	J	K	L	M	N	O	P	Q	R
1	Dataset	Run	Fold	Scheme	Scheme options	Number of training instances	Number of testing instances	Number correct	Number incorrect	Number unclassified	Percent correct	Percent incorrect	Percent unclassified	Kappa statistic	Mean absolute error	Root mean squared error
2	iris	1	1	trees.J48	'-C 0.25 -M 2'	135	15	14	1	0	93	7	0	1	0	0
3	iris	1	2	trees.J48	'-C 0.25 -M 2'	135	15	15	0	0	100	0	0	1	0	0
4	iris	1	3	trees.J48	'-C 0.25 -M 2'	135	15	15	0	0	100	0	0	1	0	0
5	iris	1	4	trees.J48	'-C 0.25 -M 2'	135	15	15	0	0	100	0	0	1	0	0
6	iris	1	5	trees.J48	'-C 0.25 -M 2'	135	15	14	1	0	93	7	0	1	0	0
7	iris	1	6	trees.J48	'-C 0.25 -M 2'	135	15	15	0	0	100	0	0	1	0	0
8	iris	1	7	trees.J48	'-C 0.25 -M 2'	135	15	13	2	0	87	13	0	1	0	0
9	iris	1	8	trees.J48	'-C 0.25 -M 2'	135	15	13	2	0	87	13	0	1	0	0
10	iris	1	9	trees.J48	'-C 0.25 -M 2'	135	15	15	0	0	100	0	0	1	0	0
11	iris	1	10	trees.J48	'-C 0.25 -M 2'	135	15	14	1	0	93	7	0	1	0	0
12	iris	2	1	trees.J48	'-C 0.25 -M 2'	135	15	13	2	0	87	13	0	1	0	0
13	iris	2	2	trees.J48	'-C 0.25 -M 2'	135	15	14	1	0	93	7	0	1	0	0
14	iris	2	3	trees.J48	'-C 0.25 -M 2'	135	15	14	1	0	93	7	0	1	0	0
15	iris	2	4	trees.J48	'-C 0.25 -M 2'	135	15	15	0	0	100	0	0	1	0	0
16	iris	2	5	trees.J48	'-C 0.25 -M 2'	135	15	15	0	0	100	0	0	1	0	0
17	iris	2	6	trees.J48	'-C 0.25 -M 2'	135	15	13	2	0	87	13	0	1	0	0
18	iris	2	7	trees.J48	'-C 0.25 -M 2'	135	15	15	0	0	100	0	0	1	0	0
19	iris	2	8	trees.J48	'-C 0.25 -M 2'	135	15	14	1	0	93	7	0	1	0	0
20	iris	2	9	trees.J48	'-C 0.25 -M 2'	135	15	13	2	0	87	13	0	1	0	0
21	iris	2	10	trees.J48	'-C 0.25 -M 2'	135	15	15	0	0	100	0	0	1	0	0
22	iris	3	1	trees.J48	'-C 0.25 -M 2'	135	15	15	0	0	100	0	0	1	0	0
23	iris	3	2	trees.J48	'-C 0.25 -M 2'	135	15	14	1		93	7		1		

Sum=0

SCRL   CAPS   NUM

Ready

Experiment1.txt

(c)

FIGURE 13.1, cont'd

compare with the baseline methods *OneR* and *ZeroR* on this dataset? For that we need the *Analyze* panel.

Analyzing the Results

The reason that we generated the output in CSV format was to show the spreadsheet in Figure 13.1(c). The Experimenter normally produces its output in ARFF format. You can also leave the file name blank, in which case the Experimenter stores the results in a temporary file.

The *Analyze* panel is shown in Figure 13.2. To analyze the experiment that has just been performed, click the *Experiment* button at the top right; otherwise, supply a file that contains the results of another experiment. Then click *Perform test* (near the bottom left). The result of a statistical significance test of the performance of the first learning scheme (*J48*) versus the other two (*OneR* and *ZeroR*) will be displayed in the large panel on the right.

We are comparing the percent correct statistic: This is selected by default as the comparison field shown toward the left in Figure 13.2. The three methods are

FIGURE 13.2

Statistical test results for the experiment of Figure 13.1.

displayed horizontally, numbered *(1)*, *(2)*, and *(3)*, as the heading of a little table. The labels for the columns are repeated at the bottom—*trees.J48*, *rules.OneR*, and *rules.ZeroR*—in case there is insufficient space for them in the heading. The inscrutable integers beside the scheme names identify which version of the scheme is being used. They are present by default to avoid confusion among results generated using different versions of the algorithms. The value in brackets at the beginning of the *iris* row *(100)* is the number of experimental runs: 10 times tenfold cross-validation.

The percentage correct for the three schemes is shown in Figure 13.2: 94.73% for method 1, 93.53% for method 2, and 33.33% for method 3. The symbol placed beside a result indicates that it is statistically better (*v*) or worse (***) than the baseline scheme—in this case *J48*—at the specified significance level (0.05, or 5%). The corrected resampled *t*-test from Section 5.5 (page 159) is used here. As shown, method 3 is significantly worse than method 1 because its success rate is followed by an asterisk. At the bottom of columns 2 and 3 are counts (*x/y/z*) of the number of times the scheme was better than (*x*), the same as (*y*), or worse than (*z*) the baseline scheme on the datasets used in the experiment. In this case there is only one dataset; method 2 was equivalent to method 1 (the baseline) once, and method 3 was worse than it once. (The annotation (*v/ /**) is placed at the bottom of column 1 to help you remember the meanings of the three counts (*x/y/z*).

13.2 SIMPLE SETUP

In the *Setup* panel of Figure 13.1(a) we left most options at their default values. The experiment type is a tenfold cross-validation repeated 10 times. You can alter the number of folds in the box at center left and the number of repetitions in the box at center right. The experiment type is classification; you can specify regression instead. You can choose several datasets, in which case each algorithm is applied to each dataset, and change the order of iteration using the *Data sets first* and *Algorithm first* buttons. The alternative to cross-validation is the holdout method. There are two variants depending on whether the order of the dataset is preserved or the data is randomized. You can specify the percentage split (the default is two-thirds training set and one-third test set).

Experimental setups can be saved and reopened. You can make notes about the setup by pressing the *Notes* button, which brings up an editor window. Serious Weka users soon find the need to open up an experiment and rerun it with some modifications, perhaps with a new dataset or a new learning algorithm. It would be nice to avoid having to recalculate all the results that have already been obtained! If the results have been placed in a database rather than an ARFF or CSV file, this is exactly what happens. You can choose *JDBC database* in the results destination selector and connect to any database that has a JDBC driver. You need to specify the database's URL and enter a username and password. To make this work with your database you may need to modify the *weka/experiment/DatabaseUtils.props* file in the Weka distribution. If you alter an experiment that uses a database, Weka will reuse previously computed results whenever they are available. This greatly simplifies the kind of iterative experimentation that typically characterizes data mining research.

13.3 ADVANCED SETUP

The Experimenter has an advanced mode. Click near the top of the panel shown in Figure 13.1(a) to obtain the more formidable version of the panel shown in Figure 13.3. This enlarges the options available for controlling the experiment, including, for example, the ability to generate learning curves. However, the advanced mode is hard to use, and the simple version suffices for most purposes. For example, in the advanced mode you can set up an iteration to test an algorithm with a succession of different parameter values, but the same effect can be achieved in simple mode by putting the algorithm into the list several times with different parameter values.

One thing you can do in advanced mode but not in simple mode is run experiments using clustering algorithms. Here, experiments are limited to those clusterers

FIGURE 13.3

Setting up an experiment in advanced mode.

that can compute probability or density estimates, and the main evaluation measure for comparison purposes is the log-likelihood. To set this up quickly, first click the *Result generator* to bring up an object editor for the *CrossValidationResultProducer*. Then click the *Choose* button for the split evaluator and select *DensityBasedClus-tererSplitEvaluator* from the list. At this point the panel on the lower right that contained the list of classifiers goes blank and the *Generator properties* dropdown box displays *Disabled*. Reenable this, and a new window appears with a list of properties (Figure 13.4(a)). Expand the *splitEvaluator* entry, select *clusterer* (as shown in the figure), and click the *Select* button. Now the active list will reappear in the bottom right panel, along with the ability to add clustering schemes, just as we did with classifiers.

Figure 13.4(b) shows a setup with two clustering schemes configured: *EM* and *MakeDensityBasedClusterer* wrapped around *SimpleKMeans*. After running this experiment, these two can be compared in the *Analyze* panel. The comparison field is not set up with a meaningful default, so choose *Log_likelihood* from the dropdown box before pressing the *Perform test* button. Figure 13.4(c) shows the results for these clustering algorithms.

Another thing you may need the advanced mode for is to set up distributed experiments, which we describe in Section 13.5 (page 515).

13.4 THE ANALYZE PANEL

Our walkthrough used the *Analyze* panel to perform a statistical significance test of one learning scheme (*J48*) versus two others (*OneR* and *ZeroR*). The test was on the error rate—the *Comparison* field in Figure 13.2. Other statistics can be selected from the dropdown menu instead: percentage incorrect, percentage unclassified, root mean-squared error, the remaining error measures from Table 5.8, and various entropy figures. Moreover, you can see the standard deviation of the attribute being evaluated by ticking the *Show std deviations* checkbox.

Use the *Test base* menu to change the baseline scheme from *J48* to one of the other learning schemes. For example, selecting *OneR* causes the others to be compared with this scheme. In fact, that would show that there is a statistically significant difference between *OneR* and *ZeroR* but not between *OneR* and *J48*. Apart from the learning schemes, there are two other choices in the *Select base* menu: *Summary* and *Ranking*. The former compares each learning scheme with every other scheme and prints a matrix with cells that contain the number of datasets on which one is significantly better than the other. The latter ranks the schemes according to the total number of datasets that represent wins (>) and losses (<) and prints a league table. The first column in the output gives the difference between the number of wins and the number of losses.

The *Row* and *Column* fields determine the dimensions of the comparison matrix. Clicking *Select* brings up a list of all the features that have been measured in the experiment—in other words, the column labels of the spreadsheet in Figure 13.1(c).

FIGURE 13.4

An experiment in clustering: (a) generator properties, (b) two clustering schemes, and (c) result panel.

FIGURE 13.5

Rows and columns of Figure 13.2: (a) row field, (b) column field, (c) result of swapping the row and column selections, and (d) substituting *Run* for *Dataset* as the rows.

You can select which to use as the rows and columns of the matrix. (The selection does not appear in the *Select* box because more than one parameter can be chosen simultaneously.) Figure 13.5 shows which items are selected for the rows and columns of Figure 13.2. The two lists show the experimental parameters (the columns of the spreadsheet). *Dataset* is selected for the rows (and there is only one in this case, the iris dataset), and *Scheme, Scheme options,* and *Scheme_version_ID* are selected for the column (the usual convention of shift-clicking selects multiple entries). All three can be seen in Figure 13.2—in fact, they are more easily legible in the key at the bottom.

If the row and column selections were swapped and the *Perform test* button pressed again, the matrix would be transposed, giving the result in Figure 13.5(c). There are now three rows, one for each algorithm, and one column, for the single dataset. If instead the row of *Dataset* were replaced by *Run* and the test were performed again, the result would be as in Figure 13.5(d). *Run* refers to the runs of the cross-validation, of which there are 10, so there are now 10 rows. The number in parentheses after each row label (100 in Figure 13.5(c) and 10 in Figure 13.5(d)) is the number of results corresponding to that row—in other words, the number of measurements that participate in the averages displayed by the cells in that row.

There is a button that allows you to select a subset of columns to display (the baseline column is always included) and another that allows you to select the output format: plaintext (default), output for the LaTeX typesetting system, CSV format, HTML, data and script suitable for input to the GNUPlot graph plotting software, and just the significance symbols in plaintext format. It is also possible to show averages and abbreviate filter class names in the output.

There is an option for choosing whether to use the paired corrected *t*-test or the standard *t*-test for computing significance. The way that the rows are sorted in the results table can be changed by choosing the *Sorting (asc.) by* option from the dropdown box. The default is to use natural ordering, presenting the rows in the order in which the user entered the dataset names in the *Setup* panel. Alternatively, the rows can be sorted according to any of the measures that are available in the *Comparison field*.

13.5 DISTRIBUTING PROCESSING OVER SEVERAL MACHINES

A remarkable feature of the Experimenter is that it can split up an experiment and distribute it across several processors. This is for advanced Weka users and is only available from the advanced version of the *Setup* panel. Some users avoid working with this panel by setting up the experiment on the simple version and switching to the advanced version to distribute it, because the experiment's structure is preserved when you switch. However, distributing an experiment *is* an advanced feature and is often difficult. For example, file and directory permissions can be tricky to set up.

Distributing an experiment works best when the results are all sent to a central database by selecting *JDBC database* as the results destination in Figure 13.1(a). It uses the RMI facility and works with any database that has a JDBC driver. It has been tested on several freely available databases. Alternatively, you could instruct each host to save its results to a different ARFF file and merge the files afterwards.

To distribute an experiment, each host must (1) have Java installed, (2) have access to whatever datasets you are using, and (3) be running the *weka.experiment. RemoteEngine* experiment server. If results are sent to a central database, the appropriate JDBC drivers must be installed on each host. Getting all this right is the difficult part of running distributed experiments.

To initiate a remote engine experiment server on a host machine, first copy *remoteExperimentServer.jar* from the Weka distribution to a directory on the host. Unpack it with

```
jar -xvf remoteExperimentServer.jar
```

It expands to three files: *remoteEngine.jar*, an executable *jar* file that contains the experiment server; *remote.policy*; and *remote.policy.example*.

The *remote.policy* file grants the remote engine permission to perform certain operations, such as connecting to ports or accessing a directory. It needs to be edited to specify correct paths in some of the permissions; this is self-explanatory when you examine the file. By default, it specifies that code can be downloaded on HTTP port 80 from anywhere on the Web, but the remote engines can also load code from a file URL instead. To arrange this, either uncomment the example in *remote.policy* or tailor *remote.policy.example* to suit your needs. The latter file contains a complete example for a fictitious user (*johndoe*) under a Linux operating system. The remote engines also need to be able to access the datasets used in an experiment (see the first entry in *remote.policy*). The paths to the datasets are specified in the Experimenter (i.e., the client), and the same paths must be applicable in the context of the remote engines. To facilitate this, it may be necessary to specify relative path names by selecting the *Use relative paths* tick box shown in the *Setup* panel of the Experimenter.

To start the remote engine server, type

```
java -classpath remoteEngine.jar:<path_to_any_jdbc_drivers>
-Djava.security.policy=remote.policy weka.experiment.RemoteEngine
```

from the directory containing *remoteEngine.jar*. If everything is going well, you will see this message (or something like it):

```
user@ml:remote_engine>Host name : ml.cs.waikato.ac.nz
Attempting to start RMI registry on port 1099 …
RemoteEngine bound in RMI registry
```

This indicates that the remote engine has started the RMI registry on port 1099 and is running successfully. You can run more than one remote engine on a given machine, and it makes sense to do so if the machine in question has multiple processors or a multicore processor. To do so, start each remote engine as before, but instead of the default port (1099), specify a different one using a command-line option (–p) to the remote engine. Repeat the process for all hosts.

Now start the Experimenter by typing

```
java -Djava.rmi.server.codebase=<URL_for_weka_code> weka.gui.
experiment.Experimenter
```

The URL specifies where the remote engines can find the code to be executed. If it denotes a directory (i.e., one that contains the Weka directory) rather than a *jar* file, it must end with a path separator (e.g., /).

The Experimenter's advanced *Setup* panel shown earlier in Figure 13.3 contains a small pane at center left; it determines whether an experiment will be distributed or not. This is normally inactive. To distribute the experiment click the checkbox, which will activate the *Hosts* button; a window will pop up asking for the machines over which to distribute the experiment. Host names should be fully qualified (e.g., *ml.cs.waikato.ac.nz*).

If a host is running more than one remote engine, enter its name into the window multiple times, along with the port number if it is not the default. For example:

```
ml.cs.waikato.ac.nz
ml.cs.waikato.ac.nz:5050
```

This tells the Experimenter that the host *ml.cs.waikato.ac.nz* is running two remote engines, one at the default port of 1099 and a second at port 5050.

Having entered the hosts, configure the rest of the experiment in the usual way (better still, configure it before switching to the advanced setup mode). When the experiment is started using the *Run* panel, the progress of the subexperiments on the various hosts is displayed, along with any error messages.

Distributing an experiment involves splitting it into subexperiments that RMI sends to the hosts for execution. By default, experiments are partitioned by dataset, in which case there can be no more hosts than there are datasets. Then each subexperiment is self-contained: It applies all schemes to a single dataset. An experiment with only a few datasets can be partitioned by run instead. For example, a 10 times tenfold cross-validation would be split into 10 subexperiments, 1 per run.

The Command-Line Interface

Lurking behind Weka's interactive interfaces—the Explorer, the Knowledge Flow, and the Experimenter—lies its basic functionality. This can be accessed more directly through a command-line interface. Select *Simple CLI* from the interface choices at the right of Figure 11.3(a) to bring up a plain textual panel with a line at the bottom on which you enter commands. Alternatively, use the operating system's command-line interface to run the classes in *weka.jar*, in which case you must first set the *CLASSPATH* environment variable as explained in Weka's *README* file.

14.1 GETTING STARTED

At the beginning of Section 11.1 (page 410) we used the Explorer to invoke the J4.8 learner on the weather data. To do the same thing in the command-line interface, type the following into the line at the bottom of the text panel:

```
java weka.classifiers.trees.J48 -t data/weather.arff
```

This incantation calls the Java virtual machine (in the Simple CLI, Java is already loaded) and instructs it to execute J4.8. Weka is organized in *packages* that correspond to a directory hierarchy. The program to be executed is called *J48* and resides in the *trees* package, which is a subpackage of *classifiers*, which is part of the overall *weka* package. The next section gives more details on the package structure. The *–t* option signals that the next argument is the name of the training file: We are assuming that the weather data resides in a *data* subdirectory of the directory from which you fired up Weka. The result resembles the text shown in Figure 11.5. In the Simple CLI it appears in the panel above the line where you typed the command.

14.2 THE STRUCTURE OF WEKA

We have explained how to invoke filtering and learning schemes with the Explorer interface and connect them together with the Knowledge Flow interface. To go further, it is necessary to learn something about how Weka is put together. Detailed, up-to-date information can be found in the online documentation included in the distribution.

This is more technical than the descriptions of the learning and filtering schemes given by the *More* button in the Explorer and Knowledge Flow's object editors. It is generated directly from comments in the source code using Sun's Javadoc utility. To understand its structure, you need to know how Java programs are organized.

Classes, Instances, and Packages

Every Java program is implemented as a class or collection of classes. In object-oriented programming, a *class* is a collection of variables along with some *methods* that operate on them. Together, they define the behavior of an object belonging to the class. An *object* is simply an instantiation of the class that has values assigned to all the class's variables. In Java, an object is also called an *instance* of the class. Unfortunately, this conflicts with the terminology used in this book, where the terms *class* and *instance* appear in the quite different context of machine learning. From now on, you will have to infer the intended meaning of these terms from their context. This is not difficult—and sometimes we'll use the word *object* instead of Java's *instance* to make things clear.

In Weka, the implementation of a particular learning algorithm is encapsulated in a class, and it may depend on other classes for some of its functionality. For example, the *J48* class described previously builds a C4.5 decision tree. Each time the Java virtual machine executes *J48*, it creates an instance of this class by allocating memory for building and storing a decision tree classifier. The algorithm, the classifier it builds, and a procedure for outputting the classifier are all part of that instantiation of the *J48* class.

Larger programs are usually split into more than one class. The *J48* class, for example, does not actually contain any code for building a decision tree. It includes references to instances of other classes that do most of the work. When there are a lot of classes—as in Weka—they become difficult to comprehend and navigate. Java allows classes to be organized into packages. A *package* is just a directory containing a collection of related classes; for example, the *trees* package mentioned previously contains the classes that implement decision trees. Packages are organized in a hierarchy that corresponds to the directory hierarchy: *trees* is a subpackage of the *classifiers* package, which is itself a subpackage of the overall *weka* package.

When you consult the online documentation generated by Javadoc from your web browser, the first thing you see is an alphabetical list of all the packages in Weka, as shown in Figure 14.1(a). (If you view the Javadoc with frames, you will see more than this. Click on *NO FRAMES* to remove the extra information.) Here we introduce a few of them in order of importance.

The *weka.core* Package

The *core* package is central to the Weka system, and its classes are accessed from almost every other class. You can determine what they are by clicking on the *weka.core* hyperlink, which brings up the web page shown in Figure 14.1(b).

This web page is divided into several parts, the main ones being the *interface summary* and the *class summary*. The latter is a list of classes contained within the package, and the former lists the interfaces it provides. An interface is similar to a class, the only difference being that it doesn't actually do anything by itself—it is merely a list of methods without actual implementations. Other classes can declare

Packages	
weka.associations	weka.core.converters
weka.associations.gsp	weka.core.logging
weka.associations.tertius	weka.core.mathematicalexpression
weka.attributeSelection	weka.core.matrix
weka.classifiers	weka.core.neighboursearch
weka.classifiers.bayes	weka.core.neighboursearch.balltrees
weka.classifiers.bayes.blr	weka.core.neighboursearch.covertrees
weka.classifiers.bayes.net	weka.core.neighboursearch.kdtrees
weka.classifiers.bayes.net.estimate	weka.core.pmml
weka.classifiers.bayes.net.search	weka.core.stemmers
weka.classifiers.bayes.net.search.ci	weka.core.tokenizers
weka.classifiers.bayes.net.search.fixed	weka.core.xml
weka.classifiers.bayes.net.search.global	weka.datagenerators
weka.classifiers.bayes.net.search.local	weka.datagenerators.classifiers.classification
weka.classifiers.evaluation	weka.datagenerators.classifiers.regression
weka.classifiers.functions	weka.datagenerators.clusterers
weka.classifiers.functions.neural	weka.estimators
weka.classifiers.functions.pace	weka.experiment
weka.classifiers.functions.supportVector	weka.experiment.xml
weka.classifiers.lazy	weka.filters
weka.classifiers.lazy.kstar	weka.filters.supervised.attribute
weka.classifiers.meta	weka.filters.supervised.instance
weka.classifiers.meta.ensembleSelection	weka.filters.unsupervised.attribute
weka.classifiers.meta.nestedDichotomies	weka.filters.unsupervised.instance
weka.classifiers.mi	weka.filters.unsupervised.instance.subsetbyexpression
weka.classifiers.mi.supportVector	weka.gui
weka.classifiers.misc	weka.gui.arffviewer
weka.classifiers.pmml.consumer	weka.gui.beans
weka.classifiers.rules	weka.gui.beans.xml
weka.classifiers.rules.part	weka.gui.boundaryvisualizer
weka.classifiers.trees	weka.gui.ensembleLibraryEditor
weka.classifiers.trees.adtree	weka.gui.ensembleLibraryEditor.tree
weka.classifiers.trees.ft	weka.gui.experiment
weka.classifiers.trees.j48	weka.gui.explorer
weka.classifiers.trees.lmt	weka.gui.graphvisualizer
weka.classifiers.trees.m5	weka.gui.sql
weka.classifiers.trees.xml	weka.gui.sql.event
weka.clusterers	weka.gui.streams
weka.clusterers.forOPTICSAndDBScan.Databases	weka.gui.treevisualizer
weka.clusterers.forOPTICSAndDBScan.DataObjects	weka.gui.visualize
weka.clusterers.forOPTICSAndDBScan.OPTICS_GUI	weka.gui.visualize.plugins
weka.clusterers.forOPTICSAndDBScan.Utils	
weka.core	

(a)

FIGURE 14.1

Using Javadoc: (a) the front page and (b) the *weka.core* package (see next page).

Overview **Package** Class Tree Deprecated Index Help Weka's home
PREV PACKAGE NEXT PACKAGE   FRAMES NO FRAMES All Classes

Package weka.core

Interface Summary

AdditionalMeasureProducer	Interface to something that can produce measures other than those calculated by evaluation modules.
CapabilitiesHandler	Classes implementing this interface return their capabilities in regards to datasets.
Copyable	Interface implemented by classes that can produce "shallow" copies of their objects.
DistanceFunction	Interface for any class that can compute and return distances between two instances.
Drawable	Interface to something that can be drawn as a graph.
EnvironmentHandler	Interface for something that can utilize environment variables.
JythonObject	An indicator interface for Jython objects.
JythonSerializableObject	An indicator interface for serializable Jython objects.
Matchable	Interface to something that can be matched with tree matching algorithms.
MultiInstanceCapabilitiesHandler	Multi-Instance classifiers can specify an additional Capabilities object for the data in the relational attribute, since the format of multi-instance data is fixed to "bag/NOMINAL,data/RELATIONAL.class".
OptionHandler	Interface to something that understands options.
Randomizable	Interface to something that has random behaviour that is able to be seeded with an integer.
RevisionHandler	For classes that should return their source control revision.
Summarizable	Interface to something that provides a short textual summary (as opposed to toString() which is usually a fairly complete description) of itself.
TechnicalInformationHandler	For classes that are based on some kind of publications.
Undoable	Interface implemented by classes that support undo.
WeightedInstancesHandler	Interface to something that makes use of the information provided by instance weights.

(b1)

Class Summary

AbstractStringDistanceFunction	Represents the abstract ancestor for string-based distance functions, like EditDistance.
AlgVector	Class for performing operations on an algebraic vector of floating-point values.
AllJavadoc	Applies all known Javadoc-derived classes to a source file.
Attribute	Class for handling an attribute.
AttributeExpression	A general purpose class for parsing mathematical expressions involving attribute values.
AttributeLocator	This class locates and records the indices of a certain type of attributes, recursively in case of Relational attributes.
AttributeStats	A Utility class that contains summary information on an the values that appear in a dataset for a particular attribute.
BinarySparseInstance	Class for storing a binary-data-only instance as a sparse vector.
Capabilities	A class that describes the capabilites (e.g., handling certain types of attributes, missing values, types of classes, etc.) of a specific classifier.
ChebyshevDistance	Implements the Chebyshev distance.
• • •	
Instance	Class for handling an instance.
InstanceComparator	A comparator for the Instance class.
Instances	Class for handling an ordered set of weighted instances.
• • •	
TechnicalInformation	Used for paper references in the Javadoc and for BibTex generation.
TechnicalInformationHandlerJavadoc	Generates Javadoc comments from the TechnicalInformationHandler's data.
Tee	This class pipelines print/println's to several PrintStreams.
TestInstances	Generates artificial datasets for testing.
Trie	A class representing a Trie data structure for strings.
Trie.TrieIterator	Represents an iterator over a trie
Trie.TrieNode	Represents a node in the trie.
Utils	Class implementing some simple utility methods.
Version	This class contains the version number of the current WEKA release and some methods for comparing another version string.

(b2)

FIGURE 14.1, cont'd

that they "implement" a particular interface and then provide code for its methods. For example, the *OptionHandler* interface defines those methods that are implemented by all classes that can process command-line options, including all classifiers.

The key classes in the *core* package are *Attribute*, *Instance*, and *Instances*. An object of class *Attribute* represents an attribute. It contains the attribute's name, its type, and, in the case of a nominal or string attribute, its possible values. An object of class *Instance* contains the attribute values of a particular instance; an object of class *Instances* holds an ordered set of instances—in other words, a dataset. You can learn more about these classes by clicking their hyperlinks; we return to them in Chapter 15 page 536 and 538) when we show how to invoke machine learning schemes from other Java code. However, you can use Weka from the command-line interface without knowing the details.

Clicking the *Overview* hyperlink in the upper left corner of any documentation page returns you to the listing of all the packages in Weka, shown in Figure 14.1(a).

The *weka.classifiers* Package

The *classifiers* package contains implementations of most of the algorithms for classification and numeric prediction described in this book. (Numeric prediction is included in *classifiers*: It is interpreted as prediction of a continuous class.) The most important class in this package is *Classifier*, which defines the general structure of any scheme for classification or numeric prediction. *Classifier* contains three methods: *buildClassifier()*, *classifyInstance()*, and *distributionForInstance()*. In the terminology of object-oriented programming, the learning algorithms are represented by subclasses of *Classifier* and therefore automatically inherit these three methods. Every scheme redefines them according to how it builds a classifier and how it classifies instances. This gives a uniform interface for building and using classifiers from other Java code. Thus, for example, the same evaluation module can be used to evaluate the performance of any classifier in Weka.

To see an example, click on *weka.classifiers.trees* and then on *DecisionStump*, which is a class for building a simple one-level binary decision tree (with an extra branch for missing values). Its documentation page, shown in Figure 14.2, shows the fully qualified name of this class, *weka.classifiers.trees.DecisionStump*, near the top. You have to use this rather lengthy name whenever you build a decision stump from the command line. The class name is sited in a small tree structure showing the relevant part of the class hierarchy. As you can see, *DecisionStump* is a subclass of *weka.classifiers.Classifier*, which is itself a subclass of *java.lang.Object*. The *Object* class is the most general one in Java: All classes are automatically subclasses of it.

After some generic information about the class—brief documentation, its version, and the author—Figure 14.2 gives an index of the constructors and methods of this class. A *constructor* is a special kind of method that is called whenever an object of that class is created, usually initializing the variables that collectively define its state. The index of methods lists the name of each one, the type of parameters it takes,

Overview Package Class Tree Deprecated Index Help Weka's home
PREV CLASS NEXT CLASS   FRAMES NO FRAMES All Classes
SUMMARY: NESTED | FIELD | CONSTR | METHOD   DETAIL: FIELD | CONSTR | METHOD

weka.classifiers.trees
Class DecisionStump

```
java.lang.Object
  └weka.classifiers.Classifier
     └weka.classifiers.trees.DecisionStump
```

All Implemented Interfaces:
    java.io.Serializable, java.lang.Cloneable, Sourceable, CapabilitiesHandler, OptionHandler,
    RevisionHandler, WeightedInstancesHandler

```
public class DecisionStump
extends Classifier
implements WeightedInstancesHandler, Sourcable
```

Class for building and using a decision stump. Usually used in conjunction with a boosting
algorithm. Does regression (based on mean-squared error) or classification (based on entropy).
Missing is treated as a separate value.

Typical usage:

```
java weka.classifiers.meta.LogitBoost -I 100 -W
weka.classifiers.trees.DecisionStump -t training_data
```

Valid options are:

```
-D
 If set, classifier is run in debug mode and
 may output additional info to the console
```

Version:
    $Revision: 5535 $
Author:
    Eibe Frank (eibe@cs.waikato.ac.nz)
See Also:
    Serialized Form

Constructor Summary
DecisionStump()

Method Summary	
void	**buildClassifier**(Instances instances) Generates the classifier.
double[]	**distributionForInstance**(Instance instance) Calculates the class membership probabilities for the given test instance.
Capabilities	**getCapabilities**() Returns default capabilities of the classifier.
java.lang.String	**getRevision**() Returns the revision string.
java.lang.String	**globalInfo**() Returns a string describing classifier
static void	**main**(java.lang.String[] argv) Main method for testing this class.
java.lang.String	**toSource**(java.lang.String className) Returns the decision tree as Java source code.
java.lang.String	**toString**() Returns a description of the classifier.

Methods inherited from class weka.classifiers.Classifier
classifyInstance, debugTipText, forName, getDebug, getOptions, listOptions, makeCopies, makeCopy, setDebug, setOptions

(a)   (b)

FIGURE 14.2

DecisionStump, a class of the *weka.classifiers.trees* package.

---

and a short description of its functionality. Beneath those indexes, the web page gives more details about the constructors and methods. We return to these details later.

As you can see, *DecisionStump* overwrites the *distributionForInstance*() method from *Classifier*; the default implementation of *classifyInstance*() in *Classifier* then uses this method to produce its classifications. In addition, it contains the methods *getCapabilities*(), *getRevision*(), *globalInfo*(), *toSource*(), *toString*(), and *main*(). We discuss *getCapabilities*() shortly. The *getRevision*() method simply returns the revision number of the classifier. There is a utility class in the *weka.core* package that prints it to the screen; it is used by Weka maintainers when diagnosing and debugging problems reported by users. The *globalInfo*() method returns a string describing the classifier, which, along with the scheme's options, is displayed by the *More* button in the generic object editor (see Figure 11.7(b)). The *toString*() method returns a textual representation of the classifier, used whenever it is printed on the screen, while the *toSource*() method is used to obtain a source code representation of the learned classifier. The *main*() method is called when you ask for a decision stump from the command line—in other words, every time you enter a command beginning with

```
java weka.classifiers.trees.DecisionStump
```

The presence of a *main*() method in a class indicates that it can be run from the command line: All learning methods and filter algorithms implement it.

The *getCapabilities*() method is called by the generic object editor to provide information about the capabilities of a learning scheme (Figure 11.9(d)). The training data is checked against the learning scheme's capabilities when the *buildClassifier*() method is called, and an error is raised when the classifier's stated capabilities do not match the data's characteristics. The *getCapabilities*() method is present in the *Classifier* class and, by default, enables all capabilities (i.e., imposes no constraints). This makes it easier for new Weka programmers to get started because they need not learn about and specify capabilities initially. Capabilities are covered in more detail in Chapter 16 (page 555).

Other Packages

Several other packages listed earlier in Figure 14.1(a) are worth mentioning: *weka.associations*, *weka.clusterers*, *weka.datagenerators*, *weka.estimators*, *weka. filters*, and *weka.attributeSelection*. The *weka.associations* package contains association-rule learners. These learners have been placed in a separate package because association rules are fundamentally different from classifiers. The *weka. clusterers* package contains methods for unsupervised learning. Artificial data can be generated using the classes in *weka.datagenerators*. The *weka.estimators* package contains subclasses of a generic *Estimator* class, which computes different types of probability distribution. These subclasses are used by the Naïve Bayes algorithm (among others).

In the *weka.filters* package, the *Filter* class defines the general structure of classes containing filter algorithms, which are all implemented as subclasses of *Filter*. Like classifiers, filters can be used from the command line—we will see how shortly. The *weka.attributeSelection* package contains several classes for attribute selection. The classes are used by the *AttributeSelectionFilter* in *weka.filters.supervised.attribute*, but can also be invoked separately.

Javadoc Indexes

As mentioned previously, all classes are automatically subclasses of *Object*. To examine the tree that corresponds to Weka's hierarchy of classes, select the *Overview* link from the top of any page of the online documentation. Click *Tree* to display the overview as a tree that shows which classes are subclasses or superclasses of a particular class—for example, which classes inherit from *Classifier*.

The online documentation contains an index of all of the classes, packages, publicly accessible variables (called *fields*), and methods in Weka—in other words, all fields and methods that you can access from your own Java code. To view it, click *Overview* and then *Index*.

Suppose you want to check which Weka classifiers and filters are capable of operating incrementally. Searching for the word *incremental* in the index would soon lead you to the keyword *UpdateableClassifier*. In fact, this is a Java interface; interfaces are listed after the classes in the overview tree. You are looking for all classes that implement this interface. Clicking any occurrence of it in the documentation brings up a page that describes the interface and lists the classifiers that implement it. To find the filters is a little trickier unless you know the keyword *StreamableFilter*, which is the name of the interface that streams data through a filter; again, its page lists the filters that implement it. You would stumble across that keyword if you knew any example of a filter that could operate incrementally.

14.3 COMMAND-LINE OPTIONS

In the preceding example, the *–t* option was used on the command line to communicate the name of the training file to the learning algorithm. There are many other options that can be used with any learning scheme and also scheme-specific ones that apply only to particular schemes. If you invoke a scheme with the *–h* or *–help* option, or without any command-line options at all, it displays the applicable options: first the general options, then the scheme-specific ones. In the command-line interface, type

```
java weka.classifiers.trees.J48 -h
```

You'll see a list of the options common to all learning schemes, shown in Table 14.1, followed by those that apply only to *J48*, shown in Table 14.2. A notable one is *–info*, which outputs a very brief description of the scheme. We will explain the generic options and then briefly review the scheme-specific ones.

Generic Options

The options in Table 14.1 determine which data is used for training and testing, how the classifier is evaluated, and what kind of statistics are displayed. For example, the *–T* option is used to provide the name of the test file when evaluating a learning scheme on an independent test set. By default, the class is the last attribute in an ARFF file, but you can declare another one to be the class using *–c* followed by the position of the desired attribute—1 for the first, 2 for the second, and so on.

When cross-validation is performed (the default if a test file is not provided), the data is randomly shuffled first. To repeat the cross-validation several times, each time reshuffling the data in a different way, set the random number seed with *–s* (default value 1). With a large dataset you may want to reduce the number of folds for the cross-validation from the default value of 10 using *–x*. If performance on the training data alone is required, *–no-cv* can be used to suppress cross-validation; *–v* suppresses output of performance on the training data. As an alternative to cross-validation, a train-test split of the data specified with the *–t* option can be performed

Table 14.1 Generic Options for Learning Schemes in Weka

Option	Function
h or –help	Print help information
–synopsis or –info	In combination with –h or –help, prints the information from the "More" button in a classifier's generic object editor
–t <training file>	Specify training file
–T <test file>	Specify test file. If none, a cross-validation is performed on the training data.
–c <class index>	Specify index of class attribute
–x <number of folds>	Specify number of folds for cross-validation
–s <random number seed>	Specify random-number seed for cross-validation
–no-cv	Don't perform cross-validation
–split-percentage <training percentage>	Specify percentage of the data to use for the training set in a train-test split
–preserve-order	Preserve original order of the data when performing a train-test split
–m <cost matrix file>	Specify file containing cost matrix
–l <input file>	Specify input file for model
–d <output file>	Specify output file for model
–v	Output no statistics for training data
–o	Output statistics only, not the classifier
–i	Output information retrieval statistics for two-class problems
–k	Output information-theoretic statistics
–p <attribute range>	Output predictions for test instances
–distribution	In combination with –p, output the full probability distribution for discrete class data instead of just the predicted label
–r	Output cumulative margin distribution
–z <class name>	Output the source representation of the classifier
–g	Output the graph representation of the classifier
–xml <filename> I <xml string>	Set scheme-specific options from XML-encoded options stored in a file or in a supplied string
–threshold-file <file>	Save threshold data (for ROC curves, etc.) to a file
–threshold-label <label>	Class label for the threshold data

Table 14.2 Scheme-Specific Options for the *J48* Decision Tree Learner

Option	Function
-U	Use unpruned tree
-C <pruning confidence>	Specify confidence threshold for pruning
-M <number of instances>	Specify minimum number of instances in any leaf
-R	Use reduced-error pruning
-N <number of folds>	Specify number of folds for reduced-error pruning; one fold is used as pruning set
-B	Use binary splits only
-S	Don't perform subtree raising
-L	Retain instance information
-A	Smooth probability estimates using Laplace smoothing
-Q	Seed for shuffling data

by supplying a percentage to use as the new training set with *–split-percentage* (the remaining data is used as the test set). Randomization of the data can be suppressed when performing a train-test split by specifying *–preserve-order*.

In the Explorer interface, cost-sensitive evaluation is invoked as described in Section 11.1 (page 403). To achieve the same effect from the command line, use the *–m* option to provide the name of a file containing the cost matrix. Here is a cost matrix for the weather data:

```
2  2    % Number of rows and columns in the matrix
0  10   % If true class yes and prediction no, penalty is 10
1  0    % If true class no and prediction yes, penalty is 1
```

The first line gives the number of rows and columns—that is, the number of class values. Then comes the matrix of penalties. Comments introduced by % can be appended to the end of any line.

It is also possible to save and load models. If you provide the name of an output file using *–d*, Weka saves the classifier generated from the training data. To evaluate the same classifier on a new batch of test data, you load it back using *–l* instead of rebuilding it. If the classifier can be updated incrementally, you can provide both a training file and an input file, and Weka will load the classifier and update it with the given training instances.

If you wish only to assess the performance of a learning scheme, use *–o* to suppress output of the model. Use *–i* to see the performance measures of precision, recall, *F*-measure, and area under the ROC curve (see Section 5.7, page 172). Use *–k* to compute information-theoretic measures from the probabilities derived by a learning scheme (see Section 5.6, page 161).

People often want to know which class values the learning scheme actually predicts for each test instance. The *–p* option prints each test instance's number, the index of its class value and the actual value, the index of the predicted class value and the predicted value, a "+" if the class was misclassified, and the probability of the predicted class value. The probability predicted for each of the possible class labels of an instance can be output by using the *–distribution* flag in conjunction with *–p*. In this case, "*" is placed beside the probability in the distribution that corresponds to the predicted class value. The *–p* option also outputs attribute values for each instance and must be followed by a specification of the range (e.g., 1–2)— use 0 if you don't want any attribute values. You can also output the *cumulative margin distribution* for the training data, which shows the distribution of the margin measure (see Section 8.4, page 361). Finally, you can output the classifier's source representation, and a graphical representation if the classifier can produce one.

Data relating to performance graphs such as ROC and recall–precision curves can be sent to a file using the *–threshold-file* option. The class label to treat as the positive class for generating the data can be specified with *–threshold-label*. The next section discusses how scheme-specific options are supplied on the command line; they can also be set from an XML file or string using the *–xml* option.

Scheme-Specific Options

Table 14.2 shows the options specific to *J48*. You can force the algorithm to use the unpruned tree instead of the pruned one. You can suppress subtree raising, which increases efficiency. You can set the confidence threshold for pruning and the minimum number of instances permissible at any leaf—both parameters were described in Section 6.1 (page 201). As well as C4.5's standard pruning procedure, reduced-error pruning (see Section 6.2, page 206) can be performed. The *–N* option governs the size of the holdout set: The dataset is divided equally into that number of parts and the last is held out (default value 3). You can smooth the probability estimates using the Laplace technique, set the random number seed for shuffling the data when selecting a pruning set, and store the instance information for future visualization. Finally, to build a binary tree instead of one with multiway branches for nominal attributes, use *–B*.

Embedded Machine Learning

When invoking learning schemes from the graphical user interfaces or the command-line interface, there is no need to know anything about programming in Java. In this section we show how to access these algorithms from your own code. In doing so, the advantages of using an object-oriented programming language will become clear. From now on, we assume that you have at least some rudimentary knowledge of Java. In most practical applications of data mining, the learning component is an integrated part of a far larger software environment. If the environment is written in Java, you can use Weka to solve the learning problem without writing any machine learning code yourself.

15.1 A SIMPLE DATA MINING APPLICATION

We present a simple data mining application for learning a model that classifies text files into two categories: *hit* and *miss*. The application works for arbitrary documents, which are referred to as *messages*. The implementation uses the *StringToWordVector* filter mentioned in Section 11.3 (page 439) to convert messages into attribute vectors in the manner described in Section 7.3 (page 328). We assume that the program is called every time a new file is to be processed. If the user provides a class label for the file, the system uses it for training; if not, it classifies it. The decision tree classifier *J48* is used to do the work.

Figure 15.1 shows the source code for the application program, implemented in a class called *MessageClassifier*. The command-line arguments that the *main()* method accepts are the name of a text file (given by *–m*), the name of a file holding an object of class *MessageClassifier* (*–t*), and, optionally, the classification of the message in the file (*–c*). If the user provides a classification, the message will be converted into an example for training; if not, the *MessageClassifier* object will be used to classify it as *hit* or *miss*.

The *main()* method reads the message into a Java *StringBuffer* and checks whether the user has provided a classification for it. Then it reads a *MessageClassifier* object from the file given by *–t*, and creates a new object of class *MessageClassifier* if this file does not exist. In either case the resulting object is called *messageCl*. After checking for illegal command-line options, the program calls the

```java
/**
 * Java program for classifying text messages into two classes.
 */

import weka.classifiers.Classifier;
import weka.classifiers.trees.J48;
import weka.core.Attribute;
import weka.core.FastVector;
import weka.core.Instance;
import weka.core.Instances;
import weka.core.SerializationHelper;
import weka.core.Utils;
import weka.filters.Filter;
import weka.filters.unsupervised.attribute.StringToWordVector;

import java.io.FileNotFoundException;
import java.io.FileReader;
import java.io.Serializable;

public class MessageClassifier implements Serializable {

/** The training data gathered so far. */
  private Instances m_Data = null;

  /** The filter used to generate the word counts. */
  private StringToWordVector m_Filter = new StringToWordVector();

  /** The actual classifier. */
  private Classifier m_Classifier = new J48();

  /** Whether the model is up to date. */
  private boolean m_UpToDate;

  /** For serialization. */
  private static final long serialVersionUID = -123455813150452885L;

  /**
   * Constructs empty training dataset.
   */
  public MessageClassifier() {
    String nameOfDataset = "MessageClassificationProblem";

    // Create vector of attributes.
    FastVector attributes = new FastVector(2);

    // Add attribute for holding messages.
    attributes.addElement(new Attribute("Message", (FastVector) null));

    // Add class attribute.
    FastVector classValues = new FastVector(2);
    classValues.addElement("miss");
    classValues.addElement("hit");
    attributes.addElement(new Attribute("Class", classValues));
```

FIGURE 15.1

Source code for the message classifier *main()*.

```
  // Create dataset with initial capacity of 100, and set index
     of class.
  m_Data = new Instances(nameOfDataset, attributes, 100);
  m_Data.setClassIndex(m_Data.numAttributes() - 1);
}

/**
 * Updates model using the given training message.
 *
 * @param message          the message content
 * @param classValue       the class label
 */
public void updateData(String message, String classValue) {
  // Make message into instance.
  Instance instance = makeInstance(message, m_Data);

  // Set class value for instance.
  instance.setClassValue(classValue);

  // Add instance to training data.
  m_Data.add(instance);
  m_UpToDate = false;
}

/**
 * Classifies a given message.
 *
 * @param message          the message content
 * @throws Exception       if classification fails
 */
public void classifyMessage(String message) throws Exception {

  // Check whether classifier has been built.
  if (m_Data.numInstances() == 0) {
    throw new Exception("No classifier available.");
  }

  // Check whether classifier and filter are up to date.
  if (!m_UpToDate) {
    // Initialize filter and tell it about the input format.
    m_Filter.setInputFormat(m_Data);

    // Generate word counts from the training data.
    Instances filteredData  = Filter.useFilter(m_Data, m_Filter);

    // Rebuild classifier.
    m_Classifier.buildClassifier(filteredData);

    m_UpToDate = true;
  }

  // Make separate little test set so that message
  // does not get added to string attribute in m_Data.
  Instances testset = m_Data.stringFreeStructure();

  // Make message into test instance.
  Instance instance = makeInstance(message, testset);
```

FIGURE 15.1, cont'd

Continued

```
      // Filter instance.
      m_Filter.input(instance);
      Instance filteredInstance = m_Filter.output();

      // Get index of predicted class value.
      double predicted = m_Classifier.classifyInstance(filteredInstance);

      // Output class value.
      System.err.println("Message classified as : " +
            m_Data.classAttribute().value((int) predicted));
   }

   /**
    * Method that converts a text message into an instance.
    *
    * @param text      the message content to convert
    * @param data      the header information
    * @return          the generated Instance
    */
   private Instance makeInstance(String text, Instances data) {

      // Create instance of length two.
      Instance instance = new Instance(2);

      // Set value for message attribute
      Attribute messageAtt = data.attribute("Message");
      instance.setValue(messageAtt, messageAtt.addStringValue(text));

      // Give instance access to attribute information from the dataset.
      instance.setDataset(data);

      return instance;
   }

   /**
    * Main method. The following parameters are recognized:
    *
    *    -m messagefile
    *       Points to the file containing the message to classify or use
    *       for updating the model.
    *    -c classlabel
    *       The class label of the message if model is to be updated.
    *       Omit for classification of a message.
    *    -t modelfile
    *       The file containing the model. If it doesn't exist, it will
    *       be created automatically.
    *
    * @param args      the commandline options
    */
   public static void main(String[] args) {

      try {
```

FIGURE 15.1, cont'd

```
      // Read message file into string.
      String messageName = Utils.getOption('m', args);
      if (messageName.length() == 0) {
        throw new Exception("Must provide name of message
          + file ('-m <file>').");

      }

      FileReader m = new FileReader(messageName);
      StringBuffer message = new StringBuffer();
      int l;
      while ((l = m.read()) != -1) {
        message.append((char) l);
      }
      m.close();

      // Check if class value is given.
      String classValue = Utils.getOption('c', args);

      // If model file exists, read it, otherwise create new one.
      String modelName = Utils.getOption('t', args);
      if (modelName.length() == 0) {
        throw new Exception("Must provide name of model
          + file ('-t <file>').");
      }
      MessageClassifier messageCl;
      try {
        messageCl =
        (MessageClassifier) SerializationHelper. read(modelName);
      } catch (FileNotFoundException e) {
        messageCl = new MessageClassifier();
      }

      // Check if there are any options left
      Utils.checkForRemainingOptions(args);

      // Process message.
      if (classValue.length() != 0) {
        messageCl.updateData(message.toString(), classValue);
      } else {
        messageCl.classifyMessage(message.toString());
      }

      // Save message classifier object only if it was updated.
      if (classValue.length() != 0) {
        SerializationHelper.write(modelName, messageCl);
      }
    } catch (Exception e) {
      e.printStackTrace();
    }
  }
}
```

FIGURE 15.1, cont'd

Continued

method *updateData()* message to update the training data stored in *messageCl* if a classification has been provided; otherwise, it calls *classifyMessage*() to classify it. Finally, the *messageCl* object is saved back into the file because it may have changed. In the following, we first describe how a new *MessageClassifier* object is created by the constructor *MessageClassifier*() and then explain how the two methods *updateData*() and *classifyMessage*() work.

MessageClassifier()

Each time a new *MessageClassifier* is created, objects for holding the filter and classifier are generated automatically. The only nontrivial part of the process is creating a dataset, which is done by the constructor *MessageClassifier*(). First, the dataset's name is stored as a string. Then an *Attribute* object is created for each attribute, one to hold the string corresponding to a text message and the other for its class. These objects are stored in a dynamic array of type *FastVector*. (*FastVector* is Weka's own implementation of the standard Java *Vector* class and is used throughout Weka for historical reasons.)

Attributes are created by invoking one of the constructors in the class *Attribute*. This class has a constructor that takes one parameter—the attribute's name—and creates a numeric attribute. However, the constructor we use here takes two parameters: the attribute's name and a reference to a *FastVector*. If this reference is null, as in the first application of this constructor in our program, Weka creates an attribute of type *string*. Otherwise, a nominal attribute is created. In that case, it is assumed that the *FastVector* holds the attribute values as strings. This is how we create a class attribute with two values, *hit* and *miss*—by passing the attribute's name (*class*) and its values, stored in a *FastVector*, to *Attribute*().

To create a dataset from this attribute information, *MessageClassifier*() must create an object of the class *Instances* from the *core* package. The constructor of *Instances* used by *MessageClassifier*() takes three arguments: the dataset's name, a *FastVector* containing the attributes, and an integer indicating the dataset's initial capacity. We set the initial capacity to 100; it is expanded automatically if more instances are added. After constructing the dataset, *MessageClassifier*() sets the index of the class attribute to be the index of the last attribute.

updateData()

Now that you know how to create an empty dataset, consider how the *MessageClassifier* object actually incorporates a new training message. The method *updateData*() does this job. It first converts the given message into a training instance by calling *makeInstance*(), which begins by creating an object of class *Instance* that corresponds to an instance with two attributes. The constructor of the *Instance* object sets all the instance's values to be *missing* and its weight to 1. The next step in *makeInstance*() is to set the value of the string attribute holding the text of the message. This is done by applying the *setValue*() method of the *Instance* object, providing it with the attribute whose value needs to be changed, and a second parameter that corresponds to the new value's index in the definition of the string attribute. This index is returned by the *addStringValue*() method, which adds the message text as a new value to the string attribute and returns the position of this new value in the definition of the string attribute.

Internally, an *Instance* stores all attribute values as double-precision floating-point numbers regardless of the type of the corresponding attribute. In the case of nominal and string attributes this is done by storing the index of the corresponding attribute value in the definition of the attribute. For example, the first value of a nominal attribute is represented by 0.0, the second by 1.0, and so on. The same method is used for string attributes: *addStringValue*() returns the index corresponding to the value that is added to the definition of the attribute.

Once the value for the string attribute has been set, *makeInstance*() gives the newly created instance access to the data's attribute information by passing it a reference to the dataset. In Weka, an *Instance* object does not store the type of each attribute explicitly; instead, it stores a reference to a dataset with the corresponding attribute information.

Returning to *updateData*(), once the new instance has been returned from *makeInstance*(), its class value is set and it is added to the training data. We also initialize *m_UpToDate*, a flag indicating that the training data has changed and the predictive model is therefore not up to date.

classifyMessage()

Now let's examine how *MessageClassifier* processes a message of which the class label is unknown. The *classifyMessage*() method first checks whether a classifier has been built by determining whether any training instances are available. It then checks whether the classifier is up to date. If not (because the training data has changed), the classifier must be rebuilt. However, before doing so, the data must be converted into a format appropriate for learning using the *StringToWordVector* filter. First, we tell the filter the format of the input data by passing it a reference to the input dataset using *setInputFormat*(). Every time this method is called, the filter is initialized—that is, all its internal settings are reset. In the next step, the data is transformed by *useFilter*(). This generic method from the *Filter* class applies a filter to a dataset. In this case, because *StringToWordVector* has just been initialized, it computes a dictionary from the training dataset and then uses it to form a word vector. After returning from *useFilter*(), all the filter's internal settings are fixed until it is initialized by another call of *inputFormat*(). This makes it possible to filter a test instance without updating the filter's internal settings (in this case, the dictionary).

Once the data has been filtered, the program rebuilds the classifier—in our case a *J48* decision tree—by passing the training data to its *buildClassifier*() method. Then it sets *m_UpToDate* to *true*. It is an important convention in Weka that the *buildClassifier*() method completely initializes the model's internal settings before generating a new classifier. Thus, we do not need to construct a new *J48* object before we call *buildClassifier()*.

Having ensured that the model stored in *m_Classifier* is current, we proceed to classify the message. Before *makeInstance()* is called to create an *Instance* object from it, a new *Instances* object is created to hold the new instance and it is passed as an argument to *makeInstance()*. This is done so that *makeInstance()* does not add the text of the message to the definition of the string attribute in *m_Data*. Otherwise, the size of the *m_Data* object would grow every time a new message was classified, which is clearly not desirable—it should only grow when training instances are added. Thus, a temporary *Instances* object is created and discarded once the instance has been processed. This object is obtained using the method *stringFreeStructure()*, which returns a copy of *m_Data* with an empty string attribute. Only then is *makeInstance()* called to create the new instance.

The test instance must also be processed by the *StringToWordVector* filter before being classified. This is easy: The *input()* method enters the instance into the filter object, and the transformed instance is obtained by calling *output()*. Then a prediction is produced by passing the instance to the classifier's *classifyInstance()* method. As you can see, the prediction is coded as a *double* value. This allows Weka's evaluation module to treat models for categorical and numeric prediction similarly. In the case of categorical prediction, as in this example, the *double* variable holds the index of the predicted class value. To output the string corresponding to this class value, the program calls the *value()* method of the dataset's class attribute.

There is at least one way in which our implementation could be improved. The classifier and the *StringToWordVector* filter could be combined using the *Filtered-Classifier* metalearner described in Section 11.5 (page 443). This classifier would then be able to deal with string attributes directly, without explicitly calling the filter to transform the data. We didn't do this because we wanted to demonstrate how filters can be used programmatically.

Writing New Learning Schemes

Suppose you need to implement a special-purpose learning algorithm that is not included in Weka. Or suppose you are engaged in machine learning research and want to investigate a new learning scheme. Or suppose you just want to learn more about the inner workings of an induction algorithm by actually programming it yourself. This section uses a simple example to show how to make full use of Weka's class hierarchy when writing classifiers.

Weka includes the elementary learning schemes listed in Table 16.1, mainly for educational purposes. None take any scheme-specific command-line options. They are all useful for understanding the inner workings of a classifier. As an example, we describe the *weka.classifiers.trees.Id3* scheme, which implements the ID3 decision tree learner from Section 4.3 (page 99). Other schemes, such as clustering algorithms and association rule learners, are organized in a similar manner.

16.1 AN EXAMPLE CLASSIFIER

Figure 16.1 gives the source code of *weka.classifiers.trees.Id3*, which extends the *Classifier* class, as you can see from what is shown in the eight-page figure that follows the next page. Every classifier in Weka does so, whether it predicts a nominal class or a numeric one. It also implements two interfaces, *Technical-InformationHandler* and *Sourcable*, which, respectively, allow the implementing class to provide bibliographical references for display in Weka's graphical user interface and a source code representation of its learned model.

The first method in *weka.classifiers.trees.Id3* is *globalInfo()*: We mention it here before moving on to the more interesting parts. It simply returns a string that is displayed in Weka's graphical user interface when this scheme is selected. Part of the string includes information generated by the second method, *getTechnicalInformation()*, which formats a bibliographic reference for the ID3 algorithm. The third method, *getCapabilities()*, returns information on the data characteristics that *Id3* can handle, namely nominal attributes and a nominal class—and the fact that it can deal with missing class values and data that contains no instances (although the latter does not produce a useful model!). Capabilities are described in Section 16.2.

Table 16.1 Simple Learning Schemes in Weka		
Scheme	**Description**	**Book Section**
weka.classifiers.bayes.NaiveBayesSimple	Probabilistic learner	4.2
weka.classifiers.trees.Id3	Decision tree learner	4.3
weka.classifiers.rules.Prism	Rule learner	4.4
weka.classifiers.lazy.IB1	Instance-based learner	4.7

buildClassifier()

The *buildClassifier*() method constructs a classifier from a training dataset. In this case, it first checks the data's characteristics against *Id3*'s capabilities. Characteristics of the training data, such as numeric attributes or missing attribute values, will cause the *Capabilities* class to raise an exception, because the ID3 algorithm cannot handle these. It then makes a copy of the training set (to avoid changing the original data) and calls a method from *weka.core.Instances* to delete all instances with missing class values, because these instances are useless in the training process. Finally, it calls *makeTree*(), which actually builds the decision tree by recursively generating all subtrees attached to the root node.

makeTree()

The first step in *makeTree*() is to check whether the dataset is empty. If it is, a leaf is created by setting *m_Attribute* to null. The class value *m_ClassValue* assigned to this leaf is set to be missing, and the estimated probability for each of the dataset's classes in *m_Distribution* is initialized to 0. If training instances are present, *makeTree*() finds the attribute that yields the greatest information gain for them. It first creates a Java *enumeration* of the dataset's attributes. If the index of the class attribute is set—as it will be for this dataset—the class is automatically excluded from the enumeration.

Inside the enumeration, each attribute's information gain is computed by *computeInfoGain*() and stored in an array. We will return to this method later. The *index*() method from *weka.core.Attribute* returns the attribute's index in the dataset, which is used to index the array. Once the enumeration is complete, the attribute with the greatest information gain is stored in the instance variable *m_Attribute*. The *maxIndex*() method from *weka.core.Utils* returns the index of the greatest value in an array of integers or doubles. (If there is more than one element with maximum value, the first is returned.) The index of this attribute is passed to the *attribute*() method from *weka.core.Instances*, which returns the corresponding attribute.

You might wonder what happens to the array field corresponding to the class attribute. We need not worry about this because Java automatically initializes all elements in an array of numbers to 0, and the information gain is always greater

```
package weka.classifiers.trees;

import weka.classifiers.Classifier;
import weka.classifiers.Sourcable;
import weka.core.Attribute;
import weka.core.Capabilities;
import weka.core.Instance;
import weka.core.Instances;
import weka.core.NoSupportForMissingValuesException;
import weka.core.RevisionUtils;
import weka.core.TechnicalInformation;
import weka.core.TechnicalInformationHandler;
import weka.core.Utils;
import weka.core.Capabilities.Capability;
import weka.core.TechnicalInformation.Field;
import weka.core.TechnicalInformation.Type;

import java.util.Enumeration;

/**
 * Class implementing an Id3 decision tree classifier.
 */
public class Id3 extends Classifier
  implements TechnicalInformationHandler, Sourcable {

  /** for serialization */
  static final long serialVersionUID = -2693678647096322561L;

  /** The node's successors. */
  private Id3[] m_Successors;

  /** Attribute used for splitting. */
  private Attribute m_Attribute;

  /** Class value if node is leaf. */
  private double m_ClassValue;

  /** Class distribution if node is leaf. */
  private double[] m_Distribution;

  /** Class attribute of dataset. */
  private Attribute m_ClassAttribute;

  /**
   * Returns a string describing the classifier.
   * @return a description suitable for the GUI.
   */
  public String globalInfo() {

    return "Class for constructing an unpruned decision tree "
      + "based on the ID3 algorithm. Can only deal with "
      + "nominal attributes. No missing values allowed. "
      + "Empty leaves may result in unclassified instances. "
      + "For more information see: \n\n"
      + getTechnicalInformation.toString();
  }
```

Continued

FIGURE 16.1

Source code for the ID3 decision tree learner.

```
/**
 * Returns an instance of a TechnicalInformation object, containing
 * detailed information about the technical background of this class,
 * e.g., paper reference or book this class is based on.
 *
 * @return the technical information about this class
 */
public TechnicalInformation getTechnicalInformation() {
  TechnicalInformation result;

  result = new TechnicalInformation(Type.ARTICLE);
  result.setValue(Field.AUTHOR, "R. Quinlan");
  result.setValue(Field.YEAR, "1986");
  result.setValue(Field.TITLE, "Induction of decision trees");
  result.setValue(Field.JOURNAL, "Machine Learning");
  result.setValue(Field.VOLUME, "1");
  result.setValue(Field.NUMBER, "1");
  result.setValue(Field.PAGES, "81-106");
  return result;
}

/**
 * Returns default capabilities of the classifier.
 *
 * @return      the capabilities of this classifier
 */
public Capabilities getCapabilities() {
  Capabilities result = super.getCapabilities();
  result.disableAll();

  // attributes
  result.enable(Capability.NOMINAL_ATTRIBUTES);

  // class
  result.enable(Capability.NOMINAL_CLASS);
  result.enable(Capability.MISSING_CLASS_VALUES);

  // instances
  result.setMinimumNumberInstances(0);

  return result;
}

/**
 * Builds Id3 decision tree classifier.
 *
 * @param data the training data
 * @exception Exception if classifier can't be built successfully
 */
public void buildClassifier(Instances data) throws Exception {

  // can classifier handle the data?
  getCapabilities().testWithFail(data);

  // remove instances with missing class
  data = new Instances(data);
  data.deleteWithMissingClass();
```

FIGURE 16.1, cont'd

```
    makeTree(data);
}

/**
   * Method for building an Id3 tree.
   *
   * @param data the training data
   * @exception Exception if decision tree can't be built successfully
   */
  private void makeTree(Instances data) throws Exception {

    // Check if no instances have reached this node.
    if (data.numInstances() == 0) {
      m_Attribute = null;
      m_ClassValue = Instance.missingValue();
      m_Distribution = new double[data.numClasses()];
      return;
    }

    // Compute attribute with maximum information gain.
    double[] infoGains = new double[data.numAttributes()];
    Enumeration attEnum = data.enumerateAttributes();
    while (attEnum.hasMoreElements()) {
      Attribute att = (Attribute) attEnum.nextElement();
      infoGains[att.index()] = computeInfoGain(data, att);
    }
    m_Attribute = data.attribute(Utils.maxIndex(infoGains));

    // Make leaf if information gain is zero.
    // Otherwise create successors.
    if (Utils.eq(infoGains[m_Attribute.index()], 0)) {
      m_Attribute = null;
      m_Distribution = new double[data.numClasses()];
      Enumeration instEnum = data.enumerateInstances();
      while (instEnum.hasMoreElements()) {
        Instance inst = (Instance) instEnum.nextElement();
        m_Distribution[(int) inst.classValue()]++;
      }
      Utils.normalize(m_Distribution);
      m_ClassValue = Utils.maxIndex(m_Distribution);
      m_ClassAttribute = data.classAttribute();
    } else {
      Instances[] splitData = splitData(data, m_Attribute);
      m_Successors = new Id3[m_Attribute.numValues()];
      for (int j = 0; j < m_Attribute.numValues(); j++) {
        m_Successors[j] = new Id3();
        m_Successors[j].makeTree(splitData[j]);
      }
    }
  }

/**
 * Classifies a given test instance using the decision tree.
 *
 * @param instance the instance to be classified
 * @return the classification
 * @throws NoSupportForMissingValuesException if instance has missing
   values
 */
public double classifyInstance(Instance instance)
  throws NoSupportForMissingValuesException {
```

FIGURE 16.1, cont'd

Continued

```
    if (instance.hasMissingValue()) {
      throw new NoSupportForMissingValuesException("Id3: no missing values, "
                                                   + "please.");
    }
    if (m_Attribute == null) {
      return m_ClassValue;
    } else {
      return m_Successors[(int) instance.value(m_Attribute)].
        classifyInstance(instance);
    }
  }

  /**
   * Computes class distribution for instance using decision tree.
   *
   * @param instance the instance for which distribution is to be computed
   * @return the class distribution for the given instance
   * @throws NoSupportForMissingValuesException if instance
   * has missing values
   */
  public double[] distributionForInstance(Instance instance)
    throws NoSupportForMissingValuesException {

    if (instance.hasMissingValue()) {
      throw new NoSupportForMissingValuesException("Id3: no missing values, "
                                                   + "please.");
    }
    if (m_Attribute == null) {
      return m_Distribution;
    } else {
      return m_Successors[(int) instance.value(m_Attribute)].
        distributionForInstance(instance);
    }
  }

  /**
   * Prints the decision tree using the private toString method from below.
   *
   * @return a textual description of the classifier
   */
  public String toString() {

    if ((m_Distribution == null) && (m_Successors == null)) {
      return "Id3: No model built yet.";
    }
    return "Id3\n\n" + toString(0);
  }

  /**
   * Computes information gain for an attribute.
   *
   * @param data the data for which info gain is to be computed
   * @param att the attribute
   * @return the information gain for the given attribute and data
   * @throws Exception if computation fails
   */
  private double computeInfoGain(Instances data, Attribute att)
    throws Exception {
```

FIGURE 16.1, cont'd

```
   double infoGain = computeEntropy(data);
   Instances[] splitData = splitData(data, att);
   for (int j = 0; j < att.numValues(); j++) {
     if (splitData[j].numInstances() > 0) {
       infoGain -= ((double) splitData[j].numInstances() /
                    (double) data.numInstances()) *
         computeEntropy(splitData[j]);
     }
   }
   return infoGain;
}

/**
 * Computes the entropy of a dataset.
 *
 * @param data the data for which entropy is to be computed
 * @return the entropy of the data's class distribution
 * @throws Exception if computation fails
 */
private double computeEntropy(Instances data) throws Exception {

  double [] classCounts = new double[data.numClasses()];
  Enumeration instEnum = data.enumerateInstances();
  while (instEnum.hasMoreElements()) {
    Instance inst = (Instance) instEnum.nextElement();
    classCounts[(int) inst.classValue()]++;
  }
  double entropy = 0;
  for (int j = 0; j < data.numClasses(); j++) {
    if (classCounts[j] > 0) {
      entropy -= classCounts[j] * Utils.log2(classCounts[j]);
    }
  }
  entropy /= (double) data.numInstances();
  return entropy + Utils.log2(data.numInstances());
}

/**
 * Splits a dataset according to the values of a nominal attribute.
 *
 * @param data the data which is to be split
 * @param att the attribute to be used for splitting
 * @return the sets of instances produced by the split
 */
private Instances[] splitData(Instances data, Attribute att) {

  Instances[] splitData = new Instances[att.numValues()];
  for (int j = 0; j < att.numValues(); j++) {
    splitData[j] = new Instances(data, data.numInstances());
  }
  Enumeration instEnum = data.enumerateInstances();
  while (instEnum.hasMoreElements()) {
    Instance inst = (Instance) instEnum.nextElement();
    splitData[(int) inst.value(att)].add(inst);
  }
  for (int i = 0; i < splitData.length; i++) {
    splitData[i].compactify();
  }
  return splitData;
}
```

Continued

FIGURE 16.1, cont'd

```
/**
 * Outputs a tree at a certain level.
 *
 * @param level the level at which the tree is to be printed
 * @return the tree as string at the given level
 */
private String toString(int level) {

  StringBuffer text = new StringBuffer();

  if (m_Attribute == null) {
    if (Instance.isMissingValue(m_ClassValue)) {
      text.append(": null");
    } else {
      text.append(": " + m_ClassAttribute.value((int) m_ClassValue));
    }
  } else {
    for (int j = 0; j < m_Attribute.numValues(); j++) {
      text.append("\n");
      for (int i = 0; i < level; i++) {
        text.append("|   ");
      }
      text.append(m_Attribute.name() + " = " + m_Attribute.value(j));
      text.append(m_Successors[j].toString(level + 1));
    }
  }
  return text.toString();
}

/**
 * Adds this tree recursively to the buffer.
 *
 * @param id          the unqiue id for the method
 * @param buffer      the buffer to add the source code to
 * @return            the last ID being used
 * @throws Exception  if something goes wrong
 */
protected int toSource(int id, StringBuffer buffer) throws Exception {
  int              result;
  int              i;
  int              newID;
  StringBuffer[]   subBuffers;

  buffer.append("\n");
  buffer.append("  protected static double node"
    + id + "(Object[] i) {\n");

  // leaf?
  if (m_Attribute == null) {
    result = id;
    if (Double.isNaN(m_ClassValue)) {
      buffer.append("    return Double.NaN;");
    } else {
      buffer.append("    return " + m_ClassValue + ";");
    }
    if (m_ClassAttribute != null) {
      buffer.append(" // " + m_ClassAttribute.value((int) m_ClassValue));
    }
    buffer.append("\n");
    buffer.append("  }\n");
```

FIGURE 16.1, cont'd

```
    } else {
      buffer.append("    checkMissing(i, "
        + m_Attribute.index() + ");\n\n");
      buffer.append("    // " + m_Attribute.name() + "\n");

      // subtree calls
      subBuffers = new StringBuffer[m_Attribute.numValues()];
      newID = id;
      for (i = 0; i < m_Attribute.numValues(); i++) {
        newID++;

        buffer.append("    ");
        if (i > 0) {
          buffer.append("else ");
        }
        buffer.append("if (((String) i[" + m_Attribute.index()
          + "]).equals(\"" + m_Attribute.value(i) + "\"))\n");
        buffer.append("      return node" + newID + "(i);\n");

        subBuffers[i] = new StringBuffer();
        newID = m_Successors[i].toSource(newID, subBuffers[i]);
      }
      buffer.append("    else\n");
      buffer.append("      throw new IllegalArgumentException
        (\"Value '\" + i[" + m_Attribute.index() + "]
        + \"' is not allowed!\");\n");
      buffer.append("  }\n");

      // output subtree code
      for (i = 0; i < m_Attribute.numValues(); i++) {
        buffer.append(subBuffers[i].toString());
      }
      subBuffers = null;
      result = newID;
  }

  return result;
}

/**
 * Returns a string that describes the classifier as source. The
 * classifier will be contained in a class with the given name (there
 * may be auxiliary classes),
 * and will contain a method with the signature:
 * <pre><code>
 * public static double classify(Object[] i);
 * </code></pre>
 * where the array <code>i</code> contains elements that are either
 * Double, String, with missing values represented as null. The
 * generated code is public domain and comes with no warranty. <br/>
 * Note: works only if class attribute is the last attribute in the
 * dataset.
 * @param className the name that should be given to the source class.
 * @return the object source described by a string
 * @throws Exception if the source can't be computed
 */
public String toSource(String className) throws Exception {
  StringBuffer      result;
  int               id;
```

Continued

FIGURE 16.1, cont'd

```
      result = new StringBuffer();

      result.append("class " + className + " {\n");
      result.append("  private static void checkMissing(Object[]
                  i, int index) {\n");
      result.append("    if (i[index] == null)\n");
      result.append("      throw new IllegalArgumentException (\"Null values "
        + "are not allowed!\");\n");
      result.append("  }\n\n");
      result.append("  public static double classify(Object[] i) {\n");
      id = 0;
      result.append("    return node" + id + "(i);\n");
      result.append("  }\n");
      toSource(id, result);
      result.append("}\n");

      return result.toString();
    }

    /**
     * Returns the revision string.
     *
     * @return  the revision
     */
    public String getRevision() {
      return RevisionUtils.extract("$Revision: 6404 $");
    }

    /**
     * Main method.
     *
     * @param args the options for the classifier
     */
    public static void main(String[] args) {
      runClassifier(new Id3(), args);
    }
}
```

FIGURE 16.1, cont'd

than or equal to 0. If the maximum information gain is 0, *makeTree*() creates a leaf.
In that case, *m_Attribute* is set to null, and *makeTree*() computes both the distribution
of class probabilities and the class with the greatest probability. (The *normalize*()
method from *weka.core.Utils* normalizes an array of doubles to sum to 1.)

When it makes a leaf with a class value assigned to it, *makeTree*() stores the class
attribute in *m_ClassAttribute*. This is because the method that outputs the decision
tree needs to access this to print the class label.

If an attribute with nonzero information gain is found, *makeTree*() splits the
dataset according to the attribute's values and recursively builds subtrees for each
of the new datasets. To make the split it calls the method *splitData*(). This creates
as many empty datasets as there are attribute values, stores them in an array (setting
the initial capacity of each dataset to the number of instances in the original dataset),
and then iterates through all instances in the original dataset and allocates them to

the new dataset that corresponds to the attribute's value. It then reduces memory requirements by compacting the *Instances* objects. Returning to *makeTree()*, the resulting array of datasets is used for building subtrees. The method creates an array of *Id3* objects, one for each attribute value, and calls *makeTree()* on each one by passing it the corresponding dataset.

computeInfoGain()

Returning to *computeInfoGain()*, the information gain associated with an attribute and a dataset is calculated using a straightforward implementation of the formula in Section 4.3 (page 104). First, the entropy of the dataset is computed. Then, *split-Data()* is used to divide it into subsets, and *computeEntropy()* is called on each one. Finally, the difference between the former entropy and the weighted sum of the latter ones—the information gain—is returned. The method *computeEntropy()* uses the *log2()* method from *weka.core.Utils* to obtain the logarithm (to base 2) of a number.

classifyInstance()

Having seen how *Id3* constructs a decision tree, we now examine how it uses the tree structure to predict class values and probabilities. Every classifier must implement the *classifyInstance()* method or the *distributionForInstance()* method (or both). The *Classifier* superclass contains default implementations for both methods. The default implementation of *classifyInstance()* calls *distributionForInstance()*. If the class is nominal, it predicts the class with maximum probability, or a missing value if all probabilities returned by *distributionForInstance()* are 0. If the class is numeric, *distributionForInstance()* must return a single-element array that holds the numeric prediction, and this is what *classifyInstance()* extracts and returns. Conversely, the default implementation of *distributionForInstance()* wraps the prediction obtained from *classifyInstance()* into a single-element array. If the class is nominal, *distributionForInstance()* assigns a probability of 1 to the class predicted by *classifyInstance()* and a probability of 0 to the others. If *classifyInstance()* returns a missing value, all probabilities are set to 0. To give you a better feeling for just what these methods do, the *weka.classifiers.trees.Id3* class overrides them both.

Let's look first at *classifyInstance()*, which predicts a class value for a given instance. As mentioned in the previous section, nominal class values, like nominal attribute values, are coded and stored in *double* variables, representing the index of the value's name in the attribute declaration. This is used in favor of a more elegant object-oriented approach to increase the speed of execution. In the implementation of ID3, *classifyInstance()* first checks whether there are missing attribute values in the instance to be classified; if so, it throws an exception. The class attribute is skipped in this check, or the classifier would not be able to make predictions for new data, where the class is unknown. Otherwise, it descends the tree recursively, guided by the instance's attribute values, until a leaf is reached. Then it returns the class value *m_ClassValue* stored at the leaf. Note that this might be a missing value, in which case the instance is left unclassified. The method *distributionForInstance*() works in exactly the same way; that is, it returns the probability distribution stored in *m_Distribution*.

Most machine learning models, and in particular decision trees, serve as a more or less comprehensible explanation of the structure found in the data. Accordingly, each of Weka's classifiers, like many other Java objects, implements a *toString*() method that produces a textual representation of itself in the form of a *String* variable. *Id3*'s *toString*() method outputs a decision tree in roughly the same format as *J48* (see Figure 11.5). It recursively prints the tree structure into a *String* variable by accessing the attribute information stored at the nodes. To obtain each attribute's name and values, it uses the *name*() and *value*() methods from *weka.core.Attribute*. Empty leaves without a class value are indicated by the string *null*.

toSource()

weka.classifiers.trees.Id3 implements the *Sourcable* interface. Classifiers that implement this interface can produce a source code representation of the learned model, which can be output on the command line by using the –*z* option (see Section 14.3, Table 14.1, page 527). Weka produces a Java class (the name of which is provided by the –*z* option) that can be used to make predictions independently of the Weka libraries. Also output is a class called *WekaWrapper* that extends *Classifier* and uses the named class to make predictions. This class can be used for testing the source code representation of the model within the Weka framework—that is, it can be run from the command line or used in the Explorer interface. Because the actual classifier is hard-coded, the *buildClassifier*() method of the *WekaWrapper* does nothing more than check the data against the capabilities.

Figure 16.2 shows the source code produced by *weka.classifiers.trees.Id3* when run on the nominal-attribute version of the weather data. The name *Id3Weather* was provided with the –*z* option, and a class of this name is shown in Figure 16.2(a). All its methods are static, meaning that they can be used without having to instantiate an *Id3Weather* object. The first method is called *classify* and takes as argument an array of Objects that give the attribute values for the instance to be classified. Each node in the ID3 tree that has been learned is represented in the source code by a static method. The *classify* method passes the instance to be classified to the method corresponding to the root of the tree—*node0*. The *node0* method corresponds to a test on the *outlook* attribute. Because it is not a leaf, it calls a node representing one of the subtrees—which one depends on the value of *outlook* in the instance being classified. Processing of a test instance continues in this fashion until a method corresponding to a leaf node is called, at which point a classification is returned.

Figure 16.2(b) shows the *WekaWrapper* class that uses *Id3Weather*. Its *classifyInstance* method constructs an array of objects to pass to the *classify* method in *Id3Weather*. The attribute values of the test instance are copied into the array and mapped to either String objects (for nominal values) or Double objects (for numeric

```
package weka.classifiers;

class Id3Weather {
  private static void checkMissing(Object[] i, int index) {
    if (i[index] == null)
      throw new IllegalArgumentException("Null values are not allowed!");
  }

  public static double classify(Object[] i) {
    return node0(i);
  }

  protected static double node0(Object[] i) {
    checkMissing(i, 0);

    // outlook
    if (((String) i[0]).equals("sunny"))
      return node1(i);
    else if (((String) i[0]).equals("overcast"))
      return node4(i);
    else if (((String) i[0]).equals("rainy"))
      return node5(i);
    else
      throw new IllegalArgumentException("Value '" + i[0]
                                  + "' is not allowed!");
  }

  protected static double node1(Object[] i) {
    checkMissing(i, 2);

    // humidity
    if (((String) i[2]).equals("high"))
      return node2(i);
    else if (((String) i[2]).equals("normal"))
      return node3(i);
    else
      throw new IllegalArgumentException("Value '" + i[2]
                                  + "' is not allowed!");
  }

  protected static double node2(Object[] i) {
    return 1.0; // no
  }

  protected static double node3(Object[] i) {
    return 0.0; // yes
  }

  protected static double node4(Object[] i) {
    return 0.0; // yes
  }

  protected static double node5(Object[] i) {
    checkMissing(i, 3);

    // windy
    if (((String) i[3]).equals("TRUE"))
      return node6(i);
    else if (((String) i[3]).equals("FALSE"))
      return node7(i);
    else
      throw new IllegalArgumentException("Value '" + i[3]
                                  + "' is not allowed!");
  }

  protected static double node6(Object[] i) {
    return 1.0; // no
  }

  protected static double node7(Object[] i) {
    return 0.0; // yes
  }
}
```

(a)

FIGURE 16.2

Source code produced by *weka.classifiers.trees.Id3* for the weather data: (a) *Id3Weather* class and (b) *WekaWrapper* class.

```
package weka.classifiers;

import weka.core.Attribute;
import weka.core.Capabilities;
import weka.core.Capabilities.Capability;
import weka.core.Instance;
import weka.core.Instances;
import weka.core.RevisionUtils;
import weka.classifiers.Classifier;

public class WekaWrapper
  extends Classifier {

  /**
   * Returns only the toString() method.
   *
   * @return a string describing the classifier
   */
  public String globalInfo() {
    return toString();
  }

  /**
   * Returns the capabilities of this classifier.
   *
   * @return the capabilities
   */
  public Capabilities getCapabilities() {
    weka.core.Capabilities result = new weka.core.Capabilities(this);

    result.enable(weka.core.Capabilities.Capability.NOMINAL_ATTRIBUTES);
    result.enable(weka.core.Capabilities.Capability.NOMINAL_CLASS);
    result.enable(weka.core.Capabilities.Capability.MISSING_CLASS_VALUES);

    result.setMinimumNumberInstances(0);

    return result;
  }

  /**
   * only checks the data against its capabilities.
   *
   * @param i the training data
   */
  public void buildClassifier(Instances i) throws Exception {
    // can classifier handle the data?
    getCapabilities().testWithFail(i);
  }

  /**
   * Classifies the given instance.
   *
   * @param i the instance to classify
   * @return the classification result
   */
  public double classifyInstance(Instance i) throws Exception {
    Object[] s = new Object[i.numAttributes()];
```

(b)

FIGURE 16.2, cont'd

```
      for (int j = 0; j < s.length; j++) {
        if (!i.isMissing(j)) {
          if (i.attribute(j).isNominal())
            s[j] = new String(i.stringValue(j));
          else if (i.attribute(j).isNumeric())
            s[j] = new Double(i.value(j));
        }
      }

      // set class value to missing
      s[i.classIndex()] = null;

      return Id3Weather.classify(s);
    }

    /**
     * Returns the revision string.
     *
     * @return          the revision
     */
    public String getRevision() {
      return RevisionUtils.extract("1.0");
    }

    /**
     * Returns only the classnames and what classifier it is based on.
     *
     * @return a short description
     */
    public String toString() {
      return "Auto-generated classifier wrapper, based on
      weka.classifiers.trees.Id3 (generated with Weka 3.6.2).\n" +
        this.getClass().getName() + "/Id3Weather";
    }

    /**
     * Runs the classfier from commandline.
     *
     * @param args the commandline arguments
     */
    public static void main(String args[]) {
      runClassifier(new WekaWrapper(), args);
    }
  }
```

FIGURE 16.2, cont'd

---

values). If an attribute value is missing in the test instance, its corresponding entry in the array of Objects is set to *null*.

main()

Apart from *getRevision()*, which is optional and simply returns a version identifier, the only method in *Id3* that hasn't been described is *main()*, which is called whenever the class is executed from the command line. As you can see, it's simple: It calls the method *runClassifier()* from its superclass (*Classifier*) with a new instance of *Id3* and the given command-line options. *runClassifier*() tells Weka's *Evaluation* class to evaluate the supplied classifier with the given command-line options and prints the resulting string. The one-line expression in *runClassifier*() that does this calls the *evaluation*() method in Weka's evaluation class and is enclosed in a *try-catch* statement, which catches the various exceptions that can be thrown by Weka's routines or other Java methods.

The *evaluation*() method in *weka.classifiers.Evaluation* interprets the generic scheme-independent command-line options described in Section 14.3 (page 526) and acts appropriately. For example, it takes the *–t* option, which gives the name of the training file, and loads the corresponding dataset. If there is no test file, it performs a cross-validation by creating a classifier object and by repeatedly calling *buildClassifier*() and *classifyInstance*() or *distributionForInstance*() on different subsets of the training data. Unless the user suppresses output of the model by setting the corresponding command-line option, it also calls the *toString*() method to output the model built from the full training dataset.

What happens if the scheme needs to interpret a specific option such as a pruning parameter? This is accomplished using the *OptionHandler* interface in *weka.core*. A classifier that implements this interface contains three methods—*listOptions*(), *setOptions*(), and *getOptions*()—which can be used to list all the classifier's scheme-specific options, to set some of them, and to get the options that are currently set. The *evaluation*() method in *Evaluation* automatically calls these methods if the classifier implements the *OptionHandler* interface. Once the scheme-independent options have been processed, it calls *setOptions*() to process the remaining options before using *buildClassifier*() to generate a new classifier. When it outputs the classifier, it uses *getOptions*() to output a list of the options that are currently set. For a simple example of how to implement these methods, look at the source code for *weka.classifiers.rules.OneR*.

OptionHandler makes it possible to set options from the command line. To set them from within the graphical user interfaces, Weka uses the JavaBeans framework. All that is required are *set...*() and *get...*() methods for every parameter used by the class. For example, the methods *setPruningParameter*() and *getPruningParameter*() would be needed for a pruning parameter. There should also be a *pruningParameterTipText*() method that returns a description of the parameter for the graphical user interface. Again, see *weka.classifiers.rules.OneR* for an example.

Some classifiers can be incrementally updated as new training instances arrive; they don't have to process all the data in one batch. In Weka, incremental classifiers implement the *UpdateableClassifier* interface in *weka.classifiers*. This interface declares only one method, namely *updateClassifier*(), which takes a single training instance as its argument. For an example of how to use this interface, look at the source code for *weka.classifiers.lazy.IBk*.

If a classifier is able to make use of instance weights, it should implement the *WeightedInstancesHandler*() interface from *weka.core*. Then other algorithms, such as those for boosting, can make use of this property.

In *weka.core* there are many other useful interfaces for classifiers—for example, interfaces for classifiers that are *randomizable*, *summarizable*, *drawable*, and *graphable*. For more information on these and other interfaces, look at the Javadoc for the classes in *weka.core*.

16.2 CONVENTIONS FOR IMPLEMENTING CLASSIFIERS

There are some conventions that you must obey when implementing classifiers in Weka. If you do not, things will go awry. For example, Weka's evaluation module might not compute the classifier's statistics properly when evaluating it. The *Check-Classifier* class can be used to check the basic behavior of a classifier, although it cannot catch all problems.

The first convention has already been mentioned: Each time a classifier's *build-Classifier()* method is called, it must reset the model. The *CheckClassifier* class performs tests to ensure that this is the case. When *buildClassifier()* is called on a dataset, the same result must always be obtained regardless of how often the classifier has previously been applied to the same or other datasets. However, *build-Classifier()* must not reset instance variables that correspond to scheme-specific options because these settings must persist through multiple calls of *buildClassi-fier()*. Also, calling *buildClassifier()* must never change the input data.

Two other conventions have also been mentioned. One is that when a classifier cannot make a prediction, its *classifyInstance()* method must return *Instance. missingValue()* and its *distributionForInstance()* method must return probabilities of zero for all classes. The ID3 implementation shown earlier in Figure 16.1 does this. Another convention is that with classifiers for numeric prediction, *classifyInstance()* returns the numeric value that the classifier predicts. Some classifiers, however, are able to predict nominal classes and their class probabilities, as well as numeric class values—*weka.classifiers.lazy.IBk* is an example. These implement the *distribution-ForInstance()* method, and if the class is numeric it returns an array of size 1, whose only element contains the predicted numeric value.

Another convention—not absolutely essential but useful nonetheless—is that every classifier implements a *toString()* method that outputs a textual description of itself.

Capabilities

We close this chapter with a closer look at the idea of "capabilities." As mentioned earlier, these allow a learning scheme to indicate what data characteristics it can handle. This information is displayed in the object editor when the user presses the *Capabilities* button; it also serves to disable the application of a scheme in the Explorer interface when the current data does not match its stated capabilities.

To ease the programming burden for those new to developing with Weka, the superclasses of the major types of learning scheme—*Classifier, AbstractClusterer,* and *AbstractAssociator*—disable all capabilities constraints by default. This allows programmers to focus on the main task of implementing the learning functionality without having to bother with capabilities. However, once satisfied that the scheme is working correctly, the programmer should specify capabilities that reflect the scheme's ability to handle various data characteristics by overriding the superclass's *getCapabilities()* method. This method returns a *weka.core.Capabilities* object that encapsulates the characteristics that the scheme can handle.

In Figure 16.1, *Id3*'s *getCapabilities()* method first obtains a *Capabilities* object by calling *super.getCapabilities()*. This returns a *Capabilities* object without any constraints. The best way to proceed is to call the *disableAll()* method on the *Capabilities* object and then enable the relevant characteristics—those that the scheme

Enum Constant Summary
BINARY_ATTRIBUTES can handle binary attributes
BINARY_CLASS can handle binary classes
DATE_ATTRIBUTES can handle date attributes
DATE_CLASS can handle date classes
EMPTY_NOMINAL_ATTRIBUTES can handle empty nominal attributes
EMPTY_NOMINAL_CLASS can handle empty nominal classes
MISSING_CLASS_VALUES can handle missing values in class attribute
MISSING_VALUES can handle missing values in attributes
NO_CLASS can handle data without class attribute, eg clusterers
NOMINAL_ATTRIBUTES can handle nominal attributes
NOMINAL_CLASS can handle nominal classes
NUMERIC_ATTRIBUTES can handle numeric attributes
NUMERIC_CLASS can handle numeric classes
ONLY_MULTIINSTANCE can handle multi-instance data
RELATIONAL_ATTRIBUTES can handle relational attributes
RELATIONAL_CLASS can handle relational classes
STRING_ATTRIBUTES can handle string attributes
STRING_CLASS can handle string classes
UNARY_ATTRIBUTES can handle unary attributes
UNARY_CLASS can handle unary classes

FIGURE 16.3

Javadoc for the *Capability* enumeration.

can handle. *Id3* does just this, enabling the ability to handle nominal attributes, a nominal class attribute, and missing class values. It also specifies that a minimum of zero training instances are required. For the most part, individual capabilities are turned on or off by calling the *enable*() or *disable*() method of the *Capabilities* object. These methods take constants that are defined in the enumeration shown in Figure 16.3, which is part of the *Capabilities* class.

Tutorial Exercises for the Weka Explorer

17

The best way to learn about the Explorer interface is simply to use it. This chapter presents a series of tutorial exercises that will help you learn about Explorer and also about practical data mining in general. The first section is introductory, but we think you will find the exercises in the later sections quite thought-provoking.

We begin with a quick, guided tour of the Explorer interface, examining each of the panels and what they can do, which largely parallels the introduction given in Chapter 11. Our screenshots are from Weka 3.6, although almost everything is the same with other versions.

17.1 INTRODUCTION TO THE EXPLORER INTERFACE

Invoke Weka from the Windows Start menu (on Linux or the Mac, double-click *weka.jar* or *weka.app*, respectively). This starts up the Weka GUI Chooser (shown in Figure 11.3(a)). Click the *Explorer* button to enter the Weka Explorer. The Pre-process panel (shown in Figure 11.3(b)) opens up when the Explorer interface is started.

Loading a Dataset

Load a dataset by clicking the *Open file* button in the top left corner of the panel. Inside the *data* folder, which is supplied when Weka is installed, you will find a file named *weather.nominal.arff*. This contains the nominal version of the standard "weather" dataset in Table 1.2. Open this file (the screen will look like Figure 11.3(b)).

As the result shows, the weather data has 14 instances, and 5 attributes called *outlook*, *temperature*, *humidity*, *windy*, and *play*. Click on the name of an attribute in the left subpanel to see information about the selected attribute on the right, such as its values and how many times an instance in the dataset has a particular value. This information is also shown in the form of a histogram. All attributes in this dataset are "nominal"—that is, they have a predefined finite set of values. The last attribute, *play*, is the "class" attribute; its value can be *yes* or *no*.

Familiarize yourself with the Preprocess panel by doing the following exercises.

Exercise 17.1.1. What are the values that the attribute *temperature* can have?

Exercise 17.1.2. Load a new dataset. Click the *Open file* button and select the file *iris.arff*, which corresponds to the iris dataset in Table 1.4. How many instances does this dataset have? How many attributes? What is the range of possible values of the attribute *petallength*?

The Dataset Editor

It is possible to view and edit an entire dataset from within Weka. To do this, load the *weather.nominal.arff* file again. Click the *Edit* button from the row of buttons at the top of the Preprocess panel. This opens a new window called Viewer, which lists all instances of the weather data (see Figure 17.1).

Exercise 17.1.3. What is the function of the first column in the Viewer window?

Exercise 17.1.4. What is the class value of instance number 8 in the weather data?

Exercise 17.1.5. Load the iris data and open it in the editor. How many numeric and how many nominal attributes does this dataset have?

Relation: weather.symbolic

No.	outlook Nominal	temperature Nominal	humidity Nominal	windy Nominal	play Nominal
1	sunny	hot	high	FALSE	no
2	sunny	hot	high	TRUE	no
3	overcast	hot	high	FALSE	yes
4	rainy	mild	high	FALSE	yes
5	rainy	cool	normal	FALSE	yes
6	rainy	cool	normal	TRUE	no
7	overcast	cool	normal	TRUE	yes
8	sunny	mild	high	FALSE	no
9	sunny	cool	normal	FALSE	yes
10	rainy	mild	normal	FALSE	yes
11	sunny	mild	normal	TRUE	yes
12	overcast	mild	high	TRUE	yes
13	overcast	hot	normal	FALSE	yes
14	rainy	mild	high	TRUE	no

FIGURE 17.1

The data viewer.

Applying a Filter

As you know, Weka "filters" can be used to modify datasets in a systematic fashion—that is, they are data preprocessing tools. Reload the *weather.nominal* dataset, and let's remove an attribute from it. The appropriate filter is called *Remove*; its full name is

```
weka.filters.unsupervised.attribute.Remove
```

Examine this name carefully. Filters are organized into a hierarchical structure of which the root is *weka*. Those in the *unsupervised* category don't require a class attribute to be set; those in the *supervised* category do. Filters are further divided into ones that operate primarily on attributes (the *attribute* category) and ones that operate primarily on instances (the *instance* category).

Click the *Choose* button in the Preprocess panel to open a hierarchical menu (shown in Figure 11.9(a)) from which you select a filter by following the path corresponding to its full name. Use the path given in the full name above to select the *Remove* filter. The text "Remove" will appear in the field next to the *Choose* button.

Click on the field containing this text. The Generic Object Editor window, which is used throughout Weka to set parameter values for all of the tools, opens. In this case it contains a short explanation of the *Remove* filter (shown in Figure 11.9(b))—click *More* to get a fuller description (Figure 11.9(c)). Enter *3* into the *attribute-Indices* field and click the *OK* button. The window with the filter options closes. Now click the *Apply* button on the right, which runs the data through the filter. The filter removes the attribute with index 3 from the dataset, and you can see that this has happened. This change does not affect the dataset in the file; it only applies to the data held in memory. The changed dataset can be saved to a new ARFF file by pressing the *Save* button and entering a file name. The action of the filter can be undone by pressing the *Undo* button. Again, this applies to the version of the data held in memory.

What we have described illustrates how filters are applied to data. However, in the particular case of *Remove*, there is a simpler way of achieving the same effect. Instead of invoking a filter, attributes can be selected using the small boxes in the Attributes subpanel and removed using the *Remove* button that appears at the bottom, below the list of attributes.

Exercise 17.1.6. Load the *weather.nominal* dataset. Use the filter *weka. unsupervised.instance.RemoveWithValues* to remove all instances in which the *humidity* attribute has the value *high*. To do this, first make the field next to the *Choose* button show the text *RemoveWithValues*. Then click on it to get the Generic Object Editor window, and figure out how to change the filter settings appropriately.

Exercise 17.1.7. Undo the change to the dataset that you just performed, and verify that the data has reverted to its original state.

The Visualize Panel

Now take a look at Weka's data visualization facilities. These work best with numeric data, so we use the iris data. Load *iris.arff*, which contains the iris dataset of Table 1.4 containing 50 examples of three types of Iris: *Iris setosa*, *Iris versicolor*, and *Iris virginica*.

Click the *Visualize* tab to bring up the Visualize panel (shown in Figure 11.17). Click the first plot in the second row to open up a window showing an enlarged plot using the selected axes. Instances are shown as little crosses, the color of which depends on the instance's class. The *x*-axis shows the *sepallength* attribute, and the *y*-axis shows *petalwidth*.

Clicking on one of the crosses opens up an Instance Info window, which lists the values of all attributes for the selected instance. Close the Instance Info window again.

The selection fields at the top of the window containing the scatter plot determine which attributes are used for the *x*- and *y*-axes. Change the *x*-axis to *petalwidth* and the *y*-axis to *petallength*. The field showing *Color: class (Num)* can be used to change the color coding.

Each of the barlike plots to the right of the scatter plot window represents a single attribute. In each bar, instances are placed at the appropriate horizontal position and scattered randomly in the vertical direction. Clicking a bar uses that attribute for the *x*-axis of the scatter plot. Right-clicking a bar does the same for the *y*-axis. Use these bars to change the *x*- and *y*-axes back to *sepallength* and *petalwidth*.

The *Jitter* slider displaces the cross for each instance randomly from its true position, and can reveal situations where instances lie on top of one another. Experiment a little by moving the slider.

The *Select Instance* button and the *Reset*, *Clear*, and *Save* buttons let you modify the dataset. Certain instances can be selected and the others removed. Try the Rectangle option: Select an area by left-clicking and dragging the mouse. The *Reset* button changes into a *Submit* button. Click it, and all instances outside the rectangle are deleted. You could use *Save* to save the modified dataset to a file. *Reset* restores the original dataset.

The Classify Panel

Now we apply a classifier to the weather data. Load the weather data again. Go to the Preprocess panel, click the *Open file* button, and select *weather.nominal.arff* from the data directory. Then switch to the Classify panel (shown in Figure 11.4(b)) by clicking the *Classify* tab at the top of the window.

Using the C4.5 Classifier

As you learned in Chapter 11 (page 410), the C4.5 algorithm for building decision trees is implemented in Weka as a classifier called *J48*. Select it by clicking the *Choose* button near the top of the *Classify* tab. A dialog window appears showing various types of classifier. Click the *trees* entry to reveal its subentries, and click *J48* to choose that classifier. Classifiers, like filters, are organized in a hierarchy: *J48* has the full name *weka.classifiers.trees.J48*.

The classifier is shown in the text box next to the *Choose* button: It now reads *J48 –C 0.25 –M 2*. This text gives the default parameter settings for this classifier, which in this case rarely require changing to obtain good performance.

For illustrative purposes we evaluate the performance using the training data, which has been loaded in the Preprocess panel—this is *not* generally a good idea because it leads to unrealistically optimistic performance estimates. Choose *Use training set* from the *Test options* part of the Classify panel. Once the test strategy has been set, the classifier is built and evaluated by pressing the *Start* button. This processes the training set using the currently selected learning algorithm, C4.5 in this case. Then it classifies all the instances in the training data and outputs performance statistics. These are shown in Figure 17.2(a).

Interpreting the Output

The outcome of training and testing appears in the Classifier Output box on the right. Scroll through the text and examine it. First, look at the part that describes the decision tree, reproduced in Figure 17.2(b). This represents the decision tree that was built, including the number of instances that fall under each leaf. The textual representation is clumsy to interpret, but Weka can generate an equivalent graphical version.

Here's how to get the graphical tree. Each time the *Start* button is pressed and a new classifier is built and evaluated, a new entry appears in the Result List panel in the lower left corner of Figure 17.2(a). To see the tree, right-click on the entry *trees.J48* that has just been added to the result list and choose *Visualize tree*. A window pops up that shows the decision tree in the form illustrated in Figure 17.3. Right-click a blank spot in this window to bring up a new menu enabling you to auto-scale the view. You can pan around by dragging the mouse.

Now look at the rest of the information in the Classifier Output area. The next two parts of the output report on the quality of the classification model based on the chosen test option.

This text states how many and what proportion of test instances have been correctly classified:

```
Correctly Classified Instances   14   100%
```

This is the accuracy of the model on the data used for testing. In this case it is completely accurate (100%), which is often the case when the training set is used for testing.

At the bottom of the output is the confusion matrix:

```
=== Confusion Matrix ===

 a b   <- classified as
 9 0 | a = yes
 0 5 | b = no
```

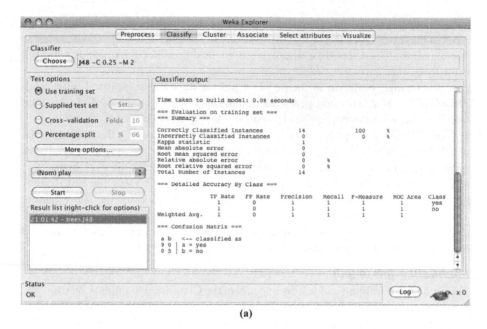

(a)

```
J48 pruned tree
------------------

outlook = sunny
|   humidity = high: no (3.0)
|   humidity = normal: yes (2.0)
outlook = overcast: yes (4.0)
outlook = rainy
|   windy = TRUE: no (2.0)
|   windy = FALSE: yes (3.0)

Number of Leaves  :   5

Size of the tree :    8
```

(b)

FIGURE 17.2

Output after building and testing the classifier: (a) screenshot and (b) decision tree.

Each element in the matrix is a count of instances. Rows represent the true classes, and columns represent the predicted classes. As you can see, all 9 *yes* instances have been predicted as *yes*, and all 5 *no* instances as *no*.

Exercise 17.1.8. How would this instance be classified using the decision tree?

outlook = sunny, temperature = cool, humidity = high, windy = TRUE

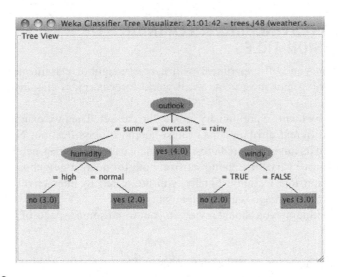

FIGURE 17.3

The decision tree that has been built.

Setting the Test Method

When the *Start* button is pressed, the selected learning algorithm is run and the dataset that was loaded in the Preprocess panel is used with the selected test protocol. For example, in the case of tenfold cross-validation this involves running the learning algorithm 10 times to build and evaluate 10 classifiers. A model built from the *full* training set is then printed into the Classifier Output area: This may involve running the learning algorithm one final time. The remainder of the output depends on the test protocol that was chosen using test options; these options were discussed in Section 11.1.

> **Exercise 17.1.9.** Load the iris data using the Preprocess panel. Evaluate C4.5 on this data using (a) the training set and (b) cross-validation. What is the estimated percentage of correct classifications for (a) and (b)? Which estimate is more realistic?

Visualizing Classification Errors

Right-click the *trees.J48* entry in the result list and choose *Visualize classifier errors*. A scatter plot window pops up. Instances that have been classified correctly are marked by little crosses; ones that are incorrect are marked by little squares.

> **Exercise 17.1.10.** Use the *Visualize classifier errors* function to find the wrongly classified test instances for the cross-validation performed in Exercise 17.1.9. What can you say about the location of the errors?

17.2 NEAREST-NEIGHBOR LEARNING AND DECISION TREES

In this section you will experiment with nearest-neighbor classification and decision tree learning. For most of it, a real-world forensic glass classification dataset is used.

We begin by taking a preliminary look at the dataset. Then we examine the effect of selecting different attributes for nearest-neighbor classification. Next we study class noise and its impact on predictive performance for the nearest-neighbor method. Following that we vary the training set size, both for nearest-neighbor classification and for decision tree learning. Finally, you are asked to interactively construct a decision tree for an image segmentation dataset.

Before continuing you should review in your mind some aspects of the classification task:

- How is the accuracy of a classifier measured?
- To make a good classifier, are all the attributes necessary?
- What is class noise, and how would you measure its effect on learning?
- What is a learning curve?
- If you, personally, had to invent a decision tree classifier for a particular dataset, how would you go about it?

The Glass Dataset

The glass dataset *glass.arff* from the U.S. Forensic Science Service contains data on six types of glass. Glass is described by its refractive index and the chemical elements that it contains; the the aim is to classify different types of glass based on these features. This dataset is taken from the UCI datasets, which have been collected by the University of California at Irvine and are freely available on the Web. They are often used as a benchmark for comparing data mining algorithms.

Find the dataset *glass.arff* and load it into the Explorer interface. For your own information, answer the following exercises, which review material covered in the previous section.

Exercise 17.2.1. How many attributes are there in the dataset? What are their names? What is the class attribute? Run the classification algorithm *IBk* (*weka.classifiers.lazy.IBk*). Use cross-validation to test its performance, leaving the number of folds at the default value of 10. Recall that you can examine the classifier options in the Generic Object Editor window that pops up when you click the text beside the *Choose* button. The default value of the KNN field is 1: This sets the number of neighboring instances to use when classifying.

Exercise 17.2.2. What is the accuracy of *IBk* (given in the Classifier Output box)? Run *IBk* again, but increase the number of neighboring instances to $k = 5$ by entering this value in the KNN field. Here and throughout this section, continue to use cross-validation as the evaluation method.

Exercise 17.2.3. What is the accuracy of *IBk* with five neighboring instances ($k = 5$)?

Attribute Selection

Now we investigate which subset of attributes produces the best cross-validated classification accuracy for the *IBk* algorithm on the glass dataset. Weka contains automated attribute selection facilities, which are examined in a later section, but it is instructive to do this manually.

Performing an exhaustive search over all possible subsets of the attributes is infeasible (why?), so we apply the backward elimination procedure described in Section 7.1 (page 311). To do this, first consider dropping each attribute individually from the full dataset, and run a cross-validation for each reduced version. Once you have determined the best eight-attribute dataset, repeat the procedure with this reduced dataset to find the best seven-attribute dataset, and so on.

Exercise 17.2.4. Record in Table 17.1 the best attribute set and the greatest accuracy obtained in each iteration. The best accuracy obtained in this process is quite a bit higher than the accuracy obtained on the full dataset.

Exercise 17.2.5. Is this best accuracy an unbiased estimate of accuracy on future data? Be sure to explain your answer. (*Hint:* To obtain an unbiased estimate of accuracy on future data, we must not look at the test data *at all*

Table 17.1 Accuracy Obtained Using *IBk*, for Different Attribute Subsets

Subset Size (No. of Attributes)	Attributes in "Best" Subset	Classification Accuracy
9		
8		
7		
6		
5		
4		
3		
2		
1		
0		

when producing the classification model for which the estimate is being obtained.)

Class Noise and Nearest-Neighbor Learning

Nearest-neighbor learning, like other techniques, is sensitive to noise in the training data. In this section we inject varying amounts of class noise into the data and observe the effect on classification performance.

You can flip a certain percentage of class labels in the data to a randomly chosen other value using an unsupervised attribute filter called *AddNoise*, in *weka. filters.unsupervised.attribute*. However, for this experiment it is important that the test data remains unaffected by class noise. Filtering the training data without filtering the test data is a common requirement, and is achieved using a metale-arner called *FilteredClassifier*, in *weka.classifiers.meta*, as described near the end of Section 11.3 (page 444). This metalearner should be configured to use *IBk* as the classifier and *AddNoise* as the filter. *FilteredClassifier* applies the filter to the data before running the learning algorithm. This is done in two batches: first the training data and then the test data. The *AddNoise* filter only adds noise to the first batch of data it encounters, which means that the test data passes through unchanged.

> **Exercise 17.2.6.** Record in Table 17.2 the cross-validated accuracy estimate of *IBk* for 10 different percentages of class noise and neighborhood sizes $k = 1$, $k = 3$, $k = 5$ (determined by the value of k in the k-nearest-neighbor classifier).
>
> **Exercise 17.2.7.** What is the effect of increasing the amount of class noise?
>
> **Exercise 17.2.8.** What is the effect of altering the value of k?

Table 17.2 Effect of Class Noise on *IBk*, for Different Neighborhood Sizes

Percentage Noise	$k = 1$	$k = 3$	$k = 5$
0%			
10%			
20%			
30%			
40%			
50%			
60%			
70%			
80%			
90%			
100%			

Table 17.3 Effect of Training Set Size on *IBk* and *J48*

Percentage of Training Set	IBk	J48
10%		
20%		
30%		
40%		
50%		
60%		
70%		
80%		
90%		
100%		

Varying the Amount of Training Data

This section examines learning curves, which show the effect of gradually increasing the amount of training data. Again, we use the glass data, but this time with both *IBk* and the C4.5 decision tree learners, implemented in Weka as *J48*.

To obtain learning curves, use *FilteredClassifier* again, this time in conjunction with *weka.filters.unsupervised.instance.Resample*, which extracts a certain specified percentage of a given dataset and returns the reduced dataset.[1] Again, this is done only for the first batch to which the filter is applied, so the test data passes unmodified through the *FilteredClassifier* before it reaches the classifier.

> **Exercise 17.2.9.** Record in Table 17.3 the data for learning curves for both the one-nearest-neighbor classifier (i.e., *IBk* with *k* = 1) and *J48*.
> **Exercise 17.2.10.** What is the effect of increasing the amount of training data?
> **Exercise 17.2.11.** Is this effect more pronounced for *IBk* or *J48*?

Interactive Decision Tree Construction

One of Weka's classifiers is interactive: It lets the user—you!—construct your own classifier. Here's a competition: Who can build a classifier with the highest predictive accuracy?

Follow the procedure described in Section 11.2 (page 424). Load the file *segment-challenge.arff* (in the data folder that comes with the Weka distribution). This dataset

---

[1]This filter performs sampling with replacement, rather than sampling without replacement, but the effect is minor and we will ignore it here.

has 20 attributes and 7 classes. It is an image segmentation problem, and the task is to classify images into seven different groups based on properties of the pixels.

Set the classifier to *UserClassifier*, in the *weka.classifiers.trees* package. We use a separate test set (performing cross-validation with *UserClassifier* is incredibly tedious!), so in the *Test options* box choose the *Supplied test set* option and click the *Set* button. A small window appears in which you choose the test set. Click *Open file* and browse to the file *segment-test.arff* (also in the Weka distribution's data folder). On clicking *Open*, the small window updates to show the number of attributes (20) in the data. The number of instances is not displayed because test instances are read incrementally (so that the Explorer interface can process larger test files than can be accommodated in main memory).

Click *Start*. *UserClassifier* differs from all other classifiers: It opens a special window and waits for you to build your own classifier in it. The tabs at the top of the window switch between two views of the classifier. The *Tree visualizer* shows the current state of your tree, and the nodes give the number of class values there. The aim is to come up with a tree of which the leaf nodes are as pure as possible. To begin with, the tree has just one node—the root node—containing all the data. More nodes will appear when you proceed to split the data in the *Data visualizer*.

Click the *Data visualizer* tab to see a two-dimensional plot in which the data points are color-coded by class, with the same facilities as the Visualize panel discussed in Section 17.1. Try different combinations of *x*- and *y*-axes to get the clearest separation you can find between the colors. Having found a good separation, you then need to select a region in the plot: This will create a branch in the tree. Here's a hint to get you started: Plot *region-centroid-row* on the *x*-axis and *intensity-mean* on the *y*-axis (the display is shown in Figure 11.14(a)); you can see that the red class (*sky*) is nicely separated from the rest of the classes at the top of the plot.

There are four tools for selecting regions in the graph, chosen using the dropdown menu below the *y*-axis selector. *Select Instance* identifies a particular instance. *Rectangle* (shown in Figure 11.14(a)) allows you to drag out a rectangle on the graph. With *Polygon* and *Polyline* you build a free-form polygon or draw a free-form polyline (left-click to add a vertex and right-click to complete the operation).

When you have selected an area using any of these tools, it turns gray. (In Figure 11.14(a) the user has defined a rectangle.) Clicking the *Clear* button cancels the selection without affecting the classifier. When you are happy with the selection, click *Submit*. This creates two new nodes in the tree, one holding all the instances covered by the selection and the other holding all remaining instances. These nodes correspond to a binary split that performs the chosen geometric test.

Switch back to the *Tree visualizer* view to examine the change in the tree. Clicking on different nodes alters the subset of data that is shown in the *Data visualizer* section. Continue adding nodes until you obtain a good separation of the classes—that is, the leaf nodes in the tree are mostly pure. Remember, however, that you should not overfit the data because your tree will be evaluated on a separate test set.

When you are satisfied with the tree, right-click any blank space in the *Tree visualizer* view and choose *Accept The Tree*. Weka evaluates the tree against the test set and outputs statistics that show how well you did.

Exercise 17.2.12. You are competing for the best accuracy score of a hand-built *UserClassifier* produced on the *segment-challenge* dataset and tested on the *segment-test* set. Try as many times as you like. When you have a good score (anything close to 90% correct or better), right-click the corresponding entry in the Result list, save the output using *Save result buffer*, and copy it into your answer for this exercise. Then run *J48* on the data to see how well an automatic decision tree learner performs on the task.

17.3 CLASSIFICATION BOUNDARIES

In this section we examine the classification boundaries that are produced by different types of models. To do this, we use Weka's *Boundary Visualizer*, which is not part of the Explorer interface. To find it, start up the Weka GUI Chooser as usual from the Windows Start menu (on Linux or the Mac, double-click *weka.jar* or *weka.app*, respectively) and select *BoundaryVisualizer* from the *Visualization* menu at the top.

The boundary visualizer shows a two-dimensional plot of the data and is most appropriate for datasets with two numeric attributes. We will use a version of the iris data without the first two attributes. To create this, start up the Explorer interface, load *iris.arff* using the *Open file* button, and remove the first two attributes (*sepallength* and *sepalwidth*) by selecting them and clicking the *Remove* button that appears at the bottom. Then save the modified dataset to a file (using *Save*) called, say, *iris.2D.arff*.

Now leave the Explorer interface and open this file for visualization using the boundary visualizer's *Open file* button. Initially, the plot just shows the data in the dataset.

Visualizing 1R

The purpose of the boundary visualizer is to show the predictions of a given model for every possible combination of attribute values—that is, for every point in the two-dimensional space. The points are color-coded according to the prediction the model generates. We will use this to investigate the decision boundaries that different classifiers generate for the reduced iris dataset.

Start with the 1R rule learner. Use the *Choose* button of the boundary visualizer to select *weka.classifiers.rules.OneR*. Make sure you tick *Plot training data*; otherwise, only the predictions will be plotted. Then click the *Start* button. The program starts plotting predictions in successive scan lines. Click the *Stop* button once the plot has stabilized—as soon as you like, in this case—and the training data will be superimposed on the boundary visualization.

> **Exercise 17.3.1.** Explain the plot based on what you know about 1R. (*Hint:* Use the Explorer interface to look at the rule set that 1R generates for this data.)
>
> **Exercise 17.3.2.** Study the effect of the *minBucketSize* parameter on the classifier by regenerating the plot with values of 1, and then 20, and then some critical values in between. Describe what you see, and explain it. (*Hint:* You could speed things up by using the Explorer interface to look at the rule sets.)

Now answer the following questions by thinking about the internal workings of 1R. (*Hint:* It will probably be fastest to use the Explorer interface to look at the rule sets.)

> **Exercise 17.3.3.** You saw earlier that when visualizing 1R the plot always has three regions. But why aren't there more for small bucket sizes (e.g., 1)? Use what you know about 1R to explain this apparent anomaly.
>
> **Exercise 17.3.4.** Can you set *minBucketSize* to a value that results in less than three regions? What is the smallest possible number of regions? What is the smallest value for *minBucketSize* that gives this number of regions? Explain the result based on what you know about the iris data.

Visualizing Nearest-Neighbor Learning

Now let's examine the classification boundaries created by the nearest-neighbor method. Use the boundary visualizer's *Choose* button to select the *IBk* classifier (*weka.classifiers.lazy.IBk*) and plot its decision boundaries for the reduced iris data.

OneR's predictions are categorical: For each instance, they predict one of the three classes. In contrast, *IBk* outputs probability estimates for each class, and the boundary visualizer uses them to mix the colors red, green, and blue that correspond to the three classes. *IBk* estimates class probabilities by looking at the set of k-nearest neighbors of a test instance and counting the number in each class.

> **Exercise 17.3.5.** With $k = 1$, which is the default value, it seems that the set of k-nearest neighbors could have only one member and therefore the color will always be pure red, green, or blue. Looking at the plot, this is indeed almost always the case: There is no mixing of colors because one class gets a probability of 1 and the others a probability of 0. Nevertheless, there is a small area in the plot where two colors are in fact mixed. Explain this. (*Hint:* Examine the data carefully using the Explorer interface's Visualize panel.)
>
> **Exercise 17.3.6.** Experiment with different values of k, say 5 and 10. Describe what happens as k increases.

Visualizing *NaïveBayes*

Turn now to the *NaïveBayes* classifier. Its assumption that attributes are conditionally independent given a particular class value means that the overall class probability is obtained by simply multiplying the per-attribute conditional probabilities together (and taking into account the class prior probabilities as well). In other words, with two attributes, if you know the class probabilities along the x- and y-axes (and the class prior), you can calculate the value for any point in space by multiplying them together (and then normalizing). This is easy to understand if you visualize it as a boundary plot.

Plot the predictions of *NaïveBayes*. But first discretize the attribute values. By default, Weka's *NaiveBayes* classifier assumes that the attributes are normally distributed given the class. You should override this by setting *useSupervisedDiscretization* to *true* using the Generic Object Editor window. This will cause *NaïveBayes* to discretize the numeric attributes in the data with a supervised discretization technique. In most practical applications of *NaïveBayes*, supervised discretization works better than the default method. It also produces a more comprehensible visualization, which is why we use it here.

> **Exercise 17.3.7.** The plot that is generated by visualizing the predicted class probabilities of *NaïveBayes* for each pixel location is quite different from anything we have seen so far. Explain the patterns in it.

Visualizing Decision Trees and Rule Sets

Decision trees and rule sets are similar to nearest-neighbor learning in the sense that they are quasi-universal: In principle, they can approximate any decision boundary arbitrarily closely. In this section, we look at the boundaries generated by *JRip* and *J48*.

Generate a plot for *JRip*, with default options.

> **Exercise 17.3.8.** What do you see? Relate the plot to the output of the rules that you get by processing the data in the Explorer.
>
> **Exercise 17.3.9.** The *JRip* output assumes that the rules will be executed in the correct sequence. Write down an equivalent set of rules that achieves the same effect regardless of the order in which they are executed. Generate a plot for *J48*, with default options.
>
> **Exercise 17.3.10.** What do you see? Again, relate the plot to the output that you get by processing the data in the Explorer interface. One way to control how much pruning *J48* performs is to adjust the minimum number of instances required in a leaf, *minNumObj*.
>
> **Exercise 17.3.11.** Suppose you want to generate trees with 3, 2, and 1 leaf node, respectively. What are the exact ranges of values for *minNumObj* that achieve this, given default values for the other parameters?

Messing with the Data

With the Boundary Visualizer you can modify the data by adding or removing points.

> **Exercise 17.3.12.** Introduce some noise into the data and study the effect on the learning algorithms we looked at above. What kind of behavior do you observe for each algorithm as you introduce more noise?

17.4 PREPROCESSING AND PARAMETER TUNING

Now we look at some useful preprocessing techniques, which are implemented as filters, as well as a method for automatic parameter tuning.

Discretization

As we know, there are two types of discretization techniques: *unsupervised* ones, which are "class blind," and *supervised* ones, which take the class value of the instances into account when creating intervals. Weka's main unsupervised method for discretizing numeric attributes is *weka.filters.unsupervised.attribute.Discretize*. It implements these two methods: equal-width (the default) and equal-frequency discretization.

Find the glass dataset *glass.arff* and load it into the Explorer interface. Apply the unsupervised discretization filter in the two different modes explained previously.

> **Exercise 17.4.1.** What do you observe when you compare the histograms obtained? The one for equal-frequency discretization is quite skewed for some attributes. Why?

The main *supervised* technique for discretizing numeric attributes is *weka.filters. supervised.attribute.Discretize*. Locate the iris data, load it, apply the supervised discretization scheme, and look at the histograms obtained. Supervised discretization strives to create intervals within which the class distribution is consistent, although the distributions vary from one interval to the next.

> **Exercise 17.4.2.** Based on the histograms obtained, which of the discretized attributes would you consider to be most predictive? Reload the glass data and apply supervised discretization to it.
>
> **Exercise 17.4.3.** For some attributes there is only a single bar in the histogram. What does that mean?

Discretized attributes are normally coded as nominal attributes, with one value per range. However, because the ranges are ordered, a discretized attribute is actually on an ordinal scale. Both filters have the ability to create binary attributes rather than multivalued ones, by setting the option *makeBinary* to *true*.

Exercise 17.4.4. Choose one of the filters and use it to create binary attributes. Compare the result with the output generated when *makeBinary* is *false*. What do the binary attributes represent?

More on Discretization

Here we examine the effect of discretization when building a *J48* decision tree for the data in *ionosphere.arff*. This dataset contains information about radar signals returned from the ionosphere. "Good" samples are those showing evidence of some type of structure in the ionosphere, while for "bad" ones the signals pass directly through the ionosphere. For more details, take a look at the comments in the ARFF file. Begin with unsupervised discretization.

Exercise 17.4.5. For *J48*, compare cross-validated accuracy and the size of the trees generated for (1) the raw data, (2) data discretized by the unsupervised discretization method in default mode, and (3) data discretized by the same method with binary attributes.

Now turn to supervised discretization. Here a subtle issue arises, discussed near the end of Section 11.3 (page 432). If Exercise 17.4.5 were simply repeated using a supervised discretization method, the result would be overoptimistic. In effect, because cross-validation is used for evaluation, *the data in the test set has been taken into account when determining the discretization intervals*. This does not give a fair estimate of performance on fresh data.

To evaluate supervised discretization fairly, use *FilteredClassifier* from Weka's metalearners. This builds the filter using the training data only, and then evaluates it on the test data using the discretization intervals computed for the training data. After all, that is how you would have to process fresh data in practice.

Exercise 17.4.6. Using *FilteredClassifier* and *J48*, compare cross-validated accuracy and the size of the trees generated for (4) supervised discretization in default mode, and (5) supervised discretization with binary attributes.
Exercise 17.4.7. Compare these with the results for the raw data from Exercise 17.4.5. How can decision trees generated from discretized data possibly be better predictors than ones built from raw numeric data?

Automatic Attribute Selection

In most practical applications of supervised learning not all attributes are equally useful for predicting the target. For some learning schemes, redundant and/or irrelevant attributes can result in less accurate models. As you found in Section 17.2, it is tedious to identify useful attributes in a dataset manually; automatic attribute selection methods are usually more appropriate.

Attribute selection methods can be divided into filter and wrapper methods (see Section 7.1, page 308). The former apply a computationally efficient heuristic to measure the quality of a subset of attributes; the latter measure the quality of an attribute subset by building and evaluating an actual classification model, which is more expensive but often delivers superior performance.

The Explorer interface's Select attributes panel applies attribute selection methods to datasets. The default is to use *CfsSubsetEval*, described in Section 11.8 (page 488), which evaluates subsets of attributes. An alternative is to evaluate attributes individually using an evaluator like *InfoGainAttributeEval* (see Section 11.8, page 491) and then rank them by applying a special "search" method, namely the *Ranker*, as described Section 11.8 (page 490).

Exercise 17.4.8. Apply the ranking technique to the labor negotiations data in *labor.arff* to determine the four most important attributes based on information gain.[2]

CfsSubsetEval aims to identify a subset of attributes that are highly correlated with the target while not being strongly correlated with one another. It searches through the space of possible attribute subsets for the "best" one using the *BestFirst* search method by default, although other methods can be chosen. In fact, choosing *GreedyStepwise* and setting *searchBackwards* to *true* gives backward elimination, the search method you used manually in Section 17.2.

To use the wrapper method rather than a filter method, such as *CfsSubsetEval*, first select *WrapperSubsetEval* and then configure it by choosing a learning algorithm to apply and setting the number of cross-validation folds to use when evaluating it on each attribute subset.

Exercise 17.4.9. On the same data, run *CfsSubsetEval* for correlation-based selection, using the *BestFirst* search. Then run the wrapper method with *J48* as the base learner, again using the *BestFirst* search. Examine the attribute subsets that are output. Which attributes are selected by both methods? How do they relate to the output generated by ranking using information gain?

More on Automatic Attribute Selection

The *Select attributes* panel allows us to gain insight into a dataset by applying attribute selection methods to it. However, as with supervised discretization, using this information to reduce a dataset becomes problematic if some of the reduced data is used for testing the model (as in cross-validation). Again, the reason is that we have

---

[2]Note that most evaluators, including *InfoGainAttributeEval* and *CfsSubsetEval*, discretize numeric attributes using Weka's supervised discretization method before evaluating them.

looked at the class labels in the test data while selecting attributes, and using the test data to influence the construction of a model biases the accuracy estimates obtained.

This can be avoided by dividing the data into training and test sets and applying attribute selection to the training set only. However, it is usually more convenient to use *AttributeSelectedClassifer*, one of Weka's metalearners, which allows an attribute selection method and a learning algorithm to be specified as part of a classification scheme. *AttributeSelectedClassifier* ensures that the chosen set of attributes is selected based on the training data only.

Now we test the three attribute selection methods from above in conjunction with *NaïveBayes*. *NaïveBayes* assumes independence of attributes, so attribute selection can be very helpful. You can see the effect of redundant attributes by adding multiple copies of an attribute using the filter *weka.filters.unsupervised. attribute.Copy* in the Preprocess panel. Each copy is obviously perfectly correlated with the original.

> **Exercise 17.4.10.** Load the diabetes classification data in *diabetes.arff* and add copies of the first attribute. Measure the performance of *NaïveBayes* (with *useSupervisedDiscretization* turned on) using cross-validation after you have added each one. What do you observe?

Do the above three attribute selection methods, used in conjunction with *AttributeSelectedClassifier* and *NaïveBayes*, successfully eliminate the redundant attributes? Run each method from within *AttributeSelectedClassifier* to see the effect on cross-validated accuracy and check the attribute subset selected by each method. Note that you need to specify the number of ranked attributes to use for the *Ranker* method. Set this to 8 because the original diabetes data contains 8 attributes (excluding the class). Specify *NaïveBayes* as the classifier to be used inside the wrapper method because this is the classifier for which we want to select a subset.

> **Exercise 17.4.11.** What can you say regarding the performance of the three attribute selection methods? Do they succeed in eliminating redundant copies? If not, why?

Automatic Parameter Tuning

Many learning algorithms have parameters that can affect the outcome of learning. For example, the decision tree learner C4.5 has two parameters that influence the amount of pruning (we saw one, the minimum number of instances required in a leaf, in Section 17.3). The k-nearest-neighbor classifier *IBk* has a parameter (k) that sets the neighborhood size. But manually tweaking parameter settings is tedious, just like manually selecting attributes, and presents the same problem: The test data must not be used when selecting parameters; otherwise, the performance estimate will be biased.

Weka's metalearner *CVParameterSelection* searches for the best parameter settings by optimizing cross-validated accuracy on the training data. By default, each setting is evaluated using tenfold cross-validation. The parameters to optimize are specified using the *CVParameters* field in the Generic Object Editor window. For each parameter, three pieces of information must be supplied: (1) a string that names it using its letter code (which can be found in the Javadoc for the corresponding classifier—see Section 14.2, page 525); (2) a numeric range of values to evaluate; and (3) the number of steps to try in this range (note that the parameter is assumed to be numeric). Click on the *More* button in the Generic Object Editor window for more information and an example.

For the diabetes data used in the previous section, use *CVParameterSelection* in conjunction with *IBk* to select the best value for the neighborhood size, ranging from 1 to 10 in 10 steps. The letter code for the neighborhood size is *K*. The cross-validated accuracy of the parameter-tuned version of *IBk* is directly comparable with its accuracy using default settings because tuning is performed by applying inner cross-validation runs to find the best parameter value for each training set occurring in the outer cross-validation—and the latter yields the final performance estimate.

Exercise 17.4.12. What accuracy is obtained in each case? What value is selected for the parameter-tuned version based on cross-validation on the full data set? (*Note:* This value is output in the Classifier Output text area because, as mentioned earlier, the model that is output is the one built from the full dataset.)

Now consider parameter tuning for *J48*. If there is more than one parameter string in the *CVParameters* field, *CVParameterSelection* performs a grid search on the parameters simultaneously. The letter code for the pruning confidence parameter is *C*, and you should evaluate values from 0.1 to 0.5 in five steps. The letter code for the minimum leaf size parameter is *M*, and you should evaluate values from 1 to 10 in 10 steps.

Exercise 17.4.13. Run *CVParameterSelection* to find the best parameter value setting. Compare the output you get to that obtained from *J48* with default parameters. Has accuracy changed? What about tree size? What parameter values were selected by *CVParameterSelection* for the model built from the full training set?

17.5 DOCUMENT CLASSIFICATION

Next we perform some experiments in document classification. The raw data is text, and this is first converted into a form suitable for learning by creating a dictionary of terms from all the documents in the training corpus and making a numeric attribute for each term using Weka's unsupervised attribute filter *StringToWord-Vector*. There is also the class attribute, which gives the document's label.

Data with String Attributes

The *StringToWordVector* filter assumes that the document text is stored in an attribute of type *String*—a nominal attribute without a prespecified set of values. In the filtered data, this is replaced by a fixed set of numeric attributes, and the class attribute is put at the beginning, as the first attribute.

To perform document classification, first create an ARFF file with a string attribute that holds the document's text—declared in the header of the ARFF file using @*attribute document string*, where *document* is the name of the attribute. A nominal attribute is also needed to hold the document's classification.

> **Exercise 17.5.1.** Make an ARFF file from the labeled mini-documents in Table 17.4 and run *StringToWordVector* with default options on this data. How many attributes are generated? Now change the value of the option *minTermFreq* to 2. What attributes are generated now?
>
> **Exercise 17.5.2.** Build a *J48* decision tree from the last version of the data you generated.
>
> **Exercise 17.5.3.** Classify the new documents in Table 17.5 based on the decision tree generated from the documents in Table 17.4. To apply the same

Table 17.4 Training Documents

Document Text	Classification
The price of crude oil has increased significantly	yes
Demand for crude oil outstrips supply	yes
Some people do not like the flavor of olive oil	no
The food was very oily	no
Crude oil is in short supply	yes
Use a bit of cooking oil in the frying pan	no

Table 17.5 Test Documents

Document Text	Classification
Oil platforms extract crude oil	unknown
Canola oil is supposed to be healthy	unknown
Iraq has significant oil reserves	unknown
There are different types of cooking oil	unknown

filter to both training and test documents, use *FilteredClassifier*, specifying the *StringToWordVector* filter and *J48* as the base classifier. Create an ARFF file from Table 17.5, using question marks for the missing class labels. Configure *FilteredClassifier* using default options for *StringToWordVector* and *J48*, and specify your new ARFF file as the test set. Make sure that you select *Output predictions* under *More options* in the Classify panel. Look at the model and the predictions it generates, and verify that they are consistent. What are the predictions?

Classifying Actual Documents

A standard collection of newswire articles is widely used for evaluating document classifiers. *ReutersCorn-train.arff* and *ReutersGrain-train.arff* are training sets derived from this collection; *ReutersCorn-test.arff* and *ReutersGrain-test.arff* are corresponding test sets. The actual documents in the corn and grain data are the same; only the labels differ. In the first dataset, articles concerning corn-related issues have a class value of 1 and the others have 0; the aim is to build a classifier that identifies "corny" articles. In the second, the labeling is performed with respect to grain-related issues; the aim is to identify "grainy" articles.

> **Exercise 17.5.4.** Build classifiers for the two training sets by applying *FilteredClassifier* with *StringToWordVector* using (1) *J48* and (2) *NaiveBayesMultinomial*, evaluating them on the corresponding test set in each case. What percentage of correct classifications is obtained in the four scenarios? Based on the results, which classifier would you choose?

Other evaluation metrics are used for document classification besides the percentage of correct classifications: They are tabulated under *Detailed Accuracy By Class* in the Classifier Output area—the number of true positives (TP), false positives (FP), true negatives (TN), and false negatives (FN). The statistics output by Weka are computed as specified in Table 5.7; the *F*-measure is mentioned in Section 5.7 (page 175).

> **Exercise 17.5.5.** Based on the formulas in Table 5.7, what are the best possible values for each of the output statistics? Describe when these values are attained.

The Classifier Output also gives the ROC area (also known as AUC), which, as explained in Section 5.7 (page 177), is the probability that a randomly chosen positive instance in the test data is ranked above a randomly chosen negative instance, based on the ranking produced by the classifier. The best outcome is that all positive examples are ranked above all negative examples, in which case the AUC is 1. In the worst case it is 0. In the case where the ranking is essentially random, the AUC is 0.5, and if it is significantly less than this the classifier has performed anti-learning!

Exercise 17.5.6. Which of the two classifiers used above produces the best AUC for the two Reuters datasets? Compare this to the outcome for percent correct. What do the different outcomes mean?

The ROC curves discussed in Section 5.7 (page 172) can be generated by right-clicking on an entry in the result list and selecting *Visualize threshold curve*. This gives a plot with FP Rate on the *x*-axis and TP Rate on the *y*-axis. Depending on the classifier used, this plot can be quite smooth or it can be fairly irregular.

Exercise 17.5.7. For the Reuters dataset that produced the most extreme difference in Exercise 17.5.6, look at the ROC curves for class 1. Make a very rough estimate of the area under each curve, and explain it in words.
Exercise 17.5.8. What does the ideal ROC curve corresponding to perfect performance look like?

Other types of threshold curves can be plotted, such as a precision–recall curve with Recall on the *x*-axis and Precision on the *y*-axis.

Exercise 17.5.9. Change the axes to obtain a precision–recall curve. What is the shape of the ideal precision–recall curve, corresponding to perfect performance?

Exploring the *StringToWordVector* Filter

By default, the *StringToWordVector* filter simply makes the attribute value in the transformed dataset 1 or 0 for all single-word terms, depending on whether the word appears in the document or not. However, as mentioned in Section 11.3 (page 439), there are many options:

- *outputWordCounts* causes actual word counts to be output.
- *IDFTransform* and *TFTransform*: When both are set to *true*, term frequencies are transformed into TF × IDF values.
- *stemmer* gives a choice of different word-stemming algorithms.
- *useStopList* lets you determine whether or not stopwords are deleted.
- *tokenizer* allows different tokenizers for generating terms, such as one that produces word *n*-grams instead of single words.

There are several other useful options. For more information, click on *More* in the Generic Object Editor window.

Exercise 17.5.10. Experiment with the options that are available. What options give a good AUC value for the two datasets above, using *NaiveBayesMulti-nomial* as the classifier?

Not all of the attributes (i.e., terms) are important when classifying documents. The reason is that many words are irrelevant for determining an article's topic. Weka's *AttributeSelectedClassifier*, using ranking with *InfoGainAttributeEval* and the *Ranker* search, can eliminate less useful attributes. As before, *FilteredClassifier* should be used to transform the data before passing it to *AttributeSelectedClassifier*.

Exercise 17.5.11. Experiment with this, using default options for *StringToWordVector* and *NaiveBayesMultinomial* as the classifier. Vary the number of the most informative attributes that are selected from the information gain–based ranking by changing the value of the *numToSelect* field in the *Ranker*. Record the AUC values you obtain. How many attributes give the best AUC for the two datasets discussed before? What are the best AUC values you managed to obtain?

17.6 MINING ASSOCIATION RULES

In order to get some experience with association rules, we work with *Apriori*, the algorithm described in Section 4.5 (page 144). As you will discover, it can be challenging to extract useful information using this algorithm.

Association-Rule Mining

To get a feel for how to apply *Apriori*, start by mining rules from the *weather. nominal.arff* data that was used in Section 17.1. Note that this algorithm expects data that is purely nominal: If present, numeric attributes must be discretized first. After loading the data in the Preprocess panel, click the *Start* button in the Associate panel to run *Apriori* with default options. It outputs 10 rules, ranked according to the confidence measure given in parentheses after each one (they are listed in Figure 11.16). As we explained in Chapter 11 (page 430), the number following a rule's antecedent shows how many instances satisfy the antecedent; the number following the conclusion shows how many instances satisfy the entire rule (this is the rule's "support"). Because both numbers are equal for all 10 rules, the confidence of every rule is exactly 1.

In practice, it can be tedious to find minimum support and confidence values that give satisfactory results. Consequently, as explained in Chapter 11, Weka's *Apriori* runs the basic algorithm several times. It uses the same user-specified minimum confidence value throughout, given by the *minMetric* parameter. The support level is expressed as a proportion of the total number of instances (14 in the case of the weather data), as a ratio between 0 and 1. The minimum support level starts at a certain value (*upperBoundMinSupport*, default 1.0). In each iteration the support is decreased by a fixed amount (*delta*, default 0.05, 5% of the instances) until either a certain number of rules has been generated (*numRules*, default 10 rules) or the support reaches a certain "minimum minimum" level (*lowerBoundMinSupport*, default 0.1)—because rules are generally uninteresting if they apply to less than 10% of the dataset. These four values can all be specified by the user.

This sounds pretty complicated, so we will examine what happens on the weather data. The Associator output text area shows that the algorithm managed to generate 10 rules. This is based on a minimum confidence level of 0.9, which is the default and is also shown in the output. The *Number of cycles performed*, which is shown as 17, indicates that *Apriori* was actually run 17 times to generate these rules, with 17 different values for the minimum support. The final value, which corresponds to the output that was generated, is 0.15 (corresponding to $0.15 \times 14 \approx 2$ instances).

By looking at the options in the Generic Object Editor window, you can see that the initial value for the minimum support (*upperBoundMinSupport*) is 1 by default, and that delta is 0.05. Now, $1 - 17 \times 0.05 = 0.15$, so this explains why a minimum support value of 0.15 is reached after 17 iterations. Note that *upperBoundMinSupport* is decreased by delta *before* the basic *Apriori* algorithm is run for the first time.

The Associator output text area also shows how many frequent item sets were found, based on the last value of the minimum support that was tried (0.15 in this example). In this case, given a minimum support of two instances, there are 12 item sets of size 1, 47 item sets of size 2, 39 item sets of size 3, and six item sets of size 4. By setting *outputItemSets* to *true* before running the algorithm, all those different item sets and the number of instances that support them are shown. Try it out!

Exercise 17.6.1. Based on the output, what is the support for this item set?

outlook = rainy humidity = normal windy = FALSE play = yes

Exercise 17.6.2. Suppose you want to generate all rules with a certain confidence and minimum support. This can be done by choosing appropriate values for *minMetric*, *lowerBoundMinSupport*, and *numRules*. What is the total number of possible rules for the weather data for each combination of values in Table 17.6?

Table 17.6 Number of Rules for Different Values of Minimum Confidence and Support

Minimum Confidence	Minimum Support	Number of Rules
0.9	0.3	
0.9	0.2	
0.9	0.1	
0.8	0.3	
0.8	0.2	
0.8	0.1	
0.7	0.3	
0.7	0.2	
0.7	0.1	

Apriori has some further parameters. If *significanceLevel* is set to a value between 0 and 1, the association rules are filtered based on a χ^2 test with the chosen significance level. However, applying a significance test in this context is problematic because of the multiple comparison problem: If a test is performed hundreds of times for hundreds of association rules, it is likely that significant effects will be found just by chance—that is, an association seems to be statistically significant when really it is not. Also, the χ^2 test is inaccurate for small sample sizes (in this context, small support values).

There are alternative measures for ranking rules. As well as confidence, *Apriori* supports *lift*, *leverage*, and *conviction*, which can be selected using *metricType*. More information is available by clicking *More* in the Generic Object Editor window.

> **Exercise 17.6.3.** Run *Apriori* on the weather data with each of the four rule-ranking metrics, and default settings otherwise. What is the top-ranked rule that is output for each metric?

Mining a Real-World Dataset

Now consider a real-world dataset, *vote.arff*, which gives the votes of 435 U.S. congressmen on 16 key issues gathered in the mid-1980s, and also includes their party affiliation as a binary attribute. This is a purely nominal dataset with some missing values (corresponding to abstentions). It is normally treated as a classification problem, the task being to predict party affiliation based on voting patterns. However, association-rule mining can also be applied to this data to seek interesting associations. More information on the data appears in the comments in the ARFF file.

> **Exercise 17.6.4.** Run *Apriori* on this data with default settings. Comment on the rules that are generated. Several of them are quite similar. How are their support and confidence values related?
>
> **Exercise 17.6.5.** It is interesting to see that none of the rules in the default output involve *Class = republican*. Why do you think that is?

Market Basket Analysis

In Section 1.3 (page 26) we introduced market basket analysis—analyzing customer purchasing habits by seeking associations in the items they buy when visiting a store. To do market basket analysis in Weka, each transaction is coded as an instance of which the attributes represent the items in the store. Each attribute has only one value: If a particular transaction does not contain it (i.e., the customer did not buy that item), this is coded as a missing value.

Your job is to mine supermarket checkout data for associations. The data in *supermarket.arff* was collected from an actual New Zealand supermarket. Take a look at this file using a text editor to verify that you understand the structure. The main point of this exercise is to show you how difficult it is to find any interesting patterns in this type of data!

Exercise 17.6.6. Experiment with *Apriori* and investigate the effect of the various parameters described before. Write a brief report on the main findings of your investigation.

Abe, N., Zadrozny, B., & Langford, J. (2006). Outlier detection by active learning. In *Proceedings of the 12th ACM SIGKDD International Conference on Knowledge Discovery and Data Mining* (pp. 767–772). New York: ACM Press.

Adriaans, P., & Zantige, D. (1996). *Data mining.* Harlow, England: Addison-Wesley.

Agrawal, R., & Srikant, R. (1994). Fast algorithms for mining association rules in large databases. In J. Bocca, M. Jarke, & C. Zaniolo (Eds.), *Proceedings of the International Conference on Very Large Data Bases* (pp. 478–499). Santiago, Chile. San Francisco: Morgan Kaufmann.

Agrawal, R., Imielinski, T., & Swami, A. (1993a). Database mining: A performance perspective. *IEEE Transactions on Knowledge and Data Engineering*, 5(6), 914–925.

———. (1993b). Mining association rules between sets of items in large databases. In P. Buneman, & S. Jajodia (Eds.), *Proceedings of the ACM SIGMOD International Conference on Management of Data* (pp. 207–216). Washington, DC. New York: ACM Press.

Aha, D. (1992). Tolerating noisy, irrelevant, and novel attributes in instance-based learning algorithms. *International Journal of Man-Machine Studies*, 36(2), 267–287.

Almuallin, H., & Dietterich, T. G. (1991). Learning with many irrelevant features. In *Proceedings of the Ninth National Conference on Artificial Intelligence* (pp. 547–552). Anaheim, CA. Menlo Park, CA: AAAI Press.

———. (1992). Efficient algorithms for identifying relevant features. In *Proceedings of the Ninth Canadian Conference on Artificial Intelligence* (pp. 38–45). Vancouver, BC. San Francisco: Morgan Kaufmann.

Andrews, S., Tsochantaridis, I., & Hofmann, T. (2003). Support vector machines for multiple-instance learning. In *Proceedings of the Conference on Neural Information Processing Systems* (pp. 561–568). Vancouver, BC. Cambridge, MA: MIT Press.

Ankerst, M., Breunig, M. M., Kriegel, H.-P., & Sander, J. (1999). OPTICS: Ordering points to identify the clustering structure. In *Proceedings of the ACM SIGMOD International Conference on Management of Data* (pp. 49–60). New York: ACM Press.

Appelt, D. (1999). An introduction to information extraction. *Artificial Intelligence Communications*, 12(3), 161–172.

Arthur, D., & Vassilvitskii, S. (2007). K-means++: The advantages of careful seeding. In *Proceedings of the Eighteenth Annual ACM-SIAM Symposium on Discrete Algorithms* (pp. 1027–1035). New Orleans. Philadelphia: Society for Industrial and Applied Mathematics.

Asuncion, A., & Newman, D. J. (2007). *UCI Machine Learning Repository* [*http://www.ics.uci.edu/~mlearn/MLRepository.html*]. Irvine: University of California, School of Information and Computer Science.

Asmis, E. (1984). *Epicurus' scientific method*. Ithaca, NY: Cornell University Press.

Atkeson, C. G., Schaal, S. A., & Moore, A. W. (1997). Locally weighted learning. *AI Review*, 11, 11–71.

Auer, P., & Ortner, R. (2004). A boosting approach to multiple instance learning. In *Proceedings of the European Conference on Machine Learning* (pp. 63–74). Pisa, Italy. Berlin: Springer-Verlag.

Barnett, V., & Lewis, T. (1994). *Outliers in Statistical Data*. West Sussex, England: John Wiley, & Sons.

Bay, S. D. (1999). Nearest neighbor classification from multiple feature subsets. *Intelligent Data Analysis*, 3(3), 191–209.

Bay, S. D., & Schwabacher, M. (2003). Near linear time detection of distance-based outliers and applications to security. In *Proceedings of the Workshop on Data Mining for Counter Terrorism and Security*. San Francisco. Philadelphia: Society for Industrial and Applied Mathematics.

Bayes, T. (1763). An essay towards solving a problem in the doctrine of chances. *Philosophical Transactions of the Royal Society of London*, 53, 370–418.

Beck, J. R., & Schultz, E. K. (1986). The use of ROC curves in test performance evaluation. *Archives of Pathology and Laboratory Medicine*, 110, 13–20.

Bergadano, F., & Gunetti, D. (1996). *Inductive logic programming: From machine learning to software engineering*. Cambridge, MA: MIT Press.

Berry, M. J. A., & Linoff, G. (1997). *Data mining techniques for marketing, sales, and customer support*. New York: John Wiley.

Beygelzimer, A., Kakade, S., & Langford, J. (2006). Cover trees for nearest neighbor. In *Proceedings of the 23rd International Conference on Machine Learning* (pp. 97–104). New York: ACM Press.

Bifet, A., Holmes, G., Kirkby, R., & Pfahringer, B. (2010). MOA: Massive online analysis. *Journal of Machine Learning Research*, 9, 1601–1604.

Bigus, J. P. (1996). *Data mining with neural networks*. New York: McGraw-Hill.

Bishop, C. M. (1995). *Neural networks for pattern recognition*. New York: Oxford University Press.

———. (2006). *Pattern recognition and machine learning*. Springer-Verlag.

BLI (Bureau of Labour Information) (1988). *Collective Bargaining Review (November)*. Ottawa: Labour Canada, Bureau of Labour Information.

Blockeel, H., Page, D., & Srinivasan, A. (2005). Multi-instance tree learning. In *Proceedings of the 22nd International Conference on Machine Learning* (pp. 57–64). Bonn. New York: ACM Press.

Blum, A., & Mitchell, T. (1998). Combining labeled and unlabeled data with co-training. In *Proceedings of the Eleventh Annual Conference on Computational Learning Theory* (pp. 92–100). Madison, WI. San Francisco: Morgan Kaufmann.

Bouckaert, R. R. (1995). *Bayesian belief networks: From construction to inference*. Ph.D. Dissertation, Computer Science Department, University of Utrecht, The Netherlands.

———. (2004). Bayesian network classifiers in Weka. Working Paper 14/2004, Department of Computer Science, University of Waikato, New Zealand.

———. (2010). DensiTree: Making sense of sets of phylogenetic trees. *Bioinformatics*, 26(10), 1372–1373.

Brachman, R. J., & Levesque, H. J. (Eds.) (1985). *Readings in knowledge representation*. San Francisco: Morgan Kaufmann.

Brefeld, U., & Scheffer, T. (2004). Co-EM support vector learning. In R. Greiner, & D. Schuurmans (Eds.), *Proceedings of the Twenty-First International Conference on Machine Learning* (pp. 121–128). Banff, AB. New York: ACM Press.

Breiman, L. (1996a). Stacked regression. *Machine Learning*, 24(1), 49–64.

———. (1996b). Bagging predictors. *Machine Learning*, 24(2), 123–140.

———. (1996c). [Bias, variance, and] arcing classifiers. Technical Report 460. Department of Statistics, University of California, Berkeley.

———. (1999). Pasting small votes for classification in large databases and online. *Machine Learning*, 36(1–2), 85–103.

———. (2001). Random forests. *Machine Learning*, 45(1), 5–32.

Breiman, L., Friedman, J. H., Olshen, R. A., & Stone, C. J. (1984). *Classification and regression trees*. Monterey, CA: Wadsworth.

Brin, S., Motwani, R., Ullman, J. D., & Tsur, S. (1997). Dynamic itemset counting and implication rules for market basket data. *ACM SIGMOD Record*, 26(2), 255–264.

Brin, S., & Page, L. (1998). The anatomy of a large-scale hypertext search engine. *Computer Networks and ISDN Systems*, 33, 107–117.

Brodley, C. E., & Friedl, M. A. (1996). Identifying and eliminating mislabeled training instances. In *Proceedings of the Thirteenth National Conference on Artificial Intelligence* (pp. 799–805). Portland, OR. Menlo Park, CA: AAAI Press.

Brownstown, L., Farrell, R., Kant, E., & Martin, N. (1985). *Programming expert systems in OPS5*. Reading, MA: Addison-Wesley.

Buntine, W. (1992). Learning classification trees. *Statistics and Computing*, 2(2), 63–73.

Burges, C. J. C. (1998). A tutorial on support vector machines for pattern recognition. *Data Mining and Knowledge Discovery*, 2(2), 121–167.

Cabena, P., Hadjinian, P., Stadler, R., Verhees, J., & Zanasi, A. (1998). *Discovering data mining: From concept to implementation*. Upper Saddle River, NJ: Prentice-Hall.

Cardie, C. (1993). Using decision trees to improve case-based learning. In P. Utgoff (Ed.), *Proceedings of the Tenth International Conference on Machine Learning* (pp. 25–32). Amherst, MA. San Francisco: Morgan Kaufmann.

Califf, M. E., & Mooney, R. J. (1999). Relational learning of pattern-match rules for information extraction. In *Proceedings of the Sixteenth National Conference on Artificial Intelligence* (pp. 328–334). Orlando. Menlo Park, CA: AAAI Press.

Cavnar, W. B., & Trenkle, J. M. (1994). N-Gram-based text categorization. In *Proceedings of the Third Symposium on Document Analysis and Information Retrieval* (pp. 161–175). Las Vegas: UNLV Publications/Reprographics.

Ceglar, A., & Roddick, J. F. (2006). Association mining. *ACM Computing Surveys*, 38(2). New York: ACM Press.

Cendrowska, J. (1987). PRISM: An algorithm for inducing modular rules. *International Journal of Man-Machine Studies*, 27(4), 349–370.

Chakrabarti, S. (2003). *Mining the web: discovering knowledge from hypertext data*. San Francisco: Morgan Kaufmann.

Chang, C.-C., & Lin, C.-J. (2001). LIBSVM: A library for support vector machines. Software available at *http://www.csie.ntu.edu.tw/~cjlin/libsvm*.

Chawla, N. V., Bowyer, K. W., Hall, L. O., & Kegelmeyer, W. P. (2002). SMOTE: Synthetic minority over-sampling technique. *Journal of Artificial Intelligence*, 16, 321–357.

Cheeseman, P., & Stutz, J. (1995). Bayesian classification (AutoClass): Theory and results. In U. M. Fayyad, G. Piatetsky-Shapiro, P. Smyth, & R. Uthurusamy (Eds.), *Advances in Knowledge Discovery and Data Mining* (pp. 153–180). Menlo Park, CA: AAAI Press.

Chen, M. S., Jan, J., & Yu, P. S. (1996). Data mining: An overview from a database perspective. *IEEE Transactions on Knowledge and Data Engineering*, 8(6), 866–883.

Chen, Y., Bi, J., & Wang, J. Z. (2006). MILES: Multiple-instance learning via embedded instance selection. *IEEE Transactions on Pattern Analysis and Machine Intelligence*, 28(12), 1931–1947.

Cherkauer, K. J., & Shavlik, J. W. (1996). Growing simpler decision trees to facilitate knowledge discovery. In E. Simoudis, J. W. Han, & U. Fayyad (Eds.), *Proceedings of the Second International Conference on Knowledge Discovery and Data Mining* (pp. 315–318). Portland, OR. Menlo Park, CA: AAAI Press.

Chevaleyre, Y., & Zucker, J.-D. (2001). Solving multiple-instance and multiple-part learning problems with decision trees and rule sets: Application to the mutagenesis problem. In *Proceedings of the Biennial Conference of the Canadian Society for Computational Studies of Intelligence* (pp. 204–214). Ottawa. Berlin: Springer-Verlag.

Cleary, J. G., & Trigg, L. E. (1995). K*: An instance-based learner using an entropic distance measure. In A. Prieditis, & S. Russell (Eds.), *Proceedings of the Twelfth International Conference on Machine Learning* (pp. 108–114). Tahoe City, CA. San Francisco: Morgan Kaufmann.

Cohen, J. (1960). A coefficient of agreement for nominal scales. *Educational and Psychological Measurement*, 20, 37–46.

Cohen, W. W. (1995). Fast effective rule induction. In A. Prieditis, & S. Russell (Eds.), *Proceedings of the Twelfth International Conference on Machine Learning* (pp. 115–123). Tahoe City, CA. San Francisco: Morgan Kaufmann.

Cooper, G. F., & Herskovits, E. (1992). A Bayesian method for the induction of probabilistic networks from data. *Machine Learning*, 9(4), 309–347.

Cortes, C., & Vapnik, V. (1995). Support vector networks. *Machine Learning*, 20(3), 273–297.

Cover, T. M., & Hart, P. E. (1967). Nearest neighbor pattern classification. *IEEE Transactions on Information Theory*, IT-13, 21–27.

Cristianini, N., & Shawe-Taylor, J. (2000). *An introduction to support vector machines and other kernel-based learning methods*. Cambridge, UK: Cambridge University Press.

Cypher, A. (Ed.), (1993). *Watch what I do: Programming by demonstration*. Cambridge, MA: MIT Press.

Dasgupta, S. (2002). Performance guarantees for hierarchical clustering. In J. Kivinen, & R. H. Sloan (Eds.), *Proceedings of the Fifteenth Annual Conference on Computational Learning Theory* (pp. 351–363). Sydney. Berlin: Springer-Verlag.

Dasu, T., Koutsofios, E., & Wright, J. (2006). Zen and the art of data mining. In *Proceedings of the KDD Workshop on Data Mining for Business Applications* (pp. 37–43). Philadelphia. Proceedings at: *http://labs.accenture.com/kdd2006_workshop/dmba_proceedings.pdf*

Datta, S., Kargupta, H., & Sivakumar, K. (2003). Homeland defense, privacy-sensitive data mining, and random value distortion. In *Proceedings of the Workshop on Data Mining for Counter Terrorism and Security*. San Francisco. Philadelphia: Society for International and Applied Mathematics.

Day, W. H. E., & Edelsbrünner, H. (1984). Efficient algorithms for agglomerative hierarchical clustering methods. *Journal of Classification*, 1(1), 7–24.

Demiroz, G., & Guvenir, A. (1997). Classification by voting feature intervals. In M. van Someren, & G. Widmer (Eds.), *Proceedings of the Ninth European Conference on Machine Learning* (pp. 85–92). Prague. Berlin: Springer-Verlag.

de Raedt, L. (2008). *Logical and relational learning.* New York: Springer-Verlag.

Devroye, L., Györfi, L., & Lugosi, G. (1996). *A probabilistic theory of pattern recognition.* New York: Springer-Verlag.

Dhar, V., & Stein, R. (1997). *Seven methods for transforming corporate data into business intelligence.* Upper Saddle River, NJ: Prentice-Hall.

Diederich, J., Kindermann, J., Leopold, E., & Paass, G. (2003). Authorship attribution with support vector machines. *Applied Intelligence*, 19(1), 109–123.

Dietterich, T. G. (2000). An experimental comparison of three methods for constructing ensembles of decision trees: Bagging, boosting, and randomization. *Machine Learning*, 40(2), 139–158.

Dietterich, T. G., & Bakiri, G. (1995). Solving multiclass learning problems via error-correcting output codes. *Journal of Artificial Intelligence Research*, 2, 263–286.

Dietterich, T. G., & Kong, E. B. (1995). Error-correcting output coding corrects bias and variance. In *Proceedings of the Twelfth International Conference on Machine Learning* (pp. 313-321). Tahoe City, CA. San Francisco: Morgan Kaufmann.

Dietterich, T. G., Lathrop, R. H., & Lozano-Perez, T. (1997). Solving the multiple-instance problem with axis-parallel rectangles. *Artificial Intelligence Journal*, 89(1-2), 31–71.

Domingos, P. (1997). Knowledge acquisition from examples via multiple models. In D. H. Fisher (Ed.), *Proceedings of the Fourteenth International Conference on Machine Learning* (pp. 98–106). Nashville. San Francisco: Morgan Kaufmann.

————. (1999). MetaCost: A general method for making classifiers cost-sensitive. In U. M. Fayyad, S. Chaudhuri, & D. Madigan (Eds.), *Proceedings of the Fifth International Conference on Knowledge Discovery and Data Mining* (pp. 155–164). San Diego. New York: ACM Press.

Domingos, P., & Hulten, G. (2000). Mining high-speed data streams. In *International Conference on Knowledge Discovery and Data Mining* (pp. 71–80). Boston. New York: ACM Press.

Dong, L., Frank, E., & Kramer, S. (2005). Ensembles of balanced nested dichotomies for multi-class problems. In *Proceedings of the Ninth European Conference on Principles and Practice of Knowledge Discovery in Databases* (pp. 84-95). Porto, Portugal. Berlin: Springer-Verlag.

Dougherty, J., Kohavi, R., & Sahami, M. (1995). Supervised and unsupervised discretization of continuous features. In A. Prieditis, & S. Russell (Eds.), *Proceedings of the Twelfth International Conference on Machine Learning* (pp. 194–202). Tahoe City, CA. San Francisco: Morgan Kaufmann.

Drucker, H. (1997). Improving regressors using boosting techniques. In D. H. Fisher (Ed.), *Proceedings of the Fourteenth International Conference on Machine Learning* (pp. 107–115). Nashville. San Francisco: Morgan Kaufmann.

Drummond, C., & Holte, R. C. (2000). Explicitly representing expected cost: An alternative to ROC representation. In R. Ramakrishnan, S. Stolfo, R. Bayardo, & I. Parsa (Eds.), *Proceedings of the Sixth International Conference on Knowledge Discovery and Data Mining* (pp. 198–207). Boston. New York: ACM Press.

Duda, R. O., & Hart, P. E. (1973). *Pattern classification and scene analysis.* New York: John Wiley.

Duda, R. O., Hart, P. E., & Stork, D. G. (2001). *Pattern Classification* (2nd ed.). New York: John Wiley.

Dumais, S. T., Platt, J., Heckerman, D., & Sahami, M. (1998). Inductive learning algorithms and representations for text categorization. In *Proceedings of the ACM Seventh*

International Conference on Information and Knowledge Management (pp. 148–155). Bethesda, MD. New York: ACM Press.

Efron, B., & Tibshirani, R. (1993). *An introduction to the bootstrap.* London: Chapman and Hall.

Egan, J. P. (1975). *Signal detection theory and ROC analysis. Series in Cognition and Perception.* New York: Academic Press.

Ester, M., Kriegel, H.-P., Sander, J., & Xu, X. (1996). A density-based algorithm for discovering clusters in large spatial databases with noise. In *Proceedings of the Second International Conference on Knowledge Discovery and Data Mining (KDD-96)* (pp. 226–231). Menlo Park, CA: AAAI Press.

Fan, R.-E., Chang, K.-W., Hsieh, C.-J., Wang, X.-R., & Lin, C.-J. (2008). LIBLINEAR: A library for large linear classification. *Journal of Machine Learning Research, 9,* 1871–1874.

Fayyad, U. M., & Irani, K. B. (1993). Multi-interval discretization of continuous-valued attributes for classification learning. In *Proceedings of the Thirteenth International Joint Conference on Artificial Intelligence* (pp. 1022–1027). Chambery, France. San Francisco: Morgan Kaufmann.

Fayyad, U. M., & Smyth, P. (1995). From massive datasets to science catalogs: Applications and challenges. In *Proceedings of the Workshop on Massive Datasets* (pp. 129–141). Washington, DC: NRC, Committee on Applied and Theoretical Statistics.

Fayyad, U. M., Piatetsky-Shapiro, G., Smyth, P., & Uthurusamy, R. (Eds.), (1996). *Advances in knowledge discovery and data mining.* Menlo Park, CA: AAAI Press/MIT Press.

Fisher, D. (1987). Knowledge acquisition via incremental conceptual clustering. *Machine Learning, 2*(2), 139–172.

Fisher, R. A. (1936). The use of multiple measurements in taxonomic problems. *Annual Eugenics, 7* (part II), 179–188. Reprinted in *Contributions to Mathematical Statistics,* 1950. New York: John Wiley.

Fix, E., & Hodges, J. L. Jr. (1951). Discriminatory analysis; non-parametric discrimination: Consistency properties. Technical Report 21-49-004(4), USAF School of Aviation Medicine, Randolph Field, TX.

Flach, P. A., & Lachiche, N. (1999). Confirmation-guided discovery of first-order rules with Tertius. *Machine Learning, 42,* 61–95.

Fletcher, R. (1987). *Practical methods of optimization* (2nd ed.). New York: John Wiley.

Foulds, J., & Frank, E. (2008). Revisiting multiple-instance learning via embedded instance selection. In *Proceedings of the Australasian Joint Conference on Artificial Intelligence* (pp. 300–310). Auckland. Berlin: Springer-Verlag.

———. (2010). A review of multi-instance learning assumptions. *Knowledge Engineering Review, 25*(1), 1–25.

Fradkin, D., & Madigan, D. (2003). Experiments with random projections for machine learning. In L. Getoor, T. E. Senator, P. Domingos, & C. Faloutsos (Eds.), *Proceedings of the Ninth International Conference on Knowledge Discovery and Data Mining* (pp. 517–522). Washington, DC. New York: ACM Press.

Frank E. (2000). *Pruning decision trees and lists.* Ph.D. Dissertation, Department of Computer Science, University of Waikato, New Zealand.

Frank, E., & Hall, M. (2001). A simple approach to ordinal classification. In L. de Raedt, & P. A. Flach (Eds.), *Proceedings of the Twelfth European Conference on Machine Learning* (pp. 145–156). Freiburg, Germany. Berlin: Springer-Verlag.

Frank, E., Hall, M., & Pfahringer, B. (2003). Locally weighted Naïve Bayes. In U. Kjærulff, & C. Meek (Eds.), *Proceedings of the Nineteenth Conference on Uncertainty in Artificial Intelligence* (pp. 249–256). Acapulco. San Francisco: Morgan Kaufmann.

Frank, E., Holmes, G., Kirkby, R., & Hall, M. (2002). Racing Committees for Large Datasets. In S. Lange, K. Satoh, & C. H. Smith (Eds.), *Proceedings of the Fifth International Conference on Discovery Science* (pp. 153–164). Lübeck, Germany. Berlin: Springer-Verlag.

Frank, E., & Kramer, S. (2004). Ensembles of nested dichotomies for multi-class problems. In *Proceedings of the Twenty-First International Conference on Machine Learning* (pp. 305–312). Banff, AB. New York: ACM Press.

Frank, E., Paynter, G. W., Witten, I. H., Gutwin, C., & Nevill-Manning, C. G. (1999). Domain-specific key phrase extraction. In *Proceedings of the Sixteenth International Joint Conference on Artificial Intelligence* (pp. 668–673). Stockholm. San Francisco: Morgan Kaufmann.

Frank, E., Wang, Y., Inglis, S., Holmes, G., & Witten, I. H. (1998). Using model trees for classification. *Machine Learning*, 32(1), 63–76.

Frank, E., & Witten, I. H. (1998). Generating accurate rule sets without global optimization. In J. Shavlik (Ed.), *Proceedings of the Fifteenth International Conference on Machine Learning* (pp. 144–151). Madison, WI. San Francisco: Morgan Kaufmann.

———. (1999). Making better use of global discretization. In I. Bratko, & S. Dzeroski (Eds.), *Proceedings of the Sixteenth International Conference on Machine Learning* (pp. 115–123). Bled, Slovenia. San Francisco: Morgan Kaufmann.

Frank, E., & Xu, X. (2003). Applying propositional learning algorithms to multi-instance data. Technical Report 06/03, Department of Computer Science, University of Waikato, New Zealand.

Freitag, D. (2002). Machine learning for information extraction in informal domains. *Machine Learning*, 39(2/3), 169–202.

Freund, Y., & Mason, L. (1999). The alternating decision tree learning algorithm. In I. Bratko, & S. Dzeroski (Eds.), *Proceedings of the Sixteenth International Conference on Machine Learning* (pp. 124–133). Bled, Slovenia. San Francisco: Morgan Kaufmann.

Freund, Y., & Schapire, R. E. (1996). Experiments with a new boosting algorithm. In L. Saitta (Ed.), *Proceedings of the Thirteenth International Conference on Machine Learning* (pp. 148–156). Bari, Italy. San Francisco: Morgan Kaufmann.

———. (1999). Large margin classification using the perceptron algorithm. *Machine Learning*, 37(3), 277–296.

Friedman, J. H. (1996). Another approach to polychotomous classification. Technical report, Department of Statistics, Stanford University, Stanford, CA.

———. (2001). Greedy function approximation: A gradient boosting machine. *Annals of Statistics*, 29(5), 1189–1232.

Friedman, J. H., Bentley, J. L., & Finkel, R. A. (1977). An algorithm for finding best matches in logarithmic expected time. *ACM Transactions on Mathematical Software*, 3(3), 209–266.

Friedman, J. H., Hastie, T., & Tibshirani, R. (2000). Additive logistic regression: A statistical view of boosting. *Annals of Statistics*, 28(2), 337–374.

Friedman, N., Geiger, D., & Goldszmidt, M. (1997). Bayesian Network Classifiers. *Machine Learning*, 29(2), 131–163.

Fulton, T., Kasif, S., & Salzberg, S. (1995). Efficient algorithms for finding multiway splits for decision trees. In A. Prieditis, & S. Russell (Eds.), *Proceedings of the Twelfth*

International Conference on Machine Learning (pp. 244–251). Tahoe City, CA. San Francisco: Morgan Kaufmann.

Fürnkranz, J. (2002). Round robin classification. *Journal of Machine Learning Research*, 2, 721–747.

———. (2003). Round robin ensembles. *Intelligent Data Analysis*, 7(5), 385-403.

Fürnkranz, J., & Flach, P. A. (2005). ROC 'n' rule learning: Towards a better understanding of covering algorithms. *Machine Learning*, 58(1), 39–77.

Fürnkranz, J., & Widmer, G. (1994). Incremental reduced-error pruning. In H. Hirsh, & W. Cohen (Eds.), *Proceedings of the Eleventh International Conference on Machine Learning* (pp. 70–77). New Brunswick, NJ. San Francisco: Morgan Kaufmann.

Gaines, B. R., & Compton, P. (1995). Induction of ripple-down rules applied to modeling large data bases. *Journal of Intelligent Information Systems*, 5(3), 211–228.

Gama, J. (2004). Functional trees. *Machine Learning*, 55(3), 219–250.

Gärtner, T., Flach, P. A., Kowalczyk, A., & Smola, A. J. (2002). Multi-instance kernels. In *Proceedings of the International Conference on Machine Learning* (pp. 179–186). Sydney. San Francisco: Morgan Kaufmann.

Genkin, A., Lewis, D. D., & Madigan, D. (2007). Large-scale Bayesian logistic regression for text categorization. *Technometrics*, 49(3), 291–304.

Gennari, J. H., Langley, P., & Fisher, D. (1990). Models of incremental concept formation. *Artificial Intelligence*, 40, 11–61.

Ghani, R. (2002). Combining labeled and unlabeled data for multiclass text categorization. In C. Sammut, & A. Hoffmann (Eds.), *Proceedings of the Nineteenth International Conference on Machine Learning* (pp. 187–194). Sydney. San Francisco: Morgan Kaufmann.

Gilad-Bachrach, R., Navot, A., & Tishby, N. (2004). Margin based feature selection: Theory and algorithms. In R. Greiner, & D. Schuurmans (Eds.), *Proceedings of the Twenty-First International Conference on Machine Learning* (pp. 337–344). Banff, AB. New York: ACM Press.

Giraud-Carrier, C. (1996). FLARE: Induction with prior knowledge. In J. Nealon, & J. Hunt (Eds.), *Research and Development in Expert Systems XIII* (pp. 11–24). Cambridge, England: SGES Publications.

Gluck, M., & Corter, J. (1985). Information, uncertainty and the utility of categories. In *Proceedings of the Annual Conference of the Cognitive Science Society* (pp. 283–287). Irvine, CA. Hillsdale, NJ: Lawrence Erlbaum.

Goldberg, D. E. (1989). *Genetic algorithms in search, optimization and machine learning*. Reading, MA: Addison-Wesley.

Good P. (1994). *Permutation tests: A practical guide to resampling methods for testing hypotheses*. New York: Springer-Verlag.

Grossman, D., & Domingos, P. (2004). Learning Bayesian network classifiers by maximizing conditional likelihood. In R. Greiner, & D. Schuurmans (Eds.), *Proceedings of the Twenty-First International Conference on Machine Learning* (pp. 361–368). Banff, AB. New York: ACM Press.

Groth, R. (1998). *Data mining: A hands-on approach for business professionals*. Upper Saddle River, NJ: Prentice-Hall.

Guo, Y., & Greiner, R. (2004). *Discriminative model selection for belief net structures*. Canada: Department of Computing Science, TR04-22, University of Alberta.

Gütlein, M., Frank, E., Hall, M., & Karwath, A. (2009). Large-scale attribute selection using wrappers. In *Proceedings of the IEEE Symposium on Computational Intelligence and Data Mining* (pp. 332–339). Nashville. Washington, DC: IEEE Computer Society.

Guyon, I., Weston, J., Barnhill, S., & Vapnik, V. (2002). Gene selection for cancer classification using support vector machines. *Machine Learning*, 46(1–3), 389–422.

Hall, M. (2000). Correlation-based feature selection for discrete and numeric class machine learning. In P. Langley (Ed.), *Proceedings of the Seventeenth International Conference on Machine Learning* (pp. 359–366). Stanford, CA. San Francisco: Morgan Kaufmann.

Hall, M., Holmes, G., & Frank, E. (1999). Generating rule sets from model trees. In N. Y. Foo (Ed.), *Proceedings of the Twelfth Australian Joint Conference on Artificial Intelligence* (pp. 1–12). Sydney. Berlin: Springer-Verlag.

Hall, M., & Frank, E. (2008). Combining Naïve Bayes and decision tables. In *Proceedings of the 21st Florida Artificial Intelligence Research Society Conference* (pp. 318–319). Miami. Menlo Park, CA: AAAI Press.

Han, J., Pei, J., & Yin, Y. (2000). Mining frequent patterns without candidate generation. In *Proceedings of the ACM-SIGMOD International Conference on Management of Data* (pp. 1–12). Dallas. New York: ACM Press.

Han, J., Pei, J., Yin, Y., & Mao, R. (2004). Mining frequent patterns without candidate generation: A frequent-pattern tree approach. *Data Mining and Knowledge Discovery*, 8(1), 53–87.

Han, J., & Kamber, M. (2006). *Data mining: Concepts and techniques* (2nd ed.). San Francisco: Morgan Kaufmann.

Hand, D. J. (2006). Classifier Technology and the Illusion of Progress. *Statistical Science*, 21(1), 1–14.

Hand, D. J., Manilla, H., & Smyth, P. (2001). *Principles of Data Mining*. Cambridge, MA: MIT Press.

Hartigan, J. A. (1975). *Clustering algorithms*. New York: John Wiley.

Hastie, T., & Tibshirani, R. (1998). Classification by pairwise coupling. *Annals of Statistics*, 26(2), 451–471.

Hastie, T., Tibshirani, R., & Friedman, J. (2009). *The elements of statistical learning* (2nd ed.). New York: Springer-Verlag.

Heckerman, D., Geiger, D., & Chickering, D. M. (1995). Learning Bayesian networks: The combination of knowledge and statistical data. *Machine Learning*, 20(3), 197–243.

Hempstalk, K., Frank, E., & Witten, I. H. (2008). One-class classification by combining density and class probability estimation. In *Proceedings of the European Conference on Machine Learning and Principles and Practice of Knowledge Discovery in Databases* (pp. 505–519). Antwerp. Berlin: Springer-Verlag.

Hempstalk, K., & Frank, E. (2008). Discriminating against new classes: One-class versus multi-class classification. In *Proceedings of the Twenty-first Australasian Joint Conference on Artificial Intelligence*. Auckland (pp. 225–236). New York: Springer-Verlag.

Ho, T. K. (1998). The random subspace method for constructing decision forests. *IEEE Transactions on Pattern Analysis and Machine Intelligence*, 20(8), 832–844.

Hochbaum, D. S., & Shmoys, D. B. (1985). A best possible heuristic for the k-center problem. *Mathematics of Operations Research*, 10(2), 180–184.

Hoerl, A. E., & Kennard, R. W. (1970). Ridge regression: applications to nonorthogonal problems. *Technometrics*, 12(1), 69–82.

Holmes, G., & Nevill-Manning, C. G. (1995). Feature selection via the discovery of simple classification rules. In G. E. Lasker, & X. Liu (Eds.), *Proceedings of the International Symposium on Intelligent Data Analysis* (pp. 75–79). Baden-Baden, Germany: International Institute for Advanced Studies in Systems Research and Cybernetics. Baden-Baden.

Windsor, Ont: International Institute for Advanced Studies in Systems Research and Cybernetics.

Holmes, G., Pfahringer, B., Kirkby, R., Frank, E., & Hall, M. (2002). Multiclass alternating decision trees. In T. Elomaa, H. Mannila, & H. Toivonen (Eds.), *Proceedings of the Thirteenth European Conference on Machine Learning* (pp. 161–172). Helsinki. Berlin: Springer-Verlag.

Holte, R. C. (1993). Very simple classification rules perform well on most commonly used datasets. *Machine Learning*, 11, 63–91.

Huffman, S. B. (1996). Learning information extraction patterns from examples. In S. Wertmer, E. Riloff, & G. Scheler (Eds.), *Connectionist, statistical, and symbolic approaches to learning for natural language processing* (pp. 246–260). Berlin: Springer-Verlag.

Jabbour, K., Riveros, J. F. V., Landsbergen, D., & Meyer, W. (1988). ALFA: Automated load forecasting assistant. *IEEE Transactions on Power Systems*, 3(3), 908–914.

Jiang, L., & Zhang, H. (2006). Weightily averaged one-dependence estimators. In *Proceedings of the 9th Biennial Pacific Rim International Conference on Artificial Intelligence* (pp. 970–974). Guilin, China. Berlin: Springer-Verlag.

John, G. H. (1995). Robust decision trees: Removing outliers from databases. In U. M. Fayyad, & R. Uthurusamy (Eds.), *Proceedings of the First International Conference on Knowledge Discovery and Data Mining* (pp. 174–179). Montreal. Menlo Park, CA: AAAI Press.

———. (1997). *Enhancements to the data mining process*. Ph.D. Dissertation, Computer Science Department, Stanford University, Stanford, CA.

John, G. H., Kohavi, R., & Pfleger, P. (1994). Irrelevant features and the subset selection problem. In H. Hirsh, & W. Cohen (Eds.), *Proceedings of the Eleventh International Conference on Machine Learning* (pp. 121–129). New Brunswick, NJ. San Francisco: Morgan Kaufmann.

John, G. H., & Langley, P. (1995). Estimating continuous distributions in Bayesian classifiers. In P. Besnard, & S. Hanks (Eds.), *Proceedings of the Eleventh Conference on Uncertainty in Artificial Intelligence* (pp. 338–345). Montreal. San Francisco: Morgan Kaufmann.

Johns, M. V. (1961). An empirical Bayes approach to nonparametric two-way classification. In H. Solomon (Ed.), *Studies in item analysis and prediction*. Palo Alto, CA: Stanford University Press.

Kass, R., & Wasserman, L. (1995). A reference Bayesian test for nested hypotheses and its relationship to the Schwarz criterion. *Journal of the American Statistical Association*, 90, 928–934.

Keerthi, S. S., Shevade, S. K., Bhattacharyya, C., & Murthy, K. R. K. (2001). Improvements to Platt's SMO algorithm for SVM classifier design. *Neural Computation*, 13(3), 637–649.

Kerber, R. (1992). Chimerge: Discretization of numeric attributes. In W. Swartout (Ed.), *Proceedings of the Tenth National Conference on Artificial Intelligence* (pp. 123–128). San Jose, CA. Menlo Park, CA: AAAI Press.

Kibler, D., & Aha, D. W. (1987). Learning representative exemplars of concepts: An initial case study. In P. Langley (Ed.), *Proceedings of the Fourth Machine Learning Workshop* (pp. 24–30). Irvine, CA. San Francisco: Morgan Kaufmann.

Kimball, R., & Ross, M. (2002). *The data warehouse toolkit* (2nd ed.). New York: John Wiley.

Kira, K., & Rendell, L. (1992). A practical approach to feature selection. In D. Sleeman, & P. Edwards (Eds.), *Proceedings of the Ninth International Workshop on Machine Learning* (pp. 249–258). Aberdeen, Scotland. San Francisco: Morgan Kaufmann.

Kirkby, R. (2007). *Improving Hoeffding trees*. Ph.D. Dissertation, Department of Computer Science, University of Waikato, New Zealand.

Kittler, J. (1978). Feature set search algorithms. In C. H. Chen (Ed.), *Pattern recognition and signal processing* (pp. 41–60). Amsterdam: Sijthoff an Noordhoff.

Kivinen, J., Smola, A. J., & Williamson, R. C. (2002). Online learning with kernels. *IEEE Transactions on Signal Processing*, 52, 2165–2176.

Kleinberg, J. (1998). Authoritative sources in a hyperlinked environment. In *Proceedings of the ACM-SIAM Symposium on Discrete Algorithms* (pp. 604–632). Extended version published in *Journal of the ACM* 46 (1999).

Koestler, A. (1964). *The act of creation*. London: Hutchinson.

Kohavi, R. (1995a). A study of cross-validation and bootstrap for accuracy estimation and model selection. In *Proceedings of the Fourteenth International Joint Conference on Artificial Intelligence* (pp. 1137–1143). Montreal. San Francisco: Morgan Kaufmann.

————. (1995b). The power of decision tables. In N. Lavrac, & S. Wrobel (Eds.), *Proceedings of the Eighth European Conference on Machine Learning* (pp. 174–189). Iráklion, Crete. Berlin: Springer-Verlag.

————. (1996). Scaling up the accuracy of Naïve Bayes classifiers: A decision-tree hybrid. In E. Simoudis, J. W. Han, & U. Fayyad (Eds.), *Proceedings of the Second International Conference on Knowledge Discovery and Data Mining* (pp. 202–207). Portland, OR. Menlo Park, CA: AAAI Press.

Kohavi, R., & John, G. H. (1997). Wrappers for feature subset selection. *Artificial Intelligence*, 97(1–2), 273–324.

Kohavi, R., & Kunz, C. (1997). Option decision trees with majority votes. In D. Fisher (Ed.), *Proceedings of the Fourteenth International Conference on Machine Learning* (pp. 161–191). Nashville. San Francisco: Morgan Kaufmann.

Kohavi, R., & Provost, F. (Eds.), (1998). Machine learning: Special issue on applications of machine learning and the knowledge discovery process. *Machine Learning*, 30(2/3), 127–274.

Kohavi, R., & Sahami, M. (1996). Error-based and entropy-based discretization of continuous features. In E. Simoudis, J. W. Han, & U. Fayyad (Eds.), *Proceedings of the Second International Conference on Knowledge Discovery and Data Mining* (pp. 114–119). Portland, OR. Menlo Park, CA: AAAI Press.

Komarek, P., & Moore, A. (2000). A dynamic adaptation of AD-trees for efficient machine learning on large data sets. In P. Langley (Ed.), *Proceedings of the Seventeenth International Conference on Machine Learning* (pp. 495–502). Stanford, CA. San Francisco: Morgan Kaufmann.

Kononenko, I. (1995). On biases in estimating multi-valued attributes. In *Proceedings of the Fourteenth International Joint Conference on Artificial Intelligence* (pp. 1034–1040). Montreal. San Francisco: Morgan Kaufmann.

Koppel, M., & Schler, J. (2004). Authorship verification as a one-class classification problem. In R. Greiner, & D. Schuurmans (Eds.), *Proceedings of the Twenty-First International Conference on Machine Learning* (pp. 489–495). Banff, AB. New York: ACM Press.

Krogel, M.-A., & Wrobel, S. (2002). Feature selection for propositionalization. In *Proceedings of the International Conference on Discovery Science* (pp. 430–434). Lübeck, Germany. Berlin: Springer-Verlag.

Kubat, M., Holte, R. C., & Matwin, S. (1998). Machine learning for the detection of oil spills in satellite radar images. *Machine Learning*, 30, 195–215.

Kuncheva, L. I., & Rodriguez, J. J. (2007). An experimental study on rotation forest ensembles. In *Proceedings of the Seventh International Workshop on Multiple Classifier Systems* (pp. 459–468). Prague. Berlin/Heidelberg: Springer-Verlag.

Kushmerick, N., Weld, D. S., & Doorenbos, R. (1997). Wrapper induction for information extraction. In *Proceedings of the Fifteenth International Joint Conference on Artificial Intelligence* (pp. 729–735). Nagoya, Japan. San Francisco: Morgan Kaufmann.

Laguna, M., & Marti, R. (2003). *Scatter search: Methodology and implementations in C.* Dordrecht, The Netherlands: Kluwer Academic Press.

Landwehr, N., Hall, M., & Frank, E. (2005). Logistic model trees. *Machine Learning*, 59(1–2), 161–205.

Langley, P. (1996). *Elements of machine learning.* San Francisco: Morgan Kaufmann.

Langley, P., Iba, W., & Thompson, K. (1992). An analysis of Bayesian classifiers. In W. Swartout (Ed.), *Proceedings of the Tenth National Conference on Artificial Intelligence* (pp. 223–228). San Jose, CA. Menlo Park, CA: AAAI Press.

Langley, P., & Sage, S. (1994). Induction of selective Bayesian classifiers. In R. L. de Mantaras, & D. Poole (Eds.), *Proceedings of the Tenth Conference on Uncertainty in Artificial Intelligence* (pp. 399–406). Seattle. San Francisco: Morgan Kaufmann.

Langley, P., & Simon, H. A. (1995). Applications of machine learning and rule induction. *Communications of the ACM*, 38(11), 55–64.

Lavrac, N., Motoda, H., Fawcett, T., Holte, R., Langley, P., & Adriaans, P. (Eds.), (2004). Special issue on lessons learned from data mining applications and collaborative problem solving. *Machine Learning*, 57(1/2).

Lawson, C. L., & Hanson, R. J. (1995). *Solving least squares problems.* Philadelphia: SIAM Publications.

le Cessie, S., & van Houwelingen, J. C. (1992). Ridge estimators in logistic regression. *Applied Statistics*, 41(1), 191–201.

Li, M., & Vitanyi, P. M. B. (1992). Inductive reasoning and Kolmogorov complexity. *Journal of Computer and System Sciences*, 44, 343–384.

Lieberman, H. (Ed.), (2001). *Your wish is my command: Programming by example.* San Francisco: Morgan Kaufmann.

Littlestone, N. (1988). Learning quickly when irrelevant attributes abound: A new linear-threshold algorithm. *Machine Learning*, 2(4), 285–318.

———. (1989). *Mistake bounds and logarithmic linear-threshold learning algorithms.* Ph, D. Dissertation, University of California, Santa Cruz.

Liu, B. (2009) *Web data mining: Exploring hyperlinks, contents, and usage data.* Berlin: Springer-Verlag.

Liu, B., Hsu, W., & Ma, Y. M. (1998). Integrating classification and association rule mining. In *Proceedings of the Fourth International Conference on Knowledge Discovery and Data Mining (KDD-98)* (pp. 80–86). New York. Menlo Park, CA: AAAI Press.

Liu, H., & Setiono, R. (1996). A probabilistic approach to feature selection: A filter solution. In L. Saitta (Ed.), *Proceedings of the Thirteenth International Conference on Machine Learning* (pp. 319–327), Bari, Italy. San Francisco: Morgan Kaufmann.

———. (1997). Feature selection via discretization. *IEEE Transactions on Knowledge and Data Engineering*, 9(4), 642–645.

Luan, J. (2002). Data mining and its applications in higher education. *New directions for institutional research*, 2002(113), 17–36.

Mann, T. (1993). *Library research models: A guide to classification, cataloging, and computers.* New York: Oxford University Press.

Marill, T., & Green, D. M. (1963). On the effectiveness of receptors in recognition systems. *IEEE Transactions on Information Theory*, 9(11), 11–17.

Maron, O. (1998). *Learning from ambiguity*. Ph.D. Thesis, Massachusetts Institute of Technology, Cambridge, MA.

Maron, O., & Lozano-Peréz, T. (1997). A framework for multiple-instance learning. In *Proceedings of the Conference on Neural Information Processing Systems* (pp. 570–576). Denver. Cambridge, MA: MIT Press.

Martin, B. (1995). *Instance-based learning: Nearest neighbour with generalisation*. M.Sc. Thesis, Department of Computer Science, University of Waikato, New Zealand.

McCallum A., & Nigam, K. (1998). A comparison of event models for Naïve Bayes text classification. In *Proceedings of the AAAI-98 Workshop on Learning for Text Categorization* (pp. 41–48). Madison, WI. Menlo Park, CA: AAAI Press.

Medelyan, O., & Witten, I. H. (2008). Domain independent automatic keyphrase indexing with small training sets. *Journal of the American Society for Information Science and Technology*, 59, 1026–1040.

Mehta, M., Agrawal, R., & Rissanen, J. (1996). SLIQ: A fast scalable classifier for data mining. In P. Apers, M. Bouzeghoub, & G. Gardarin (Eds.), *Proceedings of the Fifth International Conference on Extending Database Technology* (pp. 18–32). Avignon, France. New York: Springer-Verlag.

Melville, P., & Mooney, R. J. (2005). Creating diversity in ensembles using artificial data. *Information Fusion*, 6(1), 99–111.

Michalski, R. S., & Chilausky, R. L. (1980). Learning by being told and learning from examples: An experimental comparison of the two methods of knowledge acquisition in the context of developing an expert system for soybean disease diagnosis. *International Journal of Policy Analysis and Information Systems*, 4(2).

Michie, D. (1989). Problems of computer-aided concept formation. In J. R. Quinlan (Ed.), *Applications of expert systems (Vol. 2)* (pp. 310–333). Wokingham, UK: Addison-Wesley.

Minsky, M., & Papert, S. (1969). *Perceptrons*. Cambridge, MA: MIT Press.

Mitchell, T. M. (1997). *Machine Learning*. New York: McGraw-Hill.

Mitchell T. M., Caruana, R., Freitag, D., McDermott, J., & Zabowski, D. (1994). Experience with a learning personal assistant. *Communications of the ACM*, 37 (7), 81–91.

Moore, A. W. (1991). *Efficient memory-based learning for robot control*. Ph.D. Dissertation, Computer Laboratory, University of Cambridge, UK.

———. (2000). The anchors hierarchy: Using the triangle inequality to survive high-dimensional data. In C. Boutilier, & M. Goldszmidt (Eds.), *Proceedings of the Sixteenth Conference on Uncertainty in Artificial Intelligence* (pp. 397–405). Stanford, CA. San Francisco: Morgan Kaufmann.

Moore, A. W., & Lee, M. S. (1994). Efficient algorithms for minimizing cross validation error. In W. W. Cohen, & H. Hirsh (Eds.), *Proceedings of the Eleventh International Conference on Machine Learning* (pp. 190–198). New Brunswick, NJ. San Francisco: Morgan Kaufmann.

———. (1998). Cached sufficient statistics for efficient machine learning with large datasets. *Journal Artificial Intelligence Research*, 8, 67–91.

Moore, A. W., & Pelleg, D. (2000). X-means: Extending k-means with efficient estimation of the number of clusters. In P. Langley (Ed.), *Proceedings of the Seventeenth International Conference on Machine Learning* (pp. 727–734). Stanford, CA. San Francisco: Morgan Kaufmann.

Mutter, S., Hall, M., & Frank, E. (2004). Using classification to evaluate the output of confidence-based association rule mining. In *Proceedings of the Seventeenth Australian Joint Conference on Artificial Intelligence* (pp. 538–549). Cairns, Australia. Berlin: Springer-Verlag.

Nadeau, C., & Bengio, Y. (2003). Inference for the generalization error. *Machine Learning*, 52(3), 239–281.

Nahm, U. Y., & Mooney, R. J. (2000). Using information extraction to aid the discovery of prediction rules from texts. In *Proceedings of the Workshop on Text Mining at the Sixth International Conference on Knowledge Discovery and Data Mining* (pp. 51–58). Boston. Workshop proceedings at: *http://www.cs.cmu.edu/~dunja/WshKDD2000.html*

Niculescu-Mizil, A., & Caruana, R. (2005). Predicting good probabilities with supervised learning. In *Proceedings of the 22nd International Conference on Machine Learning* (pp. 625–632). Bonn. New York: ACM Press.

Nie, N. H., Hull, C., Jenkins, H., Steinbrenner, J. G. K., & Bent, D. H. (1970). *Statistical package for the social sciences*. New York: McGraw-Hill.

Nigam, K., & Ghani, R. (2000). Analyzing the effectiveness and applicability of co-training. In *Proceedings of the Ninth International Conference on Information and Knowledge Management* (pp. 86–93). McLean, VA. New York: ACM Press.

Nigam, K., McCallum, A. K., Thrun, S., & Mitchell, T. M. (2000). Text classification from labeled and unlabeled documents using EM. *Machine Learning*, 39(2/3), 103–134.

Nilsson, N. J. (1965). *Learning machines*. New York: McGraw-Hill.

Nisbet, R., Elder, J., & Miner, G. (2009). *Handbook of statistical analysis and data mining applications*. New York: Academic Press.

Oates, T., & Jensen, D. (1997). The effects of training set size on decision tree complexity. In *Proceedings of the Fourteenth International Conference on Machine Learning* (pp. 254–262). Nashville. San Francisco: Morgan Kaufmann.

Ohm, P. (2009). Broken promises of privacy: Responding to the surprising failure of anonymization. University of Colorado Law Legal Studies Research Paper No. 09-12, August.

Omohundro, S. M. (1987). Efficient algorithms with neural network behavior. *Journal of Complex Systems*, 1(2), 273–347.

Paynter G. W. (2000). *Automating iterative tasks with programming by demonstration*. Ph.D. Dissertation, Department of Computer Science, University of Waikato, New Zealand.

Pearson, R. (2005). Mining imperfect data. *Society for Industrial and Applied Mechanics*, Philadelphia.

Pei, J., Han, J., Mortazavi-Asi, B., Wang, J., Pinto, H., Chen, Q., et al. (2004). Mining sequential patterns by pattern-growth: The PrefixSpan approach. *IEEE Transactions on Knowledge and Data Engineering*, 16(11), 1424–1440.

Piatetsky-Shapiro, G., & Frawley, W. J. (Eds.) (1991). *Knowledge discovery in databases*. Menlo Park, CA: AAAI Press/MIT Press.

Platt, J. (1998). Fast training of support vector machines using sequential minimal optimization. In B. Schölkopf, C. Burges, & A. Smola (Eds.), *Advances in kernel methods: Support vector learning* (pp. 185–209). Cambridge, MA: MIT Press.

Power, D. J. (2002). What is the true story about data mining, beer and diapers? *DSS News*, 3(23); see *http: //www.dssresources.com/newsletters/66.php*.

Provost, F., & Fawcett, T. (1997). Analysis and visualization of classifier performance: Comparison under imprecise class and cost distributions. In D. Heckerman, H. Mannila, D. Pregibon, & R. Uthurusamy (Eds.), *Proceedings of the Third International Conference on Knowledge Discovery and Data Mining* (pp. 43–48). Huntington Beach, CA. Menlo Park, CA: AAAI Press.

Pyle, D. (1999). *Data preparation for data mining.* San Francisco, CA: Morgan Kaufmann.

Quinlan, J. R. (1986). Induction of decision trees. *Machine Learning,* 1(1), 81–106.

———. (1992). Learning with continuous classes. In N. Adams, & L. Sterling (Eds.), *Proceedings of the Fifth Australian Joint Conference on Artificial Intelligence* (pp. 343–348). Hobart, Tasmania. Singapore: World Scientific.

———. (1993). *C4.5: Programs for machine learning.* San Francisco: Morgan Kaufmann.

———. (1996). Improved use of continuous attributes in C4.5. *Journal of Artificial Intelligence Research,* 4, 77–90.

Ramon, J., & de Raedt, L. (2000). Multi instance neural networks. In *Proceedings of the ICML Workshop on Attribute-Value and Relational Learning* (pp. 53–60). Stanford, CA.

Ray, S., & Craven, M. (2005). Supervised learning versus multiple instance learning: An empirical comparison. In *Proceedings of the International Conference on Machine Learning* (pp. 697–704). Bonn. New York: ACM Press.

Read, J., Pfahringer, B., Holmes, G., & Frank, E. (2009). Classifier chains for multi-label classification. In *Proceedings of the 13th European Conference on Principles and Practice of Knowledge Discovery in Databases and 20th European Conference on Machine Learning* (pp. 254–269). Bled, Slovenia. Berlin: Springer-Verlag.

Rennie, J. D. M., Shih, L., Teevan, J., & Karger, D. R. (2003). Tackling the poor assumptions of Naïve Bayes text classifiers. In T. Fawcett, & N. Mishra (Eds.), *Proceedings of the Twentieth International Conference on Machine Learning* (pp. 616–623). Washington, DC. Menlo Park, CA: AAAI Press.

Ricci, F., & Aha, D. W. (1998). Error-correcting output codes for local learners. In C. Nedellec, & C. Rouveird (Eds.), *Proceedings of the European Conference on Machine Learning* (pp. 280–291). Chemnitz, Germany. Berlin: Springer-Verlag.

Richards, D., & Compton, P. (1998). Taking up the situated cognition challenge with ripple-down rules. *International Journal of Human-Computer Studies,* 49(6), 895–926.

Rifkin, R., & Klautau, A. (2004). In defense of one-vs.-all classification. *Journal of Machine Learning Research,* 5, 101–141.

Ripley, B. D. (1996). *Pattern recognition and neural networks.* Cambridge, UK: Cambridge University Press.

Rissanen, J. (1985). The minimum description length principle. In S. Kotz, & N. L. Johnson (Eds.), *Encyclopedia of Statistical Sciences (Vol. 5)* (pp. 523–527). New York: John Wiley.

Rodriguez, J. J., Kuncheva, L. I., & Alonso, C. J. (2006). Rotation forest: A new classifier ensemble method. *IEEE Transactions on Pattern Analysis and Machine Intelligence,* 28(10), 1619–1630.

Rousseeuw, P. J., & Leroy, A. M. (1987). *Robust regression and outlier detection.* New York: John Wiley.

Russell, S., & Norvig, P. (2009). *Artificial intelligence: A modern approach* (3rd ed.). Upper Saddle River, NJ: Prentice-Hall.

Sahami, M., Dumais, S., Heckerman, D., & Horvitz, E. (1998). A Bayesian approach to filtering junk e-mail. In *Proceedings of the AAAI-98 Workshop on Learning for Text Categorization* (pp. 55–62). Madison, WI. Menlo Park, CA: AAAI Press.

Saitta, L., & Neri, F. (1998). Learning in the "real world." *Machine Learning,* 30(2/3), 133–163.

Salzberg, S. (1991). A nearest hyperrectangle learning method. *Machine Learning*, 6(3), 251–276.

Schapire, R. E., Freund, Y., Bartlett, P., & Lee, W. S. (1997). Boosting the margin: A new explanation for the effectiveness of voting methods. In D. H. Fisher (Ed.), *Proceedings of the Fourteenth International Conference on Machine Learning* (pp. 322–330). Nashville. San Francisco: Morgan Kaufmann.

Scheffer, T. (2001). Finding association rules that trade support optimally against confidence. In L. de Raedt, & A. Siebes (Eds.), *Proceedings of the Fifth European Conference on Principles of Data Mining and Knowledge Discovery* (pp. 424–435). Freiburg, Germany. Berlin: Springer-Verlag.

Schölkopf, B., Bartlett, P., Smola, A. J., & Williamson, R. (1999). Shrinking the tube: A new support vector regression algorithm. *Advances in Neural Information Processing Systems*, 11, 330–336. Cambridge, MA: MIT Press.

Schölkopf, B., Williamson, R., Smola, A., Shawe-Taylor, J., & Platt, J. (2000). Support vector method for novelty detection. *Advances in Neural Information Processing Systems*, 12, 582–588. Cambridge, MA: MIT Press.

Schölkopf, B., & Smola, A. J. (2002). *Learning with kernels: Support vector machines, regularization, optimization, and beyond.* Cambridge, MA: MIT Press.

Sebastiani, F. (2002). Machine learning in automated text categorization. *ACM Computing Surveys*, 34(1), 1–47.

Seewald A. K. (2002). How to make stacking better and faster while also taking care of an unknown weakness. In *Proceedings of the Nineteenth International Conference on Machine Learning* (pp. 54–561). Sydney. San Francisco: Morgan Kaufmann.

Seewald, A. K., & Fürnkranz, J. (2001). An evaluation of grading classifiers. In F. Hoffmann, D. J. Hand, N. M. Adams, D. H. Fisher, & G. Guimarães (Eds.), *Proceedings of the Fourth International Conference on Advances in Intelligent Data Analysis* (pp. 115–124). Cascais, Portugal. Berlin: Springer-Verlag.

Shafer, R., Agrawal, R., & Metha, M. (1996). SPRINT: A scalable parallel classifier for data mining. In T. M. Vijayaraman, A. P. Buchmann, C. Mohan, & N. L. Sarda (Eds.), *Proceedings of the Second International Conference on Very Large Databases* (pp. 544–555). Mumbai (Bombay). San Francisco: Morgan Kaufmann.

Shalev-Shwartz, S., Singer, Y., & Srebro, N. (2007). Pegasos: Primal estimated sub-gradient solver for SVM. In *Proceedings of the 24th international conference on Machine Learning* (pp. 807–814). New York: ACM Press.

Shawe-Taylor, J., & Cristianini, N. (2004). *Kernel methods for pattern analysis.* Cambridge, UK: Cambridge University Press.

Slonim, N., Friedman, N., & Tishby, N. (2002). Unsupervised document classification using sequential information maximization. In *Proceedings of the 25th International ACM SIGIR Conference on Research and Development in Information Retrieval* (pp. 120–136). New York: ACM Press.

Smola, A. J., & B. Schölkopf. (2004). A tutorial on support vector regression. *Statistics and Computing*, 14(3), 199–222.

Soderland, S., Fisher, D., Aseltine, J., & Lehnert, W. (1995). Crystal: Inducing a conceptual dictionary. In *Proceedings of the Fourteenth International Joint Conference on Artificial Intelligence* (pp. 1314–1319). Montreal. Menlo Park, CA: AAAI Press.

Srikant, R., & Agrawal, R. (1996). Mining sequential patterns: Generalizations and performance improvements. In P. M. Apers, M. Bouzeghoub, & G. Gardarin (Eds.), *Proceedings of the Fifth International Conference on Extending Database Technology.* Avignon, France. Lecture Notes in Computer Science. Vol. 1057 (pp. 3–17). London: Springer-Verlag.

Stevens, S. S. (1946). On the theory of scales of measurement. *Science*, 103, 677–680.

Stone, P., & Veloso, M. (2000). Multiagent systems: A survey from a machine learning perspective. *Autonomous Robots*, 8(3), 345–383.

Stout, Q. F. (2008). Unimodal regression via prefix isotonic regression. *Computational Statistics and Data Analysis*, 53, 289–297.

Su, J., Zhang, H., Ling, C. X., & Matwin, S. (2008). Discriminative parameter learning for Bayesian networks. In *Proceedings of the 25th International Conference on Machine Learning* (pp. 1016–1023). Helsinki. New York: ACM Press.

Swets, J. (1988). Measuring the accuracy of diagnostic systems. *Science*, 240, 1285–1293.

Ting, K. M. (2002). An instance-weighting method to induce cost-sensitive trees. *IEEE Transactions on Knowledge and Data Engineering*, 14(3), 659–665.

Ting, K. M., & Witten, I. H. (1997a). Stacked generalization: When does it work? In *Proceedings of the Fifteenth International Joint Conference on Artificial Intelligence* (pp. 866–871). Nagoya, Japan. San Francisco: Morgan Kaufmann.

———. (1997b). Stacking bagged and dagged models. In D. H. Fisher (Ed.), *Proceedings of the Fourteenth International Conference on Machine Learning* (pp. 367–375). Nashville. San Francisco: Morgan Kaufmann.

Turney, P. D. (1999). *Learning to extract key phrases from text*. Technical Report ERB-1057, Institute for Information Technology, National Research Council of Canada, Ottawa.

U.S. House of Representatives Subcommittee on Aviation (2002). Hearing on aviation security with a focus on passenger profiling, February 27, 2002; see *http: //www.house.gov/ transportation/aviation/02-27-02/02-27-02memo.html.*

Utgoff, P. E. (1989). Incremental induction of decision trees. *Machine Learning*, 4(2), 161–186.

Utgoff, P. E., Berkman, N. C., & Clouse, J. A. (1997). Decision tree induction based on efficient tree restructuring. *Machine Learning*, 29(1), 5–44.

Vafaie, H., & DeJong, K. (1992). Genetic algorithms as a tool for feature selection in machine learning. In *Proceedings of the International Conference on Tools with Artificial Intelligence* (pp. 200–203). Arlington, VA: IEEE Computer Society Press.

van Rijsbergen, C. A. (1979). *Information retrieval*. London: Butterworths.

Vapnik, V. (1999). *The nature of statistical learning theory* (2nd ed.). New York: Springer-Verlag.

Vitter, J. S. (1985). Random sampling with a reservoir. *ACM Transactions on Mathematical Software*, 1(11), 37–57.

Wang, J., & Zucker, J.-D. (2000). Solving the multiple-instance problem: A lazy learning approach. In *Proceedings of the International Conference on Machine Learning* (pp. 1119–1125). Stanford, CA. San Francisco: Morgan Kaufmann.

Wang, J., Han, J., & Pei, J. (2003). CLOSET+: Searching for the best strategies for mining frequent closed itemsets. In *Proceedings of the International Conference on Knowledge Discovery and Data Mining* (pp. 236–245). Washington, DC. New York: ACM Press.

Wang, Y., & Witten, I. H. (1997). Induction of model trees for predicting continuous classes. In M. van Someren, & G. Widmer (Eds.), *Proceedings of the of the Poster Papers of the European Conference on Machine Learning* (pp. 128–137). University of Economics, Faculty of Informatics and Statistics, Prague. Berlin: Springer.

————. (2002). Modeling for optimal probability prediction. In C. Sammut, & A. Hoffmann (Eds.), *Proceedings of the Nineteenth International Conference on Machine Learning* (pp. 650–657). Sydney. San Francisco: Morgan Kaufmann.

Webb, G. I. (1999). Decision tree grafting from the all-tests-but-one partition. In *Proceedings of the Sixteenth International Joint Conference on Artificial Intelligence* (pp. 702–707). San Francisco: Morgan Kaufmann.

————. (2000). MultiBoosting: A technique for combining boosting and wagging. *Machine Learning*, 40(2), 159–196.

Webb, G. I., Boughton, J., & Wang, Z. (2005). Not so naïve Bayes: Aggregating one-dependence estimators. *Machine Learning*, 58(1), 5–24.

Weidmann, N., Frank, E., & Pfahringer, B. (2003). A two-level learning method for generalized multi-instance problems. In *Proceedings of the European Conference on Machine Learning* (pp. 468–479). Cavtat, Croatia. Berlin: Springer-Verlag.

Weiser, M., & Brown, J. S. (1997). The coming age of calm technology. In P. J. Denning, & R. M. Metcalfe (Eds.), *Beyond calculation: The next fifty years* (pp. 75–86). New York: Copernicus.

Weiss, S. M., & Indurkhya, N. (1998). *Predictive data mining: A practical guide*. San Francisco: Morgan Kaufmann.

Wettschereck, D., & Dietterich, T. G. (1995). An experimental comparison of the nearest-neighbor and nearest-hyperrectangle algorithms. *Machine Learning*, 19(1), 5–28.

Wild, C. J., & Seber, G. A. F. (1995). *Introduction to probability and statistics*. Department of Statistics, University of Auckland, New Zealand.

Winston, P. H. (1992). *Artificial intelligence*. Reading, MA: Addison-Wesley.

Witten, I. H. (2004). Text mining. In M. P. Singh (Ed.), *Practical handbook of Internet computing* (pp. 14-1–14-22). Boca Raton, FL: CRC Press.

Witten, I. H., Bray, Z., Mahoui, M., & Teahan, W. (1999a). Text mining: A new frontier for lossless compression. In J. A. Storer, & M. Cohn (Eds.), *Proceedings of the Data Compression Conference* (pp. 198–207). Snowbird, UT. Los Alamitos, CA: IEEE Press.

Witten, I. H., Moffat, A., & Bell, T. C. (1999b). *Managing gigabytes: Compressing and indexing documents and images* (2nd ed.). San Francisco: Morgan Kaufmann.

Wolpert, D. H. (1992). Stacked generalization. *Neural Networks*, 5, 241–259.

Wu, X. V., Kumar, J. R., Quinlan, J., Ghosh, Q., Yang, H., Motoda, G. J., et al. (2008). Top 10 algorithms in data mining. *Knowledge and Information Systems*, 14(1), 1–37.

Wu, X., & Kumar, V. (Eds.), (2009). *The top ten algorithms in data mining*. New York: Chapman and Hall.

Xu, X., & Frank, E. (2004). Logistic regression and boosting for labeled bags of instances. In *Proceedings of the 8th Pacific-Asia Conference on Knowledge Discovery and Data Mining* (pp. 272–281). Sydney. Berlin: Springer-Verlag.

Yan, X., & Han, J. (2002). gSpan: Graph-based substructure pattern mining. In *Proceedings of the IEEE International Conference on Data Mining* (pp. 721–724). Maebashi City, Japan. Washington, DC: IEEE Computer Society.

Yan, X., & Han, J. (2003). CloseGraph: Mining closed frequent graph patterns. In *Proceedings of the Ninth ACM SIGKDD International Conference on Knowledge Discovery and Data Mining* (pp. 286–295). Washington, DC. New York: ACM Press.

Yan, X., Han, J., & Afshar, R. (2003). CloSpan: Mining closed sequential patterns in large datasets. In *Proceedings of the SIAM International Conference on Data Mining* (pp. 166–177). San Francisco. Philadelphia: Society for Industrial and Applied Mathematics.

Yang, Y., & Webb, G. I. (2001). Proportional *k*-interval discretization for Naïve Bayes classifiers. In L. de Raedt, & P. Flach (Eds.), *Proceedings of the Twelfth European Conference on Machine Learning* (pp. 564–575). Freiburg, Germany. Berlin: Springer-Verlag.

Yang, Y., Guan, X., & You, J. (2002). CLOPE: A fast and effective clustering algorithm for transactional data. In *Proceedings of the Eighth ACM SIGKDD International Conference on Knowledge Discovery and Data Mining* (pp. 682–687). Edmonton, AB. New York: ACM Press.

Yurcik, W., Barlow, J., Zhou, Y., Raje, H., Li, Y., Yin, X., et al. (2003). Scalable data management alternatives to support data mining heterogeneous logs for computer network security. In *Proceedings of the Workshop on Data Mining for Counter Terrorism and Security*. San Francisco. Philadelphia: Society for International and Applied Mathematics.

Zadrozny, B., & Elkan, C. (2002). Transforming classifier scores into accurate multiclass probability estimates. In *Proceedings of the Eighth ACM International Conference on Knowledge Discovery and Data Mining* (pp. 694–699). Edmonton, AB. New York: ACM Press.

Zaki, M. J., Parthasarathy, S., Ogihara, M., & Li, W. (1997). New algorithms for fast discovery of association rules. In *Proceedings Knowledge Discovery in Databases* (pp. 283–286). Newport Beach, CA. Menlo Park, CA: AAAI Press.

Zhang, H., Jiang, L., & Su, J. (2005). Hidden Naïve Bayes. In *Proceedings of the 20th National Conference on Artificial Intelligence* (pp. 919–924). Pittsburgh. Menlo Park, CA: AAAI Press.

Zhang, T., Ramakrishnan, R., & Livny, M. (1996). BIRCH: An efficient data clustering method for very large databases. In *Proceedings of the ACM SIGMOD International Conference on Management of Data* (pp. 103–114). Montreal. New York: ACM Press.

Zhang, T. (2004). Solving large scale linear prediction problems using stochastic gradient descent algorithms. In *Proceedings of the 21st International Conference on Machine Learning* (pp. 919–926). Banff, AB. Madison, WI: Omnipress.

Zheng, F., & Webb, G. (2006). Efficient lazy elimination for averaged one-dependence estimators. In *Proceedings of the 23rd International Conference on Machine Learning* (pp. 1113–1120). New York: ACM Press.

Zheng, Z., & Webb, G. (2000). Lazy learning of Bayesian rules. *Machine Learning*, 41(1), 53–84.

Zhou, Z.-H., & Zhang, M.-L. (2007). Solving multi-instance problems with classifier ensemble based on constructive clustering. *Knowledge and Information Systems*, 11(2), 155–170.

Index

Note: Page numbers followed by "f" indicates a figure, "t" indicates a table, and "b" indicates entry is inside boxed text.

CPSIA information can be obtained at www.ICGtesting.com
Printed in the USA
LVOW03s2154111214

418124LV00003B/7/P